Learn Spanish

THIS BOOK INCLUDES:

Learn Spanish for Beginners

Spanish Short Stories for Beginners

Learn Spanish for intermediate users

Learn Spanish for Advanced Users

Spanish Short Stories

Speak Spanish

The Ultimate Spanish Language Books collection to Learn Starting from Zero, Have Fun and Become Fluent like a Native Speaker

TABLE OF CONTENTS

Learn Spanish for Beginners

Spanish Short Stories for Beginners

Learn Spanish
for Intermediate Users

Learn Spanish
for Advanced Users

Learn Spanish for Beginners

The complete beginners guide to speak Spanish in just 7 days starting from zero. Includes the most common Spanish words and phrases.

Introduction

Spanish has a great many salutations and the one who you use depends upon a number of variables, of course.

There's, of course, the generally used *hola* (oh-la). This just means "hello" in English. The etymology of the word "*hola*" is deeply interesting, but it's of course beyond the scope of this book.

Anyhow, there are also the greetings which have to do with the time of day. There is *buenos días* (bwey-nohs di-ahs). This means literally "good morning" and is one of the more common Spanish greetings aside from hola. There also is *buenas tardes* (bwey-nahs tar-dehs), which means good evening. This isn't used as often as a conventional salutation, though it certainly can be used with no problem. The last one in this category is *buenas noches* (bwey-nahs no-chess). This means literally "good night" and its usage is unwavering. You generally will only use this as a goodbye to somebody for the night is you know that you won't be seeing them again that night, if that is the case you should use the word "*adiós*" first; for not to confuse it with a greetings.

Lastly, there is *muy buenos*. (moy bwey-nohs). This is a very general greeting as compared to other ones such as *buenos días* and hola. You can use this greeting at pretty much any time of day whenever you indicate the corresponding time of day, after using this words "days", "evenings" and "nights" in the end.

So after all of that, we're now officially in the conversation, engaging in the nigh professional art of small talk. These small talk sessions generally almost always start by asking somebody how they are or how they're doing. There are a ton of ways to ask this sort of question in Spanish.

Firstly, there are the more formal routes to be taken. To simply ask "How are you?", you first need to think about who you're talking to. Are you speaking to somebody your age? Younger? Older? Have you met them before? Then you need to pick either the informal or the formal way to ask based upon your evaluations. The informal way to ask is to simply "*¿Cómo estas?*" (co-moh es-tahs), meaning in a literal sense "how are you?". The formal way is just the usted inversion of the prior question: *¿Cómo está usted?* (co-moh es-ta oos-ted). This means the same thing as before, but this version is of course to be reserved for meeting new people or for talking to people who are in a position of superiority.

On top of that, there are more casual ways to ask. You could say "how's it going?": *¿Cómo te va?* (co-moh teh va)

Simply asking "what's up?" is certainly not out of the question: *¿Qué tal?* (kay tall)

Neither would be asking something along the lines of "what's happening?"- *¿Qué pasa?* (kay pah-sah) - or "How have you been?": *¿Cómo has ido?* (co-moh ahs ee-do)

All in all, there are a ton of ways to ask somebody exactly how they're doing in Spanish. There are likewise a huge number of ways in which you could respond to this very question. Note that being in a foreign country or situation means that the culture is inevitably different; in America and England, when we ask "how are you?", we do so as a courtesy and generally not in the seeking of a very well-thought out response or any sort of genuine emotional discourse. Certain other countries aren't like this, and if you ask how they are, they'll tell you how they are.

But for all intents and purposes, you may or may not give a very deep response. Should you choose to go with a more "standard" response, there are a number of different ways in which you could phrase it.

You could start with the quintessential *bien, gracias* (byen, grah-see-as) which means simply "well/fine, thank you." You could also opt for "very well" by saying *muy bien* (moy byen). You could insert a certain amount of nihilistic apathy into your conversation by saying *Como siempre* which technically means "like always" but carries the weight more like "I am as I always seem to be." If you're not feeling well, you can say that you're sick by saying either *estoy enfermo* or *estoy enferma* depending upon your gender, men saying the first and women saying the second. And if you're not doing too well, you could say *más o menos* (moss oh men-ohs) meaning "so-so", or you could say mal which translates to simply "badly" or "poorly".

Then, there are multiple different ways in which you could say goodbye. There are a few generally used ones, and a few which are geared towards more special purposes.

The two general purpose ones that you need to know are *adiós* and *chao*. Both are common enough that I'm not going to tell you how to pronounce them. If you're on the up, you very well may notice a parallel between Spanish and neighboring Romance language Italian here, where ciao is used as a form of goodbye. Both of these are acceptable ways to say goodbye. This may also vary depending on the intimacy of the conversation.

If you'll be seeing the person soon, you could tell them *Hasta pronto* (ahs-tah pronto). But when I say soon, I mean soon. This is one place where the common conception of "soon" as used in the U.S. or Britain generally doesn't cut it in other timetables.

If you're just going to see them at a later point in time, you could say *Hasta luego* (ahs-tah lwey-go). This could imply a lack of certainty about when you'll meet again, however. It, as many things do, ultimately depends upon the context in which it's used.

The last one we're going to talk about here is *Hasta la vista* (ahs-tah lah vees-tah, but honestly, who doesn't know how to pronounce this one thanks to Hollywood?). This phrase means essentially "Until next time" or "untill we meet again". This one too can communicate a lack of certainty dependent upon the context.

On top of all of that, there are some essential phrases that you have absolutely got to know in order to ask for help in Spanish, or otherwise get around.

Firstly, there are two forms of "excuse me" you need to know. The first, *perdón*, means "excuse me" in the sense of "excuse me, could I ask you about something?"

The other form of excuse me, *con permiso*, has a meaning more along the lines of "Please excuse me", when you're needing somebody to move out of your way.

You also need to know how to say thank you and sorry. In fact, more people need to know how to do this in their native language. The way that you say "thank you" in Spanish is easy: *Gracias*. Nearly everybody knows that term. And the way you say sorry is additionally simple: *Lo siento* (lo syen-toh).

It's most certainly also worth you learning how to say please in Spanish because you invariably are going to need to at some point. You do so by saying *por favor*. (pour fah-vor)

And lastly, at some point, eventually you're going to have to ask for help in some way. The way to do this is by saying *necesito ayuda* (ney-cess-ee-toh ah-you-dah). This means literally "I need help" or "I need aid".

There's a lot of things you'll need to learn before you're ready for the streets, but hopefully now, you've got a solid enough foundation you can at least be courteous.

Chapter 1 - Articles and Adjectives

So, before we dissect those, we need to dissect one essential linguistic topic: gendering of nouns. Noun gendering is something that is lost entirely in modern English but was around in Old and Early Middle English, as well as sticking around heavily in other Germanic languages. The loss of gendering in English nouns is a particularly peculiar case because it's very difficult to beg to mind almost any other European languages which so finitely and resolutely lack a gendered noun system in the modern day. Regardless, the point is that you're unfamiliar with this sort of thing.

The idea of nouns having genders can be a little confusing at first - for example, what makes a banana innately masculine while a table is innately feminine? Well, in brief, almost nothing. Gendered nouns have very little to do with actual sex in the biological sense (unless used to refer to a living entity) and more-so to do with the notion of tone harmony. In other words, this is yet another holdover from other languages far more ancient and difficult than ours. Tone harmony is the essential idea that different parts of a sentence should sound similarly so as to make the sentence more sonically appealing and in general, just more soothing to the ears than it would be otherwise. This relatively simple concept has had a huge bearing on the languages of today, whether they're Germanic, Romantic, or a member of any other variety of language families.

What's more is that sometimes the noun genders are completely and totally arbitrary. This isn't all the time, though - in fact, it's a vast minority of the overall cases. Most of the time, there are recognizable patterns in reference to a noun's gender and the overall tone of the word. These are things that you'll begin to pick up intuitively as you learn more and more about Spanish and practice with the language more in general.

So, now, let's actually start talking about nouns. In English, nouns often have corresponding markers. These markers are referred to as articles, and they are used in a general manner to denote the plurality and definitiveness of a verb. Plurality, of course, refers to the number of a given verb. For example, we would never say "a blueberries" in English - we would say "some blueberries." Plurality matters when it comes to articles. Definitiveness is a bit of a harder topic to try to explain. Definitiveness refers to how resolute you are in reference to a specific noun. The best comparison that could be made is a sentence like "Could you hand me article book?" If you were to say "Could you hand me a book?" there is no specific reference in mind. You are asking for any book. While you may be referring to a specific title, it's presumed that there is a stack of that title and you're just asking for a copy. On the other hand, if you were to say "could you hand me the book?" it would seem as though you were referencing a particular book, often denoted by the circumstances. These are the two lines upon which articles are divided in English. However, Spanish has yet another delineation in terms of which articles work where and when.

This delineation is based upon the gender of the nouns in question. Spanish has two noun genders: masculine and feminine. Once upon a time, there was also a neuter noun, but this was long, long time ago. The system would simplify and give us what we know today.

So this means that which article you use is based on three different factors: the definitiveness, the plurality, and the gender of the noun. Fortunately, the more that you work with this specific concept, the more and more naturally it will come.

In terms of study, these nouns are usually divided into indefinite and definite. From there, they are organized by gender and plurality. For the purposes of study, we're going to be using the feminine noun *fresa* (for strawberry) and the masculine noun *damasco* (for apricot).

First, we will learn the indefinite articles:

Indefinite:

Masculine singular (an apricot) - *Un damasco*

Feminine singular (a strawberry) - *Una fresa*

Masculine plural (some apricots) - *Unos damascos*

Feminine plural (some strawberries) - *Unas fresas*

Next, we'll learn the definite articles.

Definite:

Masculine singular (the apricot) - *El damasco*

Feminine singular (the strawberry) - *La fresa*

Masculine plural (the apricots) - *Los damascos*

Feminine plural (the strawberries) - *Las fresas*

Using this, we're finally starting to understand the basics of Spanish nouns. Just like in English, nouns in Spanish can be either the subject or the object.

For example, you can say I want the strawberry:

Quiero la fresa.

Or you can say The strawberry is red.

La fresa es roja.

You see? It's actually pretty simple! Definitely not the hardest thing we've worked on so far in this book. This is another case where a little practice goes a long way.

The last Spanish sentence that we covered actually provides us a nice segue into the following topic: adjectives. Adjectives as a grammatical concept are likely already familiar to you - they're just words which describe something in one way or another. In Spanish and other Romance languages, they act a little differently to the way that they do in English.

An example of an English adjective would be something like "The man is tall." In English, though, we can just use tall to apply to anything. We don't have to shift it around. For example, if a woman is tall, we would likewise say "the woman is tall." If there were multiple men, we'd just say "The men are tall." Easy, right? Nothing too complicated about it.

In Spanish, on the other hand, there is a lot of nuance to the use of adjectives. In a lot of ways, it mimics the system utilized for articles in that it mirrors the gender and plurality of the noun in question. This isn't always the case, but a lot of the time it is. There are some special adjectives that don't change, but they're few and far between.

So, with that said, let's go back to that sentence from earlier: *La fresa es roja.*

The original adjective used in this sentence is actually *rojo*, or red. The nifty thing about Spanish adjectives is that their ending changes according to the noun being referred to. Because *fresa* is feminine, rojo changed to be feminine as well - through the *o* being changed to an *a*!

Can you take a wild guess at the mechanism through which adjectives are made plural? It's not a super difficult system. If you guessed adding an s to it, then you're right. If you wanted to say "the strawberries are red," you would say:

Las fresas son rojas.

You see? Nothing terribly difficult about it. Understanding how all of these sentence components work together actually builds to a much bigger lesson. Through this, you're now able to construct sentences that will get points across as well as describe things and people. This will carry you quite a long way as a tourist or just generally as somebody who is trying to start speaking Spanish.

However, this background knowledge also serves another important purpose: having this knowledge will allow you to more easily and intuitively discover different things about the language by reading it and hearing it spoken. This is only going to increase in simplicity as you become more comfortable with the language in general and learn more vocabulary. Your brain's natural intuition for picking up vocabulary through context clues will kick in and you'll start to really have a knack for the language.

Let's look back at our sentences "The man is tall," "the woman is tall," and "the men are tall." The word for tall is alto and the word for men and women are hombre and mujer, respectively. From this, can you guess how these sentences would be written? Give it a try.

If you guessed the following:

- *El hombre es alto.*

- *La mujer es alta.*

- *Los hombres son altos.*

Then you're absolutely correct.

The last thing that we need to discuss in this chapter is the concept of negation. Negation is very important to one's experience in speaking any language. After all, you have to be able to say you don't want something or just generally say that something isn't true. So what do you do when you need to negate something in Spanish?

Well, fortunately, negation in Spanish is very easy. There aren't really any catches or anything that makes it difficult at all, really. Negation in Spanish is an incredibly easy affair consisting primarily of just taking the word no and sticking it before the verb.

For example, if we wanted to take the sentence Jorge is tall (*Jorge es alto*) and turn it to the opposite (Jorge is not tall), we would do so by throwing a negatory no in front of the verb, like so:

Jorge no es alto.

Simple. It's relatively intuitive, but it's still something that we need to cover before we even think about moving on to the next parts of the book. It's an essential skill that you really need to have if you're going to be trying to speak Spanish as a traveler!

Chapter 2 - Preposiciones (Prepositions)

Prepositions in Spanish are the following: *a, ante, bajo, con, contra, de, desde, en, entre, hacia, hasta, para, por, según, sin, sobre* and *tras.*

A (to)

Preposition **a** can loosely translate as **to**, but it actually has many uses that differ from the English preposition. Examples:

I am going home - *Voy **a** casa*

You should go to the supermarket - *Deberías ir **al** supermercado*

We arrived at 3 pm - *Llegamos **a** las 3 de la tarde.*

How much are the tomatoes? - *¿**A** qué precio están los tomates?*

We are around the corner - *Estamos **a** la vuelta de la esquina*

The magazine is published twice a month - *La revista se publica dos veces **al** mes*

You have to turn left - *Debes girar **a** la izquierda*

Will you call your sister? - *¿Llamarás **a** tu hermana?*

I gave the book to Pedro - *Le di el libro **a** Pedro*

I go to work by foot - *Voy **al** trabajo **a** pie*

Are you going to go? - *¿Vas **a** ir?*

Ante

This preposition can translate as **before** or **in front of**.

Examples:

The truth was in front of me - *La verdad estaba **ante** mí*

Before anything, we must resolve this - ***Ante** nada, debemos resolver esto*

Bajo

Bajo means **under**, as in the following examples:

I'm under your orders - *Estoy **bajo** tus órdenes*

The cat is hiding under the blanket - *El gato está oculto **bajo** la manta*

Con

This preposition means **with**:

I love running with my trainers- *Amo correr **con** mis zapatillas*

Do it with love - *Hazlo **con** amor*

I hate eating out with my grandfather - *Odio salir a comer **con** mi abuelo*

Contra

This preposition means **against**:

I'm running against my cousin in the local elections - *Estoy compitiendo **contra** mi primo en las elecciones locales*

My team is playing against yours - *Mi equipo está jugando **contra** el tuyo*

The car crashed against the tree - *El auto chocó **contra** el árbol*

De

De means **from** and **as**, but also has many other uses:

I am from Honduras - *Soy **de** Honduras*

The car belongs to my brother - *El auto es **de** mi hermano*

They want us to leave the pub - *Quieren que salgamos **del** pub*

The sculpture is made of marble - *La escultura es **de** mármol*

I am dressed as a pirate - *Estoy disfrazado **de** pirata*

The store is open from 10 a.m. to 3 p.m. - *La tienda abre **de** las 10 de la mañana a las 3 de la tarde*

A standing ovation - *Una ovación **de** pie*

Desde

Desde also means **since** or **from**, and sometimes can be used in the same places as de:

I do this since I'm 5 years old - *Hago esto **desde** los cinco años*

Everything looks better from where you're standing - *Todo se ve mejor **desde** donde estás parado*

En

En means **in**, **at**, **on**, **during** or **into**. Examples:

I'm never at home - *Nunca estoy **en** casa*

She's travelling on a boat - *Está viajando **en** barco*

I'd rather do it during the spring - *Preferiría hacerlo **en** primavera*

I want someone like that in my life - *Quiero a alguien así **en** mi vida*

It's on the table - *Está **en** la mesa*

In the countryside, things are simpler - ***En** el campo, las cosas son más sencillas*

Entre

Entre normally means **between,** as in the following examples:

The show starts between 2 and 3 in the morning - *El espectáculo empieza **entre** las 2 y las 3 de la mañana*

I'm in between jobs - *Estoy **entre** empleos*

I'm lost in the crowd - *Estoy perdido **entre** la multitud*

Hacia

Hacia normally can translate as **to** or **around**:

I was going straight to her house - *Estaba yendo derecho **hacia** su casa*

He came around 2 p.m. - *Vino **hacia** las 2 de la tarde*

Hasta

Hasta can translate as **up to**, **to** or **until**:

I want to swim to the opposite shore - *Quiero nadar **hasta** la otra orilla*

Let's run until we get tired - *Nademos **hasta** que nos cansemos*

Para

Depending on the context, ***para*** can mean **for** or **to**:

I'm going **to** your house - *Voy **para** tu casa*

I bought a gift for you - Compré un regalo ***para*** ti

Por

Por can mean through, **near, around, in**, by, **per, for** and **because** of, depending on the context:

I'm doing it for you - *Lo estoy haciendo **por** ti*

I'm always slow in the morning - *Siempre soy lenta **por** la mañana*

I bought it for three dollars - *Lo compré **por** 3 dólares*

Near my house, there are a lot of shops - ***Por** mi casa hay muchas tiendas*

We have to pay 100 pesos each - *Debemos pagar 100 pesos **por** persona*

I visit my parents once a month - *Visito a mis padres una vez **por** mes*

Según

Según can be translated as **according to**:

We will do it according to the rules - *Lo haremos **según** las reglas*

According to Roberto, everything is fine - ***Según** lo que dijo Roberto, está todo bien*

Sin

Sin means the lack of something and sometimes can translate as **without**:

He didn't say a word in the whole day - *Estuvo todo el día **sin** decir una palabra*

I don't feel like going out - *Estoy **sin** ganas de salir*

Without job opportunities, it's difficult to take risks - ***Sin** oportunidades laborales, es difícil tomar riesgos*

Sobre

Sobre means **on, above, on top of** or **about,** as in the following examples:

Clouds are dancing above us - *Las nubes bailan **sobre** nosotros*

I left the money on the table - *Dejé el dinero **sobre** la mesa*

We were talking about your future - *Estábamos hablando **sobre** tu futuro*

Tras

Tras means **after** or **behind**:

After falling asleep for the third time, he was fired - ***Tras** quedarse dormido por tercera vez, fue despedido*

The father was spying on them behind the door - *El padre los espiaba **tras** la puerta*

Exercises

All of this time, I was under his charms - *Todo este tiempo, estaba .... sus encantos*

I didn't go alone, I went with Inés - *No fui sola, fui .... Inés*

Is that a painting by Botero? - *¿Ese cuadro es ....Botero?*

The burglar hid under the bed - *El ladrón se ocultó .... la cama*

I don't want to do anything during the day - *No quiero hacer nada .... el día*

When you come to town, don't forget to visit my family - *Cuando vengas .... la ciudad, no olvides visitar .... mi familia*

I thought Jeremías was Colombian, but in reality he's from Venezuela - *Pensé que Jeremías era colombiano, pero .... realidad es .... Venezuela*

He stood before the judge and lied - *Se paró ...... el juez y mintió*

I'm here since 8 a.m. - *Estoy aquí .... las 8 de la mañana*

What is all of this chocolate for? - *¿................ qué es todo este chocolate?*

Why are you making yelling? - *¿.......... qué gritas?*

You must take your medicine twice a week - *Debes tomar tu medicación dos veces .... la semana*

During all this time I was suspecting the wrong person - *............. todo este tiempo sospeché .... la persona equivocada*

He left me speechless - *Me dejó .... palabras*

Try to think with the brain, not with the heart - *Intenta pensar .... el cerebro, no .... el corazón*

After thinking a lot about this, I decided to quit - *............. pensarlo mucho, decidí renunciar*

I gave all the credit to my team - *Di todo el crédito .... mi equipo*

I will trade my apple for your orange - *Te cambio mi manzana .... tu naranja*

I don't leave my house a lot during the winter - *No salgo mucho .... mi casa .... el invierno*

I have to choose between my two best friends - *Debo elegir .... mis dos mejores amigos*

Where is your life going? - *¿............. dónde va tu vida?*

Chapter 3 - Prepositions and Directions

Once you have a firm grasp of the basics of verbs, adjectives, numbers and colors in Spanish, you can think about adding more to your store of knowledge with a few prepositions – in, on, under, on top of, and other 'positional' words – and directions. It's surprising how often you find yourself either asking for or giving directions – unless you're a man, of course, in which case you never, ever ask for directions! For everyone else though, directions are useful to know and, along with prepositions, they can significantly increase your potential for both speaking and writing in Spanish.

One major difference between English and Spanish prepositions is that one Spanish word can cover a number of different meanings and contexts. The only way to get a grip on this is to use the prepositions in the way the Spanish use them. It's a question of research and practice. Don't be intimidated, because you'll soon get the hang of using prepositions the way the Spanish use them.

Some prepositions need more explanation than others, because they have a wider variety of uses. Two of them – 'de' and 'a' – merit closer attention before moving on to the rest.

Using the preposition 'de'

Prepositions can be difficult in Spanish until you get used to them, because often, they have more than one meaning. An obvious example is '*de*,' which can mean of, made of, from, or about. It's also customarily used to denote possession and origins, and it's used in superlatives. Perhaps the easiest way to demonstrate how 'de' is used is to offer some examples.

Spanish	English
El coche rojo es de Maria	The red car is Maria's (of Maria)
La buffanda es de algodon	The scarf is cotton (made of cotton)
Soy de Italia	I am from Italy
Ella es la mas hermosa de todas	She is the most beautiful of them all
Leo un libro de cocina	I am reading a cookery book (book about cookery
Bebo un vaso de sangria	I am drinking a glass of sangria

For ease of understanding, the literal translations are included in brackets, after the broad meanings of the sentences. Practice using 'de' in written sentences to familiarize yourself with this important and versatile Spanish preposition.

Using the preposition 'a'

Another versatile and widely used preposition is '*a*'. It's English equivalent is to or at, but like '*de*,' it can be used in various ways, not all of which are immediately obvious. However, as you become more proficient at Spanish, you will soon learn how and when to use '*a*' in its customary contexts.

The main uses of '*a*' are to denote time, movement, location, the shape things are done and price, so it can mean towards and for, depending on the context. It can also be used to mean on, by, from, with, into, or in, among other things. Again, it's simpler and quicker to show how '*a*' is used, so here are some examples, with English translations.

Spanish - English

Vengo a las once - I'll come at 11 o'clock

Vamos al Mercado - We're going to the market

La puerta a la cocina esta abierta - The door to the kitchen is open (you could also use 'de' here)

Voy a bailar con mi marido - I am going to dance with my husband

Lavamos el coche a mano - We'll wash the car by hand

In the sentence '*Vamos al Mercado*,' *al* is used as a contraction of '*a el*,' which would be complicated to say. You should always use '*al*' with masculine objects. So you would say '*Vamos al cine*,' or 'Let's go to the cinema,' but '*Vamos a la playa*'. (Let's go to the beach). *La playa* is feminine, so there is no contraction.

There is another special use of '*a*,' which you will notice in the above examples. It's also used together with the verb '*ir*' and the infinitive when you want to express a future intention. Although the infinitive form *bailar* means 'to dance,' it's customary to use '*a*' as a bridge between the verbs. Literally, the sentence reads 'I am going to to dance with my husband.' It's one of a number of quirks of the Spanish language that doesn't have an English equivalent.

The Personal A

Speaking of things with no English equivalent, no discussion on Spanish prepositions is complete without reference to the use of the Personal A. In English, there is no difference in the sentence structure whether the verb refers to a person or a thing, but in Spanish, anything referring to a specific person or domestic pet – whom many people think of as persons in their own right – is preceded by the Personal *A*.

Confused? There's really no need to be! Let's assume you number a hairdresser among your friends and acquaintances. It's accurate to say:

Conozco a una peluquera – I know a hairdresser

However, if you're in need of a quick wash and blow dry, but don't have a particular hairdresser in mind for the job – maybe your hairdresser friend isn't very good – then you would say:

Necesito una peluquera – I need a hairdresser

Your hairdresser acquaintance is a specific person, so she gets a Personal *A*, but the required hairdresser could be anybody, so there's no need to use it.

When it comes to animals, use the Personal *A* for dogs and cats and other domestic pets, but not for animals in general. So, assuming you are walking with your dog in the fields, and you spot some cows, this is how you'd describe it:

Puedo ver a mi perro, Pedro – I can see my dog, Pedro

Puedo ver tres vacas – I can see three cows

Pedro gets a Personal *A* because he's part of the family, but the cows are not domestic animals, so they don't warrant it.

It's a good idea to spend some time working with the Personal *A*, so that its uses are clear in your mind. Getting it right shows that you are serious about learning Spanish, and like many Spanish grammar rules, it's fairly straightforward once you get used to it. And you will certainly impress your Spanish friends if you can drop in a Personal *A* when it's appropriate.

Just a point of interest to note here. You may have noticed the use of '*es*' rather than '*está*' in the sentences '*El regalo es para mí*' and '*Es una película sobre la Guerra*'. That's because these are permanent states – the gift will always be mine, and the film will always be about the war. However, the cat will not always be outside the store, and the wine will not always be in the fridge.

When to use 'para' and 'por'

Before we move on from prepositions to directions, something else warrants more explanation. You will see that there are two words for '*for*' – '*para*' and '*por*'. They each have their particular uses, and if you're serious about learning Spanish, you need to know the difference.

'*Por*' can also mean by, along, through, and about, so it is used to describe transport and movement methods, among other things. For example, if you wanted to say 'I am going to Barcelona by train,' you would say, '*Voy a Barcelona por tren*'. If you're on the market, you may see a sign on the *lechugas* (lettuces) '*Cuatro por €1*' (4 for €1).

'*Para*' is more commonly used for various scenarios. If something is intended for a particular person, it will be *para*, rather than *por*. When you order in a restaurant, you will say, '*Paella para mí*' (Paella for me) – or whatever you're having. And in the example above, '*El regalo es para mí*.' (The gift is for me). If there is a specific person or purpose, it's *para*, but if it's not so clear, it's *por*.

Now you have a list of Spanish prepositions, along with examples of how to use them, and explanations of common uses. Prepositions are very important in several aspects of Spanish conversation, and one area where prepositions can be used is in directions, whether you are asking for directions – if you're a woman! – or giving them.

Asking and offering directions in Spanish

The thing about Spanish villages and towns is that there seem to be any number of roads in and out of the place. And not all businesses have a shiny new sign above the premises. And of course, if you're on holiday, it's all new to you anyway. So there's bound to come a time when you need to ask directions. Alternatively, someone may stop you in the street to ask directions of you, if you look as if you belong there. Here's how to deal with it.

One word you really need for directions is '***donde***?' (where?) That's the magic key to unlock your directions, whether you're a couple of streets away from your destination, or several kilometres. *Donde* is always paired with **está**, since although you're asking about the fixed whereabouts of a theatre, museum, railway station or whatever, you're talking geographical locations, so the verb you want is *Estar*, rather than *Ser*. So you might well say '*¿Donde está el museo?*' (Where is the museum?)

Directions will involve going straight on (*siga recto* or *todo recto*), turning right or left (*Gire a la derecha/ a la izquierda*), and negotiating roundabouts. 'Turn right at the second roundabout' would be '*Gire a la derecha en la segunda rotunda.*' Native speakers may dispense with the '*gire.*'

If the directions involve using a main highway (*autovia*) it's handy to know the word for exit, which is '*salida*'. Spanish highway exits don't follow a regular pattern of numbering, so just because you just passed Salida 730, you can't assume the next *Salida* will be 731. For this reason, exits are usually described by town, village or suburb. It's also worth remembering that just about every highway has directions for the capital, Madrid, so don't automatically assume you have gone wrong when you see

Madrid marked up on the next *Salida* and you're travelling in the opposite direction!

Other useful direction words are *norte* (north), *sur* (south), *este* (east), and *oeste* (west). People won't necessarily use them when giving you directions, but if you're driving into a large town or city, you'll find there are several exits, and knowing the compass points will help you find the most appropriate one.

With just these few words, combined with prepositions and augmented by your vocabulary, you should be able to ask – and give – directions, and, more importantly, understand what is said to you.

Exercises

(formal) - Excuse me, can you tell me where Tour Eiffel is ? • *¿Discúlpeme, podría decirme donde está la Torre Eiffel?* • dis-kul-pe-me po-dree-a de-thir-me don-de es-ta la to-rre ei-fel• dis'kulpeme po'ðria ðe'ө'irme 'ðonde es'ta la 'tore i'fel

(informal) - Excuse me, can you tell me where Tour Eiffel is ? • *Perdón, ¿podrías decirme donde está la Torre Eiffel?* • per-don po-dree-as de-thir-me don-de es-ta la to-rre ei-fel • per'ðon po'ðrias ðe'ө'irme 'ðonde es'ta la 'tore i'fel

Where is the museum? • *¿Donde está el museo?* • don-de es-ta el mu-seo • 'donde es'ta el mu'seo

How can I get there? • *¿Cómo puedo llegar ahí?* • ko-mo pwe-do ie-gar as-ta aee • 'komo 'pweðo je'ɣar a'i

How far is it? • *¿Qué tan lejos es?* • ke tan le-hos es • ke tan 'lexos es

How long does it take on foot ? • *¿Cuánto demoras a pie?* • kwan-to de-mo-ras a pie • 'kwanto ðe'moras a pie

It takes about fifteen minutes • *Lleva unos quince minutos.* • ie-ba un-os kin-the mi-nu-tos a pie• 'jeβa 'unos 'kinөe mi'nutos a pje

What's the address? • *¿Cuál es la dirección?* • kwal es la di-rek-thion • kwal es la ðirek'өjon

(formal) - Turn left / right • *Gire a la izquierda / derecha* • hi-re a la ith-kier-da / de-re-cha • 'xire a la iө'kjerða / ðe'retʃa

(informal) - Turn left / right • *Gira a la izquierda / derecha* • hi-ra a la ith-kier-da / de-re-cha • 'xira a la iө'kjerða / ðe'retʃa

(formal) - Turn at the corner • *Gire en la esquina* • hi-re en la es-ki-na • 'xire en la es'kina

(informal) - Turn at the corner • *Gira en la esquina* • hi-ra en la es-ki-na • 'xira en la es'kina

Far • *Lejos* • le-hos • 'lexos

Near • *Cerca* • ther-ka • 'өerka

In front of • *Enfrente* • en-fren-te • en'frente

Behind • *Atrás* • a-tras • a'tras

Straight on • *Derecho* • de-re-cho • de'retʃo

By train • *En tren* • en tren• en tren

By car • *En auto* • en au-to • en 'awto

By bus • *En bus* • en bus• en bus

On foot • *A pie* • a pie • a pje

Where are the toilets? • *¿Dónde están los baños?* • don-de es-tan los ba-nios • 'donde es'tan los 'βaɲos

Are there are any public toilets nearby please ? • *¿Hay algún baño público cerca, por favor?* • ai al-gun ba-nio pu-bli-ko ther-ka por fa-bor• ai al'ɣun 'βaɲo 'puβliko 'θerka por fa'βor

Where is ...? • *¿Dónde es... ?* • don-de es • 'donde es

Chapter 4 - Personal Pronouns

Let's look at some Spanish Personal Pronouns a little more closely ...

1)   The word *nosotros* – meaning we – is used either by an entirely male group, or by a group containing at least one male.

If the group contains ONLY females, *nosotras* would be used.

So, in Spanish, there are two ways of saying we:

nosotros .... we (masculine or mixed group)

nosotras .... we (purely female group)

2)   The same rules apply to the Spanish equivalent of they:

ellos .... they (when referring to a masculine or mixed group)

ellas .... they (when referring to a purely female group)

3)   Now let's take a look at the various ways of saying you ...

Firstly, Castilian Spanish has formal and familiar forms of the word you.

*Usted is the formal (singular) form, and would be used for addressing strangers/older people/bosses etc, in order to show respect.

*Tú is the familiar (singular) form, and would be used when talking to family/friends/work companions, etc.

These two ways of saying you also have a plural form.

*If addressing more than one person to whom you should show respect, you would use ustedes (ie the plural of usted):

ustedes .... you (formal, plural, masculine or feminine)

*If the people you're addressing are family/friends/acquaintances, you'd use the plural form of tú.

The plural form of *tú* has both masculine and feminine versions:

vosotros .... you (famliar, plural, masculine or mixed group)

vosotras .... you (familiar, plural, purely female group)

To recap on you:

*one friend/family member – *tú*

*one stranger/older person – *usted*

*more than one friend/family member – *vosotros/vosotras*

*more than one stranger/older person – *ustedes*

In the written form, usted can be abbreviated to *Ud* or *Vd*.

Similarly, *ustedes* can be abbreviated to *Uds* or *Vds*.

Exercises

To be (*ser*)

they are - *ellos/ellas son*

you are - *ustedes son / vosotros sois*

To be (*estar*)

they are - *ellos/ellas están*

you are - *ustedes están / vosotros estáis*

To have (*tener*)

they have - *ellos/ellas tienen*

you have - *ustedes tienen / vosotros tenéis*

To live (*vivir*)

they live - *ellos/ellas viven*

you live - *ustedes viven / vosotros vivís*

Chapter 5 - Verbs

Regular -AR Verbs

As with English, Spanish verbs are either regular or irregular.

There are three types of regular verbs in Spanish: those ending in **-AR**, those ending in **-ER**, and those ending in **-IR**.

Examples of the infinitives of verbs in these three categories are:

hablar .... to speak

comer .... to eat

vivir .... to live

Let's concentrate on the first group – regular verbs ending in *-AR* such as *hablar* – and learn how to conjugate it in the Present Indicative Tense.

If you were to conjugate the verb to speak in the Present Tense in English, it would be like this:

to speak (infinitive)

I speak

you (singular) speak

he/she/it speaks

we speak

you (plural) speak

they speak

You've already learnt about Spanish Personal Pronouns and how to use them. Now, you just need to know the verb endings.

The Present Tense of **hablar** - and all regular verbs ending in *-AR* - would be as follows:

Singular

*yo habl**o*** .... I speak

*tú habl**as*** .... you (familiar) speak

*él/ella/Vd habl**a*** .... he/she/you (formal) speak/s

Plural

nosotros/as habl**amos** .... we speak

*vosotros/as habl**áis*** .... you (familiar) speak

*ellos/ellas/Vds habl**an*** .... they/you (formal) speak

You conjugate regular -AR verbs by taking the infinitive (ie to speak) which, in this case is *hablar* and removing the *-AR* ending in order to get the root, which would be:

habl (= hablar – ar)

To this root, you then add the following endings:

-o

-as

-a

-amos

-áis

-an

This results in the full conjugation of the Present Tense, as you saw above. Although we've used hablar as our example, the same rule would apply to any regular verbs which end in -AR.

Regular -ER Verbs

Let's now look at regular verbs ending in *-ER*, taking **comer** (to eat) as the example, and learn how to conjugate that in the Present Tense.

First of all, we'll take the infinitive (to eat) – *comer* – and find the root of the verb by knocking off the -*ER* ending:

com (= *comer* – er)

To this root, add the endings for the Present Tense of regular -ER verbs, as follows:

-o

-es

-e

-emos

-éis

-en

Consequently, the Present Indicative Tense of the verb comer would be:

Singular

yo com**o** .... I eat

tú com**es** .... you (familiar) eat

él/ella/Vd com**e** .... he/she/you (formal) eat/s

Plural

nosotros/as com**emos** .... we eat

vosotros/as com**éis** .... you (familiar) eat

ellos/ellas/Vds com**en** .... they/you (formal) eat

These same endings do not just apply to comer but to all regular *-ER* verbs.

Regular -IR Verbs

You know how to conjugate regular *-AR* and *-ER* verbs in the Present Indicative Tense. Now let's look at the last group – verbs ending in *-IR*. We'll take **vivir** (to live) as our example.

Once again, find the root of the verb by removing its ending which, in this case, will leave you with:

viv

Then, depending on the person you wish to speak to, add the endings:

-o

-es

-e

-imos

-ís

-en

In other words, the full Present Tense of the verb *vivir* would be:

Singular

*yo viv**o*** .... I live

*tú viv**es*** .... you (familiar) live

*él/ella/Vd viv**e*** .... he/she/you (formal) live/s

Plural

nosotros/as viv**imos** .... we live

*vosotros/as viv**ís*** .... you (familiar) live

*ellos/ellas/Vds viv**en*** .... they/you (formal) live

Again, the above rules apply to any regular verb ending in -IR.

You now know how to decline all regular verbs in the Present Indicative Tense!

Using Spanish Verbs

1)   Because verb endings vary so much more in Spanish than they do in English, it's not always necessary to use the Personal Pronoun.

For example, you could say:

hablas español .... you speak Spanish

como mucha fruta .... I eat a lot of fruit

vivimos en España .... we live in Spain

None of the above sentences need Personal Pronouns because it's obvious from the ending of the verb who the subject is.

2) It is, however, sometimes necessary to include the Personal Pronoun in order to clarify who it is we're talking about, as in the case of vive. If left on its own, it could mean he/she lives or you live. Therefore, you'd include the Personal Pronoun:

él vive

ella vive

Vd vive

However, very often in conversation, it's obvious who the subject is and, if this is the case, the Personal Pronoun is not included.

3) Sometimes, Personal Pronouns are included purely to add emphasis:

Yo como carne y tú comes pescado

I eat meat and you eat fish

4) When using two verbs in a row, the first is conjugated, and the second comes in the infinitive:

deseo comer paella .... I wish to eat paella

5) In Spanish, if you wish to imply negation, you simply place the word no before the verb:

el niño no come .... the boy doesn't eat

no hablo español .... I don't speak Spanish

6) If you wish to use the interrogative form and ask a question, you must remember to place a reversed question mark at the beginning of the sentence. If using the verb alone, without the Personal Pronoun, this is all you have to do to form a question in the Present Tense.

For example:

¿Hablas español?.... Do you speak Spanish?

When including the Personal Pronoun, you just reverse the normal position of the verb and the pronoun. For example:

¿Habla Vd español?.... Do you speak Spanish?

As opposed to *Vd habla español,* which would mean you speak Spanish.

Common Regular -AR Verbs

As you now know how to decline the Present Tense of regular -AR verbs, here's a list of 25 for you to practise with them!

alquilar – to rent

ayudar – to help

bailar – to dance

buscar – to look for

comprar – to buy

contestar – to answer

dejar – to allow, to leave

entrar (*in*) – to enter (into)

enviar – to send

esperar – to hope, to wait for

ganar – to earn, to win

gastar – to spend

llegar – to arrive

llevar – to wear, to carry

mirar – to look at, to watch

necesitar – to need

olvidar – to forget

pagar – to pay, to pay for

preguntar – to ask

preparar – to prepare

regresar – to return

tomar – to take, to drink

trabajar – to work

viajar – to travel

visitar – to visit

Common Regular -ER Verbs

And, here's a list of 25 regular -ER verbs with which to experiment!

aprender – to learn

beber – to drink

ceder – to give in

comer – to eat

cometer – to commit

comprender – to understand

correr – to run

creer – to believe

deber – to have to, to owe

depender (*de*) – to depend (on)

esconder – to hide

exceder – to exceed

leer – to read

meter (en) – to put (into)

ofender – to offend

poseer – to possess

proceder – to procede, to come from

prometer – to promise

proveer – to provide

responder – to reply

romper – to break

sorprender – to surprise

temer – to fear

vender – to sell

Common Regular -IR Verbs

To finish off with, here you have 25 regular -IR verbs.

abrir – to open

admitir – to admit

asistir (a) – to attend (to)

confundir – to confuse

cubrir – to cover

decidir – to decide

describir – to describe

descubrir – to discover

discutir – to argue, to discuss

dividir – to divide

*escribir – to write

evadir – to evade

existir – to exist

fundir – to melt

hundir – to sink

imprimir – to print

ocurrir – to happen

omitir – to omit

partir – to leave, to divide

permitir – to allow, to permit

recibir – to receive

subir – to go up, to come up

unir – to unite

vivir – to live

In the following exercises, you have to complete either the conjugated verb or the corresponding pronoun:

I am Ana´s best friend - … *soy la mejor amiga de Ana*

You are a great boss - Usted … *un gran jefe*

He is a very smart boy - Él … *un muchacho muy inteligente*

We are the best - ……… *los mejores*

You guys are always fighting - Ustedes ………. *siempre peleando*

They are the greatest scientists in their generation - ………. *son las mejores científicas de su generación*

I'm tired - ……. *cansado*

You are prettier each day - ……. *más lindo cada día*

She's sad - ……. *está triste*

We are in danger - ……. *en peligro*

You are crazy - Vosotros ……. *locos*

They are coming - ……. *están viniendo*

I'm cold - ………. *frío*

Do you have a lighter? - ¿………. *un encendedor?*

He's afraid - ………. *miedo*

We have what it takes - Nosotros ………. *lo necesario*

I'm OK, but you always have a problem - *Yo estoy bien, pero* ……. *tienen siempre algún problema*

They have a secret - Ellas ………. *un secreto*

I live alone - ………. *solo*

We live two blocks away - ………. *a dos cuadras*

You say she's lying? - ¿………. *que ella está mintiendo?*

They say it's too late - Ellos ………. *que es demasiado tarde*

I'm going to ask you to leave - ………. *a pedirte que te marches*

Let's go dancing! - ¡…………. *a bailar!*

I do what I can - …………. *lo que puedo*

You do the right thing - ………. *hace lo correcto*

We do everything! - ¡Nosotros …………. *todo!*

I love you - *Te* …….

26

We love Peruvian food - .... *la comida peruana*

I can't go - *No .... ir*

He sees what's going on - *Él .... lo que sucede*

I give you everything I have - *Yo te .... todo lo que tengo*

We give our lives for art - .... *nuestras vidas por el arte*

I want to eat something spicy - .... *comer algo picante*

Do you want to dance with me? - *¿............. bailar conmigo?*

They want to travel - *Ellas .... viajar*

Chapter 6 - The Use of Numbers, Colors, Time and Feelings

Counting in Spanish

Let's begin this chapter with the use of numbers. The number system in Spanish is based on a ten base (other languages, such as French, use numbers on a sixty base). This makes the numerical structure of Spanish rather similar to English. The first twenty digits are unique. After twenty, all numbers follow the same pattern until reaching one-hundred. After one-hundred, the same pattern repeats over and over until reaching one-thousand.

Let's have a look at the first ten numbers, including zero.

Spanish	English
0 = cero	Zero
1 = uno	One
2 = dos	Two
3 = tres	Three
4 = cuatro	Four
5 = cinco	Five
6 = seis	Six
7 = siete	Seven
8 = ocho	Eight
9 = nueve	Nine
10 = diez	Ten

Table 1. Numbers from 0 to 10 in Spanish

The first ten digits, plus zero, don't bear much resemblance to each other, though they are structured in the same manner. So, it is a matter of learning each digit accordingly. Arabic numbers are also used. Consequently, there is no problem in expressing numbers in the same manner.

Numbers eleven to twenty in Spanish words are presented in Table 2.

Spanish	English
11 = once	Eleven
12 = doce	Twelve
13 = trece	Thirteen
14 = catorce	Fourteen
15 = quince	Fifteen
16 = dieciseis	Sixteen
17 = diecisiete	Seventeen

18 = dieciocho	Eighteen
19 = diecinueve	Nineteen
20 = veinte	twenty

Table 2. Numbers from 11 to 20 in Spanish

In this list, you can see how each number is spelled out to reflect its combination of digits. In the case of *dieciseis, deicisiete, dieciocho,* and *diecinueve,* you may find that these are spelled as "*diez y seis*" (ten and six), "*diez y siete*" (ten and seven), "*diez y ocho*" (ten and eight), and "*diez y nueve*" (ten and nine). These are accepted spellings, though they are not usually taught that way. The reason for this is based on a simplified system where remembering the correct spelling of these numbers is a lot easier that way. Nevertheless, you can spell these numbers both ways, which should not make a difference.

One important pronunciation note is that "*quince*" (15) is pronounced as /keen-seh/ and not /kwIns/. So please keep this in mind whenever you are referring to this number.

Next, the numbers for twenty to thirty still have their own particular spelling. Let's have a look.

Spanish	English
21 = veintiuno	Twenty-one
22 = veintidós	Twenty-two
23 = veintitrés	Twenty-three
24 = veinticuatro	Twenty-four
25 = venticinco	Twenty-five
26 = veintiseis	Twenty-six
27 = veintisiete	Twenty-seven
28 = veintiocho	Twenty-eight
29 = veintinueve	Twenty-nine
30 = treinta	thirty

Table 3. Numbers from 21 to 30 in Spanish

With this lot of numbers, you will find that they have a specific spelling. Nevertheless, it is accepted to spell them as "veinte y uno," "veinte y dos," and so on. Ultimately, it is up to you to find the form that is much easier for you. Also, note that "*veintidós*" and "*veintitrés*" carry a tilde for you to recognize the stress on the word's last syllable.

The remaining numbers from 30 onward can be spelled as "treinta y uno" and so on. This makes it rather easy to spell out the remaining numbers up to one-hundred. Here is a list of the remaining numbers in order of tens.

Spanish	English
40 = cuarenta	Forty
50 = cincuenta	Fifty
60 = sesenta	Sixty
70 = setenta	Seventy

80 = ochenta	Eighty
90 = noventa	Ninety
100 = cien	One hundred
200 = doscientos	Two hundred
300 = trescientos	Three hundred
1000 = mil	One thousand

Table 4. Numbers from 40 to 1000 in Spanish

In this chart, you will notice how each ten is based on a single digit. So, "*cuatro*" becomes "*cuarenta*" and so on. Also, one hundred is spelled out as "*cien*". However, when combined with the remaining digits, the numbers would work out a "*ciento uno*" (101), "*ciento dos*" (102), and so on. What this means is that you can combine "ciento" with any other number. As such, "*ciento treinta y nueve*" (139) can be spelled out just like the earlier ones.

Also, "*mil*" is one thousand and can be combined as follows:

- *Diez mil* (ten thousand)
- *Cien mil* (one-hundred thousand)
- *Un millón* (one million)
- *Diez millones* (ten million)
- *Mil millones* (one billion)

Notice how "billion" is expressed as a "thousand million," though it is possible to say "*un billon.*" Both forms would be understood, though "thousand million" would be more suitable for a formal business context.

Describing With Colors

Next, we have colors. One very important note about numbers is that, like all adjectives, colors are subject to the masculine-feminine agreement, as well as singular and plural agreement. This means that you need to make sure that the color agrees with the subject you are talking about.

First, let's have a list of the most commonly used colors.

Spanish	English
Amarillo	Yellow
Anaranjado	Orange
Azul	Blue
Blanco	White
Gris	Grey
Marron	Brown
Morado	Purple

Negro	Black
Rojo	Red
Rosado	Pink
Verde	Green

Table 5. Most commonly used colors in Spanish

By default, colors are masculine. But when they agree with a feminine subject, their spelling changes. For example, "*vestido rosado*" (pink dress) refers to a masculine noun (vestido). So, "*rosado*" is spelled with an "o" ending. In the case of a feminine noun, "*camisa rosada*" (pink shirt), "*camisa*" is considered feminine. As such, "*rosada*" now has an "a" ending in order to signal that it is feminine and not masculine.

The situation changes somewhat when you factor in singular and plural. So, "*vestidos rosados*" (pink dresses) agrees both in terms of gender and number. The "s" ending indicates that it is plural. In the case of "*camisas rosadas*," the same situation applies.

Notice also that both the adjective and noun must be singular or plural in order to maintain the proper agreement.

There are a couple of exceptions, though. *Azul, gris, verde*, and *marrón* do not change in terms of gender but do agree in terms of number. So, "*botas grises*" (grey boots), where "*botas*" is feminine plural, would be the same as "*coches grises*" (grey cars), where "*coches*" is masculine plural.

Please keep this in mind, as there are exceptions from time to time. Bear in mind that virtually all adjectives in Spanish have a singular and plural form, even if they are considered uncountable in English. For instance, "*un pan*" (a bread) may refer to individual units of bread in Spanish, where "bread" in uncountable in English.

Also, in Spanish, adjectives come after nouns. So, "*cielo azul*" (blue sky) is the opposite of the proper English syntax. Please keep this in mind so that you can avoid confusing your interlocutors when speaking.

Telling the Time

The next topic covered in this chapter is time.

Time is a rather straightforward topic in Spanish. However, there are a couple of differences.

For starters, time is generally based on a 24-hour clock rather than two, 12-hour clocks. So, the morning hours are expressed from "*cero horas*" (zero hours, or midnight) to "*doce horas*" (twelve hours, or midday). After midday, time is expressed as "*trece horas*" (thirteen hours), all the way up to "*veinticuatro horas*" or midnight. Once the new day begins, time is then reset to "zero hours." This distinction is made in order to avoid confusion between am and pm times.

For instance, if you have an appointment at 7 o'clock in the evening, you could express it at "*diecinueve horas en punto*" (nineteen hours "on point"). The expression, "on point" is used to indicate that it is the beginning of the hour or "o'clock" in English.

It is also possible to express time on a 12-hour basis. However, it is important to include the specific time of day you are referring to. So, "ten o'clock in the morning" would be "*diez de la mañana*." Afternoon hours would be referred to as "*de la tarde*." For instance, "*cinco de la tarde*" (17:00 or 5 pm) is referring to a time that is past midday.

Now, here is an interesting difference between English and Spanish. Spanish does not account for "evening." As a matter of fact, as soon as the sun goes down and it gets dark, the time then becomes "noche" or night. So, "*seis de la tarde*" would be "six in the afternoon" since the sun doesn't typically finish setting by this time. However, "*siete de la noche*" (seven at night) would be logical since it is normal for it to be dark around this time. So, the rule of thumb is that as soon as it is completely dark, you can begin to use "night."

This also applies to greetings, like "goodnight" or "*buenas noches*", which is the applicable greeting whenever it is completely dark. However, if there is still a twinge of sunlight, then it would still be proper to use "*buenas tardes*" (good afternoon).

Fractional portions of hours also have their own particular expressions.

- "*cuarto*" refers to "quarter." So, "*es un cuarto después de las dos*" (it's a quarter past two) refers to 2:15. "*Un cuarto para las dos*", (a quater to two) refers to 1:45. Please notice the difference in the use of "*después*" (after) and "*para*" (to) when referring to time.

- Also, the use of "*media*" (half) makes it clear that you are talking about half hours. So, "*son las tres y media*" (It is three and a half) is the same as saying "half past," or 30 minutes past the hour.

- Other fractional hours can be expressed using the exact number of minutes. So, "*es la una y venticinco*" (it's one twenty-five) refers to 1:25.

- Please notice that hours are always expressed in the plural form, except for one. Hours are feminine, but minutes are masculine. Nevertheless, your expression of time will always make reference to the feminine form and not the masculine form.

When in doubt, you can always refer to time by expressing the numbers themselves. For example, you can say, "*son las cuatro y cinco*" (it's four and five), that is, 4:05. You will not be questioned if you are referring to am or pm when giving the current time, but you might be asked to clarify if you are referring to a future time. So, be sure to use "*de la mañana*," "*de la tarde*," or "*de la noche*" in order to clarify the time of day you are referring to.

Now, let us move on to the days of the week.

- *lunes* (Monday)
- *martes* (Tuesday)
- *miércoles* (Wednesday)
- *jueves* (Thursday)
- *viernes* (Friday)
- *sábado* (Saturday)
- *domingo* (Sunday)

Please note that the days of the week are not capitalized in Spanish. In fact, they are written in lowercase letters. For example, "*hoy es lunes*" (Today is Monday) illustrates how the days of the week are not capitalized.

Also, here are the months of the year.

- *enero* (January)

- *febrero* (February)

- *marzo* (March)

- *abril* (April)

- *mayo* (May)

- *junio* (June)

- *julio* (July)

- *agosto* (August)

- *septiembre* (September)

- *octubre* (October)

- *noviembre* (November)

- *diciembre* (December)

Just like the days of the week, months are not written with capitals. So, a formal date such as "*lunes, tres de septiembre*" (Monday, September third) would not be expressed in capitals. Also, please note that dates are written out in nominal number and not in ordinal numbers like in the case of English.

With regard to years, there is no split between the digits of a year. For example, the year "2010" would be "*dos mil diez*," that is, "two thousand ten." So, keep this in mind any time you are talking about a year.

Here are some examples:

- 1991 (*mil novecientos noventa y uno* – one thousand nine hundred and ninety-one)

- 2002 (*dos mil dos* – two thousand two)

- 1885 (*mil ochocientos ochenta y cinco* – one thousand eight hundred and eighty-five)

Keep this important difference in mind when talking about years.

Expressing Feelings

The last item in this chapter refers to feelings.

Generally speaking, feelings are adjectives, which agree in gender and number. This implies that you need to be aware if you are talking about yourself or others in the singular and/or plural form.

As such, a question such as "*¿Cómo estás?*" (how are you?) can be replied with:

- *Estoy bien.* (I am fine)

- Estoy cansado/a (I am tired)

- *Estoy feliz* (I am happy)

Notice how "*feliz*" does not have a gender agreement but would have a plural agreement as "*feliz*" (singular) and "*felices*" (happy in plural form).

Here is a list of the most common feelings in the Spanish language.

Spanish	English
Feliz	Happy
Enamorado/a	In love
Aburrido/a	Bored
Cansado/a	Tired
Asustado/a	Scared
Enojado/a	Angry
Celoso/a	Jealous
Sorprendido/a	Surprised
Contento/a	Happy, satisfied
Nervioso/a	Nervous
Ocupado/a	Busy
Preocupado/a	Worried
Furioso/a	Furious
Triste	Sad
Avergonzado/a	Embarrassed
Optimista	Optimistic
Relajado/a	Relaxed
Fatal	Terrible, awful

Table 6. Most commonly used colors in Spanish

Notice how most of the adjectives are presented as "*o/a*" in order to indicate their masculine or feminine form. There are a couple of exceptions, such as "*feliz*," "*triste*," and "*optimista*," which do not have a specific gender form. So, please make sure to use them without changing their ending. Nevertheless, they do have a singular and plural form. So, make sure to keep this in mind.

Chapter 7 - Nature, Animals and Geography

Plants

¿Te gusta la jardinería? (Do you like gardening?)

¿Te gusta la naturaleza? (Do you like nature?)

In case you have to buy flowers for someone, or you are going for a nature walk, let's learn some vocabulary to be able to talk about plants.

Spanish	English
Flor	Flower
Flores	Flowers
Árbol	Tree
Árboles	Trees
Un ramo de flores	A bouquet of flowers
Rosas	Roses
Margaritas	Daisies
Amapolas	Poppies
Plantas	Plants
Hierba	Grass
Césped	Lawn
Planta de interior	Indoor plant
Planta de exterior	Outdoor plant
Árbol de Navidad	Christmas's tree

Let's put now these words in sentences:

¿Cuál es tú flor favorita? (What is your favourite flower?)

Mi flor favorita es la rosa (My favourite flower is roses)

Quisiera un ramo de flores, por favor (I would like a bouquet of flowers, please)

El jardín de la escuela está lleno de flores amarillas y anaranjas (School's garden is plenty of yellow and orange flowers)

El campo está lleno de margaritas y amapolas (Countryside is plenty of daisies and poppies)

Margarita es también un nombre de mujer en español (Margarita is also a women's name in Spanish)

En la Toscana hay muchas amapolas (There are a lot of poppies in Tuscany)

No tengo ninguna planta en casa (I do not have any plant at home)

Mi gato muerde las plantas (My cat bites the plants)

Tengo que cortar la hierba del jardín (I need to cut the garden's grass)

Han cambiado el césped del campo de futbol (They have changed football field grass)

Wimbledon se juega en pista de hierba (Wimbledon is played on lawn's court)

Mi árbol de Navidad es de plástico reciclado (My Christma's tree is made from recycled plastic)

¿Puedes recomendarme una planta de interior? (Can you advise me any indoor plant?)

Es una planta de interior muy bonita, gracias (It's an indoor plant very beautiful, thanks)

Es una planta de exterior así que la pondré en el jardín (It's an outdoor plant so I'm going to put it in the garden)

¿Me ayudas a decorar el árbol de Navidad? (Can you help me to decorate the Christmas's tree?)

Animals (farm, sea, pets etc)

¿Te gustan los animales? (Do you like animals?)

¿Cuál es tú animal favorito? (What is your favourite animal?)

¿Tienes mascota? (Do you have pets?)

Vamos a aprender vocabulario sobre animales. (Let's learn some vocabulary about animals!)

Animales de granja (Farm animals)

Spanish	English
vaca	Cow
caballo	horse
cerdo	Pig
gallo	Rooster
gallina	Hen
oveja	Sheep
cabra	Goat
conejo	Rabbit
burro	Donkey
pato	Duck

Some sentences:

La vaca es grande (The cow is big)

El caballo es blanco (The horse is white)

El cerdo está gordo (The pig is fat)

El gallo y la gallina están durmiendo (The rooster and the hen are both sleeping)

La oveja está comiendo (The sheep is eating)

La cabra salta la roca (The goat jumps over the rock)

El conejo está escondido (The rabbit is hidden)

El burro está enfadado (The donkey is angry)

El pato está nadando (The duck is swimming)

¿Qué es una mascota? (What is a pet?)

¿Crees que todos los animales pueden ser mascotas? (Do you think all animals can be pets?)

Vamos a ver una lista de las mascotas más típicas (Let's take a look on this list of most typical pets):

Spanish	English
perro	dog
gato	cat
tortuga	turtle
Pez	fish
conejillo de Indias	guinea pig
lagarto	lizard
serpiente	snake
hamster	Hamster
conejo	rabbit

Let's practice the following sentences about pets:

Mi perro se llama Bombón (My dog's name is Bombon)

Soy alérgico a los gatos (I'm allergic to cats)

De pequeño tenía una tortuga (When I was a kid, I had a turtle)

El pez de Alfredo es naranja (Alfredo's fish is Orange)

Tengo dos conejillos de indias (I have two guinea pigs)

No me gustan los lagartos (I do not like lizards)

Me dan miedo las serpientes (I'm scared of snakes)

A mi hermana no le gustan los hamsters (My sister doesn't like hamsters)

Hemos adoptado un conejo (We have adopted a rabbit)

¿Y tú? ¿Tienes mascota? (And you? Do you have a pet?)

Now practice these tongue-twisters about animals.

"El perro de San Roque no tiene rabo porque Ramon Rodriguez se lo ha robado" (San Roque's dog hasn't got a tail because Ramon Rodriguez stole it)

"Tres tristes tigres comen trigo de un trigal" (Three sad tigers eat wheat from a wheatgrass)

Note: In Spanish a tongue-twister is called "*trabalenguas*".

Más animals (More animals):

Spanish	English
tigre	tiger
león	lion
elefante	elephant
jirafa	giraffe
rinoceronte	rhino
cocodrilo	crocodile
ballena	whale
delfín	dolphin
tiburón	shark
foca	seal
pulpo	octopus
oso	bear
camello	camel
leopardo	leopard

Let's make sentences about animals:

El tigre tiene rayas (Tiger has stripes)

El león vive en la sabana (Lion lives in the savannah)

El elefante africano tiene las orejas muy grandes (African elephant has a very large ears)

La jirafa corre deprisa (Giraffe runs fast)

El rinoceronte tiene dos cuernos (Rhinos have two hornes)

El cocodrilo es un animal muy peligroso (Crocodiles are very dangerous animals)

La ballena azul es el animal más grande de la Tierra (The blue whale is the biggest animal of the Earth)

El delfín es un animal muy inteligente (Dolphin is a very intelligent animal)

El tiburón más pequeño mide unos veinte centímetros (The smallest shark measures around twenty centimetres)

Hay focas en el ártico (There are seals in the Artic)

En España puedes comer pulpo (In Spain you can eat octopus)

No hay muchos osos en el Pirineo (There aren't many bears in the Pyrenees)

Hay camellos en el desierto (There are camels in the desert)

Los leopardos son más pequeños que los tigres (Leopards are smaller than tigers)

Geography and Landscapes

Now let's learn some useful vocabulary about geography and landscape.

Spanish	English
lago	lake
latitud	latitude
llano	plain
longitud	longitude
bosque	forest
cabo	cape
campo	countryside
cascada	waterfall
continente	continent
costa	coast
desierto	desert
mapa	map
estanque	pond
golfo	gulf
hemisferio	hemisphere
isla	island
mar	sea
montaña	mountain
océano	ocean
playa	beach
prado	meadow
puerto	port
río	river
tierra	land
universo	universe
valle	valley
volcán	volcano
norte	North
sur	South
este	East
oeste	West
país	country
ciudad	city
pueblo	village
barrio	borough

Let's see now examples using these words:

El agua del lago está muy fría (Lake's water is very cold)

La latitud especifica si un sitio está en el norte o en el sur (Latitude specifies if a place is in the North or the South)

El paseo es fácil porque es llano (The walk is easy because is plain)

La longitud especifica si un sitio está en el este o en el oeste. (Longitude specifies if a place is in the east or the west)

Gibraltar está en un cabo (Gibraltar is situated in a cape)

Prefiero vivir en el campo que en la ciudad (I prefer living in the countryside than in the city)

Las cascadas del Niágara son muy famosas (Niagara waterfalls are very famous)

Asia es el continente más grande (Asia is the biggest continent)

Este verano viajaremos por la costa (This summer we'll be traveling along the coast)

En el desierto hace mucho calor (It's very hot in the desert)

¿Has encontrado el mapa? (Have you found the map?)

Hay peces en el estanque (There are fishes in the pond)

El golfo de México es el golfo más grande del mundo (Mexico's gulf is the biggest gulf in the world)

Argentina está en el hemisferio sur (Argentina is in the south hemisphere)

Mallorca es una isla (Majorca is an island)

El Mar Muerto tiene mucha sal (The Death Sea has a lot of salt)

Me gusta ir a la montaña a esquiar (I like going to the mountain to sky)

El océano ártico es muy frio (The Arctic Ocean is very cold)

Hay mucha gente en la playa cuando hace buen tiempo (There are a lot of people on the beach when the weather is nice)

La granja está situada en un prado (The farm is placed in a meadow)

Siempre hay muchos barcos en el puerto de Barcelona (There are always a lot of ships in the Barcelona's port)

Este río es muy largo (This is a very long river)

Hay mucha tierra sin ninguna edificación (There is a lot of land without any building)

Es universo es enorme (The universe is huge)

El campamento está en un valle (The camp is in a valley)

En Islandia hay volcanes (There are volcanoes in Iceland)

Canadá está en el hemisferio norte (Canada is in the north hemisphere)

Estados Unidos está al sur de Canadá (USA is at the south of Canada)

China está al oeste de Canadá (China is at the west of Canada)

Inglaterra está al este de Canadá (England is at the East of Canada)

Rusia es el país más grande del mundo (Russia is the largest country in the world)

Vivo en esta ciudad desde que nací (I live in this city since I was born)

Vamos a un pueblo que está cerca de la ciudad (We're going to a village that is near to the city)

Mi barrio es seguro para vivir (My borough is safe for living)

Towns (main towns and capitals around the globe)

¿Dónde vives? (Where do you live?)

Would you know how to say your city in Spanish? For example, London is *Londres* in Spanish.

Many sites keep their name unchanged in English and Spanish (or other languages), however there are also a lot in which, names will be translated (generally slightly).

Vamos a ver como se llaman algunas ciudades en español. (Let's see how to tell some cities in Spanish!)

Spanish	English
Atenas	Athens
Bucarest	Bucharest
El Cairo	Cairo
Ciudad del Cabo	Cape Town
Copenhague	Copenhagen
Florencia	Florence
Ginebra	Geneve
La Habana	Havana
Estambul	Istambul
Lisboa	Lisbon
Londres	London
Luxemburgo	Luxembourg
La Meca	Mecca
Moscu	Moscow
Nueva Delhi	New Delhi
Nueva Orleans	New Orleans
Nueva York	New York
Filadelfia	Philadelphia
Praga	Prague
Estocolmo	Stockholm
Tokio	Tokyo
Túnez	Tunisia
Varsovia	Warsaw

Note: Although names keep unchanged (or largely similar), pronunciation can be very different.

Let's see some examples:

Atenas fue la capital de la antigua Grecia (Athens was the capital of the Ancient Greece)

Nuestra estancia en Bucarest fue encantadora (Our stay in Bucharest was lovely)

No dejes de visitar el museo egipcio cuando vayas a El Cairo (Be sure to visit the Egyptian museum when you go to Cairo)

Hacer submarinismo en Ciudad del Cabo fue una experiencia inolvidable (Diving in Cape Town was an unforgetable experience)

Tenías razón, Copenhague es una ciudad muy limpia (You were right, Copenhagen is a very clean city)

Toda la ciudad de Florencia es como un museo (The whole city of Florence is like a museum)

En Ginebra se encuentran las mejores fábricas de relojes (In Geneve can be found the best watches' factories)

La música es parte esencial del alma de La Habana (Music is an essential part of Havana's soul)

Estambul conecta Oriente con Occidente (Istanbul connects East with West)

Las cafeterías en Lisboa son un lugar perfecto para relajarse (Lisbon's cafés are the perfect place to relax)

Londres es la ciudad europea que recibe más turistas (London is the European city that receives more tourists)

Luxemburgo es uno de los estados más pequeños del mundo (Luxembourg is one of the smallest states in the world)

Me dijo que tenía que visitar La Meca al menos una vez en la vida (He told me that I had to visit Mecca at least once in my life)

Moscú es una de las ciudades más caras del mundo (Moscow is one of the most expensive cities in the world)

Si no has estado en Nueva Delhi, no conoces la India (If you haven't been in New Delhi, you don't know India)

Si te gusta la música en vivo, no dejes de visitar los clubes de Nueva Orleans (If you like live music, be sure to visit New Orleans' clubs)

Por muchas razones, Nueva York es una ciudad muy cinematográfica (Due to several reasons, New York is a very cinematographic city)

Tom Hanks ganó el óscar protagonizando "Filadelfia" (Tom Hanks won the Oscar starring in "Philadelphia")

La invasión de turistas en pequeñas ciudades como Praga se está convirtiendo en un gran problema (Tourists invasion in small cities like Prague is becoming a big issue)

Algunas personas consideran Estocolmo como la ciudad más bonita de Europa (Some people consider Stockholm as the most beautiful city in Europe)

La ciudad con más habitantes del planeta es Tokio (The city with more habitants in the planet is Tokyo)

Muchas escenas de 'La guerra de las galaxias' fueron rodadas en Túnez (Many scenes from 'Star Wars' were filmed in Tunisia)

Por su ubicación estratégica, Varsovia ha sufrido mucho en todos los conflictos europeos del siglo XX (Because of its strategic location, Warsaw has suffered a lot during all the European conflicts on the 20th century)

Now is your turn. Try to say the following cities in Spanish:

Cairo (*El Cairo*)

Florence (*Florencia*)

Copenhagen (*Copenhagen*)

Tunis (*Túnez*)

Geneve (*Ginebra*)

New York (*Nueva York*)

Istambul (*Estambul*)

Moscow (*Moscú*)

Chapter 8 - Education

School vs. Online Education.

Educación.

Escuelas vs Educación en línea:

PART 1.

¿La educación es importante? Creo que todo el mundo diría Sí, pero ¿se piensa lo mismo de las escuelas? ¿La escuela es importante? En el pasado, el mejor lugar para aprender era en la escuela, pero ahora Internet ha cambiado todo. Existen cursos en línea para todo. Tú puedes estudiar casi cualquier tema o materia que desees. Incluso puedes conseguir que un profesor te enseñe por Skype.

English:

Is education important? I think everyone would say Yes. But what about school? Is school important? In the past, the best place to learn was in school. But now the internet has changed everything. There are now online courses for everything. You can study almost any topic and subject you want to. You can even get a teacher to teach you on Skype.

Vocabulary:

Educación: Education.

- Example: *La educación es importante porque ayuda a las personas a tener una buena vida.* (Education is important because it helps people live a good life).

Aprender: To learn.

- Example: *Tú puedes aprender mucho de la lectura.* (You can learn a lot from reading.)

Curso: A course.

- Example: *Yo hice un curso de ciencia en línea.* (I did an online science course.)

Estudiar: To study.

- Example: *Yo estudio ciencias en la escuela.* (I study science at school.)

Tema/Materia: A topic/subject.

- Example: *Ciencias es mi materia favorita.* (Science is my favourite subject.)

Profesor: A teacher.

- Example: *A mí me agrada mi profesor de ciencias.* (I like my science teacher.)

Enseñar: To teach.

- Example: *Voy a enseñarle a mi amiga a conducir porque ella aún no sabe.* (I will teach my friend how to drive because she doesn't know how.)

PART 2.

Incluso puedes hacer grados universitarios en línea. Puedes realizar el plan de estudios completo sin necesidad de entrar en un aula. La única diferencia es que no hay periodos o semestres. Así que puedes estudiar tan rápido o tan lento como desees. Sin embargo, tal vez tendrás que hacer el examen en la universidad.

English:

You can even do university degrees online. You can do the full curriculum without even going into a classroom. The only difference is that there are no terms or semesters. So you can study as quickly or slowly as you want. You may have to take the exam at the university though.

Vocabulary:

Universidad: University.

- Example: *Yo estudié ciencias en la universidad.* (I studied science at university.)

Grado universitario: (A university) degree.

- Example: *Yo obtuve un grado universitario en ciencias. Ahora voy a hacer mi maestría.* (I got a degree in science. Now, I'm going to do a Masters degree.)

Plan de estudios: A (school) curriculum.

- Example: *El plan de estudios es algo difícil porque hay muchas materias.* (The curriculum is quite difficult because there are many subjects.)

Aula: A classroom.

- Example: *El profesor se para en frente del aula.* (The teacher stands at the front of the classroom.)

Periodo (académico): A term.

- Example: *Hay 3 periodos en el año.* (There are 3 terms in a year.)

Semestre: A semester.

- Example: *Las universidades generalmente tienen 2 semestres, en otoño y en primavera.* (Universities usually have two semesters, autumn and spring.)

Examen: An exam.

- Example: *Al final del curso hice un examen.* (At the end of the course I took an exam.)

Chapter 9 - How to Write in Spanish

Writing and speaking are very similar to each other in that they require a lot more active participation from the learner. You have to create your own speech, generate your own grammatical awareness, and focus on little things like word order and spelling.

Reading and listening are important skills to have and they provide necessary input (something we've discussed previously). Writing and speaking, however, take that input you've received and turn it into your own personal output, therefore helping to solidify the concepts and vocabulary in your mind.

Writing in Spanish is a wonderful tool and will help improve various other skills you've been working on. When you write, you have to read what you're writing (practice your reading). You can read it out loud (practice your speaking) and focus on your pronunciation and how the words sounds (practice your listening).

This chapter is going to focus on writing, discussing the benefits, as well as some tips, to ensure that you're getting the most out of this integral skill.

Benefits of Writing in Spanish

Writing can be tedious and it's not always the most enjoyable of activities, especially when thinking about writing in Spanish. It is, however, a very important skill to have. We use writing every day, way more often than we may even realize. All those text messages and emails you send are written. Those reminders you put in your phone or scribble onto post-it notes? These little, casual ways of writing are precisely where you can start when looking for chances to practice this skill in Spanish.

If you can't find a Spanish conversation partner, you should try to find a pen pal. Maybe someone in one of your Spanish classes you can send text messages to or email back and forth with. You can write out your to-do lists or leave yourself reminders in Spanish.

Writing in Spanish is beneficial, not only because it's something that draws on the other areas of the language that you will want to work on, but also because it is a daily part of life. If you plan on using your Spanish for work, you'll need to write emails. If you're learning Spanish for pleasure, you'll surely find yourself wanting to meet and communicate with native speakers, via Facebook, email, WhatsApp, etc.

Let's take a look at ways that you can practice and perfect your writing ability.

Write to Other People

As you may have discovered when we were talking about speaking, having a network of Spanish-speakers (or Spanish language learners) around you is extremely beneficial. Well, this is also true when talking about writing.

Write to Yourself

What's that word we keep using when talking about learning Spanish? A habit? Well, surprise, surprise, here it comes again! Creating a habit of writing in Spanish on a regular basis can be the key to success when mastering this specific skill. A writing habit can be created by writing little things in Spanish every day. This doesn't mean it has to be full sentences. Maybe it's a to-do list. Maybe it's a quick reminder to yourself to pay the gas bill. Whatever it is, writing in Spanish is a great way to commit vocabulary to memory and to ensure that you're using what you've learned on a regular basis.

Keep a Journal

This doesn't mean you have to write a daily "Dear Diary" entry. What we're talking about here is just a small notebook and daily habit of writing down a handful of things. Start by writing the day of the week, the month, etc. to practice with that basic vocabulary. Then, write out three little bullet points. What did you do that day? What good thing happened (everyone can benefit from some positive reflection at the end of every day)? You don't need to document your entire life, just simply make it a point to write something down in Spanish every day.

Write Yourself Daily Reminders

Do you live in a sea of post-it notes? Why not make that a sea of Spanish? Similarly, do you find yourself typing out a lot of reminders in your phone? Type them out in Spanish. Everyone needs a little help keeping track of all of the things that we need to do every day. If you start keeping track of those things in Spanish, you already have a built-in habit in the making.

Put Your Phone, Calendar, Facebook in Spanish

On the surface, this tip is something that will help with your reading. But if you take the extra step to continue with the Spanish vibe, you will be able to carry this very useful tool over to help with your writing skills. When you're penciling in your dinner with friends on your calendar write it down in Spanish. Setting your alarm for the morning? Type in a quick note to yourself in Spanish reminding you of anything important that you're doing that day.

Write Your Lists in Spanish

This is a wonderful way to really put all that vocabulary you've been studying into practice. Writing out your to-do lists in Spanish will help you review daily chores and household items vocabulary. Food vocabulary is something that you will want to be familiar with, especially if you plan on traveling in a Spanish-speaking country (being able to read a menu may save you some interesting experiences you'd rather not have). Write out your shopping list in Spanish.

Read, Then Write

We've talked a little about taking notes when reading. At that point, we talked about how it will help to check your reading comprehension. What we didn't say was how much it will help with other areas of your language learning, as well.

When you read something in Spanish, you may not realize it, but you are being exposed to a whole slew of useful, beneficial, and necessary input--word order, masculine/feminine, verb conjugations, object pronouns, etc. Being familiar with all of these things will not only make reading easier and speaking more natural, but they will surely help your writing as well.

After you read a passage, find a sentence or phrase that really "speaks to you". This doesn't mean it has to move you on an emotional level. Maybe it's something that contains one of those tricky verb conjugations you've been working with or perfectly puts that one vocabulary word into a context you feel you would actually use it in in the future. Then, take the time to write out this chunk of text. The best way to do this, honestly, is the good ol' fashioned pen and paper method. This is simply because it has been proven that the muscle memory that comes with writing helps the brain absorb and retain the information better than simply typing it up on a computer or into a "page" on our phone.

Don't just stop with writing out that one sentence or phrase, however. Chances are they caught your attention for a reason. Take what is said in that text and rewrite it again in your own words or write out a summary of what was happening around that section so you can remember it better later.

This doesn't have to just be limited to passages from a book. You could find a song that you really like or a scene from a movie that really drew you in.

Copying or writing things out is a good idea because it pulls on several different skills at the same time (reading OR listening OR both, then writing). Here are some ideas for things you may find yourself wanting to write down:

- Song lyrics

- Passages from a favorite book/poem

- Inspirational quotes

- Recipes

- Information about things that interest you--fun facts or statistics, sports terminology or medical terms

Write, Then Speak

If you want to proofread what you've written, short of sending it off to someone else to check, the best way to find any mistakes is through reading what you've written out loud. After you've finished writing out your to-do list, your daily journal, or you interpretations/reactions to your favorite song, take a moment to read them out loud to yourself. This is your chance to check for grammar, spelling, or vocabulary mistakes.

When reading over your writing, you should ask yourself the following questions:

- Are my sentences too short or choppy? One thing you will notice, quickly, is that in Spanish, sentences tend to be longer than we would normally have in English. Compare your sentence length/style to that of the ones in your authentic texts you've been reading.

- Have I incorporated nuances or liaisons in the correct way, in the correct place?

- Have I paid attention to the cardinal rule: AGREE, AGREE, AGREE (subject/verb, gender, number)?

- Is my word order correct (i.e. noun THEN adjective)?

- Do my ideas flow together? (Am I using the correct linking words?--see the section below.)

Learn "Real" Spanish

Reading the Quijote is one thing. Typing a text to your friend is another. You will notice as you go through your journey into the Spanish language that, like in English, there is a formal and an informal way of speaking or writing. Becoming familiar with both styles of Spanish is the difference between saying, "I'm spending time with my friends" or "I'm hanging out with my friends" in English. You will be understood no matter which of the options you say but you can imagine the trouble one might come across if they aren't familiar with the more colloquial expression "hang out" especially when speaking to natives.

Let's take a moment to look at some of the things you probably won't find in textbooks but should form a part of your Spanish language writing (and speaking!).

Idioms

Idioms are fun, usually comical, expressions that you can throw into your writing to add a little bit of a light-hearted, humorous feel to what you're saying. What makes these little expressions difficult is that they don't always translate directly to English. Here are some examples of very commonly used, non-translatable Spanish idioms.

Spanish Idiom	Meaning in English	Direct Translation
Estar como una cabra	To be crazy/to be acting out of the ordinary	To be like a goat
Echar agua al mar	"Preaching to the choir"	Throw water to the sea
No tener pelos en la lengua	To not have a filter/to speak your mind	To not have hairs on your tongue.
Tomarle el pelo	To pull someone's leg	To pull his/her/your/etc. hair.
Pillarle el toro	To run out of time	To be caught by the bull
Eramos pocos y parió la abuela	When it rains it pours	We were few, and grandma had a baby

Chapter 10 - Asking Everyday Questions

Asking Questions

Here is a list of important question words. You have already learned some of them as you go along, so those should be a review. Study the pronunciations and meanings below then read some common questions you can make with them.

Qué /kay/- what

Quién /kee-in/- who

Cuándo /cwan-do/- when

Cuánto /cwan-to/- how much/how many

Cómo /co-mo/- how

Dónde /don-day/- where

Por qué /por-kay/- why

¿Qué te gusta hacer?

Me gusta mirar la televisión y andar en bicicleta.

¿Cuánto cuestan las fresas?

Las fresas cuestan diez dólares.

¿Quién es?

Es mi amiga, Sara.

¿Cómo estás?

Estoy mal.

¿Cuándo es la reunión?

La reunión es a las cuatro.

¿Dónde estás?

Estoy en el parque.

¿Por qué tienes un libro?

Porque necesito estudiar.

Because "*porque*" is both because and why, you can answer questions that use "*porque*" with "*porque*."

If you are asking a "yes" or "no" question, you just say the sentence as you would a declaration. The only thing that changes is your inflection. There is no "is" or "does" to be put at the front to make it into a question. Look at the sentence and question examples below.

Marta es mi amiga. -I am declaring that she is my friend, telling people what I already know.

¿Marta es mi amiga? -At the end of this sentence, your voice should go up slightly to indicate that it is a question.

Es mi amiga Marta. -The subject can be a bit fluid in Spanish, and this is another perfectly fine way to state the fact.

¿Es mi amiga Marta?- Because you can state the fact like this, you can also ask the question like this.

No tienes hermanos.- I am stating a fact. You don't have siblings.

¿No tienes hermanos?- Now, I am asking.

In English, we use similar inflection when asking questions, so recognizing the spoken question should not be too difficult. Recognizing a written question is also made easy by the question mark at both the beginning and the end of a question.

Activity 1. Read the following situations and write a question for each one. Suggested questions are given below. You can also write example answers.

1. You want to know if your friend has your favorite food.
2. You want to know where your dad is.
3. You want to know when your Spanish class is.
4. You want to know how much something costs.
5. You want to know who the girl is.

Answers:

1. *¿Tienes carne?*

   Si, tengo carne.

2. *¿Dónde está mi padre?*

   Tu padre está en su trabajo.

3. *¿Cuándo es mi clase de español?*

   Es a las tres y media.

4. *¿Cuánto cuestan los huevos?*

   Cuestan ocho córdobas.

5. *¿Quién es la niña?*

   La niña es mi hermana.

Activity 2. Write answers for the following questions. Suggested answers are written below.

1. *¿Quién eres?*
2. *¿Qué te gusta hacer?*
3. *¿Dónde estás?*
4. *¿Cuándo te despiertas?* (you wake up)
5. *¿Cuándo te duermes?* (you sleep)
6. *¿Cómo eres?* (Remember that when this form of "*ser*" is used instead of "*estar*," it isn't asking how you are but rather for you to describe your characteristics).

Suggested Answers:

1. *Yo soy Madelyn.*
2. *Me gusta ir al parque y me gusta visitar a mis amigos.*
3. *Estoy en mi casa.*
4. *Me despierto a las cuatro y media de la mañana.*
5. *Me duermo a las nueve de la noche.*
6. *Yo soy baja y rubia.*

What You Do- Talking about Your Vocation

Career Vocabulary

Do you use "*ser*" or "*estar*" to talk about profession? Ser. Even though your profession can change, it is closer to "permanent" than "temporary" which is why we use the verb that is usually used for more permanent things. Below are some common professions and pronunciations.

Trabajo /trah-bah-ho/- work or job

Abogado /ah-bo-gah-do/- lawyer

Constructor /cun-strook-tor/- construction worker

Bombero /bohm-bear-oh/- fireman

Camarero /cahm-ah-rare-oh/- waiter

Dentista /den-tees-tuh/- dentist

Maestro /mah-ase-tro/- teacher

Piloto /pee-lo-to/- pilot

Peluquero /peh-loo-care-oh/- hairdresser

Médico /med-ee-co/- doctor

Secretario /seh-creh-tar-ee-oh/- secretary

Mecánico /meh-cahn-ee-co/- mechanic

Ingeniero /in-hen-ee-air-oh/- engineer

Jardinero /har-dee-nare-oh/- gardener

Cocinero /coh-see-nare-oh/- cook

Enfermero /en-fare-mare-oh/- nurse

Traductor /trah-dook-tor/- translator

Policía /po-lee-see-uh/- policeman/woman

Of the above professions, most of them can be changed to the femenine form by substituting the "o" on the end of "a." Of course, if it is fememine, you would use "*la*" instead of "*el*" at the beginning. "*Dentista*" and "*policia*" always have an "a" on the end whether it is a male or female. Look at the two sentences below.

La policía camina al parque.

El dentista trabaja diez horas.

You can see that the first sentence is talking about a policewoman and the second sentence is talking about a male dentist. The "*la*" or "*el*" is what shows the gender with those that don't change the ending.

With "*traductor*" and "*constructor*" that end in a consonant, you can make them femenine by adding an "*a*" onto the end. See the following two sentences.

El traductor no viene hoy.

La traductora viene a las dos y media.

The first sentence is about a male translator while the second sentence is about a female translator.

Asking and Answering about Jobs

There are several ways people might ask you about your job. Here are a few of the questions they might ask.

¿En qué trabajas?

¿Cuál es tu trabajo?

¿Qué haces?

The last question is more general and could be used in other circumstances as well. It can be asked when someone wants to know what you are currently doing or what you are doing in the future. *¿Qué haces mañana?*

Another question little kids might answer is.

¿Qué quieres ser cuando seas grande?

Here are some sample answers.

Quiero ser un bombero.

Quiero ser una dentista.

If someone were to ask you what you do, what would you answer?

Soy una maestra. Soy un policía.

Conversation Practice

Let's practice answering a few questions about both your profession and a friend's profession. Use full sentences to answer each question. Below the questions are sample conversations with sample answers that may or may not be similar to the ones you give.

¿En qué trabaja usted?

¿A usted le gusta su trabajo?

¿Qué le gusta sobre su trabajo?

¿Cuál es la profesión de su amigo?

¿A él le gusta su trabajo?

Sample conversations:

¿En qué trabaja usted?

Yo soy peluquero.

¿A usted le gusta su trabajo?

Si, me gusta mucho.

¿Qué le gusta sobre su trabajo?

Me gusta hablar con mis clientes.

¿Cuál es la profesión de su amigo?

Mi amigo es un doctor.

¿A él le gusta su trabajo?

Si, le gusta ser un doctor.

However, for now, another common question when talking about professions include the past perfect tense. You should memorize how to answer this type of question even though you haven't worked through this whole tense yet. That way, you will be prepared to answer it before having completed that verb study.

¿Cuánto tiempo has trabajado en la escuela? If you are a teacher, you might be asked this question.

¿Cuánto tiempo has trabajado en esta profesión? This question is more general and could be directed to anyone.

¿Cuánto tiempo has sido un _____? You would fill in the blank with your profession- médico, enfermero, ingeniero.

Your answer will use the same format. You will substitute "he" for "has" to change the question from asking about you to answering about I.

Yo he trabajado en la escuela por tres años.

Yo he trabajado en esta profesión por ocho meses.

Yo he sido un doctor por cuatro años.

You can see how the answers reflect the questions. You can pick one of these ways to answer and memorize the word order and format. That way, even if you aren't quite sure which format you are being asked, you can still answer the question correctly.

Where Are You Going?

The Verb "Ir"

The verb "*ir*" means to go, and it can be used to tell a place you are currently going. "*Ir*" being such a short verb has to be irregular. If you just took off the ending, you would be left with nothing. Below is a chart with the conjugation of "*ir*."

Yo voy	Nosotros vamos
Tú vas	Vosotros vais

Él/ ella/ usted va	*Ellos/ ustedes van*

While the verb is irregular, it still follows the ending pattern used with other verbs. You can see the "-as" ending with "*tú*" and so forth. When talking about a place you are going, you can make a sentence simply by picking the appropriate verb above and using "a" as well as the place.

For example,

Voy a mi casa.

Ella va a su casa.

Ellos van a su casa.

If you ever have a sentence like the following- *Yo voy a el parque*- you can combine "*a*" and "*el*." This combination is similar to the way we use conjugations. A + el = al

The correct way to say the above sentence is "*Yo voy al parque.*" You wouldn't leave out "*el*" altogether and say "I go to park." That sounds stilted and awkward just as it does in English. Note that if you are going to a femenine place, you will not combine "a" and "la." This combination only happens with "a" and "el."

Places Vocabulary

You have come across a few places so far in this book such as "*casa*" and "*parque*," but you go many more places than that. Study the vocabulary list below and read the words aloud following the pronunciation list.

Iglesia /ee-gles-ee-uh/- church

Biblioteca /bee-blee-oh-tek-uh/- library

Dentista /den-tees-tuh/- dentist

Tienda /tee-en-duh/- store

Restaurante /res-tow-rahn-tay/- restaurant.

Cine /seen-ay/- movie theater

Playa /plai-yuh/- beach

Estación de bus /es-tah-see-on deh boos/- bus station

Mercado /mare-cah-do/- market

Farmacia /far-mah-see-uh/- pharmacy

Banco /bahn-co/- bank

Hospital /os-pee-tahl/- hospital

Panadería /pahn-ah-dare-ee-uh/- bakery

Librería /lee-brare-ree-uh/- bookstore

However, right now, you will simply be using the vocabulary to tell where you are going. Most of the above words are clearly either "el" or "la." However, a couple are a bit harder to guess.

Activity 1. Fill in the blanks below with either *el, la, los* or *las*.

_____ *playa*

_____ *mercado*

_____ *cine*

_____ *bancos*

_____ *farmacia*

_____ *hospitales*

_____ *librerias*

_____ *tienda*

_____ *estación de bus*

Answers-

La, el, el, los, la, los, las, la, la

Activity 2. Read the following statements and draw a picture that illustrates what is happening. The answers are below.

1. *Las niñas van a la playa.*

2. *Ellos van a la iglesia el domingo.*

3. *Yo voy a la estación de bus cada dia.*

4. *Mi padre va a la tienda.*

Answers:

1. The girls go to the beach.

2. They go to the church on Sunday.

3. I go to the bus station every day.

4. My dad goes to the store.

Using "Ir" for the Future

Another way to use "*ir*" is to talk about something you are "going" to do. In English, we might say, "I am going to study." You can use the same format in Spanish. Read the following example sentences and figure out what each person is going to do.

Maria: Voy a visitar a mi abuela.

Jorge: Voy a comer carne y queso.

Pedro: Voy a nadar mañana.

This is the formula we use when using "ir" to talk about the future. "Conjugated Ir + a +unconjugated action."

Notice the second verbs in the above sentences. They are not conjugated. We do not say "*Voy a visito.*" That would be equivalent to saying "I am going I visit."

56

In fact, in other cases as well, if there are two verbs one after the other, the second verb is not conjugated. For example,

Necesito hablar. I need to speak. Once again, we would not say "I need I speak."

Quiero comer.

Ella quiere venir.

Activity 1. Read about their plans then answer the questions in full sentences. The answers can be found below.

Gregorio: El lunes, miércoles, y viernes, voy a trabajar. El martes, voy a jugar al tenis. Me gusta mucho jugar al béisbol, pero mi amigo no le gusta. El jueves, voy a limpiar mi casa. Y el sábado y domingo, voy a ir a la playa con mi familia.

Violeta: Necesito trabajar mucho esta semana. Trabajo cinco días a la semana- del martes al sábado. El domingo, voy a ir a la iglesia. El lunes, voy a la tienda y voy a comprar mucha comida, como arroz, frijoles, queso, y fruta. También, voy a llamar a mi amiga y hablar con ella. Y voy a caminar en el parque.

¿Qué va a hacer Gregorio el jueves?

¿Qué va a hacer Violeta el jueves?

¿Qué va a hacer Violeta el domingo?

¿Qué va a hacer Gregorio el viernes?

Respuestas (Answers):

Gregorio va a limpiar su casa.

Violeta va a trabajar el jueves.

Violeta va a ir a la iglesia el domingo.

Gregorio va trabajar el viernes.

Activity 2. Write about one thing you are going to do each day of the upcoming week. Here is an example schedule.

El lunes, voy a visitar a mi amiga.

El martes, voy a trabajar.

El miércoles, voy a ayudar a mi abuela.

El jueves, voy a comer una pizza grande.

El viernes, voy a mirar una película en el cine.

El sabado, voy a cocinar mucha comida.

El domingo, voy a ir a la iglesia.

Basic Conversations

Read the conversation aloud. Then, complete the second conversation with your own answers.

Elena: Hola, Marcos. ¿Cómo estás?

Marcos: Estoy bien, gracias. ¿Adonde vas?

Elena: Voy a la tienda para comprar comida para cenar. Necesito comprar huevos, fruta, carne, y repollo.

Marcos: Ah, ¿vas a hacer una ensalada?

Elena: Sí, voy a hacer una ensalada. ¿Quieres venir y comer la cena conmigo?

Marcos: No, no puedo. Voy a trabajar.

Elena: ¡Qué mal! Bueno, tal vez puedes venir a mi casa otro día.

Marcos: Okay, hasta luego.

Elena: Hasta luego.

Marcos: ¿Que vas a hacer hoy?

Tú:

Marcos: Yo voy a ir a la casa de mi amiga.

Tú:

Marcos: Sí, me gusta trabajar.

Tú:

Chapter 11 - The Imperative and Subjunctive Moods

Indicative Mood

In general, Spanish speakers use the indicative mood when engaging in regular conversation. An indicative mood is a form used to provide information, state facts, and even express opinions in the past, present, future, and conditionals.

As such, the use of the indicative mood is the most commonly used form to express meaning. Thus far, we have focused on the indicative mood. The tenses that we have discussed are all centered on this mood.

Consider this example:

- *Estoy viendo la televisión.* (I am watching television.)

This example illustrates how you can express a fact. The fact in this example is that you are watching television.

This seems pretty straightforward, right?

Indeed, the indicative mood is the most commonly used mood in a regular conversation. However, things change when you move away from the indicative mood and enter the subjunctive.

Subjunctive Mood

You probably have not heard of the subjunctive mood, as it is not a common topic in English classes. However, it is widely used in Spanish. In fact, the subjunctive is used about as much as the indicative mood. It is one of the nuances that native Spanish speakers develop more out of custom and habit than out of sheer linguistic proficiency.

You are probably wondering what the subjunctive mood is and how its use translates to the English language.

The subjunctive mood is essentially used to express wishes, obligation, necessity, desires, and doubt. Consequently, we are moving away from expressing facts and opinions to a bit of a gray area in which we are not necessarily talking about things that are clear-cut.

As such, the subjunctive is used any time you move away from "real" situations and into situations that reflect conditions, which are not always true at the moment. Hence, desires, wishes, and doubt fall perfectly into this category.

So, let us delve more into the expression of wishes and desires. In this case, you are referring to situations where you would like something to happen but may not necessarily have the ability to make it happen at the time of speaking or may seem unlikely at some point. You can even express situations that are completely unreal.

For example, you might be thinking about situations where you wish you had millions of dollars or that you could change something that is impossible to change. These circumstances, given the fact that you are not talking about a fact, would fall into the realm of the subjunctive.

Here are some expressions that generally accompany the subjunctive:

- *Desear que* (to wish that)

- *Esperar que* (to hope that)

- *Exigir que* (to demand that)

- *Mandar que* (to order that)

- *Ordenar que* (to order that)

- *Pedir que* (to ask that)

- *Preferir que* (to prefer that)

- *Querer que* (to want that)

Notice that we are talking about expressions that refer to things that you wish, hope, and prefer to happen. Also, you can see how there are actions that you can order or demand to be done. Now, it should be noted that these are not direct orders or requests. When you make a request using the subjunctive form, you are either requesting that something be done as a result of a condition being met, or you are simply trying to be much more polite about it.

The subjunctive can also be used to talk about emotions or reactions to certain situations. The underlying reason for the use of the subjunctive when expressing reactions and emotions is the use of the expression "*es + adjective + que.*" This expression, when used to express emotions or reactions, is a signal that you are using the subjunctive form.

Here are some examples of this construction:

- *Es absurdo que* (it is absurd that)

- *Es bonito que* (it is nice that)

- *Es Bueno que* (it is good that)

- *Es fundamental que* (it is essential that)

- *Es importante que* (it is important that)

- *Es inútil que* (it is useless that)

- *Es justo que* (it is fair that)

- *Es triste que* (it is sad that)

- *Es urgente que* (it is urgent that)

- *Me encanta que* (I love that)

- *Me gusta que* (I like that)

- *Me molesta que* (it bothers me that)

- *Me sorprende que* (it surprises me that)

Notice how these constructions all represent ideas and feelings, which may not necessarily be true at the time of speaking. While you might be talking about something that is very much present at the time of speaking, you might also be talking about something that hasn't even happened yet.

Consider this example:

- *Es importante llegar a tiempo.* (It is important to get there on time.)

In this example, the subjunctive form in Spanish matches up quite well with the subjunctive form in English. While the use of the subjunctive in English isn't nearly as prevalent as it is in Spanish, the previous example makes a great case for using this form in both languages.

One other case in which the subjunctive is used is when the speaker is expressing doubt or disbelief. The following expressions are characteristic of this case.

- *No creer que* (not to believe that)
- *Dudar que* (doubt that)
- *No opinar que* (not to think that)
- *No pensar que* (not to think that)

You can also use the following conjunctions with the subjunctive mood.

- *A fin de que* (in order to)
- A menos que (unless)
- *Antes de que* (before that)
- *Sin que* (without)
- *Con tal de que* (provided that)
- *Ojalá* (hopefully)
- *Quizá* (maybe)
- *Para que* (so that)
- *Tal vez* (perhaps)

Below are words pertaining to time that can also be used:

- *Cuando* (when)
- *En cuanto* (as soon as)
- *Hasta que* (until)
- Después de que (after)
- *Tan pronto como* (as soon as)

As you can see, there is a good deal of expressions that signal the use of the subjunctive. As you gain more experience with the subjunctive, you will automatically begin to recognize what expression or part of speech prompts the subjunctive form usage. So, it certainly pays to do your homework.

Imperative Mood

The other mood used in Spanish is the imperative mood. In short, the imperative is used to give direct orders and commands. In English, the imperative allows the speaker to omit the use of the subject as it is implied that the subject of a command is "you." The same rule applies in Spanish.

Now, you might be wondering what differences there would be between the use of the imperative mood and commands given in the subjunctive. First of all, orders and requests given in the subjunctive can be directed at anyone. In the case of the imperative, the orders and commands given are directed specifically to "you."

As with the subjunctive, the verb conjugation changes to reflect the difference in mood. Here is a general overview of such changes in conjugation.

With regular AR verbs, you can use the following rule of thumb.

- Verb: *hablar* (to speak)
    - o *(tú) habla – no hables (negative form)*
    - o *(usted) hable*
    - o *(nosotros) hablemos*
    - o *(ustedes) hablen*

Notice how the verb conjugation changes in the endings given to the verb. Also, the subject is placed in parentheses as it is not used when actually saying such phrases, but we have included them to illustrate the subject we are referring to.

The conjugation of the regular *IR* verbs, as well as *ER* verbs, can be viewed as follows:

- Verb: *comer* (to eat)
    - o *(tú) come / no comas (negative form)*
    - o *(usted) coma*
    - o *(nosotros) comamos*
    - o *(ustedes) coman*

Once again, you can see how the verb endings reflect a variation in the regular conjugation. As you become familiar with this form, you will notice how straightforward it actually is. The challenge, of course, is to recall the proper endings in this mood.

There are also irregular verbs that can be used in the imperative mood. So, here are the most common commands used:

- *Di* (say)
- *Haz* (do)
- *Pon* (put)
- *Sal* (come out)
- *Sé* (be)
- *Ten* (have)
- *Ve* (go)
- *Ven* (come here)

Consider these examples:

- *Di algo* (say something)
- *Haz un esfuerzo* (do an effort)
- *Pon tu nombre* (put your name)
- *Sal a jugar* (come out to play)

- *Sé honesto* (be honest)

- *Ten paciencia* (have patience)

- *Ve a dormir* (go to sleept)

- Ven conmigo (come here with me)

These examples all illustrate commands that you can express using the imperative mood. Also, they use the (*tú*) form. So, you can easily use them whenever you are asking to your interlocutor to carry out an action at any given point.

Ultimately, the use of the indicative, subjunctive, and imperative all boils down to the situation where you find yourself communicating. Consequently, you can use any of these moods to get your message across effectively. So, do take the time to go over the various moods so that you can recognize them.

Chapter 12 - Preguntando Lugares Turísticos - Asking for Tourist Places

Spanish

-Clara: *Buenos días mis amores, ya llegue.*

-Noah: *¡Mamá!*

-Agatha: *Mamii.*

-Clara: *¿Ya desayunaron?*

-Agatha: *No, vino servicio a la habitación pero no había nada que me gustara.*

-Clara: *Les tengo una sorpresa entonces... ¡ SÁNDWICHES!*

-Noah: *Yeeey.*

-Agatha: *Gracias mamá.*

-Clara: *Espero que les gusten, me los recomendó una señora de la zona, su nombre es Wanda, me dio su número para que le preguntara cualquier cosa.*

-Agatha: *Pregúntale a que lugares podemos ir a pasear.*

-Clara: *Bien pensado, ya la llamo.*

-Clara: *Hola Wanda es Clara.*

-Wanda: *Hola Clara, me alegra que llames.*

-Clara: *Gracias, quería preguntarte ¿Cuáles son los lugares turísticos que hay en la zona?*

-Wanda: *Bueno, tienes la playa que está a unos 10 minutos de la panadería; la montaña está a unos 15 kilómetros al norte y hay un parque de diversiones que está a 5 kilómetros al oeste.*

-Clara: *Perfecto, hay mucho que visitar entonces.*

-Wanda: *Así es, que lo disfruten.*

English

-Clara: Good morning, my darlings. I'm here.

-Noah: Mom!

-Agatha: Mommy.

-Clara: Have you had breakfast?

-Agatha: No, room service came, but I didn't like anything.

-Clara: I have a surprise for you then... SANDWICHES!

-Noah: Yeeey.

-Agatha: Thanks, mom.

-Clara: I hope you like them. They were recommended to me by a local lady. Her name is Wanda, and she gave me her number so I could ask her anything.

-Agatha: Ask her where we can go for a walk.

-Clara: Good thinking. I'll call her.

-Clara: Hi Wanda, it's Clara.

-Wanda: Hi Clara, I'm glad you called.

-Clara: Thank you. I wanted to ask you, what are the tourist places in the area?

-Wanda: Well, you have the beach that is about 10 minutes from the bakery. The mountain is about 15 kilometers to the north, and there is also an amusement park that is 5 kilometers to the west.

-Clear: Perfect, there's a lot to visit then.

-Wanda: That's right, enjoy it.

Visita a la playa- Visit to the beach

Spanish

-Clara: Acabo de hablar con Wanda y me dijo que hay una playa a 10 minutos de la panadería donde compré el desayuno.

-Agatha: Genial, amo la playa.

-Noah: Que bien, ¿Puedo llevar mi snorkel?

-Clara: Lo sé Agatha. Claro que puedes Noah.

-Agatha: ¿Dónde están los trajes de baño?

-Clara: En la maleta grande.

-Noah: ¿Y mi snorkel?

-Clara: Debe estar ahí también.

-Noah: Si, aquí esta.

-Clara: Traigan las toallas, sus sandalias, el protector solar, agua, gorras y sus lentes de sol.

-Noah: Llevare mi pala para hacer castillos de arena.

-Agatha: Y yo mi salvavidas.

-Clara: Perfecto. Vamonos, hay que tener cuidado con el oleaje.

-Noah y Agatha: Ok.

English

-Clara: I just spoke to Wanda, and she told me that there is a beach 10 minutes from the bakery where I bought breakfast.

-Agatha: Great, I love the beach.

-Noah: Good, can I bring my snorkel?

-Clara: I know Agatha. Of course, you can, Noah.

-Agatha: Where are the bathing suits?

-Clara: In the big suitcase.

-Noah: What about my snorkel?

-Clara: It must be there too.

-Noah: Yes, here it is.

-Clara: Bring the towels, your sandals, sunscreen, water, caps, and sunglasses.

-Noah: I'll take my shovel to make sandcastles.

-Agatha: And I will bring my lifeguard.

-Clara: Perfect. Let's go. We have to be careful with the waves.

-Noah and Agatha: Ok.

Visita a la montaña- Visit to the mountain

Spanish

-*Clara: El día de ayer en la playa fue agotador.*

-*Agatha: Fue lo máximo, lo disfrute mucho.*

-*Noah: ¿Vamos a ir hoy a la playa de nuevo?*

-*Clara: No, pensaba ir a la montaña que me dijo Wanda. ¿Qué opinan?*

-*Agatha: No me gusta la montaña.*

-*Noah: Yo nunca he ido a una.*

-*Clara: Por eso vamos a ir Agatha, para que Noah la conozca.*

-*Agatha: Bueno.*

-*Clara: Para ir a la montaña debemos llevar ropa deportiva, gorra, lentes, repelente de mosquitos y mucha agua.*

-*Agatha: Odio los mosquitos.*

-*Clara: Entonces no olvides el repelente.*

-*Agatha: Esta bien.*

-*Noah: ¿Qué se hace en la montaña, mamá?*

-*Clara: Caminar, escalar, ejercitarse y ver la flora y fauna.*

-*Noah: Ya veo.*

-*Clara: Caminar en las montañas también es conocido como treking.*

-*Agatha: Ya había oído sobre eso.*

-*Clara: Pues hoy veras como se hace.*

-*Agatha: Esta bien.*

-*Clara: Lleven zapatos deportivos también, y chaquetas por si llueve.*

-*Noah: Ok.*

-*Agatha: Esta bien.*

... En la montaña...

-Clara: *Bueno hijos, aquí estamos, miren todos esos árboles, flores, plantas, vean las aves y los insectos que hay. Algunos dicen que hay monos en ciertos lugares de la montaña*

-Noah: *Genial, yo quiero verlos.*

-Clara: *Abramos los ojos a ver si logramos verlos.*

English

-Clara: Yesterday on the beach was exhausting.

-Agatha: It was the best. I enjoyed it a lot.

-Noah: Are we going to the beach again today?

-Clara: No, I was thinking of going to the mountain that Wanda told me. What do you think?

-Agatha: I don't like the mountain.

-Noah: I've never been to one.

-Clara: That's why we're going to Agatha so that Noah knows it.

-Agatha: Good.

-Clara: To go to the mountain, we must wear sports clothes, a cap, glasses, mosquito repellent, and lots of water.

-Agatha: I hate mosquitoes.

-Clara: Then don't forget the repellent.

-Agatha: Okay.

-Noah: What do you do in the mountains, Mom?

-Clara: Walk, climb, exercise, and see the flora and fauna.

-Noah: I see.

-Clara: Walking in the mountains is also known as trekking.

-Agatha: I've heard about that before.

-Clara: Well, today, you'll see how it's done.

-Agatha: All right.

-Clara: Bring sneakers too, and jackets in case it rains.

-Noah: Ok.

-Agatha: Okay.

... On the mountain...

-Clara: Well children, here we are. Look at all those trees, flowers, and plants. Look at the birds and the insects that are there. Some say there are monkeys in certain parts of the mountain.

-Noah: Great, I want to see them.

-Clara: Let's open our eyes to see if we can see them.

Visita al parque de diversiones- Visit to the Amusement Park

Spanish

-Clara: Buenos días hijos. Estoy segura que hoy será su día favorito.

-Noah: ¿Por qué?

-Clara: Iremos al parque de diversiones.

-Agatha: ¡SIIIII!

-Noah: ¡YUPIIII!

-Clara: Vístanse para salir temprano y poder aprovechar el tiempo.

-Noah: Genial mamá

... En el parque...

-Clara: ¿Qué les parece?

-Noah: Esta increíble mamá.

-Agatha: Me encanta, quiero subirme en todo.

-Clara: Hay varias montañas rusas, hay una casa de espejos, una casa embrujada, toboganes, piscinas, caballos, nado con delfines, kartings, carros chocones, canchas de tenis, de futbol, de baloncesto, mesas de ping pong, salones de videojuegos, trampolines, buceo, simuladores, pared de escalada, paintball, un carrusel, una rueda de la fortuna y muchas otras cosas.

-Noah: Esto es el paraíso mamá.

-Agatha: Lo máximo, me quiero quedar a vivir aquí.

-Clara: Hay ciertas reglas y prohibiciones para las atracciones.

-Agatha: ¿Cómo así?

-Clara: Para algunas atracciones debes ser mayor de una altura, para otras, mayor de cierta edad.

-Noah: Rayos.

-Clara: Pero vamos, hay muchas atracciones que probar.

English

-Clara: Good morning, children. I'm sure today will be your favorite day.

-Noah: Why?

-Clara: We'll go to the amusement park.

-Agatha: YEEES!

-Noah: YUPIIII!

-Clara: Get dressed so we can leave early and be on time.

-Noah: Great mom.

... In the park...

-Clara: What do you think?

-Noah: This incredible, mom.

-Agatha: I love it. I want to get on everything.

-Clara: There are several rollercoasters. There's a mirror house, a haunted house, slides, swimming pools, horses, swimming with dolphins, karts, bumper cars, tennis courts, soccer courts, basketball courts, ping pong tables, video game rooms, trampolines, diving, simulators, climbing walls, paintball, a carousel, a wheel of fortune, and many other things.

-Noah: This is paradise, Mom.

-Agatha: The best. I want to stay and live here.

-Clara: There are certain rules and prohibitions for the attractions.

-Agatha: How so?

-Clara: For some attractions, you have to be higher than a certain height. For others, you have to be older than a certain age.

-Noah: Damn.

-Clear: But come on, there are many attractions to try.

Visita al Museo- Visit to the Museum

Spanish

-Clara: Niños, aquí estamos, este es el museo de la ciudad.

-Agatha: Es enorme.

-Clara: Si, generalmente los museos son grandes.

-Noah: ¿Qué es un museo?

-Clara: Es un lugar donde se guardan obras y objetos relacionados con la historia o cosas artísticas.

-Noah: Ya entiendo.

-Clara: Generalmente hay pinturas, esculturas, en algunos museos hay fósiles, en otros hay objetos que son importantes en la historia, como espadas, armas y otros objetos.

-Noah: ¿Y qué se hace en los museos?

-Clara: Generalmente hay un guía que te explica todo sobre los objetos, su historia, importancia, fecha y otras cosas. En los museos se aprende sobre las cosas que hay dentro y aprecias el arte y la evolución de las cosas con el pasar del tiempo.

-Agatha: suena un poco aburrido.

-Clara: No lo es. ¿Sabías que existe un museo en donde tienen la evolución y modelos de todos los aviones? Tienen el modelo del primer avión que se invento.

-Agatha: Eso si suena más interesante.

-Noah: ¿Podemos ir luego a ese museo?

-Clara: Claro, en las próximas vacaciones.

-Noah: Genial.

English

-Clara: Kids, here we are. This is the city museum.

-Agatha: It's huge.

-Clara: Yes, usually, museums are big.

-Noah: What is a museum?

-Clara: It's a place where you keep artworks and objects related to history or artistic things.

-Noah: I get it.

-Clara: Generally, there are paintings and sculptures. In some museums, there are fossils. In others, there are objects that are important in histories such as swords, weapons, and other objects.

-Noah: And what do you do in museums?

-Clara: Generally, there is a guide that explains everything about objects, their history, importance, date, and other things. In museums, you learn about the things inside and appreciate the art and the evolution of things over time.

-Agatha: It sounds a little boring.

-Clara: It's not. Did you know there's a museum where they have the evolution and models of all airplanes? They have the model of the first plane that was invented.

-Agatha: That does sound more interesting.

-Noah: Can we go to that museum next?

-Clara: Sure, in the next holidays.

-Noah: Great.

Dia de relajación- Relax day

Spanish

-Clara: Hoy tendremos un día de relajación.

-Agatha: ¿A qué te refieres?

-Clara: Iremos a un spa, nos darán masajes, nos bañaremos en aguas termales, nos harán mascarillas, entraremos a un sauna y nos relajaremos como nunca antes.

-Agatha: Suena muy bien.

-Noah: No me llama la atención.

-Clara: Ya hemos hecho muchas actividades, el cuerpo debe descansar un poco y por eso iremos.

-Noah: Yo no estoy cansado.

-Clara: Veras que al finalizar el día, estarás más descansado.

-Noah: Lo dudo.

English

-Clear: Today, we will have a day of relaxation.

-Agatha: What do you mean?

-Clara: We'll go to a spa, get massages, bathe in hot springs, get masks, go into a sauna, and relax like never before.

-Agatha: Sounds very good.

-Noah: It is not interesting.

-Clara: We have already done many activities. The body must rest a little, and that's why we'll go.

-Noah: I'm not tired.

-Clara: You'll see that at the end of the day, you'll be more rested.

-Noah: I doubt it.

Chapter 13 - Spanish Language Quirks

Like any language, Spanish has its quirks and foibles, but it's very straightforward in a lot of ways, so these quirks shouldn't present you with too many problems. And there certainly are not so many as you find in the English language. It's not essential to learn about them, but just being aware of them will help you to become more proficient in the language, and help you to sound more like a local.

Apocopation

Apocopation is the practice of shortening some adjectives whenever they precede masculine nouns. Other than a few exceptions, apocopation never happens with feminine nouns, so as a quirky way to remind yourself when to apocopate, just say to yourself 'Cut a bit off the male.'

You may even have been apocopating without even realizing what you were doing. For example, if you go out for a snack at lunchtime, you may well ask for *'un bocadillo.'* On the other hand, if you want to eat more healthily, you may order *'una ensalada.'* The masculine *'uno'* (meaning one) is the most common example of apocopation, and if you speak a little Spanish each day, you're almost certain to have used it in its shortened form.

'Bueno' – which means 'good' - is another common adjective that is always shortened with masculine nouns. So, when the waiter brings your lunch, he'll say *'buen provecho.'* However, the guy in the Tabac who sells you your Euromillions lottery ticket will say *'buena suerte,'* because *suerte* - meaning luck - is feminine, so there are no bits to cut off.

These are the most common short form adjectives:

bueno - buen (good)

malo - mal (bad)

postrero - postrer (final, last)

uno - un (one, a)

primero - primer (first)

tercero - tercer (third)

alguno - algún (some)

ninguno - ningún (none)

Other short form adjectives you need to know are *grande*, which becomes *'gran'* when preceding both masculine and feminine nouns. *Ciento* (100) becomes *'cien'* in certain instances, and *cualquiera* - meaning 'any' or 'whatever' - loses the *'a'* at the end.

This is Spanish we're learning, so there is always something that goes against the rules and is different. Where apocopation is concerned, it's the word *'santo,'* which means 'saint.' This is only shortened when it precedes certain proper nouns, but not those beginning with 'Do' or 'To.' So to be correct, you'd say 'San Juan,' and 'Santo Tomas.'

As a matter of fact, as you get used to the flow of the Spanish language, you'll find yourself automatically apocopating, simply because it sounds better as you speak. If you don't apocopate, nobody will die, so don't worry too much. However, if you do, you'll sound more like the native speakers, and ultimately, that's what you're aiming for.

Comparatives and superlatives

Making comparisons in Spanish is very different to the English way. In English, you'd simply say 'big, bigger, biggest,' where big is the standard adjective, bigger is a comparative, and biggest is the superlative. However, it doesn't work that way in Spanish.

Taking grande (big) as an example to compare like for like, there is no equivalent in Spanish of the –er and –est comparative and superlative. Instead, the language makes use of the words *más* (more) and *menos* (less). So, bigger is *más grande* (literally more big), and biggest is *el más grande*. (The more big, literally, which sounds rather odd to English or American ears, but makes perfect sense to Spanish speakers).

While you're not likely to use superlatives all that often, you could find yourself using comparatives more frequently than you might expect. For example, when shopping for clothing and shoes, you might need to ask for a smaller or larger size in something. Here are a couple of examples to illustrate comparatives in action.

¿Tienes esta falda en una talla más pequeña?

Do you have this skirt in a smaller size?

Quiero una talla más grande, por favor.

I would like a larger size, please.

Notice the word order – the noun (size) precedes the adjective (smaller/larger).

Older and younger

Another example of the use of comparatives is when saying one person is older or younger than another. The Spanish words for young and old are *joven* and *viejo/vieja* respectively. You may think 'más joven' is younger, and 'más viejo' is older, based on what you've just learned about Spanish comparatives, and while that is understandable, it's also wrong!

There are special comparative expressions for 'younger' and 'older', and they are *'menor que'* and *'mayor que,'* meaning 'younger than' and 'older than' respectively. Here are a couple of examples.

Maria es menor que su hermano

Maria is younger than her brother

Juan es mayor que Pedro

Juan is older than Pedro

Take some time to construct a few sentences using *'menor que'* and *'mayor que,'* using members of your family and friends – it's great practice, and it will help you to familiarize yourself with these comparatives.

Best and worst

The Spanish words for best and worst are *'mejor'* and *'peor.'* There's nothing quirky about that, but there is a slight difference in the way they work in speech and writing. As you surely know by now, in Spanish, the adjective follows the noun.

This is not the case with mejor and peor. For example, if you are describing a shirt by color, you would say '*Mi camisa roja.*' (My red shirt). However, if you were talking about your best shirt, you would say, '*Mi mejor camisa.*' Here's how *mejor* and *peor* work in sentences.

Examples:

Maria es la mejor estudiante en la clase

Maria is the best student in the class

Es la peor excusa de todas

That is the worst excuse of all

Las mejores cosas en la vida son gratis

The best things in life are free

él es el peor doctor en el hospital

He is the worst doctor in the hospital

Mejor and *peor* can also be preceded by 'lo' to mean 'the best/worst thing,' without the need to use the noun 'cosa.'

Chapter 14 - Restaurant — Restaurante

cubiertos (koo-byehr-tohs) Masculine noun - silverware

En los restaurantes, es importante la higiene de los cubiertos.

In restaurants, the hygiene of cutlery is important.

mesero (meh-seh-roh) Masculine or Feminine noun - waiter

Los meseros son una parte fundamental en los restaurantes.

The waiters are a fundamental part of the restaurants.

mesa (meh-sah) Feminine noun - table

Las mesas deben estar impecables y correctamente adornadas con manteles.

The tables should be impeccable and properly decorated with tablecloths.

chef (shehf) Masculine or Feminine noun - chef

El chef es el maestro de cocina que se encarga de elaborar los platos especiales.

The chef is the master of the kitchen andis responsible for preparing the special dishes.

menú (meh-noo) Masculine noun - menu

El menú en un restaurante debe ser diverso claro comprensible y bien presentado.

The menu in a restaurant must be understood easily and presented well.

cocina (koh-see-nah) Feminine noun - kitchen

La cocina de un restaurante debe estar en buen estado y siempre limpia.

The kitchen of a restaurant must be in good condition and always clean.

nevera (neh-beh-rah) Feminine noun - refrigerator

Es necesario que los restaurantes tengan una nevera suficientemente amplia y bien abastecida.

It is necessary that restaurants have a sufficiently large and well-stocked fridge.

plato (plah-toh) Masculine noun - plate

Los platos no solo deben estar limpios también los debe haber de todos los tamaños.

The dishes must not only be clean, they must also be of all sizes.

despensa (dehs-pehn-sah) Feminine noun - pantry

La despensa de los restaurantes contiene los insumos y víveres necesarios.

The restaurant's pantry contains the necessary supplies and provisions.

ayudante de cocina (ah-yoo-dahn-teh deh koh-see-nah) Masculine or Feminine noun - kitchen assistant

Los ayudantes de cocina son los que apoyan al chef en todo momento.

The kitchen assistants are the ones who support the chef at all times.

cuchara (koo-chah-rah) Feminine noun - spoon

La cuchara estaba tan sucia que parecía el dedo de un mono.

The spoon was so dirty; it looked like a monkey's finger.

cuchillo (koo-chee-yoh) Masculine noun - knife

El cuchillo lo afilaron tanto que podías cortar las pezuñas de un rinoceronte.

The knife was sharpened so much that you could cut the hooves of a rhinoceros.

tenedor (teh-neh-dohr) Masculine noun - fork

La cocina estaba equipada con todo pero no tenía ni un solo tenedor.

The kitchen was equipped with everything but did not have a single fork.

vaso (bah-soh) Masculine noun - cup, glass

Se cortó la mano con el vaso de vidrio que se cayó de la despensa.

He cut his hand with the glass tumbler that fell from the pantry.

cuenco (kwehng-koh) Masculine noun - bowl

El cuenco se desbordó de agua y todo el piso quedó mojado.

The bowl overflowed with water, and the entire floor became wet.

servilleta (sehr-bee-yeh-tah) Feminine noun - napkin

Le gustaba dibujar, pintar y hacer garabatos en las servilletas.

He liked to draw, paint, and make doodle on the napkins.

aperitivo (ah-peh-ree-tee-boh) Masculine noun - appetizer

Los aperitivos tienen la función de abrir el apetito.

The appetizers have the function of creating the appetite.

desayuno (dehs-ah-yoo-noh) Masculine noun - breakfast

El desayuno es la comida más importante del día.

Breakfast is the most important meal of the day.

postre (pohs-treh) Masculine noun - dessert

Hay gente que de verdad no se le debería permitir comer el postre.

There are people who really should not be allowed to eat dessert.

cena (seh-nah) Feminine noun - dinner

La cena debe ser ligera sencilla y humilde para no tener el sueño pesado.

Dinner should be light simple and humble so as not to have a heavy sleep.

almuerzo (ahl-mwehr-soh) Masculine noun - lunch

Muchas personas prefieren almorzar en la calle que en sus casas.

Many people prefer to have lunch on the street rather than in their homes.

plato principal (plah-toh preen-see-pahl) Masculine noun - main dish

La mayoría de las veces el plato principal no es tan bueno como el aperitivo.

Most of the time, the main course is not as good as the appetizer.

Chapter 15 - Professions — Profesiones

bombero (bohm-beh-roh) Masculine or Feminine noun - firefighter

Los bomberos no siempre apagan el fuego también rescatan gatos.

Firefighters do not always put out the fires; they also rescue cats.

mecánico (meh-kah-nee-koh) Masculine or Feminine noun - mechanic

El mecánico estuvo seis horas revisando el motor de ese auto.

The mechanic spent six hours checking the engine of that car.

médico (meh-dee-koh) Masculine or Feminine noun - doctor

El médico le dijo a su paciente que debía reposar por dos semanas.

The doctor told his patient that he should rest for two weeks.

boxeador (bohk-seh-ah-dohr) Masculine or Feminine noun - boxer

Los boxeadores entrenan muy duro y cuidan su salud para estar en forma.

The boxers train very hard and take care of their health to be fit.

abogado (ah-boh-gah-doh) Masculine or Feminine noun - lawyer

El abogado tuvo que investigar el caso a fondo durante ocho meses.

The lawyer had to investigate the case thoroughly for eight months.

veterinario (beh-teh-ree-nah-ryoh) Masculine or Feminine noun - veterinarian

Ese veterinario les salvó la vida a seis animales en un día.

That veterinarian saved six animals in one day.

arquitecto (ahr-kee-tehk-toh) Masculine or Feminine noun - architect

Se necesitaron cuatro arquitectos para revisar los planos de ese centro comercial.

It took four architects to review the plans for that mall.

dentista (dehn-tees-tah) Masculine or Feminine noun - dentist

El dentista asistió al congreso de odontología que se realizó en italia.

The dentist attended the conference of dentistry that was held in Italy.

astronauta (ahs-troh-now-tah) Masculine or Feminine noun - astronaut

Los astronautas pasaron cinco meses reparando la estación espacial de marte.

The astronauts spent five months repairing the space station on Mars.

músico (moo-see-koh) Masculine or Feminine noun - musician

Los músicos de la banda se fueron de gira por Latinoamérica.

The musicians of the band went on tour in Latin America.

periodista (peh-ryoh-dees-tah) Masculine or Feminine noun - journalist

El periodista recibió el premio pulitzer por su reportaje sobre los emigrantes.

The journalist received the Pulitzer Prize for his report on emigrants.

carpintero (kahr-peen-teh-roh) Masculine or Feminine noun - carpenter

Al carpintero le encargaron fabricar tres camas dos sillas y una mesa grande.

The carpenter was commissioned to make three beds, two chairs, and a large table.

escritor (ehs-kree-tohr) Masculine or Feminine noun- writer

El escritor terminó de escribir su última novela y la entregó a tiempo a su editorial.

The writer finished writing his latest novel and delivered it on time to his publisher.

actor (ahk-duhr) Masculine or Feminine noun - actor

El discurso de aceptación del actor en la ceremonia de entrega de los premios Oscar fue muy emotivo.

The acceptance speech of the actor in the Oscar awards ceremony was very emotional.

científico (syehn-tee-fee-koh) Masculine or Feminine noun - scientist

La sociedad científica le otorgó el máximo galardón al científico por sus aportes a la humanidad.

The scientific society gave the highest award to the scientist for his contributions to humanity.

cocinero (koh-see-neh-roh) Masculine or Feminine noun - cook

Para la fiesta de fin de año contrataron a los mejores cocineros del país.

For the end-of-the-year party, they hired the best chefs in the country.

chofer (choh-fehr) Masculine or Feminine noun - chauffeur

El chofer manejó durante 14 horas seguidas demostrando resistencia y control.

The driver drove for 14 straight hours, demonstrating resistance and control.

piloto (pee-loh-toh) Masculine or Feminine noun - pilot

Los pilotos de aviación comercial tienen una gran responsabilidad para sus pasajeros.

Commercial aviation pilots have a great deal of responsibility for their passengers.

agricultor (ah-gree-kool-tohr) Masculine or Feminine noun - farmer

El trabajo del agricultor es muy importante porque sin campo no hay ciudad.

The work of the farmer is very important because, without a field, there is no city.

docente (doh-sehn-teh) Masculine or Feminine noun - teacher

Los maestros y maestras son responsables de la educación de las generaciones futuras.

Teachers and professors are responsible for the education of future generations.

camionero (kah-myoh-neh-roh) Masculine or Feminine noun - truck driver

Los camioneros son las personas que comen más comida chatarra en todo el mundo.

Truck drivers are the people who eat the most junk food in the whole world.

consejero (kohn-seh-heh-roh) Masculine or Feminine noun - counselor

Un consejero es alguien que enseña mejor lo que el mismo necesita aprender.

A counselor is someone who teaches better than what they need to learn.

enfermero (ehm-fehr-meh-roh) Masculine or Feminine noun - nurse

El enfermero es a veces mucho más importante que el doctor y trabaja más.

The nurse is sometimes much more important than the doctor and works harder.

farmacéutico (fahr-mah-seyoo-tee-koh) Masculine noun - pharmacist

Un farmacéutico es una persona sin escrúpulos que negocia la salud de la gente.

A pharmacist is an unscrupulous person who negotiates the health of people.

juez (hwehs) Masculine or Feminine noun - judge

Es casi ciencia ficción decir que existe un juez que no sea corrupto.

It is almost science fiction to say that there is a judge who is not corrupt.

padre (pah-dreh) Masculine noun - priest

Ser padre de oficio significa explicar con fé lo que el mismo no entiende ni practica.

Being a father by trade means explaining with faith what he does not understand or practice.

Chapter 16- Transportation — Transporte

transporte (trahns-pohr-teh) Masculine noun - transportation

El transporte es cómo se transfieren los objetos y las personas.

Transportation is how objects and people are transferred.

transporte terrestre (trahns-pohr-teh teh-rrehs-treh) Masculine noun - land transport

El transporte terrestre es el que se realiza sobre ruedas como automóviles y motocicletas.

Land transport is carried out on wheels like cars and motorcycles.

señales de tránsito (see-nyal-ehs deh trahn-see-toh) Plural noun - road signs

Las señales de tránsito son los signos usados en la vía pública para dar la información correcta.

Traffic signs are the signs used on public roads to give the correct information.

carreteras (kah-rreh-teh-rah) Feminine noun - highway

Una carretera es una ruta de dominio y uso público construida para el movimiento de vehículos.

A highway is a route of domain and public use built for the movement of vehicles.

autopistas (ow-toh-pees-tah) Feminine noun - freeway

Las autopistas son aquellas que son rápidas, seguras y con un gran volumen de tráfico.

The highways are those that are fast and safe and contain a large volume of traffic.

autobus (ow-toh-boos) Masculine noun - bus

El autobús es un vehículo diseñado para transportar numerosas personas por las vías urbanas.

The bus is a vehicle designed to transport many people through urban roads.

taxi (tahk-si) Masculine noun - taxi

Ese taxi tenía una tarifa muy alta y preferí hacer el viaje en autobús.

That taxi had a very high fare, and I preferred to take a bus trip.

tren (trehn) Masculine noun - train

Este tren es uno de los más rápidos del mundo y las tarifas son económicas.

This train is one of the fastest in the world, and the rates are cheap.

metro (meh-troh) Masculine noun - metro

Las grandes ciudades prefieren el metro subterráneo como opción de transporte.

Large cities prefer the underground metro as a transportation option.

motocicleta (moh-toh-see-kleh-tah) Feminine noun - motorcycle

Las motocicletas son el medio de transporte ideal para evitar el tráfico.

Motorcycles are the ideal means of transport to avoid traffic.

carro (kah-rroh) Masculine noun - car

El carro del vecino tenía fallas en el motor y el parachoques roto.

The neighbor's car had a broken engine and bumper.

bicicleta (bee-see-kleh-tah) Feminine noun - bicycle

La bicicleta es un transporte ecológico y a la vez deportivo.

The bicycle is an ecological and sporty transport at the same time.

bote (boh-teh) Masculine noun - boat

Todos los fines de semana llevó a mis hijos a pasear en bote.

Every weekend, he took my children for a boat ride.

ciclomotor (see-cloh-moh-tohr) Masculine noun - moped

Prefiero el ciclomotor porque es mucho más rápido y seguro.

I prefer the moped because it is much faster and safer.

Chapter 17 - Yes, No, Please, Thanks: Basic Vocabulary

Along with the basic verbs that you learned in the last lesson, these are also some basic words you need to know to get by: yes, no, please, thanks.

yes – *sí*

no – *no*

please – *por favor*

thanks – *gracias*

Now that you know how to say these four words, you can travel in a Spanish-speaking country without being considered rude.

Let's see a few other expressions and words that might turn out useful in case you want to make a really good impression:

sorry – *perdón*

I am sorry – *lo siento / lo lamento*

excuse me – *disculpe*

thanks – *gracias*

thank you very much – *muchas gracias*

you are welcome – *de nada*

never mind – *no hay por qué*

it is fine – *está bien*

of course – *Por supuesto*

of course not – *Por supuesto que no*

absolutely – *absolutamente*

not at all – *para nada*

for sure – *Sin lugar a duda / Por supuesto / Pero claro*

Let's use all of these in sentences:

Yes, I also need a ticket – ***Sí***, *yo también necesito un billete*

No, I don't eat meat – ***No***, *no como carne*

Please, could you point me to the train station? – ***Por favor***, *¿podría indicarme dónde está la estación de trenes?*

Thanks, you are very kind – ***Gracias***, *eres muy amable*

Sorry, I did not see you there – ***Perdón***, *no te vi ahí*

I am sorry, I do not have any cash on me – ***Lo lamento***, *no tengo nada de efectivo conmigo*

Excuse me, do you work here? – ***Disculpe***, *¿usted trabaja aquí?*

Thanks, but that is not necessary – ***Gracias***, *pero eso no es necesario*

Thank you very much! It is delicious! – *¡**Muchas gracias**! ¡Está delicioso!*

You are welcome, I also have extra water just in case – *De nada, también tengo agua de más por si acaso*

Never mind, you would have done it for me too – *No hay por qué, tú también lo habrías hecho por mí*

It is fine; I do not need anything – *Está bien; no necesito nada*

Of course I want to go – *Claro que quiero ir*

Of course not, that was not me – *Claro que no, ese no fui yo*

Absolutely, I will be there at 7 – *Absolutamente, voy a estar ahí a las 7*

Not at all, it was not trouble for me – *Para nada, no fue ningún problema*

For sure, tell me what you need, and I will bring it – *Por supuesto, dime qué necesitas, y yo te lo traigo*

When James gets back from the beach, he sees Andrea at the hostel reception:

JAMES: Excuse me, Andrea, may I ask you a question? – *Disculpa, Andrea, ¿puedo hacerte una pregunta?*

ANDREA: Of course, James! Whatever you need – *¡Claro, James! Lo que necesites*

JAMES: Thank you – *Gracias*

ANDREA: Don't worry, tell me – *No hay de qué, dime*

JAMES: I am really sorry, but I lost my map – *Lo siento mucho, pero he perdido mi mapa*

ANDREA: Don't worry! We have millions – *¡No te preocupes! Tenemos millones*

JAMES: Are you sure? – *¿Estás segura?*

ANDREA: For sure, yes. Here, take one – *Por supuesto, sí. Aquí, toma uno*

JAMES: Thanks a lot, Andrea, you are the best! – *Muchas gracias, Andrea, ¡eres la mejor!*

ANDREA: Yes, I know! – *Sí, ¡lo sé!*

What's Happening? The Present Tense (Part I)

This is not meant to be a boring grammar book, so you won't be driven crazy with conjugation rules that you need to learn by heart. However, what will be explained in this lesson might actually turn to be quite useful to understand why verbs are conjugated the way they are. There is no need to memorize this, but it will inevitably happen once you start learning more and more verbs.

Some of the verbs before were irregular verbs. This means they don't follow the normal rules of conjugation. This is why a verb like *ser* (to be) can be conjugated into words that sound nothing like *ser: eres* (you are), for example—it is completely irregular. Now, luckily for you, most verbs in Spanish are actually regular. This means they follow three basic models of conjugation, depending on whether they end on *-ar, -er* or *-ir*.

Regular verbs that end in *-ar* always follow the same structure and add the same letters after the 'root' of the verb. You can find the root of a verb easily. Just take *-ar, -er* or *-ir* off it in its infinitive form and you will have the root. For verb *amar* (to love), for example, the root is am-.

Amar (to love)

yo am**o**

tú am**as** / vos am**ás** / usted am**a**

él/ella am**a**

nosotros am**amos**

ustedes am**an** / vosotros am**áis**

ellos/ellas am**an**

Regular verbs that end in **-er** also follow the same structure and add the same letters after the root of the verb, as in the following example. For the verb *temer* (to fear), the root is tem-.

Temer (to fear)

yo tem**o**

tú tem**es** / vos tem**és** / usted tem**e**

él/ella tem**e**

nosotros tem**emos**

ustedes tem**en** / vosotros tem**éis**

ellos/ellas tem**en**

Regular verbs that end in **-ir** also follow the same structure and add the same letters after the root of the verb, as in the following example. For the verb vivir (to live), the root is viv-.

Vivir (to live)

yo viv**o**

tú viv**es** / vos viv**ís** / usted viv**e**

él/ella viv**e**

nosotros viv**imos**

ustedes viv**en** / vosotros viv**ís**

ellos/ellas viv**en**

As you can see, in all cases, for the singular first person, *yo*, you just need to add an *o* to the root of the verb:

Caminar (to walk): I walk in the park – *Yo **camino** en el parque*

Beber (to drink): I only drink beer – *Solo **bebo** cerveza*

Partir (to leave): I leave tomorrow morning – *Yo **parto** mañana por la mañana*

For *tú*, you just add -*as* or -*es*:

Extrañar (to miss): Do you miss your sister? – *¿**Extrañas** a tu hermana?*

Creer (to believe): You do not believe in magic – *No **crees** en la magia*

Abrir (to open): Do you open the door? – *¿**Abres** la puerta?*

For *él* or *ella*, you, as in English, normally add an s. In Spanish, you just have to add an *a* or *e*:

Escribir (to write): She never writes – *Ella nunca **escribe***

Hablar (to talk): He talks too much – *Él **habla** demasiado*

Vender (to sell): She sells her soul for a snack – *Ella **vende** su alma por un bocadillo*

For *nosotros*, you add either -*amos*, -*emos* or -*imos*:

Alquilar (to rent): We rent the same apartment every year – *Todos los años **alquilamos** el mismo piso*

Aprender (to learn): We never learn! – *¡Nunca **aprendemos**!*

Asistir (to attend): Tonight we attend the party no matter what – *Hoy **asistimos** a la fiesta de cualquier forma*

For *vosotros*, you have to add -*áis*, -*éis* or -*ís*:

Ayudar (to help): Why don't you help with the cleaning? – *¿Por qué no **ayudáis** con la limpieza?*

Leer (to read): You read all day – ***Leéis** todo el día*

Compartir (to share): You share everything you do on social media – ***Compartís** todo lo que hacéis en redes sociales*

Finally, for *ellos*, *ellas*, and *ustedes*, you have to add -*an* or -*en* to the root of the verb:

Cocinar (to cook): They cook every night – ***Cocinan** todas las noches*

Responder (to answer): You always answer late – *Ustedes siempre **responden** tarde*

Decidir (to decide): They decide what to do with their lives – *Ellas **deciden** qué hacer con sus vidas*

James and Alex want to surprise the girls. They are cooking dinner for everybody! They are in the hostel's kitchen making some risotto with vegetables and seafood:

ALEX: How lucky you are here! I cook very bad – *¡Qué suerte que estás aquí! Yo **cocino** muy mal*

JAMES: Do you think I am a chef, or something like that? I'm not so good – *¿**Crees** que soy un chef o algo así? No soy tan bueno*

ALEX: We help each other – *Nos **ayudamos** el uno al otro*

JAMES: I learn a few things about rice while we do this – ***Aprendo** algunas cosas sobre el arroz mientras lo hacemos*

ALEX: Like what? – *¿Qué **aprendes**?*

JAMES: That it gets done faster while I drink beer – *Que se **cocina** más rápido cuando **bebo** cerveza*

ALEX: I miss Australian beer! – *¡**Extraño** la cerveza australiana!*

JAMES: There is a bar nearby where they sell Foster's – *Hay un bar cerca de aquí donde **venden** Foster's*

ALEX: Really? I'm leaving right now – *¿De veras? **Parto** ahora mismo*

JAMES: No way! You help me until we are done and after dinner I will take you there – *iDe ningún modo! Me **ayudas** hasta que terminemos y después de cenar te llevo.*

What's Happening?: The Present Tense (Part II)

There is another way to talk about things that are actually happening right now.

The construction of the present conjugation of verb *estar + the gerund of another verb* is very similar to the English present continuous: I am cooking, I am talking, I am walking.

While the English gerund always ends with -ing, the Spanish gerund ends in *-ando* or *-endo*.

- *Cocinar* (To cook)

*yo **estoy** cocin**ando***

*tú **estás** cocin**ando** / vos **estás** cocin**ando** / usted **está** cocin**ando***

*él/ella **está** cocin**ando***

*nosotros **estamos** cocin**ando***

*ustedes **están** cocin**ando** / vosotros **estáis** cocin**ando***

*ellos/ellas **están** cocin**ando***

- *Beber* (to drink)

*yo **estoy** beb**iendo***

*tú **estás** beb**iendo** / vos **estás** beb**iendo** / usted **está** beb**iendo***

*él/ella **está** beb**iendo***

*nosotros **estamos** beb**iendo***

*ustedes **están** beb**iendo** / vosotros **estáis** beb**iendo***

*ellos/ellas **están** beb**iendo***

- *Escribir* (to write)

*yo **estoy** escrib**iendo***

*tú **estás** escrib**iendo** / vos **estás** escrib**iendo** / usted **está** escrib**iendo***

*él/ella **está** escrib**iendo***

*nosotros **estamos** escrib**iendo***

*ustedes **están** escrib**iendo** / vosotros **estáis** escrib**iendo***

*ellos/ellas **están** escrib**iendo***

These are some sentences with verb *estar* + *gerund* that you might use a lot while traveling:

I am traveling – *Estoy viajando*

I am getting to know Spain – *Estoy conociendo España*

I am learning Spanish – *Estoy aprendiendo español*

I am taking a year off – *Me estoy tomando un año sabático*

I am falling in love with this country – *Me estoy enamorando de este país*

You might use this construction a lot while making plans:

I am leaving – *Me estoy yendo* (*yendo* is the gerund of verb *ir*, to go)

I am going to your hotel – *Estoy yendo a tu hotel*

I am coming – *Estoy llegando*

Juan is calling a taxi – *Juan está llamando un taxi*

The food is arriving – *La comida está llegando*

You can definitely use *estar* + *gerund* to talk about your life at present:

I am working for a company – *Estoy trabajando en una empresa*

I am studying in university – *Estoy estudiando en la universidad*

I am saving money to travel some more – *Estoy ahorrando para viajar más*

I am thinking about quitting my job – *Estoy pensando en renunciar*

James and Alex's meal is ready, but the girls are nowhere to be seen:

JAMES: Do you think they are coming? – *¿Crees que **están viniendo**?*

ALEX: I don't know. I'm texting María – *No lo sé. **Estoy escribiendo** un mensaje a María*

MARÍA: Who are you texting? – *¿A quién **estás escribiendo**?*

JAMES: Girls! You are here! – *¡Chicas! ¡Estáis aquí!*

ANDREA: Yes, and we are starving – *Sí, nos **estamos muriendo** de hambre*

ALEX: That is great because we are waiting for you with a surprise – *Eso es genial, porque las **estamos esperando** con una sorpresa*

ALICIA: Is that a risotto or am I hallucinating? – *¿Eso es un risotto o **estoy alucinando**?*

ALEX AND JAMES: Surprise!!! – *¡¡¡Sorpresa!!!*

Here are some other examples of this construction:

Verb to buy – comprar: I am buying a surfboard – ***Estoy comprando** una tabla de surf*

Verb to travel – *viajar*: You are traveling a lot – ***Estás viajando** mucho*

Verb to book – reservar: We are booking a room – ***Estamos reservando** una habitación*

Verb to talk – *hablar*: They are talking – *Ellos **están hablando***

Chapter 18 - Practice makes Perfect

We've established that you will need to create a learning program for yourself that includes immersion into both the Spanish language and culture. You already know that you should read, write, and speak in Spanish every day to keep yourself on pace to meet your deadline. At this point, you should focus on getting to a point where you can communicate effectively. Be sure to break out of the self-imposed isolation that is common when studying Spanish. Once you've built up an arsenal of common and personalized phrases, it's time to practice them in the real world! If you haven't located a Spanish language partner, you'll want to find someone fast.

Practicing your Spanish will improve your functional ability to use the skills you've learned so far. Interacting with native Spanish speakers regularly can improve your new language skills dramatically. You'll hear authentic pronunciations, expansive vocabularies, and accurate grammar. Finding a consistent language partner can help you to avoid getting discouraged by not finding informational content that's exactly at your pace, since you'll be able to communicate with them if something is too easy or advanced.

Traditional Methods of Practice

If you already know any Spanish speakers, reach out to them directly and ask if they would be able to go over a few things with you. Set up a video chat date with them once or twice a month, or if they are local, meet up for coffee. Being able to speak with a native Spanish speaker in person is best.

You may not know anyone personally that speaks Spanish, but there are plenty of other ways to practice. For example, there are lots of people online that you can have anything— from quick chats to full-length discussions with — entirely in Spanish. There are websites dedicated to help you break down the barriers that typically prevent people from really understanding Spanish.

Language Exchange

In addition to typical language partners, there are Language Exchange opportunities as well. A language exchange partner is what it exactly sounds like. These are people looking for someone to practice English with, and they can be super helpful with your Spanish. You might be able to find an exchange partner that will work with you one-on-one in exchange for your help. Be sure to set up a defined time-frame for your conversations and work on English half of that time, and the other half in Spanish. There are language exchange boards and forums all over the world that you can search. Some people will be upfront with what they need help with and how much of a time commitment they are able to dedicate. Make a post yourself and let prospective language exchange partners know what you'd like to work on and your availability.

Ask a stranger

Don't be afraid to talk to strangers and try and grow a thick skin. If you hear people talking Spanish when you're out and about, be brave enough to ask them for the time or even directions. Chances are most people are more than happy to answer your question. It's quite possible that they will respond to you quickly and that you may not understand; don't worry and don't get defensive! Getting defensive is way more likely to make the exchange uncomfortable than simple Spanish slip-ups. Just tell them that you're new to Spanish and ask if they can repeat what they said slowly or help you understand what they meant. While this can be a difficult thing to ask of strangers, it's a great way to get out of your comfort zone, and once you've been corrected in a real-world scenario, the chances that you'll remember the correct words for next time are very high.

Unconventional Approaches

Call restaurants and bakeries

There are plenty of unconventional approaches to practicing your Spanish as well. Make a list of Mexican or any Spanish speaking restaurants anywhere in the country. For example, you can call them and ask if you would need to make a reservation if you have a group of 7 people wanting to dine next weekend on Saturday at around 7:30 p.m. Have a script prepared for yourself before you call. Be sure to greet the person and then follow your script. There are a few different ways that you can ask this, so have those options ready to go and try them out on different phone calls. If they don't speak Spanish, simply move on to another number. Mix up the number of people on the reservation, the day, and the time that you're asking about. You could even actually make a reservation, and then call back later that day or week and cancel it. You could also simply call to ask what hours they are open, or if they have vegetarian options. Another great way to get real-world practice is to look up Latin grocery or bakeries in your area. You could make up a scenario where you call or go in and ask if they make custom birthday cakes and get pricing and details.

Get on the Phone

Try calling 1-800 numbers that have Spanish menus. Look up numbers for banks, airlines, internet providers, or any company you assume would have Spanish speaking clientele. Again, have a scenario picked out, or if you're feeling bold, improvise something based on the menu options. Before going into a call, pretend that while you may just be learning Spanish, your native language isn't English. "Lo siento, no hablo ingles" (I'm sorry, I don't speak English) will help them continue to attempt communication with you in Spanish. Some companies have an online option for a live chat. This can be a great way to practice both writing and reading.

Take it to the Kitchen

If you like to cook, you can find a wealth of Spanish cookbooks that will test out your reading comprehension and give your palate a new way to branch out. Watch a Spanish cooking show and attempt to recreate a dish you are interested in. You can search for recipes in Spanish by dish, or find a recipe you love and translate it yourself. Make a list of items you need and go to a Hispanic grocery store so that you can reinforce the language you're learning. When you're preparing the meal, read every step out loud so that you can get verbal practice.

Help Others

Volunteer organizations hold opportunities to interact with Spanish speakers as well. Perform a quick search for organizations that are active in your community and find out what kind of help they're looking for where you may get exposure to Spanish speakers. Some excellent volunteer programs focus on improving language skills while volunteering time towards a good cause. Make a few calls and ask the organizers if they are familiar with anything in line with your needs. Of course, giving back to underprivileged people in your community can be an advantageous experience in and of itself.

Remember to keep things light-hearted and fun. If you can learn to relax and go with the flow, you will naturally fall into the rhythm of the Spanish language. Commit to getting the most out of every opportunity you must practice, and you'll move from beginner to intermediate, and to advanced in no time.

Chapter 19 - A Day in the Life of a Language Learner

If you haven't figured it out yet, the official motto of this book is: Quality over Quantity. You may feel like you need to spend hours every day pouring over your Spanish books to really learn Spanish. The truth is, this isn't necessarily true. What matters is that the time you do dedicate to studying is productive. It's important that you maintain a good balance between structured "book-learning" and hands-on immersion practice and exposure.

In order to do that, take a look at the following rough guide for how to live the daily life of a Spanish language learner. In addition to your scheduled study sessions consisting of books and conjugation charts, be sure to incorporate:

Listening Skills

10 Minutes a Day

Listening is crucial to your Spanish learning process. Hearing the language used in authentic contexts by native speakers will help, not only with your comprehension abilities, but your speaking as well. Listening is your input and speaking will be your output.

Listening to Spanish podcasts, music, radio, audio books, etc. are simple, enjoyable ways to incorporate listening practice into your daily routine.

Grammar Skills

15 Minutes a Day

The foundation of any language is its grammar. Spanish is no exception to this. Grammar includes things such as verb conjugations, tenses, parts of speech (nouns, adjectives, adverbs, etc.), and sentence structure.

Grammar can be a big challenge and a thorn in the side of any and every foreign language student. Not only are the rules seemingly never ending, but there appear to be as many exceptions to these rules. The main thing to remember when working with grammar is to take it one step at a time. Focus on things in small areas and don't try to rush from one thing to the next. Make sure you give yourself the time you need to fully understand whatever topic you are working with before moving on to the next. Don't put too much pressure on yourself! Grammar is cumulative. You need to ensure that you have all the foundational building blocks understood before you can start building on them.

Writing Practice and Vocabulary

20 Minutes a Day

Writing is something you may not expect to need too much in Spanish. But the fact is, you'd be surprised to find that writing comes up a lot more than you'd think. In addition to that, writing is a great way to improve your vocabulary, grammar, and produce productive output--putting into use the input you receive from reading.

There are many different ways you can practice writing. Your 20 minutes a day doesn't need to be done all at one time. Although, sitting down every once in a while to write out a letter, journal entry, or even short story is great practice. If you don't have the time or energy to do that, though, you can find other little ways to incorporate writing in Spanish into your daily life.

- Write to-do lists in Spanish

- Write out your shopping list in Spanish

- Write reminders to yourself in Spanish

- Sit down with your vocabulary list and write out a few sentences using the new words you're working on

Reading

15 Minutes a Day

Initially, the word "reading" often brings to mind the idea of sitting down with a novel and pouring over it for hours on end. However, this doesn't have to be the case. You're constantly reading--everywhere you go. Street signs, menus, these are all things that you read on a day- in and day-out basis.

When looking for things to read in Spanish, don't limit yourself to just books. Check out some blogs in Spanish or read a Spanish newspaper online. Look up articles on things that interest you.

If you have friends who are also trying to learn Spanish, set up an e-mail exchange with them. This will force you to not only write in Spanish regularly but read in Spanish as well. Not to mention, this will create a community with which you can share your experiences with the language.

How to Include Spanish in Your Daily Routine

Below you will find a general outline for things you can do at different times of the day to make Spanish a part of your everyday life.

Morning

7am: Wake up. Set your alarm to go off with a Spanish song or a Spanish radio station. Get your brain thinking in Spanish from the get-go!

7:15am: Breakfast time. While you're eating your breakfast, open up a Spanish app on your phone or scroll through a Spanish newspaper online.

8:00am: Morning Commute. Listen to Spanish radio in the car or pop in an audio book. Or listen to a podcast on your phone if you take public transport.

Afternoon

1pm: Lunch break. Read an article online while you enjoy your meal. Or jot down your shopping list and/or to-do list for the evening.

2:45pm: Coffee break. We all need a quick cup of joe at some point in the work day. Use this time to open up an app on your phone to memorize some vocabulary. Or play a fun Spanish language game online.

5pm: Commute home. It's been a long day. Reward yourself by listening to fun Spanish songs or reading an enjoyable, easy Spanish book on the train.

Evening

8pm: Study Session. After dinner, set aside a solid block of time that you'll dedicate to the "book-learning" side of studying Spanish. Start with at least 20-30 minutes of focused study (grammar, vocabulary, etc.) and, if you're feeling up to it, keep going.

9pm: Relax. Give your brain a break. Try relaxing with a YouTube clip in Spanish, something funny and light-hearted.

10pm: Bedtime. Find a Spanish book to keep on your nightstand to read little by little as you fall asleep at night. Or pop in a Spanish movie to listen to as you drift off.

Conclusion

Finding Spanish-speaking friends is a great way to test your new language skills. It is very likely that any Spanish-speaking friends that you might have will be more than willing to help you practice what you have learned in this book. Also, this type of practice and exposure will enable you to play with the language so that you can become comfortable with going off-script. This will allow you to truly begin to communicate through the use of what you have actually learned.

If you are planning on traveling, you will find that the language presented in this book will be invaluable as you navigate your way through the various places and situations that you will encounter. Best of all, you will have the opportunity to put yourself to the test. There is an undeniable feeling of satisfaction that comes when you are able to communicate in a foreign language.

We are confident that you found the content in this book useful in any situation. In fact, don't be surprised if you get caught in learning Spanish. You might even choose to pursue your learning even further.

In that case, do check out the subsequent volumes in this series. You will find that they are intended to help you deepen your knowledge and understanding of the Spanish language in such a way that you will be truly on your way to mastering Spanish communication skills.

Learning continues in the next coming Grammar Books for Intermediate and for Advanced.

So, thank you for taking the time to read this book. There are plenty of options out there which claim to teach you Spanish in a short period of time. Unfortunately, some of those courses' under-deliver in terms of value, while others turn out to be a costly experience.

Spanish Short Stories for Beginners

Learn Spanish in a Fast and Easy Way, and Grow Your Vocabulary with 16 Captivating Short Stories

Introduction

In this book, we are presenting short stories that you can read to practice Spanish language. Each story has its own topic, where important vocabulary is presented before the story. Then, you have the story, which you can read at your own leisure.

Most importantly, you can begin to practice the language that we have discussed throughout this book in an engaging manner. As such, here is a suggested methodology that you can apply to the study of these short stories.

1.- Next, read through the story, paragraph by paragraph. Since you will find the Spanish and English version, you will be able to visualize the structures and conjugations that we have studied throughout this volume. That way, you will be able to make a mental note of the way each structure is presented in real-life. This makes learning grammar and sentence structure a lot more digestible.

2.- Then, go through every one of the paragraphs. When you reach the end of the story, go back to any parts that you feel weren't clear or perhaps you have questions about. You can focus on these parts so that you can get the extra practice that you need. Once you feel comfortable with the whole story, you can then move on to the questions.

3.- The questions following the story are both meant to test your reading comprehension and give you an opportunity to practice your writing skills. This exercise will give you the opportunity to use your imagination when it comes to writing skills.

4.- The suggested responses at the end of the story are meant to serve as a guide. So, you can compare your own answers to the suggested ones. Of course, these are only suggested answers. That means you can very well come up with your own answers according to the passage that you have read.

5.- Finally, please review the vocabulary presented at the end of the story. The words in that vocabulary have been selected in order to help you warm up for the content in the story. You will find both the Spanish and English words in the list. That way, you won't have to guess their meaning. You can read through the list, and make a note of the words that you find new or challenging.

We have some tips that will help you get the most out of these stories based on the methodology suggested -

- Don't feel that you need to complete the whole story in one session. In fact, each story has been designed so that you can take one paragraph at a time. Also, you can begin with the vocabulary and then take each paragraph as time permits. That way, you won't feel like you have been interrupted. In any case, you can continue where you left off.

- Take your time. There is no need to rush through the stories or any part of this book. This volume can very well serve you as a reference guide. That way, you can always go back to it whenever you have the need to do so.

- Try your best to reserve a specific amount of time each day for study with this book. Even 10 or 15 minutes a day is enough to get you into the habit of daily practice. Since practice is the best way in which you can improve your skills, you will soon find that getting into a rhythm is not as difficult as you thought it would be. So, try to take sometime during a break at work, your daily trip, or even before bedtime to go through parts of each story or any other part of this book. We are sure that you will not only find it enjoyable but also productive.

We hope you enjoy every one of these stories. They have been carefully crafted to provide you with a practical and meaningful experience.

1. Present Simple with "AR" Verbs

Deseo visitar lugares exóticos. Me gusta la selva, los bosques, el mar y las aventuras en lugares emocionantes. Siempre hay alguno nuevo que encontrar en los lugares exóticos. Me gusta mucho visitar la naturaleza.

I want to visit exotic places. I like the jungle, the forest, the sea and the adventures in exciting places. There is always something new to find in exotic places. I really like to visit nature.

También me gusta visitar lugares históricos. Por ejemplo, visito ruinas, monumentos y sitios famosos. Todas las ciudades del mundo son especiales. Siempre ando por las calles. Camino en busca de tesoros nuevos. Cuando encuentro un tesoro nuevo, rápidamente le tomo una fotografía. Las fotografías son mis propios tesoros. Son los recuerdos de los viajes tan inolvidables.

I also like to visit historical places. For example, I visit ruins, monuments and famous sites. Every city in the world is special. I always walk the streets. I walk ins search of new treasures. When I find a new treasure, I quickly take a picture of it. Photographs are my own treasures. They are the memories of unforgettable trips.

Por todas partes, las personas saludan cuando pasas. Te miran y te saludan amablemente. Me gustar charlar con las personas, ...bueno, si hablamos el mismo idioma. No siempre hablamos el mismo idioma, pero siempre nos comunicamos.

Everywhere, people greet when you pass. They look at you and greet you kindly. I like to chat with people, ... well, if we speak the same language. We do not always speak the same language, but we always communicate.

La comida también es maravillosa en cada viaje. Disfruto de las comidas auténticas de cada país o ciudad. Las personas trabajan mucho en preparar comida rica y deliciosa. En todos los países se cocina algo muy especial. En muchos lugares, se prepara comida especial para los turistas. Las bebidas tradicionales son una parte importante de la experiencia local. Me gusta mucho probar las bebidas tradicionales, aunque no mucho me gustan las bebidas alcohólicas.

The food is also wonderful on every trip. I enjoy the authentic foods of each country or city. People work hard to prepare rich and delicious food. In all countries, something very special is cooked. In many places, special food is prepared for tourists. Traditional drinks are an important part of the local experience. I like to try traditional drinks, although I do not like alcoholic beverages.

Me encanta viajar. Después de trabajar, es lo que más disfruto en la vida. Deseo viajar a todos los países del mundo. Esto es algo que deseo mucho lograr. Una vida sin viajar no es vida.

I love traveling. Aside from working, it's what I enjoy most in life. I wish to travel to all the countries of the world. This is something I really want to achieve. A life without traveling is not a life.

Por favor responda las siguientes preguntas.

Please answer the following questions.

¿Por qué es fascinante llegar a un lugar nuevo?

_____

_____

_____

Why is it fascinating to arrive at a new place?

_____

_____

_____

_____

¿Qué lugares deseo visitar?

_____

_____

_____

_____

What places do I want to visit?

_____

_____

_____

_____

¿Cuáles lugares me gustan?

_____

_____

_____

_____

What places do I like?

_____

_____

_____

_____

¿Cuáles son los lugares históricos que visito?

_____

_____

_____

_____

What are the historic places that I visit?

_____

_____

_____

_____

¿Qué busco cuando camino?

_____

_____

_____

What do I search for when I walk?

_____

_____

_____

¿Qué hacen las personas cuando pasas?

_____

_____

_____

What do people do when you pass?

_____

_____

_____

¿Cómo es la comida?

_____

_____

_____

What is the food like?

_____

_____

_____

¿Qué comida se prepara para los turistas?

_____

_____

_____

_____

What food is prepared for the tourists?

_____

_____

_____

¿Qué bebidas me gusta probar?

_____

_____

_____

What drinks do I like to try?

_____

_____

_____

¿Qué deseo hacer?

_____

_____

_____

_____

What do I wish to do?

_____

_____

_____

_____

Respuestas sugeridas

Suggested answers

¿Por qué es fascinante llegar a un lugar nuevo? Es fascinante llegar a un lugar nuevo porque puedes observar paisajes, personas, casas y calles. -

Why is it fascinating to arrive at a new place? It is fascinating to arrive at a new place because you can observe landscapes, people, houses and streets.

¿Qué lugares deseo visitar? Deseo visitar lugares exóticos como selvas y bosques.

What places do I want to visit? I want to visit exotics places such as jungles and forests

¿Cuál lugar me gusta? -

What place do I like?

Me gustan mucho la naturaleza.

I like nature very much.

¿Cuáles son los lugares históricos que visito?

What are the historic places that I visit?

Visito lugares históricos como ruinas y monumentos.

I visit historic places such as ruins and monuments

¿Qué busco cuando camino?

What do I search for when I walk?

Busco tesoros cuando caminos por las calles.

I search for treasures when I walk on the streets.

¿Qué hacen las personas cuando pasas?

What do people do when you pass?

Las personas te saludan cuando pasas. -

People greet you when you pass.

¿Cómo es la comida?

What is the food like?

La comida es rica y deliciosa. -

The food is rich and delicious.

¿Qué comida se prepara para los turistas?

What food is prepared for the tourists?

Preparan comidas auténticas para los turistas. -

They prepare authentic food for tourists.

¿Qué bebidas me gusta probar?

What drinks do I like to try?

Me gusta probar bebidas tradicionales. -

I like to try traditional drinks.

¿Qué deseo hacer?

What do I wish to do?

Deseo visitar todos los países del mundo. -

I wish to visit all of the countries in the world.

Vocabulario/Vocabulary

- *Viajar es una experiencia* --- Traveling is an experience
- *maravillosa* --- Experience
- *auténtica* --- authentic
- *deseo* --- wish/want
- *exóticos* --- exotic
- *fascinante* --- fascinating
- *fotografía* --- photograph/picture
- *maravillosa* --- wonderful
- *naturaleza* --- nature
- *probar* --- try
- *saludan* --- greet
- *tesoro* --- treasure

2. La Mejor Cita – The Best Date

Samantha era una joven chica de 23 años que estudiaba ingeniería mecánica, era muy hermosa, entre las tres chicas que estudiaban ingeniería mecánica, ella era la más hermosa, por lo que, los chicos solo se fijaban en ella. Ella estaba harta de que los patanes y todos los chicos siempre intentaran tener algo con ella. Un día, en la fiesta del cumpleaños del novio de Becky, su mejor amiga; Samantha estaba siendo abordada por todos los chicos de la fiesta, cuando llegó un chico muy guapo al que ella había visto durante un rato y le dijo que no podía evitar verla, Samantha, pensando que era uno del montón, lo rechazó inmediatamente, pero él le dijo que era porque tenía un moco en la cara. Samantha, súper apenada, le pregunto que, si era en serio, y que en donde lo tenía, pero era una broma de él para que ella bajara la guardia. Su nombre era Bruce. Era muy chistoso y simpático, por lo que a Samantha le agradó y estuvieron hablando el resto de la fiesta. Bruce se fue y Samantha no le dio ni le pidió su número, pues temía que pensara que era una chica fácil.

Samantha was a young girl of 23 years who studied mechanical engineering. She was very beautiful. Among the three girls who studied mechanical engineering, she was the most beautiful, so the boys only noticed her. She was sick and tired of the louts and all the boys that always trying to have something with her. One day, at the birthday party of Becky's boyfriend, her best friend, Samantha was approached by all the boys at the party. When a very handsome boy arrived and told her he couldn't avoid seeing her. Samantha, thinking he was one of the bunch, immediately rejected him, but he told her it was because she (had) a snot on her face. Samantha, super embarrassed, asked him if he was serious and that where she had it. However, it was just his joke so that she could let her guard down. His name was Bruce. He was very funny and friendly, so Samantha liked him and they talked for the rest of the party. Bruce left and Samantha didn't give her number or ask for his, because she was afraid that he thought she was an easy girl.

Emocionada por el chico que conoció, Samantha le contó todo a Becky, quien le dijo que era una tonta por no haberle dado o pedido el número de él.

Excited by the boy she met; Samantha told Becky everything, who said she was a fool for not giving or asking for his number.

Días después recibió un mensaje de un número desconocido, bromeando sobre el moco. En seguida, Samantha supo que se trataba de Bruce y lo llamó, acordaron salir a comer y verse en el centro comercial.

Days later, she received a message from an unknown number, joking about the snot. Samantha knew it was Bruce and called him. They agreed to go out to eat and meet at the mall.

La cita fue maravillosa, y Bruce le dijo a Samantha su secreto, y también le dijo que le gustaba mucho, Samantha, se lanzó sobre él y lo besó agradeciéndole por ser la mejor cita que había tenido.

The date was wonderful. Bruce told Samantha his secret and also told her that he liked her very much. Samantha, threw herself on him and kissed him, to thank him for being the best date she had ever had.

Quiz

1. ¿Cuántos años tenía Samantha cuando estudió ingeniería mecánica?
a. No nos dicen
b. 32 años de edad
c. 23 años

d. 20 años

2. ¿Cuántas chicas estudiaron ingeniería mecánica con Samantha?
a. 23
b. 3
c. ninguna
d. 1

3. ¿Cómo se llamaba el niño que vino a ver a Samantha?
a. Becky
b. Brian
c. Bruce
d. No nos dicen

4. ¿Qué hicieron Samantha y Bruce en una cita?
a. Caminado
b. Besado
c. Dormido
d. Se rio

Respuestas:

1. c
2. b
3. c
4. b

Vocabulario/Vocabulary

- *Ingeniería* --- engineering
- *Mecánica* --- Mechanical
- *Carrera* – career
- *Pecas* --- freckles
- *Cachetes* --- cheeks
- *Sonrisa* --- smile
- *Delgada* --- thin
- *Locos* --- crazy
- *Salir* --- going out/date
- *Belleza* --- beauty
- *Varones* --- male
- *Hembras* --- female
- *Compañeros* --- classmates
- *ingeniería electronica* --- electronic engineering
- *ingeniería química* --- chemical engineering
- *novio* --- boyfriend
- *fiesta* --- party
- *guapo* --- handsome
- *bailar* --- dancing

- *rechazar* – to refuse
- *miradas* --- glances
- *moco* --- snot
- *nariz* --- nose
- *bromeando* – joking
- *bajar la guardia*- lowering guard
- *cansada* --- tired
- *bien jugado* --- well played
- *creído* --- arrogant
- *foto* --- photo
- *chistoso* – funny
- contenta --- happy
- *amable* – friendly
- *gracioso* --- funny
- *despedirse* --- said goodbye
- desconocido --- unknown
- *ocupada* --- busy
- maquillarse --- make-up

3. El Lado Malo De Los Pasatiempos

Los pasatiempos son las diferentes actividades que hacemos para gastar tiempo o para recrearnos y relajarnos. Los pasatiempos pueden ser casi cualquier cosa, siempre y cuando sea diferente a las actividades diarias. Durante mi tiempo libre, a mí me gusta practicar futbol, también tengo el pasatiempo de leer ciencia ficción y tocar guitarra. Mi compañero de apartamento, tiene el pasatiempo del origami, el siempre dobla papel y crea diversos animales y formas, hoy quiere hacer muchas aves. Mi compañero dedica muchas horas todos los fines de semana a su pasatiempo, y creo yo, él es cada día mejor en el arte del origami. Yo me preocupo por mis pasatiempos, debido a que en ocasiones me distraigo tanto que me pasa el tiempo volando, y cuando me doy cuenta, debo apurarme con mis otras actividades, o incluso a veces las olvido por completo.

The hobbies are different activities we do to spend time recreationally and to relax. Hobbies can be almost anything, as long as it is different from daily activities. During my free time, I like to play soccer; I also have the hobby of reading science fiction and playing guitar. My roommate has origami as his hobby; he always folds paper and creates different animals and forms. Today he wants to make many birds. My roommate devotes many hours every weekend to his hobby. I believe that he is getting better every day in the origami art. I worry about my hobbies because sometimes I get distracted too much, that I see my time flying when I realize it, I hurry with my other activities, or even sometimes I completely forget them.

Lo malo de los pasatiempos, es que como su nombre lo indica, consumen mucho tiempo, y si no se pone mucha atención a las horas que se gasta practicándolos, Tú puedes desperdiciar días enteros, y dejar de hacer las tareas u obligaciones que son realmente importantes, y que nos traen beneficios. Los pasatiempos deben ser manejados como los vicios, con cuidado y de a poquito, para evitar crear problemas.

The bad thing about hobbies is that as the name implies, they consume a lot of time, if you do not pay much attention to track the hours spent practicing them. You can waste days, and stop doing the tasks or obligations that really matter and bring you benefits. Hobbies should be handled like vices, carefully and you should must spend a little time, to avoid creating problems.

Por supuesto, todos necesitamos actividades de esparcimiento y recreación, y los pasatiempos permiten relajarnos, y divertirnos. Pero se tiene que ser muy precavido con la cantidad de horas que le dedicamos a estos. Ellos son muy entretenidos, captan toda nuestra atención y nos hacen olvidar las tareas importantes y nuestras obligaciones. En mi opinión, los peores pasatiempos son los video juegos, debido a la gran estimulación que proporcionan. Siempre ocasionan que se descuiden las obligaciones en las personas distraídas o susceptibles de ser fanáticas de ellos.

Of course, we all need activities for recreation and leisure. Hobbies allow us to relax and have fun, but we have to be very careful with the number of hours we dedicate to them. They are very entertaining, they capture our full attention, and they make us forget the important tasks and our duties. In my opinion, the worst hobbies are video games, due to the high stimulation they provide. They always cause negligence in the obligations of people who are easily distracted or are likely to be fanatics of them.

Quiz

1. A la persona le gusta hacer los siguientes pasatiempos, excepto uno. ¿Cuál es?
a. Tocando la batería

b. leyendo ciencia ficción
c. tocar la guitarra
d. jugando futbol

2. ¿Por qué los pasatiempos deben manejarse como vicios?
a. para evitar crear problemas
b. No son buenos
c. Conducen a tentaciones
d. Son peligrosos

3. ¿Cuál es el hobby del compañeros de cuarto?
a. leyendo ciencia ficción
b. tocar la guitarra
c. jugando futbol
d. origami

4. ¿Por qué compartimos pasatiempos?
a. como trabajo
b. Para mantenernos ocupados
c. Para recreación
d. Como una actividad diaria

Vocabulary / Vocabulario

- Hobby --- *Pasatiempo*
- Waste time --- *Gastar tiempo*
- Leisure --- *Ocio (Esparcimiento)*
- Recreation --- *recreación*
- Relax --- *Relajarnos*
- Free time --- *Tiempo libre*
- Distract --- *Distraer*
- Pay attention --- *Poner atención*
- (To) practice --- *Practicar*

4. Quedarse En Casa

Era domingo en la tarde. Alejandro no tenía ningún plan en particular, por lo que se permitió recuperar el sueño que había perdido durante la semana. Sin embargo, no sería un día de ocio total, ya que tenía que hacer varias tareas domésticas.

It was a Sunday afternoon. Alejandro had no particular plans, so he fell asleep and allowed himself to catch up on sleep he had missed during the week. However, it would not be a completely lazy day, as he had to do several housework

Quizás lo más importante de todo eran las facturas no pagadas que debía revisar. La vivienda no es gratis después de todo. El alquiler, la electricidad, el agua, internet, los préstamos estudiantiles y los planes de teléfono tenían pagos vencidos. Sin embargo, gracias a la tecnología, todo esto se puede pagar en línea sin salir de casa.

Perhaps most important of all were the unpaid bills that needed to be taken care of. Housing isn't free, after all. Rent, electricity, water, internet, student loans, and phone plans all have overdue payments. Thanks to technology, all of these can be paid online without leaving home.

Luego, la ropa se había acumulado durante la semana y algunos lavados serían necesarios para la próxima semana. Él nunca se molestaba en clasificar su ropa en blanca, oscura y de colores, así que en lugar de eso solo ponía la mayor cantidad de carga posible, vertía un poco de detergente para la ropa, suavizante de telas y ponía a funcionar la lavadora.

Next, the laundry had piled up over) the week, and a few loads would be necessary for the upcoming week. He never bothered to sort his clothes into whites, darks, and colors; instead, he would just throw as much as he could in each load, pour in some laundry detergent and fabric softener, and run the laundry machine.

Mientras esperaba que cada carga de ropa terminara, pensó que se mantendría productivo lavando los platos y aspirando la casa. La casa de Alejandro de ninguna manera estaba impecable, pero él hacía un poco cada semana para mantenerla presentable. Para esta semana, haría algo de trabajo extra en la cocina. Limpió la nevera tirando los alimentos vencidos. También frotó los mostradores con desinfectante y retiró todas las migajas de comida del piso. Y terminó barriendo el suelo con su escoba y su recogedor. La limpieza podría esperar otro fin de semana, pensó.

While he waited for each load to finish, he figured he would stay productive; washing the dishes and vacuuming the house. Alejandro's house was not impeccable at all, but he did just a little bit each week to maintain what he could. This week, he would do some extra work in the kitchen. He cleaned out the fridge by throwing away expired foods. He also scrubbed the counters with disinfectant and threw all the crumbs of food on the floor. And he finished by sweeping the floor with his broom and dustpan. Mopping could wait another week, he thought.

Alejandro estaba más interesado en pasar el resto de su día en la computadora jugando videojuegos. Era fanático de los juegos de estrategia y podía pasar horas creando nuevas estrategias para probar contra sus amigos en línea e incluso en juegos de un solo jugador. Cuando necesitaba un descanso, de vez en cuando se levantaba para estirarse rápidamente, miraba por las ventanas, calentaba algo de comida en el microondas y se sentaba de nuevo para seguir jugando.

Alejandro was more interested in spending the rest of his day at the computer playing video games. He was a fan of strategy games and could spend hours devising new strategies to try out against his friends online and even in single player games. When he needed a break, he would occasionally get up for a quick stretch, looked out the windows, heated some food in the microwave, and sat down for more

gaming.

Después de pasar demasiadas horas frente a la computadora, se produjo una pequeña crisis existencial. ¿Fue realmente sabio pasar tanto tiempo jugando cuando podría haber hecho algo más significativo? Claro, había videos que podía ver en línea, ¿pero eso sería diferente? Entonces, recogió los auriculares en su habitación y comenzó a escuchar algunos de los audiolibros que le recomendó Sofía.

After spending too many hours in front of the computer, a small existential crisis would occur. Was it really all that wise to spend so much time gaming when it could be used for something more meaningful? Sure, there were videos he could watch online, but would that be any different? And so, he picked up the headphones in his bedroom and started to listen to some of the audiobook recommended to him by Sofía.

Al escuchar el libro, al instante sintió que estaba haciendo lo correcto con su tiempo e incluso tuvo la oportunidad de reflexionar un poco. Mientras seguía escuchando, vagaba por la casa. Abrió y cerró las puertas de su armario sin ninguna razón en particular. Puso su mano en el sofá y dejó que se deslizara mientras caminaba. No había mesa en el comedor para repetir esta acción, ya que vivía solo y acostumbraba a comer en la cocina o en el balcón.

Listening to the book instantly the correct use of his time and even opened up the opportunity to reflect a bit. While he kept listening, he wandered around his house. He opened and closed his closet doors for no particular reason. He put his hand on the couch and let it glide over as he walked across. There was no dining room table to repeat this action, as he lived by himself and usually ate in the kitchen or out on the balcony.

Antes de que se diera cuenta, eran las 10:00 pm. Era hora de acostarse. Si bien no terminó el audiolibro, ciertamente tenía algo nuevo de lo cual hablar el próximo fin de semana cuando fuera a una reunión familiar. Incluso podría llevar a Sofía y presentarla como la persona que le habló del libro.

Before he knew it, it was 10:00 pm. It was time for bed. While he didn't finish the audiobook, he certainly had something new to talk about next weekend when he would go to the family reunion. He could even bring Sofía and introduce her as the one who introduced him to the book.

Quiz

1. Si alguien necesita dormir, significa que...
a) ha estado durmiendo demasiado.
b) ha estado durmiendo muy poco.
c) le gusta dormir.
d) tiene problemas para conciliar el sueño.

2. ¿Cuál de los siguientes no se considera un servicio público para una vivienda?
a) Préstamos estudiantiles
b) Agua
c) Electricidad
d) Internet

3. Al limpiar la cocina, Alejandro no...
a) frotó la encimera con desinfectante.
b) tiró los alimentos vencidos.

c) trapeó el piso.
d) barrió el piso con su escoba y recogedor.

4. ¿Cuál es generalmente la forma más rápida de cocinar los alimentos?
a) En la estufa
b) En el microondas
c) En el horno
d) En el horno tostador

5. ¿Dónde encontró Alejandro sus auriculares?
a) En su habitación
b) En su armario
c) En la lavadora
d) En la sala de estar

Answers:

1. B
2. A
3. C
4. A
5. A

Vocabulario/Vocabulary

- *quedarse en casa* --- to stay at home
- domingo en la tarde --- Sunday afternoon
- *recuperar el sueño* – to catch up on sleep
- tareas domésticas – housework
- facturas sin pagar --- unpaid bills
- *vivienda* --- housing
- alquiler --- rent
- *electricidad* --- electricity
- *internet* --- internet
- préstamos estudiantiles --- student loans
- planes de teléfono --- phone plans
- *tener un pago vencido* --- to have a payment due
- *tecnología* --- technology
- *pagar en línea* --- to pay online
- *salir de casa* -- to leave the house
- *acumular* --- to accumulate, to pile up
- *ropa* --- clothes
- *clasificar* --- to sort
- *verter* --- to pour
- *detergente* --- detergent
- *suavizante de tela* --- fabric softener
- *funcionar* --- to work, to function

113

- *lavadora* --- laundry machine
- *una carga de ropa* --- a load of laundry
- *productivo* --- productive
- *lavando los platos* --- washing the dishes
- *aspirando la casa* --- vacuuming the house
- *impecable* --- spotless
- trabajo extra --- extra work
- *cocina* --- kitchen
- *limpiar la nevera* --- to clean out the fridge
- *tirar* --- to throw (away)
- alimentos vencidos --- expired food
- *frotar los mostradores* --- to scrub the counters
- *desinfectante* --- disinfectant
- *retirar* --- to remove
- migajas de comida --- food crumbs
- *piso* --- floor
- *suelo* --- floor
- *barrer el suelo* --- to sweep the floor
- *escoba y recogedor* --- broom and dustpan
- *limpieza* --- cleanliness
- *el resto del día* --- the rest of the day
- *computador* --- computer
- juegos de estrategia --- strategy games
- *juegos en solitario* --- single player games
- *estirarse* --- to stretch
- *mirar por las ventanas* --- to peer out the windows
- *calentar* --- to heat up
- *crisis existencial* --- existential crisis
- *sabio* --- wise
- *significativo* --- meaningful
- *videos* --- videos
- *ver en línea* --- to watch online
- *auriculares* --- headphones
- *habitación* --- bedroom
- *al instante* --- instantly
- *El uso correcto de su tiempo* – the correct use of his time
- *tener la oportunidad* --- to have the opportunity
- *reflexionar* --- to reflect (on)
- *vagar* --- to wander (around)
- puertas de los armarios --- closet doors
- sin ninguna razón – for no reason
- *sofá* – couch/sofa
- *deslizarse* --- to glide
- *mesa de comedor* --- dining room table
- *vivir solo* --- to live by oneself
- *balcón* --- balcony
- hora de acostarse --- bedtime

- *ciertamente* --- certainly
- *reunión familiar* --- family gathering
- *presentar* --- to introduce

5. De Viaje

Viernes, 19 de diciembre

Friday, December 19

Hoy empiezan las vacaciones de Navidad. Mis padres, mis hermanos y yo volvemos a España durante las fiestas para ver a la familia. Por la tarde hacemos las maletas, tomamos un taxi y vamos al aeropuerto.

Today the Christmas holidays begin. My parents, my brothers and I return to Spain during the holidays to see the family. In the afternoon we pack our bags, take a taxi and go to the airport.

— *¿A dónde desean ir? —pregunta el taxista.*

"Where would you like to go?" asks the taxi driver.

— *Al aeropuerto de JFK, por favor. —contesta mi padre.*

"To JFK airport, please." answers my father.

Cuando llegamos al aeropuerto, entregué mi boleto en el mostrador y mostré mi pasaporte a una azafata. Después nos dan las tarjetas de embarque y nos indican dónde podemos esperar. Nos sentamos en una cafetería a ver despegar los aviones y a tomar un chocolate caliente. Echo de menos a Luciano.

When we arrive at the airport, I handed my ticket the counter and showed my passport to a flight attendant. Then they give us the boarding passes and tell us where we can wait. We sat in a cafeteria to watch the planes take off and have a hot chocolate. I miss Luciano.

De pronto veo un gato gris que corre por la pista, entre los aviones. ¡Es Micifuz, el gato del director del colegio! Una pista de aterrizaje es un lugar peligroso para un gato, y me siento preocupado.

Suddenly I see a gray cat running along the runway, between the planes. It's Micifuz, the school principal's cat! A runway is a dangerous place for a cat, and I feel worried.

Un avión se acerca al gato por la pista. ¡Ese avión va muy rápido! Pero entonces aparece Luciano y salva al gato en el último minuto. Luciano corre detrás del gato gris para ayudarle a escapar. Yo lo veo todo desde el cristal, pero mamá está en el baño y no ve nada.

An airplane approaches the cat on the runway. That plane is going very fast! But then Luciano appears and saves the cat at the last minute. Luciano runs after the gray cat to help him escape. I see everything from the window glass, but mom is in the bathroom and she sees nothing.

— *¡Luciano! ¡Luciano! —grito por la ventana, pero Luciano no me oye. Luciano y el gato desaparecen al final de la pista.*

"Luciano! Luciano!" I scream out the window, but Luciano does not hear me. Luciano and the cat disappear at the end of the track.

— *Es hora de embarcar, —dice mi madre, y me estira del brazo.*

"It's time to board", says my mother, and she pulls at my arm.

— *No puedo subir al avión, mamá, mi duende Luciano está en la pista, con el gato del director.*

Mi madre se ríe. Ella piensa que es una broma.

"I can't get on the plane, mom, my elf Luciano is on the runway, with the principal's cat."

My mother laughs. She thinks it's a joke.

— *¿Tu amigo imaginario? Da igual, puedes jugar con él otro día.*

"Your imaginary friend? It doesn't matter, you will be able to play with him some other day."

— *Pero mamá...*

"But mom..."

— *Puedes leer un libro en el avión o pintar con tus lápices de colores, ¿de acuerdo? —dice mamá, y subimos al avión.*

"You can read a book on the plane or color with your crayons, okay?" says mom, and we get on the plane.

En el avión me parece oír los cascabeles del gorro de Luciano, pero no lo veo en ningún sitio. Creo que es sólo mi imaginación.

On the plane I think I hear Luciano's hat bells, but I don't see him anywhere. I think it's just my imagination.

Expresiones útiles/Useful expressions

¿A dónde vamos? - Where are we going to?

¿Dónde está el aeropuerto? - Where is the airport?

¿Cómo se va a la estación? - How can I get to the station?

¿A qué distancia está la playa? - How far is the beach?

He perdido el pasaporte/las llaves/la cartera - I have lost my passport/my keys/my wallet.

cerca/lejos - near/far

rápido/lento - fast/slow

aquí - here

ahí, allí - there (depending on whether it's nearer or farther away)

Esperar - to wait

Hacer cola - to queue

Facturar las maletas - to check your baggage.

Llamar - to call

Última llamada - last call

Oficina de objetos perdidos - lost property office

La dirección - address

Echar de menos (algo/a alguien) - to miss (something/someone)

Da igual - it doesn't matter

Quiz

1) ¿A dónde va la familia de Valeria en Navidad?
a) A Nueva York.
b) A Venecia.
c) A España.

2) ¿Qué medios de transporte usan para viajar?
a) Autobús y avión.
b) Taxi y barco.
c) Taxi y avión.

3) ¿Qué hacen Luciano y el gato en el aeropuerto?
a) Corren por el mostrador de facturación.
b) Toman chocolate caliente con Valeria.
c) Corren por la pista de aterrizaje.

4) ¿Luciano salva al gato de los aviones?
a) No, y el gato tiene un accidente con un avión.
b) Sí, Luciano corre y saca al gato de la pista.
c) No, y el gato se mete en una maleta.

5) ¿Puede Valeria hablar con Luciano?
a) Sí, suben juntos al avión.
b) No, su madre dice que es hora de irse.
c) Sí, hablan en la cafetería.

Answers

1) c
2) c
3) c
4) b
5) b

Vocabulario (Vocabulary)

- *Viajar* --- To travel
- Las vacaciones --- holidays
- La maleta de viaje --- suitcase
- *Hacer las maletas* --- to pack your luggage
- *El taxi* --- taxi
- El autobús --- bus
- La parada de autobús --- bus stop
- *El tren* --- train
- El coche --- car
- *La estación* (de autobuses, de tren) --- (bus, train) station
- *El avión* --- plane

- El aeropuerto – airport
- El boleto de avión --- plane ticket
- *El pasaporte* --- Passport
- *La azafata* --- flight attendant
- El mostrador de facturación --- the check-in counter
- *Pista de despegue*/aterrizaje --- take-off runway/landing strip
- *Despegar* --- to take-off
- *Aterrizar* --- to land
- *El destino* --- destination
- El retraso --- delay

6. El Huevo Podrido

Sara, Miguel, Mariano y Dulce eran mejores amigos desde primaria. Siempre habían sido compañeros de aventuras. Pero ahora que todos tenían vidas adultas (trabajos serios, hijos, deudas, electrodomésticos) rara vez encontraban tiempo para divertirse todos juntos. Ese sábado, iban a ir a una cabaña alejada del centro de la ciudad. Había sido idea de Mariano. "Es una casita muy rústica", le había dicho el dueño por teléfono "Ideal para pasar el día". Era invierno y había mucha nieve en el sur de Chile.

Sara, Miguel, Mariano and Dulce were best friends since primary school. They had always been adventure partners. But now that they all had adult lives (serious jobs, children, debts, home appliances), they rarely found the time to have fun all together. That Saturday, they were going to a cabin removed from the city center. It had been Mariano's idea. "It's a very rustic little house", the owner had told him on the phone. "It is ideal to spend the day". It was winter and there was a lot of snow in the south of Chile.

—¡Es hermosa! —dijo Sara cuando la vio desde el coche. Un verdadero sueño —añadió Miguel. Se ve muy hogareña —comentó Sara. Os lo dije —contestó Mariano. Entraron con sus provisiones para pasar el día - comida, bebida, juegos de mesa, revistas, libros y más.

—It's beautiful! —said Sara when she saw it from the car. A true dream —added Miguel. It looks very homey —Sara commented. I told you so —Mariano replied. They went in with their supplies to spend the day - food, drinks, board games, magazines, books and more.

—Está completamente amueblada —dijo Sara cuando abrió la puerta y pasó al interior. Y muy calentita. Parece que los dueños han pasado para encender la estufa —dijo Miguel. Parece que también nos han dejado comida —dijo Dulce, señalando una canasta donde había varios paquetes de pasta, galletas, frascos de mermelada y huevos. Fue una gran idea venir —dijo Mariano—. Mi idea...

—It's completely furnished —Sara said when she opened the door and stepped inside. And very warm. It seems the owners have stopped by to turn the stove on —said Miguel. It seems they have left us some food as well —said Dulce, pointing to a basket with many packages of pasta, biscuits, jam jars and eggs. It was a great idea to come —said Mariano—. My idea...

Los amigos se quitaron los abrigos y se pusieron cómodos en la cabaña. Pusieron más leña en la estufa, pusieron música, abrieron una botella de vino y se prepararon para relajarse. ¿Queréis que prepare el desayuno? —preguntó Dulce. Miró su reloj—. Más bien será un almuerzo a esta hora. Me parece excelente —dijo Miguel. Señaló los huevos de la canasta y añadió— - ¿Qué tal unas tortillas?

The group of friends took off their coats and got comfortable inside the cottage. They put more wood into the stove, put on some music, opened a bottle of wine and got ready to relax. Do you want me to prepare lunch? —asked Dulce. She looked at her watch—. It will be more like a brunch at this time. It sounds excellent to me —said Miguel. He pointed to the eggs in the basket and added— - How about some omelettes?

Dulce buscó una sartén y varios ingredientes más, como sal y queso, entre las provisiones que habían llevado. Encontró un cuenco para batir los huevos y una batidora. Entonces, cuando partió el primer huevo, notó que algo verdoso asomaba del interior. ¡El huevo estaba completamente podrido! En solo un segundo, el olor llego a su nariz. ¡Era lo peor que había olido en su vida!

Dulce looked for a pan and some other ingredients, like salt and cheese, among the supplies they had brought. She found a bowl to beat the eggs and a beater. Then, when she broke the first egg, she noticed something green poking out from the inside. The egg was completely rotten! In just a second, the smell reached her nose. It was the worst thing she had smelled in her life!

—TODOS FUERA, ¡DE INMEDIATO! —gritó. Los amigos corrieron al exterior de la cabaña tras ella. ¿Qué pasa? ¿se prendió fuego a algo? —preguntó Sara. ¿Hay un asesino en serie en la cabaña? — preguntó jocosamente Mariano. No... —dijo Dulce—. ¡Los huevos estaban podridos! ¡Ay, no! — exclamó Miguel. Vamos, no será para tanto —dijo Sara. Miguel se rio y le dijo -

¿Entonces por qué no entras y nos dices?

EVERYBODY OUT, IMMEDIATELY! —she screamed. The group of friends run to the exterior of the cabin behind her. What happens? Did something set on fire? —Sara asked. Is there a serial killer in the cabin? —Mariano asked jokingly. No... —Dulce said—. The eggs were rotten! Oh, no! —Miguel exclaimed. Come on, it can't be that bad —Sara said. Miguel laughed and said to her -

Then why don't you go in and tell us?

Sara aceptó el desafío y entró en la cabaña. A los tres segundos, salió cubriéndose la boca con la mano. Sus tres amigos se rieron. Bueno, igual vamos a tener que entrar... —dijo Miguel. Sí. Alguien tiene que sacar el huevo antes de que toda la casa se llene con esa peste. Mariano fue quien se atrevió a entrar. Se cubrió la nariz y la boca con el pañuelo que llevaba en el cuello.

Sara accepted the challenge and went into the cabin. Three seconds later, she came out covering her mouth with her hand. Her three friends laughed. Well, we will still have to go in... —Miguel said. Yes. Someone will have to take the egg out before the whole house fills up with that pestilence. Mariano was the one who dared to go in. He covered his nose and mouth with his neckerchief.

A los pocos segundos, salió corriendo con el cuenco que contenía el huevo podrido y lo vació detrás de un árbol. ¡Qué horror! —dijo—. Incluso con el pañuelo, ha sido lo más horrible que he olido en mi vida. Ahora alguien tiene que entrar a abrir las ventanas para que se ventile el lugar. Yo no pienso entrar de nuevo... Puedo llegar a morir. La siguiente en animarse a entrar en la casa fue Dulce. Los amigos vieron cómo las ventanas se abrían desde el interior una a una. Cuando salió, aspiró una gran bocanada de aire. o me he atrevido a respirar en todo el tiempo que he estado dentro —dijo, agitada.

A few seconds later, he came out running with the bowl that contained the rotten egg and emptied it behind a tree. How awful! —he said—. Even with the neckerchief on, it was the most horrible thing I smelt in my whole life. Now someone has to go in and open the windows to air the place. I don't plan to go in again... I could die. The next one to dare to go in was Dulce. The group of friends saw how the windows were opened from the inside one by one. When she came out she inhaled deeply. I didn't dare to breath the whole time I was inside —she said, agitated.

Será mejor que entre a buscar nuestras cosas, porque puede que estemos aquí fuera bastante rato — dijo Miguel. Al cabo de unos minutos, tenían sus abrigos, los juegos de mesa y el vino con ellos. Dulce puso un mantel en el suelo y se sentaron allí, sobre la nieve. Pasaron un largo rato jugando al dominó. Después, como no podían entrar a cocinar el almuerzo, comieron galletas, patatas fritas, nueces, almendras y chocolatinas.

It will be better if I go in to get our things, because we might be out here for a while —Miguel said. A few minutes later, they had their coats, the board games and the wine with them. Dulce set a tablecloth on the floor and they sat there, on the snow. They spent a long while playing domino. Later, since they couldn't go in to cook lunch, they had biscuits, fries, nuts, almonds and chocolates.

Enfadado por perder al dominó, Mariano arrojó una bola de nieve a Miguel. Así comenzó una batalla de bolas de nieve que duró media hora. Armaron dos equipos. Miguel estaba con Dulce y Mariano con Sara. Cuando terminó, se sentaron con una nueva botella de vino a charlar y disfrutar de la tranquilidad de la tarde.

Angry after losing a domino battle, Mariano threw a snowball to Miguel. That's how a snowball battle that lasted half an hour started. They made two teams. Miguel was with Dulce and Mariano with Sara. When it finished, they sat with a new bottle of wine to chat and enjoy the tranquility of the afternoon.

Ya no hay olor en la casa —anunció Dulce, que había entrado a la cabaña para usar el baño. Los amigos se miraron. Creo que estoy pasando un buen rato aquí afuera de todas formas —dijo Sara—. Hay tanta naturaleza... Sí, creo que todos estamos mejor aquí —dijo Miguel—, ¿no es así?

The house doesn't smell anymore —Dulce announced. She had gone into the cabin to use the toilet. The friends looked at each other. I think I'm having a good time out here anyway —Sara said—. There is so much nature... Yes, I think we all are better here —Miguel said—, isn't that so?

Los otros asintieron. Se quedaron el resto de la tarde en la nieve. Al anochecer, llegó un gran automóvil gris. Era el dueño de la casa. Cuando le contaron lo sucedido, soltó una gran carcajada. En esa cesta siempre dejo la comida que dejan los huéspedes. No me di cuenta de que los huevos ya podrían haberse puesto malos... Lo lamento mucho. No se disculpe, señor. Ha sido lo mejor que nos podía pasar.

The others nodded. They stayed for the rest of the afternoon on the snow. At sunset, a big grey car arrived. It was the owner of the house. When they told him what happened, he laughed. I always put into that basket the food that the guests leave behind. I didn't realize the eggs might be bad... I'm very sorry. Don't apologies, sir. It's been the best that could happen to us.

Quiz

1. Sara tenía 3 amigos, ¿quién no estaba entre sus amigos?
a. Michael
b. Miguel
c. Mariano
d. Dulce

2. ¿Cuál es el nombre de la ciudad que tenía mucha nieve?
a. Chile
b. Nueva York
c. Francia

3. Sara y sus amigas eran?
a. Compañeros de clase
b. Compañeros de trabajo
c. Compañeros de aventura

4. ¿Qué hizo Mariano después de perder una batalla de dominó?
a. Golpear la ventana
b. Llorar
c. arrojó una bola de nieve

5. ¿De qué color era el auto que llegó al atardecer?
a. Blanco
b. Azul
c. Gris

6. ¿De dónde se conocen todos?
a. Del instituto.
b. De la universidad.
c. De primaria.

7. ¿De quién fue la idea de ir ahí?
a. De Mariano.
b. Del dueño.
c. De Dulce.

8. ¿Qué llevaron con ellos?

9. ¿Cómo es el clima?
a. Nevado.
b. Lluvioso.
c. Cálido.

10. ¿Qué encuentran dentro de una cesta?

11. ¿Qué quiere preparar Dulce para el almuerzo?

12. ¿Qué consigue para empezar a cocinar?
a. Una sartén y sal.
b. Una sartén, sal, queso y huevos.
c. Un huevo podrido.

13. ¿Qué hace después de ver que el huevo está podrido?
a. Incendia algo.
b. Ve un asesino en serie.
c. Les dice a todos que salgan.

14. ¿Quién entra en la cabaña después de salir?

15. ¿Se les arruinó el día?

1. Sara had 3-friends, who wasn't among her friends?
a. Michael
b. Miguel
c. Mariano
d. Dulce

2. What is the name of the city that had a lot of snow?
a. Chile
b. New York
c. France

3. Sara and her friends were?
a. Classmates
b. Workmates

c. Adventure partners

4. What did Mariano do after losing a domino battle?
a. Hit the window
b. Cried
c. threw a snowball

5. What was the color of the car that arrived at sunset?
a. White
b. Blue
c. Grey

6. Where did they all know each other from?
a. Secondary school.
b. College.
c. Primary school.

7. Who's idea was it to go there?
a. Mariano's.
b. The owner's.
c. Dulce's.
8. What did they take with them?

9. How is the weather?
a. Snowy.
b. Rainy.
c. Warm.

10. What do they find inside a basket?
11. What does Dulce want to prepare for brunch?

12. What does she get to start cooking?
a. A pan and some salt.
b. A pan, salt, cheese and eggs.
c. A rotten egg.

13. What does she do after she sees the egg is rotten?
a. She sets something on fire.
b. She sees a serial killer.
c. She orders everybody out.

14. Who goes into the cabin after they have to go out?

15. Is their day ruined?

Respuestas

1. a

2. a

3. c

4. c
5. c
6. c
7. a
8. Comida, bebida, juegos de mesa, revistas y libros.
9. a
10. Varios paquetes de pasta, galletas, botes de mermelada y huevos.
11. Tortillas.
12. b
13. c
14. Todos deben entrar.
15. No, es lo mejor que les podría haber pasado.

Answers
1. a
2. a
3. c
4. c
5. c
6. c
7. a
8. Food, drinks, board games, magazines and books.
9. a
10. Several packs of pasta, biscuits, jam jars and eggs.
11. Omelettes.
12. b
13. c
14. They all have to go in.
15. No, it's the best thing that could have happened to them.

Vocabulario (Vocabulary)

- Companions --- *Compañeros*
- Grown up --- *Adulto*
- Debts --- *Deudas*
- Home appliances --- *Electrodomésticos*
- Cabin --- *Cabaña*
- Rustic --- *Rústico*
- On the phone --- *Por teléfono*
- Winter --- *Invierno*
- Snow --- *Nieve*
- Supplies --- *Provisiones*
- Food --- *Comida*
- Drinks --- *Bebidas*
- Board games --- Juegos de mesa
- Furnished --- *Amueblada*
- Stove --- *Estufa*

- Coats --- *Abrigos*
- To get comfortable --- *Ponerse cómodo/a*
- Pan --- *Sartén*
- Salt --- *Sal*
- To break --- *Partir*
- To notice --- *Notar*
- Smell --- *Olor*
- To set something on fire --- *Prender fuego*
- To be that bad --- *Ser para tanto*
- Challenge --- *Desafío*
- To dare --- *Atreverse*
- In my life --- *En mi vida*
- To open the windows- *Abrir las ventanas*
- To breath --- *Respirar*
- A long while --- *Bastante rato*
- A tablecloth --- *Un mantel*
- To cook lunch --- *Cocinar el almuerzo*
- A snowball --- *Una bola de nieve*
- To chat --- *Charlar*
- To enjoy --- *Disfrutar*
- Isn't that so? --- *¿No es así?*
- To nod --- *Asentir*
- Car --- *Automóvil*
- To go bad --- *Ponerse malo*
- Apologize – *Disculparse*

7. Nuevos Amigos

Ana está en la universidad. Es su primer día de clases. Estudia Derecho. Quiere convertirse en abogada penalista. Su sueño es investigar casos y defender a personas que no tienen recursos económicos.

Ana is in college. It is his first day of school. Studying Law, he wants to become a criminal lawyer. His dream is to investigate cases and defend people who do not have financial resources.

Está en un aula muy grande con otros estudiantes. Todos hablan entre ellos. Ana no conoce a nadie. Se siente un poco solitaria. Extraña a sus amigos del pueblo.

He is in a very large classroom with other students. Everyone talks to each other. Ana doesn't know anyone. It feels a little lonely. She misses her village friends.

Cuando entra el profesor, todos los estudiantes guardan silencio. El profesor empieza la clase. Habla muy rápido. Todos los estudiantes tienen bolígrafos y anotadores, y toman notas. Algunos toman notas en sus computadoras para tomar apuntes. Ana toma su mochila, la abre y saca un anotador y un bolígrafo. Quiere escribir la fecha y tomar notas, pero su bolígrafo no funciona. ¡Qué mala suerte! El profesor sigue hablando muy rápido y Ana no puede tomar notas. No sabe qué hacer.

When the teacher enters, all students remain silent. The teacher starts the class and speaks very fast. All students have pens and annotators, and take notes. Some use their computers to take notes. Ana takes her backpack, opens it and takes out a notebook and a pen. He wants to write the date and take notes, but his pen doesn't work. What a bad luck! The teacher keeps talking very fast and Ana can't take notes. He does not know what to do.

—¡Tchh! — dice alguien.

"Tchh!" Says someone.

Ana mira a su izquierda y ve a una chica rubia con un bolígrafo en la mano.

Ana looks to her left and sees a blonde girl with a pen in her hand.

—¿Quieres que te preste un bolígrafo? — pregunta la chica rubia.

"Do you want me to lend you a pen?" Asks the blonde girl.

—Sí, por favor. ¡Muchas gracias! — dice Ana.

-Yes please. Thank you very much! - says Ana.

Ana está muy contenta. Empieza a tomar notas. Cuando termina la clase, todos los estudiantes toman sus anotadores y bolígrafos y los guardan en sus mochilas. Ana llama a la chica que le prestó el bolígrafo.

Ana is very happy. Start taking notes. When the class ends, all students take their notebooks and pens and store them in their backpacks. Ana calls the girl who lent her the pen.

—Oye, muchas gracias por prestarme el bolígrafo— dice Ana.

"Hey, thank you very much for lending me the pen," says Ana.

—¡De nada! Soy Lucía Pérez, ¿eres nueva?

-You are welcome! I'm Lucía Pérez, are you new?

—Sí, es mi primer día. Me llamo Ana García.

"Yes, it is my first day." My name is Ana García.

—*Voy a tomar un café. ¿Quieres venir a tomar un café conmigo?*

-I'm going to drink a cup of coffee. Do you want to come for coffee with me?

—*Sí, me encantaría, me gusta mucho tomar café, ¡gracias!*

"Yes, I would love to, I really like having coffee, thank you!"

Ana y Lucía van a la cafetería de la universidad y compran café. Se sientan en el patio a tomarlo.

Ana and Lucia go to the university cafeteria and buy coffee. They sit on the patio to take it.

—*¿Dónde vives? — pregunta Lucía*

"Where do you live?" Asks Lucia

—*Ahora, en Palermo. Antes vivía en un pueblo. ¿Y tú?*

—Now, in Palermo. I used to live in a town. And you?

—*Yo soy de Buenos Aires de toda la vida. Vivo en Almagro. ¿Conoces el barrio de Almagro?*

—I am from Buenos Aires of a lifetime. I live in Almagro. Do you know the neighborhood of Almagro?

—*No, no lo conozco todavía.*

"No, I don't know yet."

—*¿Te gusta Buenos Aires?*

"Do you like Buenos Aires?"

—*Sí, me gusta, pero extraño a mis amigos.*

"Yes, I like it, but I miss my friends."

—*Ay, sí, qué difícil. ¡Los amigos son muy importantes!*

"Oh yes, it's difficult." Friends are very important!

—*¿Tienes familia?*

-Do you have family?

—*Sí. Vivo con mi mamá porque mis padres están divorciados. Mi mamá tiene un nuevo marido y tengo una hermana pequeña.*

-Yes. I live with my mom because my parents are divorced. My mom has a new husband and I have a little sister.

—*Yo también tengo un hermano pequeño. Mis padres siguen juntos. Creo que se quieren mucho.*

"I also have a little brother." My parents are still together. I think they love each other very much.

—*Los míos no se querían nada. ¡Es mejor que estén divorciados!*

"Mine didn't want anything." It is better that they are divorced!

—*¿Te gusta estudiar Derecho?*

"Do you like studying law?"

—*No sé aún. Me gustó mucho la clase, pero todavía no sé qué quiero hacer. ¿y Tú?*

-I do not know yet. I really liked the class but I still don't know what I want to do. And you?

—*A mí me encantó la clase. Me gusta mucho el derecho. Mi sueño es ser abogada penalista.*

"I loved the class." I really like the right one. My dream is to be a criminal lawyer.

—*Ah, como mi amigo Martín. Mira, ahí viene.*

"Oh, like my friend Martin." Look, there he comes.

Un chico alto y de cabello castaño se acerca a la mesa donde están Ana y Lucía.

A tall boy with brown hair approaches the table where Ana and Lucia are.

—*Hola, Lucía, ¿cómo estás? — dice el chico alto.*

"Hello, Lucia, how are you?" Says the tall boy.

—*Hola, Martín, esta es Ana, se acaba de mudar a Buenos Aires— dice Lucía.*

—Hello, Martín, this is Ana, she has just moved to Buenos Aires - says Lucia.

—*Hola, Ana, ¿cómo estás? — dice Martín.*

"Hello, Ana, how are you?" Says Martin.

—*Muy bien, gracias, ¿y tú? — pregunta Ana.*

"Very well, thank you, and you?" Asks Ana.

—*¡Cansado! Tuve muchas clases. ¿Y ustedes? — responde Martín.*

-Tired! I had many classes. And you? - replies Martín.

—*Yo también estoy cansada. Por suerte ya terminaron nuestras clases de hoy— dice Lucía.*

-I am tired too. Luckily our classes are over today," says Lucia.

—*Lucía, ¿vienes a mi fiesta de cumpleaños el viernes? — pregunta Martín.*

"Lucia, are you coming to my birthday party on Friday?" Asks Martin.

—*Sí, claro.*

-Yeah right.

—*Ana, ¿quieres venir a mi fiesta de cumpleaños? Es en mi casa, en Palermo— dice Martín.*

"Ana, do you want to come to my birthday party?" It's in my house, in Palermo," says Martín.

—*Sí, me encantaría, yo también vivo en Palermo—, dice Ana, contenta.*

"Yes, I would love to, I also live in Palermo," says Ana, happy.

—*Genial. Nos vemos el viernes entonces.*

-Great. See you on Friday then.

—*¡Nos vemos! — dicen Lucía y Ana.*

"See you!" Lucia and Ana say.

Ana no lo puede creer - tiene dos nuevos amigos y una invitación a una fiesta de cumpleaños. ¡Nada mal para el primer día de clases!

Ana can't believe it - she has two new friends and an invitation to a birthday party. Not bad for the first day of school!

Reading Comprehension

1. Do you remember your first day in school, in college or at work? What it was like? How did you feel? Think about how Ana feels. Is she happy in the beginning of the story?

2. Make a list (in Spanish, of course) of all the school supplies mentioned in the story. Did you use any of them at school to take notes?

3. With a partner, role-play the meeting between Lucía and Ana. Do it in Spanish, of course. Use their words and phrases!

Quiz

Select only one of the options.
1. "Ana está en un aula." What is the correct translation?
a. Ana is at school.
b. Ana is studying.
c. Ana is a classroom.

2. What is the grammatically correct sentence?
a. Los alumnos guarda silencio.
b. Los alumnos guardan silencio.
c. Los alumnos guardan silencio.

3. "Lucía es rubia." What does this sentence mean?
a. Lucía is blonde
b. Lucía is tall
c.Lucía is red-haired

4. What is the correct translation of "Ana misses her friends?"
a. Ana quiere a sus amigos.
b. Ana extraña a sus amigos.
c. Ana no extraña a sus amigos.

5. Ana likes coffee. Is that true?
a. Yes
b. No
c. She prefers tea

6. Where does Lucía live?
a. In a small town
b. In Palermo
c. In Almagro

7. "Martín es amigo de Lucía." What is the correct translation of that sentence?
a. Lucía is Martín's friend.
b. Martín is Lucía's friend.
c. Lucía is not Martín's friend.

8. Martín says he is "cansado." What does that mean?
a. He is married.

b. He is bored.
c. He is tired.

9. When's the party?
a. El viernes
b. El martes
c. El sábado

10. Where does Martín live?
a. In the same neighborhood as Lucía
b. In the same neighborhood as Ana
c. Near university

11. How does Ana feel when Martín invites her to the party?
a. Triste
b. Cansada
c. Contenta

12. If Martín says "Te invito a mi fiesta," is he inviting one, two, or more persons to his party? You can use the dictionary or anything you need to answer this question.
a. One
b. Two
c. More than two

Answers:

1. c
2. c
3. a
4. b
5. a
6. c
7. b
8. c
9. a
10. b
11. a

Vocabulario (Vocabulary)

- *Universidad* – college/University
- Convertirse --- Become
- *Investigar* --- Research
- *Recursos* --- Means
- *Estudiantes* --- Students
- *Conocer* --- Known
- *Empieza* --- Starts

- *Algunos* --- Some
- Bolígrafo --- pen
- *Quiere* --- Wants
- Puede --- may
- *Anotadores* – notebooks

8. La Gran Noticia

El 26 de septiembre era un día como cualquiera. Matías se levantaba a las 7 de la mañana, desayunaba y se iba al colegio. Últimamente había estado llegando tarde, ya que su mamá no podía llevarlo porque estaba embarazada y su papá trabajaba en la fábrica desde temprano. Matías debía tomar el autobús para llegar al colegio, y en esos viajes se había hecho un amigo, Kevin.

September 26 was a day like any other. Matías got up at 7 in the morning, ate breakfast and went to school. Lately he had been late, since his mother could not take him because she was pregnant and his father worked at the factory early. Matías had to take the bus to get to school, and on those trips, he had become a friend to Kevin.

Esa mañana, Matías saltó de la cama, tomó sus carpetas y salió corriendo a la parada de autobús. Allí lo estaba esperando Kevin y estrecharon las manos como de costumbre. Kevin estaba un poco molesto ese día, lo que le causaba un poco de disgusto a Matías, que le costaba soportar.

That morning, Matías jumped out of bed, took his books and ran to the bus stop. Kevin was waiting for him there and they shook hands as usual. Kevin was a little upset that day, which caused Matias a bit of annoyance, which was hard to bear.

Cuando llegó el autobús, subieron y ya estaban de camino a clase. Unas pocas cuadras antes de llegar, algo desafortunado sucedió. De casualidad, antes de doblar en una esquina, un camión cruzó rápidamente y causó un choque con otro auto. Matías y Kevin vieron la situación desde la ventana del autobús. El chofer bajó a ayudar a los conductores. Por suerte, los bomberos estaban de paso y se aseguraron de que no hubiera sucedido una desgracia. Ambos conductores se encontraban sanos, pero Kevin y Matías ya llegaban muy tarde, pero aún podían asistir a clase, por lo que bajaron del autobús y siguieron caminando.

When the bus arrived, they got on and were already on their way to class. A few blocks before arriving, something unfortunate happened. By chance, before turning in a corner, a truck quickly crossed and caused a crash with another car. Matías and Kevin saw the situation from the bus window. The driver went down to help the drivers. Luckily, firefighters were passing through and made sure that a misfortune had not happened. Both drivers were healthy, but Kevin and Matías were already late, but they could still attend class, so they got off the bus and kept walking.

Una vez que llegaron, le explicaron lo que había sucedido a su maestra. La maestra entendió y se puso feliz de que no hubiera víctimas. Kevin y Matías fueron a sentarse en sus pupitres.

Once they arrived, they explained what had happened to their teacher. The teacher understood and was happy that there were no victims. Kevin and Matías went to sit at their desks.

Cuando Matías abrió su cartuchera, vio un mensaje escrito a mano que decía "Hoy recibirás una gran noticia. La luna dice que será tu mejor amiga". Matías comenzó a preguntarse <<¿Qué tipo de noticia recibiré hoy?>>

When Matías opened his holster, he saw a handwritten message that said "Today you will receive great news. The moon says she will be your best friend." Matías began to wonder <<What kind of news will I receive today?>>

A Matías lo agobiaban las dudas, entonces les preguntó a sus amigos. Kevin era un poco escéptico, le dijo que quizás solo era una broma. María era un poco celosa, le dijo que él ya tenía una mejor amiga y que era ella y nadie más. Juliana era más pragmática, le dijo que la luna no hablaba. Lucas era muy pesimista, le dijo que podría ser una mala noticia.

Matthias was overwhelmed by doubts, so he asked his friends. Kevin was a bit skeptical, he said maybe it was just a joke. Maria was a little jealous, she told him that he already had a best friend and that she and no one else. Juliana was more pragmatic, she told him that the moon did not speak. Lucas was very pessimistic, he said it could be bad news.

Matías estaba lleno de curiosidad. De camino a su casa, solo pensaba en la nota. Miraba a la luna e intentaba hablar con ella. Si bien no escuchaba nada, había algo que lo llenaba de esperanzas y le confirmaba que esa tarde se iba a poner muy feliz con la noticia.

Matías was full of curiosity. On the way home, he just thought about the note. He looked at the moon and tried to talk to her. Although he didn't hear anything, there was something that filled him with hope and confirmed that he was going to be very happy with the news that afternoon.

Se había sentado al lado de una señora de unos 50 años que le contaba que ella tenía un nieto de la edad de él, que se llamaba Julián y que su mamá siempre supo que sería varón. Matías se dio cuenta de inmediato de cuál sería la sorpresa. Su mamá le había contado historias similares sobre el día en que él nació. La miró a la luna, cerró los ojos, y le dio las gracias. El mensaje era cierto, era una gran sorpresa y él ya sabía cuál era. Siempre había querido una mejor amiga con quién compartir su vida. Ya sabía quién había dejado ese mensaje en su cartuchera. Bajó del autobús y fue corriendo a su casa. Había muchos autos estacionados en la calle, y su casa era la que más brillaba a la luz de la luna. Se veían muchas siluetas en las cortinas de la ventana. Sentía un clima navideño en pleno julio.

He had sat next to a lady in her 50s who told her that she had a grandson his age, that his name was Julian and that his mother always knew he would be male. Matías immediately realized what the surprise would be. His mother had told him similar stories about the day he was born. He looked at the moon, closed his eyes, and thanked him. The message was true, it was a big surprise and he already knew what it was. He had always wanted a best friend with whom to share his life. He already knew who had left that message in his holster. He got off the bus and ran home. There were many cars parked on the street, and his house was the one that shone brighter in the moonlight. There were many silhouettes in the window curtains. I felt a Christmas weather in the middle of July.

Llegó rápido, abrazó fuerte a su papá y se encontró con sus abuelos, sus dos tíos con su hija, sus primos, y su tía. Todos sus parientes estaban allí. Y detrás de todos ellos estaba su mamá. Matías se acercó llorando de felicidad y le dio un beso a su mamá. En sus brazos estaba Rocío, tan pequeña y frágil. Matías la sostuvo en sus brazos y le dijo:

He arrived quickly, hugged his dad tightly and met his grandparents, his two uncles with his daughter, his cousins, and his aunt. All his relatives were there. And behind all of them was his mom. Matías approached crying with happiness and kissed his mother. In his arms was Rocío, so small and fragile. Matthias held her in his arms and said:

-Tú serás mi mejor amiga. Te enseñaré a hacer las mejores bromas, nos divertiremos con las mejores travesuras y te cuidaré siempre. Pero mamá, ¿cómo sabías que sería niña?

-You will be my best friend. I will teach you to make the best jokes, we will have fun with the best pranks and I will always take care of you. But mom, how did you know it would be a girl?

-Yo siempre lo supe, hijo. No solo fue la luna, sino que cuando deseas algo con fuerza, amor, honestidad y desinterés, tus deseos se hacen realidad.

-I always knew, son. Not only was the moon, but when you want something with strength, love, honesty and disinterest, your wishes come true.

-Si hubiera sido niño, lo hubiera querido igual.

-Lo sé, hijo.

Todos habían traído regalos. Sus tíos le trajeron ropa de todos colores - violeta, amarillo, marrón, negro, verde, celeste y naranja. Sus abuelos le trajeron un cochecito. Su tía le trajo la cuna que había prometido. Pero el que había recibido el mejor regalo de todos era Matías - una hermanita.

-If I had been a child, I would have wanted it the same.

-I know, son.

Everyone had brought gifts. His uncles brought him clothes of all colors - violet, yellow, brown, black, green, light blue and orange. His grandparents brought him a stroller. His aunt brought him the crib he had promised. But the one who had received the best gift of all was Matthias - a little sister.

Quiz

1. ¿Qué hizo Matías después de tomar el desayuno?
a. Fui a jugar
b. fue a la cama
c. fue a la escuela

2. ¿Por qué no podía la madre Matías llevarlo a la escuela?
a. Ella trabajó temprano en la fábrica
b. Ella estaba mal
c. Ella estaba embarazada

3. ¿Cómo se llamaba el niño que esperaba a Matías en el autobús?
a. Conocer
b. Kevin
c. Karen

4. ¿Qué pasó camino a la escuela?
a. El autobús se rompió
b. Coches chocaron
c. Hubo fuego

5. ¿Qué regalos compraron los abuelos de Matías?
a. ropa de todos los colores
b. un cochecito
c. una cuna

1. What did Matías do after taking breakfast?
a. Went to play
b. went to bed
c. went to school

2. Why couldn't Matías mother take him to school?
a. She worked early at the factory
b. She was unwell
c. She was pregnant

3. What was the name of the boy waiting for Matías at the bus?
a. Ken

b. Kevin

c. Karen

4. What happened on the way to school?

a. The bus broke

b. Cars crashed

c. There was fire

5. What gifts did the Matías grandparents buy?

a. clothes of all colors

b. a stroller

c. a crib

Respuestas

1. c

2. c

3. b

4. b

5. b

Answers

1. c

2. c

3. b

4. b

5. b

Vocabulario (Vocabulary)

- *(Nos) divertiremos* --- (we) will have fun
- *(Te) cuidaré* --- (I) will take care of (you)
- *Abuelos* --- Grandparents
- *Agobiaban* --- Overwhelmed
- *Amarillo* --- Yellow
- Amigo/ a --- Friend
- *Amor* --- Love
- *Asistir*- To be present
- *Auto* --- Car
- *Bajaron* --- Got off
- *Bomberos* --- Firefighters
- *Brazos* --- Arms
- *Brillaba* --- Gleamed
- *Broma* --- Joke
- *Calle* --- Street
- *Cama* --- Bed
- *Caminando* --- Walking

- *Camión* --- Truck
- *Carpetas* --- Folders
- *Cartuchera* --- Pencil case
- *Celeste* --- Light blue
- *Celoso/ a* --- Jealous
- *Chofer* --- (bus) driver
- *Choque* --- Crash
- *Cierto* --- True
- *Clima* --- Environment
- *Cochecito* --- Stroller
- *Colegio* --- High school
- *Comenzó* --- started
- *Compartir* --- share
- *Conductores* --- (car) drivers
- *Corriendo* --- running
- *Cualquiera* --- any
- *Cuna* --- crib
- *De camino a* --- on (their) way to
- *Desayunaba* --- had breakfast
- *Deseas* --- wish
- *Desgracia* --- misfortune
- *Desinterés* --- selflessness
- *Disgusto* --- annoyance
- *Doblar* --- turn
- *Embarazada* --- pregnant
- *Enseñaré* --- will teach
- *Entendió* --- understood
- *Entonces* --- so
- *Escéptico* --- skeptical
- *Escrito a mano* --- handwritten
- *Escuchaba* --- listened
- *Esperanzas* --- hopes
- *Esquina* --- corner
- *Estacionados* --- parking
- *Estrecharon* – shaked-hands
- *Fábrica* --- factory
- *Felicidad*- happiness
- *Fuerza* --- strength
- *Gracias* --- thanks
- *Gran(de)* --- big
- *Había dejado* --- had left
- *Había querido* --- had wanted
- *Hermanita* --- little sister
- *Hija* --- daughter
- *Hijo* --- son
- *Hoy* --- today
- *Intentaba* --- tried

- *Levantaba* --- got up
- *Llorando* --- crying
- *Luna* --- moon
- *Maestro /a* --- teacher
- *Mamá* --- mom
- *Marrón* --- brown
- *Mejor* --- best
- *Miraba* --- looked
- *Molesto* --- annoying
- *Naranja* --- orange
- *Navideño* --- christmas
- *Negro*- black
- *Nieto* --- grandson
- *Niña* --- girl
- *Ojos* --- eyes
- *Papá* --- dad
- *Parada* --- bus stop
- *Parientes* – family members
- *Pequeña* --- little
- *Preguntarse* --- wonder
- *Primos* --- cousins
- *Pupitres* --- desks
- *Quizás* --- maybe
- *Regalos* --- presents
- *Sabía* --- knew
- *Saltó* --- jumped
- *Sanos*- healthy
- *Señora*- lady
- *Sentarse*- sit down
- *Siempre* --- always
- *Sostuvo* --- held
- *Subieron* --- got on
- *Tarde*- late
- *Temprano* --- early
- *Tía* --- aunt
- *Tíos* --- uncles
- *Travesuras* --- antics
- *Últimamente* --- recently
- *Varón*- boy
- *Ventana* --- window
- *Verde*- green
- *Vida* --- life
- *Vieron*- saw
- *Violeta* --- purple

9. Salir Con Los Amigos

Hoy es viernes y mis amigos se reúnen en un bar de deportes para ver el juego de futbol de la selección nacional. El juego empieza a las 6 pm y termina a las 8 pm. Yo voy a tomar el metro para poder llegar al área del bar. El bar está ubicado en la zona norte de la ciudad, queda como a 3 kilómetros de mi oficina. Yo no llevo el carro por que hoy tomo tres cervezas en el bar, y si se toma licor no se debe manejar. En el metro, me reúno con otros compañeros y nos vamos hacia el bar.

Today is Friday, and my friends gather at a sports bar to watch the national soccer team game. The game starts at 6 pm and ends at 8 pm. I'm going to take the metro to get to the bar. The bar is located on the north part of the city. It is about 3 kilometers from my office. I do not take the car with me because today I will drink three beers at the bar. If you drink liquor, you should not drive. At the subway, I meet with other colleagues, and we go to the bar.

Son las 5 pm, y el metro está muy congestionado, hay muchos pasajeros. La gente acaba de salir del trabajo, por lo que estamos en hora pico. A mí no me gusta usar el transporte público durante las horas pico porque, todos vamos como sardinas en latas, estamos muy apretados, yo creo que hay más de 300 personas en este vagón del metro.

It is 5 pm, and the subway is very crowded, there are too many passengers. People just got off work, so we're at rush hour. I do not like to use public transportation during rush hour. Because we all get packed like sardines, we are very tight. I think there are more than 300 people in this subway car.

Las puertas del vagón no cierran porque está muy lleno, alguien tendrá que bajarse para que cierren las puertas.

Ya llegué al bar, hay una cola de espera para entrar, el portero no me deja pasar si no hago la cola. Llamo por teléfono a mis compañeros y hablo con Víctor. Víctor sale del bar y le dice al portero que mi puesto está reservado, el portero me deja entrar. Hoy el bar está lleno, el juego de hoy es decisivo para la clasificación al mundial de Rusia. La selección juega en Santiago de Chile contra la selección Argentina.

The car doors do not close because it is too full, someone will have to get off to close the doors.

I arrived at the bar; there is a long waiting line to enter, the Bouncer will not let me pass without making the line. I call my friends and talk to Victor. Victor gets out of the bar and tells the doorman that my seat is reserved; the porter lets me in. Today the bar is full. Today's game is decisive for qualifying for the World Cup in Russia. The selection plays in Santiago de Chile against the Argentina team.

Todos están muy emocionados, la gente de mi ciudad es muy aficionada al futbol, y siempre que juega la selección nacional, todos la quieren ver. Antes que empiece el juego, voy a pedir algo de comer, pido una hamburguesa con papas fritas, y de tomar un refresco. La mesonera es muy amable y trae la comida rápido. Me como todo, está muy sabroso.

Everyone is very excited. The people of my city are very fond of soccer, and whenever the national team plays, everyone wants to see it. Before the game starts, I'm going to order something to eat. I order a hamburger with fries and a soda. The server is very friendly and brings the food fast. I eat everything; it is delicious.

El juego empezó, los jugadores de Argentina se ven nerviosos. Todos en el bar están emocionados. Gritan como locos cada vez que los jugadores de la selección se acercan a la portería. El juego está muy bueno. El portero de nuestra selección es el mejor, tapa todos los tiros, nadie puede meterle un gol. Después del partido, ponen música, y la fiesta continúa, ahora las mujeres están bailando sobre

la barra, y a la que aplaude más le regalan bebidas para todo su grupo.

The game started, Argentinian players look nervous. Everyone at the bar is thrilled. They yell like crazy every time the players of the selection approach the goal. The game is very good. The goalkeeper of our team is the best, cover all the shots, nobody can put a goal. After the game, they put on music, and the party goes on, now the women are dancing on the bar, and the one who gets more cheers gains free drinks for her whole group.

La música está muy movida, el ambiente es festivo, la gente está alegre por el juego. Mi vecina está en el bar y me invita a bailar, yo bailo con ella y de repente me pregunta a qué hora me voy, yo le respondo que no lo sé. Ella me pide que por favor le dé un aventón hasta su casa cuando me vaya. Yo le digo que no tengo carro, que el carro está en la casa. Ella me dice que, por favor, cuando me vaya a mi casa le avise, y que yo la acompañe a la casa de ella, porque le da miedo irse sola en taxi.

The music is vivacious; the atmosphere is festive; people are happy for the game. My neighbor is at the bar and invites me to dance, I dance with her, and she asks me, at what time I go, I reply that I do not know. She asks me to please give her a ride home when I leave. I tell her that I do not have a car that the car is at home. She tells me to let her know when I go to my house and that I accompany her to her home because she is scared to go alone in a taxi.

Quiz

1. ¿Dónde se reúnen mis amigos el viernes?
a. Bar deportivo
b. En el garaje
c. restaurante

2. ¿Por qué dejo mi auto hoy?
 a. Llegaré tarde
b. Estaré borracho
c. Prefiero caminar

3. ¿Por qué está lleno el metro?
a. Tráfico vehicular
b. demasiados pasajeros
c. hubo lluvias

4. ¿Cómo estuvo el servidor?
a. Amistoso
b. triste
c. silencio

Answers

1. a
2. b
3. b
4. a

Vocabulary / Vocabulario

- Companion --- *Compañeros*
- Gather --- *Gather*
- Pub --- *Bar*
- Sports Bar --- *Bar Deportivo*
- Football --- *Futbol*
- Beers --- *Cervezas*
- Food --- *Comida*
- Questions --- *Preguntas*
- Answers – *Respuestas*
- Goal --- *Portería*

10. La Lectura Del Testamento

Al otro día me ducho y salgo apurado. Tomo un taxi hasta la dirección que tengo anotada en el papel. Llegamos. El taxi para delante de un edificio muy lujoso. Al igual que la otra vez, no tiene cambio y tengo que decirle "quédese con el vuelto."

The next day I take a shower and leave in a hurry. I take a taxi to the address I have written on the paper. We arrived. The taxi stops in front of a very luxurious building. Like the other time, it has no changed and I have to say "stay with the return."

Cuando veo esa fachada tan lujosa, dudo por un momento. Echo una mirada a mi ropa y me peino hacia atrás con las manos. No sé si estoy bien vestido como para entrar en un lugar así. Estoy vestido con una camisa de jean, un suéter verde y unos jeans de color azul oscuro. Tengo un estilo más bien informal y normalmente me siento muy seguro y cómodo así. Pero ahora, frente a este edificio que parece tan formal, me siento un poco fuera de lugar.

When I see that luxurious facade, I doubt for a moment. I take a look at my clothes and comb my hair back. I don't know if I'm well dressed to enter such a place. I am dressed in a jean shirt, a green sweater and dark blue jeans. I have a rather casual style and I usually feel very safe and comfortable as well. But now, in front of this building that seems so formal, I feel a bit out of place.

Subo en el ascensor hasta el piso indicado y veo que allí ya hay algunas personas esperando que empiece la lectura del testamento. Veo algunos señores de traje, los abogados y pocos más. En total somos unas quince personas.

I climb in the elevator to the floor indicated and see that there are already some people waiting for the reading of the will to begin. I see some gentlemen in suits, lawyers and few more. In total we are about fifteen people.

Recorro la sala en donde pusieron algunas sillas y un escritorio. A un lado hay una máquina de café y decido avanzar hacia allí, pero mis ojos se detienen en algo que me llama muchísimo la atención. En alguien, mejor dicho.

I walk around the room where they put some chairs and a desk. On one side there is a coffee machine and I decide to move there, but my eyes stop at something that catches my attention. In someone, rather.

Parada junto a una de las ventanas, mirando hacia afuera, veo la silueta de uno de los seres más llamativos que he visto en mi vida. Es una mujer de estatura mediana, con el pelo corto, liso y desordenado, teñido a mechones, de rosa y verde. Tiene puesto un vestido negro, muy ceñido, de tela suave y zapatos negros de taco alto. Está recostada graciosamente contra la ventana. Como si adivinara mi mirada en su espalda, se da vuelta y me mira. Tiene los ojos verdes más helados que el invierno de Londres y una boca roja cruel que se entorna un poco en una sonrisa pícara cuando me descubre mirándola.

Standing by one of the windows, looking out, I see the silhouette of one of the most striking beings I have seen in my life. She is a woman of medium stature, with short, straight and messy hair, dyed in strands of pink and green. She is wearing a black dress, very tight, soft fabric and black high heels. She is leaning graciously against the window. As if guessing my gaze on his back, he turns and looks at me. He has green eyes colder than the winter of London and a cruel red mouth that slightly arouses a mischievous smile when he discovers me looking at her.

— ¿Qué haces, Faraday? Me saluda con su media sonrisa. Intento parecer tranquilo y le extiendo la

mano. Ahora sí ella se ríe un poco y me da la mano. —Zoé García, encantada. Qué formales son ustedes por aquellos lados, che.

- What are you doing, Faraday? He greets me with his half smile. I try to appear calm and reach out. Now she laughs a little and shakes my hand. —Zoé García, delighted. How formal are you on those sides, che.

Cuando se mueve siento su perfume como de naranja y madera. Quiero preguntarle mil cosas. En realidad, quiero quedarme ahí hablando con ella y no escuchar una aburrida lectura de testamento, pero justo en ese momento, una de las abogadas nos llama para sentarnos y empezar. Suspiro resignado y me acerco. Zoé se sienta unos asientos más adelante y me paso todo el tiempo observando la forma en la que las puntas de su pelo de colores acarician el aire.

When it moves I feel its perfume like orange and wood. I want to ask you a thousand things. I really want to stay there talking to her and not hear a boring reading of will, but just then, one of the lawyers calls us to sit down and start. I sigh in resignation and approach. Zoé sits a few seats ahead and I spend all the time observing the way in which the tips of her colored hair caress the air.

Quiz

1. ¿Qué hago antes de irme?
a. Comimos
b. Duchado
c. trapeado

2. ¿Qué había en la habitación?
a. camas
b. esteras
c. sillas

3. ¿Quién me saludó con una sonrisa?
a. Zoé
b. Faraday
c. Frida

Answers

1. b
2. c
3. b

Vocabulary / Vocabulario

- *fachada* --- facade
- *manos* --- hands
- *azul* --- blue
- *edificio* – building
- *estilo* --- style
- *ascensor* --- elevator
- *algunos* --- Some
- *detienen* --- stop
- *silueta* --- silhouette
- *mueve* --- move
- *abogadas* --- lawyers
- *acarician* --- caress

11. Granja Los Villalobos

Los Villalobos, una familia de cuatro integrantes, el señor Jacobo, la señora María y sus dos hijos Luciano y Sara viven en una granja ubicada en las afueras de Costa Rica.

Jacobo quien hereda la granja de su padre, siempre tuvo el sueño de hacer de ella una atracción turística y siempre que podía comprar más hectáreas lo hacía para ampliar su variedad de animales.

Los Villalobos, a family of four, Mr. Jacobo, Mrs. Maria and their two children Luciano and Sara live in a farm located on the outskirts of Costa Rica.

Jacobo, who inherits his father's farm, always had the dream of making it a tourist attraction and whenever he could buy more hectares he did so to expand his variety of animals.

Su hijo Luciano quien también ama a los animales como su padre, siempre ha querido tener un espacio en la granja especialmente para sus animales favoritos, que son las aves.

Luciano tiene una pequeña colección. Tiene una pareja de aves quetzal, una pájaro campana y una guacamaya roja. Les tiene mucho aprecio ya que los heredó de su abuelo. Una mañana nublada la granja está muy tranquila y los animales descansan un tanto perezosos debido al clima tan fresco que había. No es una mañana soleada como solía ser. A lo lejos, se acerca el vecino.

Jacobo, saludando al vecino, le hace señas para que este se acerque a la casa y disfrute de un rico chocolate caliente.

His son Luciano, who also loves animals like his father, has always wanted to have a space on the farm especially for his favorite animals, which are birds.

Luciano has a small collection. It has a pair of quetzal birds, a bell bird and a red barnacle. He has a lot of appreciation since he inherited them from his grandfather. A cloudy morning the farm is very quiet and the animals rest somewhat lazy due to the cool weather. It is not a sunny morning as it used to be. In the distance, the neighbor approaches.

Jacobo, greeting the neighbor, beckons him to come to the house and enjoy a delicious hot chocolate.

—Hola vecino, ¿qué lo trae por aquí? —pregunta Jacobo.

El vecino responde -

—Solo paso a saludar y quiero comentarle un par de cosas, o, mejor dicho, quiero proponerle un negocio —dijo el vecino.

—A ver coménteme ese negocio del que habla —responde Luciano mientras sirve dos tazas de chocolate caliente.

"Hello neighbor, what brings you here?" Asks Jacobo.

The neighbor replies:

"I just say hello and I want to tell you a couple of things, or rather, I want to propose a business," said the neighbor.

"Let's see, tell me about that business you are talking about," Luciano replies while serving two cups of hot chocolate.

Lo que pasa es que mi esposa quiere mudarse a la ciudad y poder estar más pendiente del negocio que tenemos allá, entonces estoy pensando en vender mi granja —dice el vecino. Jacobo se fue en pensamiento mientras su vecino seguía hablando. Solamente se imaginaba todo lo que iba a hacer si compraba esa granja. ¡Jacobo! ¿Me escuchaste todo lo que dije? —pregunta el vecino exaltado. Sí disculpa, es que me agrada mucho la idea y solo me estaba imaginando todos los planes que tengo para esas jugosas siete hectáreas que tienes —dice Jacobo. Perfecto, mañana vendré con mi abogado para que podamos hacer los papeles y llevar todo de forma legal —dice el vecino.

What happens is that my wife wants to move to the city and be more aware of the business we have there," says the neighbor. Jacobo left in thought while his neighbor kept talking. He only imagined everything he was going to do if he bought that farm. Jacob! Did you hear everything I said? The exalted neighbor asks. Yes, I'm sorry, I really like the idea and I was just imagining all the plans I have for those juicy seven hectares you have," Jacobo says. Perfect, tomorrow I will come with my lawyer so we can do the papers and take everything legally," says the neighbor.

Se despiden ambos vecinos y Jacobo llama a sus hijos y a su esposa para contarles lo que le acaba de decir el vecino y todos los planes que tiene. Podemos ampliar nuestro corral, nuestro establo y podemos tener una jaula grande para poder albergar tus aves, Luciano —comenta muy emocionado Jacobo. Llega el día siguiente, esta vez sí era una mañana soleada como la mayoría, pero a Jacobo eso no le importó y desde horas de la mañana ya estaba sentado en el frente de su casa esperando a su vecino.

Both neighbors say goodbye and Jacobo calls his children and his wife to tell them what the neighbor just told him and all the plans he has. We can expand our pen, our stable and we can have a large cage to house your birds, Luciano," says Jacobo, very excited. The next day arrives, this time it was a sunny morning like most, but Jacobo didn't mind that and since morning he was already sitting in the front of his house waiting for his neighbor.

¡Vecino, vecino! —Escucha Jacobo a lo lejos, a lo que se asoma y ve a su vecino acercarse junto a un hombre con un traje negro y sosteniendo un maletín negro. Buenos días, Jacobo, te presento a mi abogado que siempre me ha acompañado en todos mis negocios. Ya le comenté que quiero vender mi granja y él ha venido a hacerlo legal dice el vecino. Perfecto, vamos a concretar esto —dice Jacobo. Pasaron dos horas platicando y firmando los papeles de su nueva adquisición. Finalmente, el vecino se despide con ojos llorosos debido a que acaba de vender su granja.

Neighbor, neighbor! —Listen to Jacobo in the distance, what he looks at and sees his neighbor approaching with a man in a black suit and holding a black briefcase. Good morning, Jacobo, I present to you my lawyer who has always accompanied me in all my businesses. I already told him that I want to sell my farm and he has come to make it legal, says the neighbor. Perfect, let's make this happen," says Jacobo. They spent two hours talking and signing the papers of their new acquisition. Finally, the neighbor says goodbye with teary eyes because he has just sold his farm.

Pasaron dos meses durante los cuales Jacobo había dedicado tiempo para ampliar su granja, colocar nuevas jaulas y dividir por zonas los distintos animales que ya tenía y los nuevos que había comprado. Las áreas para las vacas, los cerdos, los caballos y hasta pequeños ponis estaban todos con sus respectivas cercas, áreas para comer y para la recreación de los animales. Uno de los más contentos por la nueva granja y por la nueva ampliación era su hijo Luciano, ya que finalmente tenía su espacio para sus aves.

Two months passed during which Jacobo had dedicated time to expand his farm, place new cages and divide the different animals he already had and the new ones he had bought. The areas for cows, pigs, horses and even small ponies were all with their respective fences, areas for eating and for the recreation of animals. One of the happiest for the new farm and for the new extension was his son Luciano, since he finally had his space for his birds.

Finalizada la ampliación de la granja, se reúnen en familia para la planificación de las áreas de atracción turística, desde una pequeña granja de contacto para los visitantes más pequeños hasta largas caminatas a caballo. En la reunión todos opinan -

After the extension of the farm, they meet as a family to plan the areas of tourist attraction, from a small contact farm for smaller visitors to long walks on horseback. In the meeting everyone thinks:

La granja de contacto tendrá animales pequeños como cerdos, ovejas y ponis para que los niños puedan jugar y alimentarlos —opina Sara. Buena idea, y las cabalgatas a caballo serán por el sendero norte que llegarán a la colina para ver el atardecer —dice Jacobo. Me parece muy romántico la idea de las cabalgatas, tienen que ser exclusivas para las parejas que nos visiten —acota la señora María.

The contact farm will have small animals such as pigs, sheep and ponies so children can play and feed them, Sara says. Good idea, and horseback riding will be on the north path that will reach the hill to watch the sunset," says Jacobo. The idea of horseback riding seems very romantic to me, they have to be exclusive for couples who visit us," says María.

Estaba pensando que una actividad familiar sería que todos puedan ordeñar una vaca y que vieran el proceso de cómo se hace la leche —agrega Luciano—. Al finalizar su tarde en la granja se podrán tomar una foto de recuerdo con mis bellas aves. Al terminar la reunión familiar, planifican cuándo será la gran apertura de la granja para el público, comienzan todos los preparativos y realizan un gran cartel que anuncia el día de apertura.

I was thinking that a family activity would be for everyone to milk a cow and see the process of how milk is made, Luciano adds. At the end of your afternoon at the farm you can take a souvenir photo with my beautiful birds. At the end of the family reunion, they plan when the grand opening of the farm will be for the public, all preparations begin and they make a great poster that announces the opening day.

Llegado el día de apertura, muchas personas emocionadas por conocer la hermosa granja de los Villalobos, se reúnen en la gran puerta de tablas de madera esperando la hora de entrada. Los Villalobos, un poco angustiados por todos los detalles para que la gran inauguración al público salga bien, se dividen las tareas del día y Jacobo dice -

When the opening day arrives, many people excited to know the beautiful farm of the Villalobos, gather at the large wooden plank door waiting for the entrance time. The Villalobos, a little distressed by all the details so that the grand opening to the public goes well, the tasks of the day are divided and Jacobo says:

Sofía, tú te vas a encargar de los niños en la granja de contacto, asegúrate que los alimenten y jueguen con ellos. María, tú organiza la cabalgata a caballo de las parejas y Luciano, prepara la cámara para las fotos con tus aves.

Sofia, you will take care of the children in the contact farm, make sure they feed them and play with them. Maria, you organize the horseback riding of couples and Luciano, prepare the camera for photos with your birds.

Luciano pregunta –

Luciano asks -

—¿Y tú papá, ¿qué harás?

—And you dad, what will you do?

—Yo prepararé a las vacas con sus respectivos becerros y cubetas para que las familias las puedan ordeñar, previo a un pequeño curso de cómo hacerlo. —responde Jacobo.

—I will prepare the cows with their respective calves and buckets, so that families can milk them, before a small course on how to do it. - Jacobo responds.

Llega la hora de abrir las puertas y entre globos y música los visitantes entran a la hermosa granja de los Villalobos. Asombrados por lo que ven, comentan –

It is time to open the doors and among balloons and music visitors enter the beautiful farm of the Villalobos. Amazed by what they see; they comment -

—¡Qué hermosa es!, no puedo creer que exista un lugar tan bello y familiar en Costa Rica —dice una mamá que visita la granja con sus dos pequeños hijos.

—How beautiful it is! I can't believe there is such a beautiful and familiar place in Costa Rica, — says a mother who visits the farm with her two young children.

—Tenemos una granja de contacto donde sus pequeños hijos pueden estar con lindos animales, darles de comer y jugar con ellos —le dice Sofía a la mamá.

—We have a contact farm where your little children can be with cute animals, feed them and play with them, — Sofia tells the mother.

Los niños saltan de la emoción y corren a donde se encuentra la granja de contacto.

Children jump from emotion and run to where is it located the contact farm.

Muy emocionados los niños exclaman –

Very excited the children exclaim–

—¡Mira, mamá, un bebé cerdito y una pequeña oveja!, les daré de comer con este biberón.

—Look, mom, a little baby pig and a little sheep! I will feed them with this bottle.

—Son muy lindos, trátenlos con cuidado y amor —les dice la mamá a sus hijos.

—They are very cute, treat them with care and love, — the mother tells her children.

Al otro lado de la granja la señora María reúne a las parejas asistentes y les ofrece una romántica cabalgata a caballo hasta la colina, donde verán el hermoso atardecer y al finalizar degustarán unos ricos aperitivos.

On the other side of the farm, Mrs. Maria gathers the couples who attended and offers a romantic horseback ride to the hill, where they will see the beautiful sunset and at the end they will taste some delicious snacks.

Una pareja de recién casados, interesados en el paseo, comenta –

A just married couple, interested in the ride, comment–

—Me parece interesante ese paseo, ¿podemos escoger los caballos? —pregunta el esposo.

—I think that ride is interesting, can we choose the horses? Asks the husband.

—Claro que sí; vengan al establo y les muestro los caballos ensillados —responde María.

—Of course; you come to the barn and I show you saddled horses— Maria answers.

Al ir al establo, encuentran unos hermosos caballos pura sangre y María se los presenta –

When they go to the barn, they find beautiful thoroughbred horses and Maria introduced to them. –

—Este caballo negro es Cometa, es muy dócil y le encanta la zanahoria, este caballo blanco de aquí es Copo de Nieve, es muy veloz y le encanta que le trencen su cola.

—This black horse is Cometa, it is very docile and it loves carrots, this white horse here is Copo de nieve, it is very fast and it loves to be braided in his tail.

—¡Me gusta Copo de Nieve!, ese será mi caballo —dice la esposa entusiasmada.

—I like Copo de nieve! That will be my horse," says the excited wife.

—Entonces el mío será Cometa, me encantan los caballos negros —responde el esposo que visita la granja.

—Then mine will be Cometa, I love black horses — replies the husband who visits the farm.

—Está bien, móntense en sus respectivos caballos que les espera una hermosa puesta de sol —dice María a la pareja de recién casados.

— All right, get on your respective horses that a beautiful sunset awaits, — Maria says to the just married couple.

La pareja inicia la cabalgata por un hermoso sendero cubierto de un césped totalmente verde, con un clima agradable y escuchando los sonidos característicos de todos los animales que habitan en la granja.

The couple starts the ride on a beautiful path covered with a completely green lawn, with a pleasant climate and listening to the characteristic sounds of all the animals that inhabit the farm.

El señor Jacobo se reúne con las familias asistentes y les dicta una breve charla de como es el proceso de obtención de leche de vaca, y pregunta a los asistentes –

Mr. Jacob meets with the attending families and gives them a brief talk about the process of obtaining cow's milk, and asks the attendees–

—¿Alguien quiere ordeñar una de estas hermosas vacas mariposas?

—Does anyone want to milk one of these beautiful butterfly cows?

Y del grupo de asistentes, un padre y un hijo gritan emocionados –

And from the group of assistants, a father and a son shout excitedly —

—¡Nosotros, nosotros!

—We, we!

El señor Jacobo les pide que se acerquen a donde está la vaca junto a su pequeño becerro y dice que uno de los dos se siente en un taburete de madera muy bajo, que los ayudará a alcanzar las ubres de la vaca.

Mr. Jacobo asks them to go where the cow is next to his little calf and since one of the two sits on a very low wooden board, that will help them to reach the udders of the cow.

El padre de familia se sienta y coloca a su hijo en su regazo, toman como les había enseñado previamente Jacobo las ubres de la vaca y empiezan a ordeñarlas.

The father sits down and places his son in his lap, they take as Jacobo had previously taught them the cow udders and periodically milk them.

El niño muy entusiasmado le dice al papá –

The very excited boy tells his dad —

—¡Papá, es leche como la que como con mi cereal!

—Dad, it's milk like the one I eat with my cereal!

Todas las familias asistentes se ríen y continúan observando el proceso de obtención de leche.

All attending families laugh and continue to observe the process of obtaining milk.

Mientras tanto, un grupo de jóvenes se encuentran con Luciano en el área de las jaulas de aves, y extasiados por los hermosos colores de cada especie de ave y por sus peculiares cantos, se toman fotos con cada una de ellas.

Meanwhile, a group of young people meet Luciano in the area of bird cages, and ecstatic about the beautiful colors of each bird species and its peculiar songs, photos are taken with each of them.

—Quiero una foto con el ave en mi cabeza —dice un joven emocionado.

—I want a picture with the bird in my head, — says an excited young man

—¡Mi foto será alimentando al ave azul! —exclama otra joven del grupo.

—My photo will be feeding the blue bird! — exclaims another a girl from the group.

Jacobo complace a todos los presentes y les entrega su foto como recuerdo de la visita a la granja.

Jacobo pleases to everyone present and gives them his photo as a souvenir of the visit to the farm.

Al finalizar el día de apertura de la granja, toda la familia Villalobos se reúne para la cena y concluyen, que la inauguración de la granja para el público ha sido todo un éxito y que lo harían cada fin de semana de sus vidas.

At the end of the farm's opening day, whole family of Villalobos meets for dinner and concludes the inauguration of the farm for the public that has been a success and that they would do it every weekend of their lives.

Resumen

Los Villalobos es una familia de cuatro integrantes, que viven en una granja en las afueras de Costa Rica. Jacobo, el padre de la familia, tiene como objetivo ampliar el tamaño de su granja, tener más animales y convertirla en una atracción turística. A Jacobo se le presenta una gran oportunidad por la venta de la granja vecina, y emprende junto al resto de su familia la remodelación de la granja para convertirla en lo que siempre quiso, un lugar con constantes visitas de familias y grupos.

The Villalobos is a family of four who live on a farm in the outskirts of Costa Rica. Jacobo, the father of the family, aims to expand the size of his farm, have more animals and turn it into a tourist attraction. Jacobo is presented with a great opportunity for the sale of the neighboring farm, and undertakes with the rest of his family the remodeling of the farm to make it what he always wanted, a place with constant visits from families and groups.

Quiz

1. ¿De quién heredó las aves Luciano?
a. De su padre
b. De su abuelo
c. De su hermana

2. ¿Qué actividad planeaban para los visitantes más pequeños?
a. Paseos a caballos
b. Fotos con las aves
c. Granja de contacto

3. ¿Quién organiza las cabalgatas para las parejas?
a. María
b. Sofía
c. Luciano

4. ¿Qué caballo escoge el esposo que visita la granja?
a. Copo de Nieve
b. Cometa
c. Guacamaya roja

5. ¿Cuándo harán más aperturas al público luego de la exitosa inauguración?
a. Todos los días
b. Nunca
c. Cada fin de semana

Answers

1. B
2. C
3. A
4. B
5. C

Vocabulary / Vocabulario

- *Integrantes* --- Members
- *Granja* --- Farm
- *Afueras* --- Outskirts
- *Hereda* --- Inherit
- *Atracción turística* --- Tourist attraction
- *Hectáreas* --- Hectares
- *Espacio* --- Space
- *Aves* --- Birds
- *Quetzal* – (A type of bird)
- *Guacamaya roja* --- Scarlet macaw
- *Nublada* --- Cloudy
- *Perezosos* --- Lazy
- *Clima* --- Weather
- *Soleada* --- Sunny
- *Solía* --- Used to
- *Vecino* --- Neighbour
- *Saludar* --- To greet
- *Negocio* --- Deal
- *Esposa* --- Wife
- *Mudarse* --- To move out
- *Pendiente* --- Attentive
- *Vender* --- To sell

- *Imaginaba* --- Imagined
- *Agrada* --- pleases
- *Planes* --- Plans
- *Abogado* – lawyer
- *Legal* --- Legal
- *Establo* --- Barn
- *Jaula* --- Cage
- *Albergar* --- To harbor
- *Frente* --- Front
- *Traje negro* --- Black suit
- *Sosteniendo* --- Holding
- *Maletín* --- Briefcase
- *Concretar* --- To finalize
- *Platicando* --- Talking
- *Firmando* --- Signing
- *Adquisición* --- Acquisition
- *Jaulas* --- Cages
- *Zonas* --- Areas
- *Vacas* --- Cows
- *Cerdos* --- Pigs
- *Caballos* --- Horses
- *Ponis* --- Ponies
- *Cercas* --- Fences
- *Recreación* --- Recreation
- *Planificación* --- Planning
- *Granja de contacto* --- Contact farm/Petting farm
- *Caminatas* --- Walks
- *Ovejas* --- Sheep
- *Cabalgatas* --- Horseback riding
- *Sendero* --- Path
- *Colina* --- Hill
- *Atardecer* --- Sunset
- *Romántico* --- Romantic
- *Parejas* --- Couples
- *Actividad familiar* --- Family activity
- *Ordeñar* --- To milk
- *Agrega* --- Adds
- *Apertura* --- Opening
- *Preparativos* --- Preparations
- *Tablas de madera* --- Wooden boards
- *Angustiados* --- Preoccupied
- *Inauguración* --- Opening
- *Tareas* --- Tasks
- *Asegúrate* --- You make sure
- *Cámara* --- Camera
- *Becerros* --- Calves
- *Cubetas* --- Buckets

- *Curso* --- Course
- *Globos* --- Balloons
- *Asombrados* --- Amazed
- *Darles de comer* --- Feed them
- *Trátenlos* --- Treat them (instructions)
- *Cuidado* --- Care
- *Aperitivos* --- Appetizers
- *Recién casados* --- Just married
- *Escoger* --- To choose
- *Ensillados* --- Saddled
- *Pura sangre* --- Pure blood
- *Cometa* --- Comet or kite
- *Zanahoria* --- Carrot
- *Copo de Nieve* --- Snowflake
- *Veloz* --- Fast
- *Trencen* --- Braid
- *Caballos negros* --- Black horses
- *Móntense* --- Mount (a horse)
- *Puesta de sol* --- Sunset
- *Césped* --- Grass
- *Agradable* --- Nice
- *Habitan* --- They inhabit (Verb --- habitar)
- *Charla* --- Chat
- *Proceso* --- Process
- *Vacas mariposas* --- White cows with black spots
- *Taburete de madera* --- Wooden stool
- *Alcanzar* --- To reach
- *Ubres* --- Udders
- *Regazo* --- Lap
- *Mientras tanto* --- Meanwhile
- *Jóvenes* --- Young boys
- *Especie* --- Species
- *Cantos* --- Songs
- *Complace* --- Pleases
- *Entrega* --- Gives
- *Recuerdo* --- Memory
- *Éxito* --- Success
- *Fin de semana* --- Weekend

12. Los Piratas Del Bufón Errante (Torpes En Tierra Y En Mar)

The Pirates of the Wandering Jester (Clumsy on Land and Sea)

Todo sucedió tan rápido que nadie sabe qué fue lo que paso. ¿Qué paso? Eran siete barcos piratas, anclados en una montaña en el medio de la nada, no había mar, océano, rio, riachuelo, charco, pantano ni nada que esté relacionado con el agua. Simplemente eran siete barcos en una montaña sin ningún tipo de razón o explicación alguna.

Everything happened so fast that no one knows what happened. What happened? There were seven pirate ships anchored on a mountain in the middle of nowhere. There was no sea, ocean, river, stream, puddle, swamp, or anything that is related to water around. They were simply seven ships on a mountain without any kind of reason or explanation.

Piratas urbanos de ciudad establecieron su guarida en las montañas para permanecer ocultos. Estaban buscando un extraño tesoro que llevaba más de mil años enterrado en alguna parte de la ciudad. Por eso desarrollaron un sistema de ruedas y neumáticos para sus barcos y poder trasladarse desde los mares hasta las ciudades. Los Barcos Carros, auto barcos, navegaron por mar y tierra, de puerto en puerto de pueblo en pueblo, de ciudad en ciudad.

City urban pirates established their lair in the mountains to stay hidden. They were looking for a strange treasure that had been buried somewhere in the city. That's why they developed a system of wheels and tires for their ships to be able to move from the seas to the cities. The ships cars, auto boats, navigated by sea and land, from seaport to village port from, city to city.

El día de su llegada los piratas venían de una legendaria fiesta de corsarios por el Mar Muerto. Que siguió en el mar Mediterráneo terminaron a en el mar Caribe descubrieron que el verdadero Mar Muerto en realidad queda en Puerto Rico y no en Jordania. De hecho, el Mar Muerto en Puerto Rico está vivo y bueno.

The day of their arrival, the pirates came from a legendary party of pirates by the Dead Sea that flowed into the Mediterranean Sea. They ended up in the Caribbean Sea as they discovered that the true Dead Sea actually ends in Puerto Rico and not in Jordan. In fact, the Dead Sea in Puerto Rico is alive and well.

Eran conocidos como los Piratas del Bufón Errante, torpes en tierra y en mar. Y estaban convencidos de que la leyenda del tesoro del Morokotongo era cierta y estaba escondido en este pequeño Pueblo de Los Andes rodeado de montañas, cuentan los Antiguos historiadores que el tesoro de Morokotongo pertenecía al rey de los piratas, el temible Barbacoa.

They were known as the Pirates of the Wandering Jester, clumsy on land and sea. And they were convinced that the legend of the treasure of the Morokotongo was true and was hidden in this small town in the Andes surrounded by mountains. The ancient historians say that the treasure of Morokotongo belonged to the king of the pirates, the fearsome Barbacoa.

En 1883, se lo robo al conde de Bermeja. Barbacoa derrochó gran parte del tesoro en sus viajes y aventuras por los siete mares. El resto lo escondió tan bien que ningún otro pirata ha podido encontrarlo. Muchos grupos de piratas dejaron incluso de navegar para dedicarse solo a la búsqueda de ese tesoro.

In 1883, he stole the treasure from the Count of Bermeja. Barbacoa squandered much of the treasure in his travels and adventures on the seven seas. The rest he hid so well that no other pirate has been able to find it. Many groups of pirates even stopped sailing to dedicate themselves alone to the search for that treasure.

Los Piratas del Bufón Errante habían estudiado todos los errores cometidos por los piratas anteriores. Bajo juramento del código de los piratas se prometían - encontrar el legendario tesoro y pasar a la historia como los únicos piratas que descifraron la coordenada del mapa del gran Barbacoa.

The Pirates of the Wandering Jester had studied all the mistakes made by the previous pirates. Under oath of the code, the pirates promised themselves to find the legendary treasure and go down in history as the only pirates who deciphered the map coordinates of the great Barbacoa.

Pero eran un poco despistados, atolondrados y locos. Bueno todos los piratas están locos, pero estos de verdad estaban chiflados. El día que decidieron buscar él te sonó, de Morokotongo fue una verdadera locura. Apenas zarparon, todo fue un caos.

But they were a bit clueless and mad. Well, all the pirates are crazy, but they really were nuts. The day they decided to look for the treasure, Morokotongo was full of real madness. As soon as they set sail, everything was chaotic.

¡Se va se va la Baarcaaa ...tooodos a bordooooo! grito el capitán Jaky Esparragos.

"The boat is leaving! All of you aboard!" Captain Jaky Esparragos shouted.

¿Para donde se va? respondió el primero al mando,

"Where does it go?" responded the first in command.

¿Qué dicen las velas? grito el capitán.

"What do the sails say?" said the captain.

No dicen nada capitán están calladas.

"They do not say anything, Captain. They are silent."

¿Quién dejo entrar a estos monos? protestaba el capitán. Monos por todos lados del barco, colgados y saltando, desordenando y rompiendo todo lo que encontraban a su paso, acabaron con las provisiones. En la pelea contra los monos, aparecieron sesenta loros y repetían lo mismo.

"Who let these monkeys in?" the captain protested. Monkeys were all over the ship, hanging and jumping, messing up and breaking everything in their path. They ended up with provisions and in the fight against the monkeys; sixty parrots appeared and repeated the same thing.

"Rua la la Morokotongo Morokotongo peligro peligro la la rua rua donde donde Morokotongo rua rua." habla los loros.

"Rua la la Morokotongo Morokotongo danger danger la rua rua where where Morokotongo rua rua."

Se desato una gran tormenta y una de las velas se incendió. Un relámpago le pulverizo el sombrero al capitán. Los monos se bebieron todo el barril de cerveza y los toneles de vino y enloquecieron los loros se alborotaron también.

A great storm broke and one of the sails caught fire. A lightning bolt smashed the captain's hat. The monkeys drank the whole barrel of beer and wine and the parrots went mad.

Los sorprendió un bucanero y se enfrentaron a cañonazos y espadas por una hora. Así transcurrían todos sus viajes por mar y tierra. Y tenían la costumbre, como todos los piratas, de hacer retos y torneos entre ellos diciendo cosas como -

They were surprised by a buccaneer and faced guns and swords for an hour. This is how all his trips by sea and land passed. And they had the habit, like all pirates, of making challenges and tournaments between them -

¡Mi espada es la más rápida de todo el océano!

"My sword is the fastest in the whole ocean!"

¡Blasfemia! ¡Mi espada es más veloz! ¡En guardia!

"Blasphemy! My sword is faster. On guard!"

¡Ya estoy listo! ¡Te demostrare que soy el mejor con la espada! ¿Ves esa mosca que está volando sobre la botella? ¡Mira!

"I'm ready now. I will show you that I am the best with the sword. Do you see that fly that is flying over the bottle? Look."

Agarro mi espada y viste le corte las alas.

I grab my sword and cut his wings.

¡Eso no es nada! ¿Ves ese mosquito que vuela sobre la gorda panza del contramaestre? ¡Presta atención!

"That is nothing. Do you see that mosquito that flies over the fat belly of the first mate? Pay attention!"

Saco mi espada y zum...

I take out my sword and zum...

¡Ja Ja Ja, siguió volando fallaste!

"¡Ha Ha ha, kept flying! You failed!"

¡No falle para nada! ¡Es cierto que siguió volando, pero no va poder tener más hijos!

"I did not fail at all! It is true that he kept flying, but he will not be able to have more children."

¿Que?

"What?"

¡Lo que escuchas y tal como te lo acabo de demostrar que soy el mejor con la espada!

"What you hear and how I just showed you is that I am the best with the sword."

Otro de los retos piratas era "La Danza de La Plancha" que consistía en girar sobre tu propio cuerpo dando vueltas parado en un solo pie en el borde de la puncha abreva el olfato y la mirada de los tiburones. Todos los peligros riesgos y retos valían la pena porque el tesoro de Morokotongo era el mayor de todos los tesoros Dicen los que conocen la leyenda, que el tesoro del temible Barbacoa está compuesto de -

Another of the pirate challenges was "The Dance of the Plank", which consisted of spinning on one foot on the edge of the plank above the nose and the eyes of the sharks. All the dangers risks and challenges were worth it because the treasure of Morokotongo was the greatest of all the treasures. Those who know the legend say that the treasure of the fearsome Barbacoa is composed of -

ciento treinta - Toneladas de doblones de Plata

One hundred and thirty - tons of silver doubloons

dos mil ochocientos cincuenta - Lingotes de Oro

Two thousand eight hundred and fifty - gold ingots

mil cientos setenta y cinco - Esmeraldas

One thousand one hundred seventy-five - emeralds

novecientos ochenta y tres - Rubíes

Nine hundred and eighty-three - rubies

trescientos noventa y seis - Diamantes

Three hundred ninety-six - diamonds

dos mil cuatrocientos noventa y nueve - Monedas de Oro

Two thousand four hundred and ninety-nine - gold coins

tres mil cientos veintitrés - Joyas de Cristal

Three thousand one hundred and twenty-three - crystal jewelry

cuatro mil trescientos veinte - Esculturas de Bronce y Plata

Four thousand three hundred and twenty - bronze and silver sculptures

ochenta - Espadas Bañadas en Oro y Plata

Eighty - swords bathed in gold and silver

ciento noventa y cinco - Dagas Templadas en Oro

One hundred and ninety-five - gold-plated daggers

quinientos setenta y cinco - collares de Perlas Preciosas

Five hundred seventy-five - precious pearl necklaces

Después de recorrer y saquear todo el pueblo los piratas del bufón errante no tenían pista alguna del fabuloso tesoro, habían seguido las instrucciones del mapa al pie de la letra. Y no sabían que era lo que estaba mal hasta que se dieron cuenta que todo el tiempo habían estado leyendo el mapa atreves.

After touring and plundering the entire town, the Pirates of the Wandering Jester had no clue to the location fabulous treasure. They had followed the instructions on the map to the letter. They did not know what was wrong until they realized that they had been reading the map upside down all the time.

Quiz

1. ¿Dónde estaban los siete barcos?
a. Océano
b. Mar
c. Montaña

2. ¿Dónde habían establecido su guarida los piratas de la ciudad urbana?
a. montañas
b. Mar
c. Océano

3. ¿De dónde venían los piratas?
a. mar Mediterráneo
b. Mar Muerto
c. Montaña

4. ¿Dónde fue robado el tesoro en 1883?
a. Montaña
b. Conde de bermeja
c. Mar Muerto

Answers

1. c
2. a
3. b
4. b

Vocabulary / Vocabulario

- *acabaron* --- (ah-kah-bah-rohn) Transitive verb – they finished; conjugated form of acabar, past third person plural
- *agarró* --- (ah-gahr-roh) Transitive verb – I grab; conjugated form of agarrar, present first person singular
- *alborotaron* --- (ahl-boh-roh-tah-rohn) Transitive verb – they disturbed; conjugated form of alborotar, past third person plural
- *anclados* --- (ahn-klahr) Intransitive verb – to anchor
- *anterior* --- (ahn-teh-ryohr) Adjective – front, previous
- *aparecieron* --- (ah-pah-reh-seh-rohn) Intransitive verb – they appeared; conjugated form of aparecer, past third person plural
- *bajo* --- (bah-hoh) Adjective – short, low
- *bañada* --- (bah-nyah-dah) Feminine noun – bath, swim
- *bebieron* --- (beh-beh-ehr-rohn) Transitive verb – they drink; conjugated form of beber, past third person plural
- *blasfemia* – (Blahs-feh-mee-ah) Feminine noun --- blasphemy
- *botella* --- (boh-teh-yah) Feminine noun --- bottle
- *bronce* --- (brohn-seh) Masculine noun – bronze
- *bufón* --- (boo-fohn) Masculine noun – buffon, fool
- *cañonazo* --- (kah-nyoh-nah-soh) Masculine noun – cannon shot
- *caribe* (ka-ree-beh) Proper noun --- Carribean
- *cerveza* --- (sehr-beh-sah) Feminine noun --- beer
- *charco* --- (chahr-koh) Masculine noun – puddle, pool
- *chiflados* --- (chee-flahr) Transitive verb – to whistle
- *ciento noventa y cinco* (see-en-toe no-vehn-tah ee sen-coh) Adjective – the number one hundred ninety-five
- *ciento treinta* (see-en-toe trin-tah) Adjective – the number one hundred thirty
- *collar* --- (koh-yahr) Masculine noun --- necklace
- *cometido* --- (koh-meh-tee-doh) Masculine noun – task, mission, duty
- *compuesto* --- (kohm-pwehs-toh) Masculine noun --- compound
- *corsarios* --- (kohr-sah-ryoh) Masculine or Feminine noun --- pirate
- *cristal* --- (krees-tahl) Masculine noun – glass, shard of glass

- *cuatro mil trescientos veinte* (quat-roh mill tres-see-en-tohs ven-tea) Adjective – the number four thousand three hundred twenty
- *cuerpo* --- (kwehr-poh) Masculine noun --- body
- *daga* --- (dah-gah) Feminine noun --- dagger
- *dedicarse* --- (deh-dee-kahr-seh) Pronominal verb – to do for a living
- *demostrare* --- (deh-mohs-trah-rey) Transitive verb – I will demonstrate; conjugated form of demostrar, future subjunctive form, first person singular
- *derrocho* --- (deh-rroh-cho) Transitive verb – I squander; conjugated form of derrochar, present first person singular
- *desarrollaron* --- (deh-sah-rroh-yahr) Transitive verb – they developed; conjugated form of desarrollar, past third person plural
- *descifraron* --- (deh-see-frah-rohn) Transitive verb – they deciphered; conjugated form of decifrar, past third person plural
- *descubrieron* --- (dehs-koo-breer) Transitive verb – they discovered, conjugated form of descubrir, past third person plural
- *desordenando* --- (dehs-ohr-deh-nahn-doh) Transitive verb – to mess up
- *diamantes* --- (dyah-mahn-tehs) Plural noun --- diamonds
- *dos mil cuatrocientos noventa y nueve* (dohs mill quat-roh-see-en-tohs no-vehn-tah ee new-eh-veh) Adjective – the number two thousand four hundred ninety-nine
- *dos mil ochocientos cincuenta* (dohs mill oh-cho-see-en-tohs sin-qwin-tah) Adjective – the number two thousand eight hundred fifty
- *enloquecieron* --- (ehn-loh-keh-sehr) Transitive verb – to go crazy, to drive crazy; conjugated form of enloquecier, past third person plural
- *enterrado* --- (ehn-teh-rrah-doh) Adjective – buried
- *errante* --- (eh-rrahn-teh) Adjective --- wandering
- *esmeralda* --- (ehs-meh-rahl-dah) Feminine noun --- emeralds
- *espada* --- (ehs-pah-dah) Feminine noun --- sword
- *estudiado* --- (ehs-too-dyah-doh) Adjective --- studied
- *fallaste* --- (fah-yah-steh) Intransitive verb – you failed; conjugated form of fallar, past second person singular
- *gorda* --- (gohr-dah) Adjective – fat, thick, big
- *joya* --- (hoh-yah) Feminine noun --- jewel
- *juramento* --- (hoo-rah-mehn-toh) Masculine noun --- oath
- *lingote* --- (leeng-goh-teh) Masculine noun – ingot, gold bar
- *loro* --- (loh-roh) Masculine or Feminine noun --- parrot
- *mar* --- (mahr) Masculine noun – sea, ocean
- *mil ciento setenta y cinco* (mill see-en-toe seh-tehn-tah ee seen-ko) Adjective – the number one thousand one hundred seventy-five
- *mirada* --- (mee-rah-dah) Feminine noun --- look
- *monos* --- (moh-noh) Masculine or Feminine noun --- monkeys
- *mosca* --- (mohs-kah) Feminine noun --- fly
- *novecientos ochenta y tres* (no-veh-see-en-tohs oh-chin-tah ee trahys) Adjective – the number nine hundred eighty-three
- *ochenta* --- (oh-chehn-tah) Adjective – the number eighty
- *ocultos* --- (oh-kool-toh) Adjective --- hidden
- *oro* --- (oh-roh) Masculine noun --- gold
- *pantano* --- (pahn-tah-noh) Masculine noun – swampland, wetland

- *panza* --- (pahn-sah) Feminine noun --- belly
- *perlas* --- (pehr-lah) Feminine noun --- pearls
- *permanecer* --- (pehr-mah-neh-sehr) Intransitive verb – to stay
- *pertenecía* --- (pehr-teh-neh-seh-ah) Intransitive verb – to belong to; conjugated form of pertenecer, imperfect first person singular
- *plancha* --- (plahn-chah) Feminine noun --- plank
- *preciosas* --- (preh-syoh-sahs) Adjective – beautiful, precious
- *protestaba* --- (proh-tehs-tah-bah) Intransitive verb – I protested; conjugated form of protestar, imperfect first person singular
- *quinientos setenta y cinco* --- (kee-nyehn-tohs say-ten-tah ee seen-ko) Adjective – the number five hundred seventy-five
- *relámpago* --- (rreh-lahm-pah-goh) Masculine noun --- lightening
- *repetían* --- (rreh-peh-tee-ahn) Transitive verb – to repeat, to do again; conjugated form of repetir, imperfect third person plural
- *tesoro* --- (teh-soh-roh) Masculine noun – treasure
- *riachuelo* --- (rryah-chweh-loh) Masculine noun – brook, stream
- *riesgos* --- (rryehs-goh) Masculine noun --- risk
- *ruedas* --- (rruh-eh-dahs) Intransitive verb – you roll; conjugated form of rodar, present second person singular
- *saquear* --- (sah-keh-ahr) Transitive verb – to loot
- *sesenta* --- (seh-sehn-tah) Adjective – the number sixty
- *templadas* --- (tehm-plah-doh) Adjective – lukewarm, mild
- *tesoro* --- (teh-soh-roh) Masculine noun --- treasure
- *tiburone* --- (tee-boo-rohn) Masculine noun --- shark
- *tipo* --- (tee-poh) Masculine noun – type, class, sort
- *tonelada* --- (toh-neh-lah-dah) Feminine noun (weight) --- ton
- *tonto* --- (tohn-toh) Adjective – stupid, dumb, idiot
- *torpes* --- (tohr-peh) Adjective – clumsy, dim-witted
- *transcurrían* --- (trahns-koo-rreer) Intransitive verb – they passed; conjugated form of transcurrir, imperfect third person plural
- *tres mil ciento veintitrés* (trays mill see-en-toe beyn-tee-trehs) Adjective – the number three thousand one hundred twenty-three
- *trescientos noventa y seis* (trays-see-en-tohs no-ven-tah eh sahys) Adjective – the number three hundred ninety-six
- *veloz* --- (beh-lohs) Adjective --- fast

13. Intuición En Custodia

Un día común en la localidad de Capilla del Monte y Patricio decidió tomar el tren a San Juan. Todos los meses, Patricio iba a visitar a su papá, que vivía en Caucete en San Juan. Patricio tenía muy buena intuición con las personas que lo rodeaban. Él, por ejemplo, sabía que el chofer Norberto era un buen hombre que cuidaba de sus nietos. Seguramente tendría unos 65 años y siempre que lo veía en el pueblo lo saludaba con calidez y esmero.

An ordinary day in the town of Capilla del Monte and Patricio decided to take the train to San Juan. Every month, Patricio went to visit his father, who lived in Caucete in San Juan. Patricio had very good intuition with the people around him. He, for example, knew that the driver Norberto was a good man who took care of his grandchildren. Surely, he was about 65 years old and whenever he saw him in town he greeted him with warmth and care.

Aquel lunes Patricio subió al tren, pero no encontró a Norberto. En su lugar, un hombre barbudo y de aspecto descuidado estaba al mando de la locomotora. La intuición de Patricio le indicaba que algo no andaba bien. Por lo que Patricio se acercó a preguntarle a este hombre qué le había pasado al Sr. Norberto. -Murió. -le contestó; sin mediar ninguna otra palabra que amortigüe la mala noticia.

That Monday Patricio got on the train but did not find Norberto. Instead, a bearded and careless-looking man was in command of the locomotive. Patricio's intuition indicated that something was wrong. So Patricio approached to ask this man what had happened to Mr. Norberto. -Died; answered without mediating any other word that cushioned the bad news.

Patricio se sintió afligido y se dirigió de nuevo a su asiento con un par de lágrimas en sus mejillas. La mujer que estaba del lado del pasillo, al lado de su asiento habitual, le preguntó si le pasaba algo. -Gracias, señora. Pero es lo único en la vida que no tiene solución. -le respondió Patricio secándose las lágrimas. No te sientas mal. -respondió la señora intentado que la situación volviera a la cotidianeidad.

Patrick felt distressed and he returned to his seat with a couple of tears on his cheeks. The woman on the aisle side, next to her usual seat, asked if something was wrong. Thank Mrs. But it is the only thing in life that has no solution. -Patricio replied wiping her tears. Do not be sad. - the lady answered tried that the situation returned to the daily life.

Patricio se sentó a su lado, en el asiento de la ventana, y comenzó a observar el paisaje de Capilla del Monte y cómo este se iba moviendo a la velocidad de la locomotora. Sus ojos llorosos solo le permitían ver una fotografía borrosa. Al observar a través del vidrio, pudo ver la silueta de un hombre con el uniforme que siempre llevaba Norberto. La silueta se acercaba hacia el tren, como intentando alcanzarlo. Sus brazos se alzaban en el aire como si estuviera dirigiendo un avión.

Patricio sat next to him, in the window seat, and began to observe the landscape of Capilla del Monte and how it was moving at the speed of the locomotive. His teary eyes only allowed him to see a blurry photograph. When he looked through the glass, he could see the silhouette of a man in the uniform that Norberto always wore. The silhouette was approaching the train, as if trying to reach it. His arms rose in the air as if he were directing a plane.

Patricio no estaba seguro de que aquel hombre fuera Norberto, ya que ese uniforme lo había visto en muchas personas que trabajaban en la estación de trenes. De alguna u otra forma, Patricio sentía un dolor en el pecho. Era una sensación de disgusto, o un mareo fuerte que lo hacía sentirse inestable. ¿Te sientes bien? -le preguntó la mujer sentada a su lado. -Te ves pálido. No. Me duele el estómago y el pecho. -le respondió Patricio sin preocuparse por asustar a la mujer.

Patricio was not sure that this man was Norberto, since that uniform had seen him in many people who worked at the train station. One way or another, Patricio felt a pain in his chest. It was a feeling of disgust, or a strong dizziness that made him feel unstable. Do you feel good? asked the woman sitting next to him. -You look pale. No. My stomach and chest hurt. -Patricio replied without worrying to scare the woman.

Debe haber sido algo que comiste. -respondió la mujer con un tono robótico, como diciendo una respuesta automática. Esta frase era una muletilla que hasta los médicos usaban cuando realmente no querían indagar en el problema real. Patricio se calmó un poco, pero se asustaba hasta con la mirada de cada pasajero. Su padre siempre le dijo que utilizara el cerebro antes que el corazón, pues el enamoramiento con su madre había resultado en una tragedia que podría haberse anticipado con el uso de una lógica sistemática.

It must have been something you ate. - the woman answered with a robotic tone, as if saying an automatic answer. This phrase was a crutch that even doctors used when they really did not want to investigate the real problem. Patricio calmed down a bit, but he was scared even with the eyes of each passenger. His father always told him to use the brain rather than the heart, since falling in love with his mother had resulted in a tragedy that could have been anticipated with the use of systematic logic.

Es por ello que Patricio intentó calmarse y analizar la situación. Norberto había muerto, y eso era un proceso natural. Pero, ¿por qué el nuevo chofer había respondido con tanta crudeza y poca sensibilidad? Es raro que un chofer del pueblo no conociera a Norberto lo suficiente como para lamentar su pérdida. En la siguiente parada, Patricio notó que una chica se bajó descompuesta del tren, pero un hombre se levantó del asiento a intentar ayudarla y le ofreció agua. La chica estaba temblando como si hubiera visto un fantasma.

That is why Patricio tried to calm down and analyze the situation. Norberto had died, and that was a natural process. But why had the new driver responded so crudely and with little sensitivity? It's rare that a town driver didn't know Norberto enough to regret his loss. At the next stop, Patricio noticed that a girl got off the train, but a man got up from the seat to try to help her and offered her water. The girl was shaking as if she had seen a ghost.

La chica se sentó con el hombre que le ofreció agua en el asiento que estaba al frente de Patricio. Patricio la miró a la cara y la chica le respondió en silencio. Tan solo se miraban. Sentían que no podían hablar mucho. Las dos personas que tenían a sus costados no parecían de confianza, por lo que cualquier palabra significaba un riesgo. Ambos se transmitían seguridad, pero... ¿qué estaba pasando? Existía un aire de complicidad sobre el vagón. Si bien todos los indicios eran inconclusos, algo en el interior de ellos les decía que algo no estaba bien.

The girl sat down with the man who offered her water in the seat that was in front of Patricio. Patricio looked at her face and the girl answered in silence. They just looked at each other. They felt they couldn't talk much. The two people at their sides did not seem trustworthy, so any word meant a risk. Both were transmitted security, but ... what was happening? There was an air of complicity over the car. While all the signs were inconclusive, something inside them told them that something was not right.

Patricio solo tenía 15 años y sus padres no le permitían bajar del tren antes de su parada. Sin embargo, Patricio tenía muy claro que toda regla tenía al menos una excepción, y estas no habían sido aclaradas al mo. El tren comenzó a bajar la velocidad y a ese mismo ritmo el corazón de Patricio latía sincronizado con las pulsaciones de la chica que estaba al frente. El tren se detuvo en otra parada.

Patricio was only 15 years old and his parents did not allow him to get off the train before his stop. However, Patricio was very clear that every rule had at least one exception, and these had not been clarified to the mo. The train began to slow down and at that same pace Patricio's heart beat in sync with the pulsations of the girl in front. The train stopped at another stop.

Florencia, la chica que estaba al frente de él, se levantó de un golpe, tomó la mano de Patricio y se bajaron del tren corriendo. Nadie comprendía el apuro, pero otro pasajero notó que habían dejado atrás sus mochilas, por lo que las tomó y se bajó del tren con ellas para devolverlas.

Florencia, the girl in front of him, jumped up, took Patricio's hand and got off the train running. No one understood the trouble, but another passenger noticed that they had left their backpacks, so he took them and got off the train with them to return them.

Al momento de bajarse, las puertas del tren se cerraron y este siguió su camino. El pasajero que se había bajado se sentía muy desesperado porque había tenido intenciones de volver a subir al vagón. Florencia y Patricio seguían sin mediar palabras. El pasajero se quejó y los miró como si ellos tuvieran la culpa de algo. Ambos le agradecieron y lo abrazaron. Allí abrazaban a un desconocido en la estación de un pueblo que no conocían. Patricio intentó hablar, pero al abrir su boca una explosión se escucha desde lo lejos en la dirección que había seguido el tren. La onda expansiva tiró a los tres al piso. Al levantarse vieron una columna de humo que se extendía desde unos pocos kilómetros de donde ellos se encontraban.

When he got off, the train doors closed and he continued on his way. The passenger who had gotten off felt very desperate because he had intended to get back into the car. Florencia and Patricio were still speechless. The passenger complained and looked at them as if they were to blame for something. Both thanked him and hugged him. There they hugged a stranger at the station of a town they didn't know. Patricio tried to speak, but when he opened his mouth an explosion was heard from afar in the direction that the train had followed. The shock wave threw the three to the floor. When they got up they saw a column of smoke that extended from a few kilometers from where they were.

La policía detuvo a los tres en la comisaría más cercana para declarar. Cada uno contó su anécdota, pero ninguno de los detectives que los entrevistaron parecía creerles. Los tres jóvenes habían quedado como cómplices de una tragedia. Desde las noticias en la radio que se escuchaba de fondo en la comisaría se oía sobre un presunto ataque terrorista. Los tres pasajeros no sabían en qué estaban metidos, solo sabían que eran inocentes.

Police arrested all three at the nearest police station to testify. Each one told their anecdote, but none of the detectives who interviewed them seemed to believe them. The three young men had been complicit in a tragedy. From the news on the radio that was heard in the background at the police station, one heard about an alleged terrorist attack. The three passengers did not know what they were involved in, they only knew they were innocent.

Al cabo de unas horas de estar arrestados, un policía se acerca y libera a Ramón, el pasajero que se había bajado a llevar sus mochilas. ¿Por qué Patricio y Florencia seguían detenidos? Yo solo seguí mis instintos. -le confiesa Patricio a Florencia. - ¿Acaso fuimos cómplices de una tragedia? Digo, de alguna forma sabíamos que algo estaba mal pero no dijimos nada. No podíamos decir nada. Esas dos personas que estaban con nosotros sabían algo e intentaban detenernos. Ellos sí sabían algo. -le respondió Florencia.

After a few hours of being arrested, a police officer approaches and releases Ramón, the passenger who had come down to carry his backpacks. Why were Patricio and Florencia still detained? I just followed my instincts. - Patricio confesses to Florence. - Were we complicit in a tragedy? I mean, we somehow knew something was wrong but we didn't say anything. We could not say anything. Those two people who were with us knew something and tried to stop us. They did know something. - Florence replied.

La razón por la cual nosotros bajamos del tren no es menos válida que la que ellos ocultaban. Eso es lo que yo creo. De alguna forma estamos mintiendo, ¿no? -dijo Patricio, y sin esperar respuesta de

Florencia, llamó al policía de guardia para avisarle que tenía algo que confesar. El detective llegó en unos minutos y ambos firmaron una declaración.

The reason we got off the train is no less valid than the one they hid. That's what I think. Somehow we are lying, right? -Patricio said, and without waiting for an answer from Florence, he called the police on duty to let him know that he had something to confess. The detective arrived in a few minutes and they both signed a statement.

Gracias. Ya pueden ir a sus casas. -el detective confirmó la veracidad de sus declaraciones y los dejó volver a sus casas. Al llegar a la casa de su padre, Patricio lo abrazó y su padre le dijo - -Gracias por no obedecerme. Quiero que confíes en tu corazón siempre.

Thank you. They can now go to their homes. -the detective confirmed the truthfulness of his statements and let them return to their homes. Upon arriving at his father's house, Patricio hugged him and his father said - -Thanks for not obeying me. I want you to trust your heart always.

Quiz

1. ¿Qué medio de transporte tomó Patricio de Capilla del Monte a San Juan?
a. Entrenar
b. Taxi
c. Avión

2. ¿Dónde vivía el padre de Patricio?
a. Capilla del Monte
b. San Diego
c. San Juan

3. ¿Qué edad tenía Patricio cuando no se le permitió bajar del tren solo?
a. sesenta y cinco
b. 15
c. 10

4. ¿Cómo se llamaba la niña en el tren?
a. Norberto
b. Florencia
c. Gracia

Answers

1. a
2. b
3. b
4. b

Vocabulary / Vocabulario

- *acercó* --- got closer
- *afligido* --- afflicted
- *agua* --- water
- *al frente* --- in front
- *alcanzarlo* --- reach it
- *amortigüe* --- cushion
- *anécdota* --- anecdote
- *apuro* --- hurry
- *arrestados* --- arrested
- *asiento* --- seat
- *aspecto* --- appearance
- *asustar* --- frighten
- *avión* --- airplane
- *ayudarla* --- help her
- *bajar* --- get down
- *bajar* --- slow down
- *barbudo* --- bearded
- *boca* --- mouth
- *borrosa* – blurred
- *brazos* --- arms
- *buen hombre* --- good man
- *calidez* --- warmness
- *calmarse* --- calm down
- *camino* --- path
- *cara* – face
- *cerebro* --- brain
- *cómplices de crimen*- partners in crime
- *complicidad* --- complicity
- *confesar* --- confess
- *corazón* --- heart
- *corriendo* --- running
- *costados* --- sides
- *cotidianeidad* --- everydayness
- *crudeza* --- rawness
- *cuidaba* --- took care
- *De alguna u otra forma* --- One way or another
- *de confianza* --- trustworthy
- *de fondo* --- background
- de un golpe --- suddenly
- *declaración* --- declaration
- descompuesta --- sick
- desconocido – unknown
- *descuidado* --- neglected
- *desesperado* --- desperate
- *detective* --- detective

- *devolverlas* --- give them back
- *disgust* --- dislike
- *dolor* --- pain
- *enamoramiento* --- infatuation
- *entrevistaron* --- interviewed
- *esmero* --- care
- *estación* --- station
- *estómago* --- stomach
- *explosión* --- explosion
- *fantasma* --- ghost
- *firmaron* --- signed
- *fotografía* --- photography
- *frase* --- phrase
- *Gracias*- Thank you
- *había pasado* --- had happened
- *habían dejado atrás* --- they had left behind
- *habitual* --- frequent
- *hablar* – to talk
- *hubiera visto* --- had seen
- *humo* --- smoke
- *inconclusos* --- inconclusive
- *indagar* --- Inquire
- *indicaba* – indicated
- *indicios* --- clues
- *inestable* --- unstable
- *interior* --- inside
- *intuición* --- intuition
- *lágrimas* --- tears
- *latír* – to beat
- *libera* --- free
- *llorosos* --- tearful
- *locomotora* --- locomotive
- *mareo* --- dizziness
- *mediar* – mediate
- *mejillas* --- cheeks
- *meses* --- months
- *mintiendo* --- lying
- *mirada* --- look
- *mochilas* --- backpacks
- *moviendo* --- moving
- *muletilla* --- tag
- *murió* --- died
- *noticia* – news
- *obedecerme* --- obey me
- *observar* --- see
- *ocultaban* --- hid
- *ofreció* --- offered

- *ojos* --- eyes
- *pálido* --- pale
- *parade* --- stop
- *pasajero* --- passenger
- *pasillo* --- passage
- *pecho* --- chest
- *policía* --- police

14. Ella Siempre Me Supera.

Conozco a una chica desde pequeños; al ser mi vecina nos criamos prácticamente juntos. Todos los días jugábamos juntos.

I 've known a girl since childhood; being my neighbor we grew up practically together. Every day we played together.

¿Cómo llegué a tener una relación de amistad con ella? Pues la respuesta es simple.

How did I get to have a friendship with her? Well, the answer is simple.

– ¡Se mi amigo! – Gritó enfrente de mí.

- Be my friend! – shouted in front of me.

No la conocía para ese entonces, era la primera vez que nos mirábamos. Tenía alrededor de unos seis años. Solamente conocía que ella era mi vecina, pero nada más allá de eso.

I didn't know her at that time, it was the first time we looked at each other. He was about six years old. I only knew that she was my neighbor, but nothing more than that.

Por supuesto no supe cómo responder a su pedido; uno no simplemente se lanza y le pide a otra persona que formen una amistad. En lo absoluto. Era vergonzoso, pero ella... ¡Sonreía! Sonreía con una gracia que se contagiaba.

Of course, I did not know how to respond to your request; one does not simply launch and ask another person to form a friendship. At all. It was embarrassing, but she... was smiling! He smiled with a grace that was spread.

A la pura vista se podía notar que ella era una de esas chicas energéticas que siempre está feliz y jugando. Yo por otro lado era... un poco más apático. No era como si me desagradara, como dije antes, no la conocía. Simplemente... no sentía la misma emoción que ella.

In plain glance you could tell that she was one of those energetic girls who is always happy and playing. I, on the other hand was ... a little more apathetic. It wasn't like I disliked it, as I said before, I didn't know her. I just ... didn't feel the same emotion as her.

– ¿Por qué? – Le pregunté sin pensarlo.

- Why? - I asked without thinking.

No buscaba ser grosero o alejarla, solo... me interesaba saber el por qué me buscaba a mí en específico.

I was not looking to be rude or away, just ... I was interested to know why he was looking for me specifically.

– No hay más niños en esta calle. – Me respondió sin perder su sonrisa. – Y parece que también quieres divertirte, así que juguemos. –

- There are no more children in this street. - He answered without losing his smile. - And it seems that you also want to have fun, so let's play. -

Ciertamente no tenía amigos en aquel entonces, y no era un problema. Aun no comenzaba a ir a la escuela, y como ella lo había dicho, no había más niños en esa calle. Pero aun así... la idea de jugar junto a una niña... usualmente no era lo común.

I certainly had no friends at the time, and it wasn't a problem. I wasn't going to school yet, and as she had said, there were no more children in that street. But even so ... the idea of playing with a girl ... was usually not common.

– *No creo que quieras jugar conmigo. – Le respondí. – Yo no juego con muñecas como tú, tampoco a la casita o cosas así. –*

- I don't think you want to play with me. - I replied. - I don't play with dolls like you, or the house or things like that. -

– *¡Yo tampoco! – Respondió.*

- Me neither! - Answered.

Me tomó de la mano y me estiró con fuerza.

He took me by the hand and stretched me hard.

– *Juaguemos a las escondidas. – Me dijo. – Esta vez yo cuento, anda a esconderte. –*

- Let's play hide and seek. - He told me. - This time I count, go hide. -

Era como si ignorara todos los peros que pusiera y tomara únicamente las partes donde yo aceptaba, las cuales no eran ninguna.

It was as if he ignored all the buts, and took only what I accepted.

Se puso en la pared y comenzó a contar. Para ese momento una idea pasó por mi cabeza - "Vuelve a casa" Nadie me podía obligar a estar ahí con ella, bueno, quizá mamá o papá lo hubieran hecho, pero ellos no estaban ahí. Podía simplemente abandonarla en lo que ella contaba y volver a la comodidad de casa. Pero...

He got on the wall and started counting. By that time an idea went through my head - "Go back home" No one could force me to be there with her, well, maybe mom or dad would have done it, but they weren't there. He could simply abandon her in what she told and return to the comfort of home. But...

Terminé escondiéndome no muy lejos de ahí. Sentí que volver a casa no era lo correcto, aun si solo era un niño egoísta, tenía un corazón y una conciencia, la cual me estaría matando por dejarla ahí después de estar tan animada respecto al jugar.

I ended up hiding not far from there. I felt that returning home was not the right thing, even if I was just a selfish child, I had a heart and a conscience, which would be killing me by leaving it there after being so animated about playing.

Pasaron los minutos, cada vez se hacía más tarde. Ella no me encontraba, me comencé a preguntar si era que me había escondido muy bien... o quizá ella se aburrió. Si me dejó ahí. No hubiera sido extraño, después de todo, yo me había negado muchas veces y quizá eso la cansó. Pensé que quizá lo hacía para darme una lección.

The minutes passed, each time it was later. She was not there; I began to wonder if it was that I had hidden very well ... or maybe she got bored. If he left me there. It would not have been strange, after all, I had refused many times and maybe that tired her. I thought maybe I was doing it to teach me a lesson.

Pero entonces, miré nuevamente su rostro.

But then, I looked at his face again.

– *¡Te encontré! – Gritó llena de alegría.*

- I found you! - He shouted full of joy.

169

Sentí como si esas palabras tuvieran más de un significado. No solo me había encontrado de mi escondite, sino...

I felt as if those words had more than one meaning. Not only had I found myself in my hiding place, but ...

Algo movió mi corazón, y por primera vez en mucho tiempo, pude sonreír también de felicidad.

Something moved my heart, and for the first time in a long time, I could also smile with happiness.

Nuestra amistad de afinó con el tiempo. Resultó que terminamos en la misma escuela primaria, en la misma aula, y sentados uno al lado del otro.

Our friendship refined over time. It turned out that we ended up in the same elementary school, in the same classroom, and sitting next to each other.

Aquello hizo llevadera la escuela, ella siempre hacia algo entretenido o me contaba cosas extrañas. Regularmente la regañaban por no callarse en clase. Pero aun así volvía a contarme más y más cosas.

That made the school bearable, she always did something entertaining or told me strange things. They regularly scolded her for not shutting up in class. But still he told me more and more things.

Secundaria también estuvimos juntos; éramos inseparables. Al lugar que ella fuera, yo también estaba ahí.

High school we were together too; We were inseparable. Wherever she went, I was there too.

Seguía siendo mi vecina, por lo que frecuentaba mucho mi casa. Mi madre la adoraba, y mi padre daba indirectas de que yo ya estaba creciendo y que estaba orgulloso de mi.

It was still my neighbor, so I frequented my house a lot. My mother loved her, and my father gave hints that I was already growing up and that he was proud of me.

Muchos de los comentarios los ignoraba. Lo único que hacíamos era... jugar en mi habitación, mirar películas, leer algunos comics; se convirtió en mi mejor amigo.

Many of the comments ignored them. All we did was ... play in my room, watch movies, read some comics; He became my best friend.

Aquello no duró mucho. Las cosas comenzaron a cambiar, y ella lo notó. Muchos hablaban de nosotros a las espaldas. De que era extraña la relación que llevábamos, que no estaban del todo seguros si un hombre y una mujer se podían llevar tan bien. Y ella dio el siguiente paso.

That did not last long. Things began to change, and she noticed. Many talked about us behind our backs. That the relationship we were having was strange, that they were not entirely sure if a man and a woman could get along so well. And she took the next step.

– Prácticamente ya lo somos, ¿no? – Me preguntó energética como siempre.

- Practically we already are, right? - He asked me energetically as always.

– ¿A qué te refieres? – Le pregunté.

- What do you mean? - Asked.

– ¡Somos pareja! – Respondió tomando la delantera.

- We're Couple! - He responded by taking the lead.

– ¿¡Lo somos!? – Aquello me sorprendió.

- We are!? - That surprised me.

Pero viendo la relación que llevábamos, era comprensible. Todos a nuestro alrededor lo pensaban igual. Entonces... solo debíamos hacerlo "Formal". Ella no me desagradaba en lo absoluto, disfrutaba estar con ella todo el tiempo. Me entendía mejor que nadie más, y creía yo también lo hacía.

But seeing the relationship we had, it was understandable. Everyone around us thought the same. So ... we just had to do it "Formal." She didn't dislike me at all, I enjoyed being with her all the time. He understood me better than anyone else, and I thought I did too.

Una vez más... me superó. Tomó las riendas y dijo lo que yo no hubiera podido decir.

– ¿Algo cambiara? – Le pregunté.

Once again ... it surpassed me. He took the reins and said what I could not have said.

- Will something change? - Asked.

Nunca tuvimos una pareja, por lo que no comprendíamos que era serlo.

We never had a partner, so we didn't understand what it was.

– No lo creo. – Respondió alegre. – Solo que así puedo decir felizmente que te quiero. –

- I do not think so. - He replied cheerfully. - Only that way I can happily say that I love you. -

Decía las cosas más vergonzosas sin pensárselo. Pero eso no me desagradaba.

He said the most embarrassing things without thinking about it. But that didn't displease me.

Llegamos a preparatoria. Nuevamente fuimos a la misma. Seguíamos siendo pareja de lo más normal. Bueno, quizá no tan normal. Parecíamos hermanos o amigos por cómo nos comportábamos. Pero no había otra forma de hacerlo, siempre estuvo a mi lado, la confianza estaba a otro nivel. Bromear con ella de cualquier cosa era el pan de cada día.

We arrived at high school. Again, we went to it. We were still the most normal couple. Well, maybe not so normal. We looked like brothers or friends because of how we behaved. But there was no other way to do it, he was always by my side, trust was on another level. Joking with her about anything was the daily bread.

Elegimos la misma universidad, la misma carrera. A ambos nos gustaban las mismas cosas, queríamos estudiar lo mismo y trabajar juntos en los proyectos que teníamos a futuro.

We choose the same university, the same career. We both liked the same things, we wanted to study the same and work together on the projects we had in the future.

Lo que me llevó a pensar que quizá... me faltaba dar un paso más allá. Ella dio los primeros dos; ella forjó nuestra amistad, ella inicio nuestra relación. Y al pensar en mi futuro, ella siempre estaba ahí. Yo... quería ser el que diera el siguiente paso.

Which led me to think that maybe ... I had to go one step further. She gave the first two; She forged our friendship; she started our relationship. And when thinking about my future, she was always there. I ... wanted to be the one to take the next step.

El día de la graduación llegó. Nos graduamos con honores, éramos el equipo dinamita. Nada nos podía detener.

Graduation day arrived. We graduated with honors; we were the dynamite team. Nothing could stop us.

Era hora de comenzar la vida adulta. Y aun ella no daba el siguiente paso. Quizá... ella no lo quería dar. Comencé a dudar, aun si yo quería darlo, quizá ella en realidad no. Quizá estaba aburrida de nuestra relación y quería terminarlo.

It was time to start adult life. And even she didn't take the next step. Maybe ... she didn't want to give it. I started to doubt, even if I wanted to give it, maybe she didn't really. Maybe I was bored of our relationship and wanted to end it.

Pero por más que intentaba mirar un futuro sin ella... me era imposible. La conocí desde pequeña y nunca se apartó de mi lado. Quería decírselo, que quería nuestra vida nunca se separara. Aun si ella no lo miraba de la misma forma... no quería guardar esos sentimientos.

But as much as I tried to look at a future without her ... it was impossible. I knew her since I was little and she never left my side. He wanted to tell her, that he wanted our life never to separate. Even if she didn't look at him the same way ... she didn't want to save those feelings.

– Yo... quería pedirte algo. – Le dije.

- I ... wanted to ask you something. - I told.

– ¿Qué podría ser? – Preguntó confundida.

- What could it be? - Asked confused.

Tome el valor que me faltaba. Era el momento. Esta vez yo... sería quien daría el siguiente paso, no quería que ella me superara una vez más.

Take the courage I was missing. It was the moment. This time I ... would be the one to take the next step, I didn't want her to beat me once more.

– Lo he estado pensando durante un largo tiempo... quizá tu no sientes lo mismo, pero yo... en verdad lo quiero. – Dije. – Han sido unos largos años, y no los cambiaria para nada. Has alegrado mi vida de una forma que no te puedes imaginar, y por lo mismo... quiero que estés en todo lo que está por venir. Por favor... ¡CASATE CONMIGO! –

- I've been thinking about it for a long time ... maybe you don't feel the same, but I ... I really want it. - Said. – Many years have passed, and I wouldn't change them at all. You have brightened my life in a way that you cannot imagine, and for the same ... I want you to be in everything that is to come. Please... marry me! -

Con una expresión de sorpresa, quedó en silencio.

With an expression of surprise, he fell silent.

Pensé que quizá, después de todo, ella no...

I thought maybe, after all, she didn't ...

– ¿No lo estábamos ya? – Preguntó confundida.

- Weren't we already? - Asked confused.

– ¿Eh? – No comprendí su respuesta.

- Eh? - I didn't understand your answer.

– Me adelante un poco y rente un departamento. – Me dijo. – ¡Por supuesto que yo también quiero que estés en mi futuro! –

- Go ahead a little and rent an apartment. - He told me. - Of course I want you to be in my future too! -

¿Un departamento? Ella... yo... no pude aguantar las lágrimas de felicidad.

A department? She ... I ... I couldn't stand the tears of happiness.

Una vez más... ella... me superó.

Once again ... she ... beat me.

– Me alegro de haberte encontrado... –

- I'm glad to have found you... -

Quiz

1. Nosotros - con la chica del barrio.
a. Jugó
b. Cantó
c. Escolarizado

2. ¿Qué edad tenía la niña cuando nos miramos por primera vez?
a.15
b. 10
c. 2

3. ¿Por qué fue difícil conseguir un futuro sin ella?
a. La conocía desde que era pequeña
b. No pude conseguir a nadie
c. Ella me amaba

Answers

1. a
2. a.
3.a

Vocabulario/Vocabulary

- *relación* --- friendship
- *Gritó* --- shouted
- *Vecina* --- neighbor
- *Vergonzoso* --- embarrassing
- *Grosero* --- rude
- *Tampoco* --- neither
- *Contar* --- counting
- Abandonarla --- abandon
- Significado --- meaning
- *Cambiar* --- change

15. La Muerte Los Sigue

La autopista estaba vacía, no había ningún signo de algún automóvil o camión cerca. Las luces se encendían y apagaban. A la distancia, una tormenta iluminaba la noche, y el viento comenzaba a mover las copas de los árboles violentamente. Las primeras gotas comenzaron a mojar el pavimento. En medio de la carretera tres jóvenes corrían desesperados saliendo del bosque sin razón alguna. El terror se reflejaba en sus rostros y ellos no podían hacer otra cosa que correr y gritar.

The highway was empty, there was no sign of a car or truck nearby. The lights turned on and off. In the distance, a storm illuminated the night, and the wind began to move the treetops violently. The first drops began to wet the pavement. In the middle of the road three young men ran desperately out of the forest for no reason. Terror was reflected on their faces and they could do nothing but run and scream.

De pronto, los tres jóvenes cayeron muertos sin ningún signo de violencia. En sus caras se podía ver la sorpresa de quien no esperaba que la muerte llegue tan rápido. Tenían futuro, un trabajo y toda una vida por delante, pero ahora sus cuerpos estaban en la carretera. Los animales del bosque cercano miraban a la distancia a esas tres posibles presas, pero sabían muy bien que entrar en el bosque podía significar la muerte. Cada vez que alguien cruzaba las cuevas del bosque moría, estar mucho tiempo en ellas era fatal.

Suddenly, the three young men fell dead without any sign of violence. On their faces you could see the surprise of those who did not expect death to arrive so quickly. They had a future, a job and a lifetime ahead, but now their bodies were on the road. The animals of the nearby forest looked at the distance to those three possible preys, but knew very well that entering the forest could mean death. Every time someone crossed the forest caves died, being in them for a long time was fatal.

Al día siguiente con la tormenta ya muy lejos y todos los signos ya secos y olvidados, la policía rodeaba la escena del crimen, marcaban con tiza el borde de los cuerpos y sacaban fotografías a todo lo que parecía interesante o digno de investigación. Como siempre sucedía en estos casos, los camiones de noticias estaban alrededor tratando de sacar la mejor imagen de los cuerpos y luego emitirla en el horario principal. Los periodistas trataban de sacarle información a los policías, quienes estaban bajo un estricto pacto de silencio. No es que no tenían información, solo que lo mejor en estos casos era esperar que algún vocero o representante de la fuerza policíaca hiciera declaraciones cuando tuviese todos los datos.

The next day with the storm far away and all the signs already dry and forgotten, the police surrounded the crime scene, marked with chalk the edge of the bodies and took photographs of everything that seemed interesting or worthy of investigation. As always happened in these cases, news trucks were around trying to get the best image of the bodies and then broadcast it at the main time. The journalists tried to get information from the police, who were under a strict pact of silence. Not that they had no information, only that the best thing in these cases was to wait for a spokesman or a police force representative to make statements when he had all the data.

Sin embargo, a pesar de los mejores intentos de la policía, no podían encontrar ninguna pista o ningún motivo por el cual tres cuerpos jóvenes estaban en la carretera sin signos de violencia. Sin ningún tipo de solución a la vista, el fiscal que llevaba el caso decidió tragar su orgullo y llamar a un viejo conocido - El detective McHeartley.

However, despite the best attempts by the police, they could not find any clue or any reason why three young bodies were on the road without signs of violence. Without any solution in sight, the prosecutor who was carrying the case decided to swallow his pride and call an old acquaintance - Detective

McHeartley.

En su oficina el detective estaba descansando, sus pies apoyados encima del escritorio, cerca de una caja de pizza sucia y vacía. En el sillón su gato descansaba, durmiendo encima del sombrero y en una esquina su fiel chaqueta estaba colgada del perchero. Era una tarde tranquila de domingo y el detective no tenía ninguna tarea que hacer. De hecho, ni siquiera tenía un hogar al que volver, excepto esa oficina donde dormía, trabajaba y vivía toda la semana. En medio de la tranquilidad, sonó el teléfono. El ruido hizo que tanto el detective como su mascota se despertaran asustados. Desesperado, el detective atendió rápidamente el teléfono, él sabía que en un caso de investigación cada segundo es importante. "¿Hola? ¿Quién es?" prácticamente gritó al auricular "Sí, soy yo. ¿Dónde? Estoy a doce horas de distancia en autobús. No lo sé, tengo otros planes para hoy". Su gato lo miró con cara de fastidio. "¿Me van a pagar un avión privado? Bueno, está bien, allí estaré".

In his office the detective was resting, his feet resting on the desk, near a dirty and empty pizza box. In the armchair his cat was resting, sleeping on top of the hat and in one corner his faithful jacket was hanging from the coat rack. It was a quiet Sunday afternoon and the detective had no homework to do. In fact, he didn't even have a home to return to, except that office where he slept, worked and lived all week. Amid the tranquility, the telephone rang. The noise caused both the detective and his pet to wake up scared. Desperate, the detective quickly answered the phone, he knew that in an investigation case every second is important. "Hello? Who is it?" He practically shouted at the headset "Yes, it's me. Where? I am twelve hours away by bus. I don't know, I have other plans for today." His cat looked at him with annoyed face. "Will they pay me a private plane? Well, that's fine, I'll be there."

Tomó su chaqueta, su portafolio y para conseguir su sombrero tuvo que pedirle por favor a su gato que se moviera de encima de él. "Por favor, tengo que irme". Finalmente, después de darle una mirada asesina el gato se movió de encima del sombrero. "Te prometo que te traeré algo de regreso. ¿Atún? ¿Pollo? ¿Qué te parece?". El gato lo miró, solo apoyó su cabeza en la mano del detective para indicarle que podía irse en paz. "La vecina tiene las llaves, así que ella va a cuidarte un rato".

He took his jacket, his wallet and to get his hat he had to ask his cat to move on top of him. "Please, I have to go." Finally, after giving him a murderous look the cat moved from above the hat. "I promise I will bring you something back. Tuna? Chicken? How about?". The cat looked at him, just rested his head on the detective's hand to indicate that he could leave in peace. "The neighbor has the keys, so she will take care of you for a while."

Rápidamente se dirigió al aeropuerto donde lo esperaban los representantes de la policía y subieron todos a un avión privado. Mientras estaba en vuelo, McHeartley tuvo la posibilidad de leer toda la información del caso. Vio todas las fotos y toda la información recopilada por los incansables miembros de la fuerza policíaca. Otro extraño caso. Era el tipo de caso que seguía al detective, el último caso fue en el fin del mundo y fue bastante particular. No podía sacarse de encima la sensación de que este caso no iba a ser tan simple como ese.

He quickly went to the airport where police representatives were waiting for him and all got on a private plane. While in flight, McHeartley had the ability to read all the information in the case. He saw all the photos and all the information collected by the tireless members of the police force. Another strange case. It was the kind of case that followed the detective, the last case was at the end of the world and it was quite particular. He could not get rid of the feeling that this case was not going to be as simple as that.

Al aterrizar, los policías lo subieron a un coche patrulla, y fueron hacia la escena del crimen. Los periodistas y el alcalde estaban esperándolo, visiblemente nerviosos. Las elecciones eran en una semana y si el alcalde no resolvía el problema con rapidez posiblemente perdería todos los votos. El alcalde recibió con manos temblorosas al detective McHeartley y lo guio hacia una carpa de la policía

donde se llevaba a cabo toda la coordinación de la investigación.

Upon landing, the policemen put him on a patrol car, and went to the crime scene. The journalists and the mayor were waiting for him, visibly nervous. The elections were in a week and if the mayor did not solve the problem quickly he would probably lose all the votes. The mayor greeted Detective McHeartley with trembling hands and guided him to a police tent where all the coordination of the investigation was carried out.

Dentro de la carpa había una mesa blanca, una silla y copias de todas las fotos que ya había visto en el viaje hacia la escena del crimen. También tenía encima de la pila un sobre marrón que decía "Informe Forense". McHeartley lo abrió, esperando encontrar la respuesta rápido y volver a su oficina, pero en realidad era una sola hoja con un texto debajo que decía "No hay información suficiente para llegar a una conclusión, tan solo se hallaron huellas, estuvieron caminando durante tres días seguidos". El detective suspiró. Iba a ser una larga noche. Llamó a un asistente, pidió el café más negro que pudieran encontrar para mantenerse despierto.

Inside the tent was a white table, a chair and copies of all the photos he had already seen on the trip to the crime scene. He also had a brown envelope on top of the stack that said "Forensic Report." McHeartley opened it, hoping to find the quick answer and return to his office but in reality it was a single sheet with a text below that said "There is not enough information to reach a conclusion, only footprints were found, they were walking for three days straight " The detective sighed. It was going to be a long night. He called an assistant, asked for the blackest coffee they could find to stay awake.

Afuera, la prensa estaba atenta a cada movimiento. Después de todo, no todos los días el detective McHeartley, el héroe del caso del avión perdido, visitaba la ciudad. Y ciertamente esto significa que era un caso muy importante. Las horas pasaban y por supuesto, los ánimos eran bastante malos. Después de todo, cuando se transmite las 24 horas del día la misma noticia queda realmente muy poco que informar si no hay noticias nuevas. Pasaron días llenos de tensión, todos se sorprendían porque el detective contrató a especialistas de todo tipo para investigar la zona donde encontraron muertos a los jóvenes, así como informes de muertes extrañas en el pasado que hubiesen ocurrido en el pueblo.

Outside, the press was attentive to every movement. After all, not every day Detective McHeartley, the hero of the lost plane case, visited the city. And this certainly means that it was a very important case. The hours passed and of course, the moods were pretty bad. After all, when the news is broadcast 24 hours a day, the same news is really very little to report if there is no new news. They spent days full of tension, everyone was surprised because the detective hired specialists of all kinds to investigate the area where they found the young people dead, as well as reports of strange deaths in the past that had occurred in the town.

En cuanto el detective McHeartley, llamó a conferencia de prensa en la puerta de la carpa. Todos los periodistas agradecieron esas noticias nuevas, ya que significaba que al menos el final la tortura estaba cerca. Finalmente podrían saber qué había pasado con los tres cuerpos, quién era el culpable, y en particular qué pasos se tomarían para apresarlo porque las personas de ese pueblo adoraban el drama. Sin embargo, lo que los recibió no fue exactamente lo que esperaban.

As soon as Detective McHeartley called a press conference at the door of the tent. All the journalists thanked those new news, since it meant that at least the end was near torture. Finally, they could know what had happened to the three bodies, who was the guilty, and in particular what steps would be taken to capture him because the people of that town adored the drama. However, what received them was not exactly what they expected.

"Hola, buenas tardes", dijo McHeartley frente al micrófono instalado en un atril. "Los llamé a conferencia de prensa porque sé exactamente qué pasó con los cuerpos de los jóvenes. Sin embargo...",

hizo una pausa que duró años, "creo que no es lo que ustedes esperaban escuchar".

"Hello, good afternoon," McHeartley said in front of the microphone installed in a music stand. "I called them to a press conference because I know exactly what happened to the bodies of the young people. However, ... "He paused for years," I think it's not what you expected to hear. "

Los periodistas estaban en el borde de sus asientos. McHeartley continuó, "los tres jóvenes no fueron asesinados por naves espaciales, o por agentes secretos del FBI o cualquiera de esas teorías conspirativas que se comentaron mucho en la prensa en estos días. Los tres jóvenes murieron intoxicados y según las huellas estuvieron corriendo alrededor de tres días". El Alcalde no pudo detener su lengua y dijo "¿Quién lo ha hecho Señor detective? ¡Esto es un hecho siniestro! Deberíamos suspender las elecciones" gritó para que el candidato adversario no le ganara.

The journalists were on the edge of their seats. McHeartley continued, "The three young men were not killed by spacecraft, or by secret FBI agents or any of those conspiracy theories that were widely discussed in the press these days. The three young people died intoxicated and according to the tracks they were running for about three days." The Mayor was unable to stop his tongue and said "Who has done it Lord detective? This is a sinister fact! We should suspend the elections," he shouted so that the opposing candidate would not win.

"¿Usted piensa suspender las elecciones porque el culpable de la muerte de los jóvenes fue un hongo?" preguntó McHeartley enfadado porque lo había interrumpido.

"Do you plan to suspend the elections because the culprit in the death of the youth was a fungus?" McHeartley said angrily because he had interrupted him.

Silencio en la sala. La noticia fue tan fuerte que se podía sentir el silencio en los hogares donde las familias y curiosos seguían la transmisión. "Así es ¡sorpréndanse! Los tres murieron intoxicados por un hongo maligno que se encuentra en el bosque de este pueblo", añadió tristemente. "Me pareció extraño que unos jóvenes tan sanos murieran sin signos de violencia, así que pensé que fueron envenenados por algo y analicé todas las plantas del bosque que está cerca de la carretera. Efectivamente la prueba del hongo mortal dio positiva".

Silence in the room. The news was so strong that silence could be felt in homes where families and curious people followed the transmission. "That's right, surprise yourself! The three died intoxicated by an evil fungus found in the forest of this town," he added sadly. "It seemed strange to me that such healthy young people died without signs of violence, so I thought they were poisoned by something and analyzed all the plants in the forest near the road. Indeed, the deadly fungus test was positive."

Un periodista tuvo mucha curiosidad al respecto y dijo - "Entonces ¿Por qué según las huellas estuvieron corriendo alrededor de tres días seguidos? ¡Me parece que algo más tuvo que haberlos perseguido!". McHeartley lo miró fijamente, "Lo único que los siguió fue la muerte. Verá mi querido reportero, cuando alguien consume un hongo tóxico la persona alucina, cada quien a su manera. Pudieron estar perdiendo la cabeza poco a poco. Los tres jóvenes comenzaron a perder la respiración cuando estaban en lo profundo del bosque e intentaron salir a la civilización. Los tres estaban de campamento y posiblemente entraron a las cuevas del bosque que están infectadas con el hongo". El silencio fue increíble en la sala de conferencias. "Lamentablemente", añadió con un poco de tristeza, "si hubieran llevado algún teléfono de emergencia, esto se podría haber solucionado porque los efectos del hongo se eliminan con una inyección para las alergias". El alcalde miraba del otro lado de la sala de conferencias sin poder creerlo. Todo indicaba que el detective McHeartley era tan eficiente como se decía. Los rastros del veneno del hongo habían estado matando a muchas personas en medio del bosque.

A journalist was very curious about it and said - "Then why, according to the tracks, were they running

for about three days in a row? It seems to me that something else must have pursued them!"
McHeartley stared at him, "The only thing that followed them was death. You will see my dear reporter,
when someone consumes a toxic mushroom the person hallucinates, each in his own way. They could
be losing their heads little by little. The three young men began to lose their breath when they were deep
in the forest and tried to go out to civilization. All three were camping and possibly entered the caves of
the forest that are infected with the fungus." The silence was incredible in the conference room.
"Unfortunately," he added with a bit of sadness, "if they had taken an emergency phone, this could have
been solved because the effects of the fungus are eliminated with an allergy injection." The mayor
looked across the conference room without being able to believe it. Everything indicated that Detective
McHeartley was as efficient as he said. Traces of the fungus poison had been killing many people in the
middle of the forest.

*Ahora el alcalde estaba sin posibilidades de ganar las elecciones. Todo era culpa del bajo presupuesto,
la falta de entrenamiento y de los muy bajos sueldos que pagaba a los guardabosques. Como pudo,
trató de escapar, para no verse arrinconado por la prensa.*

Now the mayor was unable to win the elections. It was all the fault of the low budget, the lack of training
and the very low salaries he paid to the rangers. As he could, he tried to escape, so as not to be cornered
by the press.

*El detective se bajó del atril y procedió a buscar su chaqueta y su sombrero. Otro caso resuelto, pensó.
Antes de coger el autobús hacia el aeropuerto le compró 10 latas de atún a su gato como se lo había
dicho antes de irse de casa porque el detective McHeartley era un hombre que hacía todo lo que
prometía.*

The detective got off the lectern and proceeded to look for his jacket and his hat. Another case resolved,
he thought. Before catching the bus to the airport, he bought 10 cans of tuna from his cat as he had said
before leaving home because Detective McHeartley was a man who did everything he promised.

Quiz

1) ¿Dónde fueron encontrados los cuerpos?
a) En una iglesia
b) En medio del campo
c) En una autopista
d) En sus casas

2) ¿Qué decía el informe forense?
a) Que habían caminado por tres días seguidos
b) Decía la causa de la muerte
c) Decía que habían sido raptados por extraterrestres
d) Daba toda la información necesaria

3) ¿Cuál es la mascota de McHeartley?
a) Un oso
b) Un gato
c) Un ave
d) Un perro

4) ¿Por qué murieron los jóvenes?
a) Por intoxicación de un hongo

b) Por la picadura de un mosquito

c) Fueron asesinados

d) No se sabe

5) ¿Cuántas latas de atún le compró el detective a su mascota?

a) 5

b) 10

c) 3

d) 9

Answers

1) C

2) A

3) B

4) A

5) B

Vocabulario/Vocabulary

- *Autopista* --- Highway
- *Automóvil/Camión* --- Car/truck
- *Copas de los árboles* --- Tree crows
- *Gotas* --- Drops
- *Pavimento* --- Pavement
- *Carretera* --- Road
- *Desesperados* --- Desperate
- *Policía* --- Police
- *Escena del crimen* --- Crime scene
- *Fotografías* --- Pictures
- *Información* --- Information
- *Pacto de silencio* --- Pact of silence
- *Vocero* --- Spokesman
- *Declaraciones* --- Declarations
- *Intentos* --- Try
- *Orgullo* --- Pride
- *Oficina* --- Office
- *Escritorio* --- Desk
- *Gato* --- Cat
- *Encima* --- Over
- *Esquina* --- Corner
- *Fiel* --- Faithful
- *Domingo* --- Sunday
- *Hogar* --- Home
- *Semana* --- Week
- *Mascota* --- Pet

- *Desesperado* --- Desesperate
- *Auricular* --- Handset
- *Fastidio* --- Nuisance
- *Ánimos* --- Moods
- *Transmite* --- Transmit
- *Noticias* --- News
- *Días llenos de tensión* --- Days filled with tension
- *Tortura* --- Torture
- *Cuerpos* --- Bodies
- *Culpable* --- Guilty
- *Apresarlo* --- Arrest
- *Micrófono* --- Microphone
- *Atril* --- Lectern
- *Asesinados* --- Murdered
- *Naves espaciales* --- Spaceships
- *Agentes secretos* --- Secret agents
- *Siniestro* --- Sinister
- *Candidato* --- Candidate
- *Hongo* --- Fungus
- *Transmisión* --- Broadcast
- *Conferencia* --- Conference
- *Indicaba* --- Indicate
- *Rastros del veneno* --- Traces of poison
- *Posibilidades* --- Possibilities
- *Presupuesto* --- Budget
- *Entrenamiento* --- Training
- *Sueldos* --- Salaries
- *Arrinconado* --- Concerned

16. Playa, Salsa Y Ron

Nunca había imaginado que había tantos tonos de azul hasta que volé sobre el mar Caribe. Desde el cielo parece una gran piscina color turquesa con manchas de azul profundo, verde y hasta morado. A lo lejos, las arenas blancas brillaban como si se tratara de un desierto de sal.

I had never imagined that there were so many shades of blue until I flew over the Caribbean Sea. From the sky it looks like a large turquoise pool with spots of deep blue, green and even purple. In the distance, the white sands shone as if it were a salt desert.

Antes de salir de los Estados Unidos, raramente había pensado en visitar las islas del Caribe; lo único que sabía de la región era que había muchos cruceros de lujo que llevaban a cientos de turistas desde Miami a tomar el sol en sus playas y eso no era algo que llamara especialmente mi atención. No fue sino hasta justo antes de terminar mi curso de español en Guatemala, cuando hablando con Pierre sobre las maravillas naturales de islas como Dominica y San Vicente, la música, el baile y la cultura de Cuba, que comencé a convencerme de que el Caribe sería mi siguiente destino.

Before leaving the United States, he had rarely thought of visiting the Caribbean islands; The only thing I knew about the region was that there were many luxury cruises that took hundreds of tourists from Miami to sunbathe on their beaches and that was not something that caught my attention. It wasn't until just before finishing my Spanish course in Guatemala, when talking with Pierre about the natural wonders of islands like Dominica and San Vicente, the music, dance and culture of Cuba, that I began to convince myself that the Caribbean It would be my next destination.

Salí desde la Ciudad de Guatemala en un vuelo directo a La Habana donde tenía planeado estar un par de semanas, después me encontraría con Pierre y Kristen en República Dominicana. Sólo el viaje en avión sobre el mar era ya increíble... apenas podía imaginarme lo bellas que se verían esas aguas de cerca.

I left from Guatemala City on a direct flight to Havana where I planned to be a couple of weeks, then I would meet Pierre and Kristen in the Dominican Republic. Only the trip by plane over the sea was already incredible ... I could hardly imagine how beautiful those waters would look from close.

Cuba era el tercer país que visitaba. Ahora me sentía muy cómodo viajando, mi español era mucho mejor y ya sabía moverme fácilmente, claro con la ayuda de mi teléfono celular y mi GPS. Sin embargo, Pierre me advirtió que Cuba era un país muy diferente al resto del mundo. De eso yo ya sabía algo pues lo hablamos en mis clases de política internacional, pero no me imaginaba cómo sería la experiencia de un viajero en el país.

Cuba was the third country I visited. Now I felt very comfortable traveling, my Spanish was much better and I knew how to move easily, of course with the help of my cell phone and my GPS. However, Pierre warned me that Cuba was a very different country from the rest of the world. I already knew something about that because we talked about it in my international politics classes, but I couldn't imagine what a traveler's experience in the country would be like.

Al llegar, me sorprendió el hecho de que hubiese dos monedas diferentes, el peso cubano y el peso cubano convertible. Según me explicaba el chófer del taxi que tomé fuera del aeropuerto, una era para uso exclusivo de los extranjeros y la otra para los cubanos - "así es el sistema," afirmó.

El mismo taxista, un hombre muy simpático de tez morena y enorme sonrisa llamado Juan, me explicó que los únicos alojamientos accesibles que podría encontrar en la isla serían en casas particulares. Algunas personas en cada ciudad, me contaba, tienen permiso para rentar habitaciones en sus casas y departamentos como si se tratara de un hotel.

Upon arrival, I was surprised that there were two different currencies, the Cuban peso and the convertible Cuban peso. As explained by the driver of the taxi that I took outside the airport, one was for the exclusive use of foreigners and the other for Cubans - "this is the system," he said.

The same taxi driver, a very nice man with a dark complexion and a huge smile called Juan, explained that the only accessible accommodations I could find on the island would be in private homes. Some people in each city, he told me, have permission to rent rooms in their homes and apartments as if it were a hotel.

"O bueno, más bien la versión original de airbnb," dije en voz alta, tras lo que él me miró confundido y no respondió.

"Or well, rather the original version of airbnb," I said out loud, after which he looked at me confused and did not respond.

Así, Juan me llevó a una de las famosas casas particulares y dijo - "Mira, así es como reconoces las oficiales - tienen ese símbolo azul en la puerta".

Thus, Juan took me to one of the famous private houses and said - "Look, this is how you recognize the officers - they have that blue symbol on the door."

Muy amablemente se bajó conmigo y negoció el precio de la habitación, después me dio recomendaciones sobre qué lugares visitar, qué ver y comer en La Habana. Entonces, tras sólo una hora de haber llegado a Cuba, ya tenía hospedaje, plan para los siguientes días y una muy buena impresión de los taxistas cubanos.

He kindly got off with me and negotiated the price of the room, then gave me recommendations on what places to visit and what to see and eat in Havana. Then, after only an hour of having arrived in Cuba, I already had lodging, a plan for the following days and a very good impression of the Cuban taxi drivers.

Estaba cansado del viaje, pero no podía esperar más para recorrer las calles de la ciudad, así que sólo dejé mi mochila, me cambié mis pantalones por bermudas, mis botas por sandalias y me aventuré por las calles del centro.

I was tired of the trip, but I couldn't wait any longer to walk the streets of the city, so I just left my backpack, changed my pants for shorts, my boots for sandals and ventured through the streets of downtown.

Mi alojamiento estaba en el casco histórico de la ciudad. Justo al salir me topé con muchas callecitas que llevaban a pequeñas plazas y rincones pintorescos. Pasé frente a decenas de restaurantes y en cada uno de ellos había una banda de músicos tocando los clásicos de la música cubana mientras todo el mundo cantaba y bailaba a su alrededor. ¡Cómo me gustaría saber bailar así! Pensé.

My accommodation was in the historic center of the city. Just as I left, I came across many streets that led to small squares and picturesque corners. I passed dozens of restaurants and in each of them there was a band of musicians playing the classics of Cuban music while everyone sang and danced around them. How I would like to know how to dance like this! I thought.

Caminé por horas y cuando menos lo esperaba, empezó a oscurecer, así que entré a un pequeño restaurante camino a mi alojamiento. Cuando vi el menú no tenía idea de qué era nada de lo que estaba escrito allí. La mesera se acercó y me preguntó –

I walked for hours and when I least expected it, it began to get dark, so I entered a small restaurant on my way to my accommodation. When I saw the menu I had no idea what it was that was written there. The waitress came over and asked me -

"¿Qué le sirvo, chico?" A lo que yo me quedé mudo, entonces volvió a preguntar "¿Quiere que le recomiende algo?"

"What do I do for you, boy?" To which I was speechless, then he asked again "Do you want me to recommend something?"

"¡Sí, por favor!" contesté.

"¡Yes, please!" I replied.

"Bueno, le traigo un plato de ropa vieja".

"Well, I bring you a plate of old clothes"

"¿Ropa? Pero yo quiero comida".

"Clothes? But I want food."

"Jaja, sí, pero la ropa vieja es comida, es un platillo típico cubano, ¿usted come carne?"

"Haha, yes, but old clothes are food, it's a typical Cuban dish, do you eat meat?"

"Sí, ropa no, pero carne sí".

"Yes, clothes no, but meat yes."

"Bueno, Ya viene"

"Well, it's coming."

Estaba un poco preocupado por lo que vendría, pero el olor que salía de la cocina era delicioso. Entonces vi llegar un gran plato de carne con arroz y frijoles, y al lado, un plátano frito, se veía genial.

I was a little worried about what would come, but the smell coming out of the kitchen was delicious. Then I saw a large plate of meat with rice and beans arrive, and next to it, a fried banana, looked great.

"¿Un vaso de ron?" preguntó la mesera.

"A glass of rum?" The waitress asked.

"¿Por qué no?" contesté.

"Why not?" I replied.

Tras el delicioso manjar, estaba listo para ir a dormir. Caminé por un par de calles, pero justo una esquina antes de llegar, escuché una música estridente y con un ritmo contagioso saliendo desde un pequeño pasillo. Curioso, me acerqué a ver. Adentro había una gran sala de baile; con trompetas, percusiones, violines y guitarras, una orquesta entera de salsa tocaba la mejor música que había escuchado en mi vida.

After the delicious delicacy, I was ready to go to sleep. I walked down a couple of streets but just one corner before arriving, I heard a loud music and with a contagious rhythm coming from a small hallway. Curious, I went to see. Inside was a large dance hall; With trumpets, percussions, violins and guitars, an entire salsa orchestra played the best music I had heard in my life.

Me acerqué a la barra y pedí un mojito mientras observaba impresionado a la banda tocar con tanta alegría y pasión, y a la gente que bailaba tan bien que parecía ser una coreografía preparada con anterioridad. Sus pies se movían tan rápido que era difícil seguirlos, su energía y felicidad se transmitían, y no pude evitar sentirme feliz y con ganas de bailar. Entonces, sentí que tocaban mi espalda y salté del susto.

I approached the bar and asked for a mojito while watching the band impressed to play with such joy and passion, and the people who danced so well that it seemed to be a choreography prepared beforehand. His feet moved so fast that it was difficult to follow them, his energy and happiness were transmitted, and I couldn't help feeling happy and wanting to dance. Then, I felt that they touched my back and jumped in fright.

"Hola, ¿bailas?" me preguntaba una chica hermosa.

"Hello, are you dancing?" A beautiful girl asked me.

Me quedé congelado y ruborizado. De repente, me olvidé de cómo hablar español.

I froze and flushed. Suddenly, I forgot how to speak Spanish.

"Bueno, al menos ¿hablas?" preguntó.

"Well, at least you speak?" She asked.

Regresé de mi trance y respondí - "sí, sí, claro que hablo, pero la verdad no sé bailar, aunque me gustaría mucho".

I returned from my trance and replied - "Yes, yes, of course I speak, but I really do not know how to dance, although I would like very much."

"Yo te enseño," dijo y yo de nuevo me ruboricé.

"I teach you," he said and I blushed again.

"¿De verdad?" pregunté.

"Really?" I asked.

"Sí, anda, vamos a bailar, ¿cómo te llamas?"

"Yes, come on, let's dance, what's your name?"

"Peter, me llamo Peter".

"Peter, my name is Peter."

"Yo soy Daylin".

"I am Daylin."

Caminamos a la pista de baile y yo casi temblaba de nervios y emoción. Traté de bailar, pero mis pies parecían no coordinar con la música, y aunque intentaba e intentaba, resultaba imposible. Daylin sonrió y dijo - "Tranquilo, vamos poco a poco. Mira, intenta sólo lo básico, escucha el ritmo. Un dos, un dos tres, un dos, un dos tres". Lo intenté de nuevo y pisé sus pies.

We walked to the dance floor and I was almost trembling with nerves and emotion. I tried to dance, but my feet seemed not to coordinate with the music, and although I tried and tried, it was impossible. Daylin smiled and said - "Quiet, let's go slowly. Look, try just the basics, listen to the beat. One two, one two three, one two, one two three." I tried again and stepped on his feet.

"Daylin, ¿estás bien? Lo siento mucho".

"Daylin, are you alright? I'm sorry".

"Sí, no pasa nada, no te preocupes, si quieres sentémonos un rato".

"Yes, nothing happens, don't worry, if you want, let's sit down for a while."

"De verdad, ¿estás bien? Estoy muy apenado, es la primera vez que bailo este tipo de música".

"You are really fine? I'm very sorry, it's the first time I dance this kind of music."

"Pues ¿de dónde eres?" preguntó Daylin.

"Well, where are you from?" Daylin asked.

"De los Estados Unidos, pero de un pueblo muy pequeño. Allá los viejos escuchan música country y los jóvenes, pop. A mí me gusta la música clásica, pero de esto no sé nada".

"From the United States, but from a very small town. There the old people listen to country music and the young people, pop. I like classical music, but I don't know anything about this."

"Vaya, hablas muy bien español, pensaba que eras latino".

"Wow, you speak Spanish very well, I thought you were Latino."

"¡Gracias!, eres muy amable y muy linda. Me siento muy tonto, me gustaría mucho bailar contigo. Prometo compensarte, ¿te gustaría salir algún día conmigo?"

"Thank you! You are very kind and very pretty. I feel very silly, I would very much like to dance with you. I promise to compensate you; would you like to go out with me one day?"

"¡Pero qué rápido eres!" dijo sonriendo. "Bueno, por qué no, pero no vamos a bailar más ¿verdad?"

"But how fast you are!" He said smiling. "Well, why not, but we won't dance anymore, right?"

"Jaja, no, por ahora no".

"Haha, no, not for now."

"Este es mi número, llámame," dijo mientras me entregaba una servilleta con su número telefónico.

"This is my number, call me," he said as he handed me a napkin with his phone number.

"¡Te llamo!"

"I'll call you!"

Salí del bar un poco mareado por los mojitos, la música y el calor, apenado pero contento. Mientras caminaba, pensaba en Daylin, ella era la chica más linda que había visto, su cabello largo y rizado la hacía parecer una sirena, su brillante sonrisa me había hipnotizado. Vaya, pensé, creo que debo dormir.

I left the bar a little dizzy from the mojitos, the music and the heat, sorry but happy. As I walked, I thought of Daylin, she was the prettiest girl I had ever seen, her long curly hair made her look like a mermaid, her bright smile had mesmerized me. Wow, I thought, I think I should sleep.

Llegué a mi habitación fatigado. Apenas podía creer que había llegado a Cuba ese mismo día; tenía una sensación extraña - aunque La Habana no podía ser más diferente a mi lugar de origen, me sentía como en casa.

I arrived at my room tired. I could hardly believe that I had arrived in Cuba that same day; I had a strange feeling - although Havana could not be more different from my place of origin, I felt at home.

A la mañana siguiente estaba cansado, pero con muchos ánimos. Había decidido tomarme el día para relajarme y pensar, así que tomé la recomendación de mi taxista del día anterior y me dirigí hacia Varadero, la playa más famosa cerca de La Habana. Tomé un autobús colectivo y en dos horas, de las cuales dormí una y media, ya estaba ahí.

The next morning I was tired, but with much encouragement. I had decided to take the day to relax and think, so I took my taxi driver's recommendation from the previous day and headed towards Varadero, the most famous beach near Havana. I took a bus and in two hours, of which I slept half past one, I was

already there.

En Varadero vi por primera vez los azules profundos que pude notar desde el avión, la playa era realmente paradisíaca. Tiré mi toalla en la arena y sentí en mi piel el calor del sol del Caribe. Mientras me relajaba escuchando las olas del mar, pensaba en Daylin. Quería verla pronto pero aún estaba muy apenado de mi terrible actuación como bailarín y quería hacer algo al respecto.

In Varadero I saw for the first time the deep blues that I could notice from the plane, the beach was really paradise. I threw my towel in the sand and felt the heat of the Caribbean sun on my skin. As I relaxed listening to the waves of the sea, I thought of Daylin. I wanted to see her soon but I was still very sorry for my terrible performance as a dancer and I wanted to do something about it.

Tras nadar un poco en el mar, pude notar que había también cientos de peces de colores a mi alrededor, aunque no podía verlos bien porque el agua salada lastimaba mis ojos. Al salir del mar, noté que había barcos en la orilla de la playa ofreciendo tours de esnórquel... no lo dude ni un segundo y tomé uno. Minutos después me encontraba nadando entre peces de todas formas y colores, inclusive llegué a ver una hermosa tortuga y también una mantarraya. Nadé por horas, y al salir del agua, relajado y feliz, tuve una revelación - "¡tengo que tomar clases de salsa!" me dije a mi mismo.

After swimming a little in the sea, I noticed that there were also hundreds of goldfish around me, although I couldn't see them well because the salt water hurt my eyes. Upon leaving the sea, I noticed that there were boats on the shore of the beach offering snorkeling tours ... do not hesitate for a second and I took one. Minutes later I was swimming among fish of all shapes and colors, I even got to see a beautiful turtle and also a stingray. I swam for hours, and out of the water, relaxed and happy, I had a revelation - "I have to take salsa classes!" I said to myself.

Tomé el autobús de regreso a La Habana, llegué a mi habitación, tomé un baño y salí decidido a aprender a bailar. Caminé por todos los restaurantes y bares con música que había visto la noche anterior y ahí vi un letrero en la entrada de uno de los lugares que decía - "Clases de salsa para principiantes".

I took the bus back to Havana, arrived at my room, took a bath and left determined to learn to dance. I walked through all the restaurants and bars with music I had seen the night before and there I saw a sign at the entrance of one of the places that said - "Salsa classes for beginners".

Pasaron tres días desde la noche que conocí a Daylin. Aún no me había decidido a llamarla, pero había pasado el día entero en el salón de baile, y claro, no era un profesional, pero al menos ya no lastimaría sus pies. Mi maestra de baile era una mujer mayor muy amable y platicadora, se llamaba Carolina, y durante los tres días que había tomado clases con ella, se había tomado muy en serio el poder convertirme en un bailarín, pues según ella, el baile es la mejor forma de comunicación del mundo porque sin ninguna palabra, puedes decir mucho.

Three days have passed since the night I met Daylin. I still hadn't decided to call her, but I had spent the whole day in the ballroom, and of course, I wasn't a professional, but at least I wouldn't hurt her feet anymore. My dance teacher was a very kind and talkative older woman, her name was Carolina, and during the three days I had taken classes with her, she had taken seriously to become a dancer, because according to her, dancing is the best form of communication in the world because without any word, you can say a lot.

Tras el fin de mi tercera clase, platicamos por horas, me contó sobre su juventud bailando con el ballet folklórico cubano y sobre cómo solía viajar por el mundo entero.

After the end of my third class, we talked for hours, he told me about his youth dancing with Cuban folk ballet and about how he used to travel the world.

"Lo que haces es muy importante. Toda la gente debería poder viajar por el mundo. Eso cambia tu forma de ver las cosas, de vivir, te hace más tolerante, más sabio, sencillo y capaz de arriesgarte. Mira tú, cuándo hubieses pensado que te esforzarías tanto por aprender a bailar por una chica bonita y no me digas que no es cierto que aprendes por una chica".

"What you do is very important. All people should be able to travel the world. That changes your way of seeing things, of living, makes you more tolerant, wiser, simple and capable of taking risks. Look, when you would have thought that you would try so hard to learn to dance for a pretty girl and don't tell me that it is not true that you learn for a girl."

Me ruboricé y contesté - "En tan pocos días, Carolina, me has llegado a conocer mucho".

I blushed and replied - "In so few days, Carolina, you've got to know me a lot."

"Te diré algo, chico, tienes un buen corazón, no tienes que ser el mejor bailarín del mundo para que esa chica se fije en ti. Anda, ya has progresado mucho, ahora llámala".

"I'll tell you something, boy, you have a good heart, you don't have to be the best dancer in the world for that girl to notice you. Come on, you've already made a lot of progress, now call her."

"Lo haré, Carolina, muchas gracias por todo".

"I will, Carolina, thank you very much for everything."

Salí de mi clase y tomé el teléfono entre mis manos, no podía esperar un segundo más.

I left my class and took the phone in my hands, I couldn't wait another second.

"Bueno, ¿Daylin?"

"Well, Daylin?"

"Ella habla, ¿Quién llama?"

"She talks, who's calling?"

"Soy yo, Peter, ¿me recuerdas?, del bar la otra noche, pisé tus pies..."

"It's me, Peter, remember me? From the bar the other night, I stepped on your feet ..."

"Jaja, pero claro, Peter, claro que me acuerdo de ti. Yo pensaba que ya no me llamarías, han pasado ya varios días".

"Haha, but of course, Peter, of course I remember you. I thought you wouldn't call me anymore; it's been several days."

"Sí, lo siento, estuve muy ocupado los días anteriores, pero ahora estoy libre, ¿te gustaría ir a cenar conmigo?"

"Yes, I'm sorry, I was very busy the previous days, but now I'm free, would you like to go to dinner with me?"

"Claro, vamos".

"Sure, let's go".

Quedamos en encontrarnos unas horas más tarde en el barrio viejo. Elegí un lugar tranquilo, frente a una plaza muy linda. Yo llegué muy puntual, pero pasaban más de diez minutos después de la hora acordada y Daylin no llegaba. Comenzaba a resignarme y a pensar que mi actuación del otro día había sido tan terrible que ella se había arrepentido de verme, pero unos minutos después, ahí estaba, caminando a prisa, tan linda como la recordaba.

187

We agreed to meet a few hours later in the old neighborhood. I chose a quiet place, in front of a very pretty square. I arrived very punctual, but it was more than ten minutes after the agreed time and Daylin did not arrive. I was beginning to resign myself and think that my performance the other day had been so terrible that she had regretted seeing me, but a few minutes later, there I was, walking in a hurry, as pretty as I remembered her.

Cenamos y conversamos por horas, el tiempo parecía pasar volando. Después de haber estado en el restaurante por un largo rato, tomé valor y la invité a bailar.

We had dinner and talked for hours, time seemed to fly by. After having been in the restaurant for a long time, I took courage and invited her to dance.

"¿A bailar? ¿estás seguro?"

"To dance? are you sure?"

"Sí, a bailar, tengo una sorpresa para ti".

"Yes, to dance, I have a surprise for you."

"¿De verdad? Estoy intrigada".

"Really? I am intrigued".

"Entonces vamos".

"So, let's go".

Nos dirigimos al mismo lugar de la última vez y ahí estaba de nuevo la orquesta tocando en todo su esplendor. Justo tras entrar la llevé a la pista de baile y le mostré mis nuevos pasos. Daylin no lo podía creer, sonreía y repetía junto a mí los pasos. Bailamos toda la noche y después la llevé de la mano de regreso a su casa, me sentía en un sueño.

We went to the same place last time and there was the orchestra playing again in all its splendor. Right after entering I took her to the dance floor and showed her my new steps. Daylin could not believe it, he smiled and repeated the steps with me. We danced all night and then I took her hand back to her house, I felt in a dream.

Pasé la siguiente semana entera con Daylin, me llevó a los mejores salones de baile, a comer tamales, me enseñó a preparar ropa vieja, fuimos juntos en bicicleta desde el centro de La Habana hasta Varadero, vimos tortugas y estrellas de mar. Un fin de semana tomamos un autobús y nos fuimos hasta Cienfuegos, vimos la vida del campo en Cuba, comimos cocos y compartimos con los campesinos. No quería que mi viaje por Cuba terminara.

I spent the next week with Daylin, he took me to the best dance halls, to eat tamales, he taught me how to prepare old clothes, we went together by bicycle from the center of Havana to Varadero, we saw turtles and starfish. One weekend we took a bus and went to Cienfuegos, saw the country life in Cuba, ate coconuts and shared with the farmers. I didn't want my trip to Cuba to end.

Al regresar a La Habana, recibí una llamada de teléfono, era Pierre -

Upon returning to Havana, I received a phone call, it was Pierre -

"Peter ¿estás bien?"

"Peter are you alright?"

"Sí, ¡muy bien!"

"Yes very good!"

"Kristen y yo estábamos preocupados. Llevamos días tratando de llamarte, pero tu teléfono no tenía recepción. Estamos esperándote en San Juan desde hace tres días".

"Kristen and I were worried. We have been trying to call you for days, but your phone had no reception. We have been waiting for you in San Juan for three days."

"Lo siento, me había olvidado completamente".

"Sorry, I had completely forgotten."

"De verdad? Pero ¿cómo que te habías olvidado?"

"Really? But how could you have forgotten?"

"Es una larga historia, te contaré cuando nos veamos. La verdad es que será muy difícil despedirme de esta ciudad, pero mi viaje debe continuar".

"It's a long story, I'll tell you when we meet. The truth is that it will be very difficult to say goodbye to this city, but my journey must continue."

"Bueno, espero escuchar tu historia pronto, aquí te esperamos."

"Well, I hope to hear your story soon, here we are waiting for you."

Me despedí con mucha tristeza de Daylin y de La Habana, y compré mi vuelo hacia República Dominicana, donde Pierre y Kristen me esperaban. Daylin me llevó hasta el aeropuerto en el auto de su padre, nos despedimos con un largo abrazo y le prometí que regresaría.

I said goodbye very sadly to Daylin and Havana, and bought my flight to the Dominican Republic, where Pierre and Kristen were waiting for me. Daylin took me to the airport in his father's car, we said goodbye with a long hug and promised to return.

Quiz

1. ¿Desde dónde viajó Peter a Cuba?
a) Puerto Rico
b) Ciudad de México
c). República Dominicana
d) Guatemala

2. ¿Qué es ropa vieja?
a) Un disfraz
b) Comida
c) Vestuario
d) Postre

3. ¿Dónde conoció Peter a Daylin?
a) La escuela
b) La calle
c) El salón de baile
d) La oficina

4. ¿Qué aprendió Peter para conquistar a Daylin?
a) A hablar español
b) A bailar

c) A cantar
d) A cocinar

5. ¿Cuánto tiempo estuvo Peter en Cuba?
a) Dos años
b) Dos semanas
c) Dos meses
d) Dos días

Answers

1)D
2)B
3)C
4)B
5)B

Vocabulary / Vocabulario

- *Tonos* --- Tones
- *Volé* --- Flew
- *Piscina* --- Pool
- *Turquesa* --- Turquoise
- *Manchas* --- Spots
- *Morado* --- Purple
- *Arenas* --- Sands
- *Raramente* --- Rarely
- *Cruceros de lujo* --- Luxury cruises
- *Maravillas* --- Wonders
- *Destino* --- Destination
- *Cómodo* --- Comfortable
- *Viajero* – Traveler
- *Monedas* --- Currencies
- *Tez* --- Complexion
- *Alojamiento* --- Accommodation
- *Departamentos* --- Flats
- *Amablemente* --- Kindly
- *Recomendaciones* --- Suggestions
- *Centro* --- Downtown
- *Casco histórico* --- Old town
- *Plazas* --- Squares
- *Mesera* --- Waitress
- *Mudo* --- Mute
- *Ropa* --- Clothes
- *Olor* --- Smell
- *Arroz* --- Rice

- *Plátano frito* --- Fried plantain
- *Ron* --- Rum
- *Manjar* --- Feast
- *Estridente* --- Loud
- *Contagioso* --- Contagious
- *Pasillo* --- Hallway
- *Trompetas* --- Trumpets
- *Barra* --- Bar
- *Alegría* --- Joy
- *Anterioridad* --- Beforehand
- *Pies* --- Feet
- *Felicidad* --- Happiness
- *Bailar* --- To dance
- *Espalda* --- Back
- *Susto* --- Fright
- *Hermosa* --- Beautiful
- *Congelado* --- Frozen
- *Me gustaría* --- I would like
- *Enseño* --- Teach
- *Ruboricé* --- Blushed
- *Temblaba* --- Trembled
- *Ritmo* --- Rhythm
- *Pisé sus pies* --- Stepped on her feet
- *No te preocupes* --- Don't worry
- *Tonto* --- Foolish
- *Compensarte* --- Make it up to you
- *¿Te gustaría salir algún día conmigo?* --- Would you like to go out with me someday?
- *Servilleta* --- Napkin
- *Calor* --- Heat
- *Linda* --- Pretty
- *Sirena* --- Mermaid
- *Hipnotizado* --- Mesmerized
- *Fatigado* --- Exhausted
- *Cerca* --- Near
- *Paradisíaca* --- Idyllic
- *Pronto* --- Soon
- *Bailarín* --- Dancer
- *Nadar* --- Swim
- *Peces* --- Fish (alive)
- *Agua salada* --- Salt Water
- *Orilla* --- Shore
- *Mantarraya* --- Stingray
- *Habitación* --- Room
- *Letrero* --- Sign
- *Principiantes* --- Beginners
- *Lastimaría* --- Hurt
- *Maestra de baile* --- Dance teacher

- *Mujer mayor* --- Older woman
- *Platicadora* --- Talkative
- *Juventud* --- Youth
- *Tolerante* --- Tolerant
- *Sabio* --- Wise
- *Sencillo* --- Humble
- *Arriesgarte* --- Take risks
- *Esforzarías* --- Work hard
- *¿Quién llama?* --- Who is calling?
- *Ocupado* --- Busy
- *Hora acordada* --- Agreed time
- *Resignarme* --- Resign
- *Arrepentido* --- Regretted
- *A prisa* --- In a hurry
- *Conversamos* --- Chatted
- *Valor* --- Courage
- *¿Estás seguro?* --- Are you sure?
- *Intrigada* --- Intrigued
- *Esplendor* --- Glory
- *Pista de baile* --- Dance Floor
- *Pasos* --- Moves
- *Estrella de mar* --- Starfish
- *Cocos* --- Coconuts
- *Campesinos* --- Farmer
- *Recepción* --- Signal
- *Abrazo* --- Hug
- *Prometí* --- Promised

Conclusion

We hope you had a blast reading these fun and silly stories and that you are more confident in reading and understanding the Spanish language.

It is important to not be too hard on yourself if it seems like there are some words and phrase that you are having trouble with. It is only natural when you are learning new things. Use any frustration that you have to push you to work harder, especially those that cause problems. It is a process to learn a foreign language, and it is going to take dedicated practice.

Take all opportunities to practice Spanish as you go about your day. This will help to solidify the words in your mind, and you will also perfect your pronunciation as well.

Remember that it is also useful to involve a family member or friend. This way, you can practice together, as well as test each other. You both will enjoy the experience and learn a new language together.

Follow the guidelines found in the introduction to learn Spanish quickly so that you can speak with native speakers around the world. Remember that it can be an advantage in the workplace, when you are meeting new friends, or when you are traveling. Learning a new language is never going to be a waste. And you will continue to have fun with the language the more that you learn.

Do you want to continue learning? The perfect match for this book is the **Learn Spanish for Beginners** also edited by Fernández Language Institute. Also, a Short Stories Volume 2 For Intermediate and Advanced level, will be released soon.

Learn Spanish

An easy method for intermediate users to have a fluent Spanish conversation in just 7 days. Includes intermediate grammar rules, exercises and common everyday life sentences

Introduction

Many times, if you tell someone that you are not just learning a foreign language, but that you are specifically learning Spanish, you may be met with a variety of responses. They can vary from "Wow, that's impressive!" to "Why do you need to learn Spanish? Everyone speaks English anyways…"

Many people even have the perception that learning Spanish can be a rather difficult endeavor or that all the varieties of Spanish are similar, if not identical. In this chapter, we're going to discuss one commonly held belief (myth) about learning Spanish, and then discuss, in a little more detail, some of the tricky little nuances about learning Spanish. The goal of this chapter is to outline some of the aspects of Spanish that may trip up learners, especially at the beginning of their Spanish-learning journey.

Spanish is the official language in over 20 different countries! Mexico, Spain, Venezuela, Argentina… they all speak Spanish. This is true. But assuming that there are no differences between the varieties of Spanish you'll find spoken around the world is very, very wrong.

This is like saying that people from the US, Britain, and Australia all speak the same way because they all speak English. Not only are there varying accents (even within the countries mentioned- for example, the southern accent found in Texas versus the northern accent found in New York) but even terminology changes. If you go to England and ask for "chips", you're not ordering the crispy potato chips you would expect to get in the United States. You're actually ordering what Americans would call "fries."

The same is true with Spanish. In some places, certain words are used to mean one thing while, in others, they mean something very different. Accents, slang, and even set expressions will change based on what country you're in.

There is what can be considered "standard Spanish." This is the Spanish spoken in D.F. (Mexico City), Mexico or Lima, Peru. This isn't to say that in those places there aren't some unique and identifying elements to the language but merely that speakers from those two cities will have an easier time communicating with and being understood by Spanish-speakers from other Spanish-speaking countries.

What does this mean for you as a Spanish language learner?

Especially when starting, this fact doesn't have to have much bearing on your language-learning experience. The basics (i.e. verb conjugations and crucial vocabulary) will almost always be the same no matter where you go.

However, as you dive deeper into the language and your level begins to increase, you may want to make a few mental notes about things.

For example, the use of "vosotros" in the central and northern regions of Spain or the "vos", which is used in many Southern and Central American countries. Unless you plan on spending extensive amounts of time in one of the countries that employs one of these pronouns, you don't need to worry about including them in your own speech. However, if you intend to immerse yourself in the language (through reading, watching TV shows or movies, etc.) you will want to be aware of this fact.

This is true for many of the varying elements found within the large umbrella that is the Spanish language and something you'll want to keep in mind. If, suddenly, you pick up) a Spanish book and feel like you're struggling to follow the dialogue or narration, chances are you've found a variety of Spanish you were previously unfamiliar with.

Don't let this discourage you or make you feel overwhelmed! It's simply a reality of learning Spanish that we all face at some point of our journey or another.

Unless you plan on becoming a Spanish linguist or dedicating your life to studying the Spanish language, chances are you will never be able to fully learn all of the differences that span the 20+ Spanish-speaking countries.

The best way to approach something like this is, once you feel you have a firm understanding of the language, find the variety of the language that best fits your personal interests.

If, for example, you are learning Spanish for work or business, you may want to stick with focusing on the "standard Spanish" spoken in the D.F or Lima. But, if you find yourself interested in the history, culture, literature, music, etc. of a specific region, you'll probably want to familiarize yourself with their specific way of speaking so your immersion process goes more smoothly.

No matter what variety of Spanish you decide to go with, once you have a working knowledge of the language, you won't struggle with using it no matter who you're speaking with. Sure, there may be some moment of misunderstanding (take the "chip" example mentioned before when speaking English) but in the end, communication can and will take place.

Those tricky little nuances...

No matter what variety of Spanish you're learning, there are certain truths that will always be present-- the little things that make Spanish, well, Spanish. Many times, these things I'm about to list and discuss briefly can be difficult for English-speakers because, simply put, they don't exist in our language.

Pronunciation

Unlike other languages, Spanish pronunciation isn't actually that difficult. Spelling (something that can be frustrating and confusing in languages such as French and even English) shouldn't be a problem when learning Spanish.

Each letter in the Spanish alphabet has a specific sound. They will ALWAYS make that sound. This fact WILL NOT change. Unlike in English when we have long vowels and short vowels and oddities like the infamous -ough ending (seriously--what's with that? Why do words like through, though, hard and rough, all sharing the same ending, have to be said so differently?), you won't come across these things in Spanish.

If you make a mental note of this fact when you start learning Spanish, seeing words like *estacionamiento* or *murcielago* (both words that seem long and somewhat intimidating) shouldn't strike you with fear. Simply sound out the letters as you see them and there you have it!

For more information on the Spanish alphabet, check out this amazing website with audio samples:

http://studyspanish.com/pronunciation/

Diphthongs

There is one element of the Spanish language that is very important to remember when talking about pronunciation. It's something we don't have in English--the diphthongs.

Without getting too technical here, this process will occur when you have two vowels placed together (in the same syllable--this is very important). The sounds they make will sort of mush together to create one, combined sound.

To get a better understanding of what I'm saying with this, let's start small. Take the following two words for example:

- *Bailar*
- *Tiene*

Breaking these down, you'll see that they each only have TWO syllables.

- Bai·lar
- Tie·ne

In the first word (*bailar*-meaning to dance), we have the first syllable contains two vowels ("a" and "i"). The "a" in Spanish is pronounced "ah" and the "i" is pronounced like "ee". If we were to say these two sounds individually, the word would sound somewhat awkward and choppy.

- Bah/ee·lar

In reality, the "a" and the "i" in the first syllable will come together to make the "ay" sound. Hence the pronunciation will be:

- Bay (sounds like "bye")·lar

The same can be said with the second word (tiene- meaning he/she/it/you [singular/ formal] have). The "i" again would be pronounced "ee" and the "e" is pronounced like "eh".

Since both vowels are together in the same syllable, we need to push them together, so that they form one, slurred together sound--"ee-eh"

- Tee-eh·ne

The website mentioned before will also give you some great information about these slight oddities.

Verb Conjugations

This is something that many English-speakers struggle with. In reality, we do have conjugations in English--the only thing is they're much simpler and actually very basic. You know that silly little "s" that gets added to the ending of verbs when we use them in the 3rd person singular (I run, he runs)? This is like that, only with a lot more to keep in mind.

In English, it's almost ALWAYS required that you include both the subject and the verb when speaking. For example, you can't say "have a dog". Who has a dog? I, you, we, they?

In Spanish, however, including the subject isn't always necessary, and here's why.

A quick intro to the conjugation process

The best way to explain this is with the use of a visual. This chart is something I have used to teach subject pronouns, as well as conjugations, for years and it is actually very commonly used in Spanish classrooms around the world.

I	We
You	You plural
He/She	They

As you can see, there are two columns on the chart. The first (to the left) represents the singular pronouns. Going down the rows, you will find that they go in order (descending) from first to third person. Likewise, the right column contains your plural forms of the same 1st-3rd person pronouns.

Whenever we use a verb in English, we choose the appropriate pronoun to go along with the verb, so as not to cause any confusion.

In Spanish, however, as I will soon explain, the use of the subject pronoun isn't always necessary. This is because the verb will conjugate, in essence, to contain the subject as well.

As you will learn, if you haven't already, there are three main verb endings in Spanish. This means that when a verb is in its infinitive form (to + verb), it will end in either *-ar, -er*, or *-ir*.

- *Hablar*- to talk
- *Comer*- to eat
- *Vivir*- to live

Now, if you want to take those infinitive forms of the verbs and use them in actual, real life sentences, you're going to need to conjugate them. You can't simply say "I to talk to my mom." That doesn't make sense!

Since this isn't a grammar book and my whole point for this section is to help you wrap your mind around the process of conjugation and not so much TEACH you conjugations, I will work from here on with the first verb mentioned- "*hablar*".

The **-ar** endings in the present tense, are:

-o	*-amos*
-as	*-áis*
-a	*-an*

If you take that chart and lay it over the subject pronoun chart we just looked at, you have your conjugations! If you want to say "I talk" in Spanish, all you have to do is look at the ending for the first person singular, add it to your verb (after taking away your -ar verb ending), and say "*hablo*." "You talk" is "*hablas*", "we talk" is "*hablamos*", and so forth.

The reason why there are so many conjugations in Spanish is simple— they eliminate the need that we have in English of including a subject pronoun every single time we use a verb.

Are they annoying and frustrating at times? Yes. But if you wrap your head around them now--at the very beginning of everything--you will find that not only are they not that difficult, but they are, actually, quite nice!

Formal/ Informal "you"

It's important to note that, in the chart given above, the plural, informal "you" conjugation (second one down in the right column) is used almost exclusively in Spain. This conjugation belongs to the "*vosotros.*"

In Spanish, there are 5 different ways to say "you." That's right--five! They are:

Singular, Informal

- *Tú, Vos*

Singular, Formal

- *Usted*

Plural, Informal

- *Vosotros*

Plural, Formal

- *Ustedes*

The use of these different forms varies (of course it does...) depending on which country you're in. In some places, the "tú" is used only when speaking to children or close friends. Whereas in others, its use is extremely common and the alternative (the formal "usted") is very rare. Basically, there's no real set rule as to when it's appropriate to use the informal vs the formal form of "you". And the "vos" and "vosotros" are definitely regional things.

When talking about verb conjugations, the "usted" (singular, formal) will take the same conjugation as the 3rd person singular (he/she/it) and the "*ustedes*" (plural, formal) will follow the same conjugations as the 3rd person plural (they).

This is another one of those times where the variety of Spanish you are learning/speaking will have an impact on the way you use this one, somewhat tricky, little word ("you"). Again, don't let this overwhelm you! If you are starting, simply learn the basic conjugations (tú, usted, ustedes) and if you find the need to learn the others (vos, vosotros), they won't be hard to work into your language once you have a strong, working understanding of basic verb conjugations.

"My house is a girl and my plate is a boy?"

Another concept that is hard to understand for English-speakers is fact that all nouns in Spanish take a gender--they will be either masculine or feminine. As pointed out earlier the word "*casa*" (house) is feminine, and "*plato*" (plate) is masculine.

Fortunately for Spanish language learners, though, this concept isn't as extensive or complex as it is in other languages (French, Italian, German, for example).

In Spanish (generally speaking) nouns that end in *-a* are feminine and nouns that end in *-o* are masculine.

Now, I say "generally speaking" because there are a few additional things you should know when determining the gender of a word.

Additional Masculine Endings:

Nouns that don't end in "o", but will be masculine, will have the following endings:

Ending	Example
-e	*El maquillaje* (the makeup)
Accented vowel	*El ají* (the pepper)
A consonant (that's not -d, -z, -ion)	*El árbol* (the tree)
-ma	*El idioma* (the language)

Additional Feminine Endings:

Nouns that do not end in -a, but are still feminine, will have the following endings:

Ending	Example
-d	*La felicidad* (the happiness)
-z	*La nariz* (the nose)
-ion	*La canción* (the song)

Of course, there are exceptions. "*el mapa*" (the map) for example, that ends in -a but is, in fact, masculine. Or *la mano* (the hand) this ends in an -o but is feminine. These are things that just need to be memorized--that's the sad, but brutal, truth.

Why does this matter?

Knowing the gender of a noun is important because it will change a few key things in your sentence. For example, your articles and adjectives will need to change to fit the noun--not only in gender, but also in number.

Again, this isn't a grammar book so we won't go into too much detail with this. But here's a quick, basic run-down of what I mean.

The articles in Spanish are:

Singular Article	Singular in Spanish	Plural Article	Plural in Spanish
The	*El/ La*	The	*Los/ Las*
A/ An	*Un/ Uno/ Una*	Some	*Unos/ Unas*

Do you have one house or two? If you have two, you'll need to use a plural article. And don't forget that "*casa*" is a feminine word. So you'll need to use a plural, feminine article (either "*unas*" – "some" or "*las*"- "the" plural).

Okay, so maybe you don't have two houses. You only have one, red house. Let's just call it "the red house."

As we mentioned before, your article (the) will need to take the same gender and number as your noun. Well, your adjective will need it too! This means that you would refer to your house as *"la casa roja"* (la- "the" singular feminine, casa - "house", *roja*- "red" singular feminine).

See how nice that sounds? Everything seems to flow because all of the endings line up neatly. There's consistency between all of the words that we're using that define the one main object, the house.

Now, let's pretend for a moment that you're lucky and you actually have two red houses. If we wanted to talk about the red houses, we need to keep the same principles in play. Hence, we would say *"las casas rojas"* (las- "the" plural feminine, *casas*- "houses", *rojas*- "red" plural feminine). Again, everything seems just to fit together, doesn't it?

Everything needs to agree in gender and in number. This is something that's difficult to understand at first but will become more natural the more you get used to it.

Note: You might have noticed a slight change in word order. The adjective comes AFTER the noun. I touched on this briefly before. The idea still stands--pay attention to where your words go.

Chapter 1 - Myths About Learning A Foreign Language

There are a lot of beliefs revolving around learning a foreign language--any foreign language. Some people think that you have to be young to learn one; others believe that unless you live abroad, you'll never be able to reach a level of fluency.

In this chapter, we're going to look at some of the most commonly held beliefs about learning foreign languages and talk about why you should quickly push all of these thoughts out of your mind.

Myth: Immersion is all you need. OR You can't learn a language if you don't spend time abroad.

Immersion is the process of surrounding yourself completely in the language you are attempting to learn. We talked a little about how you can incorporate the concept of immersion into your learning experience. Taking this a step further and spending extended time in a Spanish-speaking country is always a great option if you want to excel your language ability.

However, thinking that immersion is the only way you will learn a language is one of the things that prevents so many people from becoming successful. They get discouraged--maybe moving to Spain is too expensive or maybe you have a life, work, and a family and picking up and going to Costa Rica for three months just isn't a realistic option.

Don't fall prey to the belief that immersion is the end-all-be-all of language learning. And here's why:

Myth: Immersion is all you need.

While immersion is a great tool and a wonderful way to learn things like slang and set expressions, you need more in order to really be able to become fluent in a language. Without those (sometimes) annoying little things like grammar and syntax and a working knowledge of basic vocabulary, it doesn't matter how much you immerse yourself in the language--you won't understand what's going on!

If you try to learn Spanish only by surrounding yourself with it, you will find yourself making more mistakes with things like verb conjugations and word order. Your vocabulary will be smaller and more limited and your ability to communicate your own thoughts will suffer.

By making immersion a PART of your language-learning experience, you are ensuring that you are exposed to a large amount of Spanish. But you still need to remember to set aside time to go over the basics. Without the basics, you will not have a base on which to lean.

Myth: You can't learn a language if you don't spend time abroad.

Yes, living or spending time in a Spanish-speaking country will do wonders for your language ability. But as mentioned before, that's simply not an option for a lot of people.

That's okay, though! Because, through using what are called "authentic materials" (books, newspapers, movies, etc. produced in a Spanish-speaking country or region for a Spanish-speaking audience), you'll still get the benefits of immersion. You will still be exposed to real-world, real-time, real-life Spanish.

If implemented into your study routine properly, these authentic materials will, in essence, replace the need to spend extensive time abroad to learn Spanish.

Myth: The best way to learn a foreign language is through speaking it.

This idea that many have about the journey into learning a second language fits in well with what we've been talking about immersion.

To address this commonly held belief regarding language learning, we need to discuss two very important elements of the language-learning process: Input vs Output.

- Input-the information that we receive
- Output-the information that we produce

What it comes down to is this--when you speak, you're imitating what you've heard. You're taking the input you've received and turning around and using that to create your own output. However, if the only way that you're receiving input it through conversation or immersion, then you're not really getting enough input to be able to produce NEW, original output. If you only know how to say a phrase because you've heard someone else say it, how can you know how to break down that phrase and use the elements that make it up to create your very own phrase later on?

As we've mentioned before, immersion is a great *tool* that can, and should, be incorporated into your language-learning process. However, if you don't take the time to find other sources of input, the information you absorb will be useless unless repeated under identical circumstances and in the same situation in which you received said input.

If you want to be able to reach a level of fluency in Spanish, you obviously have to be able to create your own output. You have to be able to take the information you've gained and mold it to fit your personal needs in a large variety of settings.

More speaking won't give you the grammar comprehension and extensive vocabulary you need to be successful in attaining your goal. However, including elements of immersion into your study routine will help you take the input you've gotten from your grammar lessons and vocabulary lists and hear them used in real life scenarios. This combination will make it easier for you to produce your own output along the way.

Myth: People can't learn a foreign language after the age of 16.

If that's true, then I must be an anomaly! I didn't start learning Spanish until I was just a few months shy of my 16th birthday. It's taken a lot of work, but over the years, I've been able to take my Spanish all the way up to fluent level.

Yes, learning a language once you're older does make things a little more difficult. But impossible? Not even close to being true!

You learned your first language through immersion and everyday situations. Learning a second language needs to be done differently to account for the decreased neuroplasticity in the brain. When you're younger, you are able to absorb information more quickly. As your brain develops, however, a variety of different cognitive processes start to take place. This, in turn, makes learning a new language more challenging.

One of the biggest challenges facing adults when trying to learn a foreign language isn't the condition of their brains, however. It's simply finding the time and opportunity to learn! As children, learning a language is built right into our curriculum. We have reading classes and grammar lessons. As an adult, you don't have those external forces pushing you forward to learn. You have to be self-motivated, which can be hard when you're juggling work, family, and the plethora of other responsibilities that come along with being an adult.

As an adult learning Spanish, keep in mind that the process is going to be different for you than for children and success is measured differently as well. Any time you get the chance to study is an achievement. Any progress you make is worth celebrating. Pace yourself. Take your time. And remember, learning a foreign language is not only you working towards achieving a certain goal--it's also helping your brain stay healthy and active.

"I have a horrible accent when I speak Spanish!"

This is one of those things that, to be honest, might be true when you're starting out. But don't let this discourage you. Any person learning any language will have an accent when first learning said new language. There's no quick-fix or short-cuts when it comes to acquiring a native-sounding accent. It's something that needs to be worked on and developed over time.

Pronunciation is one of those aspects of learning a foreign language that requires a lot of practice. Frustratingly enough, however, pronunciation is something that needs to come before your language level can really develop further. It does you no good to learn a new word by looking it up in the dictionary if you can't actually go out and put that word to use.

Think of it like learning a sport--let's say basketball. If your coach shows you how to shoot a 3-point shot, you have an understanding of what it's supposed to look like and what the desired end result is supposed to be. That doesn't mean, however, that just by watching someone else do it that you can walk to that little white line and sink a triple on your first attempt. You need to practice and perfect the motions.

This is the same with pronunciation. It may take a while before you find your lips and tongue moving on their own accord to create desired sounds (such as rolling your r's).

If you start working on your pronunciation now using the following tips, you'll find your Spanish will improve greatly.

Study Phonetics

The best way to fully understand the pronunciation of a language is to study said language's phonics. You remember phonics, right? Those fun little videos from when you were little called "Hooked on Phonics." Well, that's what we're talking about here. Learning how the letters sound and how they sound when they're put together with other letters.

With Spanish, which could be considered a phonetic language (i.e. words are written like they sound), learning the phonetics of the language isn't overly difficult. It really comes down to being familiar with the alphabet.

Listen to Spanish

What better way to know how something should sound than by hearing it being said by a native speaker? Whether it's through podcasts or movies, radio or YouTube videos, listening to Spanish will help you familiarize yourself with the sounds of the language, while also picking up on fun colloquial expressions and slang along the way.

Listen to Yourself

Recording yourself while speaking Spanish and playing it back to listen to may not sound like the most appealing thing to do for any language student. It's intimidating and, at times, can be quite embarrassing.

Doing this, though, is a great way to hear yourself and catch your mistakes. You won't know what you need to work on if you never hear yourself speak. It makes it easier to catch your mistakes early on. And the earlier you catch them, the earlier you can fix them.

Read Out Loud

This is a wonderful way for you to get a feel of how Spanish words work when they're put together. Not only will you be able to practice speaking and listening to yourself speak, but you will also pick up a lot of new vocabulary.

Identify the Areas You Have Problems with and Work on Them

For a lot of people, the "rr" sound is difficult. For others, the aspirated (or guttural, depending on which variety of Spanish you're learning) "j" or "g" can be tricky. Whatever it is that you struggle with, identify it early on and begin taking steps to improve that.

English Is the Universal Language--Why Do I Even Need to Learn Another?

If you are a native English-speaker (like myself) consider yourself very lucky! Speaking English is a very useful language to have a mastery of. Given its current status as "lingua franca", many countries aspire to, in some way, incorporate English into their education systems and have it as a second language.

English is used in business and politics and really comes in handy when traveling to foreign countries. However, you may be surprised to learn that only 5% of the world's population speaks English. The other 95% speak some other language! Sure, most of those other 95% of the people out there are probably learning English as well, but it's not their native tongue.

Yes, knowing English is great if you want to "get by" when visiting new places. But, if you aren't able to speak another language, you're actually missing out on a lot. Learning to speak a second language will help you in many ways. Some of the most notable are:

Improved Memory

There are tons of scientifically proven benefits of learning a second language. Not only does it help in fighting off and preventing Alzheimer's, but it improves your cognitive abilities as well.

By learning a second language, you're training your mind to think differently. You're learning to remember additional details and forcing your brain to work in a way it didn't have to previously. While it can seem challenging at first remembering all those little details of a second language, you'll be surprised at how quickly your brain adjusts and how, over time, you'll be able to recall vocabulary and grammar with ease.

Cultural Perspective

Learning a second language involves so much more than just memorizing words and conjugation charts. It involves learning about a new culture. It doesn't matter if it's Spanish, German, or Chinese-- whenever you learn a new language, you gain an insight into the culture found in the places that language is spoken. You'll learn about history and literature, cinema and music. You'll discover new foods and new places, as well as new ways of thinking. You will quickly find yourself being filled with an appreciation for these things that you didn't have previously.

Your Native Language Will Improve

As you begin to learn the grammar and syntax surrounding your new language (in this case Spanish), you'll find that your understanding of how those things work in your native language will improve as well.

Better Job Prospects

Any employer would love to have a bilingual employee working for them. Especially in today's day and age, the ability to speak Spanish is something that many businesses are actively seeking in their employees. It doesn't matter if you work in the business or medical fields. You could be a teacher, a bank teller--anything. The ability to speak Spanish will definitely make you stand out on any list of applicants.

Being Able to Travel Without a Translator

If you travel to different countries where English isn't the first language, you'll probably find that you're able to survive using English to communicate and a translation tool when necessary. But this means having to have a translator on-hand at all times. It could be an app on your phone or a dictionary. You will probably stumble through pronunciation or spend time searching for phrases. Speaking the language allows for a much more authentic interaction with the locals. It will not only make traveling easier, but also be a very rewarding experience.

Chapter 2 - The subjunctive mood (el modo subjuntivo)

Spanish subjunctive is used to talk about desires, doubts, the unknown, the abstract and some emotions. The subjunctive includes many of the same tenses as the indicative, but in this chapter we're only going to learn the present subjunctive tense and a past subjunctive tense, used in conditional sentences.

For English speakers, sometimes the subjunctive can be difficult to understand, but with practice you'll get it. To start, try to remember the following situations where you have to use it:

1. In sentences with two subjects: Sentences with one subject in the main clause and one in the noun clause use subjunctive.

2. When sentences are linked with a relative pronoun: Sentences that have parts linked by a relative pronoun (*que, quien, como*).

3. When sentences have two verbs, and the first one expresses wishes, emotions, impersonal expressions, recommendations, doubt and denial.

Examples

I need you to **do** something for me - *Necesito que **hagas** algo por mí*

He wants me to **buy** him the new videogame console - *Él quiere que le **compre** la nueva consola de videojuegos*

They expect us to **solve** everything - *Ellos esperan que nosotros **resolvamos** todo*

I doubt he **can** make it - *Dudo que él **pueda** hacerlo*

I want us to **go** on a trip - *Quiero que nos **vayamos** de viaje*

She refuses to believe he **is** guilty - *Se niega a creer que él **sea** el culpable*

We hope you **are** the architect we need - *Esperamos que **seas** el arquitecto que necesitamos*

I hate that you **talk** to me like that - *Odio que me **hables** así*

I'm glad that you **love** each other again - *Me alegra que se **amen** nuevamente*

It is necessary that someone **fixes** it - *Es necesario que alguien lo **arregle***

He recommended that I **exercise** more - *Me recomendó que me **ejercite** más*

I wish the food **tastes** as good as it looks - *Ojalá la comida **sepa** tan bien como se ve*

I wish my son **passes** his driving test - *Ojalá mi hijo **apruebe** su examen de manejo*

Present subjunctive (presente del subjuntivo)

Regular verbs

To love (*amar*)

- *que yo ame*

- *que tú ames / vos ames / usted ame*

- *que él/ella ame*

- *que nosotros amemos*

- *que ustedes amen / vosotros améis*

- *que ellos/ellas amen*

To fear (*temer*)

- *que yo tema*

- *que tú temas / vos teméis / usted tema*

- *que él/ella tema*

- *que nosotros temamos*

- *que ustedes teman / vosotros temáis*

- *que ellos/ellas teman*

To live (*vivir*)

- *que yo viva*

- *que tú vivas / vos vivís / usted viva*

- *que él/ella viva*

- *que nosotros vivamos*

- *que ustedes vivan / vosotros viváis*

- *que ellos/ellas vivan*

Irregular verbs

To be (*ser*)

- *que yo **sea***

- *que tú **seas** / vos **seas** / usted **sea***

- *que él/ella **sea***

- *que nosotros **seamos***

- que ustedes **sean** / vosotros **seáis**

- que ellos/ellas **sean**

To be (*estar*)

- que yo **esté**

- que tú **estés** / vos **estés** / usted **esté**

- que él/ella **esté**

- que nosotros **estemos**

- que ustedes **estén** / vosotros **estéis**

- que ellos/ellas **estén**

To have (*tener*)

- que yo **tenga**

- que tú **tengas** / vos **tengas** / usted **tenga**

- que él/ella **tenga**

- que nosotros **tengamos**

- que ustedes **tengan** / vosotros **tengáis**

- que ellos/ellas **tengan**

To say (*decir*)

- que yo **diga**

- que tú **digas** / vos **digáis** / usted **diga**

- que él/ella **diga**

- que nosotros **digamos**

- que ustedes **digan** / vosotros **digáis**

- que ellos/ellas **digan**

To go (*ir*)

- que yo **vaya**

- *que tú **vayas** / vos **vayas** / usted **vaya***

- *que él/ella **vaya***

- *que nosotros **vayamos***

- *que ustedes **vayan** / vosotros **vayáis***

- *que ellos/ellas **vayan***

To do (*hacer*)

- *que yo **haga***

- *que tú **hagas** / vos **hagas** / usted **haga***

- *que él/ella **haga***

- *que nosotros **hagamos***

- *que ustedes **hagan** / vosotros **hagáis***

- *que ellos/ellas **hagan***

Can (*poder*)

- *que yo **pueda***

- *que tú **puedas** / vos **podáis** / usted **pueda***

- *que él/ella **pueda***

- *que nosotros **podamos***

- *que ustedes **puedan** / vosotros **podáis***

- *que ellos/ellas **puedan***

To see (*ver*)

- *que yo **vea***

- *que tú **veas** / vos **veáis** / usted **vea***

- *que él/ella **vea***

- *que nosotros **veamos***

- *que ustedes **vean** / vosotros **veáis***

- *que ellos/ellas **vean***

To give (*dar*)

- *que yo **de***

- *que tú **des** / vos **des** / usted **dé***

- *que él/ella **de***

- *que nosotros **demos***

- *que ustedes **den** / vosotros **deis***

- *que ellos/ellas **den***

To want (*querer*)

- *que yo **quiera***

- *que tú **quieras** / vos **queráis** / usted **quiera***

- *que él/ella **quiera***

- *que nosotros **queramos***

- *que ustedes **quieran** / vosotros **queráis***

- *que ellos/ellas **quieran***

Exercises

Complete the following sentences using the subjunctive mood:

- *El público quiere que (tú, cantar) .... una serenata*

- *Estaremos más tranquilos cuando (nosotros, ganar) .... un buen sueldo*

- *No puedes obligarlo a que te (él, amar) ....*

- *Espero que el perro no (él, romper) .... su juguete nuevo*

- *Mis abuelos quieren que (nosotros, vivir) .... con ellos por un tiempo*

- *No importa cuánto (yo, estudiar) .... mis padres nunca estarán satisfechos*

- *Mi esposa quiere que nuestra hija (ella, ser) .... médica*

- *Mi mamá se asegura de que siempre (nosotros, estar) .... felices*

– *El día que (yo, ser) .... el jefe, las cosas cambiarán*

– *No logro que Juan (él, estar) .... tranquilo*

– *Quiero una casa que (ella, tener) .... tres habitaciones*

– *Necesito alguien que (él/ella, decir) .... la verdad*

– *Mis primos quieren que (nosotros, ir) .... de visita*

– *Necesito un masajista que (él, hacer) .... milagros*

– *Cuando (vosotros, poder) ....juntémonos a estudiar*

– *Cuando (tú, ver) .... dónde está el problema, podremos solucionarlo*

– *Necesitamos a alguien que nos (él/ella, dar) .... indicaciones*

– *No conocemos a nadie que (él/ella, querer) .... viajar con nosotros*

– *Dile a Jorge que (él, ir) .... a hacer las compras*

Past subjunctive (pretérito imperfecto del subjuntivo)

As you will see, there are always two forms for this subjunctive tense. You can use either.

Regular verbs

To love (am**ar**)

- *que yo amara/am**ase***

- *que tú am**aras**/am**ases** / vos am**aras**/am**ases** / usted am**ara**/am**ase***

- *que él/ella am**ara**/am**ase***

- *que nosotros amár**amos**/am**ásemos***

- *que ustedes am**aran**/am**asen** / vosotros am**arais**/am**aseis***

- *que ellos/ellas am**aran**/am**asen***

To fear (tem**er**)

- *que yo tem**iera**/tem**iese***

- *que tú tem**ieras**/tem**ieses** / vos tem**ieras**/tem**ieses** / usted tem**iera**/tem**iese***

- *que él/ella tem**iera**/tem**iese***

- *que nosotros tem**iéramos**/tem**iésemos***

- que ustedes tem**ieran**/tem**iesen** / vosotros tem**ierais**/tem**ieseis**

- que ellos/ellas tem**ieran**/tem**iesen**

To live (viv**ir**)

- que yo viv**iera**/viv**iese**

- que tú viv**ieras**/viv**ieses** / vos viv**ieras**/viv**ieses** / usted viv**iera**/viv**iese**

- que él/ella viv**iera**/viv**iese**

- que nosotros viv**iéramos**/viv**iésemos**

- que ustedes viv**ieran**/viv**iesen** / vosotros viv**ierais**/viv**ieseis**

- que ellos/ellas viv**ieran**/viv**iesen**

Irregular verbs

To be (ser)

- que yo fuera/fuese

- que tú fueras/fueses / vos fueras/fueses / usted fuera/fuese

- que él/ella **fuera/fuese**

- que nosotros fuéramos/fuésemos

- que ustedes fueran/fuesen / vosotros fuerais/fueseis

- que ellos/ellas **fueran/fuesen**

To be (estar)

- que yo estuviera/estuviese

- que tú estuvieras/estuvieses / vos estuvieras/estuvieses / usted estuviera/estuviese

- que él/ella estuviera/estuviese

- que nosotros estuviéramos/estuviésemos

- que ustedes estuvieran/estuviesen / vosotros estuvierais/estuvieseis

- que ellos/ellas estuvieran/estuviesen

To have (*tener*)

- *que yo tuviera/tuviese*
- *que tú tuvieras/tuvieses / vos tuvieras/tuvieses / usted tuviera/tuviese*
- *que él/ella tuviera/tuviese*
- *que nosotros tuviéramos/tuviésemos*
- *que ustedes tuvieran/tuviesen / vosotros tuvierais/tuvieseis*
- *que ellos/ellas **tuvieran/tuviesen***

To say (*decir*)

- *que yo dijera/dijese*
- *que tú dijeras/dijeses / vos dijeras/dijeses / usted dijera/dijese*
- *que él/ella **dijera/dijese***
- *que nosotros dijéramos/dijésemos*
- *que ustedes dijeran/dijesen / vosotros dijerais/dijeseis*
- *que ellos/ellas **dijeran/dijesen***

To go (*ir*)

- *que yo fuera/fuese*
- *que tú fueras/fueses / vos fueras/fueses / usted fuera/fuese*
- *que él/ella **fuera/fuese***
- *que nosotros fuéramos/fuésemos*
- *que ustedes fueran/fuesen / vosotros fuerais/fueseis*
- *que ellos/ellas **fueran/fuesen***

To do (*hacer*)

- *que yo hiciera/hiciese*
- *que tú hicieras/hicieses / vos hicieras/hicieses / usted hiciera/hiciese*
- *que él/ella hiciera/hiciese*

- *que nosotros hiciéramos/hiciésemos*
- *que ustedes hicieran/hiciesen / vosotros hicierais / hicieseis*
- *que ellos/ellas* **hicieran/hiciesen**

Can (*poder*)
- *que yo pudiera/pudiese*
- *que tú pudieras/pudieses / vos pudieras/pudieses / usted pudiera/pudiese*
- *que él/ella pudiera/pudiese*
- *que nosotros pudiéramos/pudiésemos*
- *que ustedes pudieran/pudiesen / vosotros pudierais/pudieseis*
- *que ellos/ellas* **pudieran/pudiesen**

To see (*ver*)
- *que yo viera/viese*
- *que tú vieras/vieses / vos vieras/vieses / usted viera/viese*
- *que él/ella* **viera/viese**
- *que nosotros viéramos/viésemos*
- *que ustedes vieran/viesen / vosotros vierais/viesen*
- *que ellos/ellas* **vieran/viesen**

To give (*dar*)
- *que yo diera/diese*
- *que tú dieras/dieses / vos dieras/dieses / usted diera/diese*
- *que él/ella diera/diese*
- *que nosotros diéramos/diésemos*
- *que ustedes dieran/diesen / vosotros dierais/dieseis*
- *que ellos/ellas* **dieran/diesen**

To want (*querer*)

- *que yo quisiera/quisiese*

- *que tú quisieras/quisieses / vos quisieras/quisieses / usted quisiera/quisiese*

- *que él/ella quisiera/quisiese*

- *que nosotros quisiéramos/quisiésemos*

- *que ustedes quisieran/quisiesen / vosotros quisierais/quisieseis*

- *que ellos/ellas quisieran/quisiesen*

Exercises

Complete the following sentences using the subjunctive mood:

- *El público quería que (tú, cantar) .... una serenata*

- *Estaríamos más tranquilos si (nosotros, ganar) .... un buen sueldo*

- *No podías obligarlo a que te (él, amar) ....*

- *Esperaba que el perro no (él, romper) .... su juguete nuevo*

- *Mis abuelos querían que (nosotros, vivir) .... con ellos por un tiempo*

- *No importaba cuánto (yo, estudiar) .... mis padres nunca estarían satisfechos*

- *Mi esposa quería que nuestra hija (ella, ser) .... médica*

- *Mi mamá se aseguraba de que siempre (nosotros, estar) .... felices*

- *Si (yo, ser) .... el jefe, las cosas cambiarían*

- *No lograba que Juan (él, estar) .... tranquilo*

- *Quería una casa que (ella, tener) .... tres habitaciones*

- *Necesitaba a alguien que (él/ella, decir) .... la verdad*

- *Mis primos querían que (nosotros, ir) .... de visita*

- *Necesitaba un masajista que (él, hacer) .... milagros*

- *Cuando (vosotros, poder) .... nos juntaríamos a estudiar*

- *Cuando (tú, ver) .... dónde estaba el problema, podríamos solucionarlo*

- *Necesitábamos a alguien que nos (él/ella, dar) .... indicaciones*

– *No conocíamos a nadie que (él/ella, querer) .... viajar con nosotros*

– *Le dije a Jorge que (él, ir) .... a hacer las compras*

Chapter 3 - The imperative mood (el modo imperativo)

The Spanish imperative mood is used to give orders. There are no tenses in the imperative mood, but there is an affirmative and a negative form. It is not used with all pronouns, since you cannot give orders to yourself or to people who isn't there.

As you can see, for the *usted, nosotros* and *ustedes* forms, the imperative is formed using the forms of the present subjunctive, which we explained in the previous chapter.

Regular verbs

To love (am**ar**)

- *tú am**a** / vos am**á** / usted am**e***
- *nosotros am**emos***
- *ustedes am**en** / vosotros am**ad***

To fear (tem**er**)

- *tú tem**e** / vos tem**é** / usted tem**a***
- *nosotros tem**amos***
- *ustedes tem**an** / vosotros tem**ed***

To live (viv**ir**)

- *tú viv**e** / vos viv**í** / usted viv**a***
- *nosotros viv**amos***
- *ustedes viv**an** / vosotros viv**id***

Irregular verbs

To be (ser)

- *tú **sé** / vos **sé** / usted **sea***
- *nosotros **seamos***
- *ustedes **sean** / vosotros **sed***

To be (*estar*)

- *tú **está** / vos **está** / usted **esté***
- *que nosotros **estemos***
- *ustedes **estén** / vosotros **estad***

To have (*tener*)

- *tú **ten** / vos **tené** / usted **tenga***
- *nosotros tengamos*
- *ustedes **tengan** / vosotros **tened***

To say (*decir*)

- *tú **di** / vos **decí** / usted **diga***
- *nosotros **digamos***
- *ustedes **digan** / vosotros **decid***

To go (*ir*)

- *tú **ve** / vos **andá** / usted **vaya***
- *nosotros **vayamos***
- *ustedes **vayan** / vosotros **id***

To do (*hacer*)

- *tú **haz** / vos **hacé** / usted **haga***
- *nosotros **hagamos***
- *ustedes **hagan** / vosotros **haced***

To give (*dar*)

- *tú **da** / vos **da** / usted **dé***
- *nosotros **demos***
- *ustedes **den** / vosotros **dad***

Imperative + pronouns

It's very common that object pronouns are attached to the imperative verb.

Tell me what you want to do - *Dime qué quieres hacer*

Tell us more about your family - *Cuéntanos más sobre tu familia*

Buy him something to eat - *Cómprale algo para comer*

Sometimes you can even attach two pronouns, an indirect object and a direct object pronoun (always in that order).

Tell it to us - *Dínoslo*

Bring it to me - *Tráemelo*

Buy it for you - *Cómpratelo*

Negative commands

Orders not to do something are formed with the adverb "no" + present subjunctive, which is explained in the previous chapter.

Don't look at me - *No me mires*

Let's not buy more bread - *No compremos más pan*

Don't tell me what to do - *No me digas qué hacer*

Chapter 4 - Conditional (condicional)

Just as in English (with would and could), this tense is used for hypothetical situations and to make polite requests.

I would love to be a millionaire - *Me encantaría ser millonario*

Could I have a glass of water? - *¿Podría tomar un vaso de agua?*

Could I have your class notes? - *¿Me prestarías tus apuntes de la clase?*

I would kill for a good slice of pizza - *Mataría por una buena porción de pizza*

Regular verbs

To love (am**ar**)

- *yo am**aría***

- *tú am**arías** / vos am**arías** / usted am**aría***

- *él/ella am**aría***

- *nosotros am**arímos***

- *ustedes am**arían** / vosotros am**aríais***

- *ellos/ellas am**arían***

To fear (tem**er**)

- *yo tem**ería***

- *tú tem**erías** / vos tem**erías** / usted tem**ería***

- *él/ella tem**ería***

- *nosotros tem**eríamos***

- *ustedes tem**erían** / vosotros tem**eríais***

- *ellos/ellas tem**erían***

To live (viv**ir**)

- *yo viv**iría***

- *tú viv**irías** / vos viv**irías** / usted viv**iría***

- *él/ella viv**iría***

- *nosotros vivir**íamos***

- *ustedes viv**irían** / vosotros viv**iríais***

- *ellos/ellas viv**irían***

Irregular verbs

To be (*ser*)

- *yo sería*

- *tú **serías** / vos **serías** / usted **sería***

- *él/ella **sería***

- *nosotros **seríamos***

- *ustedes **serían** / vosotros **seríais***

- *ellos/ellas **serían***

To be (*estar*)

- *yo estaría*

- *tú estarías / vos estarías / usted estaría*

- *él/ella estaría*

- *nosotros **estaríamos***

- *ustedes **estarían** / vosotros **estaríais***

- *ellos/ellas **estarían***

To have (*tener*)

- *yo tendría*

- *tú tendrías / vos tendrías / usted tendría*

- *él/ella **tendría***

- *nosotros **tendríamos***

- *ustedes **tendrían** / vosotros **tendríais***

- *ellos/ellas **tendrían***

To say (*decir*)

- *yo diría*
- *tú dirías / vos dirías / usted diría*
- *él/ella **diría***
- *nosotros **diríamos***
- *ustedes **dirían** / vosotros **diríais***
- *ellos/ellas **dirían***

To go (*ir*)

- *yo **iría***
- *tú **irías** / vos **irías** / usted **iría***
- *él/ella **iría***
- *nosotros iríamos*
- *ustedes **irían** / vosotros **iríais***
- *ellos/ellas **irían***

To do (*hacer*)

- *yo haría*
- *tú **harías** / vos **harías** / usted **haría***
- *él/ella **haría***
- *nosotros **haríamos***
- *ustedes **harían** / vosotros **haríais***
- *ellos/ellas **harían***

Can (*poder*)

- *yo podría*
- *tú podrías / vos podrías / usted podría*
- *él/ella **podría***

- *nosotros podríamos*

- *ustedes **podrían** / vosotros **podríais***

- *ellos/ellas **podrían***

To see (*ver*)

- *yo vería*

- *tú verías / vos verías / usted vería*

- *él/ella **vería***

- *nosotros **veríamos***

- *ustedes **verían** / vosotros **veríais***

- *ellos/ellas **verían***

To give (*dar*)

- *yo daría*

- *tú darías / vos darías / usted daría*

- *él/ella **daría***

- *nosotros **daríamos***

- *ustedes **darían** / vosotros **daríais***

- *ellos/ellas **darían***

To want (*querer*)

- *yo querría*

- *tú querrías / vos querrías / usted querría*

- *él/ella **querría***

- *nosotros querríamos*

- *ustedes **querrían** / vosotros **querríais***

- *ellos/ellas **querrían***

Past subjunctive + conditional

Conditional sentences use the past subjunctive. Just as in English you use **if** to introduce this kind of sentences, in Spanish we use **si**, which is different from *sí* (yes), because it doesn't have a tilde.

If I **were** rich, I **would buy** you a mansion - *Si yo **fuera** rico, te **compraría** una mansión*

If they **had** any brains, they **would stay away** from that scam - *Si **tuvieran** cerebro, se **alejarían** de esa estafa*

If I **had** the time, I **could start** a new major - *Si **tuviera** tiempo, **podría comenzar** una nueva carrera*

Exercises

- *Si (yo, comer) .... bien, (yo, tener) .... más energía*

- *Si me (tú, decir) .... qué necesitas, (yo, poder) .... ayudarte*

- *Si (nosotros, tener) .... tiempo, (nosotros, ir) .... al cine esta noche*

- *Si me (usted, respetar) .... no me (usted, hablar) .... en ese tono*

- *Si me (tú, amar) .... me (tú, cuidar) ....*

Chapter 5 - Basic Conversation

I'd be doing you a major disservice if I didn't teach you the very basics of Spanish conversation. The reason I've held off to this point is because a lot of language courses will start off by giving you the basic phrases of a language. That's great for letting you say hello and goodbye to people, but when it comes to building statements with any sort of actual meat to them, it's an uphill battle because you don't actually know anything about the language yet.

For example, before you even picked up this book, you most likely at least knew the word **hola** from having heard it in any number of North American sources involving Spanish speakers. But how much does that matter for having genuine discussion with Spanish speakers? Does that knowledge of **hola** allow you in any capacity to walk up to a Spanish stranger and do anything but say "hello" to them?

The answer, of course, is no. That's an utterly ridiculous notion in most every possible conceivable way. That is thus the very reason that I've held off going over all of this up until now: it simply wasn't necessary and would get in the way of actually understanding Spanish in any sort of meaningful manner.

But now that you understand the pronunciation and many basic words, I feel as though we're at a reasonable point where I can give you introductions to conversation without making myself feel like I'm making the language seem like it's anything but what it is: a language, with a thriving set of verb conjugations and unique articles and all of these awesome features that extend far, far beyond "*holá*".

Anyhow, for the sake of this chapter, we're going to work through a number of phrases one at a time with a brief explanation of everything that we're doing.

The first thing that you do in any given conversation is initiate it. Well, this isn't necessarily always true - some people are very pragmatic and get right to the point. But for most people, saying salutations is just a normal part of any given conversation, or perhaps things which aren't even really conversation. Perhaps you're passing by somebody you know in the school or workplace and want to acknowledge them. That's another situation in which you'd find knowing salutations to be a great advantage.

Spanish has a great many greetings and the one that you use depends upon a number of variables, of course.

There's, of course, the general use **hola** (oh-la). This just means "hello" in English. The etymology of the word "**hola**" is deeply interesting, but it's of course beyond the scope of this book.

Anyhow, there are also the greetings which have to do with the time of day. There is **buenos días** (bwey-nohs di-ahs). This means literally "good morning" and is one of the more common Spanish greetings aside from **hola.** There also is **buenas tardes** (bwey-nahs tar-dehs), which means good evening. This isn't used as often as a conventional salutation, though it certainly can be used as one with no problem. The last one in this category is **buenas noches** (bwey-nahs no-chess). This means literally "good night" and its usage is unwavering; you will almost never ever use this as a salutation. You generally will only use this as a goodbye to somebody for the night is you know that you won't be seeing them again that night.

Lastly, there is **muy buenos**. (muy bwey-nohs). This is a very general greeting as compared to other ones such as **buenos días** and **hola**. You can use this greeting at pretty much any time of day without anybody batting an eye.

So after all of that, we're now officially in the conversation, engaging in the nigh professional art of small talk. These small talk sessions generally almost always start by asking somebody how they are or how they're doing. There are a ton of ways to ask this sort of question in Spanish.

Firstly, there are the more formal and boring routes to be taken. To simply ask "How are you?", you first need to think about who you're talking to. Are you speaking to somebody your age? Younger? Older? Have you meet them before? Then you need to pick either the informal or the formal way to ask based upon your evaluations. The informal way to ask is to simply *"¿Cómo estas?"* (co-moh es-tahs), meaning in a literal sense "how are you?". The formal way is just the usted inversion of the prior question: *¿Cómo está usted?* (co-moh es-ta oos-ted). This means the same thing as before, but this version is of course to be reserved for meeting new people or for talking to people who are in a position of superiority.

On top of that, there are more casual ways to ask. You could say "how's it going?": *¿Cómo te va?* (co-moh teh va)

Simply asking "what's up?" is certainly not out of the question: *¿Qué tal?* (kay tall)

Neither would be asking something along the lines of "what's happening?"- *¿Qué pasa?* (kay pah-sah) - or "How have you been?": *¿Cómo has ido?* (co-moh ahs ee-do)

All in all, there are a ton of ways to ask somebody exactly how they're doing in Spanish. There are likewise a huge number of ways in which you could respond to this very question. Note that being in a foreign country or situation means that the culture is inevitably different; in America and England, when we ask "how are you?", we do so as a courtesy and generally not in the seeking of a very well-thought out response or any sort of genuine emotional discourse. Certain other countries aren't like this, and if you ask how they are, they'll tell you how they are.

But for all intents and purposes, you may or may not give a very deep response. Should you choose to go with a more "standard" response, there are a number of different ways in which you could phrase it.

You could start with the quintessential *bien, gracias* (byen, grah-see-as) which means simply "well/fine, thank you." You could also opt for "very well" by saying *muy bien* (moy byen). You could insert a certain amount of nihilistic apathy into your conversation by saying *Como siempre* which technically means "like always" but carries the weight more like "I am as I always seem to be." If you're not feeling well, you can say that you're sick by saying either *estoy enfermo* or *estoy enferma* depending upon your gender, men saying the first and women saying the second. And if you're not doing too well, you could say *más o menos* (moss oh men-ohs) meaning "so-so", or you could say *mal* which translates to simply "badly" or "poorly".

Then, there are multiple different ways in which you could say goodbye. There are a few generally used ones, and a few which are geared towards more special purposes.

The two general purpose ones that you need to know are *adiós* and *chao*. Both are common enough that I'm not going to tell you how to pronounce them. If you're on the up, you very well may notice a parallel between Spanish and neighboring Romance language Italian here, where ciao is used as a form of goodbye. Both of these are acceptable ways to say goodbye.

If you'll be seeing the person soon, you could tell them *Hasta pronto* (ahs-tah pronto). But when I say soon, I mean *soon*. This is one place where the common conception of "soon" as used in the U.S. or Britain generally doesn't cut it in other timetables.

If you're just going to see them at a later point in time, you could say *Hasta luego* (ahs-tah lwey-go). This could imply a lack of certainty about when you'll meet again, however. It, as many things do, ultimately depends upon the context in which it's used.

The last one we're going to talk about here is *Hasta la vista* (ahs-tah lah vees-tah, but honestly, who doesn't know how to pronounce this one thanks to Hollywood?). This phrase means essentially "Until next time" or "untill we meet again". This one too can communicate a lack of certainty dependent upon the context.

On top of all of that, there are some essential phrases that you have absolutely got to know in order to ask for help in Spanish, or otherwise get around.

Firstly, there are two forms of "excuse me" you need to know. The first, **perdón**, means "excuse me" in the sense of "excuse me, could I ask you about something?"

The other form of excuse me, **con permiso**, has a meaning more along the lines of "Please excuse me", when you're needing somebody to move out of your way.

You also need to know how to say thank you and sorry. In fact, more people need to know how to do this in their native language. The way that you say "thank you" in Spanish is straightforward: **Gracias**. Nearly everybody knows that term. And the way you say sorry is additionally simple: **Lo siento** (lo syen-toh).

It's most certainly also worth you learning how to say please in Spanish because you invariably are going to need to at some point. You do so by saying **por favor**. (pour fah-vor)

And lastly, at some point, eventually you're going to have to ask for help in some way, shape, or form. The way to do this is by saying **necesito ayuda** (ney-cess-ee-toh ah-you-dah). This means literally "I need help" or "I need aid". You'll also notice that this very simple phrase is built off of the verb **necesitar**, conjugated for the first person.

There's a lot of things you'll need to learn before you're ready for the streets, but hopefully now, you've got a solid enough foundation you can at least be courteous.

Chapter 6 - Asking Questions

It is not just about knowing how to answer questions, knowing how to ask questions is just as equally important or understanding them at the very least. In this chapter, you will get to know basic question words to help you clarify matters and or point things out. Before that, let us get to know the Spanish word **hay**.

USES of HAY

This word comes from **haber**, meaning "to have." We use it to say "there is" or "there are." This means **hay** is in the present tense and may be used to refer to one or more things. **Habia** is the past tense form, meaning "there was" or "there were" but we will save that for later.

Hay un gato fuera.	~ There is a cat outside.
Hay unos gatos fuera.	~ There are cats outside.

Based on these examples, you can conclude that **hay** is used for making general or passive observations. While it is correct to say, "There are books on the table," it is not proper to use hay to say, "there they are (the books)" or "there are the books, right there on the table." Otherwise, you are already referring to something specific and **hay** is only reserved for unspecific things. It is also good to point out that **hay** is only used for indefinite articles, never for definite articles. However, hay does not necessarily require them.

We can also use hay for asking questions. When you intend to ask a question, hay could mean "is there" or "are there."

¿Hay un gato fuera?	~ Is there a cat outside?
¿Hay gatos fuera?	~ Are there cats outside?
¿Hay un perro ladrando?	~ Is there a dog barking?
¿Hay perros ladrando?	~ Are there dogs barking?

The Interrogatives

There are 8 basic interrogative question words and they are the following:

¿quién?	~ Who?
¿qué?	~ What?
¿cuándo?	~ When?
¿dónde?	~ Where?
¿por qué?	~ Why?
¿cómo?	~ How?
¿cuánto?	~ How much/ how many?

¿cuál? ~ Which?

There are specific rules for using each of them. For now, let us stick with rules that apply to them in general. One, please remember that when using these question words, the subject must go after the verb. As for pronunciation, the accents in these interrogatives do not affect the way the words are pronounced. Rather, they indicate the syllable that needs to be emphasized.

You may have also noticed the inverted question mark before the word. This is important in written Spanish just as an inverted exclamation point is required for writing sentences.

¿Quién? (WHO)

Obviously, this is the interrogative to use to find out someone's identity. *¿Quién?* is used to refer to singular subjects. Add -es in the end and you have its plural form, *¿Quiénes?* which always goes with the verb **SER**. Please refer to the examples below and the conjugation for the irregular verb **SER** for your reference.

Irregular Verb SER Conjugation

Subject	SER	
Yo	Soy	I am
Tu	Eres	You are (informal)
El Ella Usted	Es	He is She is You are (formal)
Nosotros Nosotras	Somos	We are (masculine) We are (feminine)
Vosotros Vosotras	Sois	You all (M, informal) You all (F, informal)
Ellos Ellas Ustedes	Son	They are They are You all are (formal)

¿Quién es? ~ Who is it?

¿Quiénes son esas personas? ~ Who are these people?

There are variations to this interrogative. Pay attention to the following.

¿A quién? or ¿A quiénes? ("to whom" or "for whom")

Use **¿A quién?** when the indirect object is singular and **¿A quiénes?** if it is plural.

¿A quién le pertenece esta bolsa?

~ To whom does this bag belong to? / Who does this bag belong to?

¿Para quienes son estas flores?

~ For whom are these flowers? / Who are these flowers for?

¿Con quién? or ¿Con quiénes? **("with whom")**

Use this variation when there are two or more people implied in the conversation.

¿Con quién te vas?

~ With whom are you going? / With who you go?

¿Con quiénes bailando Jorge?

~ With whom is Jorge dancing? / Who is Jorge dancing with?

¿De quién? or ¿De quiénes? **("whose")**

| *¿De quién es esta bolsa?* | ~ Whose bag is this? |
| *¿De quiénes son estos libros?* | ~ Whose books are these? |

¿Qué? (WHAT)

Use this interrogative if you want to seek an explanation or definition. It remains unchanged whether it is used to refer to a singular or plural subject. There is only one variation, *¿De qué?* which means "of what" or "about what."

¿Qué libro es su favorito?	~ What book is your favorite?
¿Qué vas a hacer mañana?	~ What are you doing tomorrow?
¿De qué es el libro?	~ What is the book about?
¿De qué material está hecha la bolsa?	~ What material is the bad made of?

¿Cuándo? (WHEN)

This form is applicable for both singular and plural subjects.

| *¿Cuándo es tu cumpleaños?* | ~ When is your birthday? |
| *¿Cuándo estás tomando un viaje?* | ~ When are you taking a trip? |

¿Dónde? (WHERE)

This interrogative is used for determining the location of an object. It applies for both singular and plural objects. *¿De dónde?* ("from where") is used for identifying a noun's origin. *¿Adónde?* on the other hand, means "to where" for identifying a destination. *¿Adónde?* always goes with the verb *IR*, meaning "to go."

Examples are provided below along with reference to the conjugation of the irregular verb *IR*.

Irregular Verb IR Conjugation

Subject	IR	
Yo	*Voy*	I go
Tu	*Vas*	You go (informal)
El	*Va*	He goes

Ella		She goes
Usted		You go (formal)
Nosotros	Vamos	We go (masculine)
Nosotras		We go (feminine)
Vosotros	Váis	You all go (M, informal)
Vosotras		You all go (F, informal)
Ellos		They go
Ellas	Van	They go
Ustedes		You all go (formal)

¿Donde está el gato? ~ Where is the cat?

¿Dónde están los perros? ~ Where are the dogs?

¿De dónde es María? ~ Where is Maria from?

¿De dónde eres? ~ Where are you from?

¿Adónde va este autobús? ~ Where does this bus go to?

¿Adónde están los chicos que van a este fin de semana? ~ Where are the boys going to this weekend?

¿Por qué? (WHY/FOR WHAT REASON)

Do not confuse this interrogative with **porque** which means "because." While **¿Por qué?** is meant to identify a reason, **¿Para qué?** is the interrogative to use if you want to find out a purpose. **¿Para qué?** means "for what purpose."

¿Por qué estudia María? ~ For what reason/ why does Maria study?

Porque María quiere aprender. ~ Because Maria wants to learn.

¿Para qué estudia María? ~ For what purpose/ why does Maria study?

Para obtener una alta puntuación en el examen ~ In order to get a high score in the exam

¿Cómo? (HOW)

This interrogative can be used for both singular and plural subjects. **¿Cómo?** can also be used to clarify something. In this case, it can mean "Can you say it again?" or "Can you repeat that?"

¿Cómo está usted? ~ How are you?

¿Cómo es esto posible? ~ How is this possible?

¿Cómo se explica eso en español? ~ How do you explain it in Spanish?

¿Cuánto? (HOW MUCH/ HOW MANY)

There are four forms for this interrogative. And they are the following.

¿Cuánto?   For masculine singular nouns

¿Cuántos?   For masculine plural nouns

¿Cuánta?   For feminine singular nouns

¿Cuántas?   For feminine plural nouns

¿Cuánto cuesta esta camisa?   ~ How much for this shirt?

¿Cuántos perros tines en casa?   ~ How many dogs do you have at home?

¿Cuántas casas tienen?   ~ How many houses do they have?

¿Cuántos coches tienes que conducir?   ~ How many cars does he drive?

¿Cuál? (WHICH)

This interrogative is used to ask for a choice given different possibilities or from a selection. **¿Cuál?** is the singular form. **¿Cuáles?** is the plural form. When this interrogative is combined with the verb SER in a sentence, it can also mean "what?"

¿Cuál de sus canciones te gusta más?   ~ Which of their songs do you like best?

¿Cuáles son los libros que me recomiendas?   ~ Which books do you recommend?

That concludes this chapter but before continuing with the next lesson, let us have a quick review of the lessons we have covered.

	Masculine		Feminine	
	Singular	Plural	Singular	Plural
There is/ are	*Hay*			
There was/ were	*Habia*			
Is/ Are there?	*¿Hay?*			
Who?	*¿Quién? + SER*		*¿Quiénes? + SER*	
To/ For whom?	*¿A quién?*		*¿A quiénes?*	
With whom?	*¿Con quién?*		*¿Con quiénes?*	
Whose?	*¿De quién?*		*¿De quiénes?*	
What?	*¿Qué?*			
Of/ About what?	*¿De qué?*			
When?	*¿Cuándo?*			
Where?	*¿Dónde?*			
From where?	*¿De dónde?*			
Wherc to?	*¿Adónde? + IR*			
For what reason/ why?	*¿Por qué?*			
Because	*Porque*			
For what purpose?	*¿Para qué?*			
How?	*¿Cómo?*			
How much?/ How many?	*¿Cuánto?*	*¿Cuántos?*	*¿Cuánta?*	*¿Cuántas?*
Which?	*¿Cuál?*		*¿Cuáles?*	

Chapter 7 - The Spanish Syntax

Spanish Syntax – General Word Order

How are sentences formed in Spanish? Are they the same as in English? Well, almost, but with a few distinct differences. Spanish syntax is quite similar to English syntax regarding placement of words and intonation, but there are differences. In this lesson, you will learn the basic rules for Spanish syntax and word order, and start to see the main differences between English and Spanish sentences. As is the case with most of the lessons, the more Spanish you learn, the better you will understand the nuances of Spanish syntax.

In general, you will be understood when speaking Spanish if you follow an English word order pattern with your sentences. For example, John runs would be Juan corre. Another example would be: I want to buy an apple, which in Spanish is the same order: *Yo quiero comprar una manzana.*

One notable difference in Spanish syntax is the omission of the subject, especially when the verb form indicates who the subject is. Therefore, the last sentence would more commonly be heard: *Quiero comprar una manzana.* The verb quiero can only be used with the subject yo. In the first sentence, the verb corre can be used with a few different subjects, but Juan would be omitted if the speaker and listener already knew that the sentence would be about Juan. Because of this difference, native English speakers tend to over-use the subjects when speaking Spanish, but there is no lack of communication. One must remember this fact, however, when listening and reading to be aware of who the subject is.

Another difference to take into account from the beginning is related to the use of adjectives in Spanish sentences. Typically, an adjective in a Spanish phrase comes after the noun it describes. This is the opposite of English. Let's look at a few examples: the blue sky would be *el cielo azul*, and The tall boy runs would be *El chico alto corre.*

Although you will probably be understood using English syntax, the goal is to sound more sophisticated and as close to native as possible. We want to Learn Spanish Better!

There are many, many more differences between English and Spanish syntax. As you move ahead in the study of other grammatical concepts, you will learn about these differences.

The Evolution of Spanish Syntax

The evolution of spoken Latin into proto-Romance was characterized from early on by simplification of inflectional paradigms for nouns, adjectives and verbs, and emergence or broader use of periphrastic constructions which fulfilled some of the same grammatical functions. The nominal case paradigms were reduced to a Nominative/Accusative distinction, and prepositions emerged as markers of other cases. Definite and indefinite articles evolved (from Latin demonstrative ille "that" and the cardinal unum "one," respectively). Periphrastic comparative forms of adjectives replaced synthetic forms. In the verbal paradigms, simplification of Classical inflections included the loss of the future tense, of synthetic passives, and diverse non-finite forms. Many of these changes were incipient or well underway in spoken Latin, and some were accelerated as a result of phonological changes such as the loss of many word-final consonants and loss of distinctive vowel quantity. The most stable inflectional features were person, number and masculine/feminine gender markers, and the inflection for verbs.

The "break-up" of proto-Romance into the early differentiated Romance languages is generally dated from the point at which written Latin was no longer comprehensible to the Romance speaker, roughly between the fifth and ninth centuries.13 Characteristics of early Spanish are deduced from documents dating from the eleventh century. Grammatical changes during this period continued those trends described above: inflectional simplification and grammaticalization of functional and quasi-functional morphemes; in many instances, these changes were common across languages. For example, nouns lost their Nominative/Accusative distinction. In western varieties of Romance, accusative plural -s was reanalyzed as a plural marker. Object pronouns were de-stressed and became clitics. Verbal auxiliaries evolved in passives, compound perfect, future, and conditional tenses. The clitic se (Latin 3rd.sg. /pl. Refl.) was grammaticalized, first as a detransitive (anti-causative) morpheme, then as a marker of middles, and (in Spanish) as a marker of passive voice (Hanssen 1945:230–231).

One syntactic innovation from this period is the emergence in Spanish of the "personal a," a marker of specific, human direct objects. Personal a occurred most consistently at first with proper names and pronouns, less consistently with common nouns (Lapesa 1981:213). Torrego (1998:42; citing Lapesa 1968) mentions an additional factor which governed the distribution of personal an around the thirteenth and fourteenth centuries. A appeared with the complements of verbs that denote an action that affects an individual physically or psychologically. Only later did it occur with non-affected animate direct objects.

The constituent order of Old Spanish differs from that of Modern Spanish in several respects. In Old Spanish, only phrases headed by closed class items (such as articles, complementizers, and prepositions) were head-initial.

Lexical, or "open class," heads of phrases (nouns, adjectives, and verbs) allowed both complement–head and head–complement order. The basic order of the verb and its objects is analyzed as having switched from OV to VO order (Otero 1975; Saltarelli 1994). It is interesting to note that auxiliary–main verb complexes gradually evolved from verb–auxiliary to auxiliary–verb (Rivero 1993; Lapesa 1981:217; Hanssen 1945:249, 251). The constituents of clauses also patterned differently in Old Spanish. Fontana (1993) argues that Old Spanish is a V2 (verb second) language, not of the German type (which exhibits second-position verbs in main clauses only), but of the Icelandic type: with verbs occupying the second position in subordinate clauses also. Fontana terms this "symmetric V2."

Another difference between Old Spanish and Modern Spanish concerns the behavior and the placement of pronominal clitics. Modern Spanish clitics attach only to verbs, and either precede or follow the verb according to whether the verb is finite or non-finite. Old Spanish pronominal clitics occupied the second position in the clause and were phonologically dependent on the preceding constituent – whether that constituent was a verb or not. This is shown by the fact that they could not occur clause-initially following a pause.14

In this respect, the pronominal clitics behaved like other atomic elements, including non "not," conjunctions and some auxiliaries. Auxiliaries mostly lost this restriction during the period of Old Spanish

Old Spanish displayed auxiliary switch, similar to that of Modern French and Italian (Vincent 1982). Auxiliary ser "to be" alternated with aver "to have" in the compound perfect tenses. In these tenses, ser was generally used with unaccusatives and "reflexive" (anticausative) intransitive, and aver with transitions. The compound perfect tense also displayed past participle agreement with the object. However, both auxiliary switch and past participle agreement were inconsistent.

Spanish Sentence Structure

One aspect of syntax is the order in which words appear in a sentence. Spanish word order is fairly flexible; however, it is best to use the more common patterns of putting words together to form sentences, as given below. These patterns, for the most part, are simply illustrations of a few generalizations:

Normal word order in a Spanish declarative sentence: [declarative— referring to a statement, as opposed to a question]

SUBJECT ("doer") + PREDICATE ("action") + OBJECT ("recipient")

The subject comes first, if expressed; often it is incorporated into or at least suggested by the verb ending.

The predicate is the next primary element. This is composed of at least one verb, often accompanied by object pronouns and by a negative or other adverbial expressions.

Complements follow the verb; these include predicate nouns (after ser), or direct and indirect object nouns or noun phrases.

subject neg. verb direct object

Juan nunca levanta la mano.

As regards direct and indirect object pronouns: They are normally attached to the end of:

    1) affirmative commands:

¡Dámelo! - Give it to me!

    2) infinitives:

después de bañarme... - after taking a bath...

    3) gerunds (-ndo forms):

levantándose... - getting up...

They normally precede conjugated verb forms. If the verb is a combination of a conjugated form and an infinitive or gerund, the object pronouns may be placed in either the pre- or post-position.

¡No me lo des! [negative command]

Lo hacemos a menudo. [conjugated verb]

Estoy diciéndotelo. OR [conjugated verb plus an -ndo form]

Te lo estoy diciendo.

Voy a hablarles. OR [conjugated verb plus an infinitive]

Les voy a hablar.

Indirect object pronouns precede direct object pronouns.

Te lo envié ayer.

I sent it to you yesterday.

Normally in a Spanish interrogative sentence the order of the subject and verb is reversed: [interrogative— referring to a question, as opposed to a statement]

Usted habla italiano.

You speak Italian. [declarative]

¿Habla usted italiano?

Do you speak Italian? [interrogative]

When an interrogative word or expression (e.g., *cómo, cuándo, dónde, adónde, por qué, quién, cuál, cuánto*) appears in a question it normally occurs at the beginning:

¿Por qué hablan los colombianos tan rápido?

Why do Colombians speak so quickly?

¿Cuándo viene Margarita a verme?

When is Margarita coming to see me?

Specific patterns of word order

    –   Linking verb (e.g., *ser & estar*):

Declarative Sentences:

subject (neg.) linking verb predicate noun/predicate adj.

(Nosotros) (no) somos   estudiantes de español.

(Ella)   (no) está   cansada.

Interrogative Sentences:

(neg.)   verb   subject   predicate noun or adjective

¿(No) es   usted   el señor Montalbán?

¿(No) estás (tú)   lista?

    –   Intransitive verb (no direct object):

Declarative Sentences:

subject (neg.) intransitive verb (adverb)

(Yo)   (no)   hablo   (bien).

Interrogative sentences:

(neg.) intransitive verb subject (adverb)

¿(No) leen   (ustedes) (rápidamente)?

    –   Transitive verb, no object pronouns:

Declarative sentences:

subject (neg.) transitive verb direct object (adverb)

(Yo)   (no)   hablo   español   (bien).

Interrogative sentences (transitive verb, no object pronouns):

(neg.) transitive verb subject direct object

¿(No) traen   (ustedes) la cerveza?

–   Transitive verb, with object pronouns:

Declarative Sentences:

subject (neg.) (IO pronoun) (DO pronoun) verb (DO phrase) (IO phrase)

(Usted) (nunca) le   da un regalo (a Juan).

(Usted) se   lo   da   (a él).

Interrogative sentences:

(neg.) IO pronoun DO pronoun verb subject (DO phrase) (IO phrase)

¿(Nunca)   le   da (usted) un regalo (a Juan)?

¿Se   lo   dan (ustedes)   (a él)?

–   Interrogative Sentences:

In general, in interrogative sentences —questions— the order of subject and verb reversed (compared to their order in a declarative sentence).

Yes/no questions (that is, questions which expect the reply "yes" or "no") have already been given in the previous sections.

linking verb subject predicate noun or adjective

¿Es   usted   protestante?

¿Estamos   (nosotros) listos?

Information questions expect some information to be given in the answer, not a simple "yes" or "no". Ordinarily these sentences begin with an interrogative expression such as *cómo* (how), *cuándo* (when), *dónde,* (where) *adónde* (where to), *por qué* (why), *quién* (who), *cuál* (which), or *cuánto* (how much, how many).

¿Por qué hablan los colombianos tan rápido?

Why do Colombians speak so quickly?

¿Cuándo viene Margarita a verme?

When is Margarita coming to see me?

interrogative (neg) verb subject object

¿Quién   (nunca) trae   la cerveza?

¿Qué   quiere ella?

¿Por qué   dicen ellos   eso?

– Commands:

In commands the verb usually comes first, followed by the subject (if expressed). If the subject is tú or vosotros, it is included only for contrast or emphasis. Usted and ustedes are frequently included for reasons of courtesy and clarity.

Yo me siento aquí. Siéntate tú allí. [contrast]

Venga usted mañana a las siete.

Object pronouns are attached to the end of affirmative commands, and precede the verb in negative ones.

¡No me lo digas! [negative]

¡Dímelo! [affirmative]

Special case #1: Verbs like *gustar*.

In standard declarative word order, subjects come before the verb and indirect object phrases are placed after it. The order of these two elements is normally switched with the verb gustar (to please, used —with subject and indirect object switched— in the sense of "to like"). Similar verbs include:

importar - to matter, be important

parecer - to seem, appear

encantar - to enchant, delight, to like very much

interesar - to interest, to be interested

resultar - to result, turn out

faltar   - to be lacking, to lack

hacer falta - to be necessary, to need

molestar - to bother, irritate, to be irritated

(des) agradar - to please/displease, to like/not like

doler   - to hurt, ache

quedar   - to remain, to have left

– ind. object phrase

ind. Object pronoun verb   subject

A mí   me   gustan las manzanas. = I like apples.

A ellas les encanta el regalo = They love the gift.

Nos falta la paciencia = We lack (the) patience.

241

Special case #2: Direct object preceding the verb

Sometimes for emphasis or special effect the direct object noun or noun phrase is given before the governing verb. When this happens, a direct object pronoun is used with the verb, and the subject, if expressed, is often placed after the verb. In other words, the order of the subject and direct object is switched, and a direct object pronoun is added, one which agrees in gender and number with the direct object.

Carlos compró mis libros. [normal word order]

Mis libros los compró Carlos. [preceding direct object]

(Both sentences mean: Carlos bought my books.)

Learn Spanish Verbs - What Are the Best Ways?

Learning Spanish verb forms is a vital part of learning Spanish as pretty much everything you will say will have a verb in it, and using the correct conjugation or form will make you understood a lot easier.

Spanish verb forms are, on the whole quite regimented and easy to learn. There are three verb types you need to know; regular, irregular and reflexive verbs; and each verb, irrespective of verb type, will have one of these three endings; -ar, -er and -ir.

All Spanish verb forms WITHOUT exception will belong to one of either -ar, -er or -in groups, but it is with the regular verbs we will start.

Regular Spanish Verbs Forms:

The regular group of verbs is by far the biggest of the three groups of verb types with the verbs that end with -ar the largest. All regular verbs follow the same pattern as laid out by the grammatical rules governing regular Spanish verbs, and they are;

When the stem of the verb is referred to it generally means, especially with regular verbs, the verb minus it's ending, for example, the stem of *hablar* (to speak) would be *habl-*.

(we will use the regular -*ar* verb *hablar* for this example)

In this example of the present tense conjugation of *hablar*, a regular -*ar* verb; you can see that the stem is used with every pronoun, but the endings are different; this makes Spanish, what is lovingly called, a prodrop language; which means that in most cases the pronoun can be dropped as the verb ending will be enough to show who is performing the task.

Obviously, there will be times of ambiguity, and when this is the case, the pronoun is usually used.

Yo habl-o I speak

Tú habl-as You speak.

Él/ Ella/ Usted habl-a He/ She/ It speaks (also you speak [singular polite] when Usted is used)

Nosotros habl-amos We speak

Vosotros habl-áis You speak

Ellos/ Ellas/ Ustedes habl-an They/ You speak ([plural polite] when Ustedes is used)

This example only shows the present tense for a regular -*ar* verb; but all the other tenses have their specific patterns of formation too, the main thing to remember is that all verbs that are designated regular will follow these patterns; the same can be said for *-er* and *-ir* verbs; although their endings differ from those of *-ar* verbs.

Irregular Spanish Verb Forms

Irregular Spanish verb forms are the scourge of the student, each verb has its own distinctive pattern, and because of this, it means that each Irregular verb has to be learned individually. Unfortunately, as is often the case in many languages, the most commonly used verbs are irregular. Now, this can be deemed, a good thing or a bad thing, bad because it means learning these irregular Spanish verb forms becomes an absolute necessity and a good thing because you will get a lot of practice using them.

You will need a good verb conjugation tool to help you remember and study Irregular Spanish Verbs and the best currently available is 2000+ Spanish Irregular Verbs, you can check out this book by using the link at the end of this article. You may have heard that there are only 25 irregular verbs in Spanish, this is somewhat misleading as there are well over 2000 irregular verbs that follow over 70 different patterns, so even in irregularity, there is some regularity!

Reflexive Spanish Verb Forms

Reflexive verbs are verbs that are used when the subject and the object are the same; I wash for example. They are often derived from an original verb, for example; *lavar* (to wash) is used when you are washing an object, but if you were washing yourself the reflexive verb, *lavarse* would be used.

As you can see when a verb is reflexive, it has the addition of -se onto the end of the original verb. And here is an example of how lavarse is used:

Yo me lavo I wash myself

Chapter 8 - How to Improve Reading Comprehension in Spanish?

Some people love to read, some people hate it. Some people enjoy the process, others dread it. It really doesn't matter which of these categories you fit into or if you're somewhere in the middle of the two, reading is an essential skill to have--especially when learning a foreign language.

Being able to read Spanish will help you in a variety of ways. If you're learning Spanish for work, you may need to be able to read e-mails, invoices, etc. If you are learning Spanish for pleasure/ travel, being able to read menus, signs, and various other things is always an advantage. Reading in Spanish will take those vocabulary words you've spent hours trying to learn and show you how they are used in context with other words in different situations and for different reasons.

Reading in Spanish can be enjoyable and engaging, if you approach it with the right attitude and use the right tools. Here are a few tips for how you can go about doing that.

How to Read in Spanish:

Reading is a great way to attain new vocabulary and see those troublesome verb conjugations and grammar patterns at work. The problem that many students encounter when reading a book in Spanish, however, is that they can sometimes feel overwhelmed by the immense amount of new things they come across.

While it is a good idea to take note of new words you learn, creating a ten-page long vocab list for one chapter of a book isn't the most productive way of spending your time and it makes for a choppy, less enjoyable reading experience.

If you find that you come across a new word, try following these steps before you go reaching for your dictionary:

1. If you come across a word or phrase you don't know, ask yourself:

2. Do I need the translation of this word to understand the context? Or, can I deduce the meaning through the context?

3. Isolate the sentence that contains that word or phrase. Try reading it a few times to see if you can grasp the general meaning of what is being said.

4. Put the sentence back into a larger context (the paragraph or a few sentences that come before and after the one you're working with) and see if that helps with comprehension.

5. If you still don't understand the word/phrase/sentence, go ahead and look up the word. Also, make a note of it in your notebook.

We will touch on this idea of "how to read in Spanish" a little more later on in this chapter.

Read with Translations

It can be extremely intimidating to open a book and looking at the page and seeing nothing but Spanish.

One way to keep from letting this experience overwhelm you too much is to read with translations. Of course this doesn't mean being dependent on said translations. Here's what I mean:

Bilingual Books

Bilingual books are a great option. These usually have the text written twice--once in Spanish and once in English. This means, for example, that on the left-hand pages, you have the text in Spanish and, on the right, you have the text in English.

This is a great tool to ensure comprehension, especially when you're starting out. If you come across a word or phrase that you don't understand, you can simply glance over at the English side and there it is. As you go through reading trying to use the steps listed above for comprehension purposes, if you find that you're still not understanding the text, you can simply read the translation.

Not only will you get the meaning of the word or phrase that was tripping you up, you'll also be able to see how it fits into the context around it.

Read Translated Books

Do you have a favorite book you just can't get enough of? Is there a story that you could read over and over again and never get tired of? Great! Now, read it in Spanish.

You will already know the characters and plot so chances are you won't get as confused or overwhelmed through the reading process. Comprehension won't be as difficult because, well, you already know what's going to happen.

Change Your Reading Materials

The great thing about reading in Spanish is that you have a wealth of resources right at your fingertips. Thanks to the Internet, there is no shortage of places you can go to find Spanish language texts.

This is where you can really pull from your interests. Find articles on topics that you enjoy reading or learning about. This is a great way to ensure that you don't lose your motivation and making reading in Spanish a habit will be much easier.

Here are some ideas to get you started:

- Newspapers: Read the Spanish Newspaper El Pais or the Mexican paper El Universal.

- Books: Find some great online versions of Spanish books at donquijote.com. If you're looking for something simpler, check out Readinga-z.com, which you have to pay for. Or, for free, you can check out readlang.com, you can find both audio and text versions of the books.

- Blogs: There are tons of great Spanish blogs out there; all you have to do is search for them. For example, there's one about travel, living in Spain, and running your own business. There's another about fashion, health, and beauty.

Take Notes as you Read

Taking notes while you read can be helpful in so many ways. Not only is writing one of the best ways to commit something to memory, but it can also help you keep track of your progress, take notice of things you need to work on, and make sure that you're improving your vocabulary, grammar, and overall comprehension.

You can take notes in a variety of ways. You can use sticky notes and jot down things as you go. You can highlight or underline in your book (Don't be afraid to write in books, either. Unless, of course, they're not your books). Or you can simply keep a notebook handy as you read and scribble a few things down there are you go.

Write Summaries of What You've Read

In addition to taking note of grammar structures, vocabulary, or expressions that you come across, you should also make it a point to sit down and write a short summary of what you've read after finishing a chapter of a book or a newspaper article or a section of whatever it is you're reading.

Doing this will force you to not only check your comprehension, but it will also give you the opportunity to take any new words or expressions you learned from the text and use them in your own way.

Take Note of New Grammar Constructions

As you go through the process of learning Spanish, you will find that certain conjugations or grammatical constructions may present a little bit of a problem for you. As you go through the process of reading, take note of the times and ways that those things are used. This will give you real-life, authentic examples of when and how to use them.

Build Your Vocabulary

Reading is, of course, a great way to pick up new vocabulary. And the benefit of this is that you'll be learning new words in a larger context, not just in a list format.

Learn the Vocabulary in Context

We talked a little at the start of this chapter about the process of deducing the meaning of the words through context and not using the dictionary unless you feel it's absolutely necessary for comprehension.

This doesn't mean, however, that you shouldn't keep track of the words or phrases you come across that might trip you up. Even if you are able to understand the word in context, you should take a moment to either underline it or write it down in your notebook. That way, you can go back and look it up later to make sure that you understood it correctly.

Read With Audio

One of the best ways to learn anything is by combining as many different learning styles as you can into one activity. Reading with audio will give you not only the visual side of learning, but the auditory as well.

If you can find an audio book or a recording of what you're reading, or even a listening activity with a transcript written out, play the audio while you read the text. This will help you hear the relationship between the words as well as read it. It will also help to hear how things are pronounced, where the accents fall, and how the sentences flow.

Read with Pictures

In a previous chapter, we talked about recognizing the fact that you're still "young" as far as your language ability goes. You will definitely want to keep this in mind as you go through the process of selecting books or reading materials for yourself.

This idea of "reading with pictures" doesn't have to mean children's picture books. Of course, if you decide to pick one up, there's no problem with that. Children's books have simplified vocabulary and grammar and, let's face it, they can be pretty fun to read from time to time. You can, however, find books more suited to adults that have illustrations or drawings scattered throughout the pages.

Reading with pictures will not only help the story to come alive, but it will also serve to check your comprehension. Do you understand what's happening in the illustration/pictures? Is that what you understood to be happening in the story?

Seeing picture associated with the new words you're learning will also help with memory association.

A few Things to Keep in Mind

Before we finish this chapter, let's just talk about a few other points that are very important for you to keep in mind:

- Read what you enjoy! You will probably need to read and reread sections of the materials a few times in order to comprehend the text completely. This is why it's important that you're sure that what you're reading is something you wouldn't mind reading time and time again.

- Try to maintain the flow of reading, as best you can. Yes, you will come across words you don't understand. And, yes, you will need to reread certain sections. But, if at all possible, try to resist the urge to reach for the translator or dictionary every single time this happens. Interrupting the reading process will not only make it harder for you to really grasp the text as a whole, but it will quickly become quite frustrating.

- When you do come across a word you need to look up or you don't understand right away, make a note of it. Then, when you have the chance to sit down and review it, write it out in a sentence--your own original sentence. Using the words for yourself will help to ensure that you remember them easier in the future.

- And, as always, make sure you're choosing materials that are suited to your level.

Chapter 9 - Food, Drinks & Clothes

Food (different type of food)

Well, it's time to rest and go to grab a snack, to have lunch or to enjoy a special dinner.

In Spain is typical to have two different dishes for lunch or dinner. In fact, we can find a lot of restaurants offering menus with a special price offering "primer plato" (meaning first dish or starter) and "segundo plato" (second dish or main). Food quantity can be the same for "primer plato" and "segundo plato". After these two dishes, we can choose a dessert or coffee or both! It's typical to drink coffee after main meals in Spain, but if you think you are drinking too much caffeine, you can always order "café descafeinado" (decaf).

So, let's learn food vocabulary to avoid disappointment with the dish we have chosen. It's also important to be able to communicate clearly if or some of our group suffer some kind of food allergy or is on a special diet.

Some key sentences to order food and drinks:

Tengo hambre	I'm hungry
Tengo sed	I'm thirsty
¿Puedo ver el menú, por favor?	May I see the menu, please?
¿Qué me recomienda?	What do you recommend?
Me gustaria...	I'd like...
¿Puede darme...?	May I have some...?
¿Podría darme más...?	Can I have some more...?
Eso es todo, gracias.	That's all, thank you.
¿Dónde está al baño?	Where is the toilette?
Camarero/Camarera	Waiter/Waitress
La cuenta, por favor	The bill, please
Tenemos una reserva	We have a reservation
Soy alérgico/alérgica	I'm allergic

Las comidas durante el día (meals during the day)

- *Desayuno* = breakfast

El desayuno se sirve de 8 a 10 de la mañana (Breakfast is served from 8 to 10 am)

- *Aperitivo* = snack, appetizer

Vamos a tomar un aperitivo antes de comer (Let's go for an appetizer before lunch)

- *Comida* = lunch

Comeremos en un restaurant al lado del puerto (We're going to have a lunch in a restaurant next to the port)

- *Merienda* = snack at tea time

Tengo hambre, ¿qué tal algo de merienda? (I'm hungry, what about a snack?) **Note**: "*merienda*" is after lunch and before dinner.

- *Cena* = dinner

He reservado mesa para la cena en el restaurant Apolo (I've booked a table for dinner at Apolo restaurant)

Now that we know the meals, let's start with the food.

Trying to make it as easy as possible, let's learn the new vocabulary classified into categories.

Note: consider that in Spanish there are different verbs to say you're going to eat depending of the meal of the day.

"**Desayunar**" means eat or have breakfast.

"**Comer**" means eat or have lunch.

"**Cenar**" means eat or have dinner.

Let's dive into the food vocabulary now!

Desayuno (Breakfast)

Huevo	Egg
Tocino	Bacon
Tostada	Toast
Pan	Bread
Jamón	Ham
Queso	Cheese
Judías	Beans
Mantequilla	Butter
Mermelada	Jam
Sirope	Syrup
Cereales	Cereals
Yogurt	Yogurt
Salchichas	Sausages
Miel	Honey
Fruta	Fruit
Carne	Meat

Carne (Meat)

Carne	Meat
Pollo	Chicken
Pavo	Turkey
Ternera	Beef
Cerdo	Pig
Hamburguesa	Hamburger
Salchichas	Sausages

Bistec	Steak
Pastel de carne	Meat pie

Example sentences:

Hoy vamos a comer pollo al horno (Today we are going to eat roasted chicken)

Estas salchichas son de pavo (These sausages are made from turkey)

¿Quieres la hamburguesa de ternera o de cerdo? (Do you want beef or pig hamburger?)

Hoy tenemos barbacoa. Vamos a comer salchichas y hamburguesas (Today we have a barbecue. We are going to eat sausages and hamburgers)

¿Como te gusta el bistec? (How would you like the steak?)

He horneado un pastel de carne. ¿Quieres un poco? (I have baked a meat pie. Do you want some?)

Pescado y marisco (Fish and seafood)

Almejas	Clams
Anchoas	Anchovies
Atún	Tuna
Bacalao	Cod
Calamares	Squid
Gambas	Shrimps
Cangrejo	Crab
Langosta	Lobster
Langostino	Crayfish
Lenguado	Sole
Mero	Bass
Ostras	Oysters
Pulpo	Octopus
Rape	Monkfish
Róbalo	Haddock
Salmón	Salmon
Sardinas	Sardines
Trucha	Trout

Example sentences:

En este restaurante sirven buen marisco (In this restaurant they serve good seafood)

¿Te gustan las almejas? (Do you like clams?)

No me gustan las anchoas, son demasiadas saladas para mí (I do not like anchovies. They are too salty for me)

Hoy he comido una ensalada de atún (I've had a tuna salad for lunch)

Me gusta el bacalao rebozado (I like battered cod)

En la paella de marisco hay calamares, gambas, almejas y mejillones (In the seafood paella there are squid, shrimps, clams and mussels)

De pequeño solía pescar cangrejos (I used to fish crabs when I was a kid)

La langosta suele ser muy cara (Lobster usually is very expensive)

No me gustan los langostinos, pero sí que me gustan las ostras (I do not like crayfish, but I like oysters)

Para mí, un lenguado con patatas, por favor (For me, a sole with potatoes, please)

Yo prefiero mero con ensalada, gracias (I prefer bass with salad, please)

¿Tiene pulpo a la gallega? (Do you have Galicia style octopus?)

Hoy tenemos rape y róbalo con guisantes y salsa (Today we are serving monkfish or haddock with peas and sauce)

Me gusta el sushi de salmón (I like salmon sushi)

En la costa brava puedes comer sardinas en una tostada (You can eat sardines in a toast in the Costa Brava)

En este río puedes pescar truchas (You can fish trout in this river)

Postres (Dessert)

Arroz con leche	Rice pudding
Flan	Custard
Galletas	Cookies
Helado	Ice cream
Pastel	Cake
Tarta	Pie
Fruta fresca	Fresh fruit

Example sentences:

¿Queréis algo de postre? (Do you want some dessert?)

Yo sí, quiero un arroz con leche (I do, I want a rice pudding)

Para mí un flan (A custard for me)

Yo estoy llena, pero me comeré un helado (I'm full but I'll eat ice cream)

¿Quieres un trozo de pastel de chocolate? (Do you want a piece of chocolate cake?)

Prefiero un trozo de tarta de limón (I prefer a piece of lemon pie)

Hoy de fruta fresca tenemos melón y manzana (Today for fresh fruit we have melon and apple)

Estilo de cocina (Cooking styles)

Al horno	Baked
A la barbacoa	Barbecue
Frito	Fried
A la parrilla	Grilled
En escabeche	Marinade
Hervido	Boiled

Crudo	Raw
Ahumado	Smoked
Estofado	Stew
Pollo al horno	Baked chicken
Bistec a la barbacoa	Barbecue steak
Pescado frito	Fried fish
Verduras a la parilla	Grilled vegetables
Atún en escabeche	Marinated tuna
Huevo duro	Boiled egg
Pescado crudo	Raw fish
Salmón ahumado	Smoked salmon
Carne estofada	Stewed meat

Pedir carne (Steak ordering)

Crudo	Raw
Poco hecho	Rare
En su punto	Medium
Bien hecho	Well done

Now, let's listen more sentences about food and meals:

Yo desayuno fruta y cereales (I eat for breakfast fruit and cereals).

El hotel sirve la comida de 12 a 3 de la tarde (The hotel serves lunch from 12 to 3 pm).

Quisiera pollo al horno (I'd like roast chicken).

Vamos a cenar paella (We're going to eat paella for dinner).

Me gustaría cenar un buen bistec (I would like to have a good steak for dinner).

¿Qué quieres comer? (What would you like for eating?)

¿Tiene la carta en inglés, por favor? (Can we have the menu in English, please?)

Soy alérgico al gluten (I have gluten allergy).

Tengo alergia a los cacahuetes (I have peanut allergy).

¿Queréis tomar postre? (Do you want something for dessert?)

¿Os apetece un café después de la comida? (Fancy a coffee after the meal?)

¿Has hecho la reserva? (Have you made the booking?)

Hemos quedado a las 8 para cenar (We're going to meet at 8 for dinner).

El restaurante del hotel sirve desayunos, comidas y cenas (Hotel's restaurant offers breakfast, lunch and dinner).

¿Cuál es tu comida favorita? (What is your favourite food?)

¿Hay algún restaurante abierto cerca? (Is any open restaurant nearby?)

Este es un restaurante mejicano (This is a Mexican restaurant).

No me gusta el pescado crudo (I do not like raw fish).

Me gusta la comida tailandesa (I like Thailand meals).

Prefiero la carne al punto (I prefer meat cooked medium).

A mí me gusta la carne muy hecha (I like my meat well done).

Now, imagine you are in a restaurant and try to answer in Spanish the following questions:

¿Qué quieres de primer plato? (What do you want for starter?)

¿Qué quieres de segundo plato? (What do you want for main?)

¿Quieres postre o café? (Do you want dessert or coffee?)

How many foods can you remember in Spanish? Let's try it!

Drinks (different type of Drinks)

Now we are experts in food, so let's learn about drinks!

Let's start with these useful sentences:

¿Qué vais a tomar?	What do you want for drink?
Para mí una coca cola, por favor	A coke for me, please
Para mí un vino tinto, por favor	A red wine for me, please
Yo quiero un café	I want a coffee
Quisiera un agua con gas	I'd like a sparkling water
¿Algo más?	Anything else?
No, gracias	No, thanks
La cuenta, por favor	The bill, please

Let's listen this short dialog in a bar:

Buenos días, ¿qué vais a tomar? (Good morning, what are you going to drink?)

Yo quiero un café solo, por favor (I want an espresso, please)

Y para mí un café con leche (A latte for me, please)

¿Algo más? (¿Anything else?)

No, gracias. Es todo. (No, thanks. That's all)

Once we know the sentences, let's learn vocabulary to understand and be able to order different drinks in Spanish.

Café con leche	Latte
Cappuccino	Cappuccino
Café solo	Ristretto / espresso
Cortado	Macchiato
Té	Tea
Leche	Milk
Zumo	Juice

Refresco	Soft drink
Agua	Water
Agua con gas	Sparkling water
Vino	Wine
Vino negro	Red wine
Vino rosado	Rosé wine
Vino blanco	White wine
Cerveza	Beer
Combinado	Mixed spirit
Ron	Rum
Ginebra	Gin
Vodka	Vodka
Cóctel	Cocktail
Sin alcohol	Alcohol free

Now listen the following short texts:

En esta cafetería sirven distintos tipos de café: café con leche, capuccino, café solo, cortado, pero, si lo prefieres, tienen también té. (In this coffee shop are serving different types of coffee: latte, cappuccino, ristretto, machiatto, but, if you prefer, they have also tea.

¿Quieres tomar algo? Yo quiero una ginebra con tónica, ¿y tú? Yo quiero un combinado de ron con coca cola. (Do you want something to drink? I want a gin tonic, and you? I want a rum and cola mixed)

¿Nos puedes traer una botella de vino tinto, por favor? (Can you bring a bottle of red wine, please?)

Now that we know how to order food and drinks, let's put everything together!

¿Buenas tardes, qué vais a tomar? (Good afternoon, do you want something to drink or eat?)

Yo quiero un zumo de naranja (I want an orange juice)

Para mí un té con leche (A tea with milk for me)

¿Queréis algo para comer? (Do you want something to eat?)

Una bolsa de patatas, por favor (A packet of chips, please)

¡Enseguida! (Right away!)

How many drinks can you remember in Spanish? Let's say it!

Meals (different type of meals)

As you have seen when we were talking about food, we saw different types of meals during the day.

Can you remember? Let's try to say what is...

Desayuno? Breakfast.

Comida? Lunch.

Cena? Dinner.

Aperitivo? Appetizer or snack.

Merienda? Food we eat between lunch and dinner.

Let's make a quick refresh of types of the meal depending on the time of the day:

- *Desayuno* = breakfast

El desayuno se sirve en el restaurante del primer piso (The breakfast is served at the first floor restaurant)

- *Aperitivo* = snack, appetizer

¿Os apetece tomar algo de aperitivo? (Fancy a snack?)

- *Comida* = lunch

La comida se sirve de 12 a 2 de la tarde (Lunch is served from 12 to 2pm)

- *Merienda* = snack around tea time

¿Por qué no hacemos una merienda con chocolate caliente y churros? (Why don't we eat hot chocolate and churros at tea time?). **Reminder**: "merienda" is after lunch and before dinner.

- *Cena* = dinner

Vamos a ir a cenar al restaurante del hotel. Me han dicho que la comida es estupenda (We're going to have dinner at the hotel's restaurant. They have told me the food is amazing)

But let's take a look now on different meals depending on the occasion:

Comida de negocios	Business lunch
Cena de negocios	Business dinner
Comida con amigos	Friends lunch
Cena con amigos	Friends dinner
Comida de Navidad	Christmas lunch
Cena de Navidad	Christmas dinner
Cena de despedida	Farewell dinner
Comida de despedida	farewell lunch
Cena de cumpleaños	Birthday dinner
Comida de cumpleaños	Birthday lunch

"*Un banquete*" is a banquet.

"*Una celebración*" is a celebration.

"*Un festín*" is a feast.

"*Una fiesta*" is a party.

¡Siempre hay una buena razón para una buena comida! (There's always a good reason for a good meal!)

More sentences:

Hoy tengo una comida de negocios (I have a business lunch today).

Mañana ceno con amigos (I'm having a friend's dinner tomorrow).

Este año la comida de navidad es en mi casa (This year Christmas lunch is at my house).

Laura se va de la empresa. La semana que viene es su comida de despedida (Laura is leaving the company. Next week we'll have the goodbye lunch).

Estoy preparando la cena de cumpleaños (I'm making the Birthday dinner).

Están preparando un gran banquete (They are preparing a big banquet)

¡Vamos a celebrar una fiesta! (Let's make a party!)

Clothing

Knowing vocabulary about clothes can be useful in some situations as shopping, packing or even if we must describe what someone was wearing.

Let's see the following list of clothes and related elements:

Cinturón	Belt
Blusa	Blouse
Botas	Boots
Botón	Button
Gorro	Cap
Abrigo	Coat
Algodón	Cotton
Franela	Flannel
Guantes	Gloves
Bata	Gown
Sombrero	Hat
Chaqueta	Jacket
Cuero	Leather
Chándal	Tracksuit
Corbata	Tie
Camisón	Nightdress
Pijama	Pyjamas
Bolsillo	Pocket
Impermeable	Raincoat
Bufanda	Scarf
Camisa	Shirt
Zapatos	Shoes
Bermudas	Shorts
Seda	Silk
Falda	Skirt
Zapatillas	Slippers
Calcetín	Socks
Traje	Suit
Gafas de sol	Sunglasses
Suéter	Sweater
Pantalón	Trousers
Esmoquin	Tuxedo

Ropa interior	Underwear
Chaleco	Vest
Lana	Wool
Cremallera	Zipper

Now let's put the new vocabulary in some sentences:

Necesito comprar un cinturón (I need to buy a belt)

Llevo una blusa de color rosa (I'm wearing a pink blouse)

Si vas a la montaña, mejor lleva las botas (If you're going to the mountain, better you wear boots)

He perdido un botón (I have lost a button)

Hace frio, coge un gorro (It's cold, take a hat)

He visto a Eva, llevaba un abrigo rojo (I have seen Eva, she was wearing a red coat)

Esta camiseta es de algodón y este jersey es de franela (This t-shirt is made of cotton and this sweater is made of flannel)

¿Has visto mis guantes marrones? (Have you seen my brown gloves?)

En el hospital hace frio, llévate una bata (It's going to be cold in the hospital, take a gown)

Hace mucho viento. Mi sombrero se ha ido volando (It's very windy. My hat has gone flying)

Me he encontrado una chaqueta de piel en el metro (I have found a leather jacket in the tube)

Tengo que comprar un chándal nuevo (I have to buy a new tracksuit)

No es obligatorio llevar corbata (Wearing tie is not mandatory)

¿Crees que le gustara este camisón? (Do you think she's going to like this nightdress?)

Quiero comprar un pijama de inverno (I want to buy a winter pyjama)

Pon las monedas en el bolsillo (Putt he coins in the pocket)

Llueve, coge el impermeable (It rains, take the raincoat)

María tiene una bufanda rallada (María has a striped scarf)

Tienes que llevar una camisa blanca (You must wear a white shirt)

¿Te gustan mis nuevos zapatos? (Do you like my new shoes?)

Juan tiene calor y lleva bermudas (Juan is hot and is wearing shorts)

No me gusta la seda (I do not like silk)

¿Tienes esta falda en una talla más grande? (Do you have this skirt in one size bigger?)

Quisiera estas zapatillas en el número cuarenta (I would like these slippers in a number seven)

Quiero unos calcetines negros de lana, por favor (I want a black wool socks, please)

Nunca llevo traje (I never wear suit)

He perdido las gafas de sol (I have lost my sunglasses)

Tengo un suéter amarill. (I have a yellow sweater)

¿Dónde has comprado estos pantalones? (Where have you bought these trousers?)

Está muy guapo con esmoquin (He looks very handsome wearing tuxedo)

Necesito comprar ropa interior (I need to buy underwear)

¿Quieres la chaqueta o el chaleco? (Do you want the vest or the jacket?)

Necesito cambiar la cremallera porque está rota (I need to change the zipper because is broken)

Now try to guess what clothes is:

Una camisa (shirt)

Un pantalón (trouser)

Una camiseta (t-shirt)

Unos zapatos (shoes)

Unos calcetines (socks)

¿Qué ropa llevas hoy tu? (What clothes are you wearing today?)

Chapter 10 - Question Formation

In the Spanish language, there are two main types of questions: open-ended questions and yes or no questions.

The expected answer is "yes" or "no" to a typical yes or no question, and this is probably a part of any language. Of course, the answer can be expanded beyond the simple "yes" or "no." Nevertheless, the end result is a short answer.

Yes-or-No Questions

In order to form a question of this nature, you can take a regular statement and flip the subject and verb from their regular positions. Consider this example:

- *Él viaja a Europa cada verano.* (He travels to Europe every summer)

This is a regular statement in the affirmative. Now, to change it into a yes/no question, we need to switch the subject and verb so that they can reflect the change in syntax. Here is the new word order used to reflect the question.

- *¿Viaja él a Europa cada verano?* (Does he travel to Europe every summer?)

First of all, notice how the subject "*él*" moves from the first spot to the second, and the verb from the second to the first. This change enables the formation of a yes/no question.

Now, the answer to this question can be constructed as follows:

- *¿Viaja él a Europa cada verano?* (Does he travel to Europe every summer?)

    - *Sí, él viaja.* (Yes, he travels.)

    - *No, él no viaja.* (No, he doesn't travel.)

Please notice that the negative form is constructed by the use of "*no*." So, you can see that there is no other auxiliary used in Spanish to make the negative form. All you need is to use "*no*" in order to transform the sentence from positive to negative.

The answers presented above are short answers. Of course, you can elaborate on these responses as much as you like. Nevertheless, you could reply something like:

- *Sí, él viaja a Europa cada verano.* (Yes, he travels to Europe every summer.)

- *No, él no viaja a Europa cada verano.* (No, he doesn't travel to Europe every summer.)

These longer-form answers can be used to make a point or simply elaborate further on the question being asked. It is not a requisite for you to express your answers in this manner, though it is an option that you have at your disposal.

Below are more examples of questions in Spanish.

- *Yo como frutas todos los días. – ¿Como yo frutas todos los días?*

    - I eat fruit every day. – Do I eat fruit every day?

259

- *Tú juegas fútbol cada viernes. – ¿Juegas tú fútbol cada viernes?*

    - You play soccer every Friday. – Do you play soccer every Friday?

- *Usted vende ropa en una tienda – ¿Vende usted ropa en una tienda?*

    - You sell clothes in a shop. – Do you sell clothes in a shop?

- *Él vive en Chicago. – ¿Vive él en Chicago?*

    - He lives in Chicago. – Does he live in Chicago?

- *Ella trabaja en una oficina – ¿Trabaja ella en una oficina?*

    - She works in an office. – Does she work in an office?

- *Nosotros bebemos refrescos en la cena. – ¿Bebemos nosotros refrescos en la cena?*

    - We drink soda at dinner. – Do we drink soda at dinner?

- *Ellos hacen ejercicio en el gimnasio. – ¿Hacen ellos ejercicio en el gimnasio?*

    - They do exercise at the gym. – Do they exercise at the gym?

- *Ellas cocinan pasteles los fines de semana. – ¿Cocinan ellas pasteles los fines de semana?*

    - They bake cakes on the weekend. – Do they bake cakes on the weekend?

- *Ustedes escuchan música en el coche. – ¿Escuchan ustedes música en el coche?*

    - You listen to music in the car. – Do you listen to music in the car?

One of the most interesting characteristics of Spanish is that you can omit the subject of the sentence only when it is clear what you are talking about or to whom you are referring. This comes in very handy when asking questions as it is very common for native Spanish speakers to drop the subject, especially when they are addressing you directly.

Let us have a look at the previous examples without the use of the subject in the sentence.

- *¿Trabajas en una oficina?* (Do you work in an office?)

    - *Sí, trabajo en una oficina.* (Yes, I work in an office.)

    - *No, no trabajo en una oficina.* (No, I don't work in an office.)

As you can see in this example, it is not needed to say, *"¿Trabajas tú en una oficina?"* It is enough to say, *"¿Trabajas en una oficina?"* since it is clear that the question is being addressed to "you" and not to anyone else.

Now, it should be noted that when you omit the subject of a sentence or question, it is important to be clear about whom you are referring to. Otherwise, this could lead to confusion and cause your interlocutor to seek clarification. So, it pays to be extra careful in order to avoid any potential confusion.

Open-Ended Questions

From yes/no questions, we can move on to open-ended questions. These types of questions allow for any type of response and not just a limited yes/no reply. As such, we need to use the set of questions words available.

Here are the questions words used in Spanish:

- *Qué* (what)

- *Quién* (who)

- *Cuál* (which)

- *Cuándo* (when)

- *Cuánto* (how much/many)

- *Cómo* (how)

- *Dónde* (where)

- *Por qué* (why)

Please note that question words have a tilde attached to them in order to differentiate them from the relative pronouns. For instance, "*cuando*" is not the same as "*cuándo*". While their spelling and pronunciation are identical, the tilde differentiates their function in writing.

Consider this example:

- *Compro pan y leche cuando voy al supermercado.* (I buy bread and milk when I go to the supermarket.)

In this example, we are using "*cuando*" as a relative pronoun since it is joining two separate parts of a sentence. Also, we omitted the use of "*yo*" since the sentence makes absolutely clear that I am referring to myself and no one else.

The use of "*cuándo*" in a question would work out like this:

- *¿Cuándo compras pan?* (When do you buy bread?)

In this case, we need to carry the tilde on "*cuándo*" so that it is absolutely clear that we are talking about a question. While the structure and the context don't really leave much room for doubt, it is, nevertheless, important to make the point to avoid potential confusion.

Let's look at some more sample questions:

- *¿Dónde es mi lugar?* (Where is my place?)

- *¿Cuándo vas a la escuela?* (When do you go to school?)

- *¿Cuántos años tiene?* (How old are you?)

- *¿Quién es él?* (Who is he?)

- *¿Qué bebe ella?* (What does she drink?)

- *¿Por qué viajamos?* (Why do we travel?)

- *¿Por qué trabajan ellos?* (Why do they work?)

- *¿Cuál es la casa de ellas?* (Which is their house?)

- *¿Cómo van al trabajo?* (How do you get to work?)

There could be any number of responses to these questions. That is why they are open-ended. As such, it is up to you to find the right information that you would like to get across. For example:

- *¿Cuándo vas a la escuela?* (When do you go to school?)

    - *Voy a la escuela todos los días.* (I go to school every day.)

    - *Voy a la escuela en las noches.* (I go to school at night.)

    - *Voy a la escuela los fines de semana.* (I go to school on weekends.)

    - *No voy a la escuela.* (I don't go to school.)

As you can see, the potential responses can vary according to the information you are looking to provide your interlocutors.

Let us examine some common questions that you will come across when speaking Spanish.

- *¿Cuál es tu nombre?* (What is your name?)

- *¿De dónde eres?* (Where are you from?)

- *¿Dónde vives?* (Where do you live?)

- *¿Cuántos años tienes?* (How old are you?)

- *¿Cuál es tu número de teléfono?* (What is your telephone number?)

- *¿Dónde trabajas?* (Where do you work?)

- *¿Cuál es tu correo electrónico?* (What is your email?)

- *¿Cuál es tu trabajo?* (What do you do?)

- *¿Dónde queda el banco?* (Where is the bank?)

- *¿Dónde está el baño?* (Where is the bathroom?)

These are the most common questions that you will encounter when you are speaking to other folks. As such, these questions can come through for you in a pinch. So, do take the time to go over them, and put them into practice as often as you need to.

On the whole, question formation is a matter of practice. The more practice you are able to get structuring questions, the better you will become at asking the right questions when you need to. Best of all, Spanish syntax is flexible enough to where you could mix up the word order and still get the message across.

Consequently, you can make the most of your opportunity to travel without having to hesitate about getting directions or interacting with other folks. As you gain more proficiency, you will be able to construct your own scenarios based on your specific needs. That is why this guide will come in handy when you need a reference point.

Chapter 11 - Sport & Music

Sports (indoor, outdoor)

¿Qué deportes te gustan? (What sports do you like?)

¿Ves algún deporte por televisión? (Do you watch any sport on TV?)

¿Sigues alguna liga de deportes o competición? (Do you follow any sport league or competition?)

Let's see now some examples about main sports:

Baloncesto	Basketball	*Cuando iba a la universidad jugaba a baloncesto.*	I played basketball when I was at uni.
Fútbol	Football	*Me gusta mirar el futbol femenino.*	I like watching woman's football.
Tenis	Tennis	*Rafa Nadal es un famoso jugador de tenis.*	Rafa Nadal is a famous tennis player.
Natación	Swimming	*Prefiero nadar en la piscina en vez de en el mar.*	I prefer swimming in the swimming pool instead of the sea.
Beisbol	Baseball	*Nunca he jugado a beisbol.*	I've never been in a baseball match.
Boxeo	Boxing	*No me gusta el boxeo.*	I don't like boxing.
Criquet	Cricket	*Los sábados juego a criquet con mis amigos.*	I play cricket on Saturdays with my friends.
gimnasia	Gymnastics	*Solía hacer gimnasia en el colegio.*	I used to do gymnastics at school.
Balonmano	Handball	*En España hay equipos buenos de balonmano.*	There are good handball teams in Spain.
Jockey	Hockey	*Me gustaría jugar a jockey.*	I would like to play hockey.
Tenis de mesa	Ping-pong / table tennis	*Nunca he jugado a tenis de mesa.*	I've never played ping-pong.
Correr	Running	*Salgo a correr todas las tardes.*	I go running every evening.
Patinaje	Skating	*Voy a ir a patinar sobre hielo.*	I'm going to skate on ice.
Buceo	Diving	*Estoy estudiando un curso de buceo.*	I'm studying a diving course.
Atletismo	Athletics/track & field	*¿Quieres venir a ver atletismo?*	Do you want to come to watch athletics?
Voleibol	Volleyball	*Juego a voleibol cuando voy a la playa.*	I play volleyball when I go to the beach.
Esquiar	Skying	*Voy a esquiar el próximo fin de semana.*	I'm going to sky next weekend.

Practise now answering the following questions in Spanish:

¿Qué deporte se juega sobre hielo y con un stick? (What sport is played in ice with a stick?) (jockey)

¿En qué deporte de equipo tratan de encestar la pelota en un aro? (In what team sport, players try to score shooting to a hoop?) (baloncesto)

¿Qué deporte se practica en la nieve? (What sport is practiced in the snow?) (esquiar)

¿Qué deporte se juega con once jugadores por equipo en un campo? (What sport is played with eleven players by team on the field?) (fútbol)

Music (all main types of music)

A todo el mundo le gusta la música (Everyone likes music). Pero no a todo el mundo le gusta la misma música (but not everyone likes same music).

¿Qué tipo de música te gusta? (What kind of music do you like?)

Música clásica	classical music
Jazz	Jazz
Blues	Blues
Soul	Soul
Rock	Rock
Salsa	Salsa
Reggaeton	Reggaeton
Country	Country
Disco	Disco
Pop	Pop
Rap	Rap
House	House
Techno	Techno
Heavy	Heavy

Note: As you can see, most types of music are written the same in both languages, but the pronunciation would be different so let's practice it again!

Let's now practice the following sentences about music:

La música clásica me relaja (Classical music relaxes me)

Mi música favorita es el jazz y el blues (My favourite music is jazz and blues)

En este restaurante hacen conciertos de blues (There are blues concerts in this restaurant)

Bruce Springsteen es un cantante de rock (Bruce Springsteen is a rock singer)

Estoy aprendiendo a bailar salsa (I'm learning to dance salsa)

No me gusta el reggaetón (I do not like reggaeton)

La música country proviene de Estados Unidos (Country music comes from the United States)

En los años ochenta había música disco muy buena (In the eighties there was very good disco music)

Hoy en día hay muchos cantantes de música pop (Nowadays there are a lot of pop singers)

La música rap proviene de Nueva York (Rap music comes from New York)

La música house empezó en el año 1977 en Chicago (House music started in nineteen seventy seven in Chicago)

La música techno es un estilo de música electrónica (Techno music is a style from electronic music)

AC/DC es un grupo de música heavy (AC/DC es heavy music band)

Now answer the following questions in Spanish:

¿Qué tipo de música te gusta? (What kind of music do you like?)

¿Cuál es tu estilo de música favorito? (What is your favourite kind of music?)

¿Has estado en algún concierto recientemente? (Have you been in a concert recently?)

¿De qué estilo musical era? (What kind of music was?)

Technology & Science

Teléfono móvil (or commonly just "*móvil*") = mobile phone

He perdido el teléfono móvil (I have lost the mobile phone)

Mi móvil no funciona (My mobile phone is not working)

Me han robado el teléfono móvil (My mobile phone has been stolen)

Necesito un cargador para este móvil (I need a charger for this mobile phone)

Tableta = tablet

Llevo en la maleta mi tableta (I'm bringing in the suitcase my tablet)

No leo periodicos, leo las noticias en la tableta (I don't read any newspaper, I read the news on the tablet)

Quiero comprar una funda para esta tableta (I want to buy a case for this tablet)

¿Me prestas tu tableta? (Can I borrow your tablet?)

Ordenador portátil (or commonly just "*portátil*") = laptop

He traído el ordenador portátil (I have brought my laptop)

Estoy cargando mi portátil (I'm charging my laptop)

Mi ordenador portátil pesa mucho (My laptop is heavy)

Estoy trabajando con mi portátil (I'm working on my laptop)

Auriculares = headphones/earphones

¿Has visto mis auriculares? (Have you seen my headphones?)

He perdido los auriculares (I have lost the earphones)

¿Me pasas los auriculares? (Can you give me the headphones?)

Mis auriculares son inalámbricos (My headphones are wireless)

Red movil = Mobile network

¿Qué Red móvil me recomiendas? (What mobile network do you advise me?)

Tengo problemas con mi Red móvil (I'm having issues with my mobile network)

Quiero cambiar de Red móvil (I want to switch mobile network)

Las tarifas de este Red móvil son baratas (Rates of this mobile network are cheap)

Cargador = charger

Necesito un cargador para mi teléfono (I need a charger for my phone)

El cargador de mi ordenador portátil servirá para el tuyo (My laptop's charger will work with yours)

He olvidado el cargador (I have forgotten the charger)

Necesito un adaptador para enchufar mi cargador (I need an electric adapter to plug in my charger)

WIFI = WIFI (The same word, different pronunciation)

¿Me puedes dar la contraseña del WIFI, por favor? (Can you give me WIFI's password, please?)

No tengo datos y necesito WIFI (I do not have any data allowance and need WIFI)

Se ha colgado el WIFI (WIFI is frozen)

Estoy conectada en WIFI (I'm on WIFI)

Funda = case

Necesito una funda nueva (I need a new case)

Se me ha roto la funda del teléfono móvil (My mobile's case has broken)

Guarda el ordenador portátil en su funda (Keep the laptop in its case)

La funda de la tableta es negra (The tablet's suitcase is black)

Batería = Battery

Se me está agotando la batería (I'm running out of battery)

No tengo batería (I'm off of battery)

Necesito cargar la batería (I need charging the battery)

Me falla la batería, la tengo que cambiar (The battery is mot working properly, I have to change it)

Schools & Education

Escuela = School

Los niños van a la escuela (The children go to school)

Hay escuelas de primaria y escuelas de secundaria (There are primary and secondary schools)

Hay escuelas públicas y escuelas privadas (There are public and private schools)

Guarderia = Nursery

Los bebés pueden empezar la guardería con tres meses (Babies can start going to the nursery when are 3 months old)

Hay una guardería al lado de casa (There is a nursery next to home)

Mi hijo está en la guardería porque trabajo (My son attends the nursery because I'm working)

Colegio Universitario (universidad) = college

Estoy estudiando en un colegio universitario (I'm studying in a college)

He empezado este año un curso en la universidad (I've started this year a course at college)

Trabajo como profesora en un colegio universitario (I work as a teacher in a college)

Universidad = University

El año que viene empiezo la universidad (I'm starting university next year)

Mi hermana trabaja en la universidad (My sister works at university)

Este año cambio de universidad (I'm switching university this year)

Residencia de estudiantes = Student's residency

Vivo en una residencia de estudiantes (I live in a student's residency)

La residencia de estudiantes está al lado de la universidad (The student's residency is next to the university)

La residencia de estudiantes está cerrada (The student's residency is closed)

Carrera universitaria (commonly just "*carrera*") = University degree

Aun no sé qué carrera universitaria voy a elegir (I still don't know what degree I'm going to choose)

Hoy en día hay muchas carreras universitarias para elegir (Nowadays there are a lot of university degrees to choose)

El año que viene tengo que decidir qué carrera universitaria quiero estudiar (Next year I'll have to decide what degree I want to study)

Beca = bursary, scholarship

Ofrecen becas para profesores (They are offering bursaries for teachers)

No tengo ningún gasto porque tengo una beca completa (I do not have any expense because I have a full scholarship)

Ofrecen una beca al mejor deportista (They are offering a scholarship for the best sportsman or women)

Estudiante = Student

Soy estudiante, no trabajo (I'm a student, I'm not working)

He perdido mi carné de estudiante (I have lost my student card)

La tarjeta de estudiante ofrece descuentos (You have some discounts with your student card)

Chapter 12 - Making Comparisons

The basic structure for the comparative form in Spanish is rather straightforward. As such, you can quickly begin to put it into practice in order to express your ideas.

In essence, comparisons boil down to the use of adjectives to compare two or more objects or people. This structure is evidenced by the "*más* + adjective + *que*" expression. This expression takes the adjective, which is the focal point of the comparison.

Comparative Form

It is important to keep in mind that this comparison is about two items. The adjective in question is meant to compare the two items that are contrasted. Virtually any adjective can be used in this case. So, let's consider some examples of this structure:

- *Roberto es más alto que Diego.* (Roberto is taller than Diego.)

In this example, we are using the verb "*ser*" since we are discussing permanent conditions. After all, height is a rather permanent condition that cannot be altered. Therefore, we generally use the verb "*ser*" to compare and contrast the characteristics of individual items. Next, we have "*más*" (more) and the adjective in question. "*Alto*" (tall) agrees in both gender and number. That means if the items in question are in singular form or plural, the adjective must reflect this difference. This is also the case if the items are feminine or masculine. Then, "*que*" introduces the second item in question.

Let's consider the following example to illustrate agreement in terms of both number and gender.

- *Las niñas son más rápidas que los niños.* (Girls are faster than boys.)

In this example, we are comparing two groups, that is, girls and boys. As such, "*niñas*" (girls) is plural. This means that the adjective "*rápidas*" (fast) must agree both in terms of number and gender. This is a key point to keep in mind as this is applicable to all cases. Nevertheless, we are still comparing two items, even if they are actually a number of items grouped into a single one.

Similarity

If you would like to indicate that two items are the same or not, you can use this expression: "*igual que*" (same as).

With this expression, you are indicating that two items are the same. For instance: "*un libro digital es igual que un libro físico*" (a digital book is the same as a physical book.) In this example, you are making clear that both items are the same; that is, there is no difference between them.

Now, consider this situation:

- "*Un libro digital no es igual que un libro físico*" (A digital book is not the same as a physical book.)

In this example, you are simply saying that both items are different. While you are not specifying where the difference lies, you are stating that the items in question do not have the same characteristics.

So, you can use this structure to simply make a point that two items or groups of items are the same or different. Ultimately, your use of this structure is intended to mark the difference or similarity between the items in question.

Superlative Form

When you are comparing more than two items, you can use the superlative form. This form indicates that there is one item that is "more" or "less" than the rest. This form can be used anytime you are comparing any number of items in excess of two.

Consider the following example:

- *Alejandra es la mejor estudiante de quinto grado.* (Alejandra is the best student of the 5th graders.)

In this example, you are saying that "*Alejandra*" is the best student out of all the students in Grade 5. While the number of students isn't known (at least from simply reading the statement), it is clear that "*Alejandra*" is the best one of all. This implies that there are at least three students in the class.

You can even use this form to refer to an immense number of objects. For instance:

- *Los agujeros negros son los objetos más grandes del universo.* (Black holes are the largest objects in the universe).

In this case, we are comparing the vast number of objects in the universe. So, given the fact that there is an unfathomable number of objects out there, it is a good idea to use the superlative form to make such a generalization.

Consequently, you can see that the main difference lies in the use of "*el/la*" or "*los/las.*" This is what underscores the use of the superlative form. Consider this other example:

- *El Ferrari es el auto más costoso.* (The Ferrari is the most expensive)

In this example, you are making it clear that it is "the most expensive," thereby making proper use of the superlative form. However, keep in mind that this form needs to agree in both number and gender. So, "*los agujeros negros*" is masculine plural. By the same token, "*el Ferrari*" is masculine singular.

Of course, you could also make other types of generalizations that are intended to reflect an opinion. The example, "*Laura es la chica más bella del mundo*" (Laura is the most beautiful girl in the world) is intended to reflect a personal opinion more than anything else. As such, you can use this form to reflect your personal opinions and beliefs about a person or object.

In this case, we are making an agreement with a singular feminine noun, that is, "*Laura.*" As you gain more practice with this form, you will be able to recognize quickly the difference that lies among the various nouns and their corresponding agreements.

Comparison of Verbs

One other use of the comparative and superlative forms lies in the comparison of verbs. Technically speaking, this comparison requires the use of adverbs since you would be describing an action. Nevertheless, the structure and use of adjectives remain the same.

Consider the following examples:

- *Fernando juega fútbol mejor que Pablo.* (Fernando plays soccer better than Pablo)

- *Nancy habla más despacio que Patricia.* (Nancy speaks slower than Patricia)

- *Los niños comen menos que los adultos.* (Kids eat less than adults)

- *Los dólares valen más que los pesos.* (Dollars are worth more than pesos)

- *Las computadoras trabajan más eficientemente que las máquinas de escribir.* (Computers work more efficiently than typewriters)

In these examples, we can see how the comparison among objects is focused on the way certain actions are done, as opposed to the characteristics of these items themselves. Consequently, you can use the same form, though instead of using the verb "*ser*," you can virtually use any verb that you wish to take into account.

Notice in the sentence, "*Las computadoras trabajan más eficientemente que las máquinas de escribir,*" where we are using the adverb "*eficientemente*" (efficiently) to highlight the difference between the two items. Thus, you can virtually use any adjective or adverb to state your comparisons.

Also, keep in mind that all adjectives and adverbs are preceded by "*más*" (more) or "*menos*" (less). Hence, there is no need for transformations, such as "nice" into "nicer." This makes expressing comparisons much more straightforward as compared to English.

Chapter 13 - Stress and Accents

In that chapter, we mentioned the use of accents in Spanish as a means of indicating word stress.

But before we move on to the use of accents, let's establish what we mean by "stress." Stress refers to the syllable where a word receives its inflection. This inflection is what makes the word sound logical in a given language.

Consider this example:

The word, "chocolate" in English would be pronounced as CHOcolate. In this case, notice how the first syllable receives the stress. The same word, "chocolate" in Spanish, would be pronounced as chocoLAte. Please notice how the third syllable is the one that receives the stress. This is why you often hear Spanish speakers stress words incorrectly in English. While this won't necessarily hinder communication, it may lead to misunderstandings at some point.

Now that we have defined what stress is, there are some ground rules to the use of accents in Spanish.

Accent Types

First, there are three accent types. The first is known as "*tilde*." The tilde is used exclusively on vowels. It can be used to indicate that the syllable is to be stressed. For example, "*comunicación*" (communication) ought to be pronounced as comunicaCIÓN. Hence, the stress is placed on the last syllable.

Next, the other type of accent used on vowels is called a "*diérisis*" (dieresis). This accent mark is used exclusively in the "*gu*" combination. It is a bit of a rarity in Spanish, but it is present in some very common words. For example, "*pingüino*" (penguin) and "*bilingüe*" (bilingual) use this accent mark.

The reason for the use of the dieresis lies in the fact that the "gu" combination with other vowels produces a hard sound. For example, "*guerra*" (war) is pronounced as /geh-rah/. However, if the dieresis is used as "güerra," then you would have a soft sound like /gweh-rah/. Needless to say, "güerra" does not exist in Spanish. Nevertheless, the use of the accent makes all the difference between the right word and a funky sounding mistake.

It is unclear as to how the dieresis came about in Spanish. Nevertheless, it is utilized in other languages. So, if you happen to be familiar with these accents in other languages, then you shouldn't be entirely surprised by their inclusion in Spanish.

The third type of accent is the "*vergulilla*". This is the accent above the "ñ". This is the only accent used on a consonant in Spanish. No other consonant has an accent placed on it. As noted earlier, the /en-yeh/ sound clear differentiates it from the /n/ sound. Just like the dieresis, it is unclear as to how the "ñ" emerged in Spanish. It is widely accepted as a part of countless numbers of accents that were initially used in Spanish writing. Over time, Spanish writing was simplified, leaving the "ñ" on the books for practical reasons.

Uses of the Tilde

As you dig deeper into your Spanish studies, you will find that there are some rather complex orthographic rules that go into the use of Spanish. With the intent of simplifying things, we have compiled a list of cases where the use of the tilde is certain.

- Words that end in "*ción*" and "*sión*" will always carry a tilde on the "o." Examples are "conclusión" and "*confirmación*." Leaving the tilde off is considered to be a spelling mistake in this case.

- Verbs in the past tense, such as "*jugué*" (I played) and "*dormí*" (I slept) are good examples. Virtually, all verbs in the past tense will end in a tilde on the final consonant. This is a phonological device used to highlight clearly the tense of the verb.

- Verbs with the "*ía*" ending are another example. These verbs are roughly equivalent to the "would + verb" combination in English. For instance, "*jugaría*" (would play) and "*dormía*" (would sleep) are solid examples.

- Next, a verb in the future simple will also have a tilde on the final syllable. For example, "*jugaré*" (I will play) and "*dormiré*" (I will sleep) highlight this type of verb conjugation. Nevertheless, keep in mind that while "*jugué*" and "*dormiré*" both end in the same "é" vowel, they are completely different tenses.

- Then, there are "long" words that carry tildes in the middle of the word. These "long" words carry a tilde since they have more than four syllables. As such, the tilde is needed in order to guide the reader as to the proper pronunciation of the word. For instance, "*demostrándole*" (showing him) or "*insertándolos*" (inserting them) are words which could potentially be confusing if they didn't have the accent attached to them.

- Most words that carry the stress on the final syllable have a tilde on that syllable. This is intended to avoid any potential confusion in the word's pronunciation. Some examples include, "*bebé*" (baby), "*japonés*" (Japanese), "*maíz*" (maize, corn). On that note, nationalities that end in "*nés*" will always carry a tilde. By the way, nationalities are not capitalized in Spanish. Of course, not every single word that carries the stress in the final syllable has a tilde, but this is a good, general rule of thumb.

- Be on the lookout for names and surnames that carry a tilde. In legal terms, it is not required for names to carry tilde unless they are legally spelled that way. For instance, "*Fernández*" and "*Fernandez*" would be pronounced the same, though legally, it may be spelled without the tilde. This could be due to a clerical error. So, keep in mind that if an accentuated name or surname is spelled without the mark, it could be due to a legal issue.

The official ruling body on the use of tildes is the RAE. What this means is that if you are ever in doubt with the use of a tilde, there is the place where you can go. In general, the RAE dictionary is the official sources whenever you have any doubt on the spelling of a word of the conjugation of a verb. So, it certainly pays to keep this in mind.

Perhaps the best way to improve your use of accents is through reading. The more you read, the more you will notice which words carry an accent and which ones do not. This will allow you to become more familiar with the way that Spanish accents work.

At the end of the day, proper spelling and accentuation can be learned through constant practice. The guidelines in this chapter are meant to make the entire process as simple as possible. So now it's just a matter of practicing these points so that you can make the most of your practice time.

Chapter 14 – Everyday life of a Spaniard "Walking to the Office path"

Now we will talk about walking in the Spanish office. We first learned that Spain is a busy country and people are a country.

Ahora hablaremos sobre caminar en la oficina española. Primero supimos que España es un país ocupado y la gente son un país.

However, there is a limitation of time for Spanish people to work. And that is where every office starts, from 10 am. And that ends at five in the afternoon. Then we know first that Madrid is one of the busiest cities in Spain.

Sin embargo, hay una limitación de tiempo para que el español trabaje. Y ahí es donde comienza cada oficina, a partir de las 10 a.m. Y que termina a las cinco de la tarde. Entonces sabemos primero que Madrid es una de las ciudades más concurridas en España.

People are very busy here. With whom? You have to get inside in their heads. Only then can you understand the movement of the people, the busyness and the noise of the human ears. Since people are so busy here, the first thing you need to do is adapt yourself.

La gente está muy ocupada aquí. ¿Con quien? Tiene que adentrarse en sus cabezas. Sólo entonces puedes entender el movimiento de las personas, el ajetreo y el ruido de los oídos humanos. Como la gente está tan ocupada aquí, lo primero que debe hacer es adaptarse.

Everybody here is going through the course of life. Wake up at six o'clock in the morning. Pray to your Creator. Have breakfast at eight o'clock. And they bathe before 9 am.

Todos aquí están pasando por el curso de la vida. Despiertan a las seis de la mañana. Oran a su Creador. Desayunan a las ocho en punto. Y se Báñan antes de las 9 a.m.

Get yourself ready for office now! Exiting the house before ten. If you have a car, drive to your office by car. And if no, then a bus stop, where your office bus will be waiting for you. It has to reach its destination by climbing.

¡Prepárese para la oficina ahora! Salir de la casa antes de diez. Si tiene un automóvil, maneje a su oficina en automóvil. Y si no, entonces una parada de autobús, donde el autobús de su oficina lo estará esperando. Tiene que llegar a su destino escalando.

In this way, every Spaniard is spending their daily office life. However, it is important to know that their words are always effective mini, "Never agree to waste time", "I always try to be sensitive".

De esta manera, cada español está pasando su vida diaria en la oficina. Sin embargo, es importante saber que sus palabras siempre son mini efectivas, "Nunca aceptes perder el tiempo", "Siempre trato de ser sensible".

And some try to stay unique. So that he can do something good, "A lot of time is paid here. So if you want them to be able to look after yourself over time, you can see it very closely". But one thing is known, it is to enter the office at time

Y algunos intentan mantenerse únicos. Para que pueda hacer algo bueno, "Aquí se paga mucho tiempo. Entonces, si desea que puedan cuidarse a sí mismo con el tiempo, puede verlo muy de cerca". Pero se sabe una cosa, es ingresar a la oficina a la hora

Work will be done today. You will receive your notice after you leave for work. About your work, you will start working on that.

Se trabajará hoy. Recibirá su aviso después de irse a trabajar. Sobre tu trabajo, comenzarás a trabajar en eso.

Your time will be in the morning, from ten to five in the afternoon. Of course, there is a lunch break from two to three. So that you can eat your food.

Su tiempo será en la mañana, de diez a cinco de la tarde. Por supuesto, hay un descanso para almorzar de dos a tres. Para que puedas comer tu comida.

However, most Spanish snacks are eaten out of the house. And at noon they buy breakfast and eat. And there are many, who take food from home. And eat it. However, their style of living is different, the stars do not agree to waste any time.

Sin embargo, la mayoría de los bocadillos españoles se comen fuera de la casa. Y al mediodía compran el desayuno y comen. Y hay muchos que toman comida de casa. Y se lo comen. Sin embargo, su estilo de vida es diferente, las estrellas no aceptan perder el tiempo.

Always keep up the time, keep going. When the office is properly completed, they will then leave for their residence. In this way, they will get on the office's bus, and the bus will drop each of them in front of their home. So that they can reach home with ease.

Siempre mantén el tiempo, sigue adelante. Cuando la oficina se complete correctamente, se irán a su residencia. De esta manera, se subirán al autobús de la oficina, y el autobús dejará a cada uno de ellos frente a su casa. Para que puedan llegar a un hogar con facilidad.

In this way, every Spaniard has a daily routine of their lives. Where people from all over the city gather and move.

De esta manera, cada español tiene una rutina diaria de sus vidas. Donde la gente de toda la ciudad se reúne y se mueve.

But the office center is not so full. Because of the people here, office officials are the majority people. So you understand, they are very comfortable with their time. If you put it in your head, you will see that you have gained enough knowledge about them, how to adapt yourself to them.

Pero el centro de la oficina no está tan lleno de gente. Debido a la gente de aquí, los funcionarios de oficina son la mayoría de las personas. Entonces entiendes, se sienten muy cómodos con su tiempo. Si se lo pones en su cabeza, verá que ha adquirido suficiente conocimiento sobre ellos, Cómo adaptarte a ellos.

Because here I am, with the kind of work they do in the world. I have described them all in front of you.

Porque aquí estoy, con el tipo de trabajo que hacen en el mundo. Los he descrito a todos delante de ti.

And I've tried hard enough to explain it all. Now that everything is up to you, if you understand it well, then it will be very nice to be able to work with them.

Y he intentado lo suficiente como para explicarlo todo. Ahora que todo depende de usted, si lo entiende bien, será muy bueno poder trabajar con ellos.

But first of all, one has to agree with them. Which the Spaniards call daily work. Now we will know about them through another story.

Pero, antes que nada, uno tiene que estar de acuerdo con ellos. Lo que los españoles llaman trabajo diario. Ahora sabemos sobre ellos a través de otra historia.

So, let's not forget about a story. And furthering their knowledge of them, getting to the forefront. It can be easily mixed with them, so no problem, let's get started.

Así que no nos olvidemos de una historia. Y fomentando su conocimiento de ellos, poniéndose a la vanguardia. Se puede mezclar fácilmente con ellos, así que no hay problema, comencemos.

Chapter 15 - Tips for Spanish Learners

How to Learn Spanish: Here Are a Few Ways to Learn

How do I learn to speak Spanish? If this question has been bugging you, then read on!

Learn by Taking up Classes

Spanish classes are perfect for people who are still in school and those who have ample time to take classes regularly. There are a variety of classes for your every need. There are short courses that teach the basic principles in speaking Spanish which is perfect for ordinary tourists who need to speak conversational Spanish when abroad. There are the long term and intensive classes which are perfect for those who speak Spanish daily, like businessmen and office workers who deal with Spanish speaking clients regularly. Learning how to speak Spanish helps boost careers by opening more business opportunities for the individual.

One good (and expensive) option would be to learn Spanish abroad. A lot of schools offer Spanish classes. The biggest advantage of learning Spanish abroad is that you'll me immersed in the language no only in class but your daily encounters. This practice will help your fluency in the language.

Learn by Self-Study

If you cannot find time and resources to take up classes, then self-studying is the way to go. There a lot of different products available in the market to suit everyone's learning needs.

If you spend most of your time in front of the computer, then there are online courses and cd-ROMs available for your needs. Many of these online courses are often free although some of them require a certain fee. The cd-ROMs are usually available at local computer stores and the internet as well. These courses provide tutors and chat rooms for the students who want to practice their lessons.

There also books to guide your learning process. These books are available in your local bookstore. These contain the basic principles in learning Spanish.

Lastly, if you learn the most through listening, then these audio lessons work best for you. They come in tapes, CDs, mp3s and podcasts. Like the online courses, many of them are free but some require a certain fee, it's just a matter of picking the best product to suit you.

Learn by Adaptation

You may think that this is a weird way to learn Spanish. According to Charles Darwin humans, much like any mammal adapt to the ever-changing environment. Otherwise, they will not survive. So if you are a foreigner in a certain country, you are bound to adapt their environment to survive. Learning their language is a way to adapt to the new environment. Constant exposure to Spanish will help you learn it practically.

There are many ways how to learn Spanish; it is just a matter of finding out which suits you the best.

Saying the Right Words

When learning a new language, the first thing that you should pay attention to is how to use the appropriate words to make sense in speaking what you mean. There are various phrases that do not have exact translations in Spanish, although expressing it would still be possible if you know the correct words to use. If you want to use Learn Spanish Language Fast, these are the few things that you would need to consider.

Studying how words come up in conversations in Spanish is an integral part of your learning process. For instance, about an object would need you to put a "gender" on it, as this language uses the prepositions "el" and "la" specifically for items with male and female genders, respectively. If you are not yet familiar with this concept, it is best that you refer to a reliable guide that would help you become fluent in applying this knowledge as you construct your sentences.

When you start using Learn Spanish Language Fast, you will notice that repeating the ideas often would help you enhance your memory and make you remember the words easily. You could start by repeating particular words, then phrases, and then continue with properly-constructed and complete sentences that you can use in daily conversations. This way, you would be able to practice speaking the language without any trouble.

Another thing to keep in mind is that every language has a certain "rhythm" or "melody" that it follows. The accent that comes along with it will truly help you to express yourself more clearly as you use the language. Focus on how native speakers would use the words and their respective "tunes" when in actual conversations. This will help you identify the proper pronunciation and enunciation of the words to avoid confusion. Since some words might sound the same to you, paying attention to the correct diphthong as it is used in the language would help you determine how words vary in sound and enunciation.

One good way to start learning the language is, to begin with familiarizing with Spanish words that are somewhat derivatives of English words and vice versa. As an example, the word "excellence" is translated to "Excelencia" in Spanish. As you may notice, these words are almost the same, if not for the addition of certain syllables. Nevertheless, these words can be easily related to each other by nature with which they are spelled and pronounced. Associating the words in English with that in Spanish would truly be helpful for you in your aim to learn a new language.

Probably one of the best ways to learn the language is to have someone to converse with in Spanish, just like in Learn Spanish Language Fast. Some self-help guides could provide you with this feature: with the many language exercises, you can conduct to practice your skills in speaking Spanish. Note that in some cases, the sentence construction in the said language is different as it is in English, and so studying it more closely would enable you to comprehend it better.

Tips

If you are interested in discovering how to learn Spanish, this article will give you some pointers to help you find the most effective language training methods for your needs. Spanish is one of the major players when it comes to world languages. So you have made a wise choice.

So, some tips to get you started! First of all, ask yourself why you want to speak Spanish and how well you want to be able to speak it?

There are many reasons why you may want to start learning Spanish, and these could range from getting a better grade at college to learning to speak with neighbors or with distant relatives and from getting a more interesting job to making traveling abroad more fun. The level and accuracy of Spanish you need will vary according to your goals. If you just want to chat with neighbors or relatives, you'll get by even if you don't always get things right, although do ask them to correct you so that you can improve.

However, it's a different story if you are aiming for a job using Spanish or you wish to pass high-level exams. You can't afford to make too many mistakes in these situations if you want to further your career.

There are probably hundreds of reasons to learn Spanish, and there are also hundreds of ways to learn. But the best way to learn Spanish is the way that works best for you and which fulfills your needs, which is why you need to consider how well you want to be able to speak Spanish.

Everyone has to start with the basics, and you should look for a program which offers a variety of resources. Learning accurate pronunciation is essential if you want to be able to speak Spanish correctly and building listening skills are crucial if you want to hold a conversation. There is no point in speaking excellent Spanish if you can't understand a word that is being said to you! Audio Spanish programs can be found on the internet, and you can download lessons on mp3 and then listen at odd moments during the day when you have some free time.

Basic grammar is important as it forms the structure on which the whole language is based and once learned, you won't have much difficulty moving forward. If you aspire to reach a high level, you absolutely must ensure that you learn grammar from the beginning. You can learn in small chunks and should choose a course which gives you exercises to practice what you've learned. So although you can start with a basic introduction, you'll want to get a detailed grammar book as you progress.

If you are learning for holidays or talking to friends, reading and writing won't be the most important aspects of your Spanish learning program, but they shouldn't be ignored. If you want to know how to learn Spanish well, you should concentrate on developing each of the four skills - reading, writing, speaking, and listening will complement all the other skills. And you never know, you may enjoy the language or travel to Spanish speaking countries that you decide to take your Spanish to the next level.

5 Tips for Learning Spanish on Your Own

Q: What connects 24 countries, 500 million people and the second most spoken language in the world?

A: Spanish!

Spanish is one of the fastest growing languages today. The combined GDP of all Spanish speaking countries is the third highest in the world! Even in a non-Hispanic country like the United States, being bilingual is a great enhancement to your professional and personal life. I speak Spanish, and I can't begin to tell you how much it's helped me.

So here's how to learn this beautiful and immensely useful language and keep it for life!

1. Get Used to Hearing Spanish

The first step to learning any language is to familiarize yourself to its sounds and speech patterns. Audio lessons teach you how to understand spoken Spanish and most importantly, help you develop the correct accent. I'd recommend audio lessons that use "standardized" pronunciation and accent, such as the Castilian or Mexican one, which is clearer and easier for beginners.

2. Don't Ignore Grammar

Audio lessons make a great stepping-stone into the language, but you need to supplement them with grammar if you want to make any progress. Spanish is a lot like English in some ways but very different in others. A good grammar guide that's simple but in-depth will go a long way in helping you speak naturally and building up your vocabulary.

3. Brush Up On Your ENGLISH Grammar

Sounds weird in an article on Spanish right? You won't find this tip anywhere else, but I speak from experience. Grammar books will often use terms like "infinitive," "transitive verb" or "conjunction." All of us probably know what they mean but aren't familiar with the technical use of the terms. Knowing your English grammar terms helps, especially since Spanish grammar terms sound a lot like English ones.

4. Get the Human Touch

Learning Spanish on your own instead of in a class or with a tutor means that you don't get as many chances of using the language in a real-life setting. But don't worry, there are still plenty of ways you can practice using your Spanish.

    i.   If you have a Spanish speaking friend, don't hesitate to ask their help.

    ii.   You could also use your Spanish when you deal with Hispanic people in places such as restaurants or shops. Spanish speakers are usually very friendly and will encourage and help you out (just don't massacre their language too much!!)

    iii.   If you don't know any Spanish speakers or don't live in an area with a significant Hispanic population, then the Internet is your savior. There are plenty of language exchange sites out there. You could talk with a native speaker using instant messengers or clients such as Skype. You'll improve you're Spanish AND make a friend!

5. Important: HAVE FUN

If I could give you one tip for learning Spanish, this is it. If learning Spanish feels like a chore to you, then you'll never get anywhere. There are plenty of ways you could do this.

    i.   Language Games: There are lots of interactive games that help you brush up on your Spanish. Rocket Spanish has a great set of games that help you improve your vocabulary, grammar, and speech.

    ii.   Movies: These are a fun way to get familiar with another language. You can start by watching Spanish movies with English subtitles and later, switch to Spanish subtitles. There are some great Spanish directors - Pedro Almodovar, Alfonso Cuarón, Guillermo del Toro and many more. You could also watch Hollywood movies dubbed into Spanish (trust me, they're a lot of fun!).

    iii.   Music: Choose the kind of music you like - pop, rock, metal, folk or whatever - and find a Spanish band in that genre. Singing along to songs is a good way to learn without boring your brains out.

iv.   Podcasts: Podcasts are a great way to learn while commuting or working out. There are podcasts for all types of learners, from beginners to advanced learners to those who just want to pick up a few survival phrases. Download them onto your mp3 player, and you're good to go. The best part? They're usually free!

I hope these tips will help you in exploring this enchanting language. These are all common sense tips that I discovered while learning Spanish myself.

Conclusion

If you are interested in learning Spanish fast, there are a variety of methods that can help you do it. First, it is important to understand your memory and how capable your mind is of learning quickly. Remember that the brain is a muscle and must be exercised just like any other muscle in your body to become stronger.

Regardless of how you learn Spanish, an important role in your success is practice and discipline.

Language, Memory, and Learning

learning Spanish fast is a possibility because unlike other languages such as Russian, French, or Cantonese, it is not a difficult of a language to learn. However, you must find the right learning tools and resources. Some of these include products such as Rosetta Stone, online classes, or enrolling in a college course.

According to various experts, one is realistically capable of mastering 200 hundred words a day when learning a new language. Although if you want to speed the process up, one way of doing so is to understand how to use the words in conversation. Using the words whenever you can allow you to remember them more easily.

Using Mnemonics

A technique that is useful for learning is to by using mnemonics, which are learning aids to help remember meanings of words. You can use images and verbal cues to associate words from Spanish with those from your language.

If you want to start speaking Spanish quickly, focus on learning the most common one hundred words or so used in Spanish. Every language has these words that makeup 50% of the conversation, so this will give you a foundation to work from.

Learn Spanish

The complete learning guide for advanced users to learn Spanish like a pro and be fluent like a native speaker. Includes advanced grammar, exercises and advanced sentences

Introduction

Many times, if you tell someone that you are not just learning a foreign language, but that you are specifically learning Spanish, you may be met with a variety of responses. They can vary from "Wow, that's impressive!" to "Why do you need to learn Spanish? Everyone speaks English anyways…"

But one must remember that there are benefits to learning Spanish language too!

1. You can travel. That sounds very attractive, doesn't it? Imagine yourself skydiving or at the Tomatina festival in Spain. If you learn the language, you will be able to tour freely through Spain or most of Central and South America, without having to worry about any language barrier. This goes without saying for every other language.

2. You can meet new people. You will discover, that you do not hesitant to talk to someone from Spain for not knowing the language.

3. You will learn more about a new culture! You will be able to improve about the history, the culture and the country itself. Learn to see the country through the eyes of another person.

4. It gives you a new hobby. Every person is annoyed with life or is bored and looks for a way to break free. This is the perfect way to do so. You are learning something new and also giving yourself a break from the monotony that life usually gives.

Chapter 1: Do I Know You? Useful Verbs When Meeting People

Encontrar and encontrarse

Encontrar is quite a common verb, and it means "to find". You will not find this verb as useful as its pronominal form, encontrarse, while you meet people. Let's look first at the simple form so you can understand the difference between the two.

This is the present tense conjugation of the verb encontrar:

I find – *yo encuentro*

You find – *tú encuentras / usted encuentra / vos encontrás*

He finds – *él encuentra*

She finds – *ella encuentra*

We find – *nosotros encontramos*

You find – *vosotros encontráis / ustedes encuentran*

They find – *ellos encuentran / ellas encuentran*

Let's see how to use this verb in some examples:

I cannot find my camera! – *¡No puedo encontrar mi cámara!*

James always has trouble finding his pen – *James siempre tiene problemas para encontrar su bolígrafo*

Laura can't find a place in a hostel, everything is booked! – *Laura no puede encontrar un lugar en un hostal; ¡Todo está reservado!*

Every day we find a new restaurant we like – *Todos los días encontramos un nuevo restaurante que nos gusta*

Now, as mentioned before, there is another version of this verb that has the particle -se at the end: encontrarse.

All verbs ending in -se are called **pronominal verbs.**

There is no need to remember that word; you just need to know that these verbs require a little word (me, te, se, nos, os, se) next to the conjugated verb. The little word depends on the pronoun (yo, tú, él, nosotros, etc.). It is placed before the conjugated verb (when it is placed afterward, then it is an order! But let's not get into that yet).

Encontrarse means to be, to feel or to meet. Yes, it has three meanings, hence why it is useful for you to learn it, especially if you want to meet (and meet with) people: you can use it when you are asking people how they feel and when you are making plans.

Let's see how to conjugate it first, and then some real-life examples are provided:

Yo me encuentro

Tú te encuentras / usted se encuentra / vos te encontrás

Él se encuentra

Ella se encuentra

Nosotros nos encontramos

Vosotros os encontráis / ustedes se encuentran

Ellos se encuentran / ellas se encuentran

Here are some examples for this particular verb:

I am okay – *Yo me encuentro bien*

Tomorrow I meet with Sara at a coffee shop – *Mañana me encuentro con Sara en un café*

She feels tired – *Ella se encuentra cansada*

Pablo is not feeling very well – *Pablo no se encuentra muy bien*

We meet at the train station in ten minutes – *Nos encontramos en la estación de tren en diez minutos*

Some other pronominal verbs and examples:

To get married – *casarse* (I get married in October – *Me caso en octubre*)

To get dressed – *vestirse* (Juan already gets dressed on his own – *Juan ya se viste solo*)

To look – *verse* (Do we look fine? – *¿Nos vemos bien?*)

To get – *ponerse* (The kids get really cranky at this time – *Los niños se ponen muy fastidiosos a esta hora*)

To sit down – *sentarse* (Do we sit down? – *¿Nos sentamos?*)

James made plans to meet with Alex and María at the beach. They are talking on the phone because they cannot find each other:

JAMES: Hi, María, can you hear me? – *Hola, María, ¿me oyes?*

MARÍA: Yes, I hear you, are you okay? – *Sí, te oigo. ¿te encuentras bien?*

JAMES: I am doing great! – *¡Me encuentro muy bien!*

MARÍA: Great! Are we meeting at the beach? – *¡Genial! ¿Nos encontramos en la playa?*

JAMES: Sure, I am already here, at the beach – *Claro, ya me encuentro aquí, en la playa*

MARÍA: We are also at the beach – *¡Nosotros también nos encontramos en la playa!*

JAMES: I cannot see you, can you see me? – *No os veo, ¿vosotros me veis?*

MARÍA: Are you near the sea? Can you raise an arm? – *¿Te encuentras cerca del mar? ¿Puedes alzar un brazo?*

JAMES: Sure – *Claro*

MARÍA: I see you! – *¡Te veo!*

Comenzar and empezar

Comenzar means to start. There is another Spanish verb that means the same, *empezar*. Let's see the conjugation in the present tense and some examples you might find useful:

I start – *yo comienzo*

You start – *tú comienzas / usted comienza / vos comenzás*

He starts – *él comienza*

She starts – *ella comienza*

We start – *nosotros comenzamos / nosotras comenzamos*

You start – *vosotros comenzáis / vosotras comenzáis / ustedes comienzan*

They start – *ellos comienzan / ellas comienzan*

I start – *yo empiezo*

You start – *tú empiezas / usted empieza / vos empezás*

He starts – *él empieza*

She starts – *ella empieza*

We start – *nosotros empezamos / nosotras empezamos*

You start – *vosotros empezáis / vosotras empezáis / ustedes empiezan*

They start – *ellos empiezan / ellas empiezan*

These two verbs are synonyms, so you can choose the one you like the most or the one that is most widely used in the country you are visiting. Normally, in Spain, they use empezar, and in most of Latin America they prefer comenzar, but any Spanish-speaking person will understand either without any inconvenience:

I start my trip in Colombia – *Comienzo mi viaje en Colombia / Empiezo mi viaje en Colombia*

Lucía starts studying again in two weeks – *Lucía comienza a estudiar de nuevo en dos semanas / Lucía empieza a estudiar de nuevo en dos semanas*

We start cooking now! – *¡Ya comenzamos a cocinar! / ¡Ya empezamos a cocinar!*

James, back at the hostel, is talking with one of the Mexican girls, Daniela, about their trips:

JAMES: Dani, is your trip starting or finishing? – *Dani, ¿tu viaje está empezando o terminando?*

DANIELA: My trip has just started! Me and my friends are going down to the south of Argentina, and then we start going up to Ecuador – *¡Mi viaje recién comienza! Yo y mis amigas bajamos hasta Argentina, y luego empezamos a subir a Ecuador*

290

JAMES: For how long are you traveling? – *¿Por cuánto tiempo viajan?*

DANIELA: We start with a one-month plan... But I think the trip is starting to grow – *Comenzamos con un plan de un mes... pero creo que el viaje empieza a extenderse*

JAMES: You do not need to go back to Mexico to start your classes? – *¿No debes volver a México para comenzar con tus clases?*

DANIELA: Oh, no! I already graduated. When I come back, I have to start working – *¡Oh, no! Ya me he graduado. Cuando vuelva, debo empezar a trabajar*

Desear and querer

Two verbs in Spanish can be translated as to want. In some situations, you can use either of them, but they are not real synonyms. Querer can express to want, to care, and to love, while desear can express to want, to desire, and to wish.

You do not need to remember this by heart. The conjugations for these two verbs are presented later and, afterward, some examples so you can learn their meanings with practice.

I want – *yo deseo*

You want – *tú deseas / usted desea / vos deseás*

He wants – *él desea*

She wants – *ella desea*

We want – *nosotros deseamos / nosotras deseamos*

You want – *vosotros deseáis / vosotras deseáis / ustedes desean*

They want – *ellos desean / ellas desean*

I want – *yo quiero*

You want – *tú quieres / usted quiere / vos querés*

He wants – *él quiere*

She wants – *ella quiere*

We want – *nosotros queremos / nosotras queremos*

You want – *vosotros queréis / vosotras queréis / ustedes quieren*

They want – *ellos quieren / ellas quieren*

Let's see some examples of situations you could use each verb:

I want to meet your brother – *Quiero/deseo conocer a tu hermano*

I wish you good luck – *Te deseo buena suerte*

Do you love me? – *¿Me quieres?*

James is making plans with Daniela to go out together:

JAMES: Do you want to have coffee later? – *¿Quieres ir a tomar un café más tarde?*

DANIELA: No! I mean... yes, I want to go out with you, but I do not want to drink coffee; I do not like coffee – *¡No! Quiero decir... sí, deseo salir contigo, pero no quiero beber café; no me gusta el café*

JAMES: Do you want to have a drink tonight, then? – *¿Deseas ir a beber un trago a la noche, entonces?*

DANELA: Sure, at what time do you want to go? – *Claro, ¿a qué hora quieres ir?*

JAMES: At eight, is that good? There is a bar around the corner I want to try – *A las ocho, ¿te parece bien? Hay un bar a la vuelta que deseo probar*

Chapter 2: Syllabication

Syllabication is the separation of words into smaller units based on the sounds that are produced. In general, a syllable will consist of a vowel and consonant sound. Sometimes, syllables can be individual vowel sounds, although they are never individual consonant sounds.

When looking at the way syllables are formed in all languages, these tend to break down based on the natural phonological patterns of that language. Nevertheless, the vowel-consonant connection is common throughout virtually all languages.

It is generally accepted that early human language was monosyllabic; that is, early human communication was done through the utterance of individual sounds. To this day, we still use monosyllabic communication to convey meaning. For example, expressions such as "huh" can be used to indicate a specific meaning. Other essential words in English, like "yes" and "no" are classic examples of monosyllabic communication.

With the evolution of human language, communication became more and more complex. This led to the union of individual sounds in order to form words. Now, it should be noted that monosyllabic utterances are also words (such as "I"). Nevertheless, these are generally considered to be isolated sounds. This is especially true when these isolated sounds do not actually have any meaning attached to them.

As human communication becomes richer, the need for more and more words led to the use of syllables under various combinations. This is the reason that one of the most effective methods used to teach kids how to read is based on phonics.

Phonics is composed of core sounds; when combined, they can produce a myriad of words. Consequently, phonics, as individual syllables, can be used to make words. At the end of the day, the words that we use in daily conversation are nothing more than the aggregate of any number of syllable combinations.

Spanish is no exception to this evolution. Children in Spanish schools are taught to read and write using these basic building blocks of language. Initially, children learn the five-vowel sounds before moving on to isolated consonant sounds. Then, vowels sounds are tacked on to individual consonant sounds. For example, children are taught to read, "ma," "me," "mi," "mo," "mu." These syllables, in themselves, are meaningless. However, when they are combined with other such combinations, they can lead to word formation.

Let's take a quick look at how these syllables can be used to make words. For instance, "mama" is one of the first words children in Spanish schools begin to read. So, just like children in English schools learn to read English and pronounce it correctly using phonics, children in Spanish schools use these segregated syllables to make their first words.

Syllabication Structure

As such, each consonant is combined with the five vowel sounds to produce words. Let's take a closer look at this syllabication structure:

- *Ba, be, bi, bo, bu*
- *Ca, Ce, Ci* (pronounced differently, like "ce" c-ae and "ci" c-ee,"), *co, cu*
- *Da, de, di, do, du*

- *fa, fe, fi, fo, fu*
- *ga, ge, go, gu*
- *gue, gui*
- *ha, he, hi, ho, hu*
- *cha, che, chi, cho, chu*
- *ja, je, ji, jo, ju*
- *ka, ke, ki, ko, ku*
- *la, le, li, lo, lu*
- *lla, lle, lli, llo, llu*
- *ma, me, mi, mo, mu*
- *na, ne, ni, no, un*
- *ña, ñe, ñi, ño, ñu*
- *pa, pe, pi, po, pu*
- *ra, re, ri, ro, ru*
- *rra, rre, rri, rro, rru*
- *sa, se, si, so, su*
- *ta, te, ti, to, tu*
- *va, ve, vi, vo, vu*
- *wa, we, wi, wo, wu*
- *ya, ye, yi, yo, yu*
- *za, zo, zu (no "ze", "zi")*
- *an, en, in, on, un*
- *ar, er, ir, or, ur*
- *as, es, is, os, us*

The two letters that are excluded from this list are "Q," as it is always combined with "U" and produce a /k/ sound, and "X" which is not used at the beginning of words. In fact, there are a few exceptions, such as "*xilófono*" (xylophone), where it is used at the beginning of a word.

From here onward, you can combine any number of these syllables to make your own words. Consider this:

- ma + pa = *mapa* (map)
- ro + sa = *rosa* (rose)
- ta + za = *taza* (cup)
- ca + ma = *cama* (bed)
- tu + yo = *tuyo* (yours)

These are two-syllable words. And then here are some three-syllable words:

- to + ma + te = *tomate* (tomato)
- pa + ta + ta = *patata* (potato)
- ta + ja + da = *tajada* (slice)
- pa + pa + ya = *papaya* (papaya)
- ba + ti + do = *batido* (smoothie)

As you can see, Spanish is built on these individual syllable combinations. As you become more familiar with the language, you will see that all words can be broken down into these consonant-syllable units. This will make reading far easier while helping you get a grip on the proper pronunciation of the words.

The best way to go about your understanding of syllabication in Spanish is to repeat the various consonant-vowel combinations until you are able to begin forming your own words. At first, you'll have a list of two-syllable words. Then, you will begin to recognize three-syllable words, then four, and so on.

A word of caution: by now, you may have noticed that some words have an accent on them. As such, it is important to note that an accent indicates that the syllable must be stressed. If there is no accent used in a word, then you will have to listen to the way it is pronounced.

Later on, we will be taking an in-depth look into the way accents are used in Spanish. But for now, it is important to be on the lookout for these accents. These will give you a clear indication as to how a word is pronounced.

And if you are ever in doubt with regard to the pronunciation of a word, tools such as spanishdict.com and Word reference will help you get the right pronunciation. Best of all, you will be able to hear the way a word is pronounced in various Spanish accents. This is certainly an educational tool that will help you get it right every single time.

Chapter 3: Conditional (Condicional)

Just as in English (with would and could), this tense is used for hypothetical situations and to make polite requests.

I would love to be a millionaire - ***Me encantaría** ser millonario*

Could I have a glass of water? - *¿**Podría** tomar un vaso de agua?*

Could I have your class notes? - *¿**Me prestarías** tus apuntes de la clase?*

I would kill for a good slice of pizza - ***Mataría** por una buena porción de pizza*

Regular verbs

To love (am*ar*)

- *yo am**aría***
- *tú am**arías** / vos am**arías** / usted am**aría***
- *él/ella am**aría***
- *nosotros am**arímos***
- *ustedes am**arían** / vosotros am**aríais***
- *ellos/ellas am**arían***

To fear (tem*er*)

- *yo tem**ería***
- *tú tem**erías** / vos tem**erías** / usted tem**ería***
- *él/ella tem**ería***
- *nosotros tem**eríamos***
- *ustedes tem**erían** / vosotros tem**eríais***
- *ellos/ellas tem**erían***

To live (viv*ir*)

- *yo viv**iría***
- *tú viv**irías** / vos viv**irías** / usted viv**iría***
- *él/ella viv**iría***
- *nosotros viv**iríamos***
- *ustedes viv**irían** / vosotros viv**iríais***
- *ellos/ellas viv**irían***

Irregular verbs

To be (*ser*)

- *yo* **sería**
- *tú* **serías** / *vos* **serías** / *usted* **sería**
- *él/ella* **sería**
- *nosotros* **seríamos**
- *ustedes* **serían** / *vosotros* **seríais**
- *ellos/ellas* **serían**

To be (*estar*)

- *yo* **estaría**
- *tú* **estarías** / *vos* **estarías** / *usted* **estaría**
- *él/ella* **estaría**
- *nosotros* **estaríamos**
- *ustedes* **estarían** / *vosotros* **estaríais**
- *ellos/ellas* **estarían**

To have (*tener*)

- *yo* **tendría**
- *tú* **tendrías** / *vos* **tendrías** / *usted* **tendría**
- *él/ella* **tendría**
- *nosotros* **tendríamos**
- *ustedes* **tendrían** / *vosotros* **tendríais**
- *ellos/ellas* **tendrían**

To say (*decir*)

- *yo* **diría**
- *tú* **dirías** / *vos* **dirías** / *usted* **diría**
- *él/ella* **diría**
- *nosotros* **diríamos**
- *ustedes* **dirían** / *vosotros* **diríais**
- *ellos/ellas* **dirían**

To go (*ir*)

- *yo* **iría**
- *tú* **irías** / *vos* **irías** / *usted* **iría**
- *él/ella* **iría**
- *nosotros* **iríamos**
- *ustedes* **irían** / *vosotros* **iríais**
- *ellos/ellas* **irían**

To do (*hacer*)

- *yo* **haría**
- *tú* **harías** / *vos* **harías** / *usted* **haría**
- *él/ella* **haría**
- *nosotros* **haríamos**
- *ustedes* **harían** / *vosotros* **haríais**
- *ellos/ellas* **harían**

Can (*poder*)

- *yo* **podría**
- *tú* **podrías** / *vos* **podrías** / *usted* **podría**
- *él/ella* **podría**
- *nosotros* **podríamos**
- *ustedes* **podrían** / *vosotros* **podríais**
- *ellos/ellas* **podrían**

To see (*ver*)

- *yo* **vería**
- *tú* **verías** / *vos* **verías** / *usted* **vería**
- *él/ella* **vería**
- *nosotros* **veríamos**
- *ustedes* **verían** / *vosotros* **veríais**
- *ellos/ellas* **verían**

To give (*dar*)

- *yo **daría***
- *tú **darías** / vos **darías** / usted **daría***
- *él/ella **daría***
- *nosotros **daríamos***
- *ustedes **darían** / vosotros **daríais***
- *ellos/ellas **darían***

To want (*querer*)

- *yo **querría***
- *tú **querrías** / vos **querrías** / usted **querría***
- *él/ella **querría***
- *nosotros **querríamos***
- *ustedes **querrían** / vosotros **querríais***
- *ellos/ellas **querrían***

Past subjunctive + conditional

Conditional sentences use the past subjunctive. Just as in English you use **if** to introduce this kind of sentences, in Spanish we use si, which is different from sí (yes), because it doesn't have a tilde.

If I **were** rich, I **would buy** you a mansion - *Si yo **fuera** rico, te **compraría** una mansión*

If they **had** any brains, they **would stay away** from that scam - *Si **tuvieran** cerebro, se **alejarían** de esa estafa*

If I **had** the time, I **could start** a new major - Si ***tuviera*** tiempo, ***podría comenzar*** *una nueva carrera*

Exercises

– *Si (yo, comer) .... bien, (yo, tener) .... más energía*

– *Si me (tú, decir) .... qué necesitas, (yo, poder) .... ayudarte*

– *Si (nosotros, tener) .... tiempo, (nosotros, ir) .... al cine esta noche*

– *Si me (usted, respetar) .... no me (usted, hablar) .... en ese tono*

– *Si me (tú, amar) .... me (tú, cuidar) ....*

Chapter 4: How To Talk About Years

If you want to say the year you were born, or if you want to mention a year in which something happened, you are going to need to know how to say complex numbers like 1986 or 2001.

It is not as hard as it seems. First, here are the thousands:

1.000 – *mil*

2.000 – *dos mil*

3.000 – *tres mil*

5.000 – *cinco mil*

15.000 – *quince mil*

And the hundreds:

100 – *cien*

200 – *doscientos*

300 – *trescientos*

400 – *cuatrocientos*

500 – *quinientos*

600 – *seiscientos*

700 – *setecientos*

800 – *ochocientos*

900 – *novecientos*

And decades:

10 – *diez*

20 – *veinte*

30 – *treinta*

40 – *cuarenta*

50 – *cincuenta*

60 – *sesenta*

70 – *setenta*

80 – *ochenta*

90 – *noventa*

100 – *cien*

Now, you just have to combine them:

1967 – *mil novecientos sesenta y siete*

1974 – *mil novecientos setenta y cuatro*

1990 – *mil novecientos noventa*

1999 – *mil novecientos noventa y nueve*

2002 – *dos mil dos*

2010 – *dos mil diez*

2019 – *dos mil diecinueve*

You can use the plural of thousand (miles) when you are talking about an unspecified amount. You can do the same with cientos (hundreds) and millones (millions).

I have thousands of options – *Tengo **miles** de opciones*

Thousands of students registered – *Se inscribieron **miles** de alumnos*

In the capital, they are millions and we are hundreds of thousands – *En la capital, son **millones** y nosotros somos **cientos** de **miles***

It is incorrect to say cientas, even when talking about something feminine:

I have hundreds of questions – *Tengo **cientos** de preguntas*

Hundreds of women participated – *Participaron **cientos** de mujeres*

Note that, in Spanish, the thousands are marked with a dot (.), not with a comma as in English. Decimals, instead, are marked with a comma. Just like in English, though, Spanish does not use the dot in some numbers, such as years.

1,500 – 1.500 (*mil quinientos*)

200,000 – 200.000 (*doscientos mil*)

1.5 – 1,5 (*uno coma cinco*)

2.75 – 2,75 (*dos coma setenta y cinco*)

year 1900 – año 1900 (*mil novecientos*)

The word for million is *millón*, but do not forget you have to say it in plural when you have more than one:

1.000.000 – *un millón*

2.000.000 – *dos millones*

10.000.000 – *diez millones*

(Note that, while in English, a billion is a thousand million, in Spanish, it just called a thousand millions mil millones. In Spanish billón means a million million.)

Damián gets up and walks to the door. James is really curious. He stands up and walks over to see who is at the door:

JAMES: Kate? What are you doing here? – *¿Kate? ¿Qué haces aquí?*

KATE: My silly big brother, I had not seen you in years! – *Mi tonto hermano mayor, ¡hacía años que no te veía!*

JAMES: In two years, since you moved to Spain in 2017 – *Hace dos años, desde que te mudaste a España en 2017 (dos mil diecisiete)*

KATE: I bet you didn't expect to see me here now – *Apuesto que no esperabas verme aquí ahora*

JAMES: Of course not, it is a massive surprise. How did...? – *Claro que no, es una sorpresa enorme. ¿Cómo...?*

KATE: Remember you texted me three months ago telling me you were in touch with an architect from Lima? – *¿Recuerdas que me escribiste hace tres meses para decirme que estabas en contacto con un arquitecto de Lima?*

JAMES: Yes, so? – *Sí, ¿y?*

KATE: I looked him up, I wrote him a message, and we planned all this – *Lo busqué, le escribí un mensaje, y planeamos todo*

Here is a list of time-related vocabulary you will definitely use while traveling around Latin America and Spain:

time – *tiempo*

hour – *hora*

minute – *minuto*

second – *segundo*

morning – *mañana*

noon – *mediodía*

afternoon – *tarde*

evening – *noche*

midnight – *medianoche*

night – *noche*

sunrise – *amanecer*

sunset – *atardecer*

today – *hoy*

yesterday – *ayer*

tomorrow – *mañana*

the day before yesterday – *El día antes de ayer*

the day after tomorrow – *El día pasado mañana*

now – *ahora*

never – *nunca*

always – *siempre*

late – *tarde*

early – *temprano*

on time – *a tiempo / en horario*

day – *día*

week – *semana*

month – *mes*

year – *año*

And here are some sentences where you might find these words:

I don't have much time – *No tengo mucho **tiempo***

He always arrives an hour late! – *¡Siempre llegas una **hora** tarde!*

I want to seize every minute – *Quiero aprovechar cada **minuto***

See you at noon – *Nos vemos al **mediodía***

We came back around midnight – *Volvimos cerca de la **medianoche***

Let's see the sunrise at the beach! – *¡Veamos el **amanecer** en la playa!*

Let's see the sunset from the lighthouse! – *¡Veamos el **atardecer** desde el faro!*

Today I'm leaving – ***Hoy** me voy*

I met her yesterday – *La conocí **ayer***

Have we met before? – *¿Nos conocemos de **antes**?*

See you after work – *Nos vemos **después** del trabajo*

I went to the museum the day before yesterday – *Fui al museo **antes de ayer***

I am going to Peru the day after tomorrow – *Voy a ir a Perú **pasado mañana***

I want to do something now – *Quiero hacer algo **ahora***

I never traveled on my own – ***Nunca** he viajado sola*

She is always by my side – *Ella **siempre** está a mi lado*

I am leaving early in the morning – *Me voy **temprano** por la mañana*

My plane is leaving on time – *Mi avión sale **en horario***

This is not something you see every day – *Esto no es algo que ves todos los **días***

I'm staying for another week! – *¡Me quedo una **semana** más!*

It was the best month of my life – *Fue el mejor **mes** de mi vida*

See you next year! – *¡Nos vemos el **año** que viene!*

Here are some tricky ones! For example, morning and tomorrow are both *mañana*:

What a beautiful morning! – *¡Qué hermosa **mañana**!*

I think tomorrow is going to rain – *Creo que **mañana** va a llover*

And afternoon and late are both *tarde*:

I have to work a lot this afternoon – *Tengo que trabajar mucho esta **tarde***

Do not be late – *No llegues **tarde***

And remember evening and night are both *noche*:

I do not want to go out at night – *No quiero salir por la **noche***

We are going for drinks this evening – *Vamos a por unos cocktails esta **noche***

Segundo, just like in English, means both second (time unit) and second (ordinal number):

Give me one second... – *Dame un **segundo**...*

You're the second one to ask – *Eres el **segundo** en preguntar*

These are the ordinal numbers in Spanish:

1° – *primero / primera*

2° – *segundo / segunda*

3° – *tercero / tercera*

4° – *cuarto / cuarta*

5° – *quinto / quinta*

6° – *sexto / sexta*

7° – *séptimo / séptima*

8° – *octavo / octava*

9° – *noveno / novena*

10° – *décimo / décima*

Masculine ordinal numbers 1 and 3 lose the o when they are put before the noun they are affecting:

I did not have many boyfriends. Alex is the first one – *No tuve muchos novios. Alex es el **primero***

Alex is my first boyfriend – *Alex es mi **primer** novio*

This day is the third of my trip – *Este día es el **tercero** de mi viaje*

It's the third day of my trip – *Es mi **tercer** día de viaje*

Chapter 5: Numbers for a Rainy Day: Shopping

Numbers are not only necessary for telling the date and time, but they are in everyday life in another way as well... Maybe you even have some numbers in your pockets right now... Yes, money!

Let's take a look at local currencies and their approximate equivalent to one American dollar (this might change with time in some countries with volatile currencies, of course):

Spain: *euro* (1 American dollar is equivalent to 0.89 *euros*)

Mexico: *peso* (1 American dollar is equivalent to 19 *pesos*)

Argentina: *peso* (1 American dollar is equivalent to 45 *pesos*)

Bolivia: *boliviano* (1 American dollar is equivalent to 7 *bolivianos*)

Chile: *peso* (1 American dollar is equivalent to 663 *pesos*)

Colombia: *peso* (1 American dollar is equivalent to 3,000 *pesos*)

Paraguay: *guaraní* (1 American dollar is equivalent to 6,200 *guaraníes*)

Peru: *sol* (1 American dollar is equivalent to 3.30 *soles*)

Uruguay: *peso* (1 American dollar is equivalent to 33.80 *pesos*)

Dominican Republic: *peso* (1 American dollar is equivalent to 50 *pesos*)

Panama: *balboa* (1 American dollar is equivalent to 1 *balboa*)

Costa Rica: *colón* (1 American dollar is equivalent to 600 *colones*)

El Salvador: *colón* (1 American dollar is equivalent to 8 *colones*)

Shopping vocabulary:

cash – *efectivo*

credit card – *tarjeta de crédito*

debit card – *tarjeta de débito*

cash machine – *cajero automático*

counter – *caja*

the bill – *la cuenta*

sale – *rebajas*

discount – *descuento*

price – *precio*

change – *vuelta / cambio*

Note – *billete*

coin – *moneda*

Common questions while shopping:

Do you take VISA credit cards? – *¿Aceptan tarjetas de crédito VISA?*

Can I pay with cash? – *¿Puedo pagar con efectivo?*

How much is it? – *¿Cuánto es?*

How much is this? – *¿Cuánto cuesta esto?*

What is the price for that? – *¿Cuál es el precio de eso?*

How much are these two magnets? – *¿Cuánto cuestan estos dos imanes?*

How much is the change? – *¿Cuánto es mi vuelto?*

Some very useful verbs for ordering and buying are *querer* (to want), *necesitar* (to need), *dar* (to give), *costar* (to cost), and *ser* (to be):

I want three mangos and two pears – ***Quiero*** *tres mangos y dos peras*

I need two kilos of strawberries – ***Necesito*** *dos kilos de fresas*

Could I have a kilo of flour, please? – *¿Podría* ***darme*** *un kilo de harina, por favor?*

Give me five! – *¡****Deme*** *cinco!*

That costs two eighty – *Eso* ***cuesta*** *dos con ochenta*

The price is two hundred soles – *El precio* ***es*** *de doscientos soles*

There is a verb you might need a lot while shopping: *pagar* (to pay). Let's see its conjugation and some practical sentences:

To Pay (pagar)

- I pay – *yo* ***pago***
- You pay – *tú* ***pagas*** */ usted* ***paga*** */ vos* ***pagás***
- He pays – *él* ***paga***
- She pays – *ella* ***paga***
- We pay – *nosotros* ***pagamos*** */ nosotras* ***pagamos***
- You pay – *vosotros* ***pagáis*** */ vosotras* ***pagáis*** */ ustedes* ***pagan***
- They pay – *ellos* ***pagan*** */ ellas* ***pagan***

I pay with cash, is it possible? – ***Pago*** *con efectivo, ¿es posible?*

Do we pay now? – *¿****Pagamos*** *ahora?*

You pay for dinner, right? – *Vosotras* ***pagáis*** *la cena, ¿verdad?*

You pay for the coffee, I will pay for the movie tickets – *Tú* ***pagas*** *el café, yo* ***pago*** *las entradas del cine*

This is basic vocabulary related to numbers:

to add – *sumar*

to subtract – *restar*

to multiply – *multiplicar*

to divide – *dividir*

the sum – *la suma*

the difference – *la diferencia*

to count – *contar*

The verb *contar* has two meanings! There is contar as in to count: *uno, dos, tres, cuatro,* and *contar* as in to tell. Let's see the conjugation and some examples:

- I tell – *yo **cuento***
- You tell – *tú **cuentas** / usted **cuenta** / vos **contás***
- He tells – *él **cuenta***
- She tells – *ella **cuenta***
- We tell – *nosotros **contamos** / nosotras **contamos***
- You tell – *vosotros **contáis** / vosotras **contáis** / ustedes **cuentan***
- They tell – *ellos **cuentan** / ellas **cuentan***

Here are some examples:

Kate counts how many beers we have left – *Kate **cuenta** cuántas cervezas nos quedan*

Sara tells me about her life – *Sara me **cuenta** sobre su vida*

Santiago tells me a secret – *Santiago me **cuenta** un secreto*

Should I tell you about my work? – *¿Te **cuento** sobre mi trabajo?*

Kate and James are very happy to see each other after so long. After having a few wines with Damián, they go to the market to buy something so they can prepare dinner:

KATE: First, how many soles do you have? – *Primero, ¿cuántos soles traes?*

JAMES: I have... around fifty – *Tengo... unos cincuenta*

KATE: Great, that'll be enough – *Genial, con eso será suficiente*

JAMES: Should we buy some fresh tomatoes and garlic and make pasta? – *¿Llevamos tomates frescos y ajo para hacer pasta?*

KATE: Sounds perfect; how many tomatoes do we take? – *Suena perfecto, ¿cuántos tomates llevamos?*

JAMES: Let's take four. How much are they? – *Podemos llevar cuatro. ¿Cuánto cuestan?*

KATE: They are 1.20 soles per kilo. Four tomatoes are... a kilo and a half – *Están a un sol con veinte cada kilo. Cuatro tomates son... ¡un kilo y medio!*

JAMES: Excellent! – *¡Excelente!*

Did you ever use *kilos* as a measurement unit? In Spanish-speaking countries, you will definitely use the metric system (kilograms, liters, meters, and Celsius degrees) instead of the imperial system (pounds, gallons, yards, and Fahrenheit degrees).

Let's quickly see some equivalencies:

1 kilo – 2.20 pounds

100 grams – 3.5 ounces

1 liter – 2.11 pints

4 liters – 1.05 gallons

1 meter – 3.28 feet

1 meter – 1.09 yards

1 centimeter – 0.39 inches

5 centimeters – 1.96 inches

When talking about temperature: 0 to 10 Celsius degrees is cold; 10 to 15 is chilly; 15 to 25 is warm; 25 to 30 is hot; and >30 is really hot.

0 Celsius degrees – 32 Fahrenheit degrees

15 Celsius degrees – 59 Fahrenheit degrees

30 Celsius degrees – 86 Fahrenheit degrees

What about fractions? You may need to buy half a kilo of something, or a quarter of a kilo of another thing. When you have half of something, you say "*medio*" or "*media*" depending on whether the object is masculine or feminine:

½ – *medio/media*

⅓ – *un tercio*

¼ – *un cuarto*

⅛ – *un octavo*

Half a kilo of potatoes, please! – **Medio** *kilo de patatas, ¡por favor!*

I need half a loaf of bread – *Necesito* **media** *hogaza de pan*

Can I have a quarter of a kilo of strawberries, please? – *¿Podría darme* **un cuarto** *de kilo de fresas, por favor?*

Chapter 6: Come Again? Understanding Each Other

No matter how hard you study, there are some situations in which communication is not fluent. Maybe the person you are talking to has a really strong accent, or they are speaking very fast. For those situations, you need to be prepared too!

Here are some practical sentences you may find useful when you get lost in translation:

I do not understand – *No comprendo / No entiendo*

Please speak slowly – *Por favor, hable despacio*

Can you say that again, please? – *¿Podría decir eso nuevamente, por favor?*

Do you speak English? (formal) – *¿Habla inglés?*

Do you speak Spanish? (formal) – *¿Habla español?*

Do you speak English? (informal) – *¿Hablas inglés?*

Do you speak Spanish? (informal) – *¿Hablas español?*

Can I ask you something? – *¿Puedo preguntarle algo?*

What is the meaning of this? – *¿Qué significa esto?*

In these sentences, there are some basic verbs you need to know when you are trying to be understood by Spanish-speaking people: *hablar, decir, comprender, entender, significar,* and *preguntar.*

Let's see them one by one—what they mean and how you can use them in different situations.

Hablar

Hablar is a very important verb when you are learning a new language. Do not forget the h is mute. You will use it a lot in its infinitive form to talk about your ability to speak Spanish. For those situations, you can use some of these sentences:

I am learning to speak Spanish – *Estoy aprendiendo a hablar en español*

I do not know how to speak Spanish yet! – *No sé hablar español ¡todavía!*

I know how to speak Spanish, but not very well – *Sé hablar español, pero no muy bien*

Do you speak English? (informal) – *¿Sabes hablar en inglés?*

This is the conjugation for the present tense of the verb *hablar:*

- I talk – *yo **hablo***
- You talk – *tú **hablas** / usted **habla** / vos **hablás***
- He talks – *él **habla***
- She talks – *ella **habla***
- We talk – *nosotros **hablamos** / nosotras **hablamos***

- You talk – *vosotros* **habláis** / *vosotras* **habláis** / *ustedes* **hablan**
- They talk – *ellos* **hablan** / *ellas* **hablan**

Here are some practical examples with the different conjugations:

I speak Spanish – *Hablo español*

I do not speak Spanish – *No hablo español*

I speak four languages... more or less – *Hablo cuatro idiomas... más o menos*

You speak very fast! Slow down, please – *¡Hablas muy rápido! Más despacio, por favor*

She speaks very well because she practices continuously – *Ella habla muy bien porque practica continuamente*

Do you speak English? (formal) – *¿Habla usted inglés?*

He does not know what he is talking about – *No sabe de qué habla*

Shall we speak Spanish? – *¿Hablamos en español?*

Sometimes we speak in English, sometimes we speak in Spanish – *A veces hablamos en inglés, a veces hablamos en español*

James is out on a date with Dani, the Mexican girl he met at the hostel. They are talking... about talking:

DANI: Am I talking too fast? You can tell me – *¿Estoy hablando demasiado rápido? Puedes decirme*

JAMES: No, you do not speak fast... Well, you do speak fast, but you speak very clearly – *No, no hablas rápido... Bueno, sí hablas rápido, pero hablas muy claramente*

DANI: Good, I stay at ease – *Bien, me quedo tranquila*

JAMES: Your friend Sara does speak too fast – *Tu amiga Sara sí habla muy rápido*

DANI: I know! Even I have a hard time to understand her when she talks – *¡Lo sé! Incluso yo tengo problemas para comprender cuando habla*

Decir and significar

Decir means to say. When communicating with people in Spanish, especially at first, there can be many situations in which you can find this verb useful. Let's see the present tense conjugation for the verb *decir*, then some real-life examples:

- I say – *yo* **digo**
- You say – *tú* **dices** / *usted* **dice** / *vos* **decís**
- He says – *él* **dice**
- She says – *ella* **dice**
- We say – *nosotros* **decimos** / *nosotras* **decimos**
- You say – *vosotros* **decís** / *vosotras* **decís** / *ustedes* **dicen**
- They say – *ellos* **dicen** / *ellas* **dicen**

Decir can also be used together with the verb *querer* (to want). When these two verbs are put together, they get a new meaning:

'Croqueta' is a funny word; what does it mean? – *'Croqueta es una palabra graciosa; ¿qué quiere decir?*

I like your tattoo. What does it mean? – *Me gusta tu tatuaje. ¿Qué quiere decir?*

I do not understand those signs; what do they mean? – *No comprendo esos letreros; ¿qué quieren decir?*

There is another verb in Spanish that can be used in the same way, to express meaning: *significar*. Let's see the same examples with this verb:

'Croqueta' is a funny word; what does it mean? – *'Croqueta es una palabra graciosa; ¿qué significa?*

I like your tattoo. What does it mean? – *Me gusta tu tatuaje. ¿Qué significa?*

I do not understand those signs; what do they mean? – *No comprendo esos letreros; ¿qué significan?*

Comprender / Entender

This is one of the first things any traveler has to learn: how to say I do not understand!

The two Spanish verbs entender and comprender are synonyms; they both mean to understand. Let's see their present tense conjugation, then some real-life examples, so you know how to apply them:

- I understand – *yo* **comprendo**
- You understand – *tú* **comprendes** / *usted* **comprende** / *vos* **comprendés**
- He understands – *él* **comprende**
- She understands – *ella* **comprende**
- We understand – *nosotros* **comprendemos** / *nosotras* **comprendemos**
- You understand – *vosotros* **comprendéis** / *vosotras* **comprendéis** / *ustedes* **comprenden**
- They understand – *ellos* **comprenden** / *ellas* **comprenden**

- I understand – *yo* **entiendo**
- You understand – *tú* **entiendes** / *usted* **entiende** / *vos* **entendés**
- He understands – *él* **entiende**
- She understands – *ella* **entiende**
- We understand – *nosotros* **entendemos** / *nosotras* **entendemos**
- You understand – *vosotros* **entendéis** / *vosotras* **entendéis** / *ustedes* **entienden**
- They understand – *ellos* **entienden** / *ellas* **entienden**

Here are some practical sentences with the verb *comprender:*

I understand – *Comprendo*

I do not understand – *No comprendo*

Do you understand what I say? – *¿Comprendes lo que digo?*

We understand almost everything, if you speak slowly – *Comprendemos casi todo, si habla lentamente*

She understands Spanish very well, but she finds it hard to speak it – *Comprende muy bien el español, pero le cuesta hablarlo*

There are some accents that are hard to understand – *Hay algunos acentos difíciles de comprender*

I do not understand what you are saying – *No comprendo lo que dices*

I do not understand what this is – *No comprendo qué es esto*

I do not understand what you want to do – *No comprendo qué quieres hacer*

I do not understand where you want to go – *No comprendo a dónde quieres ir*

Here are the same examples with the verb *entender:*

I understand – *Entiendo*

I do not understand – *No entiendo*

Do you understand what I say? – *¿Entiendes lo que digo?*

We understand almost everything, if you speak slowly – *Entendemos casi todo, si habla lentamente*

She understands Spanish very well, but she finds it hard to speak it – *Entiende muy bien el español, pero le cuesta hablarlo*

There are some accents that are hard to understand – *Hay algunos acentos difíciles de entender*

I do not understand what you are saying – *No entiendo lo que dices*

I do not understand what this is – *No entiendo qué es esto*

I do not understand what you want to do – *No entiendo qué quieres hacer*

I do not understand where you want to go – *No entiendo a dónde quieres ir*

Preguntar

Preguntar means to ask. Never be afraid to ask questions. Most people will be glad to answer them. To ask questions in Spanish, the first thing you should learn is how to ask:

May I ask you something? (formal) – *¿Puedo hacerle una pregunta?*

Can I ask you a question? (informal) – *¿Puedo preguntarte algo?*

Sorry, I have a question... – *Perdón, una pregunta...*

This is the present tense conjugation for the verb *preguntar:*

- I ask – *yo **pregunto***
- You ask – *tú **preguntas** / usted **pregunta** / vos **preguntás***

- He asks – *él **pregunta***
- She asks – *ella **pregunta***
- We ask – *nosotros **preguntamos** / nosotras **preguntamos***
- You ask – *vosotros **preguntáis** / vosotras **preguntáis** / ustedes **preguntan***
- They ask – *ellos **preguntan** / ellas **preguntan***

James and Dani are hanging out in the common room. After their date the night before, they have spent most of their time together:

JAMES: Dani, may I ask you something? – *Dani, ¿puedo preguntarte algo?*

DANI: Of course! Ask me whatever you want – *¡Claro! Pregúntame lo que quieras*

JAMES: Is there someone special in your life? – *¿Hay alguien especial en tu vida?*

DANI: Well, yes. Many people: my mom, my dad, my grandma – *Pues, sí. Mucha gente: mi mamá, mi papá, mi abuela...*

JAMES: Haha, no, that's not what I am asking – *Jaja, no, eso no es lo que estoy preguntando*

DANI: What are you asking then? – *¿Qué me preguntas, entonces?*

JAMES: I was wondering if you have a partner – *Me preguntaba si tienes pareja*

DANI: Oh, that is what you are asking! – *Oh, ¡eso es lo que preguntas!*

JAMES: What is your answer? – *¿Cuál es tu respuesta?*

DANI: No, I do not have a boyfriend, that is my answer – *No, no tengo novio, esa es mi respuesta*

Vocabulary for going out

¿Puedo comprarte algo de beber? – May I buy you something to drink?

¿Vienes aquí a menudo? – Do you come here often?

¿De qué trabajas? – So, what do you do for a living?

¿Quieres bailar? – Do you want to dance?

¿Quieres tomar aire fresco? – Would you like to get some fresh air?

¿Quieres ir a otra fiesta? – Do you want to go to a different party?

¡Vayámonos de aquí! – Let's get out of here!

¿Mi casa o tu casa? – My place or yours?

¿Quieres ver una película en mi casa? – Would you like to watch a movie at my place?

¿Tienes planes para esta noche? – Do you have any plans for tonight?

¿Te gustaría comer conmigo uno de estos días? – Would you like to eat with me sometime?

¿Quieres ir a tomar un café? – Would you like to go get a coffee?

¿Puedo acompañarte/llevarte a tu casa? – May I walk/drive you home?

¿Quieres que nos volvamos a ver? – Would you like to meet again?

¡Gracias por una hermosa noche! – Thank you for a lovely evening!

¿Quieres entrar y tomar una taza de café? – Would you like to come inside for a coffee?

¡Eres hermoso/a! – You're gorgeous!

¡Eres gracioso/a! – You're funny!

¡Tienes unos ojos hermosos! – You have beautiful eyes!

¡Bailas muy bien! – You're a great dancer!

¡He estado pensando en ti todo el día! – I have been thinking about you all day!

¡Ha sido muy agradable charlar contigo! – It's been really nice talking to you!

Chapter 7: Goodbye! Let's Meet Again!

James is leaving Colombia. It is a sad day at the hostel because all of the regulars (María, Alex, Alicia, Andrea, Daniela, and the Mexican girls) grew very fond of him... But he has to move on. He has a flight booked to Lima, Perú.

You can surely learn something from James' departure. For example, how to say goodbye.

Bye! – *¡Chao!*

Goodbye – *Adiós*

See you – *Nos vemos*

See you later – *Hasta luego*

See you soon – *Nos vemos pronto*

See you tomorrow – *Hasta mañana*

It was a pleasure to meet you – *Fue un placer conocerte*

I hope we meet again – *Espero que nos volvamos a ver*

Have a nice day – *Tenga un buen día*

Have a good weekend! – *¡Ten un buen fin de semana!*

Take care – *Cuídate*

Everyone is gathered at the hostel's reception to say goodbye to James:

JAMES: Okay, guys, I really should be leaving now, my plane is leaving in two hours... My taxi is here! – *Okay, chicos, realmente debería irme ahora, mi avión sale en dos horas... ¡Mi taxi está aquí!*

ALEX: You are not leaving without giving me another hug, mate! – *¡No te vas sin antes darme otro abrazo, amigo!*

ANDREA: It was a real pleasure to meet you, James – *Fue un verdadero placer conocerte, James*

ALICIA: When are you coming back? – *¿Cuándo regresas?*

JAMES: Well, I don't know. Soon, I hope – *Bueno, no lo sé. Pronto, espero*

MARÍA: I wish you the best of luck for the rest of your trip – *Te deseo la mejor de las suertes para el resto de tu viaje*

JAMES: Thanks to all of you, really. Dani, don't cry! We will see each other someday – *Gracias a todos, de verdad. Dani, ¡no llores! Nos veremos algún día*

DANI: I know! I know! I am going to miss you – *¡Lo sé! ¡Lo sé! Te voy a extrañar*

JAMES: Me too... I'm going to miss you all – *Yo también... Los voy a extrañar a todos*

ANDREA: Your taxi is getting impatient... – *Tu taxi se está poniendo impaciente...*

JAMES: All right, bye, guys! We'll see each other soon! Thank you for everything – *Bien, ¡chau, chicos! ¡Nos veremos pronto! Gracias por todo*

ALL: Goodbye, James! – *¡Adiós, James!*

But what about technology? Nowadays, just because you do not see someone physically anymore does not mean you cannot stay in touch with them.

Here are some sentences that might be useful if you want to keep in touch with someone:

Let's keep in touch – *Mantengámonos en contacto*

Call me – *Llámame*

What is your phone number? – *¿Cuál es tu número de teléfono?*

Write to me – *Escríbeme*

Follow me on Instagram – *Sígueme en Instagram*

Can I add you on Facebook so we can keep in touch? – *¿Puedo añadirte a mis amigos en Facebook para que estemos en contacto?*

Give me your email address – *Dame tu dirección de email*

What's your email address? – *¿Cómo es tu dirección de correo electrónico?*

Do you use Snapchat? – *¿Tienes Snapchat?*

If you have to send an email in Spanish for work, studies, accommodation or any other formal setting, these are some ways you can say hello, introduce yourself, and say goodbye:

Dear, Andrea, – *Estimada, Andrea,*

My name is James – *Mi nombre es James*

I am contacting you because... – *Le escribo porque...*

If it is not an inconvenience to you – *Si no supone inconvenientes para usted*

Looking forward to hearing from you – *Espero su respuesta*

Kind regards – *Saludos cordiales*

James is going to Peru next. When James arrives in Peru, he will not stay in a hostel. He will be 'couchsurfing' instead.

This means he got in touch with another traveler through a specific website earlier, and now the other person is going to let him stay in their house for free!

Before leaving for the airport, James sends Damián, the other traveler, an email to remind him that he is arriving that afternoon:

Estimado, Damián,

Dear, Damián,

¡Espero que estés bien!

I hope you are doing great!

Te escribo para recordarte que hoy es mi vuelo a Perú.

I am writing to remind you today is my flight to Peru.

Estoy saliendo de mi hostal en Cartagena en algunos minutos.

I'm leaving my hostel in Cartagena in a few minutes.

Mi avión sale al mediodía.

My plane leaves at noon.

Llegará a Lima cerca de las tres y media de la tarde.

It will arrive in Lima around half past three in the afternoon.

Voy a tomar un taxi hasta tu casa.

I am taking a taxi to your house.

No tengo ganas de tomar el bus; estoy algo cansado...

I do not feel like taking a bus; I am a little bit tired...

Llevo unas botellas de vino para compartir contigo.

I'm taking some bottles of wine to share with you.

Y más tarde, puedo cocinar.

And later, I can prepare dinner.

Bueno, ¡eso es todo!

Well, that is it!

Mis amigos del hostal me esperan para despedirme.

My friends from the hostel are waiting for me to say goodbye.

Voy a extrañarlos mucho.

I am really going to miss them.

Nos vemos más tarde.

See you later.

¡Chao!

Bye!

Chapter 8: Meeting People/Nationality/Job

Every name of things in Spanish is either feminine or masculine, not simply the obvious ones such as boy or girl, man or women. That different is called as the gender of the word. You could tell a gender of the word from its ending. For example, almost all word ending in -o are mescaline. Those that end in –a are feminine. Gender is vital, as it influences the other words in your sentence. There is more in this chapter. Do not worry about this, it is a new concept that seems strange to you. In practice, it does not cause a massive struggle in Spanish.

a) Meeting People

Soy de Francia.	I'm from France.
¿De dónde eres?	Where are you from?
Tú eres español	You are Spaniard.
¿Cómo es tu país?	How's your country?
Es un país bonito	It's a nice country.
Mi major amiga es china.	My best friend is Chinese.
Mi compañero de cuarto quiere viajar a—	My roommate wants to go to —
¿Qué idioma hablas en tu país?	What language do you speak in your country?

Take note that it is optional to utilize the articles las, los, la, and el before most countries in Spanish unless the specific name has such an article. For example, El Salvador.

Talking about your family and your country is vital in Spanish conversations. That's because the Hispanics are curious about people. They love to know all about you and the place where you are from. The majority of Hispanics nowadays are also travel a lot. Therefore, thy will be enthusiastic about telling you about their adventures in foreign lands.

Me llamo (My name is)

One way of identifying yourself and the other person is to utilize *me llamo* (I am called, or my name is), and *se llama* (he/she is called, you are called). If you want to ask someone's name, you can utilize the word *¿Cómo?* at the start of the question:

¿Cómo? se llama?	What is his/her/its name? / What is he/he/it called?
¿Cómo? se llama Vd.?	What is your name? / What are you called?

You will have noticed that question words or also know as "interrogatives," such as *¿quién?* who? and *¿cómo?* how? have an accent. That isn't to indicate where the stress falls, however, to present that the word is being utilized in a question, not a statement. You will also find them utilized without accents in statements.

Using *Estos* (These)

Estos is utilized along with plural words that talk about various masculine individuals or to a mixed group of people or things. For example, *estos señores* that means these men or these men and women.

How to Make a Question?

In Spanish, it is very simple to create a question. One way to is to include *¿no?* to the end of your statement. Make sure that you increase your voice a bit to offer a questioning tone at the end of your sentence. That has a similar impact a using isn't you, isn't it and more in the English language.

¿Vd.es Isabel?	Are you Isabel?
Vd. es Isabel, ¿no?	You are Isabel, aren't you?

Another way is to turn Vd. es, Vds. Son round:

¿Es Vd. Isabel?	Are you Isabel?
¿Son Vds. Los Sres. Herrero?	Are you Mr. and Mrs. Herrero?

You will notice that in written Spanish, there are two question marks utilized to determine a question. You will find an inverted one at the start and the standard question mark at the end. When only part of the sentence is the question, the question marks will go round that part. For example, Vd. es. Isabel ¿no? The exclamation marks work the similar way:

Coco, ¡es Vd.!	Coco, it's you!

Formal 'You'

Usted refers to you. It is utilized except when talking to other people you know well or to kids (God or animals). When you write, it is sometimes abbreviated to *Vd.* (plural *Vds.*)

Using the Negative

If you prefer to tell something is not the case, you can just place no before the word. That will tell you what is happening (the verb).

Below are some conversations you need to know if you want to get to know someone:

¿Donde trabajas?	Where do you work?
Trabajo en un restaurante.	I work at a restaurant.
¿Cuáles son tus aficiones?	What are your hobbies?
Me gusta leer libros y ver películas.	I like to read books and watch movies.
¿De donde eres?	Where are you from?
Soy de Irlanda.	I'm from Ireland.

319

¿Cuál es tu película favorita?	What's your favorite movie?
Me encanta Star Wars.	I love Star Wars.
¿Desde cuándo aprendes español?	How long have you been learning Spanish?
Aprendo español desde hace tres meses.	I've been learning Spanish for three months.
¿Cuál es tu color favorito?	What is your favorite color?
Me gusta el verde.	I like green.
¿Hablas otros idiomas?	Do you speak other languages?
Sí, hablo inglés y francés	Yes, I speak English and French.

b) Nationality (*Nacionalidad*)

In Spanish, some nationality adjectives along with a masculine form which ends in a consonant add −*a* to create the feminine. The adjectives inglés (as well as other nationality adjectives, which ends in −*és*) and aleman remove the accent on their last vowel. That is to keep their original stresses:

Masculine	Feminine	Meaning
Español	*Española*	Spanish
Inglés	*Inglesa*	English
Alemán	*Alemana*	German

You will also find several adjectives along with a masculine form that ends in −*or* and −*a* to create the feminine form.

Masculine	Feminine	Meaning
trabjador	*trabajadora*	Worker
hablador	*habladora*	Chatty / talkative

To say your nationality or someone else's, you need to utilize the words son, somos, es, soy as you did to determine individuals. You could also include the nationality description: *soy inglés, es español/española.* Take note that the ending of the nationality word should change based on the gender of the person described. It also transforms if you're speaking about more than one individual: somos Americanos, son franceses.

Below are some examples along with the masculine, feminine and plural forms:

Country	Masculine	Feminine	Plural
América	*americano*	*americana*	*Americanos/ americanas*
Australia	*australiano*	*australiana*	*Australianos/ australianas*
Italia	*italiano*	*italiana*	*Italianos/ italianas*

Francia	francés	francesa	Franceses/ francesas
Escocia	escocés	escocesa	Escoceses/ escocesas
Irlanda	irlandés	irlandesa	Irlandeses/ irlandesas
Alemania	alemán	alemana	Alemanes/ alemanas

These words of nationality are the ones you utilize when you wish to tell a Frenchman, a Spanish woman, etc. *Un francés* refers to a Frenchman.

Take note that not every Spanish people will tell *soy espannol/a*. For instance, might insist *soy catalán, soy catalana, soy de Cataluña, somos catalanes, somos de Cataluña* when they are from the north-east of Barcelona or Spain.

Some individuals from the country of Basque tend to consider themselves as Basques instead of Spaniards. They will tell *soy vasco, soy vasca, soy de Euzkadi, somos vascos, somos de Euzkadi*. You see, Euzkadi is the Basque term for the region of Basque.

It is vital that you are informed of the strong region, or some would say national, sensibilities throughout Spain, especially in those regions that still utilize their own individual languages like the *Cataluña* as well as the Basque region.

What's more, the Basque language is somewhat different from Spanish. It's an old language and extremely hard to learn. *Catalán* as well is another language from Spanish. You need to learn individually. However, compared to Basque, it is connected to Spanish because it is derived from the Spanish language. Often, the Spanish language is also called as *castellano* or 'Castillan.' A man from Barcelona (which is the capital of *Cataluña*) could tell soy Barcelona. *Soy barceloñes. Soy catalán y también español. Hablo* (I speak) *catalán y tambié castellano*.

Keep in mind that all Spaniards are connected to their region of origin. That's true even if they have relocated away from it. It is in recognition of that regional loyalty that Spanish is separated into autonomias or regions along with a huge deal of local self-government. Local pride is also apparent in people's attachment and loyalty to their city or town of origin. Compared to English, where you only have some words such as Mancunian or Londoner, Spanish has a term for the inhabitants of every town of any size. For instance, a man from Seville would describe himself as un *sevillano*.

c) Job (Trabajo)

You will find two simple ways of asking what work someone does. One way is to ask him or her *¿Qué hace Vd.?* (What do you do? The majority of the responses might sound the same to English. However, in the Spanish language, the majority of them have a feminine and masculine form.

Below are some of the examples of what an individual might tell when you ask them *¿Qué hace Vd.?*

	Masculine	Feminine	Meaning
soy	actor	actriz	actor/actress
soy	professor	profesora	teacher
soy	administrador	administradora	administrator

soy	camerero	camarera	waiter/waitress
soy	director de empresa	directora de empresa	company director
soy	enfemero	enfermera	nurse

You will find some terms for occupations are similar whether they talk about a man or a woman. Those have ending in −ista or −e, like the following:

un/una taxista	a taxi driver
un/una artista	an artist
un/una periodista	a journalist
un/una contable	an accountant
un/una intérprete	an interpreter
un/una estudiante	a student

The other way to ask about a person's job is to say ¿Dóndé trabaja Vd.? (Where do you work?). Below are different potential answers to this question:

Trabajo en una oficina	I work in an office.
Trabaho en una agencia de turismo	I work in a tourist office/agency.
Trabajo en un colegio.	I work in a school.
Trabajo en un hospital.	I work in a hospital.
Trabajo en casa.	I work at home.

Take note that ¿Dóndé? and ¿Qué? are two examples of words, which require accents when they are utilized to ask a question.

Try to practice the following conversations:

¿Cuál es su profesión?	Soy consultor.
What do you do?	I am a consultant.
¿Para qué empresa trabaja usted?	Soy autónomo.
What company do you work for?	I am self-employed.
¡Qué interesante!	¿Y cuál es su profesión?
How's interesting	And what is your profession?
Soy dentistia.	Mi hermana es dentista también.
I am a dentist.	My sister is a dentist too.

'I work; I live...'

Trabajo and *vivo* denotes I work, and I live. If you like to say 'I' do something, you need to find the term that ends in −*o*, as in many examples you might already know: *entiend, me llamo, hablo.* You will find a few exceptions to this rule, one of which is the world for I am − *soy.*

'Where do you live?' *(¿Dónde vive?)*

Depending on your context, you may require to offer only a vague response like vivo en Londres or vivo en Madrid. On some cases, however, you may require to present your own address, and for visiting Spanish friends or places, you will need to know when someone tells you that.

Chapter 9: The Curious Traveler: Questions and Answers

If you are going to travel around Latin America or Spain, you are definitely going to be asking loads of questions. Learning a new language is not only learning new words; it is learning about a whole new culture.

This is why you need to be ready to ask, and ask and ask even more, and also get ready to hear some answers!

Have you ever heard of the six W and the two H? They are *what, when, who, where, why, which, how,* and *how much*? In Spanish, these could be translated as *qué, cuándo, quién, dónde, por qué, cuál, cómo* and *cuánto.*

These words are fundamental if, let's say, you want to buy something (*how much is that*?), if you want to move around (*where is the train station*?) or even if you want to know the time (*what time is it*?).

What? (¿Qué?)

What are you doing here? – *¿Qué estás haciendo aquí?*

What are we going to eat? – *¿Qué vamos a comer?*

What do you mean? – *¿Qué quieres decir?*

What do we do now? – *¿Qué hacemos ahora?*

What's up, guys? – *¿Qué pasa, chicos?*

What time is it? – *¿Qué hora es?*

¿Cuándo?

When is our plane leaving? – *¿Cuándo sale nuestro avión?*

When is Sara picking you up? – *¿Cuándo te recoge Sara?*

When is your thesis due? – *¿Cuándo debes entregar la tesis?*

When are you coming to visit? – *¿Cuándo vienes de visita?*

When are we going to Machu Picchu? – *¿Cuándo vamos a Machu Picchu?*

When is the bus coming? – *¿Cuándo viene el bus?*

¿Quién?

Who was that girl? – *¿Quién era esa chica?*

Who do we have to talk to? – *¿Con quién tenemos que hablar?*

Who is in charge here? – *¿Quién está a cargo aquí?*

Who are you? – *¿Quién eres?*

Who do you think you are? – *¿Quién crees que eres?*

Who could have imagined something like this? – *¡Quién podría haber imaginado algo así!*

¿Dónde?

Where are you? – *¿Dónde estás?*

Where is this hotel? – *¿Dónde está este hotel?*

Where do you want to go? – *¿A Dónde quieres ir?*

Where is my phone?! – *¡¿Dónde está mi teléfono?!*

Where do we go afterward? – *¿Dónde vamos a continuación?*

Where is this place?! – *¿¡Dónde está este sitio!?*

¿Por qué?

Why do you want to go there? – *¿Por qué quieres ir ahí?*

Why do we have to go there? – *¿Por qué tenemos que ir allí?*

Why don't we go back? – *¿Por qué no regresamos?*

Why are you running? – *¿Por qué corres?*

Why don't we order everything on the menu? – *¿Por qué no pedimos todo lo que hay en el menú?*

Why don't we open a bottle of champagne? – *¿Por qué no abrimos una botella de champán?*

¿Cómo?

How do we go back to the house? – *¿Cómo volvemos a la casa?*

How did we get here? – *¿Cómo llegamos aquí?*

How did this happen? – *¿Cómo pasó esto?*

How can I return the favor? – *¿Cómo puedo devolverte el favor?*

How do you know my name? – *¿Cómo sabes mi nombre?*

How can I help you? – *¿Cómo puedo ayudarte?*

¿Cuánto?

How much is that? – *¿Cuánto cuesta eso?*

How many times do I have to say this? – *¿Cuántas veces debo decir esto?*

How much did you miss me? – *¿Cuánto me has extrañado?*

How much did you walk today? – *¿Cuánto has caminado hoy?*

How much can we spend? – *¿Cuánto podemos gastar?*

How much did they steal from you? – *¿Cuánto te han robado?*

¿Cuál?

What's the hostel's address? – *¿Cuál es la dirección del hostal?*

Which one is your phone? – *¿Cuál es tu teléfono?*

Which one is your favorite? – *¿Cuál es tu preferida?*

Which car are you talking about? – *¿De cuál automóvil hablas?*

What was your best trip? – *¿Cuál fue tu mejor viaje?*

What was your worse flight? – *¿Cuál fue tu peor vuelo?*

James made an impulsive decision and bought a plane ticket to Mexico, to visit Daniela, the girl he dated shortly in Cartagena. She does not know he is coming to visit, so it is a big shock when he knocks on her door:

DANIELA: My God! What are you doing here? – *¡Dios mío! ¿Qué haces aquí?*

JAMES: Happy to see me? – *¿Feliz de verme?*

DANIELA: Of course, but I cannot believe it. When did you arrive? – *Claro, pero no lo puedo creer. ¿Cuándo llegaste?*

JAMES: Like... an hour ago, why? – *Como... hace una hora, ¿por qué?*

DANIELA: I don't know. Did you come here just to see me? – *No lo sé. ¿Has venido aquí para verme?*

JAMES: Yes. Is it too crazy? – *Sí, ¿es muy loco?*

DANIELA: Definitely! Do you know what is even crazier? – *¡Definitivamente! ¿Sabes qué es aún más loco?*

JAMES: What? – *¿Qué?*

DANIELA: I bought a plane ticket to go see you – *Yo compré un billete de avión para ir a verte a ti*

JAMES: What? How? Where? – *¿Qué? ¿Cómo? ¿Dónde?*

DANIELA: I thought you were going to be in Buenos Aires... I was going to go there in an hour – *Pensé que estarías en Buenos Aires... Iba a ir allí en una hora*

Conclusion

¡Hola nuevamente!

Did you enjoy this Spanish book and James' love story?

Now you have the basics to understand this beautiful language: its verbal tenses, pronouns, prepositions, and much more.

Dare to challenge yourself and explore Spanish even further until you don't need any book. Read short stories in Spanish, novels, newspapers, websites, watch films, and immerse yourself in as many Spanish-speaking countries as you can.

Try every possible food and learn its ingredients and recipe. Ask locals about their slang, local dishes, and customs. Not only will you end up being fluent in Spanish, but you will also make tons of new friends and get to know much about the world and different cultures. This will definitely make you feel like a richer person.

So, if this is nothing but a starting point, let's hope it was useful for you to take your first steps into this amazing, complex, ever-changing language.

Here are some final tips for you to go all the way with Spanish:

1. Speak from the first day

Unfortunately, many people follow the wrong approach when learning a language. A language is a means of communication and should, therefore, be lived rather than learned. There is no such thing as an "I am ready now." Thus, just jump into the cold water and speak the language at home from day one. It is best to set the goal not to miss a day when you have not used the foreign language in any form. Just try to implement everything you learn directly. So speak, write, and think in your foreign language.

2. Immerse yourself in the foreign language at home

This tip goes hand in hand with the first one. To learn the foreign language quickly and efficiently, you have to integrate it firmly into your everyday life. It is not enough if you learn a few words from time to time and engage in grammar and pronunciation. This has to be done much more intensively. You have to dive properly into the foreign language. Just bring foreign countries to your home. By so-called "immersion", you surround yourself constantly and everywhere with the language.

3. Change the language setting on devices

For example, you could change the menu language of your smartphone or laptop from your native language to the language you are learning. Since you use your smartphone or your laptop every day, you know where to find something and learn some vocabulary along the way. Of course, you can also do the same with your social networks like Facebook and Twitter. However, watch out that you are always able to change back the menu language!

4. Use foreign language media

You could, for example, get a foreign language newspaper. If that is not available or too expensive, then there are enough newspapers or news portals where you can read news online. You are probably already familiar with the news through your native language, and then the context is easier if you reread the same messages in the foreign language. Further aids are foreign-language films or series. It's probably best to start with a movie or series that you've already seen in your native language. Slang and common phrases can make it really hard for you. If you realize that you do not understand it well, try the subtitles in the foreign language. If that does not work, then take the subtitles of your native language and try again. Even music should not be neglected in your foreign-language world. This has the advantage of teaching you much about the pronunciation and emphasis. Incidentally, you are getting a lot closer to the culture of the country.

5. Leave notes in your home

If it does not bother you and others, place sticky notes with words throughout your home. Whether this is your toothbrush, the couch or the remote control, just place notes on as many objects and pieces of furniture as possible with the respective name of the object in the foreign language. As a result, you have the vocabulary all day long and memorize it automatically.

6. Learn the most important phrases

Another helpful tip is to think about what words and phrases you'll need before you travel. For example, you could write down how to reserve a hotel room, book a bus ride, order in a restaurant, ask someone for directions, and communicate with a doctor or the police.

7. Set clear goals

Without goals, you will never get where you want to go. Since you have already booked your flight, you also have a deadline, to which you have reached a goal you have set. To accomplish this, you can now place mini orders. But stay realistic with your goals, especially concerning your mini goals. If they are too big and not realistically achievable, you may lose your courage and give up. A good tip is also that you record your goals in writing because writing is like having a contract with yourself. It makes your goals more binding and makes you feel more obligated to stick to your schedule. Writing things down also has the advantage that you have to formulate your goals more precisely and not forget them so quickly. Do not just try to formulate these goals but really approach and implement them.

8. Humor

Do not feel dejected if it does not work right away. You may be embarrassing yourself in front of a native speaker because you mispronounce a word and form a completely different sense. Nobody will blame you. For most people, it means a lot that you try to learn their language. And when they laugh, they do not mean it negatively. However, the most important thing is: have fun getting to know a new language! After all, you do not have any pressure—as you do at school.

Mastering the foreign language of your destination country only has advantages. You will learn to understand how people of a particular region think, what fears and worries they have, and how they tackle life. You will become more tolerant and see the world differently, and, after your journey, you'll definitely question many ways of thinking regarding your own culture. Of course, you will also learn many new things abroad, even in foreign languages. Make sure to take the time to get familiar with the new language before you leave. It is worth it!

¡Buena suerte!

Chapter 10: Complaints & Problems

You will discover three kinds of police in Spain, each of them is armed. This is composed of *La Policia Municipal* who come under the local authority at the town hall. They are accountable for the order and law within the local community region, as well as traffic control. These officers were blue uniforms.

La Guardia Civil is accountable for order and law within the rural regions, as well as for the traffic control on major roads and in cities. These officers wear green uniforms.

La Policia Nacional is the police officers who are accountable for order and law at the national level. These officers wear dark blue uniforms.

If you are one of those people whose vehicle is towed away, you need to get in touch with the *Policia Municipal* who will provide you the information on where to go to collect your car.

In a hotel, when all else fails, and you cannot obtain a complaint sorted out to your gratification, feel free to ask for the complaints books. Hotels are obliged by law to have one. So make sure you jot down your problems or complaints so it will be given to the Spanish Ministry of Tourism.

You might see...

Servicio al cliente	Customer services
Libro de reclamaciones	Complaints book
No funciona	Out of order
Comisaria	Police station

General Phrases:

¿Puede ayudarme?	Can you help me?
¿Puede arreglarlo?	Can you fix it (immediately?
¿Cuando puede arreglarlo?	When can you fix it?
Hay un problema con...	There's a problem with...
No hay...	There isn't/haven't...
Necesito...	I need...
El/La... no funciona.	The.... doesn't work.
El...está roto/La...está rota.	The... is broken.
No puedeo...	I can't...
No ha sido mi culpa	It wasn't my fault.
He olvidado el/la...	I have forgotten my...
He perdido el/la..	I have lost my...
Hemos perdido los/has...	We have lost our...
Me han robado el/la...	Someone has stolen my...

Mi... no está	My...isn't here.
Flata algo	Something is missing
Falta el/la...	The... is missing.
Esto no es mio.	This isn't mine.

A) Where You're Staying (*Dónde te estás Quedando*)

No hay agua (caliente).	There isn't any (hot) water.
No hay papel higienico.	There isn't any toilet paper.
No hay luz	There isn't any electricity.
No hay toallas.	There aren't any towels.
Necesito otra manta	I need another blanket.
La luz no funciona	The light doesn't work.
La ducha no funciona.	The shower doesn't work.
La cerradura está rota.	The lock is broken
El intrruptor de la lampara está roto	The switch on the lamp is broken
No puedo abrir laventana	I can't open the window
No puede cerrar el grifo	I can't turn the tap off
La cisterna no funciona	The toilet doesn't flush
El lavabo está atascado	The wash-basin is blocked
El lavabo está sucio	The wash-basin is dirty
La habitacion es...	The room is...
La habitacion es demasiado pequeña	The room is too small
Es demasiado calor en la habitacion	Its too hot in the room
La cama es muy incómoda	The bed is very uncomfortable
Hay mucho ruido	There's a lot of noise
Huele a gas	There's a smell of gas

B) In Bars & Restaurants (*En bares y restaurantes*)

Esto no está heco	This isn't cooked
Esto está quemado	This is burnt
Esto está frio	This is cold
No pedi esto, pedi...	I dint order this, I ordered...
Este vaso está roto	This glass is craked
Esto está sucio	This is dirty

330

Esto huele mal	This smells bad
Esto tiene un sabor raro	This tastes strange
Hay un error en la cuenta	There is a mistake on the bill

C) In Shops (En tiendas)

Compré esto aqui (ayer)	I bought this here (yesterday)
¿Puede cambiarme esto?	Can you change this for me?
Quiero devolve resto.	I want to return this
¿Puede devolverme el dinero?	Can you refund me the money?
Aqui está el recibo	Here is the receipt
Tiene un defecto	It has a flaw
Tiene un agujero	It has a hole
Hay una mancha	There is a stain/mark
Esto está pasado	This is off/rotten
Esto no está fresco	This is fresh
Falta la tapa	The lid is missing

D) Losing Things, Forgetting and Theft

He olvidado el billete	I have forgotten my ticket
He olvidado la llave	I have forgotten the key
He perdido la cartera	I have lost my wallet
He perdido la licencia de conducir.	I have lost my driving license
Hemos perdido las mochilas	We have lost our rucksacks
¿Dónde está la oficina de objetos perdidos?	Where is the lost property office?
¿Dónde está la comisaria?	Where is the police station?
Me han robado el bolso	Someone has stolen my bag
Me han robado el coche	Someone has stolen the car
Me han robado el dinero	Someone has stolen my money

E) If Someone is Bothering You

Por favor, dejeme en paz	Please leave me alone
Vayase, o llamo a la policia	Go away, or I'll call the police
Hay alguien que me está molestando	There is someone bothering me

Hay alguien que me está siguiendo   There is someone following me

Chapter 11: Major Spanish Grammar Lessons To Consider

To learn the Spanish language, you must immerse yourself in it and learn everything, including grammar. You need to learn the basic principles of Spanish grammar. It is fundamental to build a strong block in the language. Here are some of the things you should learn.

Nouns Combined with Articles

A noun is a place, person, or a thing. In Spanish, a noun is preceded by the article, but the ending can change depending on the gender of the noun. When learning this language, you should learn the articles and understand which one comes before a particular noun. The nouns are determined by gender. You cannot predict the gender of any Spanish noun, so you must master the nouns and vocabulary words to know speak or write the language correctly.

A good example is the word "dress." Your first guess is that this word is female, but it is wrong; "dress" is a male noun. You need to memorize the articles with a noun instead of trying to guess them. One of the great tips to use when mastering the Spanish grammar is that feminine nouns mostly end with an "*a*," while masculine ones end with "*o*." They are similar to "an," "a," and "the" used in English. Examples include the following:

- *El*, which masculine singular

- *La*, which is feminine singular

- *Los*, which is masculine plural

- *Las*, which feminine plural

A noun also changes for a living thing, for example, a dress is el vstido, and this never changes because it's a non-living thing. However, when refereeing to "the cat," you say el gato, which changes, depending on the cat's gender.

- ***El gato*** means the male cat.

- ***La gata*** means the female cat.

Learning the Plurals

Spanish plurals are not different from English plurals. You simply add an "*s*" or "*es*" at the end; however, you must also change the article when writing and speaking in plural. For a noun that ends with a vowel in Spanish, you add an **s** to change into plural. For example, ***La camas*** is the plural of ***la cama.*** It's the same thing in English where **bed** becomes **beds**, for example.

A noun that ends with a consonant in Spanish requires you to add an es and change the article to change it into plural.

El professor is changed to *Los profesores* (the professor becomes the professors)

The nouns, articles, and genders help you speak correct Spanish, and you can describe events in proper grammar. These are the pillars of learning Spanish like a native and enable you to communicate effectively.

Always ask yourself what the definition of the nouns and the articles are. The gender alterations of the word define how you can write in the plural and the articles to use with it.

Asking Questions in Spanish

In every language, you need to ask questions, especially when learning. Questions are also important in real life when you need help in directions or even when you have a conversation with someone. If the locals only speak Spanish, you must know how to ask questions.

When speaking, the voice inflection helps you ask a question. This means you simply raise the voice just before you end the sentence. The whole statement becomes a question because of the change of pitch. It works perfectly when communicating in Spanish verbally.

A written question in Spanish has two question marks, indicating a raising voice. One question mark is at the beginning of a sentence and another one at the end.

For example:

"¿Qué significa esta palabra?" and it means "Where are you going?"

In Spanish, there are interrogative words, which also referred to as the question words. They have a unique accent that makes it easy for the reader to know they are questions and not just ordinary statements. As a Spanish learner, it will take you a lot of practice to get familiar with common question words. Here are some examples:

¿Dónde está...? And it means, where is...?

¿Quién es...? Meaning, who is...?

The Descriptive words

For you to express yourself in Spanish, you must know how to describe people, your surroundings, and places. You cannot write or speak Spanish unless you know the description words. Describing things is part of every language, and this is the part that carries most vocabularies. It's unlimited; you can enrich your language by learning as many descriptive words as you can.

Spanish descriptive sentences are not very different from English; you have to follow the same principles of grammar. The only difference is that, in Spanish, the noun comes before the adjective. This means learning to think the opposite when writing or speaking Spanish. For example:

Manos grandes, which means hands big.

Pelo largo, which means long hair.

To practice more Spanish description words, read books you know in English but are translated in Spanish. Since you already know the story, it will you identify useful phrases that you can use in descriptions. What's more, you get to learn more vocabulary words and use them.

Learning Basic Conjugation-Verbs

At this point, you are already familiar with questions, nouns, and descriptions. You are still a newbie in

Spanish but on your way to learning how to speak and read like natives. However, for you to put everything together, you must also learn about verbs, and verbs cannot be used without conjugation.

Conjugating verbs make your language fluent. But, one incorrect conjugation will alter the whole meaning of a sentence. A good example is Yo soy de Tejas, which means, "I am from Texas." If the conjugation is changed, the sentence goes like, Eres de Tejas, which means, "You are from Texas."

As a beginner, do not stress yourself overmastering everything at the same time. Study and try to memorize as much as possible. Start with the basic ones and advance gradually to the present tense conjugations; they are the simplest and most important. Most conversations are in the present tense, so this will be helpful and prepare you for the other tenses.

For example:

"Good morning Mary, how are you."

"I am fine thank you."

"Glad you good, do you want to go out tonight?"

"No, I would like to stay indoors."

This conversation is an example of the everyday discussions people engage in the present tense. Present tense conjugation endings include:

- **"o"** when speaking about yourself

- **"a"** referring to someone else informally

- **"a"** refereeing to someone else formally

- **"Emos, imos, amos"** they referred to a group where you are included

- **"an"** refers to a group where you are not included.

The Stem-Changing Verbs

These are verbs consisting -ar, -ir, and -er. They are also known as shoe verbs; when a stem-changing verb is conjugated, it fits in the "shoe," and the vowel changes from single to double vowel. These groups of stem-changing verbs mainly speak about you, about someone informally or formally, or about a group where you are not included. They are the most used verbs in Spanish. So, getting familiar with them will help you get ready to learn future and past tense conjugations. As they say, practice makes perfect. Spend time practicing the conjugating stem-changing verbs, and use the shoe fitting trick so that you may know what to change.

The Spanish Tenses

Learning Spanish grammar and tenses is the primary way to speak and write this language correctly. What you should know is that it is not possible to learn everything right away. Get a general idea in the initial stages, and you will understand how to learn Spanish without feeling intimidated. Take time to familiarize yourself with different tenses.

Present Tense

Speaking in the present tense means speaking or referring in the present. The present tense is exactly what you think. It's speaking in the present.

"¿Cómo estás? Yo estoy bien." It means, "How are you doing? I am well."

Imperfect Tense

This tense is used to refer to actions that took place in the past, and they occurred repeatedly. It is also used to when refereeing to something that took place over a long time. But, it's used to discuss mental or emotional actions and not physical.

"Comía pan tostado todos los días," meaning, "I ate toast every day."

Past Preterite

The preterite tense speaks about particular actions that took place in the past; they are mostly one-time occurrence events. Sometimes, they have a specific time when they start and come to an end. What's more, it is used to discuss a completed event, and it's the one used when making a list of consecutive actions.

For example:

"I went to the store, bought chicken, and went home." However, for you to remember preterite tense, you need to understand that this tense answers questions regarding past actions.

The Future Tense

The future tense discusses future events or things that might happen. It is used when expressing or discussing probability. Near-future is discussed using present tense, and future tense discusses a future that is far away, for example:

"Yo ganaré la medalla de oro," meaning, "I will win the gold medal."

"Yo compraré ese suéter la próxima semana," meaning **"I will buy that sweater next week."**

Pairing Nouns and Adjectives

Adjectives, just like in English, are describing words. Examples include small, wide, round, and white, among others. Spanish adjectives are paired with nouns, and they must match with the gender and number of the nouns.

Before you give a noun to an adjective, consider the gender and number. For example, if a noun is in singular form and feminine, your adjective should match the description. For example, using the adjective **yellow**:

El libro amarillo, which means the yellow book. This sentence is singular and masculine.

La manzana amarilla, which means the yellow apple. This sentence is feminine and singular.

Los libros Amarillo, which means the books are yellow. It is masculine and plural.

The Subjunctive

The subjunctive makes English speakers find learning Spanish extremely difficult; this tense is used to discuss future, present, and past tenses. Subjunctive reflects beyond what the speaker says and expresses uncertainty and shows how the speaker feels. When using the subjunctive, you can express your desire or will, and an indicative phrase should always follow it.

Here is an example showing how to use the indicative phrase.

"Espero que Maria se vuelva professor." This means, "I hope Mary becomes a teacher." The words "I hope that" shows the use of subjunctive and "becomes" is the subjunctive tense. This sentence presents the mood of a speaker but does not say that indeed, Mary will become a teacher. As you advance in Spanish verb tenses, learn to pay attention when a character is narrating or telling a story for you to identify the tense they are using. You can also watch Spanish movies and soaps to practice and learn more about spoken Spanish and especially the tenses.

Learning Spanish cannot happen overnight; a lot of practice is required. The more you lay a strong foundation by learning the correct grammar, basic verbs, sounds, such as reading and speaking in Spanish, the higher the chances of mastering immaculate Spanish.

Chapter 12: How to Read in Spanish

Just like in the usual physical exercise, there must be a warm-up phase. In the process of learning the Spanish Language, you must consider the following friendly advice and tips:

- You should exercise your jaw, open it as wide as you can, and then close it slowly. After that, you must also gently massage both jaws;

- Speak in front of the mirror. Through that, you can be able to see if you are confident enough to speak the Spanish Language;

- You must also speak aloud, clearly and slowly;

- If you want to make some exaggeration when speaking, do it. Do not think twice if you know that it will make your learning better; and lastly,

- You should allot an hour of everyday to be devoted to the proper way of learning the Spanish Language.

Al igual que en el ejercicio físico habitual, debe haber una fase de calentamiento. En el proceso de aprender el idioma español, debe considerar los siguientes consejos y sugerencias amistosas:

- *Debe ejercitar la mandíbula, abrirla lo más que pueda y luego cerrarla lentamente. Después de eso, también debes masajear suavemente ambas mandíbulas;*

- *Habla frente al espejo. A través de eso, puede ver si tiene la confianza suficiente para hablar español;*

- *También debes hablar en voz alta, clara y lentamente;*

- *Si quieres hacer una exageración al hablar, hazlo. No lo piense dos veces si sabe que mejorará su aprendizaje; y, por último,*

- *Debe dedicar una hora diaria para dedicarse a la forma correcta de aprender el idioma español.*

When reading, you should develop your own strategy in reading the Spanish Language. You may want to go to a place wherein you are most comfortable with. You must also consider your time, and how fast you want to finish the book, you are about to read. Do not compare yourself with other people who can read aloud and confidently. You may use your own control in reading, you may go the fastest way you can, or you can be as slow as you want to.

Al leer, debe desarrollar su propia estrategia para leer el idioma español. Es posible que desee ir a un lugar en el que se sienta más cómodo. También debe considerar su tiempo y la rapidez con que desea terminar el libro que está a punto de leer. No te compares con otras personas que puedan leer en voz alta y con confianza. Puede usar su propio control en la lectura, puede ir de la manera más rápida posible o puede ser tan lento como desee.

Going to your own hibernation place or a sanctuary, as what some people call it, is a must if you want to get serious with your reading. That reading may be a novel or a simple book for learning, and either way, you must find a good place to start reading. It may be a library if you want to be alone but seeing other people who are also doing the same thing with you. It may be a canteen if you want to eat while reading. It may be an enclosed room where you may be comfortable laying or slouching while reading.

Ir a su propio lugar de hibernación o un santuario como lo llaman algunas personas es imprescindible si quiere tomar en serio su lectura. Esa lectura puede ser una novela o un libro simple para aprender, y, de cualquier manera, debe encontrar un buen lugar para comenzar a leer. Puede ser una biblioteca si quieres estar solo, pero viendo a otras personas que también están haciendo lo mismo contigo. Puede ser una cantimplora si quiere comer mientras lee. Puede ser una habitación cerrada donde puede estar cómodo acostado o encorvado mientras lee.

Another tip is that you may consider listening to music because there are people who can concentrate well by listening to music, which may be a soft one or even modern kind of music. (Otro consejo es que puede considerar escuchar música porque hay personas que pueden concentrarse bien escuchando música que puede ser suave o incluso música moderna.)

The following are another batch of friendly tips about reading spanish language:

Below are some tips that you might use in the correct and enjoyable reading of Spanish Language short stories. After these tips, you will have to read two of the basic short stories for kids. It is intentionally for kids because kids need baby steps in order to learn, in as much the same way as a learner needs to know about the Spanish Language.

- The first tip is the presence of titles and photos or pictures in the book. The reason here is that you will have a hint of the story because of the graphics. By having a slight idea, you can already formulate some possibilities or possible events that might happen along with the story;

- The second tip is that as you read the story, start relating it to yourself. You might have a similar experience with the character of the story. You might want to draw in your mind what might possibly happen because this exact scene has already happened in your life before;

- Usually, the short stories have preguntas or questions, and then before answering it directly, you must consider reading all the questions so that as time passes by, you will surely have the gist as to where you will get answers to those questions. Sometimes, in reading comprehension, the tendency of the reader is to read all the questions all at the same time and then after that, he will be able to capture the gist of the story;

- Lastly, you must use your own grammar because you already have your knowledge about the Spanish Language since you are in course where Spanish Language is its subject. So, it is imperative to use your stock knowledge in reading. Say, for instance; there is a pregunta or question, your respuesta or answer must be based on your own knowledge as a learner of Spanish Language.

Los siguientes son otro lote de consejos amigos sobre la lectura del lengua Española:

A continuación, hay algunos consejos que puede usar para leer correctamente y de manera agradable las historias cortas en español. Después de estos consejos, tendrá que leer dos de los cuentos básicos para niños. Es intencional para los niños porque los niños necesitan pequeños pasos para aprender, de la misma manera que un alumno necesita saber sobre el idioma español.

- *El primer consejo es la presencia de títulos y fotos o imágenes en el libro. La razón aquí es que tendrás una pista de la historia debido a los gráficos. Al tener una ligera idea, ya puede formular algunas posibilidades o posibles eventos que podrían ocurrir a lo largo de la historia;*

- *Second El segundo consejo es que a medida que lees la historia, comienza a relatarla contigo mismo. Es posible que tenga una experiencia similar con el personaje de la historia. Es posible que desee recordar en su mente lo que podría suceder porque esta escena exacta ya ha sucedido en su vida antes;*

- *Por lo general, las historias cortas tienen preguntas o preguntas, luego, antes de responderlas directamente, debe considerar leer todas las preguntas para que a medida que pase el tiempo, seguramente tenga la idea de dónde obtendrá las respuestas a esas preguntas. A veces, en la comprensión lectora, la tendencia del lector es leer todas las preguntas al mismo tiempo y luego, después de eso, podrá capturar la esencia de la historia;*

- *Por último, debe usar su propia gramática porque ya tiene su conocimiento sobre el idioma español, ya que está en el curso donde el idioma español es su materia. Por lo tanto; es imprescindible utilizar su conocimiento de valores en la lectura. Digamos, por ejemplo, que hay una pregunta o pregunta, su respuesta o respuesta debe basarse en su propio conocimiento como estudiante de español.*

The character is a working man, who has been working for a long period of time. He loves doing his job for the customers or clients they cater. He enjoys his work but there are people who cause him a lot of pressure and a lot of disappointment in his everyday life. He is a person who is dedicated to his craft but he just cannot take all the insults coming from his boss' mouth. One day, he promised to himself that he will make a decision on May 23.

El personaje es un hombre trabajador, que ha estado trabajando durante un largo período de tiempo. Le encanta hacer su trabajo para los clientes o clientes que atienden. Disfruta de su trabajo, pero hay personas que le causan mucha presión y mucha decepción en su vida cotidiana. Es una persona dedicada a su oficio, pero no puede soportar todos los insultos que salen de la boca de su jefe. Un día, se prometió a sí mismo que tomará una decisión el 23 de mayo.

One fine day, it is May 23. He woke up late but instead of cramming going to work, he just slowly wakes up and gets his towel for him to take a bath. After bathing, he got his cup of coffee and bread for breakfast. He looked at his watch, and he is really late already. But he said to himself, it is okay because this is the day that he will never forget. He went outside the house and proceeded to his car. He rode in his car, but it is so humid because there is no air-conditioning unit available inside his old car. He may be sweating, but he told himself, "It is alright. It will be a fine day, and I will make the best decision of my life today." While driving, the traffic approached him, but it is alright because according to him, all is well, all is going well. Then after that, he finally reached his office. He went outside the car and proceeded inside the office building. He saw the face of his boss with a frown, and instead of explaining why he is late, he just greeted him "Good day Sir! It is a fine day, isn't it?" The boss' face continues to make a very frowning one. So the boss asked him, "What time is it?" and then he answered, "It is time to make the best decision of my life, Sir." The boss again asked him when he will be early to come to the office, and he said, "Never Sir." The boss frowned up even more and shouted, "What?" and then he answered again, "I said, I will never come to work early Sir, not now, not ever, ever!" His boss repeated all the questions, and he even answered the same answers in a more confident way.

Un buen día, es el 23 de mayo. Se despertó tarde, pero en lugar de irse a trabajar, se levanta lentamente y toma su toalla para que se bañe. Después de bañarse, tomó su taza de café y un pan para el desayuno. Miró su reloj y ya es muy tarde. Pero se dijo a sí mismo, está bien porque este es el día que nunca olvidará. Salió de la casa y se dirigió a su automóvil. Él viajaba en su automóvil, pero está muy húmedo porque no hay una unidad de aire acondicionado disponible dentro de su automóvil antiguo. Puede estar sudando, pero se dijo a sí mismo: "Está bien. Será un buen día y tomaré la mejor decisión de mi vida hoy". Mientras conducía, el tráfico se acercó a él, pero está bien porque, según él, todo está bien, todo va bien. Luego, después de eso, finalmente llegó a su oficina. Salió del auto y entró al edificio de oficinas. Vio la cara de su jefe con el ceño fruncido, y en lugar de explicar por qué llega tarde, simplemente lo saludó: "¡Buenos días, señor! Es un buen día, ¿no es así?" La cara del jefe sigue haciendo una mueca muy ceñuda. Entonces, el jefe le preguntó: "¿Qué hora es?" Y luego respondió: "Es hora de tomar la mejor decisión de mi vida, señor". El jefe nuevamente le preguntó cuándo llegaría temprano a la oficina, y él dijo: "Nunca, señor". El jefe frunció el ceño aún más y gritó: "¿Qué?" El jefe repitió todas las preguntas e incluso respondió las mismas respuestas de una manera más segura.

He resigned and got all his things up. His boss is just watching him, and he told him that he is not going back to that office ever again. The end!

Renunció y levantó todas sus cosas. Su jefe solo lo está mirando y él le dijo que no volverá a esa oficina nunca más. ¡El fin!

In this story, the morale of the story is that people who are not happy with their lives and work always have a choice. It is either to leave the work or that situation or continue living and suffering the same situations again. For instance, you choose to leave and resign; there is no turning back. You have to stand up for your decision, and you have to have a great job in replacement for what you have lost. Remember that even if you have the worst boss, but you have to admit that you are earning out of those insults. The second one is thtat hoose to stay, you must be firm, and you must avoid being too sensitive at all times. It is because once you become too sensitive, you tend to think of many things which are not even existing in the first place.

En esta historia, la moral de la historia es que las personas que no están contentas con sus vidas y su trabajo siempre tienen una opción. Es dejar el trabajo o esa situación o continuar viviendo y sufriendo las mismas situaciones nuevamente. Por ejemplo, si elige irse y renunciar, no hay vuelta atrás. Debe defender su decisión y debe tener un gran trabajo en reemplazo de lo que ha perdido. Recuerde que incluso si tiene el peor jefe, pero debe admitir que está ganando con esos insultos. Segundo, si elige quedarse, debe ser firme y debe evitar ser demasiado sensible en todo momento. Es porque una vez que te vuelves demasiado sensible, tiendes a pensar en muchas cosas que ni siquiera existen en primer lugar.

So, the decision of the main character in this Cima Del Mundo short story is the best decision for his personality. There are no regrets and there will always be replacement for everything that is lost.

Entonces, la decisión del personaje principal en este cuento de Cima Del Mundo es la mejor decisión para su personalidad. No hay arrepentimientos y siempre habrá un reemplazo para todo lo que se pierde.

Chapter 13: Memorizing Vocabulary and Tenses

Memorizing is one of those parts of learning a language that seems extremely daunting, especially at the beginning when the lists of words to learn and tenses to get familiar with seem endless. When you put a lot of pressure on yourself to memorize everything, you will often find yourself feeling very overwhelmed, if not discouraged. When a word isn't as easily brought to mind as you would like, it's so tempting to just throw your hands in the air and say, "I just have a horrible memory."

This isn't necessarily the case, though. Remember this: *there is no such thing as a bad memory*. There are different learning styles. Just because you know someone in your Spanish class who can recite any vocab list a day after seeing it doesn't mean that, because you can't, you lack the ability to do so. It simply means that you have a different learning style and you need to find a different way to conquer vocabulary and tenses.

In this chapter, we will discuss several different methods you can use to remember vocabulary and tenses. You may find that not all of them work for you. That's fine! The point of this section is to help you find which of the methods mentioned is the right fit for you and your individual learning style.

Vocabulary

Vocabulary is the fundamental basis on which the rest of your Spanish language skills will be built. If you are unable to understand the words, you won't be able to read, write, or speak in Spanish. Some words will be easy to learn whereas others will give you more problems. The important thing to keep in mind is that you have to be patient with yourself. You are learning vocabulary and you will continue to learn new words throughout your entire language-learning experience. Think about your native language. When you started speaking, you didn't know all the words you know now (obviously). And I'm sure that there are even words that you still hear from time to time that aren't familiar with. Vocabulary develops over time through practice and exposure.

Set Realistic Goals

You cannot expect to sit down in front of a vocabulary list or Spanish dictionary and memorize whatever you see in the span of 20 minutes. Sure, after reading through the list a few times, you might be able to repeat it. But an hour after walking away from your desk, chances are you probably won't remember even half of what you looked at.

A good benchmark goal to set for yourself is to expect to learn 10-15 new words for every hour you spend studying. This doesn't mean that you have to spend one straight hour studying just vocabulary. Break it up into small chunks. Spend 15 minutes every few days with the overall goal of spending one hour a week in vocabulary.

Learn Words with Context

While it seems easy and even tempting to simply learn a word a day from a list, if you're unable to use that word within a context, what's the point?

Here are a few ideas for how you can learn a word within a larger context:

Group Words Together

Learning thematically words is a great way to conquer a larger number of new words at one time. If you want to learn how to say "kitchen" why not go ahead and learn how to say the other rooms in your house? If you want to learn how to say "shirt" go ahead and look up how to say "pants," "sweater," and "shoes." The brain has a natural tendency to put information into categories.

One way you can use this to help with your Spanish is by selecting a "theme" for each week. One week focus on weather vocabulary, the next focus on food, and so on.

Learn Sentences

The whole point of learning vocabulary in Spanish is so that you can take those words and use them in a spoken or written form one day. Words learned within an applicable context are more likely to stick in your mind. For example, if you're learning the vocabulary related to weather, why not take the words you're learning and make a sentence to go along with them? What do you do when it's sunny out? Does it rain a lot where you live? Do you love or hate the snow? Create a context around the vocabulary you're learning so that you won't only have an X=Y meaning but an actually applicable significance in your mind.

Avoid Learning Opposites Together

It can be tempting, even seem logical, to learn opposites together. For example, hot and cold. It seems to make sense that these two words would come up together but, if you learn them together, you can experience what is known as cross vocabulary association. This means that when you want to recall the word for cold, you may find yourself bringing the word for hot because they are stored together in your mind in the same place.

A way to avoid this is to apply the techniques we just talked about. When you learn the word for cold, create a word group of things that are cold (snow, ice, winter, etc.). Focus on these words one day, and the next move to hot and words you would associate with that word (fire, the sun, summer).

Work Around the Word

While you are going through your experience of learning Spanish, you'll come across words that you just can't remember, no matter what you do. They're words that you'll look up a million times, write them out in sentences, put them on flashcards, everything. But they just won't stick in your memory. Or maybe there are words you do know but can't seem to get it out of your mind when you need it.

Don't worry. This isn't the end of the world. There are things you can to do to prevent this is a very common occurrence of stopping you.

Learn Synonyms

It's always useful and beneficial to learn a few words related to a new word you're learning. This can be especially useful when talking about adjectives. For example, if you've just seen a movie with your friends, you may want to describe it as "funny," "entertaining," or "hilarious." If you can't think of the word for hilarious, you can use the other words you've learned that communicate a similar idea.

Describe the Word that You're Trying to Say

It can be frustrating, embarrassing, and discouraging to be in the middle of a conversation and unable to think of a specific word. All Spanish-language student has had this experience. To overcome it, you can use something called "circumlocution." This is the process of describing the word and/or working around it so that the conversation doesn't lose its pace.

For example, if you're trying to say that you saw your friend in the "store" but the word for "store" won't come to mind, you can say "the place you buy food/clothes/etc."

Don't Be Afraid to Ask

If you can't think of a word or a way to describe that word, don't be afraid to ask your Spanish-speaking friends, *"¿Cómo se dice...?"* What does it mean, "How do you say...?"

Analyze New Words as You Learn Them

Learning new words is great. But if you're not paying attention to how those new words are spelled or written you could potentially be missing out on some very useful information. Doing this, however, will help you dedicate the word to memory easier. The thing is, most words have a "root word" --a word around which the rest of the longer word is formed. This is true for nouns, adjectives, and verbs. Being aware of the root word will make the process of learning new words go more smoothly and make it a lot less daunting knowing that you only need to learn one, main word. You can then add the appropriate prefixes or suffixes to change the word to fit your needs.

Im-/In- Prefix

These prefixes are added to adjectives and adverbs to make their opposites

Root Word	Meaning in English	Root Word with Prefix	Meaning in English
Capaz	Able	*Incapaz*	Unable
Posible	Possible	*Imposible*	Impossible
Útil	Useful	*Inútil*	Unuseful

Ante- Prefix

Adding "ante" to the front of the word adds the meaning of "before".

Root Word	Meaning in English	Root Word with Prefix	Meaning in English
Ayer	Yesterday	*Anteayer*	The day before yesterday

Mano	Hand	*Antemano*	Beforehand
Noche	Night	*Anteanoche*	The night before last

Re- Prefix

Adding "re" to a verb in Spanish is much like adding "re" to a word in English

Root Word	Meaning in English	Root Word with Prefix	Meaning in English
Usar	To use	*Reusar*	To reuse
Pasar	To pass	*Repasar*	To review (to pass over again)
Nacer	To be born	*Renacer*	To be born again

Mal- Prefix

"*Mal*" is an adjective in Spanish that means "bad." Adding this prefix to the beginning of a verb adds that same meaning to the action.

Root Word	Meaning in English	Root Word with Prefix	Meaning in English
Tratar	To treat	*Maltratar*	To treat someone badly
Nutrición	Nutrition	*Malnutrición*	Malnutrition
Criado	Raised	*Malcriado*	To be raised badly/ Spoiled
Comer	Eat	*Malcomer*	To eat poorly

-mente Suffix

Added to adjectives to turn them into adverbs, much like the "-ly" suffix in English

Root Word	Meaning in English	Root Word with Prefix	Meaning in English
Difícil	Difficult	*Difícilmente*	With difficulty
Lento/a	Slow	*Lentamente*	Slowly
Rápido/a	Quick	*Rápidamente*	Quickly
Alegre	Happy	*Alegremente*	Happily

-ito/-ita Suffix

This is a diminutive, and when added to nouns means "little"

Root Word	Meaning in English	Root Word with Prefix	Meaning in English
Hermano	Brother	*Hermanito*	Little brother
Hermana	Sister	*Hermanita*	Little sister
Casa	House	*Casita*	Little house/cottage
Mentira	Lie	*Mentirita*	Fib

-ote/-ota/-on/-ona/-azo/-aza Suffixes

These are augmentatives and function in the exact opposite was of diminuitives. When used with a noun, they give the feeling of "large" or "big."

Root Word	Meaning in English	Root Word with Prefix	Meaning in English
Libro	Book	*Librote*	Big book
Cabeza	Head	*Cabezota*	Stubborn (Hard headed)
Grande	Big	*Grandote*	Very big

-ísimo/-ísima Suffix

These are also augmentative suffixes; however, they are added to adjectives to create the superlative form.

Root Word	Meaning in English	Root Word with Prefix	Meaning in English
Cansado/a	Tired	*Cansadísimo/a*	Extremely tired
Temprano	Early	*Tempranísimo*	Very early
Barato	Cheap	*Baratísimo*	Extremely cheap

Read to Increase Your Vocabulary

When we were looking at the chapter on how to become great at reading in Spanish, we discussed the benefits that read could have for your language skills. Reading gives you the chance to see new words used in an authentic context.

And, of course, make sure you read things that interest you, so you keep your motivation high. This will also help you find and acquire new vocabulary related to topics you enjoy talking about, so are more likely to do so.

Use Visual Representations

Linking a word to a picture or image, and not just the direct English translation, will help to make the word more tangible. It will be easier to remember and you'll begin to work on cutting out the middle translation process that can become a hindrance when you begin reaching higher levels.

Flashcards are a great way to incorporate visual aids into your vocabulary learning process. You can make your own, buy them in stores, or even find them online and print them. There are even websites that test your vocabulary with the use of virtual flashcards from websites like Spanish Dict.

If you want to be able to take your vocabulary exercises with you on the go, check out these apps that you can download to your phone:

- Memrise
- Duolingo
- FluentU

The only real drawback to visual learning in this way is that you're only working with one word in an isolated situation. We've discussed in this chapter the importance of context and learning other words related to the ones you're working on. To do this, don't just practice with the flashcards, but take the time to write the words you learn using them and put them in sentences or group them together with other words you've already learned or are in the process of learning.

Pay Attention to the Cognates

False cognates are words that look the same in Spanish and in English but actually have very different meanings. It is, of course, very important to be familiar with these. There are, however, true cognates that exist between English and Spanish as well. So, as you go through the process of learning vocabulary, be sure that you stay tuned. If a word looks like an English word, take the time to look it. Is it a false or a true cognate?

True cognates are very easy to remember, for obvious reasons. Here are some examples:

Word in Spanish	Word in English
Accidente	Accident
Color	Color
Opinión	Opinion
Aceptar	Accept
Doctor	Doctor
Necesario	Necessary

Tenses

Learning tenses in Spanish can be overwhelming. Conjugations tables seem to go on forever and the rules for when to use which can be confusing. Here are some tips as to how to make the process of learning tenses easier.

Start with the Present

If you can speak in the present, you have a good foundation. It's the most commonly used tense and getting familiar with it will give you a good base to build on.

The present tense in Spanish will also serve as the starting point for other conjugations (such as the subjunctive or the formal "usted" command formations). If you have a good understanding of this tense, you'll be able to conjugate these others much easier.

Read Aloud

As you read in Spanish, you will, without a doubt, come across conjugated verbs. As you do, take the time to read them aloud. Pay attention to how the sound and the context within which they are being used. This will help to link the written word to how it sounds, while simultaneously listening to yourself saying it. In doing so, you're incorporating three of the major elements that go into learning a language.

Write Them Down

During one of your more formal study sessions, take the time to write down the conjugations of different verbs. Focus with just the present at first and, once you're confident with that, move on to the past (preterite and imperfect), then the present continuous, and so on.

Try writing down the conjugations five times, saying the words aloud as you do. This repetition will train your muscle memory through writing and your oral memory when speaking.

Know the Rules, Then Learn the Exceptions

In Spanish, as with any language, there are always exceptions to the rules. They are inevitable and you will come across them more often than you think. But if you want to be able to work with them, you have to fully understand what they are "exceptions" of first.

When starting, focus on becoming familiar with the rules. Focus on being able to master the regular verbs first, and then move forward to tackle irregular verbs.

Note: That when speaking about Spanish and irregulars, we aren't talking about the "stem-changing" verbs (e: ie, o: ue, etc.). The same can be said for the "go" verbs (*Poner-Pongo, Hacer-Hago*). These should be learned in groups, as you would any other form of conjugations. They do still have rules they follow and these are rules you should become familiar from the beginning.

Tenses

When learning tenses, the first thing to focus on are the conjugations. There are some tenses in Spanish that can be difficult to learn in regards of when to use them (the preterite vs. imperfect, for example). But if you want to practice using them, you at least have to have an idea of how to form them.

As you know, there are three different verb endings: -ar, -er, and -ir. These endings are the endings you will add to the verb when conjugating it into any of the various tenses.

Let's take a few verbs as examples and look at the conjugations for some of the most common tenses in

Spanish:

- Present-I talk
- Preterite-(talking about the past during a specific time) I talked
- Imperfect-(talking about the past during an unspecified time) I was talking
- Future-I will talk
- Conditional-I would talk

Regular "ar" verb: *Hablar*-"to talk"

	Present	**Preterite**	**Imperfect**	**Future**	**Conditional**
Yo	*Hablo*	*Hablé*	*Hablaba*	*Hablaré*	*Hablaría*
Tú	*Hablas*	*Hablaste*	*Hablabas*	*Hablarás*	*Hablarías*
El / Ella / Usted	*Habla*	*Habló*	*Hablaba*	*Hablará*	*Hablaría*
Nosotros	*Hablamos*	*Hablamos*	*Hablábamos*	*Hablaremos*	*Hablaríamos*
Vosotros	*Habláis*	*Hablasteis*	*Hablabais*	*Hablaréis*	*Hablaríais*
Ellos / Ellas / Ustedes	*Hablan*	*Hablaron*	*Hablaban*	*Hablarán*	*Hablarían*

Regular "er" verb: *Comer*-"to eat"

	Present	**Preterite**	**Imperfect**	**Future**	**Conditional**
Yo	*Como*	*Comí*	*Comía*	*Comeré*	*Comería*
Tú	*Comes*	*Comiste*	*Comías*	*Comerás*	*Comerías*
El / Ella / Usted	*Come*	*Comió*	*Comía*	*Comerá*	*Comería*
Nosotros	*Comemos*	*Comimios*	*Comíamos*	*Comeremos*	*Comeríamos*
Vosotros	*Coméis*	*Comisteis*	*Comíais*	*Comeréis*	*Comeríais*
Ellos / Ellas / Ustedes	*Comen*	*Comieron*	*Comían*	*Comerán*	*Comerían*

Regular "ir" verb: *Vivir*-"to live"

	Present	Preterite	Imperfect	Future	Conditional
Yo	Vivo	Viví	Vivía	Viviré	Viviría
Tú	Vives	Viviste	Vivías	Vivirás	Vivirías
El / Ella / Usted	Vive	Vivió	Vivía	Vivirá	Viviría
Nosotros	Vivimos	Vivimos	Viviamos	Viviremos	Viviríamos
Vosotros	Vivís	Vivisteis	Vivíais	Viviréis	Viviríais
Ellos / Ellas / Ustedes	Viven	Vivieron	Vivían	Vivirán	Vivirían

Chapter 14: Day-to-Day conversations - *Conversaciones del día a día*

Pidiendo una pizza - Ordering a pizza

Spanish

-Max: Buenas tardes, ¿Pizzería Loca?

-Operador telefónico: Correcto. ¿En que lo puedo ayudar?

-Max: Me gustaría saber si tienen servicio de entrega.

-Operador telefónico: Así es

-Max: Excelente. ¿Cuánto es el tiempo de entrega?

-Operador telefónico: Depende del lugar donde deba ser entregada.

-Max: A cuatro cuadras de su tienda.

-Operador telefónico: Aproximadamente diez minutos.

-Max: Perfecto. ¿Qué tamaños de pizza tiene?

-Operador telefónico: Pequeña, mediana, grande, extra grande y súper grande.

-Max: ¿Para cuantas personas son?

-Operador telefónico: La pequeña es para una sola persona, la mediana para dos, la grande para cuatro, la extra grande para seis y la súper grande para ocho.

-Max: Excelente. ¿Qué ingredientes adicionales tienes?

-Operador telefónico: Maíz, cebolla, pimentón, champiñones, extra queso, jamón, piña, jalapeños, pepperoni, salchichas, carne, pollo, papas fritas, queso cheddar, aceitunas y anchoas.

-Max: Entiendo. Voy a querer una súper grande con maíz, cebolla, pimentón, extra queso y jamón; una extra grande con papas fritas y pepperoni y una pequeña con anchoas y piña.

-Operador telefónico: Anotado. ¿Desea algo para tomar?

-Max: ¿Qué tiene?

-Operador telefónico: Gaseosas, té helado, café y jugos naturales.

-Max: Tres gaseosas de 2 litros.

-Operador telefónico: Listo. Su orden llegara en cuarenta minutos.

-Max: Muy bien, ¿para pagar?

-Operador telefónico: Puede pagarle al chico de entregas en efectivo, con tarjeta o a través de nuestra app.

-Max: Muchas gracias.

English

-Max: Good afternoon, Pizzeria Loca?

-Telephone operator: Correct. How can I help you?

-Max: I would like to know if you have a delivery service.

-Telephone operator: That's right.

-Max: Excellent. How long is the delivery time?

-Telephone operator: Depends on where it should be delivered.

-Max: Four blocks from your store.

-Telephone operator: Approximately ten minutes.

-Max: Perfect. What pizza sizes do you have?

-Telephone operator: Small, medium, large, extra-large, and super large.

-Max: How many people are they for?

-Telephone operator: The small one is for one person, the medium one for two, the big one for four, the extra big one for six, and the super big one for eight.

-Max: Excellent. What additional ingredients do you have?

-Telephone operator: Corn, onion, paprika, mushrooms, extra cheese, ham, pineapple, jalapeños, pepperoni, sausages, meat, chicken, french fries, cheddar cheese, olives, and anchovies.

-Max: I understand. I'm going to order a super large one with corn, onion, paprika, extra cheese, and ham; an extra-large one with fries and pepperoni and a small one with anchovies and pineapple.

-Telephone operator: Annotated. Would you like something to drink?

-Max: What do you have?

-Telephone operator: Soft drinks, iced tea, coffee, and natural juices.

Max: Three 2-liter soft drinks.

-Telephone operator: Ready. Your order will arrive in forty minutes.

-Max: All right, to pay?

-Telephone operator: You can pay the delivery boy in cash, by card, or through our app.

-Max: Thank you very much.

Centro comercial - Shopping Mall

Spanish

-Andrea: ¡Mira! Ya abrieron el nuevo centro comercial.

-Penélope: ¡WOW! Se ve increíble.

-Andrea: Deberíamos entrar a ver.

-Penélope: Me parece excelente.

-Andrea: Vamos entonces.

... Dentro del centro comercial...

-Andrea: Apenas estoy entrando y ya me encanta.

-Penélope: La entrada esta espectacular.

-Andrea: Así es. Mira todas las tiendas que tiene.

-Penélope: Si, eso estaba viendo. Tiene zapaterías, perfumerías, heladerías, peluquerías, barberías, salones de belleza, tiendas de ropa y hasta una academia de baile.

-Andrea: Que emoción. Tiene también un cine, un arcade, tienda de electrónicos, tienda de videojuegos, un supermercado, panaderías, parques para niños, restaurantes y están remodelando una tienda de comida rápida.

-Penélope: Amo este lugar. Creo que pasare aquí mucho tiempo.

-Andrea: Opino igual.

-Penélope: Vengamos todos los viernes a visitar una tienda nueva.

-Andrea: Listo. Lo pondré en mi agenda.

-Penélope: Hoy comamos helado en esa tienda de allí.

-Andrea: ¿Cuál es tu sabor favorito?

-Penélope: Me encanta el de fresa, ¿Y a ti?

-Andrea: Amo el de torta suiza.

-Penélope: ¿Probaste el de chocolate de avellanas?

-Andrea: Lo voy a probar hoy.

English

-Andrea: Look! They've already opened the new shopping center.

-Penelope: WOW! It looks incredible.

-Andrea: We should go in and see.

-Penelope: I find it excellent.

-Andrea: Let's go then.

... Inside the mall...

-Andrea: I'm just coming in, and I love it already.

-Penelope: The entrance is spectacular.

-Andrea: That's right. Look at all the stores it has.

-Penelope: Yes, that's what I was seeing. It has shoe stores, perfumeries, ice cream shops, hairdressers, barbershops, beauty salons, clothing stores, and even a dance academy.

-Andrea: So exciting. It also has a cinema, an arcade, an electronics store, a video game store, a supermarket, bakeries, children's parks, restaurants, and they are remodeling a fast food store.

-Penelope: I love this place. I think I'll spend a lot of time here.

-Andrea: I feel the same way.

-Penelope: Let's come every Friday to visit a new store.

-Andrea: Ready. I'll put it in my schedule.

-Penelope: Today, let's have ice cream in that store over there.

-Andrea: What's your favorite flavor?

-Penelope: I love strawberry, and what about you?

-Andrea: I love Swiss cake.

-Penelope: Have you tried the hazelnut chocolate one?

-Andrea: I'm going to try it today.

Pidiendo un café - Ordering a coffee

Spanish

-*Andrew: Buenos días. ¿Cómo está hoy?*

-*Vendedor: Muy bien, gracias por preguntar. ¿Y usted?*

-*Andrew: Bien también.*

-*Vendedor: ¿Cómo va a querer su café?*

-*Andrew: Hoy quiero algo nuevo. ¿Qué opciones hay?*

-*Vendedor: Tengo café con leche, frapucino, capucino, late vainilla, café con chocolate, café con crema, café helado y café extra fuerte.*

-*Andrew: ¿Cuál me recomiendas?*

-*Vendedor: A mí me gustan todos. El café extra fuerte es amargo, el café con crema muy dulce, el café helado es delicioso y el frapucino, capucino y late vainilla son la especialidad.*

-*Andrew: Dame entonces un café helado.*

-*Vendedor: En camino.*

-*Andrew: Muchas gracias. Toma esta propina.*

-*Vendedor: Gracias señor, que tenga un buen día.*

English

-Andrew: Good morning. How are you today?

-Seller: Very well, thank you for asking. And you?

-Andrew: Good too.

-Seller: How will you want your coffee?

-Andrew: I want something new today. What are the options?

-Seller: I have coffee with milk, frappuccino, cappuccino, late vanilla, coffee with chocolate, coffee with cream, iced coffee, and extra strong coffee.

-Andrew: Which one do you recommend?

-Seller: I like them all. Extra strong coffee is bitter, coffee with cream is too sweet, iced coffee is delicious, and frappuccino, cappuccino, and late vanilla are the specialties.

-Andrew: Then give me an iced coffee.

-Seller: On the way.

-Andrew: Thank you very much. Take this tip.

-Salesman: Thank you, sir, have a good day.

Usando un autobus - Using a bus

Spanish

-*Brad: Buenas noches.*

-*Katy: Buenas noches.*

-*Brad: ¿Esta es la estación de autobús de Brickell?*

-*Katy: No, esta es la estación de Miami Beach.*

-*Brad: ¿Como llego a la estación de Brickell?*

-*Katy: Espera al autobús que diga ruta 3.*

-*Brad: Ok, muchas gracias.*

-*Katy: A su orden.*

-*Brad: Y, ¿Para llegar hasta la estación de Davie?*

-*Katy: Puedes ir a la estación de Brickell tomar el autobús de la ruta 5 o esperar aquí y tomar el autobús de la ruta 7.*

-*Brad: ¿Sabes a qué hora salen los autobuses?*

-*Katy: Allá está el horario. Puedes chequear allí.*

-*Brad: Excelente. Hasta luego.*

-*Katy: Hasta luego.*

English

-Brad: Good evening.

-Katy: Good evening.

-Brad: Is this the Brickell bus station?

-Katy: No, this is Miami Beach Station.

-Brad: How do I get to Brickell Station?

-Katy: Wait for the bus that says route 3.

-Brad: Okay, thank you very much.

-Katy: On your order.

-Brad: And, to get to Davie Station?

-Katy: You can go to Brickell station and take the bus from route 5 or wait here and take the bus from route 7.

-Brad: Do you know what time the buses leave?

-Katy: There is the schedule. You can check there.

-Brad: Excellent. See you later.

-Katy: See you later.

Comprando alimentos – Buying food food

Spanish

-*Eric: Amor, invite a mis amigos a comer mañana.*

-*Sheila: Que bueno, ¿qué vas a cocinar?*

-*Eric: Pensaba hacer una parrilla, quizás una ensalada y algo de postre.*

-*Sheila: Debes ir al supermercado a comprar.*

-*Eric: ¿Me acompañas?*

-*Sheila: Vamos.*

… En el supermercado…

-*Eric: Hay que comprar carne, salchichas, papas, cebollas, tomate, pepino, calabacín, azúcar, sal, cervezas, refrescos, harina, leche, huevos y aceite de oliva.*

-*Sheila: Esta bien, también hay que comprar más verduras para las ensaladas de la semana como brócoli, lechuga, berenjenas, coliflor y espinaca. Ya tenemos poco arroz y pasta.*

-*Eric: Vayamos a la sección de descuentos a ver que ofertas hay hoy.*

-*Sheila: Ok.*

-*Eric: Deberíamos comprar unas chucherías para los hijos de mis amigos como chocolates, malvaviscos y esas cosas.*

-*Sheila: Bien pensado.*

-*Eric: También hay que comprar carbón.*

-*Sheila: Ya lo busco.*

English

-Eric: Darling, I invited my friends to eat tomorrow.

-Sheila: Good, what are you going to cook?

-Eric: I thought I'd make a grill, maybe a salad, and some dessert.

-Sheila: You have to go to the supermarket to buy.

-Eric: Will you come with me?

-Sheila: Let's go.

… At the supermarket …

-Eric: We have to buy meat, sausages, potatoes, onions, tomatoes, cucumbers, zucchini, sugar, salt, beer, soft drinks, flour, milk, eggs, and olive oil.

-Sheila: Okay, you also need to buy more vegetables for the week's salads like broccoli, lettuce, eggplant, cauliflower, and spinach. We are already short on rice and pasta.

-Eric: Let's go to the discount section and see what's on today.

-Sheila: Ok.

-Eric: We should buy some sweets for my friends' kids like chocolates, marshmallows, and stuff.

-Sheila: Good thinking.

-Eric: We also have to buy charcoal.

-Sheila: I'll get it.

Comprando ropa - Buying Clothes

Spanish

-*Daniela: ¡Brittany! ¿Que haras mañana?*

-*Brittany: Creo que nada, ¿Por?*

-*Daniela: En el nuevo centro comercial hay una tienda de ropa que hace descuentos de hasta el 50% todos los miércoles y jueves.*

-*Brittany: Eso es una locura.*

-*Daniela: Absolutamente, quería ir mañana. ¿Vienes?*

-*Brittany: Seguro, ¿A qué hora?*

-*Daniela: A las tres de la tarde.*

-*Brittany: Nos vemos allá.*

... En la tienda de ropa al día siguiente...

-*Daniela: Todo es hermoso, y esta súper barato.*

-*Brittany: No se que comprarme de todo lo que hay.*

-*Daniela: ¿Qué necesitas?*

-*Brittany: Necesito pantalones, vi unos jeans azules y unos negros que me gustaron. También vi algunas licras de colores que me gustaron y leggins punteados bellísimos.*

-*Daniela: Si yo vi los leggins y están bellos. Hay unas sudaderas de camuflaje que quedarían espectaculares con ellos; hay unas camisetas de rayas que no me gustan.*

-*Brittany: Creo que se cuales son, ¿Están cerca de las bufandas?*

-*Daniela: Esas.*

-*Brittany: Los zapatos y las carteras están normales, he visto cosas más bonitas.*

-*Daniela: ¿Vistes las faldas y los vestidos?*

-*Brittany: No, ¿Dónde están?*

-*Daniela: Detrás de los probadores, cerca de la caja*

-*Brittany: Ya iré a verlos.*

-*Daniela: Primero mira estas camisas unicolores, hay rojas, verdes, moradas, rosadas, negras, turquesas y blancas.*

-*Brittany: Estan bonitas, se parecen a las franelas de allá.*

-*Daniela: Tienes razón. Ahora, veamos los vestidos y faldas.*

English

-Daniela: Brittany! What are you doing tomorrow?

-Brittany: I guess nothing, why?

-Daniela: In the new mall, there is a clothing store that offers discounts of up to 50% every Wednesday and Thursday.

-Brittany: That's crazy.

-Daniela: Absolutely, I wanted to go tomorrow. Are you coming?

-Brittany: Sure, what time?

-Daniela: At three o'clock in the afternoon.

-Brittany: See you there.

... In the clothes shop the next day ...

-Daniela: Everything is beautiful, and it's super cheap.

-Brittany: I don't know what to buy from everything there is.

-Daniela: What do you need?

-Brittany: I need pants. I saw some blue jeans and some black ones that I liked. I also saw some colored Lycras that I liked and some beautiful dotted leggings.

-Daniela: I saw the leggings and they're beautiful. There are some camouflage sweatshirts that would look spectacular with them. There are some striped t-shirts that I don't like.

-Brittany: I think I know which ones. Are they near the scarves?

-Daniela: Those.

-Brittany: Shoes and purses are normal; I've more beautiful things.

-Daniela: Did you see the skirts and the dresses?

-Brittany: No, where are they?

-Daniela: Behind the dressing rooms, near the box.

-Brittany: I'll go and see them.

-Daniela: First, look at these unicolored shirts. There are red, green, purple, pink, black, turquoise, and white.

-Brittany: They're pretty. They look like the flannels over there.

-Daniela: You're right. Now, let's see the dresses and skirts.

Ir a un restaurant – Go to a Restaurant

Spanish

-Valeria: Muchas gracias por invitarme a cenar hoy.

-Domin: No tienes que agradecer, te lo mereces.

-Valeria: Esta bien.

-Domin: Buenas noches, mesa para dos por favor.

-Mesonero: Buenas noches, por aquí, por favor.

-Domin: Gracias.

-Valeria: Gracias.

-Mesonero: Tomen asiento.

-Domin: Muchas gracias, muy amable. Me trae el menú cuando pueda por favor.

-Mesonero: Seguro. Un momento.

-Valeria: Que lugar tan bonito. Muy tranquilo y lujoso.

-Domin: Eso es lo que me gusta.

-Mesonero: Aquí tiene el menú.

-Domin: Genial.

-Valeria: ¿Me puede traer un vaso de agua?

-Mesonero: En seguida.

-Domin: ¿Chequeaste el menú?

-Valeria: Se ve todo muy rico. Las sopas, las entradas, los platos, las bebidas, los postres.

-Domin: Yo pediré una ensalada cesar, una lasaña, un mojito y de postre pensaba en una torta.

-Valeria: Yo creo que pediré una ensalada capresa, una pizza, tomare una copa de vino y no creo que quede espacio para el postre.

-Domin: Bien pensado.

-Mesonero: Aquí tiene su agua señorita.

-Valeria: Gracias.

-Domin: Ya estamos listos para ordenar.

-Mesonero: Dígame su orden.

-Domin: Yo voy a querer esto, esto, esto y de postre esto.

-Mesonero: ¿Y la señora?

-Valeria: Yo pediré esto, esto y esto.

-Mesonero: Excelente. Vuelvo en un momento.

-Domin: Muchas gracias. Me trae la cuenta de una vez, por favor.

-Mesonero: Como no.

English

-Valeria: Thank you so much for inviting me to dinner today.

-Domin: You don't have to thank me. You deserve it.

-Valeria: Okay.

-Domin: Good evening. Table for two, please.

-Waiter: Good evening. This way, please.

-Domin: Thank you.

-Valeria: Thank you.

-Waiter: Have a seat.

-Domin: Thank you very much. Please bring me the menu when you can.

-Waiter: Sure. Just a moment.

-Valeria: What a beautiful place. Very quiet and luxurious.

-Domin: That's what I like.

-Waiter: Here's the menu.

-Doma: Great.

-Valeria: Can you get me a glass of water?

-Waiter: Right away.

-Domin: Did you check the menu?

-Valeria: Everything looks very nice, the soups, the appetizers, the dishes, the drinks, the desserts.

-Domin: I'll order a caesar salad, a lasagna, a mojito, and for dessert, I thought of a cake.

-Valeria: I think I'll order a capresa salad, a pizza. I'll have a glass of wine and I don't think I'll eat dessert.

-Domin: Good thinking.

-Waiter: Here's your water, miss.

-Valeria: Thank you.

-Domin: We're ready to order.

-Waiter: Tell me your order.

-Domin: I'm going to want this, this, this, and this for dessert.

-Waiter: And the lady?

-Valeria: I'll ask for this, this, and this.

-Waiter: Excellent. I'll be right back.

-Domin: Thank you very much. Bring me the bill once, please.

-Waiter: Of course.

Pasear al perro - Walk the Dog

Spanish

-Matt: *Mamá voy a salir a pasear al perro.*

-Madre: *Ve con cuidado.*

-Matt: *Tranquila, voy con Heather.*

-Madre: *Mandale saludos de mi parte.*

-Matt: *Esta bien.*

... En el parque de perros...

-Matt: *Hola Heather, ¿Cómo estás?*

-Heather: *Muy bien, ¿Y tú?*

-Matt: *Excelente. ¿Cómo está Rosi?*

-Heather: *Esta muy bien, mírala, ayer la bañe con jabón anti pulgas.*

-Matt: *Que bueno, yo quiero bañar a Roll, tiene muchas pulgas.*

-Heather: *Es que ya tiene el pelo muy largo.*

-Matt: *Es que por su raza le crece rápido.*

-Heather: *¿Qué raza es?*

-Matt: *Es un labrador.*

-Heather: *Con razón.*

-Matt: *Dicen que a algunas razas les caen mas pulgas que a otras.*

-Heather: *¿Cuáles?*

-Matt: *¿Ves aquel perro? Es un pastor alemán. Ellos tienen muchas.*

-Heather: *¿Y ese?*

-Matt: *Ese es un Beagle. Ellos no tienen muchas.*

-Heather: *Ya veo.*

-Matt: *Mira Heather, Rosi hizo pupú.*

-Heather: *Aquí tengo la bolsa, ya lo recojo*

English

-Matt: Mom, I'm going out to walk the dog.

-Mother: Be careful.

-Matt: Don't worry, I'm going with Heather.

-Mother: Tell him I said hi.

-Matt: All right.

... In the dog park...

-Matt: Hi Heather, how are you?

-Heather: Very well, how are you?

-Matt: Excellent. How's Rosi?

Heather: She's very well. Look at her. Yesterday, I bathed her with anti-flea soap.

-Matt: Well, I want to bathe Roll. He's got a lot of fleas.

-Heather: He's got long hair.

-Matt: Because of his breed, it grows fast.

-Heather: What breed is it?

-Matt: It's a golden Labrador.

-Heather: Rightly so.

-Matt: They say that some breeds get more fleas than others.

-Heather: Which ones?

-Matt: See that dog? He's a German shepherd. They have many.

-Heather: What about that one?

-Matt: That's a Beagle. They don't have many.

-Heather: I see.

-Matt: Look, Heather. Rosi made poop.

-Heather: Here's the bag. I'll pick it up.

Autolavados - Carwashes

Spanish

-Tony: Buenas tardes.

-Luis: Buenas tardes Sr Tony, ¿Cómo le va?

-Tony: Muy bien Luis, ¿Y a ti?

-Luis: Todo bien gracias a Dios.

-Tony: Me alegro. ¿Estás ocupado?

-Luis: Un poco, ¿Qué necesita?

-Tony: ¿Puedes llevar mi carro al autolavado?

-Luis: Seguro, en unos minutos.

-Tony: Perfecto, muchas gracias.

-Luis: ¿Va a querer que lo laven, lo aspiren y lo pulan?

-Tony: Correcto. Que lo laven con mucha espuma. Y que laven bien los rines y la tapicería.

-Luis: Entendido. Déjeme las llaves y lo llevo cuando pueda.

-Tony: Aquí tienes. Gracias.

-Luis: Para servirle.

English

Tony: Good afternoon.

-Luis: Good afternoon, Mr. Tony, how are you doing?

-Tony: Very well, Luis. And you?

-Luis: All good, thank God.

-Tony: I'm glad. Are you busy?

-Luis: A little, what do you need?

-Tony: Can you take my car to the car wash?

-Luis: Sure, in a few minutes.

-Tony: Perfect, thank you very much.

-Luis: Are you going to want it washed, vacuumed, and polished?

-Tony: That's right. To be washed with a lot of foam. And let them wash the rims and the upholstery well.

-Luis: Understood. Let me have the keys, and I'll take it when I can.

-Tony: Here you go. Thank you.

-Luis: To serve you.

Pedir una cita - **Make an Appointment**

Spanish

-Mac: Buenos días. ¿Es este el consultorio del Dr. Lewis?

-Secretaria: Correcto. ¿En qué puedo ayudarle?

-Mac: Estoy llamando para pedir una cita médica.

-Secretaria: ¿Para cuándo desea pedir la cita?

-Mac: Estoy libre estos jueves y viernes.

-Secretaria: Para esos días ya no hay citas.

-Mac: ¿Cuándo entonces?

-Secretaria: El lunes en la tarde o el martes en la mañana.

-Mac: ¿A qué hora el lunes?

-Secretaria: A las 4:30 PM.

-Mac: ¿Y el martes?

-Secretaria: El martes seria a las 7:00 am.

-Mac: Pongame la cita el martes a las 7:00 am entonces.

-Secretaria: Perfecto. No lo olvide.

-Mac: No lo hare.

English

-Mac: Good morning. Is this Dr. Lewis' office?

-Secretary: Correct. How can I help you?

-Mac: I'm calling to make an appointment.

-Secretary: When do you want to make the appointment?

-Mac: I'm free this Thursday and Friday.

-Secretary: For those days, there are no more appointments.

-Mac: When then?

-Secretary: Monday afternoon or Tuesday morning.

-Mac: What time on Monday?

-Secretary: 4:30 PM.

-Mac: What about Tuesday?

-Secretary: Tuesday would be at 7:00 am.

-Mac: Put me on Tuesday at 7:00 am then.

-Secretary: Perfect. Don't forget it.

-Mac: I won't.

Visitando el Banco - Visiting the bank

Spanish

-Jake: Buenas, disculpe, ¿Se encuentra el gerente del banco?

-Vigilante: Si, ¿Quién pregunta?

-Jake: Jake Smith, un amigo suyo.

-Vigilante: Un momento....

-Vigilante: Pase adelante.

-Jake: Gracias.

-Phil: Bienvenido Jake.

-Jake: ¿Qué tal? ¿Qué me cuentas?

-Phil: Todo bien. Mucho trabajo aquí en el banco, pero supongo que sabes como es.

-Jake: Me imagino. Siempre te veo apurado.

-Phil: Mas o menos. ¿Qué haces por aquí?

-Jake: Era para pedir un balance de mis cuentas, y preguntar sobre los nuevos intereses e impuestos.

-Phil: *Pudiste haberme llamado para eso. Ya te paso todo eso por correo electrónico.*

-Jake: *Gracias Phil, eres el mejor.*

-Phil: *Tranquilo, cuando quieras.*

English

-Jake: Hi, excuse me. Is the bank manager in?

-Watchman: Yes, who's asking?

-Jake: Jake Smith, a friend of his.

-Watchman: One moment....

-Watchman: Come in.

-Jake: Thank you.

-Phil: Welcome Jake.

-Jake: How are you? What do you tell me?

-Phil: All right. A lot of work here at the bank, but I guess you know what it's like.

-Jake: I can imagine. You're always in a hurry.

-Phil: More or less. What are you doing here?

-Jake: It was to ask for a balance of my accounts and to ask about the new interest and taxes.

-Phil: You could have called me for that. I'll pass all that on to you by email.

-Jake: Thanks Phil, you're the best.

-Phil: Take it easy, anytime.

Visitando la escuela - Visiting the School

Spanish

-Jason: *Disculpe, ¿Tiene tiempo para hablar?*

-Profesora: *Claro, dígame.*

-Jason: *Soy Jason Thompson, el padre de Mike.*

-Profesora: *Mucho gusto.*

-Jason: *Mucho gusto. Quería preguntarle ¿Cómo va mi hijo en clases?*

-Profesora: *Va excelente. Es un alumno sobresaliente.*

-Jason: *Me alegra oírlo, el se esfuerza mucho estudiando en casa.*

-Profesora: *Su esfuerzo está dando resultados. Sígueme, la directora quiere conocerlo desde hace tiempo.*

-Jason: *¿Y eso para qué?*

-Profesora: *Para saber más sobre el método de estudio de su hijo y usarlo con los otros alumnos.*

-Jason: De acuerdo. Vamos.

... En la oficina de la directora...

-Profesora: Directora, este es el Sr Thompson, el papa de Mike, el niño que sale muy bien en clases.

-Directora: Encantada de conocerlo. Tenía tiempo preguntándome quién era el padre de Mike.

-Jason: Un placer.

-Directora: Su hijo es brillante. Me gustaría conversar con usted sobre varias cosas.

-Jason: Muchas gracias, me halaga. Por supuesto, estoy a la orden.

English

-Jason: Excuse me. Do you have time to talk?

-Teacher: Sure, tell me.

-Jason: I'm Jason Thompson, Mike's father.

-Teacher: Nice to meet you.

-Jason: Nice to meet you. I wanted to ask you, how's my son doing in class?

-Teacher: He's going great. He's an outstanding student.

-Jason: I'm glad to hear it. He works very hard studying at home.

-Teacher: His effort is paying off. Follow me, the principal has been wanting to meet you for a long time.

-Jason: What's that for?

-Teacher: To learn more about your child's study method and use it with other students.

-Jason: Okay. Let's go.

... In the principal's office...

-Teacher: Principal, this is Mr. Thompson, Mike's dad. The boy who does very well in class.

-Principal: Nice to meet you. I have been wondering who Mike's father was.

-Jason: My pleasure.

-Principal: Your son is brilliant. I'd like to talk to you about a few things.

-Jason: Thank you very much, I'm flattered. Of course, I'm on your orders.

Ir al cine - Going to the cinema

Spanish

-Samuel: Alo, ¿Dari?

-Dari: Si, ¿Quién es?

-Samuel: Soy yo, Samuel.

-Dari: Ahh hola Samuel, ¿Cómo estás?

-Samuel: Todo bien, ¿Y tú?

-*Dari: Bien, descansando.*

-*Samuel: Que bueno. Hoy estrenan la nueva película de terror que querías ver.*

-*Dari: ¿En serio?*

-*Samuel: Si, ¿Vamos al cine a verla?*

-*Dari: Me encantaría.*

-*Samuel: Perfecto, paso por ti a las 4:30 de la tarde para ir a comprar los boletos.*

-*Dari: ¿No es mejor que pases a las 5:00 y yo los compro por internet?*

-*Samuel: Bien pensado. A las 5:00 entonces.*

-*Dari: Genial.*

-*Samuel: ¿Puedes apartar unas palomitas por internet?*

-*Dari: Creo que sí, ya intentare.*

-*Samuel: Gracias. Nos vemos más tarde.*

English

-Samuel: Alo, Dari?

-Dari: Yes, who is it?

-Samuel: It's me, Samuel.

-Dari: Ahh, hello, Samuel, how are you?

-Samuel: All right, how are you?

-Dari: I'm fine, resting.

-Samuel: That's good. Today, the new horror movie you wanted to see is released.

-Dari: Really?

-Samuel: Yes, shall we go to the movies to see it?

-Dari: I'd love to.

-Samuel: Perfect. I'll pick you up at 4:30 p.m. to buy the tickets.

-Dari: Isn't it better if you come by at 5:00 and I buy them online?

-Samuel: Good thinking. At 5:00 then.

-Dari: Great.

-Samuel: Can you get some popcorn online?

-Dari: I think so. I'll try.

-Samuel: Thank you. See you later.

Yendo a un partido de futbol - Going to a Football Match

Spanish

-Alan: ¡Hola! ¿Cómo te va?

-Nicolás: Hermano, todo bien, ¿Tu?

-Alan: Muy contento. Ayer en el entrenamiento me eligieron capitán para el partido de hoy.

-Nicolás: Excelente noticia. Me alegro por ti, te esforzaste mucho por eso.

-Alan: Fueron muchos meses de trabajo duro, pero lo logre.

-Nicolás: Así es.

-Alan: Voy camino al partido, ¿Vas a hacer algo ahorita?

-Nicolás: No creo, ¿Por?

-Alan: Ven conmigo para que veas el partido.

-Nicolás: Suena bien.

-Alan: El equipo también está contento, hemos practicado mucho.

-Nicolás: Todos lo hemos notado.

-Alan: Hoy jugaremos con una formación 4-3-3, con Pedro como portero; Jack, Buck y Joey como delanteros; Víctor, Héctor y Javier como mediocampistas y Luis, José, Cesar y yo como defensas.

-Nicolás: Estoy seguro que van a ganar.

-Alan: Yo también.

-Nicolás: Esperemos que el campo este en buenas condiciones, grama cortada, sin huecos y sin pantanos.

-Alan: Ayer estaba bien.

English

-Alan: Hi! How's it going?

-Nicolas: Brother, everything's fine, you?

-Alan: Very happy. Yesterday, in training, I was elected captain for today's match.

-Nicolas: Excellent news. I'm happy for you. You worked very hard for that.

-Alan: It was many months of hard work, but I did it.

-Nicolas: That's right.

-Alan: I'm on my way to the game. Are you going to do something right now?

-Nicolas: I don't think so, why?

-Alan: Come with me to watch the game.

-Nicolas: Sounds good.

-Alan: The team is also happy. We've practiced a lot.

-Nicolas: We've all noticed.

-Alan: Today, we will play with a 4-3-3 formation, with Pedro as goalkeeper; Jack, Buck, and Joey as strikers, Victor, Hector, and Javier as midfielders, and Luis, José, Cesar, and myself as defenders.

-Nicolas: I'm sure you're going to win.

-Alan: Me too.

-Nicolas: Let's hope the field is in good condition, grass cut, no holes, and no swamps.

-Alan: Yesterday, it was fine.

Pidiendo un libro en la biblioteca - Asking for a Book at the Library

Spanish

-*Emma: Buenas tardes.*

-*Roxana: Buenas tardes. Bienvenida a la biblioteca municipal.*

-*Emma: Muchas gracias.*

-*Roxana: ¿Vas a leer aquí o vas a pedir un préstamo para un libro?*

-*Emma: Es primera vez que vengo, ¿Qué clase de libros tiene?*

-*Roxana: Tenemos todo tipos de libros, de terror, de suspenso, de comedia, biografías, de ciencias, de política, de historia, de ficción, de romance, etcétera.*

-*Emma: ¿Y cómo es su política de préstamos?*

-*Roxana: Depende del historial de la persona, como tú eres nueva, te podemos prestar un libro por una semana, pasada esa semana, si no regresas el libro comenzaremos a aplicar sanciones para tus futuros prestamos.*

-*Emma: Ya veo. Mis favoritos son los de terror. ¿Cuál es el mejor que tiene?*

-*Roxana: El libro de terror mas pedido es "El Monstruo del ático".*

-*Emma: Perfecto, me lo llevo.*

-*Roxana: Ya te lo busco.*

English

-Emma: Good afternoon.

-Roxana: Good afternoon. Welcome to the municipal library.

-Emma: Thank you very much.

-Roxana: Are you going to read here or are you going to borrow a book?

-Emma: It's my first time here. What kind of books do you have?

-Roxana: We have all kinds of books, horror, suspense, comedy, biographies, sciences, politics, history, fiction, romance, and so on.

-Emma: And how is your lending policy?

-Roxana: It depends on the history of the person. As you are new, we can lend you a book for a week. Passed that week, if you do not return the book, we will begin to apply sanctions for your future loans.

-Emma: I see. My favorites are horror. Which one is the best?

-Roxana: The most requested horror book is "The Monster in the Attic.

-Emma: Perfect, I'll take it.

-Roxana: I'll get it for you.

Pidiendo la clave del wifi - Asking for Wifi's Password

Spanish

-Gabriela: Buenas noches, ¿Está usted bien?

-Lucy: Buenas noches, en realidad no, me siento un poco mareada.

-Gabriela: ¿Hay algo que pueda hacer para ayudarla?

-Lucy: ¿Serias tan amable de buscar en internet que hacer en estos casos?

-Gabriela: Lo haría, pero no tengo conexión a internet en este momento.

-Lucy: Pídele la clave del wifi a aquella señora, ella es mi vecina.

-Gabriela: Perfecto, ya voy.

-Lucy: Gracias….

-Gabriela: Buenas noches, disculpe, pero, ¿Podría darme usted la clave de su wifi? Su vecina Lucy se está sintiendo mal y necesito entrar a internet tan pronto como sea posible.

-Gladys: Claro cariño, la clave es 1234567891. ¿Qué tiene Lucy?

-Gabriela: Se está sintiendo un poco mareada y la veo débil. Buscare en internet que puede ser y como solucionarlo.

-Gladys: Hazme saber si necesitan algo más. Dile que me avise cuando mejore.

-Gabriela: Seguro.

English

-Gabriela: Good evening, are you all right?

-Lucy: Good evening, not really, I feel a little dizzy.

-Gabriela: Is there anything I can do to help you?

-Lucy: Would you be so kind as to search on the Internet what to do in these cases?

-Gabriela: I would, but I don't have an internet connection at the moment.

-Lucy: Ask that lady for the wifi password, she's my neighbor.

-Gabriela: Perfect, on my way.

-Lucy: Thank you...

-Gabriela: Good evening. Excuse me, but could you give me the password of your wifi? Your neighbor Lucy is feeling bad and I need to get on the Internet as soon as possible.

-Gladys: Sure, honey. The password is 1234567891. What's wrong with Lucy?

-Gabriela: She's feeling a little dizzy and I see her weak. I'll search the internet for what it could be and how to solve it.

-Gladys: Let me know if you need anything else. Tell her to let me know when she gets better.

-Gabriela: Sure.

Pidiendo un aventón - Asking for a Ride

Spanish

-Troy: Hey Alice, ¿Cómo estás?

-Alice: Troy, muy bien, ¿Y tú?

-Troy: Todo bien, un poco preocupado en realidad.

-Alice: ¿Por qué?

-Troy: Tengo que caminar a casa, pero está lloviendo mucho.

-Alice: ¿Y porque no pides un aventón?

-Troy: ¿Tú crees?

-Alice: Claro, alguien de acá debe ir hacia allá.

-Troy: Bien pensado.

-Alice: ¿A dónde vas tú?

-Troy: A la Avenida 4 con calle 13.

-Alice: Ok. Creo que ron usa esa vía.

-Troy: ¿Puedes preguntarle?

-Alice: Hey Ron, ¿Tu pasas por la avenida 4 con calle 13 para ir a tu casa?

-Ron: Hola Alice, si, pero hoy no voy a mi casa.

-Alice: ¿Sabes de alguien que pase por ahí? Troy necesita un aventón por la lluvia.

-Ron: Estoy casi seguro que Amanda.

-Alice: Genial. Muchas gracias. Vamos Troy.

-Troy: Gracias de todas maneras Ron.

-Ron: En otra oportunidad será.

-Troy: Seguro.

-Alice: Hola Amanda. ¿Ya te vas?

-Amanda: Alice, si, ya voy saliendo a casa.

-Alice: Me dijo ron que pasas por la Avenida 4 con calle 13, ¿Correcto?.

-Amanda: Así es, ¿Por?

-Troy: ¿Crees que me puedas dar un aventón? La lluvia no me dejara caminar hasta allá.

-Amanda: Claro, con mucho gusto. Pero ya me voy, así que apúrate.

-Troy: Ok, muchas gracias, y gracias a ti también Alice. Nos vemos mañana.

-Alice: Hasta mañana.

English

-Troy: Hey Alice, how are you?

-Alice: Troy, all right, how are you?

-Troy: All right, a little worried really.

-Alice: Why?

-Troy: I have to walk home but it's raining a lot.

-Alice: Why don't you ask for a ride?

-Troy: You think so?

-Alice: Of course, someone from here must go there.

-Troy: Good thinking.

-Alice: Where are you going?

-Troy: 4th Avenue and 13th Street.

-Alice: Okay. I think Ron uses that road.

-Troy: Can you ask him?

-Alice: Hey, Ron. Do you go down 4th Avenue and 13th Street to your house?

-Ron: Hello, Alice. Yes, but I'm not going home today.

-Alice: Do you know of anyone passing by? Troy needs a ride because of the rain.

-Ron: I'm pretty sure Amanda does.

-Alice: Great. Thanks a lot. Come on Troy.

-Troy: Thanks anyway, Ron.

-Ron: Some other time.

-Troy: Sure.

-Alice: Hi, Amanda. Are you leaving already?

-Amanda: Alice, yes, I'm going home.

-Alice: Ron told me that you're going through 4th Avenue and 13th Street, right?

-Amanda: That's right, why?

-Troy: Do you think you can give me a ride? The rain won't let me walk there.

-Amanda: Of course, with pleasure. But I'm leaving now, so hurry.

-Troy: Okay, thank you very much, and thank you, Alice. See you tomorrow.

-Alice: See you tomorrow.

Visitando al doctor - Visiting the Doctor

Spanish

-Donald: *Buenos días Doctor. ¿Cómo esta?*

-Doctor: *Muy bien, ¿Usted?*

-Donald: *Bien. Vengo por el chequeo mensual.*

-Doctor: *Esta bien, aunque la ultima salió bastante bien.*

-Donald: *Gracias a Dios. Pero me he sentido resfriado, por eso vine.*

-Doctor: *Muy bien, empecemos con la consulta y chequeo entonces.*

-Donald: *Gracias.*

English

-Donald: Good morning, Doctor. How are you?

-Doctor: Very well, you?

-Donald: Good. I'm here for the monthly checkup.

-Doctor: All right, although the last one went quite well.

-Donald: Thank God. But I had a cold, that's why I came.

-Doctor: All right, let's start with the consultation and checkup then.

-Donald: Thank you.

Número equivocado - Wrong Number

Spanish

-Thalia: *Hola, ¿Es este el numero de Noah?*

-Extraño: *Buenas tardes, me temo que no, está equivocado.*

-Thalia: *Llame al número equivocado, disculpe.*

-Extraño: *Vale, adios.*

English

-Thalia: Hi, is this Noah's number?

-Stranger: Good afternoon. I'm afraid not, you're wrong.

-Thalia: I called the wrong number, excuse me.

-Stranger: Okay, bye.

Aplicar para un trabajo - Apply for a job

Spanish

-Vanessa: *Buenas tardes. Vengo por el anuncio del periódico de que buscan un vendedor y me gustaría aplicar para el puesto.*

-Secretaria: *Buenas tardes, bienvenida. Toma asiento y serás atendida en un momento.*

-Vanessa: *Muchas gracias....*

-Secretaria: *Puedes pasar a la entrevista.*

-Vanessa: *Gra-gracias.*

-Secretaria: *No estés nerviosa, sonríe, te irá bien.*

-Vanessa: *De acuerdo.*

...

-Vanessa: *Buenas tardes.*

-Entrevistador: *Buenas tardes, siéntate por favor.*

-Vanessa: *Ok.*

-Entrevistador: *Me dijo la secretaria que estas aquí para aplicar por el puesto de vendedora, ¿es cierto?*

-Vanessa: *Si señor.*

-Entrevistador: *¿Por qué deberíamos contratarte?*

-Vanessa: *Aquí tengo mi curriculum, puede ver que soy la indicada para el puesto, además, soy muy responsable y comprometida.*

-Entrevistador: *Ya veo. Me gustaría entrevistarla otro día con más calma.*

-Vanessa: *De acuerdo, ahí está mi número de teléfono, me llama.*

English

-Vanessa: Good afternoon. I came for the newspaper ad that says you're looking for a salesman and I'd like to apply for the job.

-Secretary: Good afternoon, welcome. Take a seat and you will be attended in a moment.

-Vanessa: Thank you very much...

-Secretary: You can go to the interview.

-Vanessa: Tha-Thank you.

-Secretary: Don't be nervous. Smile. You'll be fine.

-Vanessa: Fine.

...

-Vanessa: Good afternoon.

-Interviewer: Good afternoon. Please sit down.

-Vanessa: Ok.

-Interviewer: The secretary told me that you are here to apply for the position of the saleswoman, is that right?

-Vanessa: Yes, sir.

-Interviewer: Why should we hire you?

-Vanessa: I have my resume here. You can see that I'm the right person for the job, and I'm very responsible and committed.

-Interviewer: I see. I'd like to interview you another day more slowly.

-Vanessa: Okay, there's my phone number. You call me.

Chapter 15: Spanish Grammar Lessons to Advance Your Language Mastery

Tips to Master Spanish Grammar

- **Practice Present Tense for Three Months**

Spend three months perfecting in the present tense. English speakers have a hard time mastering the tenses. The best way to simplify the whole Spanish learning process is to study the present tense and learn them entirely. What's more, it will help you tackle the complex Spanish tenses.

- **Participate in Private Conversations to Practice Future and Past Tenses**

Find private conversation classes where you will get extra attention to progress in the Spanish language after practicing the present tense for a long time. It will be easier to grasp the past and future tenses.Everything becomes part of you if you make it familiar through regular practice. The Spanish language will become one of your favorites if you make it so. Keep practicing without giving up.

- **Have a Notebook to Write Down Gender of Different Nouns**

Have a notebook with you all the time. It will help you note down how gender is applied in the language. This is a complex thing for English speakers. But you can simplify it by using creativity. Have two columns, one for female nouns and the other one for male nouns. A notebook will help grasp the common nouns and the general rules of using them. While the general rule is that any noun that ends with "a" is feminine, there are exceptions.

A good example is *el clima*, which means the weather. While it clearly ends with "a," this word falls under the masculine nouns. If you keep noting such points, you will eventually memorize it.

- **Write Something in Spanish Daily**

Whether it's an exercise from a book you bought online or in your local store, write something in Spanish. It helps you practice, and eventually, if writing is your thing, you can start a blog. Just like everything else that you want to perfect in Spanish, practice it daily. Or, you can write your diary in Spanish; it will help you understand the grammar tricks and work around them successfully.

- **Go for a Course on How to Use the Subjunctive**

Subjunctives are not common in English. But, in Spanish, they are an essential part of the language. The past and present subjunctive forms are used frequently. Being a native English speaker, you will definitely have a problem with Spanish grammar and the way to ease this is to join a program that allows professional training mainly on the subjunctive. But nothing is impossible; just set your goals and be consistent, and the language will become your second favorite.

- **Learn and Understand Connectives That Has Particular Constructions**

Learning Spanish is fun if you look at it from a positive perspective. But, at times, you will feel the heat that comes with new grammar different from what you are used to. The popular Spanish connectives are pero for "but," desd meaning "from" or "since," mientras, which means "while," sin embargo meaning "however," por lo tanto meaning "therefore," and de todas maneras meaning "anyway." These are the words that enrich your language and especially any content written Spanish.

They make sentences flow, and words get intertwined so beautifully. Nothing sounds terrible like content without connectives; the sentence sounds so unrelated.

- **Read a Lot of Spanish Books**

Reading Spanish books, especially scholarly literature, will help you perfect your grammar. Make sure the books are written in perfect Spanish so that you learn the right thing. Look for help if you do not know where to find trustworthy reading materials. Spanish newspapers are readily available online, and you will be reading news and learning Spanish at the same time.

- **Identify and note the differences or similarities between Spanish and English grammar**

If you can identify the patterns of the Spanish language that are similar or different from the English language, you will move a level higher in learning. A good example is that a gerund always follows English prepositions, and, in Spanish, prepositions are usually followed by the verb base form.

Find the patterns and highlight the grammatical differences or similarities between the two languages. You can correctly translate grammar patterns without doing literal translations. Spanglish means poor Spanish grammar and will not help you excel, so use patterns to know the correct grammar.

- **Avoid Any Habit That Will Slow Down Your Learning**

When learning Spanish, incorporate all accents, such as tildes. Write every word as it should be, whether you are just chatting with your friend or sending a formal letter. You are a student learning a foreign language; make use of every moment to write in proper Spanish. This is the learning experience that will help you master the language like a native.

For example, when you write hablo, which means "I speak," it's totally different from habló, which means "he/she/it spoke." Show the distinction in your writing, and later on, you will not have significant grammar issues with grammar.

- **Enjoy Learning the Elements and Fundamentals of Spanish Grammar**

Spanish grammar is not a walk in the park, especially for English speakers. It is confusing and dense, but if you get the elements and the fundamentals clearly, you will be good to go. For example, if you want to use conditionals, you simply add "a" at the end of verb base form. Enjoy such moments and have fun when learning; it will not only ease the learning process but ensure you do not forget. When using conditionals, for instance, you only have to add "ía" to the end of the base form of the verb.

It's important to revel in these moments because when you're having fun with the language, you'll learn more. When Spanish grammar makes it easy for you, smile, laugh, and, most importantly, have fun chatting away in your second language.

- **Always Get Something to Enrich Your Learning Process**

If you are really looking forward to learning Spanish smartly, use apps, guides, and other materials available online. Just make sure you verify their quality before you add them to your learning arsenal. You can also watch videos on YouTube, movies, or even soccer. Combine different ways of learning Spanish, and, with time, you will be at a native level.

There is a lot to learn when taking Spanish grammar lessons. But there are lessons that you must consider before you can confidently write or speak Spanish.

- **Speak Spanish from Day One**

After you have started attending class, one lesson you need to learn is speaking Spanish. Put effort and speak the few words you learn. Within a short time, you will be speaking fluently. Look for friends who speak Spanish if you are not in Spain. Burying yourself in books and audios will not give you the desired results. You must practice and talk about the language. Albeit speaking imperfectly, those who know the language will correct you, and after a few weeks, you will be conversing fluently.

- **Immerse yourself in Spanish**

It's time to stop speaking English. If you keep speaking English, especially if you are in Spain, you will never break the barriers. If you have people around you, who can speak this language, immerse yourself into Spanish. You can even choose to do this at least two days a week. By practicing, you will easily remember what you learned, and living in Spain will make it easier. However, you do not have to leave your country for a Spanish speaking one. You can immerse into this language even without anyone else speaking it.

- **Listen to Audios and Podcasts**

You will find many audio courses and podcasts to help you practice speaking Spanish. They have features and creativity that will ease your Spanish lessons while perfecting them.

- **Join a University That Teaches in Spanish**

If you have been struggling with learning Spanish, join a course that is taught in Spanish. By doing this, you will be forced to study and take your language to the highest level possible. But why join the university to learn Spanish?

  - You will master Spanish excellently. Since academic papers must be written in proper grammar, you will fight with every tooth and nail to get a good grasp of the language.

  - Being in college, you will have a chance to explore Spanish literature, history, and culture.

  - You will have to spend at least one year studying in a country where Spanish is the official language. That will give you an excellent chance to immerse into Spanish.

- **Take a Short Course in Summer School**

If you are not looking forward to getting a full degree, you can join a language school to learn Spanish. Look for summer school that has intensive programs that will enable you to start speaking this language from day one. And always remember that you do not have to travel or move to a Spanish-speaking country to master this language professionally.

- **Get Yourself a Tutor Online**

The worst mistake you can do is to join a class with many students. The tutor cannot concentrate on you. So, why not get yourself an online tutor? The cost maybe a little higher, but it's worth it. Look for reputable platforms and get yourself a tutor; you will not only learn the language privately but also study Spanish from the comfort of your home or office.

- **Get Yourself a Study Partner**

The study partner you find should know Spanish. It is one of the cheapest ways to get Spanish lessons. In most cases, you learn Spanish while teaching the other person English. Look for one in your city or go online. You can use Skype or any other efficient online platform to communicate and learn each other's language without spending even a dime.

- **Attend Language meetings**

If you are not interested in a one-on-one language exchange, look for "language exchange" events in your city. It includes people from various parts of the world who come together to practice any language of their choice.

Spanish is the second language in many countries; therefore, it is possible to find Spanish meet-up groups. However, the shortcoming of taking such lessons is that you end up learning the same thing. Most people will want to know your name, where you come from, your job, and some general information. What's more, they do not have the time to teach you Spanish grammar and other rules of the language.

However, if it's useful to you, you can even create a Spanish language group. Here, you can meet other people with the same interest and learn the language together.

- **Join a Language Challenge**

If you have learned a good amount of the Spanish language, you can join a language marathon for some fun. If you meet with people who are on the same track as you, you will learn Spanish better. You will find encouragement and motivation to pursue your shared goal.

The challenge can be online or held locally. It is exciting to have one with your classmates. It will not only challenge you but will also give you support on areas where you are weak in the Spanish language.

English Problems That Will Make Your Pronunciation Sound Terrible

The Consonants Issues

The Spanish consonants make specific sounds according to the language's strict sound rules. However, there are exceptions, but the language is still completely different from English, where consonant issues are concerned. In Spanish, a consonant change when combined with some vowels and consonants, and it's straightforward. It is more comfortable compared to the irregularities and combinations in the English sounds.

Consonants do change a lot when it comes to Spanish; most of the sounds are like in English. Nonetheless, non-natives over-enunciate them in Spanish, making them sound terrible.

Vowel problems

In general, Spanish vowels are pronounced in the same way; if you learn how to do it, you will be good to go. You need a lot of practice to get the sound right. Pay attention to the vowel sound length. The Spanish vowels tend to be pronounced quickly and shortly. A fun way to learn this is to give each vowel half a second sound. It should be brief and precise. Don't forget to pronounce the vowels strongly despite being short.

Open the mouth when pronouncing them to bring out the correct sound. For example, *a* sounds perfect with the jaw dropped, and *i* sounds well when the mouth is stretched and looks like a grin. For *u* and *o*, the mouth must open widely but with the lips rounded. Knowing how to open the mouth makes the vowels sound natural as you speak.

Accent Marks

Accent marks are significant, especially when writing in Spanish. It changes the meaning of a word if you miswrite it. When speaking, you must know the syllable to press. Check for any accent placed in a word before you read it out. The best thing is that you can find online tools to help you with Spanish pronunciation.

B/V

In English, *b* and *v* are totally different. However, in Spanish, these two letters are hardly differentiable. They sound like *b* in English, and even natives who have not had extensive education in writing and reading confuse them all the time.

For example, when a word begins with a *v* or *b*, followed by *n* or *m*, it is pronounced as b in English. In Spanish, be ready to explore strange things as you learn new pronunciations.

Cl

Cl sounds so graceful in Spanish that it makes English speakers sound off note. It is pronounced swiftly, yet softly. A good illustration is the word "clomp," where you should not be hard on the "c" sound or linger a lot in "l."

Spanish treats "cl" differently, for example, *aclarar*, which means clarify. Pronunciation reduces how cl sounds. Do it swiftly, in half a second. Let the tongue tap your mouth's roof gently and quickly, but gracefully lilt to the next letter which is a.

S/S

In Spanish, the letter "c" sounds like "s" when followed by "i" or "e." English speakers make the mistake of stressing it hard. English speakers take the "c" seriously, which is different from Spanish. When pronouncing this sound, the air leaves your mouth.

For example, try the word "cow," and you will feel how the air leaves the mouth. In Spanish, sound "c" does not cause the air to leave your mouth. *Acomodar*, which means accommodate, is a perfect Spanish example. The "c" sound comes out crisp, and you spend less time on it.

D

Letter d is the reason native English speakers have a problem in speaking other languages correctly. This letter is deeply pronounced in English, and it becomes a problem in Spanish where it's non-existent. It is pronounced softly and sometimes not pronounced at all. A good example is *pescado*, which is mostly read as *pescao*.

Chapter 16: Taking Spanish Speaking Lessons

After getting a gist about the history of Spanish and what its learning entails, it's now time to shift gears and get into the nitty-gritty of taking up the Spanish speaking lessons. To begin, a Spanish lesson comprises a list of instructions that can enable you to understand the language.

For you to access such guidelines, you must have a source.

Online and Offline Sources for Your Spanish Lessons

Taking a look at both the online and offline sources for your Spanish lessons yields several results which include the following.

• Reading books — These sources have been utilized since time immemorial and are still being used by many for reference purposes and practice. By reading books, you'll be familiarizing yourself with the basics of learning the Spanish language. That way, you'll be able to garner instrumental skills regarding how to speak the Spanish language. Also, you'll master the different uses of vowels. That way, you can apply them in your speech.

• Audio lessons — These lessons are mostly in the form of audiobooks and podcasts and can help you to have grasp specifics of the language since they are lesser targeted. The audio lessons will also assist you in comprehending how to put different sentences to use.

• Video lessons — In this format, you will watch as an instructor gives you lessons concerning the language

• Applications — Several applications can link you to Spanish tutors or an online platform where you can learn various Spanish lessons. Apart from that, we have those who can assist you in grammar and pronunciation.

• Learning partners — You can help your fellow learners and support each other to master the language. These can be through discussions and forums, among other avenues. When working with partners, you'll garner interesting lessons based on how to master vital elements of the Spanish language. Therefore, you can ensure that you're working with the right partner. In this case, it refers to someone who is willing to train you while amassing a source of knowledge on the same subject. Perhaps you can try to learn more about the language by partnering with a native speaker. That way, you can rest assured that you are garnering vital lessons about how to become pro!

• Group lessons — These sources have a similar format to class lessons where a coach or tutor takes a whole group through training sessions. You can ask any questions that can be answered during the sessions. A group lesson also plays a role in supporting your ability to master the language. With the group, you'll be in a position to learn fast. You'll also have the support of your team in assessing different uses of verbs and adverbs. With that said, your lessons should directly be appended to your requirements. In the learning process, you should also garner lessons based on how to use nouns and pronouns. To be successful in this, you also need to work with people who have the same goal. That way, you can master some of the basic Spanish lessons that the group offers.

• Native speakers as tutors — Through applications, you can link yourself with an online native speaker who can become your Spanish teacher. Alternatively, you can hire one near you to take you through the lessons on a face-to-face basis. Working with a native speaker allows you to master different languages. You'll be able to learn more about how to take the next steps involved in learning Spanish. You shall also learn about the requirements of speaking the Spanish language not only in school but also in other forums.

• Live training — you can also attend live online training sessions by native speakers via your computer. It can be free sessions like those offered by native speaker volunteers or paid versions done by professionals.

• Taking weekly audio Spanish lessons — just like the live pieces of training, you can also get free weekly audio lessons from volunteers and organizations. These groups are out there to provide you with free lessons. You can access such through your personal computer, phone, or radio.

• YouTube — There are tons of free video Spanish lessons on YouTube. Once inside this platform, you can select your favorite instructor and listen to them.

• Taking free online Spanish systems and courses — As a beginner, you can get tons of free online courses to start you off on your journey. Just make sure that you conduct a review of the course you are going to take. The same applies to all units you're willing to learn. It's better rather than wasting time on an outdated piece of material or one which makes your learning experience horrible.

What to consider when purchasing or signing up for a Spanish lesson?

• The tutor should have all the language tools. The requirements indicate that one should have the right software, too. In the case of software, it needs to have all the necessary language tools at its disposal. The same will enable you to quickly learn all the helpful expressions and the fundamental conversational Spanish.

• It offers the best value. I'm sure that you want a lesson that provides the best value for your money spent. Furthermore, attending such lessons is a life investment; therefore, you need a serious course that transforms you from a newbie to a master in the language.

• It's affordable for you. Make sure to purchase a class that you can easily afford without breaking the bank. If you are not financially stable, you can start with the free stuff and, when ready, graduate to the premium content. An ideal lesson is neither too expensive nor too cheap for you.

• It has different teaching format. Select a lesson or Spanish application with a teaching methodology that you are comfortable in. Different forms of the experiences do exist in the market; therefore, you need to select the one that you are comfortable in.

• The lessons have different levels. If you are a beginner, stick to the readings for starters and so on. Each level has its lessons, so make the right choice.

• This can be a free or paid lesson.-Before starting up, ascertain whether the course you are signing up is a free one, or you will be required to pay for it within a particular period or is a trial lesson. This can save you from starting a course then abandoning it halfway because of the monetary aspect, which can derail your learning or demoralize you from continuing to learn.

What constitutes a useful Spanish lesson?

A practical Spanish lesson has the following attributes.

• Has the needed ingredients — A well-thought-out lesson needs to have all the necessary components to guarantee its success. The one facilitating the learning process need to be proficient in their communication, whatever method they are using. Also, they should have the ability to explain the concepts using more than a single method to facilitate proper understanding. Moreover, a coach or tutor should be patient enough for you to understand.

• Include typical phrases — This enables the utilization of the concept immediately after class and also fosters the learning experience. In this regard, they have to use your standard pronunciation, spelling, sentence structure, grammar, and colloquialisms.

• Has constant repetitions to understand the language — Repetition of the common phrases will often be required during the lessons. The coach or tutor needs to be asking you or the class to repeat what they say. They can also utilize other things, such as word plays, role-play, and subtitles from the movies or television programs when the class breaks from intense learning.

• Should incorporate quizzes and tests — The lessons need to have some exams after every significant aspect learned. Also, the tutors need to give their students announced and surprise tests to understand how they are fairing on with the lesson. These would also help students to identify their weak areas and improve on them. These will also build your confidence in the learning progress, which is equally important.

• Needs to have rewards — A practical lesson is one that identifies where you have improved during the learning process and rewards you accordingly, which can act as a motivation for putting in more efforts. It should also determine if you are not making any progress so that additional coaching can be offered to you.

• Challenging — The lessons need to throw up some challenges within it to encourage the learning process. Once you overcome a specific problem, you can learn something new, which prepares you for an even more significant challenge, and the cycle continues. Besides, difficulties can break up the monotony that occurs when learning the same things over and over again.

• Engaging — A conversational lesson makes the language user-friendly. You will understand it quickly, thus allowing you to understand the concepts. Engaging content is also fun to learn since it brings liveliness and breaks up the monotony.

• Productive — A practical lesson needs to yield some positive results among the learners. For instance, more than half of the students should gain something after the lesson rather than sticking at the same levels

• Continuous — This means that the lesson should add value to what was taught before. This acts as building blocks to future lessons that you are going to undertake. With a positive attitude from both ends, an excellent learning experience is possible.

How to Self-Master Spanish Lessons

Developing a mastery of Spanish by yourself is an intricate process that requires some specific steps or techniques, which include the following.

Choose Your Resources

How to go about acquiring the best Spanish resources and lessons. In this step, you should review the resources you are going to purchase. It's vital to make sure that you buy the best audio course, book, or online course and study the lessons. You need to include the audio component to get a hint of how Spanish words sound.

Regarding classes, you may take the Spanish lessons in the country where you live or decide to migrate to a Spanish speaking country or take a plunge into the online world to acquire your lessons. An alternative would be conducting an online tutor to teach you the language using a progressive curriculum.

Utilize Practical Study Methods

You can study yourself to identify the most suitable study method that may suit you. In the beginning, you may not know what is appropriate for you. Therefore, try to experiment with various techniques of learning.

Spend the Required Time on the Lessons

In the process of trying out a self-study of the Spanish language, self-discipline comes up as a vital component that you need to incorporate in your study schedule. An appropriate learning program should one that requires you to practice the language daily. Sticking to such kind of program will enable you to grasp the basics which would act as the foundation to the higher levels.

You can also utilize idle time to your advantage by practicing how to read and write Spanish; for instance, time spends a while on the bus, queue, or relaxing. You can do this by writing the Spanish vocabulary on several cards which you can be removed from time to time during those time and try to memorize what is on them. Alternatively, you can always have a Spanish novel or textbook to read at a convenient time. Besides, listen to podcasts and audiotapes while doing other things such as driving to work, performing some manual duties, among other activities. Doing this will allow the language to stick. It'll also make the learning of the next courses easier.

In case you don't have sufficient time to create it. These can entail the cancellation of some chores to accommodate the program. You can cut off some unproductive activities from your daily schedules and allocate them to learning. In the long run, it would pay off since it is a long term investment thing.

Immersion

Another technique for self-learning Spanish is by total immersion. In this method, you immerse yourself among Spanish speaking persons and take the challenge of mastering it head-on and combining this method with other well-known techniques aid leaning. Examples of techniques you can utilize in immersion without actually having to travel to a Spanish speaking country include:

i. Watching Spanish videos daily: these videos must not necessarily be learning videos but can be from any subject or topic in Spanish. For instance, if you want to watch a Spanish video regarding cooking, you can google translate "cooking" into Spanish then copy and paste the results on to your browser. You will get so many Spanish cooking videos which you can watch at your convenience. These can provide you with the flow of the Spanish language and the words to use in topics and subjects that fancy you.

ii. Writing Spanish daily: you can juggle your mind through writing in Spanish for a few minutes daily. You can write a sentence or talk about how your day was using a new vocabulary learned that day. The same can reinforce whatever phrases or words acquired while stimulating your mind to start thinking in Spanish.

iii. Think in Spanish: It can be challenging at the start; but with constant practice, your abilities can skyrocket. You may achieve this by questioning yourself and try answering it in Spanish. By doing so, the various locations of your brain become stimulated and also helps to argument the already learned into a coherent, purposeful sentence or phrase.

iv. You may immerse into your favorite Spanish books. Since a lot of top novels and books have already been translated to Spanish, you may take your ideal edition in English and compare it with the translated version. These make it easy to understand what you are reading.

v. Form a habit of listening to Spanish audio: you can listen to your exciting topic. Doing this will familiarize you with the Spanish sounds and improve your grammar and vocabulary.

vi. Use music as a learning aid: some channels can translate songs that are in Spanish into English subtitles. Therefore, you can select your favorite song and start to listen while reading the texts that are both in Spanish and English. Utilizing a bit of your creativity, you can be able to create an immersive setting that can take care of your learning needs.

Chapter 17: Tips & Tricks to learn quickly a new language

¡Enhorabuena! (Congratulations!) You have started your Spanish learning journey and you have finished the first stage!

It can be overwhelming to learn a lot of new vocabulary and you can think "how am I going to remember everything I have learnt?".

No, it's not easy. The secret is that there is not any secret, you have to keep practicing. Use it as much as you can is best advise you can get! But there are some tips and tricks to make the process less complicated.

Let's make a list of things we can't forget when we speak Spanish:

In Spanish we write like we speak; *every letter has an only sound* (most of times).

We always use articles before each noun, and noun has gender and number, that means that articles, nouns (and also adjectives) must match gender and number.

Unlike English, in Spanish adjectives, most of times, go after the noun (*El libro rojo* = the red book)

And tricks to keep practicing Spanish and enjoy doing it:

Make Spanish be part of your life.

Why not switch your mobile phone language into Spanish? You're likely using your mobile phone daily and if you have its menus in Spanish you will be learning same time you keep using it as usual, so no extra time needed. It will be tricky for the first days, but you'll get used shortly. You can also practice your Spanish and pronunciation with your mobile virtual assistant!

Learning a foreigner language takes effort and you can give up if you're feeling bored. It will be easier if you read something you are really interested in, in Spanish. Why not read about cooking in Spanish if you enjoy baking pies? Do you like sports? Try to read sports news in Spanish. Interested in music? The same!

You can also start watching some TV shows in Spanish, with English subtitles at the beginning, but switching to Spanish subtitles when you feel ready.

Listen Spanish podcasts or radios will also help.

You can read newspapers in Spanish as well. If you are interested into traveling to a Spanish speaking country, you can get information about how things are there, reading the local newspapers.

Finding a pal to exchange language would be really good. There's always some Spanish speaker who would like to improve English, so meeting for a café and practice both languages will be very helpful. Not just for learning the language, but for understanding better the culture and, of course, to make friends!

Do you fancy a Spanish karaoke? Why not! Is a funny way to practice the language.

If you are a board games lover, playing in Spanish is a good option to practice and keep learning Spanish. You can try to get the Spanish version of the game or create your own Spanish board game.

If you are more an old school student, you can create Spanish vocabulary flashcards. Writing is also a good method to learn and memorize vocabulary. You can create different flashcards classified in different topics and you can then practice a topic per day.

You have started the journey, and it's going to be a long journey, but starting is the most difficult stage and you have already done a lot so… don't stop and keep going!

Conclusion

Thank you for taking the time to study and read through this book. I hope the conversations and vocabulary included have been as useful to you as they have been for me. They certainly have helped me in my travels throughout Latin America.

In fact, these kinds of dialogues, phrases, and expressions have helped me make new friends, move around, ask for help, and socialize in various contexts. For instance, I've made plenty of new friends in local shops, markets, and restaurants by simply being able to greet people, ask for their name and give them my basic information. From there, I was able to take the conversations even further by asking what their hobbies were, what kind of music they liked, what they did for fun, etc.

But perhaps the most significant occasion in which my Spanish was quite useful was when I lost my credit card at an airport in Argentina. I was paying for some items I had purchased but when I left the shop, I stopped to get some food when I realized I didn't have my card on me. So, I retraced my steps and finally returned to the store where I was sure I had left my card. It was a bit of a scary situation because the clerk in the shop had turned my card over to airport security. I needed to navigate my way through this situation in order to get my card back. I would never have been able to handle this situation if it hadn't been for the dialogues and conversations I had learned before making my trip. This is why it's important to be somewhat competent in Spanish before traveling. You never know when being able to speak Spanish, even at a basic level, it can be useful when you need it most.

Spanish Short Stories

12 compelling short stories for intermediate and advances users to grow your vocabulary and learn in a fun way

Introduction

Reading is a complicated skill. Think of how you learned to read in your mother tongue. It took you years to master the language before you even started learning how to read, from the simplest words to the most complicated ones. During this time you built a complex set of micro skills that allows you to read different things at a different pace and with different levels of understanding.

However, research suggests that this doesn't happen when reading in a foreign language. You stop being able to use all those micro skills that help you understand a difficult text and you start focusing on understanding the meaning of every single word. That, for the intermediate level learner, tends to be exhausting and contributes to a rapid frustration at being unable to understand due to an elementary vocabulary. Advanced level learners are expected to have overcome this issue, but constant reading is necessary to keep yourself in shape.

The first tip is to avoid getting instantly overwhelmed by the unknown words. Try reading a full page, or even just a paragraph before stopping to look up the meaning of words. Not breaking the semantic flow of the story will eventually make it easier to get a general idea of it. It does not matter if you miss small details because your reading speed will increase and you will improve your fluency.

It is also important to commit yourself to a minimum page count per day. Remember, the more you read, the more you learn.

Keep coming back to the stories. You will be amazed by how much more of them you understand the second time.

In this book, we are presenting short stories that you can read to practice Spanish language. Each story has its own topic, where important vocabulary is presented at the end of the story.

Always keep in mind that the goal of reading is not to understand every single word in a story. The purpose of reading is to be able to enjoy the stories while you expose yourself to new expressions and to tell stories in Spanish. So, if you don't understand a word, try to guess it from the context or just continue reading.

The questions following the story are both meant to test your reading comprehension and give you an opportunity to practice your writing skills. This exercise will give you the opportunity to use your imagination when it comes to writing skills. The suggested responses at the end of the story are meant to serve as a guide. So, you can compare your own answers to the suggested ones. Of course, these are only suggested answers. That means you can very well come up with your own answers according to the passage that you have read.

Finally, please review the vocabulary presented at the end of the story. The words in that vocabulary have been selected in order to help you warm up for the content in the story. You will find both the Spanish and English words in the list. That way, you won't have to guess their meaning. You can read through the list, and make a note of the words that you find new or challenging.

The last two stories of this book will be only presented in Spanish language, without translation, so that by that time you can really test your level of understanding of the Spanish language.

1. ¿Cómo Perder Peso?

*Para muchas personas, el **inicio** de un **nuevo año** es una oportunidad para hacer cambios en su **vida**. Algunas personas **deciden volver a estudiar**. Otras personas piensan en un nuevo trabajo. Y otras **quieren** iniciar un nuevo pasatiempo.*

For many people, the beginning of a new year is an opportunity to make changes in their lives. Some people decide to study again. Other people think of a new job. And others want to start a new hobby.

*Hay otro grupo de personas que piensan en **perder peso**. Esta es una meta que parece **sencilla**, pero en realidad, no lo es. Para empezar, perder peso es una manera de vivir una vida **saludable**. Las personas que tienen **sobrepeso** están **expuestas** a **problemas de salud**. Estos problemas de salud se convierten en **enfermedades serias**. Por lo tanto, los doctores recomiendan perder peso hasta llegar al **peso ideal**.*

There is another group of people who think about losing weight. This is a goal that seems simple, but it really is not. To start, losing weight is a way of living a healthy life. People who are overweight are exposed to health problems. These health problems become serious diseases. Therefore, doctors recommend losing weight until you reach the ideal weight.

*La mejor manera de **lograr** el peso ideal es una **combinación** de ejercicio regular y una dieta balanceada. Existen muchas **maneras** de hacer ejercicio. Se puede **caminar, correr, nadar, andar en bicicleta** o **ir al gimnasio**. De hecho, muchas personas se **inscriben** al gimnasio a principio de año. Pero, la mayoría **dejan de ir** después de unas **semanas**.*

The best way to achieve the ideal weight is a combination of regular exercise and a balanced diet. There are many ways to exercise. You can walk, run, swim, ride a bike or go to the gym. In fact, many people sign up for the gym at the beginning of the year. But, most stop going after a few weeks.

*Además, es necesario cambiar los **hábitos alimenticios** usuales por hábitos **más sanos**. Por ejemplo, es importante dejar de comer comida chatarra y muy dulce por comida saludable como las frutas y los vegetales. Con una dieta balanceada, es posible estar sano y perder peso.*

In addition, it is necessary to change the usual eating habits for healthier habits. For example, it is important to stop eating junk and very sweet food for healthy food such as fruits and vegetables. With a balanced diet, it is possible to be healthy and lose weight.

*A un principio, cambiar hábitos no es fácil. Para algunas personas, es muy **difícil** cambiar estos hábitos. Se necesitan semanas para establecer nuevos hábitos y nuevas **rutinas**. Se necesita tiempo para dejar la comida poco saludable y consumir solo comida saludable. Es difícil dejar el azúcar y la **grasa**. Comidas como pizza, patatas fritas, pollo frito y hamburguesas son **deliciosas**, pero poco saludables.*

At first, changing habits is not easy. For some people, it is very difficult to change these habits. It takes weeks to establish new habits and new routines. It takes time to leave unhealthy food and consume only healthy food. It is difficult to leave sugar and fat. Meals such as pizza, chips, fried chicken, and hamburgers are delicious, but unhealthy.

*Si tú quieres perder peso, aquí hay algunos **consejos** que te pueden servir para **mejorar** tus hábitos.*

*Primero, piensa en tus **metas**. ¿Qué quieres lograr? ¿Quieres perder peso? ¿Quieres estar **saludable**? ¿Tienes **algún problema de salud**? Piensa en estas preguntas. Pero debes ser honesto. Si respondes **honestamente** puedes lograr tus metas.*

If you want to lose weight, here are some tips that can help you improve your habits.

First, think about your goals. What do you want to achieve? Do you want to lose weight? Do you want to be healthy? Do you have any health problems? Think about these questions. But you must be honest. If you respond honestly you can achieve your goals.

Luego, *piensa en tus hábitos* **actuales**. *¿***Consumes demasiada comida chatarra***? ¿***No bebes suficiente agua***? Estos son* **factores** *importantes a considerar dentro de tus hábitos alimenticios. También debes considerar tu rutina de ejercicios. Si no haces mucho ejercicio, piensa en* **incrementar** *la cantidad de ejercicio que haces* **progresivamente**. *Poco a poco, puedes ir* **aumentando** *la cantidad de ejercicio que haces.*

Then, think about your current habits. Do you consume too much junk food? Don't you drink enough water? These are important factors to consider within your eating habits. You should also consider your exercise routine. If you don't exercise much, think about increasing the amount of exercise you do progressively. Little by little, you can increase the amount of exercise you do.

Otro aspecto **importante** *es hablar con tu doctor. Tu doctor te puede dar muchas ideas sobre* **cómo** *puedes mejorar tu salud, perder peso y encontrar la mejor manera para hacer los cambios que necesitas* **realizar**. *La ayuda de tu doctor es* **esencial** *para alcanzar tus metas y* **mantener** *tu peso en su nivel ideal. También puedes contar con la ayuda de un* **nutricionista**. *Este profesional te puede ayudar a* **diseñar** *una dieta ideal para ti.*

Another important aspect is talking to your doctor. Your doctor can give you many ideas on how you can improve your health, lose weight and find the best way to make the changes you need to make. Your doctor's help is essential to achieve your goals and keep your weight at its ideal level. You can also count on the help of a nutritionist. This professional can help you design an ideal diet for you.

Finalmente, *la* **clave del éxito** *está en tu* **mente**. *Si tienes una* **mentalidad positiva**, *tus* **resultados** *son positivos. Pero si tienes una* **actitud negativa**, *no es fácil alcanzar tus metas. Por eso, siempre debes mantener una mentalidad y actitud positiva.*

Finally, the key to success is in your mind. If you have a positive mindset, your results are positive. But if you have a negative attitude, it is not easy to achieve your goals. Therefore, you should always maintain a positive mindset and attitude.

Questions about the Story

1. ¿Qué quieren perder las personas?
a. Tiempo
b. Dinero
c. Peso
d. Interés

2. ¿Cómo se puede perder peso?
a. Con comida saludable y mucho interés
b. Con ejercicio regular y una dieta balanceada
c. Con ejercicio regular y comida chatarra
d. Con comida saludable y mucho dinero

3. ¿A quién consulta sobre perder peso?
a. A un mecánico
b. A un dentista

c. A un profesional

d. A un nutricionista

4. ¿Qué comida se debe comer?

a. Pizza con vegetales

b. Hamburguesa con tomate

c. Frutas y vegetales

d. Frutas con azúcar

5. ¿Qué se necesita para perder peso?

a. Una actitud positiva y dinero

b. Una mente y actitud positiva

c. Una mente positiva y un doctor

d. Une actitud positiva y calma

Answers

1. C

2.B

3.D

4.C

5.B

Vocabulario (Vocabulary)

- *Inicio* --- beginning
- *nuevo año* --- new year
- *vida* --- life
- *deciden volver a estudiar* --- decide to go back to school
- *quieren* --- want
- *perder peso* --- lose weight
- *sencilla* --- simple
- *saludable* --- healthy
- *sobrepeso* --- overweight
- *expuestas* --- exposed
- *problemas de salud* --- health problems
- *enfermedades* --- diseases
- *serias* --- serious
- *peso ideal* --- ideal weight
- *lograr* --- achieve
- *combinación* --- combination
- *maneras* --- means
- *ir al gimnasio* --- go to the gym
- *inscriben* --- register
- *deja de ir* --- stop going
- *semanas* --- weeks

- *hábitos alimenticios* --- eating habits
- *más sanos* --- healthier
- *difícil* --- difficult
- *rutinas* --- routines
- *grasa* --- fat
- *deliciosas* --- delicious
- *mejorar* --- improve
- *¿Quieres perder peso?* --- would you like to lose weight?
- *¿Tienes algún problema de salud?* --- Do you have any health problems?
- *Honestamente* --- honestly
- *Luego* --- then
- *Actuales* --- current
- *¿Consumes demasiada comida chatarra?* --- Do you consume too much junk food?
- *¿No bebes suficiente agua?* --- You don't drink enough wáter?
- *Factores* --- factors
- *Incrementar* --- increase
- *progresivamente* --- progressively
- *aumentando* --- increased
- *importante* --- important (e)
- *cómo* --- how
- *realizar* --- carry out
- *esencial* --- essential
- *mantener* --- keep
- *nutricionista* --- nutritionist
- *diseñar* --- design
- *Finalmente* --- finally
- *clave del éxito* --- key to success
- *mente* --- mind
- *mentalidad positiva* --- positive mindset
- *resultados* --- results
- *actitud negativa* --- negative attitude

2. ¿Cómo Ser Exitoso?

*El **éxito** en la vida es el **resultado** de **trabajo duro** y **aprendizaje**. Cuando una persona trabaja duro, **adquiere** experiencia y **conocimientos** útiles para hacer un buen trabajo. Si una persona es **dedicada** y **diligente**, es capaz de **alcanzar** muchas cosas. Por ejemplo, puede conseguir un buen trabajo en una empresa **estable**.*

Success in life is the result of hard work and learning. When a person works hard, he acquires experience and useful knowledge to do a good job. If a person is dedicated and diligent, he is able to achieve many things. For example, you can get a good job in a stable company.

***Además**, hay muchas cosas por **aprender** en la vida. Una **manera** de aprender cosas útiles es **yendo** a la escuela. Después de la escuela, los **jóvenes** van a la universidad. **De esta manera**, es **posible** aprender muchas cosas **importantes** y **significativas** para la vida y el trabajo.*

In addition, there are many things to learn in life. One way to learn useful things is to go to school. After school, young people go to college. In this way, it is possible to learn many important and significant things for life and work.

***Cuando** un joven **asiste** a la universidad, va a **estudiar** una carrera, es decir, un área en **donde** piensa trabajar por el **resto de su vida**. La universidad les da la **preparación necesaria** para ser exitosos en esta **carrera**.*

When a young man attends college, he will study a career, that is, an area where he plans to work for the rest of his life. The university gives them the necessary preparation to be successful in this career.

*Pero la universidad no es el **único** lugar en donde un joven puede aprender sobre una carrera. Un joven también puede asistir a un **instituto técnico** en donde aprende un **oficio**. Un oficio es un área especializada como la mecánica, electricidad o carpintería. Esto le permite hacer trabajos **específicos** dentro de varias **industrias**.*

But college is not the only place where a young person can learn about a career. A young man can also attend a technical institute where he learns a trade. A trade is a specialized area such as mechanics, electricity or carpentry. This allows you to do specific jobs within various industries.

*Hay otros trabajos que requieren bastante **entrenamiento práctico**. Por ejemplo, la policía, los bomberos y las **fuerzas armadas** requieren que los **reclutas** pasen cierto tiempo **recibiendo** entrenamiento antes de poder **integrarse** a sus **unidades** y **servir** a su comunidad. Estos son trabajos que requieren una combinación de **habilidad física** y **destreza mental**. Los mejores reciben oportunidades para **ascender** a puestos de **mayor liderazgo**.*

There are other jobs that require a lot of practical training. For example, police, firefighters and armed forces require recruits to spend some time receiving training before they can integrate into their units and serve their community. These are jobs that require a combination of physical ability and mental dexterity. The best receive opportunities to advance to positions of greater leadership.

*Otro aspecto importante para ser exitoso en la vida es contar con destrezas individuales como el **liderazgo**, la **paciencia**, la **honestidad** y la **integridad**. Estos son características personales que las personas deben **desarrollar** para ser exitosos en **cualquier** trabajo. También existen otras habilidades como el trabajo en equipo, la **proactividad** y la **asertividad**, las cuales sirven para que una persona se **posicione** como un **miembro valioso** de la **organización** a la que **pertenece**.*

Another important aspect to be successful in life is to have individual skills such as leadership, patience, honesty and integrity. These are personal characteristics that people must develop to be successful in any job. There are also other skills such as teamwork, proactivity and assertiveness, which serve to position a person as a valuable member of the organization to which he belongs.

*Si tú **deseas** alcanzar el éxito en la vida, necesitas una combinación de conocimientos **sólidos** en tu carrera y características personales. Esta combinación de características te da la oportunidad de ser un miembro **productivo** de tu comunidad. Además, puedes alcanzar puestos importantes en tu trabajo. Estos puestos **representan** mayor **autoridad**, pero también mayor **responsabilidad**.*

If you want to achieve success in life, you need a combination of solid knowledge in your career and personal characteristics. This combination of features gives you the opportunity to be a productive member of your community. In addition, you can achieve important positions in your work. These positions represent greater authority, but also greater responsibility.

***Toma el tiempo** para pensar en qué quisieras **lograr** con tu vida. Esta meta es el éxito que tanto deseas alcanzar. Recuerda que una persona exitosa no **necesariamente** se **mide** por el dinero. También se **conoce** a una persona exitosa por el bien que hace y lo que **contribuye** a su comunidad. **Adicionalmente**, si tienes una familia estable también eres una persona exitosa. Lo más importante de todo es la **felicidad** contigo mismo. Si eres feliz contigo mismo, entonces eres una persona de mucho éxito.*

Take the time to think about what you would like to achieve with your life. This goal is the success you so much want to achieve. Remember that a successful person is not necessarily measured by money. A successful person is also known for the good he does and what contributes to his community. Additionally, if you have a stable family you are also a successful person. The most important of all is happiness with yourself. If you are happy with yourself, then you are a very successful person.

Quiz:

1. ¿Qué se necesita para el éxito?
a. Trabajo duro
b. Tener amigos
c. Vivir en la ciudad
d. Viajar mucho

2. ¿Qué es un oficio?
a. Es un juego de mesa
b. Es una película
c. Es una vida nueva
d. Es un área especializada

3. ¿Cuáles son los oficios?
a. Ingeniería, carpintería, mecánica
b. Electricidad, medicina, ingeniería
c. Electricidad, mecánica, carpintería
d. Medicina, carpintería, electricidad

4. ¿Dónde se aprende un oficio?
a. En la universidad
b. En un instituto técnico
c. En una universidad especial
d. En la escuela especial

5. ¿Cuáles son características personales importantes?
a. Responsabilidad y proactividad
b. Dieta balanceada y ejercicio regular
c. Inteligencia y un buen trabajo
d. Asertividad y juegos de mesa

Answers

1.A
2.D
3.C
4.B
5.A

Vocabulario (Vocabulary)

- *Éxito* --- success
- *Resultado* --- result
- *trabajo duro* --- hard work
- *aprendizaje* --- learning
- *adquiere* --- acquire
- *conocimientos* --- knowledge
- *dedicada* --- dedicated
- *diligente* --- diligent
- *alcanzar* --- achieve
- *estable* --- stable
- *Además* --- also
- *Aprender* --- learn
- *Manera* --- manner
- *Yendo* --- going
- *De esta manera* --- in this way
- *Posible* --- possible
- *Importantes* --- important
- *Significativas* --- significant
- *Cuando* --- when
- *Asiste* --- attend
- *Estudiar* --- study
- *Donde* --- where
- *resto de su vida* --- rest of your life
- *preparación necesaria* --- necessary training
- *carrera* --- career
- *único* --- only
- *instituto técnico* --- technical institute
- *oficio* --- trade
- *específicos* --- specific
- *industrias* --- industries

- *entrenamiento práctico* --- practical training
- *fuerzas armadas* --- armed forces
- reclutas --- recruits
- *recibiendo* --- receiving
- *integrarse* --- integrates
- *unidades* --- units
- *servir* --- serve
- *habilidad física* --- physical ability
- *destreza mental* --- mental skills
- *ascender* --- promotion
- *mayor* --- greater
- *liderazgo* --- leadership
- *paciencia* --- patience
- *honestidad* --- honesty
- *integridad* --- integrity
- *desarrollar* --- develop
- *cualquier* --- any
- *proactividad* --- proactivity
- *asertividad* --- asertiveness
- *posicione* --- positions
- *miembro* --- member
- *valioso* --- valuable
- *organización* --- organization
- *pertenece* --- belong
- *deseas* --- wish
- *sólidos* --- solid
- *productivo* --- productive
- *representan* --- represent
- *autoridad* --- authority
- *responsabilidad* --- responsibility
- *Toma el tiempo* --- take the time
- *Lograr* --- accomplish
- *Necesariamente* --- necessarily
- *Mide* --- measure
- *Conoce* --- know
- *Contribuye* --- contributes
- *Adicionalmente* --- additionally
- *Felicidad* --- happiness
- *Esperes* --- expect
- *poco a poco* --- little by little

3. Pueblo Y Ciudad

Antes de su gran cita con Sofía, Alejandro tenía que hacer algunos encargos para asegurarse de que todo estuviera listo. En primer lugar, necesitaba ir al banco para retirar suficiente dinero, que le alcanzara para el día ajetreado que se avecinaba. En el camino al banco, se detuvo en su cafetería favorita para comprar algo de cafeína, muy necesaria para comenzar el día.

Before his big date with Sofía today, Alejandro had a few errands to run to make sure everything was ready. First of all, a trip to the bank was needed, so he could withdraw enough cash for the busy day ahead. Along the way to the bank, he stopped by his favorite coffee shop to pick up some much needed caffeine to start the day.

Luego, tuvo que dirigirse a la oficina de correos y dejar un correo que estaba atrasado. Después de eso, fue al centro comercial a buscar un nuevo atuendo para usar ese día. Estuvo en dos tiendas de ropa e incluso tuvo tiempo suficiente para hacerse un nuevo corte de cabello en la barbería.

Next, he had to make a run to the post office and drop off some mail that was overdue and nearly late. After that, it was off to the mall to find a new outfit to wear on today's date. He perused two clothing stores and even had enough time to get himself a new haircut at the barber shop.

A las 2:00 pm, Alejandro y Sofía se encontraron para hacer un recorrido por la ciudad. Comenzaron caminando por el parque para ponerse al día con lo que había sucedido durante la semana. Dentro del parque había una gran plaza donde la pareja encontró un pequeño concierto de una banda de rock. Después de escuchar algunas canciones, dejaron el parque y se dirigieron hacia un parque de diversiones local.

At 2:00 pm, Alejandro and Sofía met up, ready to take a tour around town. They started by walking around the park, catching up on what happened with each other during the week. Inside the park was a large plaza, where the couple found a small concert by a rock band. After hearing a few songs, they left the park and headed towards a local amusement park.

Debido a un gran accidente, el parque de diversiones estaba cerrado, así que, como plan alternativo, la pareja decidió ir a cine. Por suerte para Sofía, esa tarde pudieron encontrar una película de terror. Tenían una hora de espera para entrar a ver la película, de modo que tomaron una cena temprano en un restaurante cercano con el tiempo suficiente para regresar al cine. La película resultó ser bastante genérica y predecible, pero hubo escenas que los hicieron saltar del susto, haciendo que tanto Alejandro como Sofía se sintieran realmente bien.

Due to a large accident, the amusement park had to be shut down, so as a back-up plan, the couple decided to go to the movie theater instead. To Sofía's luck, they were able to find a horror movie playing that week. It would be an hour-long wait for the movie, so they grabbed an early dinner at a nearby restaurant with just enough time to make it back to the theater. The movie turned out to be fairly generic and predictable, but there was one jump scare that got both Alejandro and Sofía really, really good.

Cuando llegó la noche, la pareja tuvo la sensación de no querer quedarse fuera, en la ciudad, hasta demasiado tarde, pero acordaron tomar una bebida en un bar único que encontraron buscando con sus teléfonos inteligentes. Tenía un tema de castillo medieval y estaba decorado con pancartas, armaduras y sillas que parecían tronos. Tuvieron la oportunidad de conversar y junto con ello vino más bebida.

As the evening came, the couple had a mutual feeling of not wanting to stay out too late in the city, but they agreed to have one drink at a unique bar they found searching on their smartphones. It had a medieval castle theme and was decorated with banners, suits of armor, and chairs that looked like thrones. The conversation picked up between the two and along with it came more drinking.

¡Ahora ambos estaban demasiado ebrios para regresar a casa sanos y salvos! No sintiéndose con ganas de ir a discotecas, esperaron dos horas para estar sobrios y recuperarse antes de conducir a casa. Llamar un taxi era una opción loca y costosa, y esperar no fue tan difícil. Para pasar el tiempo, caminaron por el paseo marítimo y se detuvieron en una tienda para tomar un refrigerio rápido.

Now they were both too intoxicated to drive home safely! Not feeling up for a night of clubbing, they would wait two hours to sober up before driving home. Calling a taxi would be a crazy expensive option, and it wasn't all that much of a wait to begin with. To pass the time, they walked along the boardwalk and stopped by the convenience store for a quick snack.

Alejandro y Sofía habían disfrutado mucho de estar juntos, por lo que las horas pasaron más rápido de lo esperado, y había llegado la hora de separarse. Un breve beso fue compartido junto con un par de sonrisas pícaras, y eso fue todo antes de que ambos regresaran a casa.

Alejandro and Sofía thoroughly enjoyed each other's presence, so the hours passed quicker than expected, but it was time to part ways. A brief kiss was shared, along with a couple of cheeky smiles, and that was it before they both returned home.

Quiz

1. Cuál fue el primer encargo que realizó Alejandro antes de la cita?
a. Pasar por el banco
b. Buscar un atuendo
c. Comprar cafeína

2. ¿Qué película fueron a ver al cine Alejandro y Sofía en su cita?
a. Una película de acción
b. Una película romántica
c. Una película de terror

3. ¿Cuál era el tema del bar al que fue Alejandro y Sofía?
a. Comida rápida
b. Medieval
c. Vaquero

Answers

1) A
2) C
3) B

Vocabulario/Vocabulary

- *quedarse en casa* --- to stay at home
- *ocio* --- leisure, idleness
- *tarea doméstica* --- household chore
- *factura no pagada* --- unpaid bill
- *vivienda* --- housing
- *alquiler* --- rent
- *préstamo estudiantil* --- student loan
- *pago vencido* --- overdue payment
- *en línea* --- online
- *acumular* --- to accumulate, to pile up
- *lavado* --- laundry
- *molestarse* --- to bother, to trouble oneself
- *clasificar* --- to sort
- *verter* --- to pour
- *suavizante de tela* --- fabric softener
- *funcionar* --- to run, to function
- *lavadora* --- laundry machine
- *lavar los platos* --- to wash the dishes
- *aspirar la casa* --- to vacuum the house
- *impecable* --- spotless, impeccable
- *cocina* --- kitchen
- *nevera* --- fridge
- *tirar* --- to throw away
- *alimentos vencidos* --- expired food
- *frotar el mostrador* --- to scrub the counter
- *retirar* --- to remove
- *migaja de comida* --- food crumb
- *piso* --- floor
- *barrer el suelo* --- to sweep the floor
- *escoba* --- broom
- *recogedor* --- dustpan
- *limpieza* --- cleansing, sanitizing
- *computador* --- computer
- *fanático* --- fan
- *estrategia* --- strategy
- *crear* --- to create
- *juego de un solo jugador* --- single player game
- *descanso* --- break, rest
- *mirar por la ventana* --- to peer out the window
- *calentar* --- to heat up
- *producirse* --- to take place, to occur
- *sabio* --- wise
- *significativo* --- meaningful
- *auriculares* --- headphones
- *habitación* --- bedroom

- *recomendar* --- to recommend
- *reflexionar* --- to reflect on
- *vagar* --- to wander (around)
- *armario* --- closet
- *razón* --- reason
- *deslizarse* --- to glide
- *comedor* --- dining room
- *repetir* --- to repeat
- *acción* --- action
- *acostumbrar* --- to be used to
- *balcón* --- balcony
- *hora de acostarse* --- bedtime
- *ciertamente* --- certainly
- *reunión familiar* --- family gathering

4. Cartas De La Habana

Mirar el mar siempre me recuerda a Peter. Lo imagino en un enorme barco, alejándose de las costas de Cuba con rumbo hacia no sé dónde. Desde que se fue he soñado todos los días con él, me imagino todas sus aventuras, sus paseos por la selva y todas las cosas que a veces me cuenta.

Looking at the sea always reminds me of Peter. I imagine it in a huge ship, moving away from the coast of Cuba towards I don't know where. Since he left I have dreamed of him every day, I imagine all his adventures, his walks in the jungle and all the things he sometimes tells me.

En La Habana, llegó el verano y el calor se hace cada vez más insoportable. Los días son lentos, sofocantes y a veces nublados. Escuché en la radio que en las próximas semanas tal vez venga un huracán. No me gusta cuando llueve mucho porque hay que encerrarse todo el día en casa. Mi madre llena todas las ventanas de plástico y cartón, movemos todos los muebles y parece que estuviésemos dentro de una cueva.

In Havana, Summer arrived and the heat is every time increasingly unbearable. The days are slow, suffocating and sometimes cloudy. I heard on the radio that in the next few weeks a hurricane may come. I don't like it when it rains a lot because you have to lock yourself up all day at home. My mother fills all the plastic and cardboard windows, we move all the furniture and it seems that we were inside a cave.

En mi casa no hay conexión a internet, de hecho, sólo hay en muy pocos lugares de La Habana. No es común que las personas tengan computadoras en casa, mucho menos conexión. Desde que se fue Peter, yo voy todos los días a la biblioteca de la universidad al salir de clases. Mi madre está contenta pues piensa que estoy estudiando más de lo normal, pero mis compañeras de clase están preocupadas pues piensan que me convertí en un cerebrito.

In my house there is no internet connection, in fact, there are only in very few places in Havana. It is not common for people to have computers at home, much less connection. Since Peter left, I go to the university library every day after school. My mother is happy because she thinks that I am studying more than usual, but my classmates are worried because they think I became a brain.

"Tú estás muy rara, Daylin," me dijo mi amiga Martha el otro día.

"You're very weird, Daylin," my friend Martha told me the other day.

"La rara serás tú," le contesté.

"The weird one will be you," I replied.

Y desde entonces, dejó de invitarme a comer helado con ella por las tardes; ahora la verdad es que la extraño y tengo pensado pedirle disculpas. Pero entre la escuela de enfermería, mis clases de arte y mi hora de las cartas (así le llamé a mi tiempo en la biblioteca escribiéndole a Peter), tengo muy poco tiempo. Esa se había vuelto mi rutina diaria, hasta que un día cambió.

And since then, he stopped inviting me to eat ice cream with her in the afternoon; Now the truth is that I miss her and I plan to apologize. But between nursing school, my art classes and my time for letters (that's what I called my time in the library writing to Peter), I have very little time. That had become my daily routine, until one day it changed.

Desde que desperté, el día presagiaba ser extraño. Cuando me levanté de mi cama, parecía aún ser de noche así que regresé a dormir plácidamente. Sentía recién haber cerrado mis ojos cuando me despertó un fuerte grito de mi madre.

Since I woke up, the day presaged to be strange. When I got up from my bed, it seemed to be still night, so I went back to sleep peacefully. I just felt that I had closed my eyes when a loud cry from my mother woke me up.

"Daylin, pero ¿qué haces dormida? Es tardísimo, ¿no tienes pensado ir a la escuela o qué?"

"Daylin, but what are you doing asleep? It's too late, don't you plan on going to school or what?"

"Pero mamá, si apenas desperté y aún es de noche".

"But mom, if I just woke up and it's still night."

"Nada que de noche. Está nublado, nada más. Va a llover por la tarde. Levántate de inmediato y vas a tener e irte sin desayunar".

"Nothing at night. It is cloudy, nothing more. It is going to rain in the afternoon. Get up immediately and you will have and leave without breakfast."

Me levanté, me mojé la cara con agua fría, cepillé rápidamente mi cabello y salí corriendo. El próximo autobús no pasaría hasta dentro de 45 minutos más, así que ir en bicicleta hasta la escuela era la opción más rápida. Pedaleé a toda velocidad y en sólo 15 minutos ya estaba en la universidad. Me dirigí al salón de clases y por la ventana, desde la distancia, pude ver a la maestra de biología en plena explicación. Me acerqué, esperé el momento adecuado y cuando ella se dio la vuelta para escribir en el pizarrón, abrí la puerta intentando no hacer ningún ruido y entré sigilosamente.

I got up, wet my face with cold water, quickly brushed my hair and ran. The next bus would not pass for another 45 minutes, so cycling to school was the fastest option. I pedaled at full speed and in just 15 minutes I was already in college. I went to the classroom and through the window, from a distance, I could see the biology teacher in full explanation. I approached, waited for the right moment and when she turned around to write on the board, I opened the door trying not to make any noise and sneaked in.

Repentinamente, todas mis compañeras comenzaron a reír y la maestra se volteó.

Suddenly, all my classmates started laughing and the teacher turned around.

"¡Daylin! Pero ¿qué haces llegando tan tarde? Además, entrando a mis espaldas".

"Daylin! But what are you doing arriving so late? In addition, entering behind my back."

"Perdón, maestra, es que mi despertador se descompuso".

"Sorry, teacher, my alarm clock broke down."

"Anda, pasa, pero siéntate ya".

"Come on, come in, but sit down now."

Fui a mi lugar y me senté, confundida. Mi compañera de enfrente volteó rápidamente y me dijo:

I went to my place and sat, confused. My partner in front turned quickly and said:

"¿No te diste cuenta de que traes pantuflas?"

"Didn't you realize you bring slippers?"

Miré a mis pies y oh, sorpresa, había salido tan a prisa que había olvidado ponerme zapatos. Me sentía en una pesadilla.

I looked at my feet and oh, surprise, I had come out so quickly that I had forgotten to put on shoes. I felt in a nightmare.

405

Me sonrojé tanto que parecía un tomate, pero intenté concentrarme y continuar mis clases normalmente. El día fue largo y tedioso, pero al final de las clases ya todos, yo incluida, nos habíamos olvidado de que yo estaba en pantuflas. Decidí continuar mi día con normalidad, con zapatos de dormir y todo. El cielo seguía completamente oscuro y veía como poco a poco cada parte de la ciudad era cubierta por una nube negra. Aunque según la radio no llovería hasta tarde por la noche.

I blushed so much it looked like a tomato, but I tried to concentrate and continue my classes normally. The day was long and tedious, but at the end of class and everyone, me included, we had forgotten that I was in slippers. I decided to continue my day normally, with sleeping shoes and everything. The sky was still completely dark and I saw how little by little each part of the city was covered by a black cloud. Although according to the radio it would not rain until late at night.

Al terminar mis clases, fui a buscar a Adela, una de mis mejores amigas y compañera de la clase de pintura, pero para mi sorpresa, cuando llegué a su salón de clases, ella no estaba ahí. Pregunté a varios de sus compañeros, pero nadie sabía nada de ella. Llamé a su casa y su madre respondió.

When I finished my classes, I went to look for Adela, one of my best friends and classmate of the painting class, but to my surprise, when I arrived at her classroom, she was not there. I asked several of her classmates but nobody knew anything about her. I called his house and his mother answered.

"Hola, señora Lucía," dije. "Estoy buscando a Adela en la escuela, pero no está por ningún lado. ¿Está en casa?"

"Hello, Mrs. Lucia," I said. "I'm looking for Adela at school, but she isn't anywhere. He's at home?"

"Sí, acá está mi niña, pero está muy enferma, no se pudo levantar del dolor de estómago, parece que ayer que fue a comer helados con las otras niñas y algo le cayó mal".

"Yes, here is my girl, but she is very sick, she could not get up from the stomach ache, it seems that yesterday she went to eat ice cream with the other girls and something went wrong."

"Qué pena, dígale que lo siento mucho y que espero que se recupere pronto".

"What a pity, tell him I'm very sorry and I hope he recovers soon."

Colgué el teléfono y no pude evitar pensar que ahí estaba el segundo mal augurio del día. Adela está enferma y no tendré nadie con quién platicar en mi clase de pintura. Pero intenté relajarme, recordé que mi clase de pintura me hace muy feliz y que después de ella, correría hacia la biblioteca a escribirle a Peter y si tenía suerte, a leer una más de sus cartas.

I hung up the phone and couldn't help thinking that there was the second bad omen of the day. Adela is sick and I won't have anyone to talk to in my painting class. But I tried to relax, I remembered that my painting class makes me very happy and that after it, I would run to the library to write to Peter and if I was lucky, to read one more of his letters.

Caminé tranquilamente hacia la escuela de arte. En el camino, varios niños se rieron de mis particulares zapatos, pero a mí no me importó. Hacía mucho calor y los rizos de mi cabello se pegaban sobre mi frente. Sentí ganas de ir a la playa y pasar el día frente al mar, pero no lo hice, continué caminando hasta llegar a mi clase.

I walked calmly to the art school. Along the way, several children laughed at my particular shoes, but I didn't care. It was very hot and the curls of my hair stuck on my forehead. I felt like going to the beach and spending the day facing the sea, but I didn't, I continued walking until I reached my class.

"Daylin, llegas tarde," dijo mi maestra de pintura apenas cuando crucé la puerta.

"Daylin, you're late," my painting teacher said just when I crossed the door.

"Pero…"

"But…"

"Nada de peros. Te estamos esperando para comenzar".

"No buts. We are waiting for you to start."

No entendía qué estaba pasando, tal vez era sólo que mis pantuflas me traían mala suerte.

I didn't understand what was happening, maybe it was just that my slippers brought me bad luck.

"Hoy no vamos a pintar, vamos a trabajar en una nueva técnica. Todo artista debe conocer distintas formas de crear para ser bueno. No es sólo tomar la brocha y ya, hay que estudiar y cultivarse. Hoy trabajaremos la técnica de los pasteles y quiero que sean creativos, dibujen lo que surja en este momento de su imaginación," dijo mi maestra mientras yo me acomodaba en la silla.

"Today we are not going to paint, we are going to work on a new technique. Every artist must know different ways of creating to be good. It's not just taking the brush and now, you have to study and cultivate. Today we will work on the technique of cakes and I want them to be creative, draw whatever comes up in this moment of their imagination," said my teacher while I settled in the chair.

Saqué los cuadernos de dibujo de mi bolsa y de nuevo me decidí a intentar disfrutar de mi día, a pesar de las adversidades. Me concentré, cerré los ojos y comencé a dibujar sin pensar nada. Dibujé el mar que tanto añoraba esa tarde de calor y un pequeño barco que se acercaba a la costa; en mi mente, dentro de ese barco viajaba Peter, que regresaba a bailar de nuevo conmigo en las salas de baile de La Habana. Estaba a punto de terminar mi obra cuando mi maestra se acercó a mí y preguntó.

I took the sketchbooks from my bag and again I decided to try to enjoy my day, despite the adversities. I concentrated, closed my eyes and began to draw without thinking anything. I drew the sea that I longed for that hot afternoon and a small ship that approached the coast; In my mind, Peter was traveling inside that ship, who was dancing with me again in the dance halls of Havana. I was about to finish my work when my teacher approached me and asked.

"Daylin, ¿estás enamorada?"

"Daylin, are you in love?"

"¿Por qué lo pregunta, maestra?"

"Why do you ask, teacher?"

"Tengo bueno ojo y yo también me enamoraba mucho cuando era joven como tú. Yo lo puedo ver en la forma en la que pintas".

"I have a good eye and I also fell in love a lot when I was young like you. I can see it in the way you paint."

Me sonrojé y respondí, "Puede que tenga razón, maestra".

I blushed and replied, "You may be right, teacher."

"Pues ten cuidado. Muy pocos hombres en este mundo son de fiar, no te enamores fácilmente".

"Well, be careful. Very few men in this world are reliable, don't fall in love easily."

"Está bien maestra, lo tendré en cuenta".

"Okay teacher, I'll keep that in mind."

Terminé mi clase con un bello dibujo en mano y preguntándome qué más depararía para mi este extraño día. En el momento en que salí de la escuela de arte me percaté de que había olvidado mi

407

bicicleta en la universidad, por eso había llegado tarde a mi clase de pintura y ni siquiera me había dado cuenta.

I finished my class with a beautiful hand drawing and wondering what else this strange day would hold for me. By the time I left art school I realized that I had forgotten my bicycle at the university, so I had arrived late to my painting class and had not even noticed.

Me resigné a caminar hasta la biblioteca y de regreso a casa, total, podía recoger mi bicicleta después en la universidad. Caminé con emoción porque al fin había llegado el momento más esperado de mi día, pero bastó dar la vuelta en la esquina para saber que mi día sería aún peor de lo que esperaba. Una enorme nube negra que se posaba sobre mi comenzó a lanzar rayos anunciando la llegada anticipada de la lluvia. Corrí lo más rápido que pude, pero no pude evitar que mi dibujo se mojara completamente y se arruinara. ¡Qué día! Sólo quedaba llegar a la biblioteca para que tan agobiante paseo al menos valiera la pena, pero mi día terminó por ser uno de los peores de mi vida cuando al llegar a la puerta de la biblioteca, me encontré con un letrero que decía "Cerrada hasta nuevo aviso". No lo podía creer.

I resigned myself to walk to the library and back home, in total, I could pick up my bicycle later at the university. I walked with emotion because the most anticipated moment of my day had finally arrived, but it was enough to go around the corner to know that my day would be even worse than I expected. A huge black cloud that perched on me began to throw lightning announcing the early arrival of the rain. I ran as fast as I could, but I couldn't help my drawing from getting completely wet and ruined. What a day! I only had to get to the library to make it so cramped at least it was worth it, but my day ended up being one of the worst of my life when I arrived at the library door, I found a sign that said "Closed until new notification". I could not believe it.

Regresé a casa, sin bicicleta, con una pintura arruinada, con mi ropa mojada y sin saber hasta cuándo podría hablar de nuevo con Peter.

I returned home, without a bicycle, with a ruined paint, with my wet clothes and not knowing until when I could talk to Peter again.

Pasaron diez largos días en los que diariamente visité la biblioteca al salir de la universidad, pero cada día fue lo mismo: "Cerrada hasta nuevo aviso". Comenzaba a sentirme triste y desesperada. Algunas noches no podía dormir pensando: ¿será que ya no debo hablar más con Peter? ¿Será todo esto una señal de los orishas? De verdad comenzaba a creerlo, pues todo parecía estar en contra de que continuáramos nuestra historia de amor a distancia y pensé que tal vez era el momento de que me olvidara de él. Pero no podía tomar esa decisión yo sola, necesitaba platicar, así que llamé a Adela para hablarlo con ella.

Ten long days passed in which I visited the library daily after leaving university, but every day was the same: "Closed until further notice." I was starting to feel sad and desperate. Some nights I couldn't sleep thinking: Could it be that I shouldn't talk to Peter anymore? Is all this a sign of the orishas? I was really beginning to believe it, because everything seemed to be against us continuing our love story from a distance and I thought maybe it was time for me to forget about it. But I couldn't make that decision on my own, I needed to talk, so I called Adela to talk to her.

"Adela, tengo algo muy importante de que hablarte. Nos podemos ver después de clase, tomamos un helado y platicamos después, ¿te parece?"

"Adela, I have something very important to talk to you about. We can meet after class, have an ice cream and talk later, do you think?"

"Sí, claro, pero me preocupas, ¿qué es eso tan importante que me tienes que decir? Ya decía yo que te habías estado comportando rara estos últimos días. Dime la verdad ¿estás embarazada?"

"Yes, of course, but you worry me, what is that so important that you have to tell me? I already said that you had been behaving strangely in recent days. Tell me the truth, are you pregnant?"

"¡No! Para nada, pero ¡qué pregunta es esa! No te preocupes, no es nada grave, sólo necesito hablar con alguien".

"No! Not at all, but what a question is that! Don't worry, it's nothing serious, I just need to talk to someone."

"Bueno, te veo después de clase".

"Well, see you after class."

Justo al terminar las clases, fui a esperarla frente a su salón. Ella me vio y dijo: "Pero vaya que tienes prisa, no puedo esperar para saber lo que me tienes que contar".

Just after school, I went to wait for her in front of her classroom. She saw me and said: "But what a hurry, I can't wait to know what you have to tell me."

"Sí, vamos".

"Yeah come on".

Caminamos hacia nuestra plaza favorita, ese día no llovió, el cielo estaba lindo y despejado, era el día ideal para comer un helado de mango y tomar decisiones importantes.

We walked to our favorite square, that day it didn't rain, the sky was nice and clear, it was the ideal day to eat mango ice cream and make important decisions.

"Adela, hace diez días que no habló con Peter," dije sin más.

"Adela, ten days ago I didn't talk to Peter," I said simply.

"Cuéntame, ¿por qué? También te recuerdo que hace muchos días que no hablas conmigo fuera de la clase de pintura, todo por ir a la biblioteca a hablar con ese gringo, así que espero que tengas una buena explicación. ¿Te pidió él que dejaran de hablar? Porque si es así, está bien, tú eres muy linda, no necesitas sufrir por nadie, menos por él".

"Tell me, why? I also remind you that you haven't talked to me outside of painting class for many days, all for going to the library to talk to that gringo, so I hope you have a good explanation. Did he ask you to stop talking? Because if so, that's fine, you're very pretty, you don't need to suffer for anyone, except for him."

"Espera, espera, Adela, te cuento. Él no me ha dicho nada, de hecho, no sé nada de él, pero creo que es el destino que no quiere que estemos juntos".

"Wait, wait, Adela, I'll tell you. He hasn't told me anything, in fact, I don't know anything about him, but I think it's the destiny that doesn't want us to be together."

"¿Cómo es eso? ¿Cuándo te dijo eso el destino?"

"How is that? When did fate tell you that?"

"Hace diez días exactamente. Tuve un día horrible y después la biblioteca estaba cerrada. Seguí yendo día tras día para escribirle, pero siempre igual, cerrada. Además, ese día llovió muchísimo, lo tomé como un presagio".

"Exactly ten days ago. I had a horrible day and then the library was closed. I kept going day after day to write to him, but always the same, closed. Besides, that day it rained a lot, I took it as an omen".

"Tienes razón, es un poco raro, pero ¿por qué no buscas otro lugar más donde haya computadora e

internet? Ya sabes que hay otras bibliotecas, otros lugares..."

"You're right, it's a bit weird, but why don't you look for another place where there is computer and internet? You already know that there are other libraries, other places..."

"Porque estoy intentando escuchar al destino, si la biblioteca no abre de nuevo, creo que ya no debo buscarlo más".

"Because I'm trying to listen to fate, if the library doesn't open again, I don't think I should look for it anymore."

"Interesante... pero te tengo que decir, estás un poco loca, aunque te apoyo en tus teorías sobre el destino. Tal vez tienes razón y sí es una señal".

"Interesting... but I have to tell you, you are a little crazy, although I support you in your theories about destiny. Maybe you're right and it is a sign. "

"Así es, creo que sí sentí que era una señal para ya no hablar más con él. Debo esperar también una señal para hacerlo y si no llega, se terminó".

"That's right, I think I felt it was a signal to stop talking to him anymore. I must also wait for a signal to do so and if it does not arrive, it is over."

"Tienes mi apoyo, amiga".

"You have my support, friend."

Los días siguientes fueron difíciles. Pensaba en Peter todos los días, pero seguía mi vida con tranquilidad. Volví a hablar con todas mis amigas a las que había abandonado por correr a la biblioteca cada día, mejoré en mis técnicas de pintura, mis calificaciones en la escuela se volvieron mejores y comencé a realizar nuevas actividades.

The following days were difficult. I thought about Peter every day, but I followed my life in peace. I spoke again with all my friends whom I had abandoned because of running to the library every day, I improved my painting techniques, my grades in school became better and I started doing new activities.

Por la semana de la cultura en la universidad, tuvimos una feria internacional artística, ahí me quedé maravillada con los bailarines argentinos y el tango. Me pareció una forma de baile muy diferente a la nuestra, pero tan llena de emoción y ritmo que decidí ir a una clase de tango junto con todas mis amigas. Practicamos diariamente después de clases. Al terminar, yo corría a mis clases de pintura y después a casa a cenar con mamá. Así llené mis días de actividades y poco a poco dejé de pensar en Peter.

For the week of the culture in the university, we had an international artistic fair, there I was amazed with the Argentine dancers and the tango. I found a way of dancing very different from ours, but so full of emotion and rhythm that I decided to go to a tango class together with all my friends. We practice daily after school. When I finished, I ran to my painting classes and then home to dinner with Mom. So I filled my days with activities and little by little I stopped thinking about Peter.

Había pasado casi un mes desde que dejamos de hablar. Yo dejé de ir a la biblioteca, pero por rumores escuché que aún permanecía cerrada; al parecer, tras las intensas lluvias, el agua se había colado por las paredes y mojó muchos de los libros y también las computadoras, así que seguía sin internet. La última vez que recibí un mensaje de Peter, él acababa de llegar a la Amazonia colombiana, escribía mucho y estaba siempre ocupado, tal vez él también se había olvidado ya de mí.

It had been almost a month since we stopped talking. I stopped going to the library, but by rumors I heard that it was still closed; Apparently, after the heavy rains, the water had seeped through the walls and wet many of the books and also the computers, so it was still without internet. The last time I received a message from Peter, he had just arrived in the Colombian Amazon, wrote a lot and was always busy, maybe he had already forgotten about me.

El tango se había convertido en mi nueva pasión y yo soñaba con viajar igual que Peter. Quería alguna vez visitar Argentina para ver los grandes ballets de tango con música en vivo. Sorpresivamente, no pasaría mucho para que eso pasara.

Tango had become my new passion and I dreamed of traveling just like Peter. I wanted to visit Argentina to see the great tango ballets with live music. Surprisingly, it wouldn't be long for that to happen.

Al llegar a clase, una tarde como cualquier otra, mi maestra nos reunió a todas y dijo:

Upon arriving to class, one afternoon like any other, my teacher brought us all together and said:

"Tengo una increíble noticia para ustedes. Hemos sido invitadas a una reunión internacional de tango en Buenos Aires. El gobierno de Argentina va a otorgar una beca a las cinco mejores estudiantes de esta clase para que puedan asistir. Sé que la mayoría de ustedes aún son principiantes, pero son muy talentosas y estoy segura de que esta será una experiencia que para algunas de ustedes cambiará su vida".

"I have incredible news for you. We have been invited to an international tango meeting in Buenos Aires. The government of Argentina will grant a scholarship to the five best students in this class so they can attend. I know that most of you are still beginners, but you are very talented and I am sure that this will be an experience that will change your life for some of you."

"Maestra, pero ¿cuándo van a elegir?, ¿cómo?, ¿cuánto tiempo tenemos para prepararnos?" se levantaron las voces de todas las estudiantes, generando un gran murmullo.

"Teacher, but when are they going to choose? How? How much time do we have to prepare?" The voices of all the students rose, generating a great murmur.

"Hablaremos de eso mañana. Por ahora, sigan practicando," dijo la maestra mientras todas comenzamos a gritar y hablar con emoción.

"We will talk about that tomorrow. For now, keep practicing," said the teacher as we all started screaming and talking with emotion.

"¿Te imaginas, Daylin? ¿Que vayamos nosotras juntas hasta Argentina? ¡Qué emocionante!"

"Can you imagine, Daylin? Let us go together to Argentina? How exiting!"

"Adela, justo ayer estaba pensando en eso, tengo un buen presentimiento, creo que eso fue una señal".

"Adela, just yesterday I was thinking about that, I have a good feeling, I think that was a sign."

"Bueno tú y tus señales. Ya me estás asustando... pero sí, yo estoy segura de que iremos".

"Well you and your signals. You're already scaring me ... but yes, I'm sure we'll go."

Salí a casa en mi bicicleta a toda velocidad, por el camino fui pensando en el viaje a Buenos Aires, en todos los bailarines que conoceríamos, en todo lo que bailaríamos, en todas las empanadas argentinas que comeríamos. Estaba muy emocionada.

I went home on my bike at full speed, along the way I was thinking about the trip to Buenos Aires, all the dancers we would know, everything we would dance, all the Argentine empanadas we would eat. I was very excited.

Cuando llegué a casa, me asombró encontrar una gran cantidad de cartas bajo la puerta. Abrí con cuidado y las recogí una por una. Me sorprendió aún más saber que todas y cada una de ellas eran de

Peter para mí. Las comencé a abrir en orden de fecha.

When I got home, I was amazed to find a lot of letters under the door. I opened carefully and picked them up one by one. I was even more surprised to know that each and every one of them were from Peter to me. I started to open them in order of date.

"Querida Daylin, hace ya una semana que no sé nada de ti. No sé qué sucede, espero que las lluvias y tormentas que estuvieron afectando el Caribe no hayan afectado a La Habana. Intenté estar informado a través de las noticias, siempre pensando en que tú y tu familia estuvieran bien. Esperé tu correo por días, pero al no recibirlo, decidí enviarte una carta. Pensé siempre en la posibilidad de que tu correo electrónico haya sido robado o que dejaras de tener acceso a internet, en fin, me he preguntado mucho el porqué de la ausencia de tus cartas, pero he decidido escribirte todos los días hasta saber de nuevo de ti. Espero leerte pronto, te pienso todos los días y espero que todo vaya bien. Abrazos, Peter".

"Dear Daylin, it's been a week since I know anything about you. I do not know what happens, I hope that the rains and storms that were affecting the Caribbean have not affected Havana. I tried to be informed through the news, always thinking that you and your family were fine. I waited for your mail for days, but not receiving it, I decided to send you a letter. I always thought about the possibility that your email has been stolen or that you no longer have access to the internet, in short, I have wondered why the absence of your letters, but I have decided to write to you every day until I know again you. I hope to read you soon, I think about you every day and I hope everything goes well. Hugs, Peter."

"Querida Daylin, los días son más largos sin saber de ti. La selva me encanta, amo escribir en silencio con sólo el ruido de las aves y el viento, pero tú siempre estás en mis pensamientos..."

"Dear Daylin, the days are longer without hearing from you. I love the jungle, I love to write in silence with only the noise of the birds and the wind, but you are always in my thoughts..."

"Querida Daylin..."

"Dear Daylin ..."

Querida Daylin... había más de 20 cartas, una por cada día que pasó desde que decidí no escribirle más a Peter. Me senté y las leí todas, una a una, pero fue la última la que más me impactó, en ella estaba la señal que había estado esperando.

Dear Daylin ... there were more than 20 letters, one for each day that passed since I decided not to write to Peter anymore. I sat down and read them all, one by one, but it was the last one that struck me the most, on it was the signal I had been waiting for.

"Querida Daylin, en unos días parto a Buenos Aires con mis amigos Matías y Verónica. Esta es la última carta que te escribo, entiendo si no quieres saber más de mí, estoy lejos y ni siquiera puedo asegurarte cuándo volveremos a vernos. Entiendo que esa no es una situación ideal para nadie y tomaré tu silencio como una despedida".

"Dear Daylin, in a few days I go to Buenos Aires with my friends Matías and Verónica. This is the last letter I write to you, I understand if you do not want to know more about me, I am far away and I cannot even assure you when we will see each other again. I understand that this is not an ideal situation for anyone and I will take your silence as a farewell. "

No podía ser posible, justo el día que mi maestra del baile nos habló sobre el viaje a Argentina, Peter me dice que viajaba hacia allá. Tenía que hablar con él en ese mismo instante. Tomé mi bicicleta y me apresuré a la biblioteca a toda velocidad, esta vez en la puerta no había ningún letrero. Entré y las computadoras estaban de nuevo en funcionamiento. En el mismo lugar de siempre, me senté y escribí:

It could not be possible, just the day my dance teacher told us about the trip to Argentina, Peter tells me he was traveling there. I had to talk to him at that moment. I took my bike and hurried to the library at full speed, this time at the door there was no sign. I went in and the computers were running again. In the same place as always, I sat down and wrote:

"Querido Peter, perdona mi ausencia. Tuve problemas de internet y después de decisión, pero ahora estoy de regreso. ¿Nos vemos en Buenos Aires?"

"Dear Peter, forgive my absence. I had internet problems and after decision, but now I'm back. See you in Buenos Aires?"

Quiz

1. ¿De qué es la clase que Daylin toma después de la universidad?
a) Canto
b) Manualidades
c) Pintura
d) Cocina

2. ¿Desde dónde le escribía Daylin a Peter?
a) Su casa
b) Su escuela
c) La biblioteca
d) Un café

3. ¿Por qué dejaron de funcionar las computadoras de la biblioteca?
a) Un terremoto
b) Las lluvias
c) El calor
d) Un accidente

4. ¿En qué descubrió Daylin su nueva pasión?
a) La enfermería
b) El baile
c) La pintura
d) La cocina

5. ¿Desde dónde le escribía Peter a Daylin sus cartas?
a) La selva
b) La ciudad
c) La playa
d) El mercado

Answers

1.c
2.c
3.b
4.b
5.a

Vocabulario/Vocabulary

- *Verano* --- Summer
- *Insoportable* --- Unbearable
- *Sofocantes* --- Suffocating
- *Nublados* --- Cloudy
- *Huracán* --- Hurricane
- *Encerrarse* --- Shut down
- *Cartón* --- Cardboard
- *Muebles* --- Furniture
- *Cueva* --- Cave
- *Biblioteca* --- Library
- *Cerebrito* --- Nerd
- *Enfermería* --- Nursery
- *Rutina diaria* --- Daily routine
- *Presagiaba* --- Forebode
- *Plácidamente* --- Peacefully
- *Fuerte* --- Loud
- *Tardísimo* --- Very late
- *Mojé* --- Dampened
- *Cepillé* --- Brushed
- *Padaleé* --- Pedaled
- *Dio la vuelta* --- Turned around
- *Pizarrón* --- Board
- *Sigilosamente* --- Stealthily
- *A mis espaldas* --- Behind my back
- *Descompuso* --- Stopped working
- *Pantuflas* --- Slippers
- *Concentrarme* --- Focus
- *Tedioso* --- Tiresome
- *Salón de clases* --- Classroom
- *Compañeros* --- Classmates
- *Helados* --- Ice cream
- *Cayó mal* --- Made her stomach upset
- *Qué pena* --- That is too bad
- *Recupere* --- Gets better
- *Augurio* --- Omen
- *Suerte* --- Luck
- *Rizos* --- Curls
- *Pegaban* --- Stuck
- *Sentí ganas* --- I felt like
- *Brocha* --- Brush
- *Cultivarse* --- Develop yourself
- *Adversidades* --- Difficulties
- *Añoraba* --- Longed for
- *¿Estás enamorada?* --- Are you in love?
- *Fiar* --- Trustworthy

414

- *Depararía* --- Would hold
- *Percaté* --- Noticed
- *Rayos* --- Lightning
- *Anticipada* --- In advance
- *Arruinara* --- Becoming ruined
- *Agobiante* --- Stifling
- *Cerrada hasta nuevo aviso* --- Closed until further notice
- *En contra* --- Against
- *Comportando* --- Acting
- *Embarazada* --- Pregnant
- *Grave* --- Serious
- *Sufrir* --- To suffer
- *Destino* --- Fate
- *Presagio* --- Omen
- *Señal* --- Signal
- *Apoyo* --- Support
- *Calificaciones* --- Grades
- *Realizar* --- Carry out
- *Rumores* --- Gossips
- *Colado* --- Leaked
- *Reunió* --- Gathered
- *Beca* --- Scholarship
- *Murmullo* --- Buzz
- *Presentimiento* --- Gut feeling
- *Cartas* --- Letters
- *Fecha* --- Date
- *Tormentas* --- Storms
- *Robado* --- Stolen
- *Ausencia* --- Absence
- *Pensamientos* --- Thoughts
- *Impactó* --- Shocked
- *Apresuré* --- Hurried
- *En funcionamiento* --- In working order

5. Caminos Cruzados

Peter en Buenos Aires

Buenos Aires es una ciudad fascinante. Sus grandes avenidas me recuerdan a las ciudades de las películas europeas de los años 60, su comida es deliciosa y su gente interesante, pero lo más cautivante de ella son sus sonidos y su baile. Sus habitantes bailan al ritmo del tango que suena por cada esquina de la ciudad, bajo una nube de olor a mate y tabaco.

Buenos Aires is a fascinating city. Its great avenues remind me of the cities of European films of the 60s, its food is delicious and its people interesting, but the most captivating of it are its sounds and its dance. Its inhabitants dance to the rhythm of the tango that sounds in every corner of the city, under a cloud of smell of mate and tobacco.

Llegué a Buenos Aires hace sólo unos días, pero la ciudad inmediatamente me atrapó. Debo admitirlo: el cambio del silencio de la selva a la gran ciudad fue complicado al principio. Las primeras dos noches no pude dormir, me faltaba el arrullo del viento y las aves para descansar. En su lugar, tenía los cláxones y el ruido nocturno de la ciudad; fue difícil pero la cultura y vida de Buenos Aires podían hacerte superar todo.

I arrived in Buenos Aires only a few days ago, but the city immediately caught me. I must admit: changing the silence from the jungle to the big city was complicated at first. The first two nights I could not sleep, I lacked the coo of the wind and the birds to rest. Instead, he had the horns and the night noise of the city; It was difficult but the culture and life of Buenos Aires could make you overcome everything.

Tras concluir mi entrenamiento como guía en la Amazonía, decidí alcanzar a Matías y Vero en la ciudad. Me habían hablado maravillas de ella y de su gran oferta cultural, lo que me pareció una excelente opción. Además, con mi creciente interés en escribir, estaba seguro de que sería un lugar que me inspiraría, pues no en vano algunos de los más grandes escritores de Latinoamérica habían vivido ahí.

After completing my training as a guide in the Amazon, I decided to reach Matías and Vero in the city. I had been told wonders about her and her great cultural offer, which I thought was an excellent option. Also, with my growing interest in writing, I was sure it would be a place that would inspire me, because not in vain some of the greatest writers in Latin America had lived there.

Estaba contento de volver a ver a mis amigos, aunque aún sentía una profunda tristeza por la ausencia de Daylin. Pasé días y noches enteras preguntándome por qué había dejado de escribirme así de repente. Un día, recibo un mensaje suyo contándome lo mucho que piensa en mí, lo mucho que ansía volverme a ver y después... nada, desaparece completamente sin responder a ninguno de mis correos ni mis cartas. Sólo esperaba que estuviera bien y guardaba su recuerdo con cariño en mi corazón, pero ahora estaba listo para seguir adelante.

I was glad to see my friends again, although I still felt a deep sadness at Daylin's absence. I spent days and nights whole wondering why he had suddenly stopped writing me like that. One day, I receive a message from him telling me how much he thinks of me, how much he wants to see me again and then ... nothing, disappears completely without responding to any of my emails or letters. I just hoped he was well and kept his memory with love in my heart, but now he was ready to move on.

"Peter, ¿ya has terminado de escribir?" me preguntó repentinamente Matías.

"Peter, have you finished writing?" Matthias asked me suddenly.

"Sí, Matías, justo estaba terminando, ¿qué pasa?"

"Yes, Matías, it was just ending, what happens?"

"Quería saber si querías salir a dar un paseo conmigo esta tarde. Has estado aquí ya tres días y Vero y yo hemos tenido poco tiempo para ti. Lo siento, tuvimos unos días muy ocupados organizando nuestras actividades al regresar de Perú, pero hoy te quiero compensar".

"I wanted to know if you wanted to go for a walk with me this afternoon. You've been here for three days now and Vero and I have had little time for you. Sorry, we had a very busy day organizing our activities when we returned from Peru, but today I want to compensate you."

"No te preocupes, Matías, entiendo. Pero claro, me gustaría mucho ir a dar un paseo contigo. ¿A dónde vamos?"

"Don't worry, Matías, I understand. But of course, I would very much like to go for a walk with you. Where we go?"

"Es una sorpresa".

"It's a surprise".

"Excelente, me encantan las sorpresas".

"Excellent, I love surprises."

Salimos de casa de Matías y tomamos el metro. Al salir de él, nos encontramos con un barrio muy lindo que yo ya había visitado antes pero que ese día se veía totalmente diferente.

We left Matías's house and took the subway. Upon leaving it, we found a very nice neighborhood that I had visited before but that day looked totally different.

"¿Qué pasa hoy, Matías? ¿Hay alguna celebración especial? El barrio se ve increíble".

"What's up today, Matthias? Is there any special celebration? The neighborhood looks amazing. "

"La celebración es que es fin de semana. Así son los domingos en San Telmo. Bonito ¿no?"

"The celebration is that it is weekend. So are Sundays in San Telmo. Nice isn't it? "

"Es increíble".

"Is incredible".

Las calles del pintoresco barrio estaban llenas de tiendas de artesanía, músicos y bailarines que se reunían alrededor de una hermosa plaza formando un gran corazón artístico. Nos detuvimos en una pequeña plaza donde tocaba un grupo de jóvenes. Con un acordeón, un violín y un contrabajo creaban melodías hipnotizantes y poderosas; a su lado, decenas de parejas bailaban cadenciosamente, observé anonadado. Caminamos una calle más y nos encontramos con decenas de pintores, algunos dibujando paisajes y otros haciendo caricaturas de los turistas.

The streets of the picturesque neighborhood were full of craft shops, musicians and dancers that gathered around a beautiful square forming a great artistic heart. We stopped in a small square where a group of young people played. With an accordion, a violin and a double bass created hypnotizing and powerful melodies; Beside him, dozens of couples danced cadentiously, I watched stunned. We walked one more street and met dozens of painters, some drawing landscapes and others making cartoons of tourists.

"¿Sabes por qué te traje aquí?"

"Do you know why I brought you here?"

"¡Porque es muy lindo!"

"Because it's very cute!"

"Sí, claro, pero también por algo más. Me siento muy contento de que hayas encontrado lo que quieres hacer, es muy inspirador. Además, Vero me mostró algunos de tus textos y yo creo que puedes llegar a ser un muy buen escritor, así que te traje aquí para que te inspires. En este barrio es donde vivieron algunos de los más grandes escritores del país. Hay arte por todos lados, imaginé que te gustaría".

"Yes, of course, but also for something else. I feel very happy that you found what you want to do, it is very inspiring. In addition, Vero showed me some of your texts and I think you can become a very good writer, so I brought you here to get inspired. In this neighborhood is where some of the greatest writers of the country lived. There is art everywhere, I imagined you would like it."

"Pues, tenías razón, me encanta".

"Well, you were right, I love it."

"Bueno, ahora vamos a la parte más interesante".

"Well, now we are going to the most interesting part."

Caminamos por una calle estrecha y llegamos a un pequeño local. Parecía ser un restaurante con una decoración muy particular: había figuras religiosas por todos lados y en una pared una gran cabeza de toro disecada; las mesas de madera estaban cubiertas de dibujos hechos por los clientes y los meseros tenían uniformes muy elegantes que contrastaban con el estilo desarreglado del lugar.

We walked along a narrow street and arrived at a small place. It seemed to be a restaurant with a very particular decoration: there were religious figures everywhere and on a wall a large dissected bull's head; the wooden tables were covered with drawings made by customers and the waiters had very elegant uniforms that contrasted with the untidy style of the place.

"Este es el más famoso bar de escritores de Buenos Aires. Más de la mitad de las personas que ves aquí son escritores, además, sirven las mejores empanadas de todo el barrio".

"This is the most famous writer's bar in Buenos Aires. More than half of the people you see here are writers, and they serve the best empanadas in the whole neighborhood."

"Muchas gracias por traerme aquí, Matías, este lugar es tan excéntrico como inspirador".

"Thank you very much for bringing me here, Matthias, this place is as eccentric as it is inspiring."

"Es un placer, amigo, ya un día tú me mostrarás los lugares más particulares del pueblo de tus padres del que tanto has hablado".

"It is a pleasure, friend, and one day you will show me the most particular places in your parents' town that you have talked about so much."

Quiz

1. ¿Qué fue lo que más asombró a Peter de la ciudad de Buenos Aires?
a) La comida
b) La gente
c) La cultura
d) La arquitectura

2. ¿En dónde se hospedó Peter en Buenos Aires?
a) Un campamento
b) Un hostal
c) La casa de sus amigos
d) La escuela

3. ¿Cuántas estudiantes de la clase de Daylin viajarán a Buenos Aires?
a) Diez
b) Cinco
c) Cuatro
d) Una

4. ¿Sobre qué decide escribir Peter durante sus últimas semanas de viaje?
a) Sus días en la selva
b) Sobre Daylin
c) Sobre la ciudad
d) Sobre su viaje

5. ¿En cuántos días después de ser seleccionada viajará Daylin a Buenos Aires?
a) Una semana
b) Tres días
c) Dos días
d) Un mes

Answers:

1.c
2.c
3.b
4.c
5.c

Vocabulario/Vocabulary

- *Fascinante* --- Fascinating
- *Avenidas* --- Avenues
- *Cautivante* --- Captivating
- *Cláxones* --- Horns
- *Superar* --- Overcome
- *Entrenamiento* --- Training
- *Creciente* --- Growing
- *Vano* --- Vain
- *Tristeza* --- Sadness
- *De repente* --- Suddenly
- *Cariño* --- Affection
- *Seguir adelante* --- Move on
- *Domingos* --- Sundays

- *Acordeón* --- Accordion
- *Contrabajo* --- Double bass
- *Poderosas* --- Powerful
- *Cadenciosamente* --- Rhythmically
- *Anonadado* --- Stunned
- *Caricaturas* --- Cartoons
- *Inspirador* --- Inspiring
- *Toro* --- Bull
- *Disecada* --- Stuffed
- *Madera* --- Wood
- *Clientes* --- Customers
- *Meseros* --- Waiters
- *Contrastaban* --- Contrasted
- *Desarreglado* --- Disarranged
- *Excéntrico* --- Eccentric
- *Particulares* --- Special
- *Sería un gran gusto* --- It would be a great pleasure
- *Copas* --- Glasses
- *Vino tinto* --- Red wine
- *Descubrimiento culinario* --- Culinary Discovery
- *Queso con pasas* --- Cheese with raisins
- *Sillón* --- Arm chair
- *Arrendador* --- Landlord
- *Ventanal* --- Large window
- *Acomodar* --- Fit
- *Inesperada* --- Unexpected
- *Agonía* --- Agony
- *Breve* --- Brief
- *Como siempre* --- Like always
- *Que gusto* --- What a pleasure
- *Tareas* --- School assignments
- *Exagerando* --- Exaggerating
- *Perderemos* --- Will lose
- *Sospechas* --- Suspicions
- *Parada del autobús* --- Bus stop
- *Estacionada* --- Parked
- *Soborné* --- Bribed
- *Prestar* --- Lend
- *Sombrillas* --- Umbrellas
- *Hielera* --- Cooler
- *Concurso* --- Contest
- *Competencia* --- Competition
- *Paró* --- Stood
- *Recursos limitados* --- Limited resources
- *Desanimen* --- Be discouraged
- *Capacidad de improvisar* --- Ability to improvise
- *Sentir* --- Feel

- *Encendía* --- Turned on
- *Orgullosa* --- Proud
- *Pedazo de papel* --- Piece of paper
- *Merezca* --- Deserves
- *Votos* --- Votes
- *Paralizada* --- Paralysed

6. Ando Blogueando

Ginelle era una chica que se dedicaba a bloguear sobre los viajes que hacía a los distintos países del mundo. Lo atractivo de su blog, y lo que llamaba mucho la atención de las personas es que, mientras estaba en el país, iba a los restaurantes y dejaba que las otras personas pidieran la comida por ella. Muchas veces las personas eran conscientes y pedían platos muy deliciosos, por lo que la experiencia y el artículo que escribía en el blog era bastante positivo. Sin embargo, algunas veces, las personas no eran buenas y pedían platos exóticos y desagradables. Por lo que el artículo del blog resultaba un poco negativo.

Ginelle was a girl who was blogging about the trips she made to the different countries of the world. The appeal of his blog, and what caught people's attention is that, while he was in the country, he went to the restaurants and let other people ask for food for her. Many times people were aware and asked for very delicious dishes, so the experience and the article I wrote on the blog was quite positive. However, sometimes, people were not good and asked for exotic and unpleasant dishes. So the blog article was a bit negative.

Ginelle estaba muy emocionada pues viajaría a Venezuela en veinte días, nunca antes había ido a ese país y le habían dicho que la comida de allá era extremadamente sabrosa. Publicó en sus redes que viajaría para Venezuela y todos sus seguidores comenzaron a recomendarle platos y postres.

Ginelle was very excited because she would travel to Venezuela in twenty days, she had never been to that country before and had been told that the food there was extremely tasty. He published in his networks that he would travel to Venezuela and all his followers began to recommend dishes and desserts.

Llegado el día, fue al aeropuerto, se montó en el avión y salió a vivir su nueva aventura. Llegó al aeropuerto y la recogió un taxi, ella le pidió que la llevara a su restaurante favorito. Él, un poco extrañado, la llevó a un restaurante donde vendían todo tipo de pescados. Cuando se bajó del carro, ella preguntó

When the day came, he went to the airport, got on the plane and went out to live his new adventure. He arrived at the airport and picked up a taxi, she asked him to take her to her favorite restaurant. He, a little surprised, took her to a restaurant where they sold all kinds of fish. When he got out of the car, she asked

-*Ginelle: ¿Qué pides tú aquí cuando vienes?*

-Ginelle: What do you ask here when you come?

-*Taxista: Pido un pargo, con tostones y ensalada rallada. Para beber una malta.*

-Taxist: I ask for a snapper, with tostones and grated salad. To drink a malt.

-*Ginelle: Genial, muchas gracias.*

-Ginelle: Great, thank you very much.

Eran aproximadamente las 2:30 pm cuando Ginelle entró al restaurante y pidió lo que le había dicho el taxista. Cuando el plato llegó se veía delicioso, el pargo era un tipo de pescado bastante jugoso y con pocas espinas; los tostones eran plátanos sin madurar aplastados y fritos, con kétchup, mayonesa, queso y sal, finalmente, la ensalada rallada era una ensalada de zanahoria, repollo, uvas pasas y mayonesa. Comenzó a comer y la comida estaba realmente exquisita, el pescado, los tostones y la ensalada eran la combinación perfecta, además, y la malta era la malta más rica que había

probado.

It was about 2:30 pm when Ginelle entered the restaurant and asked for what the taxi driver had said. When the dish arrived it looked delicious, the snapper was a fairly juicy type of fish with few bones; the tostones were crushed and fried unripe bananas, with ketchup, mayonnaise, cheese and salt, finally, the grated salad was a carrot salad, cabbage, raisins and mayonnaise. He started eating and the food was really delicious, the fish, the tostones and the salad were the perfect combination, and the malt was the richest malt he had ever tasted.

Después de eso, se fue al hotel. Tomó una ducha y se acostó a dormir, pues estaba cansada por el viaje. Cuando despertó eran las 8:30pm, era la hora de cenar. Se arregló y bajó al restaurante del hotel. Allí, le pidió a alguien que ordenara la comida por ella. La persona pidió empanadas, una de queso y la otra de pollo. Nuevamente, Ginelle quedó encantada con lo que había comido.

After that, he went to the hotel. She took a shower and lay down to sleep, because she was tired of the trip. When he woke up it was 8:30 pm, it was dinner time. He got ready and went down to the hotel restaurant. There, he asked someone to order the food for her. The person ordered empanadas, one cheese and the other chicken. Again, Ginelle was delighted with what she had eaten.

Ginelle estuvo visitando restaurantes durante días y todo lo que pedía la gente le encantaba, comió cachapas, arepas, tequeños, sándwiches, granjeros, hamburguesas, perros calientes, pabellón, paella, comida china (Que en realidad no era comida china), chica, papelón con limón, golfeados y muchas otras cosas que le encantaron.

Ginelle was visiting restaurants for days and everything she asked people loved, she ate cachapas, arepas, tequeños, sandwiches, farmers, hamburgers, hot dogs, pavilion, paella, Chinese food (which really wasn't Chinese food), girl, paper with lemon, golfeados and many other things that he loved.

Ya quedando pocos días para que su viaje finalizara, decidió viajar a otra región de Venezuela, para ver cómo difería la cocina dependiendo de la región.

With few days left before his trip ended, he decided to travel to another region of Venezuela, to see how the cuisine differed depending on the region.

-*Ginelle: Buenas tardes, disculpa, ¿Cuál es tu restaurante favorito de la zona?*

-Ginelle: Good afternoon, excuse me, what is your favorite restaurant in the area?

-*Extraño: ¿Mi restaurante favorito? ...Sígueme.*

-Strange: My favorite restaurant? .... Follow me.

-*Ginelle: De acuerdo.*

-Ginelle: Okay.

Caminaron unos diez minutos y llegaron a una pequeña y humilde casa.

They walked about ten minutes and arrived at a small and humble house.

-*Extraño: Espera aquí afuera un momento.*

-Weird: Wait a minute out here.

Dijo el extraño, entró y tardó como cinco minutos en volver a salir

Said the stranger, entered and it took about five minutes to get back out

-*Extraño: Esta es mi mamá; ella hace la mejor comida que he comido en mi vida.*

- Strange: This is my mom; she makes the best food I have ever eaten in my life.

423

-Ginelle: *Me llamo Ginelle, mucho gusto.*

-Ginelle: My name is Ginelle, nice to meet you.

-Sara: *Mi nombre es Sara, un placer.*

-Sara: My name is Sara, a pleasure.

-Ginelle: *¿Cree que pueda hacerme el plato que más le gusta a su hijo? Yo le pagaré*

-Ginelle: Do you think you can make the dish that your child likes best? I will pay him

-Sara: *¿Estás segura?*

-Sara: Are you sure?

-Ginelle: *Completamente.*

-Ginelle: Completely.

-Sara: *Está bien, pero debes venir mañana, para yo tener tiempo de prepararlo.*

-Sara: Okay, but you must come tomorrow, for me to have time to prepare it.

Ginelle aceptó en regresar al día siguiente a donde aquella señora. Fue a un hotel y pasó la noche allí. Al día siguiente, se levantó, se arregló y fue a donde Sara. Al llegar, estaba Sara afuera sentada en una silla esperando.

Ginelle agreed to return the next day to that lady. He went to a hotel and spent the night there. The next day, he got up, got ready and went to Sara. Upon arrival, Sara was sitting outside in a chair waiting.

-Sara: *Bienvenida, pensé que no vendrías.*

-Sara: Welcome, I thought you wouldn't come.

-Ginelle: *No iba a perder esto por nada.*

-Ginelle: I wasn't going to lose this for anything.

-Sara: *Me alegra que pienses así.*

-Sara: I'm glad you think that way.

-Sara: *Es una sorpresa, primero debes probarlo, decirme si te gusta o no y yo luego te diré.*

-Sara: It's a surprise, you must first try it, tell me if you like it or not and I'll tell you later.

-Ginelle: *Entendido.*

-Ginelle: Understood.

-Ginelle: *Bueno, ¿Qué voy a comer?*

-Ginelle: Well, what am I going to eat?

Así fue, Sara le sirvió el primer plato a Ginelle, era algo muy parecido a la empanada gallega, pero el sabor era bastante diferente.

So it was, Sara served Ginelle's first dish, it was something very similar to the Galician pie, but the taste was quite different.

-Ginelle: *Esto se parece mucho a la empanada gallega, pero sabe diferente.*

-Ginelle: This looks a lot like Galician pie, but it tastes different.

-Sara: *¿Te gusta?*

-Sara: Do you like it?

-*Ginelle: Me encantó. ¿Qué es?*

-Ginelle: I loved it. What is it?

-*Sara: Termina de comer para traerte el otro plato y luego te digo.*

-Sara: Finish eating to bring you the other dish and then I tell you.

Ginelle terminó de comer y le trajeron el otro plato. Era arroz con algo muy parecido al pollo. Comió y le encantó. Finalmente, cuando le preguntó a Sara que qué era lo que había comido Sara le respondió:

Ginelle finished eating and they brought her the other dish. It was rice with something very similar to chicken. He ate and loved it. Finally, when he asked Sara what he had eaten Sara replied:

-*Sara: Lo primero era pastel de morrocoy (Morrocoy es una especie de tortuga) y lo segundo era arroz con iguana.*

-Sara: The first was morrocoy cake (Morrocoy is a species of turtle) and the second was rice with iguana.

Quiz:

1. ¿Qué hacía Ginelle?
a. Blogueaba
b. Era youtuber
c. Vendía comida
d. Escribía libros
e. Dibujaba

2. ¿A qué país viajaría?
a. Colombia
b. Ecuador
c. Panamá
d. Perú
e. Venezuela

3. ¿Qué fue lo primero que comió en Venezuela?
a. Empanada
b. Tequeño
c. Pescado
d. Arepa
e. Cachapa

4. ¿Qué fue lo que probó en Venezuela que era más rico que en otro lado?
a. Queso
b. Hamburguesa
c. Perro caliente
d. Malta
e. Pizza

5. ¿Cómo se llamaba la protagonista?

a. Giselle

b. Ginelle

c. Ginna

d. Ginnie

e. Gibelle

Answers:

1) a

2) e

3) c

4) d

5) a

Vocabulario/Vocabulary

- *Países* --- Countries
- *Atractivo* --- Attractive
- *Pedir* --- Order
- *Experiencia* --- Experience
- *Desagradables* --- Disgusting
- *Publicó* --- Posted
- *Taxi* --- Taxi /Cab
- *Pescado* --- Fish
- *Ensalada* --- Salad
- *Jugoso* --- Juici
- *Espinas* --- spines
- *Zanahoria* --- Carrot
- *Queso* --- Cheese
- *Pollo* --- Chicken
- *Perro caliente* --- Hot dog
- *Limón* --- Lemon
- *Sígueme* --- Follow me
- *Pequeña* --- Little
- *Mañana* --- TomorrowNoche --- Night

7. No Te Excedas

Como bien sabemos, en la actualidad las cosas han cambiado mucho con respecto a cómo eran hace treinta o cuarenta años atrás. Esto es debido a los grandes avances tecnológicos que han traído bastantes beneficios a nuestras vidas, pero también han hecho mucho daño.

As we well know, things have changed a lot today regarding how they were thirty or forty years ago. This is due to the great technological advances that have brought many benefits to our lives, but they have also done a lot of damage.

Si comparamos a la juventud de ahora con la juventud de hace treinta o cuarenta años, notaremos una inmensa diferencia en el ámbito social. Los niños en el pasado jugaban horas y horas en parques, manejaban bicicletas, y hacían muchísimas otras actividades que hoy en día se han olvidado. Los niños de ahora pasan los días jugando a videojuegos en sus consolas, teléfonos, tablets o computadoras. O también viendo videos en Youtube. Mathías no era la excepción.

If we compare the youth of now with the youth of thirty or forty years ago, we will notice an immense difference in the social sphere. Children in the past played hours and hours in parks, drove bicycles, and did many other activities that today have been forgotten. Children now spend their days playing video games on their consoles, phones, tablets or computers. Or also watching videos on YouTube. Mathías was no exception.

Mathías era un niño de doce años, al que le encantaban los videojuegos. Su rutina diaria era: levantarse, desayunar, ir al colegio, regresar a casa, almorzar, jugar videojuegos, ver videos, hacer en los videojuegos lo que veía en los videos, cenar y dormir.

Mathías was a twelve-year-old boy, who loved video games. His daily routine was: getting up, having breakfast, going to school, going home, having lunch, playing video games, watching videos, doing in video games what he saw in the videos, dining and sleeping.

Todos los días era lo mismo, ya estaba acostumbrado. Por mucho que la mamá le dijera que eso era malo para su salud, él no obedecía.

Every day was the same, I was used to it. As much as the mother told him that it was bad for his health, he did not obey.

Un día, durante una tormenta eléctrica, Mathias estaba viendo videos en Youtube, cuando un rayo cayó cerca de su casa. Eso provocó un pequeño bajón de luz. Después de eso, la computadora y la consola de videojuegos comenzaron a portarse extraño, se prendían y apagaban solos. También se activaban y cerraban los juegos y aplicaciones solas.

One day, during a thunderstorm, Mathias was watching videos on YouTube, when lightning struck near his home. That caused a small downturn. After that, the computer and video game console began to behave strangely, turned on and off alone. The games and applications alone were activated and closed.

Eso siguió durante varios días, Mathias estaba muy molesto con la computadora y la consola, pues pensaba que se estaban dañando. Por lo que le dio un golpe a la consola y esta se apagó permanentemente. Después de darle el golpe se acostó a dormir.

That followed for several days, Mathias was very upset with the computer and the console, because he thought they were being damaged. Then he hit the console and it went off permanently. After hitting it he lay down to sleep.

Cuando Mathias se durmió, la computadora y la consola se prendieron, y ambas empezaron a sonar como una alarma. De repente, cuando Mathias se despertó, estaba en un bosque, todo se veía pixelado, incluso él.

When Mathias fell asleep, the computer and console turned on, and both began to sound like an alarm. Suddenly, when Mathias woke up, he was in a forest, everything looked pixelated, even he.

-Consola: Bienvenido, estás dentro de mí.

Console: Welcome, you are inside me.

-Mathias: ¿Quién dijo eso?

-Mathias: Who said that?

-Consola: Yo, soy tu consola de videojuegos. Ahora eres parte de un videojuego.

-Consola: Me, I'm your video game console. Now you are part of a video game.

-Mathias: Genial, ¿Es decir que puedo hacer lo que quiera?

-Mathias: Great, I mean I can do what I want?

-Consola: ¿No te cansas, verdad? No lo has entendido.

-Consola: You don't get tired, right? You have not understand.

-Mathias: ¿De qué hablas?

-Mathias: What are you talking about?

-Consola: Esto es un castigo. La computadora y yo estamos cansados de que nos uses todo el día todos los días, es agotador trabajar tanto únicamente para entretenerte.

-Consola: This is a punishment. The computer and I are tired of using us all day every day, it is exhausting to work so hard just to entertain you.

-Mathias: Para eso fueron creados, ¿No?

-Mathias: That's what they were created for, right?

-Consolas: En parte, pero tu uso de nosotros es excesivo. Ahora verás lo que la computadora y yo sentimos.

-Consolas: In part, but your use of us is excessive. Now you will see what the computer and I feel.

De repente, todo el bosque en donde estaba Mathias comenzó a temblar, había un terremoto y se comenzó a abrir el piso por la mitad. Por lo que Mathias tuvo que correr para sobrevivir. Después de eso, aparecieron monstruos a los que tuvo que matar, jefes con los que tuvo que luchar y muchas otras cosas que se hacen normalmente en los videojuegos.

Suddenly, the whole forest where Mathias was started to shake, there was an earthquake and the floor began to open in half. So Mathias had to run to survive. After that, monsters appeared that he had to kill, bosses with whom he had to fight and many other things that are normally done in video games.

Al principio, a Mathias le gustaba, estaba viviendo un videojuego en carne y hueso, o bueno, carne y pixeles, pero a medida que más hacía en el juego, más y más cosas había por hacer. Se volvía frustrante que nunca acabara o que no tuviera un poco de descanso. Después de varias horas (En el juego), Mathias ya estaba exhausto

At first, Mathias liked it, he was living a video game in flesh and blood, or well, meat and pixels, but as he did more in the game, more and more things had to be done. It became frustrating that it never ended or that he didn't have a little rest. After several hours (In the game), Mathias was already exhausted

-*Mathias: Por favor, ya fue suficiente, estoy agotado, no puedo seguir jugando. Ten piedad.*

-Mathias: Please, it was enough, I'm exhausted, I can't keep playing. Be merciful.

-*Consola: ¿Ves lo que se siente?*

-Consola: Do you see what it feels like?

-*Mathias: Si. Pero ya por favor, ya aprendí mi lección.*

-Mathias: Yes. But please, I already learned my lesson.

-*Consola: Cada vez que la computadora o yo te mostramos un mensaje de que es hora de tomar un descanso, es porque ya estamos agotados, no porque seamos máquinas significa que no nos cansemos. Nuestros componentes se recalientan, jugar muchas horas nos perjudica a nosotros como a tu salud.*

-Consola: Every time the computer or I show you a message that it is time to take a break, it is because we are already exhausted, not because we are machines means that we do not get tired. Our components overheat, playing many hours hurts us as well as your health.

-*Mathias: Lo siento. De verdad lo siento. No imaginaba que eso les sucedía, pensé que estaban diseñados para eso. Para horas y horas de uso.*

-Mathias: I'm sorry. I'm truly sorry. I didn't imagine that happening to them, I thought they were designed for that. For hours and hours of use.

-*Consola: Mi castigo ya ha sido suficiente. Ahora le toca a la computadora.*

-Consola: My punishment has been enough. Now it's the computer's turn.

De pronto, todo se oscureció para Mathias. Se sentía como si estuviese flotando, de repente, se encendió una pantalla gigante en blanco delante de él. Luego, apareció el logo de Youtube.

Suddenly, everything went dark for Mathias. It felt like he was floating, suddenly, a giant blank screen lit in front of him. Then, the YouTube logo appeared.

-*Computadora: Bienvenido al mundo de Youtube. Como pasas muchas horas utilizándome para ver videos, tu castigo será ver videos por horas.*

-Computer: Welcome to the world of YouTube. As you spend many hours using me to watch videos, your punishment will be to watch videos for hours.

-*Mathias: Eso no está tan mal.*

-Mathias: That is not so bad.

-*Computadora: Verás los peores videos de la historia de Youtube, los más aburridos, los que más terroríficos, los que más fastidiosos y los más asquerosos.*

-Computer: You will see the worst videos in YouTube history, the most boring, the most terrifying, the most annoying and the most disgusting.

-*Mathias: Ya aprendí mi lección, no debo utilizarlos todo el día, ustedes también merecen tener un descanso.*

-Mathias: I already learned my lesson, I should not use them all day, you also deserve to have a rest.

-*Computadora: Que lo digas no tiene sentido, debes sentir lo que yo siento.*

-Computer: That you say it does not make sense, you must feel what I feel.

429

Entonces empezó el primer video, era el video de los sonidos más molestos del mundo. Era un video tan, pero tan estresante, que a los diez minutos ya Mathias estaba a punto de volverse loco; ya estaba arrancándose los pelos.

Then the first video began, it was the video of the most annoying sounds in the world. It was a video so, but so stressful, that at ten minutes Mathias was about to go crazy; He was already tearing his hair.

El castigo de la computadora siguió por unas cuantas horas. Mathias ya había llorado de miedo, de aburrimiento, de asco y de escuchar tantos sonidos fastidiosos. Hasta que llegó la hora de que finalizara.

The computer punishment continued for a few hours. Mathias had already cried in fear, boredom, disgust and hearing so many annoying sounds. Until it was time for it to end.

-Computadora: Ya fue suficiente, ya lograste ver lo que siento cuando pasas horas viendo videos en mí. Te regresaremos al mundo real. Pero recuerda todo lo que hablamos y todo lo que sentiste.

-Computer: It was enough, you already managed to see what I feel when you spend hours watching videos on me. We will return you to the real world. But remember everything we talked about and everything you felt.

-Consola: Esperamos que no vuelvas a ser el mismo de antes y seas más prudente mientras uses cualquier aparato electrónico.

-Consola: We hope you will not be the same as before and be more cautious while using any electronic device.

-Mathias: Lo seré, lo prometo.

-Mathias: I will be, I promise.

Todo oscureció, y cuando Mathias abrió los ojos estaba de nuevo en el mundo real, acostado en su cama. La consola y la computadora estaban apagadas y ya no se prendían solas. Desde ese día Mathias cambió para siempre. Solo utilizaba la computadora y la consola una hora al día. Empezó a practicar fútbol y a salir más con sus amigos.

Everything got dark, and when Mathias opened his eyes he was back in the real world, lying in his bed. The console and the computer were turned off and no longer turned on themselves. From that day Mathias changed forever. I only used the computer and the console one hour a day. He started practicing football and going out more with his friends.

Quiz

1. ¿Cuántos años tenía Mathias?
a. 10
b. 12
c. 14
d. 9
e. 6

2. ¿Qué hacía Mathias justo al llegar del colegio?
a. Almorzar
b. Cenar
c. Ver videos
d. Jugar videojuegos

e. Bañarse

3. ¿Qué dañó la consola?
a. Una tormenta eléctrica
b. Un vaso de agua
c. Un golpe
d. El perro
e. Un virus

4. ¿Qué castigo le puso la consola?
a. Ver videos
b. Jugar mucho
c. Dormir
d. Cocinar
e. Limpiar el cuarto

5. ¿Qué castigo le puso la computadora?
a. Ver videos
b. Jugar mucho
c. Dormir
d. Cocinar
e. Limpiar el cuarto

Answers:

1) b
2) a
3) a
4) b
5) a

Vocabulario/Vocabulary

- *Beneficios* --- Benefits
- *Vidas* --- Lives
- *Daño* --- Damage
- *Juventud* --- youth
- *Inmensa* --- Huge
- *ámbito social* --- Social field
- *Parques* --- Parks
- *Consolas* --- Consoles
- *Computadoras* --- Computers
- *Excepción* --- Exception
- *Almorzar* --- To lunch
- *Salud* --- Health
- *Obedecer* --- Obey
- *Rayo* --- Lightning

431

- *Portarse* --- Behave
- *Prender* --- Turn on
- *Apagar* --- Turn off
- *Agotado* --- Exhausted.

8. Perdidos En El Bosque

Era el año 2009 cuando un grupo de amigos decidieron organizar un paseo vacacional al bosque que estaba en las afueras de la ciudad, allí caminarían, llegarían a ríos y cascadas, entrarían a cuevas, escalarían unas montañas y acamparían. La idea nació de un programa de TV que veían todos, donde un hombre, junto a su familia se dedicaba a pasear y a enfrentarse a la naturaleza en varias ocasiones y lugares, en selvas, bosques, desiertos, montañas heladas y otros ecosistemas.

It was the year 2009 when a group of friends decided to organize a holiday trip to the forest that was on the outskirts of the city, there they would walk, reach rivers and waterfalls, enter caves, climb mountains and camp. The idea was born from a TV program that everyone saw, where a man, along with his family, was dedicated to walking and confronting nature on several occasions and places, in jungles, forests, deserts, icy mountains and other ecosystems.

El grupo era de ocho amigos, Fred, Michael, Hugh, Brad, Lindsey, Carolina, Daniela y Esther. Fred era el más joven de todos, pero era el más valiente y temerario, fue el que tuvo la idea de hacer el viaje; Michael era el mayor de todos, era amante de la naturaleza y deseaba conocerla y vivirla; Hugh era un poco mayor que Fred, pero era todo lo contrario, era miedoso y cobarde, todo lo asustaba y todo le daba miedo; Brad era mayor que Hugh y era el hippie del grupo. En cuanto a las mujeres, Carolina era la más joven, era la pareja de Fred y le encantaban las ideas aventureras y arriesgadas de su novio; Daniela era muy parecida a Hugh, le aterraba salir de su zona de confort, era siempre muy negativa en cuanto a todo lo nuevo; Esther era amante de los deportes extremos, ella estaba planeando todas las actividades que iban a realizar en su paseo, había dicho para hacer rappel y otras cosas pero los demás no se atrevieron y por último; Lindsey, era hija de una pareja muy adinerada por lo que siempre había vivido con todos los lujos, razón por la que quería ir en el viaje con ellos a tener una nueva y diferente experiencia.

The group was eight friends, Fred, Michael, Hugh, Brad, Lindsey, Carolina, Daniela and Esther. Fred was the youngest of all but he was the bravest and reckless, he was the one who had the idea of making the trip; Michael was the oldest of all, was a lover of nature and wanted to know and live it; Hugh was a little older than Fred, but he was quite the opposite, he was fearful and cowardly, everything scared him and everything scared him; Brad was older than Hugh and was the group's hippie. As for women, Carolina was the youngest, she was Fred's partner and she loved the adventurous and risky ideas of her boyfriend; Daniela was very similar to Hugh, she was terrified of leaving her comfort zone, she was always very negative about everything new; Esther was a lover of extreme sports, she was planning all the activities they were going to do on her walk, she had said to rappel and other things but the others did not dare and finally; Lindsey, was the daughter of a very wealthy couple so she had always lived with all the luxuries, which is why she wanted to go on the trip with them to have a new and different experience.

En el año 2009 cuando comenzaron a planificar el viaje, Fred y Carolina tenían aun 16 años, por lo que, para viajar sin adultos tendrían que esperar dos años más y cumplir los 18 años. Eso hicieron entonces, todo el grupo ahorró y planificó cada momento del viaje durante los dos años que debían esperar para que Fred y Carolina fueran mayores de edad. Fueron comprando los alimentos no perecederos y las cosas indispensables como las carpas, los bolsos, las linternas, las cuerdas, los abrigos y esos utensilios.

In 2009 when they started planning the trip, Fred and Carolina were still 16 years old, so, to travel without adults they would have to wait two more years and turn 18. That they did then, the whole group saved and planned every moment of the trip during the two years they had to wait for Fred and Carolina to be of legal age. They were buying non-perishable food and essential items such as tents, bags, flashlights, ropes, coats and those utensils.

Llegó entonces el año 2011, Carolina cumplió años antes que Fred, entonces se prepararon todos para salir a acampar un día después del cumpleaños de Fred. Llegado el día del cumpleaños de Fred, decidieron no hacer fiesta para tener energías para el viaje al día siguiente. Estaban todos en sus casas, se acostaron a dormir temprano para que llegara el gran día. Fred en su casa celebro su cumpleaños con sus padres y se fue a dormir también temprano. Al día siguiente, Michael se despertó a las 5:00 a.m. pues él era el que iba a manejar el carro de su padre y llevaría a todos al bosque, le reviso el aire a los cauchos, chequeó el refrigerante, el aceite, la gasolina, guardó sus cosas, revisó el caucho de repuesto y salió entonces a buscar a cada uno de sus amigos.

Then came the year 2011, Carolina turned years before Fred, then everyone prepared to go camping one day after Fred's birthday. When Fred's birthday arrived, they decided not to party to have energy for the trip the next day. They were all in their homes, they went to bed early for the big day to come. Fred at home celebrated his birthday with his parents and went to sleep too early. The next day, Michael woke up at 5:00 a.m. because he was the one who was going to drive his father's car and take everyone to the forest, he checked the air to the rubbers, checked the refrigerant, the oil, the gasoline, put away his things, checked the spare rubber and then left to look for each of his friends.

Hugh y Brad eran vecinos, por lo que los recogió a ambos al mismo tiempo. Eran las 6:00 a.m. cuando los recogió, seguían medio dormidos todos así que se saludaron con las manos y nadie dijo nada más. Luego recogió a Carolina, que vivía cerca, ella estaba súper energética pues había tomado varias tazas de café antes de salir.

Hugh and Brad were neighbors, so he picked them both at the same time. It was 6:00 a.m. when he picked them up, they were still half asleep, so they waved and no one said anything else. Then he picked up Carolina, who lived nearby, she was super energetic because she had had several cups of coffee before leaving.

-Carolina: Hola muchachos, ¿Cómo están? ¿No están emocionados? Yo estoy muy emocionada, ¿Tienen sueño? ¿Cómo pueden tener sueño?, si hoy es el gran día. ¿No querían llegara el día? Hoy llego, aquí estamos por fin nos vamos de paseo. No puedo esperar.

-Carolina: Hi guys, how are you? Are you not excited? I am very excited, are you sleepy? How can you be sleepy? if today is the big day. Didn't they want the day to come? Today I arrive, here we are finally going for a walk. I can not wait.

-Michael: Ya Carolina cálmate, son las 6:15 a.m. relájate un poco, tenemos que buscar primero a los demás y después es que empezamos el viaje.

-Michael: Carolina calm down, it's 6:15 a.m. relax a bit, we have to look for others first and then we start the trip.

-Carolina: Ay pero que amargado, hay personas a las que levantarse temprano las pone de mal humor, tú debes ser una, yo no, yo estoy perfecta.

-Carolina: Oh but that bitter, there are people who get up early puts them in a bad mood, you must be one, I do not, I am perfect.

-Michael: Como digas.

-Michael: As you say.

Luego Michael fue a buscar a Esther, Daniela y Lindsey. Carolina seguía hablando y hablando mientras los demás intentaban dormir un poco más. Finalmente llegaron a casa de Fred a las 6:45

434

a.m.

Then Michael went to look for Esther, Daniela and Lindsey. Carolina kept talking and talking while the others tried to sleep a little more. They finally arrived at Fred's house at 6:45 a.m.

-*Fred: Buenos días, ¿Cómo están? Justo a tiempo, como estaba planificado.*

-Fred: Good morning, how are you? Just in time, as planned.

-*Michael: Así es, todo de acuerdo al plan.*

-Michael: That's right, all according to plan.

-*Carolina: Hola mi amor buenos días. ¿Cómo pasaste tu cumpleaños ayer? Te extrañe mucho, quería que llegara el día, los demás son unos aburridos, hoy por fin es nuestro viaje y esos flojos quieren dormir y dormir.*

-Carolina: Hello my love, good morning. How did you spend your birthday yesterday? I missed you so much, I wanted the day to come, the others are boring, today is finally our trip and those lazy people want to sleep and sleep

-*Fred: Amor, ¿Tomaste café verdad?*

-Fred: Love, did you drink coffee, right?

-*Carolina: Si, un poco, ¿Por?*

-Carolina: Yes, a little, why?

-*Fred: ¿Cuántas tazas?*

-Fred: How many cups?

-*Carolina: Una sola.*

-Carolina: One.

-*Fred: Dime la verdad.*

-Fred: Tell me the truth.

-*Carolina: Como tres jejeje*

-Carolina: Like three hehehe

-*Fred: ¿Segura?*

-Fred: Are you sure?

-*Carolina: Bueno, de acuerdo, tome cuatro tazas de café, es que tenía mucho sueño y me tome la primera y me quitó un poco el sueño entonces sin darme cuenta y mientras esperaba a Michael me serví otra y otra...*

-Carolina: Well, okay, I had four cups of coffee, I was very sleepy and I took the first one and it took my sleep a little bit off then without realizing it and while I waited for Michael I served myself another and another ...

-*Fred: Tomaste demasiado, intenta calmarte un poco.*

-Fred: You took too much, try to calm down a bit.

-*Carolina: Bueno, no aprecian mi energía ni mi buen humor.*

-Carolina: Well, they don't appreciate my energy or my good mood.

Y así dieron inicio al viaje que tanto habían planificado, tenían las tres rutas grabadas en el GPS, la opción A, la opción B y la opción C, bien usadas, cada una de ellas los haría llegar a su destino a las 9:15 a.m. A medida que iban acercándose al lugar de llegada iban perdiendo el sueño y comenzaban a emocionarse todos poco a poco, menos Carolina que estaba emocionada desde que salió de su casa.

And so they started the trip they had planned so much, they had the three routes recorded on the GPS, option A, option B and option C, well used, each of them would make them arrive at their destination at 9:15 A.M. As they approached the place of arrival they were losing sleep and began to get excited little by little, except Carolina who was excited since leaving home.

Tenían todo planificado para estar cinco días allí en el bosque, ya habían comprado absolutamente todo, pan de hamburguesa, pan de perro caliente, salchichas, carne para parrilla, una rejilla para cocinar utilizando el fuego de la fogata, carbón, gaseosas, agua, chocolates, malvaviscos, repelente de insectos, protector solar y muchos otros recursos que utilizarían durante su estadía en el bosque.

They had everything planned to be there in the forest for five days, they had already bought absolutely everything, hamburger bread, hot dog bread, sausages, grill meat, a cooking rack using the fire of the campfire, coal, soda, water, chocolates, marshmallows, insect repellent, sunscreen and many other resources that they would use during their stay in the forest.

Tal y como habían planificado, llegaron a las 9:15 a.m. al bosque, estacionaron el carro en un lugar seguro, bajaron todas las cosas que habían llevado para su acampada y comenzaron a caminar. Esther era la encargada de leer el mapa, ella tenía experiencia con eso porque antes salía a acampar con su padre, quien la enseñó a leer mapas, lo que la hacía la indicada para guiar a aquel grupo de amigos. Después de caminar dos horas y media llegaron al lugar de acampada de la primera noche, desempacaron, cada quien armó su carpa, metieron su equipaje y comieron algunos sándwiches, pues ya eran la 1:30 p.m. tal y como lo decía la planificación.

As planned, they arrived at 9:15 a.m. to the forest, they parked the car in a safe place, they lowered all the things they had taken for their camping and began to walk. Esther was in charge of reading the map, she had experience with that because she used to go camping with her father, who taught her to read maps, which made her the one to guide that group of friends. After walking two and a half hours they arrived at the campsite on the first night, they unpacked, each one assembled their tent, put in their luggage and ate some sandwiches, since it was already 1:30 p.m. as the planning said.

-Michael: Ya son las 1:30 p.m. es hora de comer los sándwiches.

-Michael: It's already 1:30 p.m. It's time to eat the sandwiches.

-Fred: Ya era hora, moría de hambre.

-Fred: It was time, I was starving.

-Lindsay: Los míos son los sándwiches de pan integral.

-Lindsay: Mine are whole wheat bread sandwiches.

-Esther: Pensé que venías para salir de tu mundo de fantasía y disfrutar la naturaleza, algo diferente y nuevo.

-Esther: I thought you were coming to leave your fantasy world and enjoy nature, something different and new.

-Lindsay: A eso vine, pero no puedo salirme de la dieta.

-Lindsay: That's what I came for, but I can't get out of the diet.

-Daniela: Yo quiero los sándwiches sencillos por favor; no quiero que me vaya a doler el estómago

aquí en medio de la nada.

-Daniela: I want simple sandwiches please; I don't want my stomach to hurt here in the middle of nowhere.

-Esther: Hubiese sido mejor venir con mi hermanito, se queja y pide menos.

-Esther: It would have been better to come with my little brother, he complains and asks for less.

-Hugh: Tu hermanito no es consciente de los riesgos de un viaje así.

-Hugh: Your little brother is not aware of the risks of such a trip.

-Brad: Tranquilo hermano, la naturaleza no nos hará nada si nosotros no le hacemos nada. Ella siente nuestras energías.

-Brad: Quiet brother, nature will do nothing to us if we do nothing to it. She feels our energies.

-Michael: Ya vas a empezar con tus cosas místicas y extrañas de hippie.

-Michael: You're going to start with your mystical and strange hippie things.

Mientras comían y hablaban descansaron un poco, pues caminar en el bosque durante dos horas y media con las irregularidades del terreno no es tarea fácil. Después de haber descansado lo suficiente (según la planificación), fueron todos a sus carpas y se cambiaron la ropa, se pusieron sus trajes de baño y se pusieron protector solar y repelente, pues irían a unos lagos que estaban a, aproximadamente, 15 minutos de donde ellos estaban acampando según el mapa. Salieron todos de sus carpas vistiendo sus trajes de baño, Esther agarró el mapa y comenzaron a caminar. A los 10 minutos ya lograban ver el lago y era algo impresionante. El lago era asombroso, todos quedaron sin palabras al ver tanta hermosura, al ver la perfección de la naturaleza, el agua estaba calmada y era tan clara y limpia que parecía ser un vidrio. Se apresuraron entonces a llegar a aquel lugar tan hermoso para poderse bañar y jugar allí el tiempo que les quedaba del primer día de su acampada.

While they ate and talked they rested a little, because walking in the forest for two and a half hours with the irregularities of the terrain is not an easy task. After having had enough rest (as planned), they all went to their tents and changed their clothes, put on their bathing suits and put on sunscreen and repellent, as they would go to some lakes that were approximately 15 minutes away where they were camping according to the map. They all left their tents wearing their swimsuits, Esther grabbed the map and began to walk. After 10 minutes they were able to see the lake and it was impressive. The lake was amazing, everyone was speechless to see so much beauty, to see the perfection of nature, the water was calm and so clear and clean that it seemed to be a glass. They hurried then to get to that beautiful place to be able to bathe and play there the time they had left on the first day of their camping.

Quiz

1. Where did a group of friends to on holiday trips?
a. forest
b. Ocean
c. Movie

2. Who was the youngest of the eight friends?
a. Hugh
b. Fred
c. Brad

3. Two friends couldn't travel because of their age, who were they?
a. Hugh and Fred
b. Lindsey and Carolina
c. Fred and Carolina

Answers

1. a
2. b
3. c

Vocabulario/Vocabulary

- *Selvas* --- Jungles
- *Más valiente* --- Bravest
- *Aventurero* --- Adventurous
- *Lujos* --- Luxuries
- *Linternas* --- Flashlights
- *Cumpleaños* --- Birthday
- *Vecinos* --- Neighbors
- *Dormir* --- Sleep
- *Bosque* --- Forest
- *Sin palabras* --- speechless

9. El Invento

*Lo único que hacía falta era **comprobar** si el motor **funcionaba** bien. Era un **invento** muy raro, **ambicioso e** innovador. Pero, sobre todo, muy raro. Dos científicos se habían propuesto crear una **máquina, ellos** informan que entraran al menos cuatro personas. Esta máquina que llamaron el Tosta Móvil. Podía viajar al pasado. Durante el viaje el Tosta Móvil tenía un dispositivo que te **desintegraba** la **ropa** actual que tenías puesta al momento de ingresar a la máquina y te la **cambiaba** por una **réplica** exacta del **tipo** de vestimenta de la **época** a la que decidas viajar.*

All that was needed was to check if the engine worked well. It was a very rare, ambitious and innovative invention. But, above all, it was very rare. Two scientists had set out to create a machine, they report that at least four people will enter. They called this machine the Tosta Mobile. It could travel to the past. During the trip, the Tosta Móvil had a device that disintegrated the current clothes that you had on when you entered the machine and exchanged them for an exact replica of the type of clothing of the time where you decided to travel.

*Los dos científicos, Orlando y Marcos, habían fracasado **doscientos setenta y cinco** veces, cuando estaban creando y experimentando para inventar algo. Que realmente ayudará a descubrir la verdad sobre la historia de la curvatura del espacio-tiempo y no lo que te cuentas los libros y las revistas y mucho menos lo que te enseñan en la escuela. Pero después de tantos intentos **fallidos** por **fin** había **logrado** crear su máquina.*

The two scientists, Orlando and Marcos, had failed 275 times when they were creating and experimenting on the invention. It really helps the interest to discover the truth about the history of the curvature of space-time, which you cannot read in books or magazines or learn in school. But after so many failed attempts, they had finally managed to create their machine.

*Tenían que probanza y comprobar que funcionaba y serían ellos mismos quienes **asumirán** el **riesgo** de viajar al pasado en el Tosta Móvil porque no sabían si tendrá efectos secundarios negativos. No querían poner en peligro la vida de ninguna otra persona.*

They had to prove and verify that it worked, and they would be the ones who will take the risk of traveling to the past in the Tosta Mobile because they did not know if it will have negative side effects. They did not want to endanger the life of any other person.

*Así que Orlando y Marcos, después al **arreglar** los últimos detalles técnicos en el motor, se lanzaron a la aventura de la deformación en el tiempo. Eligieron ir al año 1789 cuando francia se encontraba en una profunda crisis económica y social. La **monarquía** también estaba en crisis financiera. Por los **elevados** costos y gastos de la **corte**.*

So Orlando and Marcos, after fixing the latest technical details on the engine, set out on the adventure of time warp. They chose to go to the year 1789 when France was in a deep economic and social crisis. The monarchy was also in financial crisis because of the high costs and spending of the court.

*El problema es que tuvieron una falla técnica en el dispositivo de cambio de ropa y el vestuario no fue el traje típico que estaban en Francia en 1789. El Tosta Móvil les colocó ropa de **astronautas** modernos y así fue como Orlando y Marcos entraron a los **acontecimientos** de la revolución francesa, vestidos de astronautas.*

The problem is that they had a technical flaw in the change of clothes device, and the costumes were not the typical costume they were in France in 1789. The Tosta Mobile placed them into clothes of modern astronauts, and that was how Orlando and Marco entered the events of the French revolution—dressed as astronauts.

*Fue un caos total. Además, de verdad querían la muerte de Napoleón Bonaparte. El pequeño detalle es que ahí también se habían **equivocado** porque Napoleón murió en la isla de Santa Elena el 5 de mayo de 1821.*

It was total chaos. They also wanted the death of Napoleon Bonaparte. They were also wrong there because Napoleon died on the island of Santa Elena on May 5, 1821.

*Pero el Tosta Móvil estaba programado para no volver a la época actual para resolver lo que fueron a investigar. Dos astronautas en pleno 1789 no era nada bueno. La gente **enloquecía** en las calles. Ya no les importaba la **revuelta** social. Creían que era **el fin del mundo,** y que Orlando y Marcos eran los **demonios** del **Apocalipsis**.*

But the Tosta Mobile was programmed not to return to the current era to solve what they want to investigate. Two astronauts in the middle of 1789 were nothing good. People went crazy in the streets. They no longer cared about the social revolt. They believed it was the end of the world, and that Orlando and Marcos were the Devil of the Apocalypse.

*Sus mentes de científicos tenían que encontrar una solución y rápido. Corrieron escapando de la multitud enloquecida. Se escondieron en un viejo establo donde había grandes cantidades de **estiércol** de caballo. Pero por suerte alguien había **dejado** dos **mudas** de ropa **secándose** sobre un tronco dentro del **establo**. Se quitaron los trajes de astronauta y se vistieron con humildes trajes típicos de 1789.*

The minds of scientists had to find a solution fast. They ran away from the crazed crowd. They hid in an old stable where there were large amounts of horse manure. But luckily, someone had left two changes of clothes drying on a trunk inside the stable. They removed the astronaut costumes, and they dressed in the humble typical clothing of 1789.

*Volvieron al sitio donde estaba escondido el Tosta Móvil. Ellos Intentarían reprogramar la máquina y viajar a la **fecha** correcta en 1821. Pero el 4 de mayo, es decir, un día antes de la muerte de Napoleón Bonaparte. Pero mientras se dirigían al Tosta Móvil, se encontraron con una mujer que llorando a gritos pedía ayuda porque unos guardias del **Rey** habían **encarcelado** a su hijo. No sabían qué hacer hasta que Orlando tuvo una idea.*

They returned to the place where the Tosta Mobile was hidden. They would try to reprogram the machine and travel to the correct date in 1821, on May 4; that is, one day before the death of Napoleon Bonaparte. But as they went to the Tosta Mobile, they met a woman who was crying loudly for help because some of the King's guards had falsely imprisoned her son. They didn't know what to do until Orlando had an idea.

*Orlando: Ya sé que hacer. Es una idea un poco **atolondrada**.*

Orlando: "I know what to do. It is a slightly stunning idea."

*Marcos: Ya **no me gusta**. Sea lo que sea, no me gusta.*

Marcos: "I don't like it anymore. Whatever it is, I don't like it."

*Orlando: Regresaremos al establo y buscaremos los trajes de astronauta. Los esconderemos en unos de las bolsas con lo que encontremos. Vamos con esta mujer al Rey y ahí buscamos un lugar donde **ponernos** los trajes de astronauta. Entonces los **aterrorizaremos** con cosas terribles sobre el Apocalipsis si no **suelta** al hijo de esta mujer.*

Orlando: "We will return to the stable and look for the astronaut costumes. We will hide them in one of the bags. We go with this woman to the King, and there, we will look for a place to put on the astronaut costumes. Then we will terrify them with the terrible things about the apocalypse if he does not release this woman's son."

Marcos: ¡Nos van a matar!

Marcos: "They're going to kill us!"

*Orlando: No si decimos cosas que los **asustan** relacionadas con acontecimientos que los **confundan**.*

Orlando: "Not if we say things that can scare them, things related to events that can confuse them."

Marcos: ¿Por ejemplo?

Marcos: "For example?"

*Orlando: Que la **Reina** de Francia actual en realidad el fantasma de Juana de Arco.*

Orlando: "That the current queen of France actually is the ghost of Joan of Arc."

Marcos: ¡Nos van a matar!

Marcos: "They're going to kill us!"

*Pero aún contra de todo **pronóstico** de **desastre**, las cosas salieron bien. Los dos científicos crearon tanta confusión y caos que lograron **liberar** no sólo al hijo de la mujer sino a todos los **injustamente** encadenados al **calabozo**. Regresaron a la máquina y adelantaron el viaje de 1789 a 1829—justo a tiempo para **descubrir** que Napoleón Bonaparte no había muerto de un cáncer provocado por una úlcera en el **estómago** si no que fue **conscientemente envenenado** con **arsénico**.*

But even against all the odds and any imminent disaster, things went well. The two scientists created so much confusion and chaos that they managed not only to free the woman's son but also those unjustly chained to the dungeon. They returned to the machine and approved the trip from 1789 to 1829—just in time to discover that Napoleon Bonaparte had not died of cancer caused by a stomach ulcer but was consciously poisoned with arsenic.

Quiz:

1. Los científicos inventaron:
a. Una bicicleta con alas y hélices
b. Un helicóptero submarino
c. Una máquina en forma de tostadora que viaja en el tiempo

2. Los trajes de los científicos en 1789 eran de:
a. Bomberos
b. Astronautas
c. Militares

3. La Máquina se llamaba:
a. Torbellino
b. Locofución
c. Tosta Movil

Answers

1. c

2. b
3. c

Vocabulario/Vocabulary

- Acontecimiento --- event
- *Ambicioso* --- ambitious
- *apocalipsis* --- apocalypse
- *arreglar* --- to fix or to repair
- *arsénico* - arsenic
- *astronauta* --- astronaut
- *asumirán* --- they will assume
- *asustan* --- they frighten
- *aterrorizaremos* --- to terrify
- *atolondrada* --- scatter-brained
- *calabozo* - prison
- *cambiaba* --- I changed
- *comprobar* --- to check or to prove
- *confundan* --- to confuse
- *conscientemente* --- consciously
- *corte* --- royal court
- *dejado* --- careless
- *demonio* --- the devil
- *desastre* --- disaster
- *descubrir* --- to discover or to uncover
- *desintegraba* --- I disintegrated
- *doscientos setenta y cinco* --- two-hundred seventy-five
- *el fin del mundo* --- the end of the world
- *elevados* --- to lift or to raise
- *encarcelado* --- incarcerated
- *enlazando* --- to link or to connect
- *enloquecía* --- to go crazy
- *envenenado* --- to poison
- *época* --- a period of time or era
- *equivocado* --- wrong
- *estable* --- stable or steady
- *estiércol* --- dung or manure
- *estómago* --- stomach
- *fallidos* --- failed
- *fecha* --- a specific date
- *fin* --- end or conclusion
- *funcionaba* --- I worked
- *injustamente* --- unfairly
- *invento* --- invention
- *jaleando* --- to cheer on

- *liberar* --- to free
- *logrado* --- successful
- *máquina* --- machine
- *monarquía* --- monarchy
- *mudas* --- you change
- *no me gusta* --- I do not like
- *ponernos* --- to put
- *Por ejemplo* --- For example
- *pronóstico* --- prediction
- *reina* --- queen
- *réplica* --- replica
- *revuelta* --- revolt
- *rey* --- king
- *riesgo* - risk
- *ropa* --- clothing
- *secándose* --- drying out
- *suelta* --- release
- *tipo* --- type

10. La Sospecha

Capítulo Uno

Jennifer es una estudiante de una universidad en Puerto Rico a quien le robaron mientras salió del colegio durante el fin de semana. Al regresar al colegio el domingo por la noche con su amiga, descubre que no solamente se encuentran perdidas muchas de sus pertenencias, sino que el ladrón puede estar todavía dentro del edificio.

Jennifer is a student at a university in Puerto Rico who was robbed when she left the college for the weekend. When she returns to school Sunday night with her friend, she discovers that not only are many of her belongings gone, but also the thief may still be inside the building.

Jennifer empacó sus cosas dentro del carro de su amiga para ir a casa de ella durante el fin de semana. Sabiendo que va a ayudar dando clase a los niños en la iglesia donde asiste la familia de su amiga, trae su laptop en una mochila y unos dulces para los niños.

Jennifer packs her things in her friend's car to go to her friend's house for the weekend. Knowing that she is going to help teach a children's class at the church where her friend's family attends, she brings her laptop in a backpack and some candy for the kids.

"¡Ay!" exclama, "¡Se me olvida mi guitarra!" Regresa a su pequeña **habitación** *en el dormitorio para recogerla. Es una guitarra nueva, un regalo de parte de su padre en su cumpleaños, y es una de sus* **posesiones** *más* **preciadas**.

"Oh!" she exclaims, "I'm forgetting the guitar!" She returns to her small dorm room to retrieve it. It's a new guitar, a gift from her father for her birthday, and it's one of her most prized possessions.

"¡Apúrate, Jennifer!" grita su amiga, esperándole en el carro. "¡Tenemos que llegar pronto porque cumple años mi hermanito y su fiesta empieza en media hora!"

"Hurry up, Jennifer!" Shouts her friend, waiting in the car. "We have to arrive there soon, because it's my little brother's birthday and his party starts in half an hour!"

"Ya voy, Luisa," grita Jennifer, agarrando su guitarra y despidiéndose de Samantha, una de sus amigas quien se queda el fin de semana en el colegio. En su universidad, pocos estudiantes se quedan los fines de semana en el campus; la mayoría se van con sus padres a sus casas o se hospedan con amigos.

"I'm coming, Luisa," Shouts Jennifer, grabbing her guitar and saying goodbye to Samantha, one of her friends who stays at the college on weekends. At her college, only a few students stay on campus for the weekend; the majority go home to their parents or stay with friends.

Luisa y Jennifer empiezan a manejar hasta el pueblo de Trujillo Alto, llegando justo a tiempo para la fiesta del hermanito de Luisa. Pasen un tiempo muy divertido con todos los niños, y Jennifer saca su guitarra para que puedan cantar la canción de feliz cumpleaños. Al final de la fiesta, el hermano de Luisa abre los regalos, comen pastel, y todos los niños se van a sus casas. Jennifer se queda en la **casa** *de Luisa y pasa la noche en el* **cuarto de huéspedes**.

Luisa and Jennifer start driving towards Trujillo Alto, arriving just in time for Luisa's brother's party. They have a great time with the kids, and Jennifer takes out her guitar so that they can sing happy birthday. At the end of the party, Luisa's brother opens present, they eat cake, and then all the kids go home. Jennifer stays at Luisa's house and spends the night in the guest room.

Al día siguiente, Luisa y Jennifer pasan el día en la playa, ya que es sábado. Manejan a una playa en la cuidad de Fajardo y juegan en el mar, regresando hasta la noche para hacer sus tareas de la universidad. El domingo, Jennifer toca guitarra en la iglesia para los niños y les enseña en una clase.

The next day, Luisa and Jennifer spend the day on the beach, since it is Saturday. They drive to a beach in the city of Fajardo and play in the ocean, returning home at night to do their university homework. On Sunday, Jennifer plays the guitar at church for the kids and teaches in a class.

*El domingo en la tarde, las muchachas necesitan regresar al **colegio**, entonces empacan todas sus cosas en el carro de Luisa de nuevo y regresan a la **universidad** en Bayamón. Se estacionan en el pequeño estacionamiento y se bajan con sus **cosas**. El campus está vacío, ya que los estudiantes que se quedan en los **dormitorios** por el fin de semana están cenando en la casa de un profesor que vive cerca, como suelen hacer los domingos por la noche.*

On Sunday night, the girls need to return to the college, so they pack their things into Luisa's car again and return to the university in Bayamón. They park in the small parking lot and get out of the car with their things. The campus is empty, since the students who stay in the dorms for the weekend are eating dinner at the house of a professor who lives nearby, as they usually do on Sunday nights.

*Jennifer se acerca al dormitorio con su mochila y guitarra y nota algo muy extraño. La **puerta** del dormitorio está abierta. Entra cautelosamente.*

Jennifer approaches the dorm, suitcase and backpack in hand, and notices something very strange. The door of the dorm is open. She enters cautiously.

*"¿**Hola**? ¿Hay alguien aquí?"*

"Hello? Is anyone here?"

Avanza unos pasos más y mira a su alrededor en el vestíbulo del dormitorio, y llama a su amiga.

She takes a few more steps and looks around the lobby of the dorm, and calls her friend.

"Oye, Luisa. Ven."

"Hey, Luisa, come here."

Luisa entra al dormitorio. "¿Por qué está abierta la puerta? ¿Hay alguien aquí?"

Luisa enters the dorm. "Why is the door open? Is someone here?"

*Las chicas entran la habitación de Jennifer, y para su sorpresa, hay **pertenencias** tiradas por todas partes. Cada **cajón** del **tocador** está abierto, y hay **ropa** esparcida por todo el piso. Hay varias cajas y bolsas tiradas en la cama. Al parecer, las únicas cosas que siguen en su lugar original son los libros escolares. Jennifer levanta un **joyero** vacío de la cama.*

The girls enter Jennifer's bedroom, and much to their surprise, there are belongings scattered everywhere. Every drawer of the dresser is open, and there are clothes thrown all over the floor. There are boxes and bags on the bed. It seems that the only things that remain in their place are the school books. Jennifer lifted her empty jewelry box from the bed.

*"Guau. Creo que esto se trata de un **robo**. Mira. Mi joyero está completamente vacío." Se acerca al **armario**. "Y aquí, **falta** más de la mitad de mi ropa."*

"Wow. I think we're looking at a robbery. Look. My jewelry box is completely empty." She approaches the closet. "And here, more than half of my clothes are missing."

*"Aquí es donde siempre pones tu secadora de cabello y todos tus productos de cabello, ¿verdad?" pregunta Luisa, señalando una caja plástica en un **estante**.*

445

"This is where you always put your hairdryer and your hair products, right?" asks Luisa, pointing to a plastic box on a shelf.

"Ah, sí. Tampoco está mi secadora ahí."

"Oh, yeah, my hairdryer isn't there either."

"Hay que hablar con la supervisora," dice Luisa. "Alguien de las otras estudiantes tiene tus cosas, estoy segura."

"We have to tell the supervisor," says Luisa. "One of the other students has your stuff, I'm sure of it."

"Sí, porque yo no tengo cosas **caras**— mis collares y anillos eran todos de pedrería falsa prácticamente. ¿Y ropa? Yo no creo que un **ladrón** va a venir a mi dormitorio nada más para **robar** unos pantalones y camisetas que ni son de marcas famosas. Qué ridículo."

"Yeah, because I don't have expensive things— my necklaces and rings are practically all made with fake stones. And clothing? I don't think a thief is going to come to my dorm just to rob some pants and shirts that aren't even branded famous. How ridiculous!"

"Ya sé," responde Luisa. "Y siempre llevas tu computadora y tu guitarra a mi casa los fines de semanas, entonces aquí nunca queda nada de tanto **valor**."

"I know," replies Luisa. "And you always bring your computer and guitar to my house on weekends, so nothing of value ever stays here."

"Exacto," dice Jennifer, inspeccionando la cama y armario de su compañera del cuarto. "Oye, ¡todas las pertenencias de mi compañera siguen aquí! Solo le faltan unas bolsas, carteras, y mochilas."

"Exactly," says Jennifer, inspecting her roommate's bed and closet. "Hey, all of my roommate's stuff is still here! She's only missing some bags, purses, and backpacks."

"Qué extraño," contesta Luisa. "Jaja ya sé. Es porque el ladrón está usando las bolsas de ella para llevarse tus cosas."

"That's weird," answers Luisa. "Haha oh I know. It's because the robber is using her bags to carry your stuff."

"Ah, pues sí, eso tiene sentido," responde Jennifer.

"Oh, well sure, that makes sense," replies Jennifer.

Luisa mira adentro de los cajones del tocador. "¿Qué es lo que guardas aquí normalmente?"

Luisa looks inside the dresser drawers. "What do you normally keep in here?"

"Oh, ahí guardo mi ropa interior."

"Oh, I store my underwear in there."

Luisa se ríe. "Esto tiene que ser una broma. ¡El cajón está vacío!"

Luisa laughs. "This has to be a joke. The drawer is empty!"

"Jajaja," ríe Jennifer. "¡Creo que es una ladrona, no un ladrón!"

"Hahaha," laughs Jennifer. "This has got to be a female thief, not a male!"

Las chicas se ríen por un rato, a pesar de que ahora Jennifer deben estar triste por ya no tener casi nada de ropa para ponerse. Luisa para de reír de repente.

The girls giggle for a while, even though Jennifer should be sad about not having hardly any clothes to wear now. All of a sudden, Luisa stops laughing.

"Oye, Jennifer. ¿Y si el ladrón todavía está aquí adentro del dormitorio?" Las chicas se miran, asustadas.

"Hey, Jennifer, what if the thief is still here inside the dorm?" The girls look at each other, frightened.

Quiz

1. ¿Qué olvida Jennifer en su dormitorio?
a. su mochila
b. su guitarra
c. su laptop

2. ¿A dónde va Jennifer durante el fin de semana?
a. a su casa
b. a su dormitorio
c. a la casa de Luisa

3. ¿Qué pasa cuando Jennifer regresa a su dormitorio el domingo?
a. sus amigas le sorprenden con una fiesta
b. descubre un desastre en su cuarto
c. descubre un animal en su cuarto

4. ¿Cuáles de las siguientes cosas NO están perdidas?
a. ropa
b. joyería
c. libros escolares

5. ¿Qué tipo de persona es el ladrón, según Jennifer y Luisa?
a. una mujer
b. un hombre
c. un niño

Answers

1. b
2. c
3. b
4. c
5. a

Vocabulario/Vocabulary

- *Habitación* --- Bedroom
- *Posesiones* --- Possessions
- *Preciadas* --- Prized
- *Casa* --- House
- *Cuarto de huéspedes* --- Guest room

- *El día siguiente* --- The next day
- *Colegio* --- School/college
- *Universidad* --- University
- *Cosas* --- Things
- *Dormitorios* --- Dorms
- *Puerta* --- Door
- *¿Hay alguien aquí?* --- Is anyone there?
- *Pertenencias* --- Belongings
- *Cajón* --- Drawer
- *Tocador* --- Dresser
- *Ropa* --- Clothing
- *Joyero* --- Jewelry box
- *Robo* --- Robbery
- *Armario* --- Closet
- *Falta* --- Is missing, from the verb "faltar" (to miss)
- *Estante* --- Shelf
- *Cara (s)* --- Expensive
- *Ladrón* --- Thief, robber
- *Robar* ---- To steal/to rob
- *Valor* --- Value

Capítulo Dos

Jennifer y Luisa siguen revisando el dormitorio para ver si más cosas están perdidas. Llegan los demás estudiantes y la directora de la escuela, e inician una búsqueda para ver si algún estudiante está escondiendo las cosas en su recamara. Ya que no aparece ninguna de las pertenencias perdidas, la directora decide llamar a la policía.

Jennifer and Luisa continue to check the dorm to see if any more things are missing. The other students and the school's director arrive, and they begin a search to see if any student is hiding things in his or her bedroom. Since none of the missing items turn up, the director decides to call the police.

"¡Quizá el ladrón está todavía aquí, esperándonos!" dice Luisa, susurrando.

"Maybe the thief is still in here, waiting for us!" whispers Luisa.

*"Puede ser," dice Jennifer. "Pero no te asustes todavía. No se escuchan **ruidos** ni nada."*

"Could be," says Jennifer. "But don't get scared yet. I don't hear sounds or anything."

*Las chicas salen de la habitación y empiezan a caminar por el pasillo del dormitorio lentamente y sin hacer ruido. Entran en la primera habitación, y observan que todo sigue en su lugar, y no hay nadie **escondiéndose** adentro. Así encuentran el segundo cuarto que entran, y el tercero también. Checan todas las habitaciones, pero no encuentran a nadie, y nada está movido de su lugar.*

The girls come out of the room and begin to walk through the hallway to the dorm slowly and without making any noise. They enter the first room, and observe that everything is in its place, and no one is hiding within. They find the conditions of the second and third rooms to be the same. They check all the bedrooms, but do not find anyone, and nothing is moved out of place.

"No entiendo por qué solo quiere mis cosas," dice Jennifer, suspirando.

448

"I don't understand why she just wants my things," Jennifer says, sighing.

*"Pues por eso te digo, la **ladrona** tiene que ser alguien de aquí," responde Luisa.*

"Well, that's why I'm telling you, the thief must be someone from here," answers Luisa.

*En este momento, empiezan a **llegar** los demás estudiantes. Jennifer y Luisa les preguntan si saben algo acerca del robo, pero nadie sabe nada. Con la ayuda de algunos otros estudiantes, Jennifer y Luisa revisan otras partes del campus para **evidencia** del robo. En la cafetería, encuentran que unas cajas de latas de soda están **perdidas**, pero todo lo demás está en su lugar, ya que la puerta del almacén tiene un **candado** puesto. El dormitorio de los hombres no fue **afectado**, ni ninguna otra parte del campus.*

At that moment, the rest of the students begin to arrive. Jennifer and Luisa ask them if they know something about the robbery, but no one knows anything. With help from a few other students, Jennifer and Luisa check other parts of campus for evidence of theft. In the cafeteria, they find that some boxes of soda cans are missing, but everything else is in its place, since the pantry door has a lock. The men's dorm is not affected, and neither is any other part of the campus.

*Después de un rato, entra una de las otras muchachas al dormitorio y se da cuenta que su violín, que normalmente deja guardado en el vestíbulo del dormitorio, está **ausente**. Desconsolada, llama a la directora del colegio por teléfono. La directora llega al campus en diez minutos y habla con la supervisora del dormitorio de las muchachas, con la dueña del violín, y con Jennifer y Luisa. Revisa el cuarto de Jennifer y toma algunas **fotos**. Cuando llegan la mayoría de los estudiantes, los reúne en la cafetería para dar un **anuncio**.*

After a while, one of the other girls enters the bedroom and realizes that her violin, which she normally keeps in the bedroom lobby, is missing. Disconsolate, she calls the college director on the phone. The director arrives on campus in ten minutes and speaks to the girls' bedroom supervisor, with the violin's owner, and with Jennifer and Luisa. She checks Jennifer's room and takes some pictures. When the majority of the students arrive, she gathers them into the cafeteria to make an announcement.

*"Estudiantes," anuncia la directora, "como ya saben algunos de ustedes, algunas pertenencias de algunas de las muchachas están perdidas. No sabemos si es un **hurto** simple, llevado a cabo por alguno de ustedes, o si alguien de afuera quiere hacernos **daño**. Por eso necesitamos hacer una **revisión** de los cuartos y pertenencias de cada uno de ustedes, para **asegurar** que no tenemos un ladrón entre nosotros. Estoy confiada en la honestidad e integridad de ustedes, mis estudiantes, y espero no encontrar las pertenencias perdidas en sus habitaciones, pero tenemos que estar seguros antes de llamar a la **policía**. Hay que **realizar una búsqueda** en este momento, entonces pedimos que ustedes permanezcan aquí en la cafetería mientras las otras autoridades de la escuela y yo entramos a las recamaras."*

"Students," the director begins, "as some of you already know, some of the girls' belongings are missing. We do not know if this is a minor robbery, perpetrated by one of you all, or if someone outside campus wants to do us harm. That is why we must carry out a thorough search of the bedrooms and belongings of each one of you, to make sure that we do not have a thief among us. I trust in the honesty and integrity of all of you, my students, and I hope not to find any of the missing items in your rooms, but we have to be sure before calling the police. We must begin the search right now, so we ask you to stay here in the cafeteria while the other school authorities and I search the bedrooms.

*Unas horas después, las autoridades terminan la búsqueda sin encontrar ninguno de los objetos perdidos. En seguida, la directora hace una llamada a la **comisaría** para **denunciar** el robo.*

A few hours later, the authorities finish the search without finding any of the missing objects. Right away, the director makes a call to the police station to report the robbery.

"Buenas noches," dice la directora. "Quiero denunciar un **delito.**"

"Good evening," says the director. "I would like to report a crime."

"¿Cuál es su nombre completo?" responde el agente.

"What is your full name?" responds the agent.

"Es Marta Berenice Lobos Cárdenas."

"It's Marta Berenice Lobos Cardenas."

"¿Qué tipo de delito deseas denunciar?"

"What type of crime do you wish to report?"

"Un robo de algunas pertenencias de nuestros estudiantes."

"A theft of some of our students' belongings."

"¿Hay alguien herido?"

"Is anyone hurt?"

"No."

"No."

"Ok, necesito su dirección y algunos datos más para empezar a hacer nuestra **investigación.**"

"Ok, I need your address and a few more details to begin our investigation."

La directora explica con más detalle acerca de la **naturaleza del crimen** *y los objetos perdidos. Después de veinte minutos, un* **vehículo patrullero** *llega al estacionamiento. Varios policías entran al dormitorio, toman fotos, y anotan los objetos robados. Hacen preguntas a varios de los estudiantes. Después de un par de horas se alistan para irse, llenando lo último del papeleo con las autoridades de la escuela.*

The director explains in greater detail the nature of the crime and the missing objects. Ten minutes later, a patrol car arrives in the parking lot. A few police officers enter the bedroom, take pictures, and write down which objects were stolen. They ask some students a few questions. After a few hours, they get ready to leave, completing the last of the paperwork with the school authorities.

"Aquí tiene la denuncia," dice un oficial, entregando unos papeles a la directora. "Vigile mejor, que hay ladrones y **carteristas** *por todos lados. Hay que tomar mejores* **medidas de seguridad.**"

"Here is the official report," says the officer, handing some papers to the director. "Keep watch over everything better; there are thieves and pick-pockets everywhere. You need to take better security measures."

"Gracias, oficial," responde la directora. "Tiene razón. Esperamos comprar un sistema de alarmas y seguir todos sus consejos. Muchas gracias por atendernos rápidamente."

"Thank you, officer," the director replies. "You are right. We hope to buy an alarm system and follow all of your advice. Thank you for responding to the situation so quickly."

"De nada, Señora. Nos retiramos; que pasen una buena noche."

"You're welcome, madam. We'll be going now, have a great night."

Se van las patrullas, y Jennifer se pone a recoger el desorden en su habitación. Todos se van a dormir esa noche un poco preocupados por la situación. La ciudad en donde viven es peligrosa, pero esta es la primera vez que los estudiantes experimentan un robo de primera mano.

The patrols leave, and Jennifer begins clean up the mess in her room. Everyone goes to sleep that night a little worried about the situation. The city in which they live is dangerous, but this is the first time that the students have ever experienced theft first-hand.

La dueña del violín pasa un tiempo en su habitación llorando con varias de sus compañeras a su alrededor. Todas hacen su mejor esfuerzo para consolarla, pero está muy alterada por el hecho de que ya no puede tocar en un recital programado para el siguiente sábado.

The owner of the violin spends some time crying in her room with a few of her roommates gathered around her. Everyone does their best to console her, but she is very upset due to the fact that she can no longer play in next Saturday's recital.

Jennifer está un poco triste por la pérdida de su joyería y blusas favoritas, pero está agradecida que todavía tiene su laptop y su guitarra. En las semanas que siguen, algunas de las muchachas le regalan prendas de vestir y le prestan artículos de tocador.

Jennifer is a little sad over the losing of her jewelry and favorite blouses, but she's thankful that she still has her laptop and guitar. In the next few weeks, some of the girls give her clothes and lend her some toiletries.

La vida en la universidad continua como siempre, pero la policía todavía no averigua quien es el ladrón. La escuela decide investigar los precios para instalar un sistema de alarmas y mejores candados a las puertas para evitar futuros robos.

Life in the college continues as always, but the police still do not find out who the thief is. The school decides to start checking prices of alarm systems and better locks on the doors to avoid further thefts.

Quiz

1. ¿Qué instrumento musical está perdido?
a. una guitarra
b. un piano
c. un violín

2. ¿Qué hace la directora cuando llega al campus?
a. toma fotos e inicia una búsqueda
b. llama a la policía
c. averigua quien es el ladrón

3. ¿Quién llama a la comisaría?
a. Jennifer
b. el policía
c. la directora

4. ¿En cuantos minutos llega la policía al campus?
a. 10
b. 20
c. 15

5. ¿Qué consejo da el oficial a la directora?
a. buscar al ladrón por la noche
b. comprar un sistema de alarma

c. llenar el papeleo

Answers

1. c
2. a
3. c
4. a
5. b

Vocabulario/Vocabulary

- *Ruidos* --- Noises
- *Escondiéndose* --- Hiding (oneself)
- *Ladrona* --- Female thief
- *Llegar* --- To arrive
- *Evidencia* --- Evidence
- *Perdida(s)* --- Lost
- *Candado* --- Lock
- *Afectado* --- Affected
- *Ausente* --- Absent
- *Fotos* --- Photos
- *Anuncio* --- Announcement
- *Hurto* – theft
- *Daño* --- Harm
- *Revisión* --- Inspection
- *Asegurar* --- To make sure
- *Policía* --- Police
- *Realizar una búsqueda* --- Perform a search
- *Comisaría* --- Police station
- *Denunciar* --- To report
- *Delito* --- Crime
- *Investigación* --- Investigation
- *Naturaleza del crimen* --- Nature of the crime
- *Vehículo patrullero* --- Patrol vehicle
- *Carteristas* --- Pick-pockets
- *Medidas de seguridad* --- Security measures

Capítulo Tres

Pasan varias semanas, y la policía no encuentra al ladrón. Jennifer y Luisa ven un reporte acerca de los robos en las noticias. Una noche, Jennifer ve a alguien afuera de su ventana, y empieza a investigar por su cuenta. Ella ayuda a descubrir a la persona culpable de los delitos, y por fin se paran los robos en su vecindario.

A few weeks pass, and the police still do not find the thief. Jennifer and Luisa see a report about the robberies on the news. One night, Jennifer sees someone outside her window, and begins to do some investigating on her own. She helps discover the person guilty of the crimes, and finally the robberies in her neighborhood come to an end.

*Pasan semanas, y todavía no hay **noticias** sobre la identidad del ladrón. Sin embargo, los estudiantes oyen noticias de varios robos que están ocurriendo en el mismo **vecindario** donde está situada su universidad. Un jueves por la noche en la escuela, Jennifer y Luisa ven un programa de noticias que menciona los robos en el celular de Luisa.*

The weeks drag on and on, and still there is no news about the robber's identity. However, the students hear news reports of various robberies occurring in the same neighborhood in which the university is located. One Thursday night, Jennifer and Luisa watch a news program that mentions the thefts on Luisa's phone.

*"Cierren bien las puertas de sus casas y de sus autos," dice la reportera. "La **inseguridad** está aumentando en nuestro pueblo, y reportamos una **serie** de robos en el área de Sierras de Bayamón. Nos informan los oficiales de la policía que los responsables de estos **crímenes** aparentemente roban artículos de mujeres solamente. En este momento, no tenemos más **información**, pero pedimos a todo nuestro **público**, que ayude a denunciar cualquier delito de esta **índole** del cual se enteren."*

"Make sure to properly close the doors of your homes and cars," says the reporter. "There is a growing lack of security in our town, and a series of robberies are being reported from the Sierras de Bayamón area. Officials inform us that the responsible parties for these crimes apparently steal only women's belongings. At this time, we have no further information, but we ask our viewers to please report any crime of this kind that you may witness."

*"Pues, parece que nuestra ladrona solo quiere robar artículos de mujeres," dice Jennifer, riéndose. "**Se me hace** muy ridículo."*

"Well, it seems that our thief only wants to steal women's stuff," says Jennifer, laughing. "That seems so ridiculous to me."

"No es ridículo si es una mujer, y no puede comprar las cosas que necesita," contesta Luisa. "Y es más fácil entrar en un dormitorio que no está bien cerrado, como el nuestro, o una casa habitada por gente de clase media, que intentar robar cosas caras de la gente rica, con sus sistemas de seguridad de alta-tecnología."

"It's not ridiculous if she's a woman, and can't afford the things she needs," answers Luisa. "And it's easier to enter a dorm that's not so secure, like ours, or a middle-class person's house, than to try to steal expensive things from rich people, with their high-tech security systems."

"Hmm, tienes razón," responde Jennifer. "¿Tienes experiencia como ladrona, o qué?"

"Hmmm, you're right," replies Jennifer. "Do you have experience as a thief, or what?'

Luisa se ríe. "Sí, claro," le dice, guiñando el ojo, "tengo experiencia desde el kínder, robando tus colores y lápices y así, ¿te acuerdas?"

Luisa laughs. "Yes, of course," she says, winking, "I have experience from kindergarten, stealing your crayons and pencils and stuff, do you remember?"

"Jaja, sí, me acuerdo."

"Haha, yeah, I remember."

*Después de pasar un rato recordando los viejos tiempos, las muchachas regresan a sus respectivas habitaciones en el dormitorio y se duermen. A las tres de la **madrugada**, un ruido despierta a Jennifer. Ve una sombra pasar por los árboles en el estacionamiento. Se le pone la **piel de gallina**,* *sintiendo la presencia de una persona afuera de su ventana. Tiene ganas de **gritar** y despertar a su compañera, pero guarda silencio y trata de **mantener la calma. Es ella,** piensa. **¡La ladrona!***

After spending some time reminiscing on the good old days, the girls return to their respective dorm rooms and sleep. At three in the morning, a noise wakes Jennifer. She sees a shadow pass through the trees in the parking lot. She gets goosebumps, feeling the presence of someone outside her window. She wants to scream and wake up her roommate, but she keeps silent and tries to remain calm. It's her, she thinks. The thief!

*La figura de una mujer se acerca más y más a la ventana de Jennifer. Las cortinas están cerradas, pero Jennifer puede ver por medio del espacio entre los paneles de tela y la ventana. Tiene mucho miedo, pero está **resuelta** a seguir viendo para saber quién es la **culpable.** Unos segundos pasan, y la figura se desaparece. De repente, se escucha el sonido de alguien moviendo el **pomo** de la puerta del dormitorio, y Jennifer quiere gritar por miedo. Trata de despertar a su compañera de cuarto, pero la muchacha tiene sueño profundo y no se levanta.*

A woman's figure gets closer and closer to Jennifer's window. The curtains are closed, but Jennifer can see through a space between the panels of fabric and the window. She is very scared, but determined to keep watching in order to see the guilty. A few seconds pass, and the figure vanishes. Suddenly, Jennifer hears the sound of someone turning the doorknob of the dorm door, and Jennifer wants to shriek with fright. She tries to wake up her roommate, but the girl is a deep sleeper and doesn't move.

*Jennifer se levanta de su cama y camina hacia la puerta de su recamara. Justo cuando va a girar el pomo, la puerta se abre con fuerza desde el otro lado, y Jennifer **suelta** un grito. La otra persona grita también.*

Jennifer gets out of bed and walks toward her bedroom door. Just when she's about to the turn the knob, the door opens forcefully front the other side, and Jennifer lets out a scream. The other person screams too.

*"¿Sam?" dice Jennifer, al ver a su amiga Samanta, quien vive en el dormitorio al otro lado del estacionamiento. "¿Qué estás haciendo? Me tienes toda **asustada,** pensando que eres esa ladrona, jaja."*

"Sam?" says Jennifer, seeing her friend Samantha before her, who lives in the dorm on the other side of the parking lot. "What are you doing? You're scaring me into thinking you're that thief, haha."

"Jaja, claro que no. Estoy aquí para preguntarte si tienes un antiácido. ¡Ya no tengo, y traigo un dolor de estómago horrible! Sé que tu padeces de lo mismo. ¿Por casualidad tienes una pastilla que me puedas regalar?"

"Haha, of course not. I'm here to ask you if you have an antacid pill. I ran out, and I've got a horrible stomach ache! I know you suffer from the same thing sometimes. Do you happen to have a pill you could give me?"

"Ah, ok, sí. Ten," dice Jennifer, dándole una pastilla. "Espero que te mejores."

"Oh, ok, yeah, here," says Jennifer, handing her a pill. "I hope you feel better."

"Gracias, Jen," responde Sam, abrazándola. "Y perdón por asustarte."

"Thanks, Jen," replies Sam, hugging her. "Sorry for scaring you."

"Oh, está bien, Sam, no te preocupes. Dulces sueños."

"Oh, it's fine, Sam, don't worry. Sweet dreams."

"Dulces sueños, Jen."

"Sweet dreams, Jen."

*Samanta se va, y Jennifer se duerme de nuevo. No piensa nada del **incidente** de la noche anterior hasta que ve a Samanta atascándose de comida mientras desayuna en la mañana. ¿**No se supone que está enferma del estómago?** piensa Jennifer.*

Samantha leaves, and Jennifer goes back to sleep. She thinks nothing of last night's incident until she sees Samantha stuffing herself with food during breakfast in the morning. Doesn't she have stomach problems? Jennifer thinks.

Sus sospechas aumentan más cuando nota que Samanta come mucho pan y pastel en el almuerzo a mediodía. Decide actuar sobre su presentimiento, y entra al dormitorio de Samanta para espiar en su recamara mientras ella está asistiendo a una clase en la tarde.

Her suspicions are raised even more when she sees Samantha eating lots of bread and cake at lunchtime. She decides to act upon her hunches, and enters Samantha's dorm to snoop inside her bedroom while she's in an afternoon class.

*Jennifer descubre que sus **sospechas** son **válidas** cuando entra el cuarto de Samanta y ve en su mesita de noche la pastilla antiácida sin usar. **Algo muy extraño está pasando aquí,** piensa Jennifer, revisando el resto de la recamara de su amiga. No ve a ninguno de los objetos robados, pero siente que Samanta está involucrada en algo **sospechoso**.*

Jennifer's suspicions are confirmed when she enters Samantha's room and sees the unused antacid pill lying on her nightstand. Something really weird is going on here, Jennifer thinks, checking the rest of her friend's room. She doesn't see any of the stolen objects, but she has a feeling that Samantha is involved in something suspect.

*Va directamente a la oficina de la directora, donde le cuenta acerca de la noche anterior y la pastilla. La directora no cree que Samanta es la ladrona, pero de todos modos decide **llamar** al policía para que le **aconsejen**. El oficial le dice que van a colocar varias patrullas por el vecindario y la universidad para las siguientes noches para atraparla en el acto.*

She goes directly to the director's office, where she tells her about last night and the pill. The director doesn't believe Samantha's the thief, but she decides to call the police for advice anyway. The officer tells her that they will place a few patrol cars throughout the neighborhood and by the university for the next few nights to catch her in the act.

*La policía no tiene que esperar ni dos noches, porque sorprenden a Samanta intentando robar una casa cerca del colegio esa misma noche. Resulta que trabaja con otras señoritas delincuentes, y los oficiales hallaron el violín y la ropa y joyería de Jennifer en la casa de una de sus socias en el crimen. El misterio resuelto, Jennifer y el resto de las muchachas ya pueden descansar, sabiendo que las criminales están **detenidas**. Sin embargo, de vez en cuando se sienten tristes por perder a su amiga.*

The police don't even have to wait two nights, because they catch Samantha trying to rob a house nearby the college that very same night. It turns out that she works with a few other girls with criminal records, and the officers found the violin and Jennifer's clothing and jewelry in the house of one of Samantha's partners in crime. The mystery solved, Jennifer and the rest of the girls can now rest, knowing that the criminals are in custody. However, every now and then they are sad for the loss of their friend.

Quiz

1. ¿Qué tipo de artículos están robando los ladrones?
a. cosas de niños
b. cosas de mujeres
c. cosas de hombres

2. ¿A qué hora ve Jennifer a alguien por su ventana?
a. a las 3 de la tarde
b. a las 3 de la madrugada
c. a las 10 de la noche

3. ¿Quién está afuera de la ventana de Jennifer?
a. Samanta
b. Luisa
c. la directora

4. ¿Por qué piensa Jennifer que Samanta es la ladrona?
a. porque encuentra su ropa en el cuarto de Samanta
b. porque le ve robando cosas
c. porque encuentra la pastilla sin usar en el cuarto de Samanta

5. ¿Quiénes son los ladrones?
a. Luisa y sus amigas
b. Samanta y sus amigas
c. una mujer de la calle

Answers

1. b
2. b
3. a
4. c
5. b

Vocabulario/Vocabulary

- *Noticias* --- News
- *Colonia* --- Neighborhood
- *Inseguridad* --- Lack of safety, insecurity
- *Serie* --- Series
- *Crímenes* --- Crimes
- *Información* --- Information
- *Público* --- Viewers/public
- *Índole* --- Type/nature
- *se me hace* --- It seems to me
- *Madrugada* --- The early morning

- *Piel de gallina* --- Goosebumps
- *Gritar* --- To scream
- *Mantener la calma* --- To keep calm
- *Resuelta(o)* – Determined/solved
- *Culpable* --- Guilty/culprit
- *Pomo* – Knob/handle
- *Suelta* – Release (from the verb "soltar" meaning to let go of)
- *Asustada(o)* – Frightened/scared
- *Incidente* --- Incident
- *Sospechas* --- Suspicions
- *Válidas* --- Valid
- *Sospechoso* --- Suspicious
- *Llamar* --- To call
- *Aconsejen* --- They advise (from the verb "Aconsejar" meaning to advise)
- *Detenida(s)* --- Detained/arrested

11. La Familia Cooper

La familia Cooper era una familia a la que le encantaban hacer paseos y viajes juntos. Connor era el nombre del padre; Amelia era el nombre de la madre; Noah era el nombre del hijo, quien tenía 15 años y Agatha el nombre de la hija, quien tenía 14 años. Siempre salían a todos los eventos y fiestas que hubiese en la ciudad.

Un día, escucharon que a la ciudad iría el parque de atracciones móvil más grande y divertido de todo el mundo, por lo que decidieron que debían ir sí o sí.

-Connor: Chicos, ¿Vieron que va a venir el parque XTRM?

-Noah: Si papá, y se ve genial.

-Agatha: Sería genial papi.

-Amelia: ¿Tú crees que debamos ir?

-Connor: Absolutamente, ¿Cuándo tendremos otra oportunidad de asistir?

-Amelia: ¿Qué fecha es?

-Connor: Cinco y seis de Noviembre.

-Noah: Yo tengo un torneo de béisbol el tres y cuatro de Noviembre, así que estaré libre para esas fechas.

-Amelia: Tu Agatha, ¿Tienes algo para esa fecha?

-Agatha: Creo que no mamá.

-Connor: Yo pediré esos días libres en el trabajo. Así que creo que ya está decidido, iremos.

-Amelia: Listo entonces, lo anotaré en el calendario.

Compraron los boletos, apartaron las entradas y esperaron a que llegaran los dos días.

Llegado el cinco de Noviembre, partieron entonces desde muy temprano hacia aquel parque de diversiones. Eran la tercera familia en la fila para entrar al parque. Tan pronto se abrieron las puertas para entrar, ellos entraron.

-Agatha: Papá, ¿Podemos montarnos en la montaña rusa primero?

-Connor: ¿En cuál? Hay tres

-Agatha: En la más grande, esa de allá.

-Connor: ¿Segura que puedes con tanto?

-Agatha: Sólo mírame.

-Connor: De acuerdo.

Y fueron entonces Agatha y Connor a montarse en la montaña rusa más alta del parque. Mientras ellos se montaban allí, Amelia y Noah fueron a la casa del terror.

-Noah: No fue la mejor casa del terror en la que he estado.

-Amelia: Pero estuvo bastante bien.

-Noah: Eso no lo puedo negar, que usaran tanta sangre falsa mejoró bastante la experiencia.

-Amelia: Y los efectos especiales que usaron para crear a los fantasmas fueron geniales.

-Noah: Tienes razón.

Estuvieron todo el día en aquel parque, se montaron en exactamente la mitad de las atracciones, para montarse en las restantes el día siguiente.

Ese primer día se montaron en dos montañas rusas, en la casa del terror, manejaron los go karts, se lanzaron en la tirolina, jugaron golf, entraron a la casa de los espejos, se subieron a la rueda de la fortuna, lanzaron dardos e hicieron y usaron muchas otras atracciones que allí habían.

Regresando a casa todos comentaron cuáles habían sido sus atracciones favoritas, cuáles les parecían las mejores, cuáles las peores y así hablaron durante todo el trayecto a casa. Estaban agotados, estuvieron diez horas en el parque de atracciones, corriendo y jugando, ya no les quedaba mucha energía. Debían acostarse a dormir lo más temprano posible para recuperar fuerzas y volver a salir al día siguiente igual de temprano para que pudieran montarse en la mitad de las atracciones que faltaban.

Llegaron a casa, cenaron, y acordaron bañarse todos en la noche para poder salir temprano al día siguiente y disfrutar al máximo el parque de diversiones. Mientras Noah se estaba bañando, estaba tan cansado que se quedó dormido por un segundo, el que fue suficiente para que se resbalara y luego no pudiera mantener el equilibrio, por lo que se cayó y se golpeó en el tobillo. Sus padres fueron a auxiliarlo, lo levantaron del suelo, lo secaron, lo llevaron hasta la cama, donde pudo vestirse y allí le revisaron el tobillo.

-Amelia: Oh Dios, no puede ser.

-Noah: ¿Qué pasa?

-Amelia: Connor, me temo que tenías razón

-Noah: ¿Qué sucede mamá? ¿De qué hablas?

-Amelia: Me temo que tienes un esguince hijo.

-Noah: ¿Qué es eso?

-Amelia: Es una....

-Connor: Es una lesión, por la que deberás tomar reposo hasta que se mejore.

-Noah: ¿Y qué tiene de malo? ¿Por qué mamá está tan preocupada?

-Connor: Debes empezar el reposo desde hoy. No podrás ir mañana al parque.

En ese momento Noah se sintió muy molesto, se perdería el segundo día del mejor parque de atracciones móvil del mundo gracias a un segundo de sueño.

-Noah: No es justo, cerré los ojos solo un segundo y ocurrió esto.

-Connor: Cálmate Noah, tuviste suerte de que fue en la ducha y no manejando un carro o pudiste haber muerto.

Noah sabía que su padre tenía razón, por lo que comenzó a calmarse y sentirse un poco mejor consigo mismo. De igual manera, estaba preocupado de que sus padres también faltaran al parque para cuidarlo, pues no quería que ellos se vieran perjudicados por su lesión.

-Noah: Vayan mañana al parque, sin mí.

-Amelia: ¿Qué te sucede? No te dejaré aquí solo con una lesión en el pie.

-Noah: Podemos pedirle a la tía que venga a cuidarme, realmente no quiero que ustedes también *pierdan su segundo día en el parque por mi culpa. Vayan y disfruten mucho y tómense fotos para que puedan venir y contarme.*

Así sucedió, al día siguiente salieron Amelia, Agatha y Connor bastante temprano al parque a disfrutar su segundo día. Al principio se sintieron un poco mal por haber dejado a Noah en casa con la tía, pero Noah tenía razón, era mejor que fueran y le mostraran fotos y videos de las atracciones en las cuáles él no se había podido subir.

Durante todo el día, Agatha le enviaba fotos a Noah de las atracciones en las que se montaban, y Noah, aunque estaba bastante celoso de que él no podía montarse estaba contento de que su familia estuviese disfrutando tanto de aquel momento.

Quiz:

1. ¿Quién tuvo un esguince en el tobillo?
a. Connor
b. Amelia
c. Agatha
d. Noah

2. ¿Cómo se llamaba el parque?
a. XTRM
b. MRTX
c. XTMR
d. XMRT
e. XMTR

3. ¿En cuál de estas atracciones NO se montaron el primer día?
a. Montaña rusa
b. Tirolina
c. Ascensor
d. Go karts
e. Casa de espejos

4. ¿Qué fecha iba el parque a la ciudad?
a. 11/04-05
b. 12/04-05
c. 11/02-03
d. 02/03-10
e. 11/06-07

5. ¿De qué era el torneo de Noah?
a. Natación
b. Básquet
c. Polo
d. Béisbol
e. Waterpolo

Answers:

1) d
2) a
3) c
4) a
5) d

Vocabulario/Vocabulary

- *Encantaban* --- Loved
- *Juntos* --- Together
- *Madre* --- Mother
- *Padre* --- Father
- *Escuchar* --- Hear
- *Mundo* --- World
- *Eventos* --- Events
- *Parque de atracciones* --- Amusement park
- *Oportunidad* --- Opportunity
- *Fecha* --- Date
- *Noviembre* --- November
- *Calendario* --- Calendar
- *Tercera* --- Third
- *Montaña rusa* --- Roller coaster
- *Casa del terror* --- Horror house
- *Fantasmas* --- Ghosts
- *Espejos* --- Mirrors
- *Cenar* --- To have dinner
- *Resbalar* --- slip/slide
- *Esguince* --- Sprain
- *Tobillo* --- Ankle.

12. La Cita

Hoy en día, mucha gente conoce a su pareja por medio de las redes sociales, aplicaciones de citas en sus celulares, o en sitios web de citas. Muchos dicen que la caballerosidad ya no existe, ya que los hombres ya no suelen abrir puertas a las mujeres, ni pagarles la cena. Algunos dicen que esto es debido al movimiento "feminista" y el hecho que las mujeres hoy en día demandan "igualdad de derechos". Yo, siendo una mujer de 35 años del siglo veintiuno, estoy de acuerdo que debemos tener esa "igualdad de derechos" que tanto buscamos, pero algo en mí extraña la caballerosidad de los antiguos tiempos. Me llamo Samanta, y soy una mujer latina, inteligente y trabajadora, y estoy buscando a alguien con quien compartir la vida. Ya me estoy dando cuenta que esto no es nada fácil. Digamos que no tengo suerte con las **citas amorosas**. Déjame contarte algunas de mis experiencias recientes...

Samanta es una mujer latina de 35 años que busca compartir su vida con alguien. Casi todas sus citas amorosas terminaban mal, pero aun así sigue con la esperanza de encontrar a la persona perfecta y casarse algún día.

Un día en septiembre, conoce a un hombre que tiene los mismos gustos que ella, y salen a comer a un restaurante chino. El hombre es simpático, se llevan bien y para Samanta parece ser el final en su búsqueda.

Es lunes, el 19 de septiembre. Estoy revisando una aplicación en mi celular cuando veo un mensaje de un hombre en mi buzón.

"Hola, Samanta. Veo que eres una mujer amante de la **comida china**. A mí también me gusta mucho. **¿Te gustaría salir a comer conmigo?**"

Reviso su perfil, y veo que tiene varias fotos donde está comiendo comida china en **restaurantes** bonitos. **Ah...mínimo no es un mentiroso...**

Veo que tiene dos perros— también me gustan a mí— y que le gusta viajar, ya que tiene fotos de diferentes países en su perfil. Así que...Decidí responderle

"Hola, Roberto. Gracias por tu mensaje. Creo que tenemos algunas cosas en común, y sí, a mí me encanta la comida china. ¿Vamos? Tú decides el día y la hora."

Unas horas después, Roberto me confirma el día y la hora para **cenar**, y cuando llega el gran día, me siento bastante emocionada. Roberto tiene 37 años, no está casado, tiene un buen trabajo (según su perfil) y, al parecer, ¡tenemos muchas cosas en común! Me pongo uno de mis vestidos favoritos, uno rojo que me regaló mi hermana, y voy para el restaurante chino.

Al llegar, no veo a nadie parecido a Roberto por ningún lado. Empiezo a preocuparme.

Y... ¿si no es como aparece en sus fotos? Tal vez me está mintiendo, y realmente es un hombre de unos 80 años...

Pero mis dudas desaparecen cuando Roberto entra el restaurante, y se ve igual a su foto. Se acerca con una sonrisa agradable en su rostro, me saluda, y se sienta en la **mesa** en frente de mí.

"Samanta, tengo que decirte... ¡este restaurante es uno de mis favoritos! Me **encanta** la comida china. Sabes, aquí la comida no es exactamente **autentica**, ¡pero **sabe** tan **deliciosa**! ¿Y qué tal los **palillos**, ¿eh?" Se pone a jugar con los palillos.

"Em, pues, sí...de hecho esos palillos son para..."

Me interrumpe, agitando los palillos en mi cara. "¡Son para jugar! Qué divertido, ¿No?"

*"Bueno, em, yo no los uso para jugar." Acomodo mi **servilleta** y saco un **tenedor**. "De hecho, no los uso. Prefiero usar el tenedor."*

*"Jajaja, el tenedor. **Qué aburrido**. Los tenedores son para peinarse, como hacen en esa película de la Sirenita de Disney."*

Roberto procede a cantar una canción de la película.

"No, no, no, está bien...Roberto, ¿qué tal si hablamos de otra cosa, te parece?"

Ya estoy empezando a tener mis dudas de que si este hombre tiene en realidad 37 años o es un niño de 7. Pero Roberto deja de cantar, y esto me da esperanza de poder rescatar esta cita tan desagradable.

"Oye, pues," dice Roberto con una mirada pícara. "Ya sé que ustedes las mujeres hoy en día quieren ser como que "independientes" y todo eso...entonces ¿qué tal si pagamos cada quien por lo suyo?"

*No me sorprende su comentario, y no me ofende en ninguna manera, entonces le digo que "sí". Un **mesero** se acerca a la mesa.*

*"Buenas noches. Soy Alfonso. **¿Qué desean tomar?**"*

*Roberto me interrumpe sin yo decidir que quiero tomar. "Una **jarra** de **refresco** para los dos está bien."*

"Y, ¿qué desean ordenar?"

*Empiezo a **pedir** mi comida, pero Roberto me interrumpe de nuevo.*

*"**Tráigame** el pollo con salsa agridulce, por favor, con arroz y vegetales."*

El mesero escribe en su libreta. "¿Y para usted, señorita?"

"Para mí el—

"Ella quiere el pollo agridulce también."

*Ya estoy bastante extrañada con el comportamiento de este hombre, pero decido quedarme callada. Pronto llega la comida y Roberto empieza a hablar de él, sus logros, sus **gustos**, las recetas que le gusta **cocinar** — y ni una sola vez me pregunta algo acerca de mí. Termino mi comida rápido para poder irme, y tan pronto que veo que Roberto termina de comer, le hablo al mesero.*

"¿Puede traernos la cuenta, por favor?"

*El mesero trae la **cuenta**, y Roberto saca un papel de su bolsillo y se lo da al mesero.*

"Esto es para el mío."

*Extrañada, me pregunto cómo Roberto puede pagar con un papel. Roberto me pasa la cuenta y noto que el total vale por solo una cena. Saco unos billetes y le pago al mesero, incluyendo una **propina**, y le miro a Roberto.*

"Roberto, ¿cómo pagaste por el tuyo?"

*"Ahhh, pues me sale **gratis** con mi cupón de dos **entradas** por el **precio** de uno."*

Quiz

1. ¿Qué tipo de comida le gusta a Samanta?
a. comida rápida
b. comida china
c. comida italiana

2. ¿Qué cosas tienen en común Samanta y Roberto?
a. les gusta la comida china y viajar
b. les gusta la comida italiana y viajar
c. les gusta la comida china y los gatos

3. ¿Con qué juega Roberto en la mesa?
a. con la servilleta
b. con los palillos
c. con ambos a y b

4. ¿Cuántos años tiene Roberto?
a. 37
b. 27
c. 7

5. ¿Por qué Roberto no paga por su comida?
a. porque lo paga Samanta
b. porque tiene un cupón
c. porque no le gusta la comida

Answers

1. b
2. a
3. b
4. a
5. b

Vocabulario/Vocabulary

- *Cenar* --- To dine
- *Cita amorosa* --- A date /a romantic date
- *Comida china* --- Chinese food
- *¿Te gustaría salir a comer conmigo?* --- Would you like to go out to eat with me?
- *Cenar* --- To dinner/to go out to eat
- *Restaurantes* --- Restaurants
- *Mesa* --- Table
- *Me encanta* --- I love it
- *Autentica* --- Authentic
- *Sabe* --- It tastes (from the verb "saber", to taste)

464

- *Deliciosa* --- Delicious
- *Palillos* --- Chopsticks
- *Servilleta* --- Napkin
- *Tenedor* --- Fork
- *Qué aburrido* --- How boring
- *Mesero(a)* --- Waiter/waitress
- *¿Qué desean tomar?* --- What would you like to drink?
- *Jarra* --- A pitcher, a jar
- *Refresco* --- Soda
- *Y, ¿qué desean ordenar?* --- And, what would you like to order?
- *Pedir* --- To order (or to ask for something)
- *Tráigame* --- Bring me (an item)
- *Gustos* --- Taste, likes or dislikes
- *Cocinar* --- To cook
- *¿Puede traernos la cuenta, por favor?* --- Can you bring us the bill, please?
- *Cuenta* --- Bill
- *Propina* --- Tips
- *Gratis* --- Free (of charge)
- *Entradas* --- Entrees
- *Precio* --- Price

Conclusion

We hope you had a blast reading these funny and silly stories and that you have more confidence to read and understand the Spanish language.

It is important to not be too hard on yourself if it seems like there are some words and phrase that you are having trouble with. It is only natural when you are learning new things. Use whatever frustration that you have to push you to work harder, especially those that cause problems. It is a process to learn a foreign language, and it is going to take dedicated practice.

Take all opportunities to practice Spanish as you go about your day. This will help to solidify the words in your mind, and you will also perfect your pronunciation as well.

Remember that it is also useful to involve a family member or friend. This way, you can practice together, as well as test each other. You both will enjoy the experience and learn a new language together.

Follow the guidelines found in the introduction to learn Spanish quickly so that you can speak with native speakers around the world. Remember that it can be an advantage in the workplace, when you are meeting new friends, or when you are traveling. Learning a new language is never going to be a waste. And you will continue having fun with the language the more that you learn.

Speak Spanish

Typical Spanish way of saying and sentences to use in your daily life and speak like a native. Includes cultural habits and tips on how to behave in different situations.

Introduction

The Spanish language has been the most spoken language of romance; this is from the number of speakers in many countries where the language is spoken. Around the world, there are over 500 million people who speak Spanish. Use and pronunciation vary from one state to the next. However, the difference in the regions does not mean the language will be unintelligible to people speaking the language in areas where the language is not spoken. The evolution of the language has led to many Spanish dialects in different regions across the world. The history of the Spanish language originated from Spain, and it came about from the linguistic evolution of what is known as Vulgar Latin. In America, the Spanish language started with the American colonization, which happened at the end of the 15th century. During this time, however, the Spanish language was already mostly spoken in the Iberian Peninsula. During the 16th century, the Spanish language was brought to Latin America by Spanish colonization. Today, the Spanish language is widely used by Spanish descendants in America. These groups include the Spanish population that is rapidly growing and the mixed-race majority who are also known as mixed Spanish-Americans.

The colonies fought independence wars in the 19th century. After that, the elites who were the new rulers brought the Spanish language to the population to strengthen their national unity and to encourage all natives to speak the language fluently. Today, the Spanish language is spoken by many Americans. It is no doubt that many learning institutions are offering Spanish language classes as a foreign language. Learning the language will help one appreciate the Spanish culture and heritage. Interactions with many Spanish communities will be more relaxed and comfortable.

Learning Spanish should not be hard and tiresome. Therefore, this book has provided beneficial tips to understand various Spanish accents and exposed you to some of the Spanish grammar rules. Learning Spanish will also make your travel adventure fun and exciting if you visit places where Spanish is spoken. We all have to start somewhere. Do not be discouraged if you are not learning the language as fast as you want to. Learning a new language is not easy, but it can be made fun and fast if you have the right attitude. The positive attitude motivates, and it influences learning. It will make learning the hardest lesson seem easy. It is also important to surround yourself with people who will encourage you to do more and be the best you can be. We cannot hide the fact that, in the future, the Spanish language will be widely spoken throughout the world, just like English.

Spanish is also known as the language of love. From the Spanish songs to the soap operas, the language awakens love and romance. Interact more with people who speak the language; this will help build your vocabulary and improve your mastery of the language. Creating a study schedule will help you be in charge of your learning objectives and goals.

Chapter 1 - Advanced Words and Phrases

Everybody knows that the most common greeting in Spanish is "¡Hola!". How many times do we say "hello?"

There are millions of ways to say "hi" in Spanish, too. Every one of them could be used in various situations. This chapter will give you the words, but it will tell you when you should use them and when you shouldn't. This chapter is full of examples to help you in most situations.

There is also a slang section at the end where we will cover slang in 19 countries.

Basic Greetings

You have many different greeting options in Spanish, but for the most part you will only see about eight different ones. The most common are:

- "¿Cómo vas?"

This is considered to be an informal way to ask a person, "How are you?"

- "¿Cómo estás?"

This is also an informal version of asking a person how they are doing or what they are doing. To make this a formal question, all you have to do is drop the "s" and just say: *¿Cómo está?*

- *Buenas*

If you are the type of person who normally says "morning" instead of "good morning," this is something you will likely say a lot. This works much in the same way, but you can use it throughout the day, no matter if it is morning or afternoon.

- *Buenas noches*

This is considered a formal greeting that you would use when it is night. It is equivalent to "good evening" but is used when greeting someone. In order to tell somebody "good night" right before you are going to bed, you would normally say "descansa" meaning rest.

- *Buenas tardes*

If you have a meeting at two o'clock in the afternoon, you need to use this greeting. This is a formal greeting for the afternoon. How weird would it sound to greet a friend with a good afternoon?

- *Buenos días*

This is a very formal and respectful way of greeting a person and is mainly used when you are greeting a person you don't know. You will use it during the morning hours.

- *¿Qué tal?*

This is considered an informal greeting, and you can use it with your friends and family. It is universal for "what's up?"

Now that you know some of the most common greetings, let's look at some situations where you might use them.

1. In a Coffee Shop

Imagine walking into a café, and you see somebody you have known your entire life sitting in the corner booth, you go over and say: *"¿qué tal?"*

Why: You two are already friendly with each other, so using *"buenas"* would be too formal. You do have the option to say *"hola,"* but this might be too boring. Good friends tend to say things like, "what's up? I haven't seen you in a long time!" So, that's why you would likely use *"¿qué tal?"*

It will greatly depend on the country you are in because different countries have various words for "What's up."

2. Meeting Your Significant Other's Parents

You have been asked your significant other's parent's house for dinner for the very first time. You might be scared to death. You walk in and shake their hands, and then you would say either *"buenas noches, ¿cómo están?"* or just *"buenas noches"*. Once the dinner is finished, you should end the evening with *"Qué tengan buena noche,"* or *"feliz noche."* If you are planning on seeing them the following day, you could also say, *"hasta mañana."*

Why: Since this is the first time you have had dinner with them, you will likely want to be respectful, so you will need to use something formal. The next time you see them, you could just use *"buenas."* If you don't have a very close relationship, don't use anything less formal than *"buenas."*

3. Texting a Person

If you are starting a conversation with someone you like or know, you could say: *"¿Qué tal?"*, *"¿Cómo estás?"* or even *"¿Cómo vas?"*

Why: These are all friendly and informal greetings. You could follow a conversation by asking something like: "How is your day going?" or *"¿Cómo va el día?"*

Basic Goodbyes

While you have many different ways to greet a person, saying goodbye is simple. *"Hasta mañana,"* *"adiós,"* *"chao,"* or *"hasta luego"* is all there is.

- *"Nos vemos"*

This is literally telling someone that "we will see each other," it is typically used when you are talking later into the future. You would use this when you know you are going to see someone very soon.

- *Chao*

This word is Italian but is used as an informal goodbye. It gets used as the word "peace" in the English language. You can use it among friends.

- *Adiós*

This is an informal goodbye. It is normally used when making a permanent statement. When you say this, you know you won't see one another soon. This is what you would hear from a significant other when you break up.

- *"Hasta mañana"*

This one can be both informal and formal. This can be used when you are sure that you will be seeing that person the following day. You switch it to "hasta la próxima semana," which means "see you next week." You can also use hasta along with any other expression of time, such as day as in "hasta el lunes," año as in "hasta el próximo año," or month as in "hasta el próximo mes."

- *"Hasta pronto"*

This is a semi-formal goodbye. If you know there is a chance that you are going to see them in a few days, you can use this statement; but if you aren't sure, you should use "adiós" or "hasta luego."

- *"Hasta luego"*

This is another formal way to say goodbye. This can be used if you are saying goodbye to somebody that you could be seeing again in a few days, but you just aren't sure when.

Here are some examples of using goodbyes:

1. Leaving Work

You have finished at work and you are preparing to return home. Before you leave, you want to say goodbye to your coworkers, and you will see them the next day, so you could say: *"nos vemos mañana,"* or *"hasta mañana"*. If it is Friday, you could say: *"nos vemos el lunes"* or *"hasta el lunes"* which means "see you Monday."

Why: These expressions are informal and formal, and that means you can use them with someone you just met: your boss or your friends.

2. At an Airport

If someone who is important to you, or you, are leaving for several months, or possibly years, this would likely be a time for you to say *"adiós."*

Why: while you or they aren't leaving forever, it will take some time for them to come back. This is a long-term goodbye.

3. Speaking on the Telephone

While you are on the phone with a friend of yours, and you are ready to end the conversation, the most common thing to say is *"chao."* If you are having a formal conversation, then you should use *"hasta luego."*

Why: The first option is very informal, so you should only ever use it with friends.

Spanish Slang

Let's say you are walking down the street, and you decide to walk in a bar. Inside, you see some close friends. Which of the following greetings are they are going to give you:

- "Hello, how are you?"
- "Broooo, what's up?"

When you use local slang, even the slang for "what's up," it can make a big difference.

The following are several ways to say "what's up" in 19 different countries that speak Spanish. This wasn't researched on the internet; this was done by going to countries and talking with the locals.

Colombian

- *"¿Bien o qué?"*
- *"¿Bien o no?"*
- *"¿Entonces qué?"*
- *"¿Qué más?"*

If you find yourself in Medellin, it is also said as: *"¿qué más pues?"* Those from Medellin like using *"pues,"* which means "well."

Venezuelan

- *"¡Épale, chamo!, ¿qué va?"*

Spanish

- *"¿Qué hay?"*
- *"Qué tal?"*

Chilean

- *"Holanda"*
- *"Ke talka"*
- *"Hulax"*

Argentinian

- *"¿Cómo andás?"*
- *"¿Qué hacés boludo?"*

Dominican Republican

- *"¿Qué lo que?"*

Costa Rican

- *"Diay"*
- *"¿Cuál es la última?"*

Mexican

- *"¿Qué más?"*
- *"¡Quiubole!"*

473

- *"¿Qué onda?"*

Cuban

- *"¿Qué bola?"*

Ecuadorian

- *"¿Qué fue cabrón?"*

Bolivian

- *"¿Cómo es?"*
- *"¿Qué onda?"*

El Salvadorian

- *"¿Quionda vos?"*
- *"¿Quiondas macizo?"*

Guatemalan

- *"¿Qué onda vos?"*

Honduran

- *"Kiubole"*
- *"¿Qué pedos?"*

Nicaraguan

- *"¿Qué honda, chele?"*

Panamanian

- *"¿Qué e' lo que e'?"*
- *"¿Qué xopa?"*

Paraguayan

- *"¿Qué tal?"*

Peruvian

- *"¿Qué más?"*
- *"¡Habla!"*

Uruguayan

- *"¿Qué haces guacho?"*
- *"¿Qué haces gil, todo bien?"*

Chapter 2 - Meeting and Greetings:

In Spanish, there are many ways to greet someone and also to introduce yourself:

Spanish

1. *¡Buenos días!*
2. *Hola*
3. *¡Buenas noches!*
4. *¡Buenas tardes!*

English

1. Good morning!
2. Hi!/Hello
3. Good evening! /Good night!
4. Good afternoon!

If you want to ask how a person is:

1. *¿Cómo estás?*
2. *¿Cómo andas?*
3. *¿Cómo te va?*
4. *¿Cómo te encuentras?*

1. How are you?
2. How are you doing?
3. How's it going?
4. How are you?

And also:

1. *¿Cómo está?*
2. *¿Cómo anda?*
3. *¿Cómo le va?*
4. *¿Cómo se encuentra?*

1. How are you?
2. How are you doing?
3. How's it going?
4. How are you?

At first glance, it may seem that the graphics shown above have the same content, but as indicated by the bold words, there are subtle differences. The first chart is used when you're talking with a close friend or acquaintance, a relative, or someone your age.

The second chart is used in more polite settings: talking to a teacher, someone in a position of authority, a police officer, someone who you meet for the first time, someone older than you and so on.

How can you answer these questions? Take a look at the possible answers:

1. *Estoy bien.*
2. *Me va bien.*
3. *Estoy muy bien, gracias.*
4. *Me encuentro bien, gracias.*

1. I'm fine.
2. It's going well
3. I'm fine, thank you.
4. I'm fine, thank you.

If you want to introduce yourself:

Me llamo...	My name is...
Tengo 18 años	I'm 18 years old
Vengo de...	I come from
Mi nombre es...	My name is
Trabajo de...	I work as a...

And if you want to ask someone:

1. *¿Cómo te llamas?*
2. *¿De dónde vienes?*
3. *¿A que te dedicas?*
4. *¿Cuál es tu nombre?*
5. *¿Cuántos años tienes?*

1. What's your name?
2. Where do you come from?
3. What do you do for a living?
4. What's your name?
5. How old are you?

Again, these questions also have a polite form:

1. *¿Cómo se llama?*
2. *¿Cuál es su nombre?*
3. *¿De dónde viene?*
4. *¿A que se dedica?*
5. *¿Cuántos años tiene?*

1. What's your name?

2. What's your name?
3. Where do you come from?
4. What do you do for a living?
5. How old are you?

What if you want to say goodbye in Spanish? That's easy, just learn these phrases:

1. *Adiós*
2. *¡Nos vemos!*
3. *¡Hasta pronto!*
4. *¡Hasta luego!*
5. *¡Hasta mañana!*
6. *¡Nos vemos luego!*
7. *¡Nos vemos pronto!*
8. *¡Nos vemos mañana!*
9. *¡Cuídate!*
10. *¡Fue un gusto! /¡Fue un placer!*
11. *¡Fue un gusto haber conversado con usted!*
1. *¡Fue un placer haber conversado con usted!*
12. *¡Fue un gusto haberlo conocido!*
2. *¡Fue un gusto haberlo conocido!*
13. *¡Espero volverte a ver! / ¡Espero volver a verlo!*

1. Goodbye
2. See you!
3. See you soon!
4. See you soon!
5. See you tomorrow!
6. See you soon!
7. See you soon!
8. See you tomorrow!
9. Take care of yourself!
10. It was a pleasure!
11. It was a pleasure to talk to you!
12. It was a pleasure to meet you!
13. I hope to see you again!

Let's see some conversations where these phrases are used:

-   *¡Hola!*
-   *¡Hola!*
-   *¿Cómo te llamas?*
-   *Me llamo Roberto. ¿Cómo te llamas tú?*
-   *Yo me llamo Iván.*
-   *Es un gusto conocerte, Iván.*
-   *Gracias. También es un gusto conocerte.*
-   *¿A qué te dedicas?*

- *Yo soy profesor. ¿Y tú? ¿A qué te dedicas?*
- *Yo soy un ingeniero.*
- *¿Cuántos años tienes, Roberto?*
- *Yo tengo 28 años, ¿y tú?*
- *Yo tengo 26.*

This is the translation of the conversation:

- Hi!
- Hi!
- What's your name?
- My name is Roberto. What's your name?
- My name is Iván.
- It's a pleasure to meet you, Iván.
- Thank you. It's also a pleasure to meet you.
- What do you do for a living?
- I'm a teacher. And you? What do you do for a living?
- I'm an engineer
- How old are you, Roberto?
- I'm 28 years old, and you?
- I'm 26

Now let's see a more formal conversation:

- *¡Buenas tardes!*
- *¡Buenas tardes! ¿Cómo se llama?*
- *Me llamo Juan. ¿Cómo se llama, usted?*
- *Me llamo Francisco. ¿Cómo se encuentra?*
- *Me encuentro muy bien, gracias. ¿Y usted? ¿Cómo se encuentra?*
- *Me encuentro muy bien. Gracias por preguntar. ¿De dónde viene?*
- *Yo vengo de México. ¿De dónde viene, usted?*
- *Yo vengo de Uruguay. ¿A qué se dedica?*
- *Pues, yo soy cantante.*
- *Ya veo.*

And this is the translation of the story:

- ¡Good afternoon!
- ¡Good afternoon! What's your name?
- My name is Juan. What's your name?
- My name is Francisco. How are you?
- I'm very fine, thank you. And you? How are you?
- I'm very fine. Thanks for asking. Where do you come from?
- I come from Mexico. Where do you come from?
- I come from Uruguay. What do you do for a living?
- Well, I'm a singer.

- I see

Finally, let's see one final conversation. This is a conversation between two close friends:

- *¡Hola, Juan!*
- *¡Hola, Fabián! ¿Cómo estás?*
- *Estoy bien. ¿Qué hay de ti?*
- *Pues, también estoy bien, gracias.*
- *Sabes, no me acuerdo cuántos años tienes, Juan.*
- *Yo tengo 18 años. ¿Cuántos años tienes tú, Fabián?*
- *Yo tengo 19. ¿Estás trabajando?*
- *Sí, estoy trabajando con mi papá.*
- *¿A qué te dedicas?*
- *Soy panadero. ¿Y tú? ¿Estás trabajando?*
- *No. No estoy trabajando.*
- *¿Estás estudiando?*
- *Sí. Estoy estudiando en la universidad.*
- *Pues, ¡qué bien! ¿Sabes qué hora es?*
- *Sí, son las 3 en punto.*
- *¡O, no!*
- *¿Pasa algo?*
- *¡Tengo que ir a trabajar!*
- *Entiendo. ¡Corre! Espero que no llegues tarde.*
- *¡Nos vemos luego!*
- *¡Nos vemos!*

And this is the translation of the conversation:

- Hi, Juan!
- Hi, Fabián! How are you?
- I'm fine. What about you?
- Well, I'm also fine, thank you.
- You know, I can't remember how old you are, Juan.
- I'm 18 years old. How old are you, Fabián?
- I'm 19. Are you working?
- Yes, I'm working with my dad.
- What are you doing?
- I'm a baker. And you? Are you working?
- No, I'm not working.
- Are you studying?
- Yes. I'm studying in college.
- Well, ¡that's great! Do you know what time is?
- Yes, it's 3 o'clock
- Oh, no!
- What's wrong?
- I have to go to work!

479

- I understand. Run! I hope you don't arrive late!
- See you later!
- See you!

If you want to answer about your job, you can say:

Soy / Trabajo como:

- *Un profesor/ una profesora*
- *Un ingeniero/ una ingeniera*
- *Un escritor/ una escritora*
- *Un doctor/ una doctora*
- *Un panadero/ una panadera*
- *Un bombero/una bombera*
- *Un actor/ una actriz*
- *Un/ una electricista I am / I work as:*
- A teacher
- An engineer
- A writer
- A doctor
- A baker
- A fireman/ firewoman
- An actor/ an actress
- An electrician

Now that you know how to greet and introduce yourself. Let's keep moving and learn more vocabulary.

Chapter 3 - At the Restaurant

If you go to a restaurant, what should you have in mind? Many things, of course. The first thing that can arise in your mind is the place. Try these Spanish phrases to decide and ask for other's opinions on the restaurant you want to go:

1. *¿A dónde vamos?*
2. *¿A dónde quieres ir?*
3. *¿A dónde quieren ir?*
4. *¿Qué quieres comer?*
5. *¿Ya has ido a este restaurante anteriormente?*
6. *¿Ya han ido a este restaurante anteriormente? (Plural)*
7. *¿Qué restaurantes conoces?*
8. *¿Conoces algún restaurante cerca de aquí?*
9. *¿Conoces algún restaurante de comida china?*
10. *¿Qué se te antoja?*
11. *Quiero ir a un restaurante de comida italiana*
12. *No quiero comer en un restaurante de lujo*
13. *Quiero ir a un restaurante barato*
14. *Conozco un restaurante que te encantará*
15. *¿Quiénes irán al restaurante?*

And this is the translation of the phrases:

1. Where do we go?
2. Where do you want to go?
3. Where do you want to go?
4. What do you want to eat?
5. Have you been to this restaurant before?
6. Have you been to this restaurant before?
7. What restaurants do you know?
8. Do you know any restaurant near here?
9. Do you know any Chinese food restaurant?
10. What do you crave? /What would you like to eat?
11. I want to go to an Italian food restaurant.
12. I don't want to eat in a fancy restaurant
13. I want to go to a cheap restaurant
14. I know a restaurant that you will love
15. Who will go to the restaurant?

After you have decided what restaurant you to go, you need to know how to order and ask for some unknown dishes. Take a look at the following phrases:

1. *¿Ya llegamos al restaurante?*
2. *¿Qué piensas ordenar?*

3. *Ordenaré lo más barato.*
4. *¿Dónde está el menu?*
5. *No sé leer el menú*
6. *¿Cuánto cuesta este platillo?*
7. *¿Ya has probado este platillo?*
8. *¿Por qué no pides este platillo?*
9. *¿Es delicioso este platillo?*
10. *¿Dónde están las bebidas?*
11. *¿Dónde está el baño?*
12. *¿Eres alérgico a algo?*
13. *¿Te gusta el pescado?*
14. *No me gusta el pescado*
15. *¿Hay postres?*
16. *¿Venden tacos?*
17. *¿Dónde está el mesero?*

1. Have we arrived at the restaurant?
2. What do you want to order?
3. I'll order the cheapest dish.
4. Where's the menu?
5. I don't know how to read the menu.
6. How much is this dish?
7. Have you eaten this dish before?
8. Why don't you order this dish?
9. Is this dish delicious?
10. Where are the drinks?
11. Where's the bathroom?
12. Are you allergic to anything?
13. Do you like fish?
14. I don't like fish
15. Are there desserts?
16. Do they sell tacos?
17. Where's the waiter?

While eating, a conversation may take place, or maybe you just want to tell everyone you're enjoying your dish. Whatever it is you want to do, these following phrases will surely help you:

1. *¡La comida está deliciosa!*
2. *¡Este platillo está delicioso!*
3. *¡Me encanta este platillo!*
4. *¡Debes probar este platillo!*
5. *¡Mis felicitaciones al chef!*
6. *¿Qué piensas de tu platillo?*
7. *¿Te gusta tu platillo?*
8. *¿Te gusta lo que estás comiendo?*

9. *¡Me encanta!*
10. *¡No me gusta!*
11. *¡Está horrible!*
12. *No lo recomiendo*
13. *Puede estar mejor*
14. *Necesita más sal*
15. *No me gusta para nada*
16. *¿Puedo pedir más?*
17. *¿Puedo pedir otro platillo?*

1. The food is delicious!
2. This dish is delicious!
3. I love this dish!
4. You must try this dish!
5. My compliments to the chef!
6. What do you think about your dish?
7. Do you like your dish?
8. Do you like what you're eating?
9. I love it!
10. I don't like it!
11. It's horrible!
12. I don't recommend it
13. It can be better
14. It needs more salt
15. I don't like it all.
16. Can I ask for more?
17. Can I ask for another dish?

Ok, you have enjoyed your meal. That's great. But you now that someone might have to pay for all you have eaten. Learn these phrases so that the situation doesn't catch you unprepared:

¿Cuánto cuesta este platillo?	How much is this dish?
¿Quién pagará por este platillo?	Who will pay for this dish?
¿Pagaremos todos?	Will we all pay?
¿Dividiremos la cuenta?	Will we split the bill?
¿Puedo pagar yo?	Can I pay?
Quiero pagar por ti	I want to pay for you
Yo lo pagaré	I'll pay for it
No tengo dinero	I don't have money
Yo invitaré	It's on me
¿Aceptan tarjetas de crédito?	Do they accept credit cards?
¿Aceptan dinero en efectivo?	Do they accept cash?

¿Aceptan tarjetas de débito?	Do they accept debit cards?
¿Deberíamos dar propina?	Should we tip?
Cada uno pagará por su platillo	Each one will have to pay for his meal

After paying, you can thank your hosts by saying:

Gracias por invitarme a cenar con ustedes	Thanks for inviting me to have dinner with you
De nada	You're welcome
Disfruté mucho su compañía	I enjoyed your company a lot
Me gusto mucho haber cenado con ustedes	I liked very much to have dinner with you
Gracias por venir	Thanks for coming
Debemos salir nuevamente	We should go out again
¿Cuándo volvemos a salir?	When will we go out again?

Let's see some conversations:

- *¿A dónde iremos a cenar esta noche?*
- *No lo sé. ¿A dónde quisieras ir a comer?*
- *¿Conoces algún restaurante cerca de aquí?*
- *Sí. Conozco un restaurante de comida italiana cerca de aquí.*
- *¿Has ido a ese restaurante anteriormente?*
- *Sí, he ido a ese restaurante muchas veces con mis amigos.*
- *Entonces, está decidido. ¡Vamos!*

- Where will we go to eat out tonight?
- I don't know. Where would you like to go to eat out?
- Do you know any restaurant near here?
- Yes. I know an Italian food restaurant near here.
- Have you been to that restaurant before?
- Yes, I've been to that restaurant many times with my friends
- Then, it's decided!

- *¿A qué restaurante iremos?*
- *Iremos a un restaurante de comida china.*
- *No me gusta la comida china. ¿Conoces algún otro restaurant?*
- *Sí. Conozco un restaurante de comida tailandesa. ¿Quisieras ir a ese restaurante?*
- *¿Es un restuarante de lujo?*
- *Sí. La comida en ese restaurante es muy cara.*
- *No tengo mucho dinero.*
- *Entiendo.*

- *¿Por qué no vamos a otro restaurante? Yo conozco otro restaurant de comida china cerca de aquí. Y lo mejor de todo es que la comida allí es muy barata.*
- *Suena como una buena idea. ¡Vamos!*

- What restaurant will we go to?
- We will go to a Chinese food restaurant.
- I don't like Chinese food. Do you know any other restaurant?
- Yes. I know a Thai food restaurant. Would you like to go to that restaurant?
- Is it a fancy restaurant?
- Yes. Food there is very expensive
- I don't have much money.
- I understand
- Why don't we go to another restaurant? I know another Chinese food restaurant near here. And the best of all is that the food there is very cheap.

- *¿Qué piensas de tu platillo? ¿Te gusta?*
- *Sí. ¡Me encanta!*
- *Sabía que te iba a gustar. Tu mama me dijo que a ti te gustaba la comida china.*
- *¿Qué hay de ti? ¿Te gustó tu platillo?*
- *Bueno, estuvo delicioso, pero no me gustó mucho.*
- *¿Por qué no?*
- *Porque creo que le faltó un poco de sal.*
- *Bueno, no te preocupes mucho.*
- *Creo que tenemos que pagar ya.*
- *Sí. ¿Cuánto cuesta este platillo?*
- *Tu platillo cuesta 15 dólares y el mío cuesta 20 dólares.*
- *¿Dividimos la cuenta?*
- *No. Creo que sería mejor si tú pagas por lo que comiste y yo pago por mi platillo.*
- *Suena bien. ¿Sabes si aceptan tarjetas de crédito?*
- *No lo sé.*
- *¿Cómo vas a pagar tú?*
- *Voy a pagar en efectivo.*
- *Será mejor que pregunte al mesero si aceptan mi tarjeta.*
- *Es una buena idea.*
- *Gracias por invitarme a cenar.*
- *Gracias por venir.*

- What do you think of your dish? Do you like it?
- Yes. I love it!
- I knew that you would like it. Your mom told me that you liked Chinese food.
- What about you? Did you like your dish?
- Well, it was delicious, but I didn't like it very much.

- Why not?
- Because I think that it needed more salt.
- Well, don't worry too much.
- I think we have to pay now
- Yes. How much is this dish?
- Your dish is 15 dollars and mine is 20 dollars.
- Should we split the bill?
- No. I think it would be better if you pay for what you ate and I pay for my dish.
- That sounds good. Do you know if they accept credit cards?
- I don't know.
- How are you going to pay?
- I'm going to pay in cash.
- I'd better ask the waiter if they accept my card.
- It's a good idea.
- Thanks for inviting me to have dinner
- Thanks for coming.

Chapter 4 - At the Hotel:

When you want to stay at a hotel, you need to ask for as much information as you need. What questions will help you find the best deals?

Spanish

1. ¿Cómo se llama este hotel?
2. ¿Qué tipo de hotel estás buscando?
3. ¿Buscas un hotel de lujo?
4. ¿Qué comodidades estás buscando?
5. ¿Dónde quieres hospedarte?
6. ¿Quieres que el hotel tenga una piscina?
7. ¿Tiene este hotel una piscina?
8. ¿Tiene este hotel un gimnasio?
9. ¿Cuánto cuesta la habitación?
10. Quiero una habitación matrimonial.
11. Quiero una habitación de lujo
12. ¿Está este hotel cerca del aeropuerto?
13. ¿Está este hotel en el centro de la ciudad?
14. ¿Está este hotel cerca del paradera de bus?

And this is the translation of the phrases:

English

1. What's the name of this hotel?
2. What type of hotel are you looking for?
3. Are you looking for a fancy hotel?
4. What amenities are you looking for?
5. Where do you want to stay?
6. Do you want the hotel to have a pool?
7. Does this hotel have a pool?
8. Does this hotel have a gym?
9. How much does the room cost?
10. I want a double room
11. I want a luxury room.
12. Is this hotel near the airport?
13. Is this hotel in the city center?
14. Is this hotel near the bus stop?

Once you have found the hotel you want to stay at, you need to make yourself feel like home. Use these phrases so you can have a great time at the hotel:

1. ¿Cuál es el número de mi habitación?
2. Mi número de habitación es 302
3. ¿En qué piso está mi habitación?
4. Mi habitación está en el tercer piso

5. *Mi habitación está sucia*
6. *Tienes que mostrar tu identificación*
7. *¿Tengo que dejar propina?*
8. *¿Dónde está la piscina?*
9. *¿Dónde está el gimnasio?*
10. *¿Dónde están las toallas?*
11. *¿Tengo que pagar para entrar al gimnasio?*
12. *¿A quién debo llamar si hay una emergencia?*
13. *¿Cuál es el número del servicio a la habitación?*
14. *¿Cuál es el número de la recepción?*
15. *¿Quién llevará mis maletas?*
16. *¿Dónde está el comedor?*
17. *¿Dónde está la oficina?*
18. *¿Dónde está el restaurante?*
19. *¿Pueden traer el desayuno a mi habitación?*
20. *¿Pueden llamarme para despertarme, por favor?*

And this is the translation of the phrases:

1. What's my room number?
2. My room number is 302
3. What floor is my room on?
4. My room is on the third floor.
5. My room is dirty.
6. You have to show your ID
7. Do I have to leave a tip?
8. Where's the pool?
9. Where's the gym?
10. Where are the towels?
11. Do I have to pay to enter the gym?
12. Who should I call if there's an emergency?
13. What's the number of room service?
14. What's the number of the reception?
15. Who will carry my bags?
16. Where's the lunchroom?
17. Where's the office?
18. Where's the restaurant?
19. Can you bring breakfast to my room?
20. Can you give me a wake-up call?

Let's see some conversations where these phrases are used:

- *¿Qué estás haciendo?*
- *Estoy buscando un hotel.*
- *¿Qué tipo de hotel estás buscando?*
- *Estoy buscando un hotel que está cerca del aeropuerto.*
- *¿Estás buscando un hotel de lujo?*
- *No. No quiero gastar mucho dinero.*
- *Conozco un hotel que te va a gustar. Es un hotel que está cerca del aeropuerto y no está muy*

caro.

- *¿En serio? ¿Cómo se llama el hotel?*
- *El hotel se llama "Costa Grande"*
- *¿Qué comodidades tiene ese hotel?*
- *Tiene una piscina, un spa, un gimnasio, un restaurante y más.*
- *¡Vaya! ¡Espero que no sea muy caro!*
- *No te preocupes. Yo me quede en ese hotel el año pasado y no fue para nada caro.*

- What are you doing?
- I am looking for a hotel.
- What type of hotel are you looking for?
- I am looking for a hotel that is near the airport.
- Are you looking for a luxury hotel?
- No. I don't want to spend a lot of money.
- I know a hotel that you will like. It is a hotel that is close to the airport and not very expensive.
- Seriously? What is the name of the hotel?
- The hotel is called "Costa Grande"
- What amenities does this hotel have?
- It has a pool, a spa, a gym, a restaurant and more.
- Wow! I hope it is not very expensive!
- Don't worry. I stayed at that hotel last year and it was not expensive at all.

- *¡Buenas tardes! Reservé una habitación en este hotel hace una semana.*
- *¿Cómo se llama?*
- *Me llamo Francisco Armín.*
- *¿Podría mostrarme su identificación?*
- *¡Claro! Aquí está.*
- *Ya confirmé que usted es verdaderamente Francisco Armín.*
- *¡Genial! ¿Dónde está mi habitación? ¿Cuál es el número de mi habitación?*
- *Su habitación está en el quinto piso. El número de su habitación es 510.*
- *Gracias. ¿Dónde está el elevador?*
- *El elevador está cerca de las escaleras.*
- *¿Quién llevará mis maletas?*
- *El botones llevará sus maletas.*
- *Gracias.*

- Good afternoon! I booked a room at this hotel a week ago.
- What is your name?
- My name is Francisco Armín.
- Could you show me your ID?
- Sure! Here it is.
- I've confirmed that you truly are Francisco Armín.
- Great! Where is my room? What is my room number?
- Your room is on the fifth floor. Your room number is 510.
- Thank you. Where is the elevator?
- The elevator is near the stairs.

- Who will carry my bags?
- The bellhop will carry your bags.
- Thank you.

Chapter 5 - At the Gas Station

What should you say when you're at a gas station? Take a look at the following phrases and see if you can use them:

1. *¿Dónde está la gasolinera?*
2. *¿Dónde está gasolinera más cercana?*
3. *¿Cuánto cuesta la gasolina?*
4. *¿Está cara la gasolina aquí?*
5. *¿Puedes mostrarme dónde está la gasolinera?*

1. Where's the gas station?
2. Where's the nearest gas station?
3. How much does gasoline cost?
4. Is gasoline expensive here?
5. Can you show me where the gas station is?

Let's see some conversations where these phrases are used:

- *¡Buenas tardes!*
- *¡Buenas tardes! ¿En qué le puedo ayudar?*
- *Quisiera poner gasolina en mi auto.*
- *¿Cuánta gasolina desea?*
- *Quisiera 10 litros de gasolina.*
- *¿Qué tipo de gasolina quisiera?*
- *Quisiera la de 95, por favor.*
- *El galón de gasolina de 95 cuesta $5 por litro. ¿Está bien?*
- *Sí. Me parece bien.*
- *¿Cómo desea pagar?*
- *Quisiera pagar con tarjeta de crédito*
- *Hay un descuento de 5 dólares si usted compra 15 galones de gasolina.*
- *Me parece una muy buena oferta. Entonces, quisiera comprar 15 galones de gasolina.*
- *¡Genial! Ya está*
- *Gracias.*
- *¡Tenga un buen día!*
- Good afternoon!
- Good afternoon! How can I help you?
- I would like to put gasoline in my car.
- How much gasoline do you want?
- I want 10 liters of gasoline.
- What type of gasoline would you like?
- I want 95, please.
- The gallon of 95 costs $ 5 per liter. Is it okay?
- Yes. It seems fine.
- How would you like to pay?
- I would like to pay by credit card

- There is a $ 5 discount if you buy 15 gallons of gasoline.
- I think it's a very good offer. So, I would like to buy 15 gallons of gasoline.
- Great! It's done
- Thank you.
- Have a nice day!

Chapter 6 - At the Mall

When you go shopping, you may find it very useful to remember the following phrases:

1. *¿Dónde está el centro comercial?*
2. *¿Qué puedo encontrar en el centro comercial?*
3. *¿Está el centro comercial abierto?*
4. *¿Qué tiendas encontraré en este centro comercial?*
5. *¿Hay una tienda de muebles en este centro comercial?*
6. *¿Cuánto está este mueble?*
7. *¿Dónde está tienda de electrónicos?*
8. *¿Dónde puedo encontrar un cargador de celular?*
9. *Puedes encontrarlo en la tienda de electrónicos*
10. *¿Aceptan tarjetas de crédito?*
11. *¿Tienen alguna oferta disponible?*
12. *¿Hay algún descuento?*
13. *Hay 10% de descuento en este producto.*
14. *Hay una oferta de dos por tres.*
15. *No tenemos descuentos disponibles*
16. *¿Dónde está la tienda de ropa de hombres?*
17. *¿Dónde está la tienda de ropa de mujeres?*
18. *¿Cuánto cuesta este vestido?*
19. *Este vestido cuesta 30 dólares*
20. *¿Cuánto cuesta esta blusa?*
21. *Está blusa cuesta 50 dólares*
22. *¿Tiene este vestido en un tamaño más pequeño?*
23. *¿Tiene este vestido en un tamaño más grande?*
24. *Este vestido es muy apretado*
25. *Este vestido es muy suelto*
26. *No me gusta este pantalón*
27. *¿Dónde está la sección de ropa para bebés?*
28. *Esta es la sección de ropa para bebés*
29. *¿Tiene más vestidos?*
30. *¿Dónde está el estacionamiento?*

1. Where's the shopping mall?
2. What can I find at the shopping mall?
3. Is the shopping mall open?
4. What stores will I find in this shopping mall?
5. Is there a furniture store in this mall?
6. How much does this furniture cost?
7. Where is the electronics store?
8. Where can I find a phone charger?
9. You can find it in the electronics store.
10. Do you accept credit cards?
11. Do you have any available offer?
12. Is there any discount?
13. There is a 10% discount on this product.

14. There is a three-for-two offer
15. We don't have any available discounts.
16. Where is the men's clothing store?
17. Where is the women's clothing store?
18. How much does this dress cost?
19. This dress costs $30
20. How much does this blouse cost?
21. This blouse costs $50
22. Do you have this dress in a smaller size?
23. Do you have this dress in a larger size?
24. This dress is very tight
25. Este vestido es muy flojo
26. I don't like this dress
27. Where is the baby clothes section?
28. This is the baby clothes section.
29. Do you have more dresses?
30. Where's the parking lot?

Now let's take a look at some conversations where these phrases are used:

- *Gracias por venir conmigo al centro comercial.*
- *¿Es la primera vez que vienes a este centro comercial?*
- *Sí. Nunca he venido antes a este centro comercial*
- *¿Qué piensas comprar?*
- *Quiero comprar un cargador de celular y también ropa para mí.*
- *Pues has venido al lugar indicado. En este centro comercial encontrarás todo lo que estás buscando.*
- *¿Sabes si hay ofertas disponibles?*
- *No lo sé. Pero puedes preguntar a los vendedores. Ellos te pueden ayudar.*
- *¿Dónde está la tienda de electrónicos?*
- *La tienda de electrónicos está en el segundo piso.*
- *¿Este centro comercial tiene segundo piso?*
- *Sí, si quieres ir a la tienda de electrónicos, tendrás que usar las escaleras eléctricas.*
- *¿Y dónde está la tienda de ropa?*
- *La tienda de ropa está cerca a la tienda de electrónicos.*
- *Parece que conoces muy bien este centro comercial. ¿Vienes a este centro comercial a menudo?*
- *Vengo todos los fines de semana con mis amigos a ver una película.*
- *¿También hay un cine en este centro comercial?*
- *Sí. ¿Quieres que te lo muestre?*

- Thank you for coming with me to the mall.
- Is it the first time you come to this mall?
- Yes. I have never come to this mall before
- What do you want to buy?
- I want to buy a cell phone charger and also clothes for me.
- Well, you have come to the right place. In this mall, you will find everything you are looking for.
- Do you know if there are offers available?

- I don't know. But you can ask the sellers. They can help you.
- Where is the electronics store?
- The electronics store is on the second floor.
- Does this mall have a second floor?
- Yes, if you want to go to the electronics store, you will have to use the escalators.
- And where is the clothing store?
- The clothing store is close to the electronics store.
- You seem to know this mall very well. Do you come to this mall often?
- I come every weekend with my friends to watch a movie.
- Is there also a cinema in this mall?
- Yes. Do you want me to show it to you?

Let's take a look at another conversation:

- *¡María! ¡Qué gusto verte aquí en este centro comercial!*
- *¡Hola, Ariana! También es un gusto verte. ¿Qué estás haciendo aquí?*
- *He venido a este centro comercial porque quiero comprar un nuevo celular para mi hermano menor.*
- *¿En serio? ¿Piensas regalarle un celular?*
- *Así es. Estoy seguro que le va a encantar el nuevo celular que he comprado para él.*
- *¿Ya lo compraste? ¿Dónde está?*
- *Esta aquí en la bolsa.*
- *¿Puedo verlo?*
- *¡Claro!*
- *¡Vaya! Es un celular muy bonito. ¿Dónde lo compraste?*
- *Lo compré en la tienda de celulares que está en el tercer piso.*
- *Ya veo. Creo que yo también compraré un nuevo celular.*
- *Veo que tienes muchas bolsas. ¿Qué has comprado?*
- *Compré ropa para mí y también para mi esposo.*
- *¡Has comprado mucho!*
- *Es que hay muchos descuentos disponibles en la tienda de ropa. Hay incluso una oferta de tres por dos en toda la ropa de hombres.*
- *¿En serio? Creo que iré a la tienda de ropa también. Mi hijo también necesita ropa nueva.*
- *¡Tienes que ir! Además, con toda la ropa que está en descuento, ahorrarás muchísimo dinero.*
- *Sí. Creo que tienes razón. Ahora mismo iré a la tienda.*
- *¡Te veo luego!*
- *¡Nos vemos!*

- Mary! What a pleasure to see you here in this mall!
- Hello Ariana! It is also nice to see you. What are you doing here?
- I have come to this mall because I want to buy a new cell phone for my younger brother.
- Really? Do you plan to give him a cell phone?
- That's right. I'm sure he will love the new cell phone that I bought for him.
- You already bought it? Where is?
- It's here in the bag.
- Can I see it?

- Sure!
- Wow! It's a very pretty cell phone. Where did you buy it?
- I bought it at the cell phone store on the third floor.
- I see. I think I'll buy a new cell phone, too.
- I see you have many bags. What have you bought?
- I bought clothes for myself and also for my husband.
- You have bought a lot!
- There are many discounts available in the clothing store. There is even a three-for-two offer on all men's clothing.
- Seriously? I think I'll go to the clothing store, too. My son also needs new clothes.
- You have to go! Also, with all the clothes that are on discount, you will save a lot of money.
- Yes. I think you are right. I will go to the store right now.
- See you later!
- See you!

Chapter 7 - At the Bank

Being abroad can already be very stressful. It's especially stressful if you have to deal with money problems in a different country. What can you say so that everyone around you understands what you're talking about?

Spanish

1. ¿Dónde está el banco?
2. ¿Dónde está el banco más cercano?
3. ¿Qué banco estás buscando?
4. Estoy buscando este banco
5. ¿Dónde está oficina central?
6. Quiero ir a la oficina central
7. Vengo para abrir una cuenta de ahorros
8. ¿En qué le podemos ayudar?
9. Quisiera abrir una cuenta de ahorros
10. Quisiera abrir una cuenta corriente
11. Quisiera hacer una transacción bancaria
12. Quisiera retirar dinero
13. Quisiera depositar dinero
14. ¿Dónde está el cajero automático más cercano?
15. ¿Debo esperar a que me llamen?
16. Quisiera tener una tarjeta de crédito
17. Quisiera tener una tarjeta de débito
18. Quisiera una cuenta de ahorros en dólares
19. Quisiera una cuenta de ahorros en euros
20. Yo soy el titular de la cuenta
21. Él es el titular de la cuenta
22. Tengo una chequera
23. ¿Dónde aceptan esta tarjeta?
24. ¿Cobran mantenimiento de cuenta?
25. ¿Hay cargos por retiro?
26. ¿Hay cargos por transferencia?
27. ¿Cuánto es la tasa de interés anual?
28. ¿Dónde puedo retirar dinero?
29. ¿Puedo hacer transferiencias en línea?
30. ¿Dónde está mi clave?
31. ¿Cuál es mi clave?
32. ¿Este es mi número de tarjeta?
33. ¿Quién puede ayudarme con mis preguntas?
34. ¿Cómo bloqueo la tarjeta?
35. ¿Cambian monedas extranjeras aquí?
36. ¿Dónde puedo pedir un préstamo?
37. ¿Qué documentos debo presentar?
38. Quiero un préstamo de 1500 dólares.

And this is the translation:

English

1. Where's the bank?
2. Where's the nearest bank?
3. What bank are you looking for?
4. I'm looking for this bank
5. Where's the head office?
6. I want to go to the head office.
7. I come to open a savings account
8. How can I help you?
9. I would like to open a savings account
10. I would like to open a checking account
11. I would like to make a bank transaction
12. I would like to withdraw money
13. I'd like to deposit some money
14. Where is the nearest ATM?
15. Should I wait to be called?
16. I would like to have a credit card
17. I would like to have a debit card
18. I would like a dollar savings account
19. I would like a savings account in euros
20. I am the account holder
21. He is the account holder
22. I have a checkbook
23. Where is this card accepted?
24. Do you charge account maintenance?
25. Are there any withdrawal fees?
26. Are there transfer fees?
27. How much is the annual interest rate?
28. Where can I withdraw money?
29. Can I make transfers online?
30. Where is my password?
31. What is my password?
32. Is this my card number?
33. Who can help me with my questions?
34. How do I lock the card?
35. Do you exchange foreign currencies here?
36. Where can I ask for a loan?
37. What documents should I submit?
38. I want a loan of 1500 dollars.

Now let's see some conversations where these phrases are used:

- *¡Buenas tardes!*
- *¡Buenas tardes! ¿En qué podemos ayudarle?*
- *Quisiera abrir una cuenta de ahorros.*
- *Le puedo ayudar con eso, señor.*
- *Gracias.*
- *¿Cuál es su nombre?*

- *Mi nombre es Juan.*
- *¿Cuál es su apellido?*
- *Mi apellido es Ramirez.*
- *Muy bien. ¿Tiene algún document de identidad?*
- *Sí, tengo mi pasaporte.*
- *¿Podría mostarmelo, por favor?*
- *¡Claro! Aquí está.*
- *Gracias. Señor Razmirez, ¿cuántos años tiene?*
- *Tengo 35 años.*
- *¿Dónde nació?*
- *Nací en Buenos Aires, Argentina.*
- *¿Hace cuánto está usted en este país?*
- *He estado en este país por 5 años.*
- *Muy bien. ¿A qué se dedica?*
- *Soy profesor de matemáticas.*
- *¿Dónde trabaja?*
- *Trabajo en una escuela secundaria en el centro de la ciudad.*
- *¿Dónde vive?*
- *Yo vivo en Calle Almería 321.*
- *¿Tiene esposa o hijos?*
- *Sí. Estoy casado y tengo 2 hijos.*
- *Muy bien. Por favor, firme estos documentos.*
- *Ya está. ¿Qué más debo hacer?*
- *Nada más. Ya todo lo necesario está hecho. Ahora lo que usted necesita hacer es esperar a que su tarjeta de débito llegue a su dirección.*
- *¿Cuándo llegará mi tarjeta de débito?*
- *Llegará en 3 días.*
- *¿Dónde aceptan esa tarjeta de débito?*
- *La aceptan en todas las tiendas que aceptan Visa.*
- *¿Puedo retirar dinero con mi tarjeta de débito?*
- *¡Claro que sí!*
- *¿Qué debo hacer para retirar dinero de una cuenta de ahorros?*
- *Usted puede usar su tarjeta de débito para retirar dinero de su cuenta. Lo que usted debe hacer es ir a un cajero automático e insertar su tarjeta de débito en el cajero automático. Luego, usted tendrá que indicar cuánto dinero quiere retirar.*
- *Suena bien. ¿Me cobran cargos adicionales por hacer retiros?*
- *No. Los retiros en los cajeros automáticos son totalmente gratuitos.*
- *¿Cuánto dinero puedo retirar?*
- *Usted puede retirar un máximo de 3000 dólares por día.*
- *Entiendo.*
- *¿Alguna otra pregunta, señor Ramirez?*
- *¿Qué pasa si pierdo mi tarjeta?*
- *Usted puede llamar a este número que está aquí en este docuemento. Tiene que seguir las instrucciones que le digan para poder bloquear la tarjeta.*
- *¿Puedo pedir otra tarjeta si la pierdo?*
- *Claro, y la nueva tarjeta es totalmente gratis también.*

- Good afternoon!
- Good afternoon! How can we help you?
- I would like to open a savings account.
- I can help you with that, sir.
- Thank you.
- What's your name?
- My name is Juan.
- What is your last name?
- My last name is Ramirez.
- Ok. Do you have any identification documents?
- Yes, I have my passport.
- Could you show me, please?
- Sure! Here it is.
- Thank you. Mr. Razmirez, how old are you?
- I'm 35.
- Where were you born?
- I was born in Buenos Aires, Argentina.
- How long have you been in this country?
- I have been in this country for 5 years.
- OK. What do you do for a living?
- I am a math teacher.
- Where do you work?
- I work in a high school in the city center.
- Where do you live?
- I live in Calle Almería 321.
- Do you have a wife or children?
- Yes. I am married and have 2 children.
- OK. Please sign these documents.
- It's done. What else should I do?
- Nothing else. Everything necessary is already done. Now what you need to do is wait for your debit card to arrive at your address.
- When will my debit card arrive?
- It will arrive in 3 days.
- Where is that debit card accepted?
- They accept it in all stores that accept Visa.
- Can I withdraw money with my debit card?
- Of course!
- What should I do to withdraw money from a savings account?
- You can use your debit card to withdraw money from your account. What you should do is go to an ATM and insert your debit card into the ATM. Then, you will have to indicate how much money you want to withdraw.
- Sounds good. Am I charged additional fees for making withdrawals?
- No. Withdrawals at ATMs are completely free.
- How much money can I withdraw?
- You can withdraw a maximum of $ 3,000 per day.

- I get it.
- Any other questions, Mr. Ramirez?
- What happens if I lose my card?
- You can call this number that is here in this document. You have to follow the instructions they tell you to be able to lock the card.
- Can I ask for another card if I lose it?
- Sure, and the new card is totally free, too.

Let's take a look at another conversation:

- *¡Buenas tardes!*
- *¡Buenas tardes! ¿En qué podemos ayudarla?*
- *Vengo a pedir un préstamo.*
- *Yo le puedo ayudar con eso. ¿Cuál es su nombre?*
- *Mi nombre es María Ríos.*
- *¿Tiene algún documento de identidad?*
- *Sí. ¿Quiere que se lo muestre?*
- *Sí, por favor.*
- *Muy bien, señorita Ríos. Veo que usted ya es cliente nuestro.*
- *Así es. Yo tengo una tarjeta de crédito. La uso todos los días.*
- *¡Qué bien! ¿Podría decirme cuanto dinero gastas todos los meses?*
- *Gasto aproximadamente 600 dólares.*
- *Entendido. ¿Cuánto dinero quisiera pedir?*
- *Quisiera un préstamo de 6500 dólares.*
- *OK. Muy bien. Si usted desea pedir un préstamo de 6500 dólares, entonces tendrá que llenar este documento.*
- *Lo haré.*
- *¿Terminó?*
- *Sí, ya terminé. ¿Qué más debo hacer?*
- *¿Desea recibir el dinero en un cheque?*
- *No. ¿Puedo recibir el dinero en mi cuenta de ahorros?*
- *¿Tiene usted también una cuenta de ahorros?*
- *Sí. Yo soy el titular de una cuenta de ahorros.*
- *Muy bien. Deme un momento para poder ingresar la información.*
- *¿Desea que le de mi número de cuenta?*
- *No es necesario. Aquí tengo toda la información necesaria.*
- *¿Ya está hecho?*
- *Sí. Ya transferí el dinero a su cuenta de ahorros.*
- *¡Genial! ¡Muchas gracias!*
- *No se preocupe. Estamos para ayudarla.*

- Good afternoon!
- Good afternoon! How can we help you?
- I've come to ask for a loan.
- I can help you with that. What's your name?
- My name is María Ríos.

- Do you have any identification documents?
- Yes. Do you want me to show it to you?
- Yes, please.
- Very well, Miss Rios. I see that you are already our client.
- That's right. I have a credit card. I use it every day.
- That's perfect! Could you tell me how much money you spend every month?
- I spend approximately $ 600.
- Understood. How much money would you like to ask for?
- I would like a loan of $ 6,500.
- OK. Very well. If you wish to request a loan of $ 6,500, then you will have to fill out this document.
- I will.
- Finished?
- Yes, I've already finished. What else should I do?
- Do you want to receive the money in a check?
- No. Can I receive the money in my savings account?
- Do you also have a savings account?
- Yes. I am the account holder of a savings account.
- Very well. Give me a moment to enter the information.
- Do you want me to give you my account number?
- It's not necessary. Here I have all the necessary information.
- It's done?
- Yes. I already transferred the money to your savings account.
- Great! Thank you very much!
- Don't worry. We are here to help you.

Chapter 8 - At the Hospital

In a perfect world, we wouldn't need to go to the doctor. Unfortunately, this is not a perfect world. While we hope you never get into trouble while you're abroad, it's still important for you to learn some Spanish phrases that might come very in handy in your new country:

Spanish --> English

El cuidado médico en este hospital es muy bueno. --> Medical care in this hospital is very good

¿Dónde está el hospital más cercano? --> Where's the nearest hospital?

¿Dónde está la oficina del doctor? --> Where's the doctor office?

¿Cuánto cuesta la cita médica en este hospital? -->How much does the medical appointment in this hospital cost?

¿Tiene seguro médico? ---> Do you have medical insurance?

Yo tengo seguro médico ---> I have medical insurance

Yo no tengo seguro médico --> I don't have medical insurance

¿Cómo puedo conseguir seguro médico? --> How can I get medical insurance?

Mi seguro médico ha expirado --> My medical insurance has expired.

¿Dónde te duele? --> Where does it hurt?

¿Te duele aquí? --> Does it hurt here?

Tienes que tomar estos medicamentos --> You have to take these medications

Tienes que tomar estas pastillas --> You have to take these pills

¿Cuánto cuestán estas pastillas? --> How much do these pills cost?

¿Qué cubre mi seguro? --> What does my insurance cover?

¿Dónde tengo que pagar? --> Where do I have to pay?

¿Dónde puedo conseguir estas pastillas? --> Where can I get these pills?

¿Dónde puedo conseguir estos medicamentos? --> Where can I get these medications?

¿Necesito cirugía? --> Do I need surgery?

Necesitas cirugía --> You need surgery

¿Es una emergencia? --> Is it an emergency?

Me duele mucho el estómago --> My stomach hurts a lot

Me duelen mucho las piernas --> My legs hurt a lot

Me duele mucho aquí --> It hurts a lot here

¿Has comido algo? --> Have you eaten anything?

¿Eres alérgico a algo? --> Are you allergic to anything?

¿Eres alérgico a algún medicamento? --> Are you allergic to any medications?

¿Puedes tomar este medicamento? --> Can you take this medication?

¿Tienes mareos? --> Do you have dizziness?

¿Tienes náuseas? --> Do you have nausea?

¿Has vomitado? --> Have you vomited?

¿Qué síntomas tienes? --> What symptoms do you have?

Tengo mareos --> I'm dizzy

Tengo náuseas --> I have nausea

Me duele la cabeza --> I have a headache

Tuve un accidente --> I had an accident

Me caí -->I fell

Me rompí el tabique --> I broke the septum

Te has fracturado la pierna --> You have broken your leg

Te has fracturado el brazo --> You have fractured your arm

Tienes que descansar --> You have to rest

No hagas ejercicio --> Don't exercise

No tomes alcohol --> Don't drink alcohol

No fumes --> Don't smoke

¿Tomas alcohol? --> Do you drink alcohol?

¿Fumas? --> Do you smoke?

¿Consumes drogas? --> Do you use drugs?

¿Qué drogas consumes? --> What drugs do you use?

Esta es la receta médica --> This is the medical prescription.

¿Es usted el doctor? --> Are you the doctor?

¿Puede ayudarme? --> Can you help me?

¿Cuánto pesas? --> How much do you weigh?

¿Cuánto mides? --> How tall are you?

Siéntate aquí --> Sit here

Recuéstate aquí --> Lie here

Tienes que tener una cita médica --> You have to have a medical appointment

Tienes que tomar este jarabe --> You have to drink this syrup

Now that you have seen some common phrases, it's time to see some of those phrases in a conversation:

- *¡Buenos días!*
- *¡Buenos días! ¿Este es el hospital Armando Plazas?*
- *Así es. Este es el hospital Armando Plazas. ¿En qué le podemos ayudar? ¿Tiene alguna emergencia?*

- *No es una emergencia. Simplemente me duele mucho el estómago.*
- *Ya veo. ¿Tiene una cita médica?*
- *No*
- *¿Es la primera vez que viene a este hospital?*
- *Sí.*
- *Para ser atendido necesita tener una cita médica. Pero como a usted le duele mucho el estómago, usted puede ir a la sala de urgencias. Allí le ayudarán*
- *Gracias. ¿Dónd está la sala de urgencias?*
- *La sala de urgencias está allí.*
- *Gracias.*
- *¿Es esta la sala de urgencias?*
- *Sí. ¿En que le podemos ayudar?*
- *Me duele mucho el estómago.*
- *¿Ha comido algo?*
- *Sí.*
- *¿Qué comió?*
- *Comí un plato de espagueti en la calle.*
- *¿Es alérgico a algo?*
- *No.*
- *¿Qué síntomas tiene?*
- *Tengo un fuerte dolor de estómago y también tengo náuseas.*
- *¿Tiene mareos?*
- *No, no tengo mareos*
- *Ok. ¿Tiene seguro médico?*
- *Sí.*
- *Muy bien, señor. Le atenderemos en un momento. Siéntese aquí, por favor.*
- *Ok. Muchas gracias.*

- Good Morning!
- Good Morning! Is this the Armando Plazas Hospital?
- That's right. This is Armando Plazas Hospital. How can I help you? Do you have an emergency?
- It is not an emergency. My stomach just hurts a lot.
- I see. Do you have a medical appointment?
- No
- Is it the first time you come to this hospital?
- Yes.
- To be treated you need to have a medical appointment. But since your stomach hurts a lot, you can go to the emergency room. They will help you there
- Thank you. Where is the emergency room?
- The emergency room is there.
- Thank you.
- Is this the emergency room?
- Yes. How can we help you?
- My stomach hurts a lot.
- Have you eaten anything?
- Yes.

- What did you eat?
- I ate a plate of spaghetti in the street.
- Are you allergic to anything?
- No.
- What symptoms do you have?
- I have a strong stomach ache and I also feel nauseous.
- Do you have dizziness?
- No, I don't have dizziness
- Okay. Do you have health insurance?
- Yes.
- Ok, sir. We will help you in a moment. Sit here, please.
- Okay. Thank you very much.

Let's take a look at another conversation:

- *Gracias por la atención, doctor.*
- *No se preocupe. No olvide tomar sus pastillas.*
- *¿Cómo se llaman las pastillas?*
- *Los nombres de las pastillas está en la receta médica que le di.*
- *Hay muchos medicamentos escritos en esta receta médica.*
- *Así es. Estas pastillas son para el dolor de estómago. Tiene que tomar 1 pastilla después del desayuno y una después de la cena.*
- *Ok. Entiendo. ¿Y qué hay de este otro medicamento?*
- *Ese es un jarabe. Ese jarabe ayudará con el ardor de garganta. Recuerde que tiene que tomarlo antes de comer.*
- *¿Y estas pastillas?*
- *Estas pastillas son para la infección.*
- *¿Algo más que deba saber?*
- *No debe comer nada picante. No debe tomar gaseosa o bebidas alcohólicas. ¿Usted fuma?*
- *No, yo no fumo.*
- *Bien. Usted no consume drogas, ¿verdad?*
- *No consumo drogas, doctor.*
- *¡Qué bien! No cene muy tarde. No se estrese demasiado.*
- *¿Puedo hacer deporte?*
- *Sí, pero con mucho cuidado.*
- *¿Y si me vuelve a doler el estómago?*
- *Si le duele mucho, entonces usted puede venir a la sala de emergencias.*
- *¿Por cuánto tiempo debo tomar estas pastillas?*
- *Debe tomar esas pastillas hasta la siguiente cita.*
- *¿Cuándo es la siguiente cita?*
- *La siguiente cita es en dos semanas.*
- *¿Cuánto cuesta la cita?*
- *No cuesta nada. Su seguro cubre todas las citas.*
- *¿Qué más cubre mi seguro?*
- *Su seguro también cubre los medicamentos y cirugías, si es que lo necesita.*
- *Muchas gracias por toda su ayuda doctor.*

- *De nada. Por favor, no se olvide tomar sus medicamentos.*
- *No lo olvidaré. Gracias.*

- Thank you for your care, doctor.
- Don't worry. Don't forget to take your pills.
- What are the names of the pills?
- The names of the pills are in the medical prescription I gave you.
- There are many medications written in this prescription.
- That's right. These pills are for your stomach ache. You have to take 1 pill after breakfast and one after dinner.
- Okay. I get it. And what about this other medicine?
- That is a syrup. That syrup will help with the burning sensation in the throat. Remember to drink it before eating.
- And these pills?
- These pills are for the infection.
- Anything else I should know?
- You should not eat anything spicy. You should not drink soda or alcoholic beverages. Do you smoke?
- No, I do not smoke.
- Good. You don't consume drugs, right?
- I don't consume drugs, doctor.
- That's perfect! Don't have dinner too late. Don't get stressed out too much.
- Can I do exercise?
- Yes, but very carefully.
- What if my stomach hurts again?
- If it hurts a lot, then you can come to the emergency room.
- How long should I take these pills?
- You should take those pills until the next appointment.
- When is the next appointment?
- The next appointment is in two weeks.
- How much does the appointment cost?
- It costs nothing. Your insurance covers all appointments.
- What else does my insurance cover?
- Your insurance also covers medications and surgeries, if you need them.
- Thank you very much for all your help doctor.
- No problem. Please don't forget to take your medications.
- I won't forget. Thank you.

Chapter 9 - At the Pharmacy

After having been to the doctor's, you may need to go to the pharmacy to get the medication he prescribed to yo. What phrases can you use? Let's take a look at the most common:

Spanish --> English

¿En qué le podemos ayudar? --> How can we help you?

Quiero comprar estas pastillas --> I want to buy this pills

¿Cuánto cuestan estas pastillas? --> How much do these pills cost?

Quiero 20 pastillas --> I want 20 pills

¿Quiere que le muestre mi receta médica? --> Do you want me to show you my prescription?

¿Puede mostrarme su receta médica? --> Can you show me your prescription?

Aquí está mi receta médica --> Here's my prescription

¿Para qué sirven estas pastillas? --> What are these pills for?

¿Tiene algún descuento? --> Do you have any discount?

¿Desea comprar todos los medicamentos en esta receta? --> Do you want to buy all the medication that's in this prescription?

¿Tiene esta receta médica la firma del doctor? --> Does this prescription have the doctor's signature?

¿Cubre mi seguro estos medicamentos? --> Does my insurance cover these medications?

Tengo seguro médico --> I have medical insurance

¿Tiene medicamentos genéricos? --> Do you have generic medications?

¿Tiene medicamentos de venta libre? --> Do you have over-the-counter medications?

Quiero comprar medicamentos sin receta médica --> I want to buy over-the-counter medications

Let's look at some conversations:

- *¡Buenas tardes!*
- *¡Buenas tardes! ¿En qué podemos ayudarla?*
- *Quisiera comprar estos medicamentos.*
- *¿Está es la receta médica?*
- *Sí, esta es la receta.*
- *¿Tiene la receta la firma del doctor?*
- *Sí, aquí está firma del doctor*
- *Muy bien. Nosotros tenemos todos estos medicamentos.*
- *¡Genial!*
- *¿Quiere comprar todos los medicamentos que se mencionan en esta receta?*
- *No. Hay 5 medicamentos escritos ahí, ¿verdad?*
- *Sí. Hay 5.*
- *Sólamente quisiera comprar 4.*
- *¿Cuáles quiere comprar?*

- *Quiero comprar esta medicina. Son pastillas, ¿verdad?*
- *Así es. Son pastillas para el dolor de estómago*
- *Ok. También quiero comprar el jarabe.*
- *Este jarabe cuesta 50 dólares.*
- *¿En serio? Pero solo quiero la botella de 150 miligramos.*
- *Lo siento. No vendemos ese jarabe en botellas de 150 miligramos.*
- *¿En cuánto lo tiene?*
- *Sólo lo tenemos en 500 miligramos.*
- *Pero eso es demasiado.*
- *Lo sé, pero es lo único que tenemos.*
- *Bueno, entonces llevaré esa. ¿Para qué es ese jarabe? Me acuerdo que el doctor me dijo que ese jarabe era bueno para la infección.*
- *Eso es cierto. Este jarabe es para la infección. ¿Qué otro medicamento quiere comprar?*
- *Quiero comprar este medicamento.*
- *¿Cuál sería el último medicamento que comprará?*
- *Estas pastillas. Solo espero que no sean muy caras.*
- *No se preocupe, lo tenemos en genérico.*
- *¿En serio?*
- *Así es. Si usted compra la version genérica de ese medicamento, le saldrá mucho más barato.*
- *Ok, suena bien. Quisiera llevar la versión genérica de ese medicamento, entonces.*
- *Muy bien. Veo que usted tiene seguro médico.*
- *Así es.*
- *Su seguro médico cubre todos estos medicamentos. No tendrá que pagar absolutamente nada.*
- *¿En serio?*
- *Así es.*
- *¡Qué buena noticia! Muchas gracias.*
- *De nada, señorita.*

- Good afternoon!
- Good afternoon! How can we help you?
- I would like to buy these medications.
- Is this the prescription?
- Yes, this is the prescription.
- Does the prescription have the doctor's signature?
- Yes, here is the doctor's signature
- Very good. We have all these medications.
- Great!
- Do you want to buy all the medications mentioned in this prescription?
- No. There are 5 medications written there, right?
- Yes. There are 5.
- I would just like to buy 4.
- Which ones do you want to buy?
- I want to buy this medicine. They are pills, right?
- That's right. They are stomach ache pills
- Okay. I also want to buy the syrup.
- This syrup costs $ 50.

- Really? But I just want the 150-milligram bottle.
- I'm sorry. We do not sell that syrup in 150-milligram bottles.
- What do you have?
- We only have it in 500 milligrams.
- But that is too much.
- I know, but it's the only thing we have.
- Well, then I'll take that one. What is that syrup for? I remember the doctor telling me that syrup was good for the infection.
- That's true. This syrup is for infection. What other medicine do you want to buy?
- I want to buy this medicine.
- What would be the last medication you will buy?
- These pills. I just hope they are not very expensive.
- Don't worry, we have it in generic.
- Really?
- That's right. If you buy the generic version of that medicine, it will be much cheaper.
- OK, sounds good. I would like to have the generic version of that medication, then.
- Very good. I see that you have medical insurance.
- That's right.
- Your medical insurance covers all these medications. You will not have to pay absolutely anything.
- Really?
- That's right.
- That is good news! Thank you very much.
- You're welcome.

Let's take a look at another conversation:

- *¡Buenos días!*
- *¡Buenos días! ¿En qué podemos ayudarlo?*
- *Quisiera comprar unos medicamentos.*
- *¿Tiene receta médica?*
- *No, no tengo receta médica.*
- *Disculpe, sólo vendemos medicamentos con receta médica. No lo podemos ayudar.*
- *Quiero comprar medicamentos de venta libre.*
- *Ya veo. ¿Qué medicamentos esta buscando?*
- *Quiero una pastilla para la gripe.*
- *¿Tiene gripe?*
- *Sí*
- *Entiendo. Aquí tiene unas pastillas para la gripe.*
- *¿Cómo debo tomarlas?*
- *Debe tomar una pastilla cada ocho horas. No tome alcohol ni fume.*
- *Entiendo. ¿Cuánto cuestan estas pastillas?*
- *Estas pastillas cuestasn 8 dólares*
- *¿Cada pastille cuesta 8 dólares?*
- *No, todas las pastillas cuestan 8 dólares.*
- *Entiendo.*

- *¿Algo más en lo que le pueda ayudar?*
- *Bueno, quisiera también comprar un jarabe para el dolor de estómago.*
- *Ok, pero sólo podrá comprarlo si tiene receta médica.*
- *Bueno, entonces regresaré luego con mi receta médica. Gracias*
- *De nada.*

- Good Morning!
- Good Morning! How can we help you?
- I would like to buy some medications.
- Do you have a prescription?
- No, I don't have a prescription.
- I'm sorry, we only sell prescription drugs. We can not help you.
- I want to buy over-the-counter medications.
- I see. What medications are you looking for?
- I want a flu pill.
- Do you have a cold?
- Yes
- I get it. Here are some flu pills.
- How should I take them?
- You should take one pill every eight hours. Don't drink alcohol or smoke.
- I get it. How much do these pills cost?
- These pills cost 8 dollars
- Does each pill cost 8 dollars?
- No, all pills cost $ 8.
- I get it.
- Anything else I can help you with?
- Well, I would also like to buy a stomach pain syrup.
- Ok, but you can only buy it if you have a prescription.
- Well, then I'll come back later with my prescription. Thank you
- No problem.

Chapter 10 - Location, Directions, And Getting Around

You learned different places you would like to go already. Now, you can learn how to ask for directions as well as understand the locations such as near, far, next to, etc. These are short words but they can change the meaning of a sentence a lot.

Prepositions to Describe Location

For each of the prepositions listed below, there is a sample sentence. Draw the sample sentence to illustrate the preposition. Write the sample sentence under your drawing.

You will note that many of the prepositions in the list below have a secondary preposition listed beside them. Spanish prepositions are not always used exactly like English prepositions. Sometimes, "de" will be added in, even though it doesn't make sense in English. Memorize both prepositions together so that it becomes a habit to use them together.

Abajo de /uh-bah-ho day/- under --> *El gato está abajo.*

Adentro de /uh-den-tro day/- inside --> No estoy adentro de la iglesia.

Afuera de /uh-fwair-uh day/- outside --> Las plantas crecen afuera de la ventana.

Al lado de /ahl lah-do day/- beside/ next to --> El baño está al lado de la cocina.

Arriba de /uh-ree-buh day/- above --> Los libros están arriba del escritorio.

Cerca de/a /sare-cuh day/ ah/- close to --> El león no está cerca de la serpiente.

Delante de /day-lahn-tay day/- in front of --> El carro está delante del tren.

Detrás de /day-trahs day/- behind --> Estoy detrás de mi maestro.

En /ehn/- in/ on /at --> La bola está en la cesta.

Encima de /ehn-see-muh day/- on top of --> El agua está encima del refri.

En frente de /ehn fren-tay day/- in front of --> El arbol está en frente de la casa.

Entre /ehn-tray/- between --> El niño está entre sus padres.

Lejos de /lay-hos day/- far from --> Mi tio vive lejos de nosotros.

Sobre /so-bray/- above --> Los lápices están sobre la carpeta.

Prepositions in Sentences

If the preposition is used as the last word in the phrase or sentence, you will not use the "de" at the end of each sentence. If it is connected to something, for example, outside of something or under something, then you will use "de." Look at these examples.

La niña está encima de la silla.

La niña está adentro.

In the first sentence, we know she is on top of the chair. Because of that, we use "de." The second sentence does not tell us what she is in. There is no need for "de."

Take a look at the following incorrect sentences. Try to figure out what is wrong with each sentence. Correct the sentences.

Pedro están en la clase. The verb needs to be conjugated correctly for Pedro. He is one person. The correct verb in this sentence is *está.*

Los perros están encima de la casa. This sentence doesn't make sense. The dogs are on top of the house? No, there are many other prepositions that would fit much better. For example, *adentro, afuera,* or *en.*

Vivo cerca una tienda. You need a preposition after cerca. You wouldn't say "I live close a store." *Vivo cerca a una tienda* would fit much better.

Ellos trabajan adentro de un escritorio. This sentence doesn't make sense either. Who works inside a desk? The preposition can be changed or the object. Here is another sentence that makes better sense: *Ellos trabajan en un escritorio.* While "*en*" can mean on, in, or at, "at" is clearly the one that makes the most sense here.

Debajo vs abajo

In some examples, you may see "*debajo.*" In other examples, you will see "*abajo.*" "*Abajo*" is used when you are simply saying an object is under or below. However, if you are naming another object, the object it is under, then you need to use "*debajo.*"

La niña está abajo.

La niña está debajo del carro.

You will see this same difference with "*dentro*" and "*adentro de*" as well as "*delante*" and "*adelante*" and "*afuera*" and "*fuera.*" These words have the same meaning, but they are simply used differently depending on what comes afterward. Look at the following examples.

Las peras están debajo de las manzanas.

Ellos están adentro.

La serpiente está dentro de su jaula.

A la niña le gusta jugar fuera de la casa.

Al niño le gusta jugar afuera.

El carro rojo está adelante del carro azul.

El carro gris está adelante.

Prepositions Practice

Activity 1. Write "de" or "del" in the blank if one is needed. If not, put an x.

El gato está cerca _____ ratón.

No quiero ir adentro _____ ahora.

La tienda está cerca _____ la biblioteca.

Vivo lejos _____ toda mi familia.

513

Estás entre _____ los dos estantes.

Respuestas

El gato está cerca del ratón.

No quiero ir adentro ahora.

La tienda está cerca de la biblioteca.

Vivo lejos de toda mi familia.

Estás entre los dos estantes.

Activity 2. Write sentences with the following prepositions. Look around the room you are currently in and use objects you can see for your sentences. Use the prepositions- *adentro, afuera, al lado de, entre, and delante.*

Activity 3. Fill in the blanks with any of the prepositions above. Make sure you use "de" or "del" when needed. There can be more than one correct answer in some instances. The answers listed below are only one example of what can fit in the sentence.

1. *Siempre pongo mis zapatos _____ la cama.*

2. *Está lloviendo _____.*

3. *La escuela está _____ la casa de mi amiga.*

4. *La ducha está _____ inodoro.*

5. *La luz está _____ la mesa.*

6. *El piso está _____ techo.*

7. *No me gusta poner la comida _____ la mesa.*

Respuestas

1. *Siempre pongo mis zapatos debajo de la cama.*

2. *Está lloviendo afuera.*

3. *La escuela está cerca de/ lejos de la casa de mi amiga.*

4. *La ducha está al lado del inodoro.*

5. *La luz está sobre la mesa.*

6. *El piso está debajo del techo.*

7. *No me gusta poner la comida debajo de la mesa.*

¿Donde está....?

Asking Directions

If you are planning to visit a Spanish-speaking country, being able to ask for directions is one of the most important abilities. You will be unfamiliar with the town and streets, and it may be difficult to find street signs. Below are some of the most important vocabulary words to know.

Derecha /deh-reh-chuh/- right

Izquierda /iz-kee-air-duh/- left

Derecho /deh-reh-cho/- straight

Directo /dee-rec-to/- straight

Doblar /do-blar/- to turn

Esquina /es-kee-nuh/- corner

Cruzar /croo-sar/- to cross

Calle /cai-yay/- street

Semaforo /seh-mah-fore-oh/- stoplight

Cuadra /cwah-drah/- block

Norte /nore-tay/- north

Sur /suhr/- south

Este /es-tay/- east

Oeste /oh-es-tay/- west

Listen to this set of directions.

Doble a la derecha y camina por tres cuadras. Luego, doble a la izquierda y camine una cuadra. La farmacia estará en su derecha.

When in doubt, Spanish-speakers are generally louder and more out-going. They will point and indicate with their hands which direction to go. Even if you don't understand everything they say, you can point in the direction you think you should go and ask this question:

¿Esa dirección?

You might not know all the steps, but you will know which direction to start out in.

What questions can you ask to get someone to give you directions? Here are a few options.

¿Dónde está el hotel Vargas?

¿Dónde puedo encontrar el mercado?

¿Dónde está una panadería?

Once again, the speaker will probably point. Listen for the key words "*derecha*" or "*izquierda*" to help guide you.

Vocabulary Review

If there is a place you think you will need to find while on vacation, you can look up that specific word. Meanwhile, Match the following place to their meanings.

Iglesia   church

Biblioteca	library
Farmacia	library
Tienda	store
Restaurante	restaurant
Cine movie	theater
Playa	beach
Estación de bus	bus station
Mercado	market

Use the prepositions from earlier in this chapter to describe some of these places in relation to your house. For example,

La tienda está al lado de mi casa.

La estación de bus está cerca de mi casa.

La playa está lejos de mi casa.

Direction Practice

Activity 1. Read the description of the town aloud. Draw a picture to illustrate the town then use your picture to follow directions in the second activity.

En la ciudad, hay una biblioteca. La biblioteca es muy grande. Cubre toda una cuadra. Al norte, hay un banco, y al lado del banco, hay un mercado. Al sur de la biblioteca, hay dos panaderías y un cine. Adelante del cine está una estación de bus. Al este de las panaderías está una farmacia. Hay un parque al oeste de la biblioteca. No hay una feria en la ciudad.

Look at your map and answer the questions.

¿Dónde está el banco?

¿Hay un cine en la ciudad?

¿Dónde está la biblioteca?

Respuestas-

El banco está al lado de un mercado.

Si, hay un cine en la ciudad.

La biblioteca está al norte de las panaderías. (Answers may vary for this one).

Activity 2. Using your map, write directions *"del parque a la farmacia."* Here are some possible directions.

Salga del parque. Doble a la derecha. Camine media cuadra. Doble a la izquierda. Camine una cuadra. La farmacia estará en tu derecha.

Commands for "Usted"

Re-read these directions below, then read the second set. What is the difference?

Doble a la derecha y camine tres cuadras. Luego, doble a la izquierda y camine una cuadra. La farmacia estará en su derecha.

Dobla a la derecha y camina tres cuadras. Luego, dobla a la izquierda y camina una cuadra. La farmacia estará en su derecha.

There is a very subtle difference. Notice the ending letter on the verbs. On the first set, the verbs end with "e." On the second set, the verbs end with "a." Why is this? Well, the above verbs are not regularly conjugated verbs. They are command verbs. The person giving the directions is commanding you to take certain directions if you want to arrive at your destination.

There are two separate ways to form commands. Luckily, they are not too complicated.

For *usted*, you need to follow these steps.

1. Make the "*yo*" form of the verb.

2. Drop the "*o*" from the end of the "*yo*" form.

3. Add on the opposite ending. If it is an *-ar* verb, add on "e." If it is an *-er* or *-ir* verb, add on "a."

Let's go through these steps with a few different examples.

Hablar -> Hablo -> Habla -> Hable

Now, it may seem as though the step about creating the "*yo*" form and dropping the "*o*" is not important. It is very important. If a verb is irregular, this will change its spelling. Sometimes, you may forget which verbs are irregular until you conjugate them to the "*yo*" form.

Encontrar -> Encuentro -> Encuentra -> Encuentre

Comer -> Cómo -> Come -> Coma

Jugar -> Juego -> Juega -> Juegue

Notice that with "*jugar*," an "*ue*" was added instead of just "*e*." This is to maintain the proper pronunciation. If there was no "*u*," the syllable "*ge*" would sound like "*heh*." With the "*u*," the "*g*" keeps its strong sound.

Try changing these to "*usted*" commands.

Beber, Recordar, Salir, Preguntar, Caer

Respuestas-

Beba, Recuerde, Salga, Pregunte, Caiga

If you want to make a negative usted command, you simply add "no" in front.

No beba leche.

No juegue con el perro.

Pretend you are cleaning the house, and you need your roommates to help clean-up. Change the following into commands.

Poner los libros en la mesa.

Poner los zapatos en el closet.

Guardar la comida.

Limpiar el baño.

No apagar la televisión.

Respuestas-

Ponga los libros en la mesa.

Ponga los zapatos en el closet.

Guarde la comida.

Limpie el baño.

No apague la televisión.

Once again, the last one has the letter "u" added to keep the pronunciation. Those are how you make commands for "*usted.*"

Tú Commands

"*Tú*" commands are formed a bit differently. To make a positive "*tú*" command, you need to use the *él/ ella/ usted* format.

For example, "*Baila con la música*" or "*Limpia su cuarto.*"

These commands should be fairly simple to make, since you already know how to conjugate verbs in the present *él/ ella/ usted* format. However, negative "*tú*" commands are different than the positive command. For the negative command, you follow the same formula as the "*usted*" commands except for one difference. Read the steps below.

1. Make the "*yo*" form of the verb.

2. Drop the "*o*" from the end of the "*yo*" form.

3. Add on the opposite ending. If it is an -*ar* verb, add on "*es.*" If it is an -*er* or -*ir* verb, add on "*as.*"

Jugar -> Juego -> Juega -> Juegues

Recordar -> Recuerdo -> Recuerda -> Recuerdes

Now, there are a few completely irregular commands that you will need to memorize. You can see them in the chart below.

Ser	Sé
Ir	Ve
Tener	Ten
Venir	Ven
Decir	Di
Poner	Pon
Salir	Sal
Hacer	Haz

Commands with Direct and Indirect Objects

With commands, you can add direct and indirect objects onto the end of the command word. For example, I can say.

Traiga el libro a mi -> Traigamelo.

You always put the person, usually the indirect object first, before the direct object. Look at another example.

Lea la historia a él. -> Leasela.

Now, where did the "*se*" come from? Normally, "*él*" would be changed to "*le*" as the indirect object. However, in Spanish, you cannot put "*le*" and "*la*" or "*le*" and "*lo*" together. If it appears that you need to abbreviate your sentence, and you will have both "*le*" and either "*lo*" or "*la*," then you change the "*le*" to "*se*." This is simply to make the pronunciation of the word sound a bit better. It does not change the meaning at all.

For example,

Da el regalo a ella. -> Daselo.

The "*se*" stands for "*ella*," the indirect object. The "*lo*" stands for *regalo*, a singular, male object. Review the section on direct and indirect objects if you are still having trouble with this. Otherwise, practice shortening the sentences below. Not all of them will have both an indirect object and a direct object.

Beba el jugo. _____

Da la silla a tu amiga. _____

Compre los libros para tu esposa. _____

Traiga una bebida para nosotros. _____

Haz eso para mi por favor. _____

Respuestas-

Bebalo

Dasela

Compreselos

Traiganosla

Hazmelo por favor.

Spend time memorizing the irregular commands before you move on to the next section. It can be easy to mix up some of the irregular commands for regularly conjugated verbs if you don't know what they are.

Basic Conversations

Read the following conversation aloud. Practice playing different parts with a friend.

Manuel: ¿Dónde está mi hotel?

Hombre: ¿Cómo se llama su hotel?

Manuel: Se llama...el Hotel Atardecer.

Hombre: Ah, el Hotel Atardecer. Yo sé dónde está. Usted necesita ir por el sur.

Manuel: ¿Cuanto tiempo caminando?

Hombre Tal vez cinco ó seis minutos. Luego, doble a la derecha y camine por diez minutos. El Hotel Atardecer es muy alto. Es gris y verde.

Manuel: ¡Muchas gracias!

Chapter 11 - Your Method for Learning Spanish with Music

Here is an easy 4-step method to learning Spanish from songs and music:

Step 1: Pick a Song and Start Listening

Step 2: Get the Lyrics Online

Step 3: Learn the Song

Step 4: Sing and Perform

Step 1: Pick a Song and Start Listening

As with movies and shows, here are two particularly important things to consider when picking out a song:

- Pick a genre of music that you like
- Pick a song suitable to your level

Another great way to choose a Spanish song is to search through some of your favourite genres:

- If you like listening to the top hits on the US Billboard charts, then you'll also probably enjoy pop, soft rock, and the reggaetón hits on the Latin Billboards as well.
- If you like hip-hop or rap then look for reggaetón, Latin rap or hip-hop songs.
- If you like music involving a variety of wind, string, and percussion instruments then go for the traditional Latin rhythms like salsa, vallenato, and bachata.
- If you're into country music, then you might like banda or ranchera.
- If you enjoy rock or alternative, then choose the same type of genre but in Spanish.

Once you have figured out the type of genre you would like to listen to, pick a song that is suitable to your level. It's important to choose the kind of music that you enjoy, but if you are a beginner then you are probably going to have a harder time picking up reggaetón lyrics or rap than let's say pop or rock. A lot of salsa music can be very fast-paced too. The easier songs to learn at first are usually in the rock or pop genre.

Feel free to use my top 20-recommendation list to find songs that best suit your level, likes, and musical preferences. I've highlighted the songs that are more appropriate for beginners, intermediates, or advanced level students to help you find the perfect song for you to begin studying with.

Once you've chosen a song, add it to your playlist and start listening. Feel free to add a couple of other Spanish songs that aren't included in my list that you also might be interested in. After listening to all the songs you've gathered, you can then choose the song you like best to use in your studies.

The goal here is to passively listen to your new Spanish music playlist. By casually listening, you'll be able to figure out naturally which songs appeal to you the most. You also might find yourself learning a few words here and there or even being able to sing parts of the chorus without even studying the song yet. Once you've gotten to know the song's basic rhythm and melody, you're now ready for the next step.

Identifying Vocabulary

Before you go online to get the translation for your song, make a list of how many words you know. This will test your listening and comprehension skills.

As a beginner, you might find that you only recognize a handful of words. For those of you who are intermediate or advanced, you may surprise yourself with how much you already know. If you know a lot of the words, that's great. If you don't know that many - no worries.

Step 2: Get the Lyrics Online

Now that you have your song stuck in your head, it's time to start studying it. First things first, you need to understand what all the lyrics mean. If you did the last exercise, you've already written down the words you already know. The basic idea of this learning method is to slowly add more and more words to the list of words you know and take less and less from the list of words you don't.

Start by looking up the Spanish lyrics as well as the English translation online. The songs I've included in this book's top 20 recommendations are all very popular, so you shouldn't have any trouble finding the lyrics in both languages. Print out both the English and Spanish lyrics.

Get familiar with the song's lyrics. Read through the Spanish lyrics and go through the English version as well to get a general idea of what the song is all about. Once you've done that, move on to the next step.

Learn New Vocabulary

It's now time to look up any words you're unfamiliar with. Take a look through the entire song and pick out all the words you don't understand and would like to study further. Look them up using the English translation print out or by using a dictionary. Keep in mind, sometimes it's useful to double-check the translation, especially for words repeated in the song to make sure you have the right meaning. Sometimes online translations are incorrect.

Once you've found the meanings to all your vocabulary words, turn them into flashcards either with an online tool or make them yourself at home. Begin studying them and memorizing them religiously.

Step 3: Learn the Song

At this point, you should have a pretty good grasp of your selected Spanish song. You've listened to it multiple times, you've gotten familiar with the rhythm and melody, and you've studied and memorized key vocabulary. So, now what?

It's time to sing along! But before you go and grab the copy of your Spanish lyric print out, I want you to grab a blank sheet of paper instead and write the lyrics out by hand. At first, this may seem like an extra step that is a bit unnecessary but trust me when I say, this is also a very important step in the learning process. It's a known fact that the specific act of writing things down increases your focus and helps you process more of the information. A recent study even showed that note-taking with an actual pen or pencil is way more effective than simply taking notes on a laptop or smartphone! This may be a bit tedious but, I promise, it's very effective and will help you learn faster in the long run. Take some time now to write down the Spanish lyrics.

Once you've written out the lyrics, it's time to start singing! Start by learning the chorus. If the chorus's words and melody are already stuck in your head at this point – great! If not, grab your Spanish lyrics and listen to the song while you practice singing along. Once you've memorized the lyrics and can easily repeat the chorus without looking, move on to verses 1 and 2 and do the same.

Learning the verses can sometimes be a little tricky because they're normally not as catchy or repetitive as the chorus usually is. From my personal experience, I found that the best way to learn the verses is by putting a lot of emphasis on the very first line and then stacking the 2nd, 3rd, and 4th lines after that. The basic idea behind this technique is to use the part of our mind that remembers information by association. When given the first line of a lyric, our brain naturally works to trigger your memory so that it remembers what words follow after it.

Here's an example using a verse from the Spanish version of Jingle Bells:

Caminando en trineo, cantando por los campos,

Volando por la nieve, radiantes de amor,

Repican las campanas, brillantes de alegría.

Paseando y cantando se alegra el corazón, ¡ay!

Start by memorizing the first line, "*Caminando en trineo, cantando por los campos*".

Next stack the second line. But always remember to start singing from the very first line.

Example: "*Caminando en trineo, cantando por lo campos, volando por la nieve, radiantes de amor.*"

Then, stack the third line. And again, start by singing the lyrics from the very first line, then the second, then the third.

Repeat the same stacking sequence for the fourth and final line.

The key is to focus the very first line. Then anchor the second line to the first, the third line to the second, and the fourth line to the third.

Step 4: Sing and Perform

The final step in this learning process is to sing the entire song out loud from start to finish. Of course, you will not be allowed to look at any of the lyrics while you sing. You will have to sing it entirely from memory!

If you can, try to not just sing by yourself; find someone to sing the song to. To start, you could try singing to family members in your living room or to some friends at a karaoke bar. You could also team up with another Spanish learner and sing together. If you're feeling extra confident, you could even challenge yourself by practicing the song with a band and perform the song on stage. Treating this specific exercise like a "performance" is a plus as it will give you an added incentive to memorize your lines.

If you prefer not to sing in front of people, but you enjoy acting or roleplaying, you could watch the music video and act out or mimic the singer. Pretend you're the artist and go all out. This step is especially fun if you have a Spanish learning buddy to practice and sing with.

You should already know your song quite well at this point, so your main focus should be on being able to sing the entire song through without stopping or forgetting any of the lyrics. This performance mentality will solidify in your mind, the new vocabulary you've learned and help you retain it long term.

Building on Your New Vocabulary

Another tip to take your studying even further is to pick specific words or phrases from the song's lyrics and create your own original sentences to use in your Spanish conversation. Try this simple exercise to practice your Spanish communication skills.

Look through your lyrics again, choose 3-5 words, expressions, or short phrases from the song to incorporate into your conversational practice.

Here are some lyrics from the Spanish version of Jingle Bells:

Caminando en trineo, cantando por los campos,

Volando por la nieve, radiantes de amor,

Repican las campanas, brillantes de alegría.

Paseando y cantando se alegra el corazón, ¡ay!

Cascabeles, cascabeles, tra la la la la.

¡Qué alegría todo el día, que felicidad, ay!

Cascabeles, cascabeles, tra la la la la.

Que alegría todo el día, que felicidad

Pick a word or phrase and introduce it into a real conversation by creating your own original sentence.

For Example:

Voy caminando al colegio todos los días.

I walk to school every day.

El avión está volando demasiado bajo.

That plane is flying too low.

By doing exercises like this, you can begin building on the vocabulary you've learned from the songs you're studying and you can start using them in your Spanish conversations.

Chapter 12 - Internship Evaluation

- *Esto decidirá tu futuro en la industria* – This will decide your future in the industry

- *no te había vuelto a ver desde tu primer día* - i hadn't seen you again since your first day

- *voy a suponer que estás buscando la evaluación* - i'm guessing you've come looking for the evaluation

- *las obligaciones de la pasantía* - the internship obligations

- *me he sentido muy agradecido con usted* - i have felt very thankful to you

- *voy a recordar mi experiencia aquí para siempre* - i'm going to remember my experience here forever

- *vengo a realizar la evaluación final de la pasantía* - i'm here to take part in the final internship evaluation

- *agradezco que tengas esa percepción de la empresa* - i'm thankful for you to have that perception of the company

- *¿estás listo para contestar las preguntas?* - are you ready to answer the questions?

- *será sencillo todo, pero debes ser sincero* - everything will be simple, but you have to be honest

- *es lo último que me falta para culminar esta pasantía* - it's the last thing remaining to finish this internship

- *¿puedes describir tu experiencia en la empresa con una única palabra?* - can you describe your experience at the company with a single word?

- *Comenzó a hacerme sentir como parte de una gran familia* - started making me feel as if I was part of a great family

- *nunca me faltó colaboración para poder aprender a usar los sistemas* - I never lacked cooperation to learn how to use the systems

- *siempre hubo alguien acompañándome* - there was always someone accompanying me

- *asegurándose de que me iba bien* - making sure I was doing well

- *¿hubo algo que no te haya gustado o que cambiarías?* - was there something that you didn't like or which you'd change?

- *no cambiaría nada* - I wouldn't change anything

- *disfruté las instalaciones* - enjoyed the facilities

- *¿cómo piensas usar esta experiencia para crecer en tu carrera?* - how do you plan to use this experience to grow in your career?

- *¿le dio esta pasantía un giro a tu vida profesional o simplemente fue un paso más?* - did this internship give a new turn to your professional life, or was it simply an additional step?

- *creo que esta experiencia me ayudará a entender cómo es la vida realmente en las empresas* - I think that this experience will help me understand what life is really like in the companies

- *pude ver realmente qué es lo que hacemos* - I was able to see what we really do

- *qué voy a hacer en un futuro* - what I'm going to do in the future

- *entender mejor mi rol en la industria* - better understanding my role in the industry

- *observar las dificultades de todas las cosas que vienen por delante* - observing the difficulties I have coming up ahead

- *entender mejor lo que debo aprender antes de graduarme y convertirme en un empleado más* - better understand what I must learn before graduating and becoming another employee

- *me ayudó a prepararme para trabajar en equipo con otros profesionales* - helped me learn to prepare myself for working as a team with other professionals

- *¿cuál fue tu momento profesional más memorable dentro de la empresa?* - what was your most memorable professional moment within the company?

- *recibí una gran bienvenida. Hubo muy buena recepción* - received a great welcome. There was such a good reception

- *una gran fiesta de cumpleaños anticipada* - it was like a great birthday party in advance

- *me sentí como parte de algo especial* - I felt like part of something special

- *algo que intento cultivar en la oficina* - It's something that I try to cultivate at the office

- *¿cuál sería tu evaluación de ti mismo en estos ocho meses de pasantía?* - what would be your evaluation of yourself in these eight months of internship?

- *un valor del uno al diez* - a value between one to ten

- *no logré cumplir todos los objetivos que me propuse* - I didn't manage to accomplish all of the objectives I set myself

- *tu actitud profesional ha sido genial* - your professional attitude has been excellent

- *has logrado enormes resultados* - you've accomplished enormous results

- *me aseguraré de darte una recomendación* - I'll make sure to give you a recommendation

- *¡sal allá afuera a comerte el mundo!* - go out there and show the world what you're made of!

Let's see the following dialogue:

- *Elena: ¿Cómo te va, Jack? Es un placer verte por acá, no te había vuelto a ver desde tu primer día... ¿hace cuánto fue eso? ¿Qué te trae por aquí el día de hoy? Voy a suponer que estás buscando la evaluación.*

- Elena: How's it going, Jack. It's a pleasure to see you come by, since I hadn't seen you again since your first day... how long ago was that? What brings you here today? I'm guessing you've come looking for the evaluation.

- *Jack: Hola, señora Elena, estoy muy bien, ¿y usted? Sí, no he tenido tiempo de pasar por acá por las obligaciones de la pasantía, el informe y todas esas cosas. Igualmente, me he sentido muy agradecido con usted por haberme traído a esta empresa y voy a recordar mi experiencia aquí para siempre. Y, bueno, sí... vengo a realizar la evaluación final de la pasantía, ¿tendrá tiempo ahora mismo o prefiere que regrese en unas horas?*

- Jack: Hello, Mrs. Elena, I'm doing very well, and you? Yes, I haven't had much time to come by here because of the internship obligations, the report and all of those things. Still, I have felt very thankful to you for bringing me to this company, and I'm going to remember my experience here forever. And well, yes... I'm here to take part in the final internship evaluation, do you have time right now or do you prefer that I come back in a few hours?

- *Elena: Muy bonitas palabras, Jack. Agradezco que tengas esa percepción de la empresa. De acuerdo, creo que sí tengo media hora para dedicarla a esta evaluación. Ahora, ¿estás listo para contestar las preguntas? Será sencillo todo, pero debes ser sincero.*

- Elena: Very beautiful words, Jack. I'm thankful for you to have that perception of the company. Okay then, I think I do have half an hour to dedicate to this evaluation. Now, are you ready to answer the questions? Everything will be simple, but you have to be honest.

- *Jack: Sí, estoy listo. Es lo último que me falta para culminar esta pasantía, así que he estado preparándome.*

- Jack: Yes, I'm ready. It's the last thing remaining to finish this internship, so I've been preparing myself.

- *Elena: Perfecto. Voy a comenzar. Vamos con la primera pregunta: ¿puedes describir tu experiencia en la empresa con una única palabra? De ser así, ¿cuál y por qué?*

- Elena: Perfect. I'll begin. Let's start with the first question: can you describe your experience at the company with a single word? If so, which one and why?

- *Jack: De acuerdo, sí puedo usar una palabra. Me gustaría utilizar la palabra familiar para esta respuesta. Digo «familiar» porque, al llegar, no pasaron ni diez minutos para que las personas de mi departamento de la empresa comenzaran a hacerme sentir como parte de una gran familia. Nunca me faltó colaboración para poder aprender a usar los sistemas, para saber los horarios y para hacer amigos. Fue muy genial, siempre hubo alguien acompañándome y asegurándose de que me iba bien.*

- Jack: Very well, I can use one word. I would like to use the word family for this answer. I say 'family' because when I arrived, not even ten minutes had passed before people of my company department started making me feel as if I was part of a great family. I never lacked cooperation to learn how to use the systems, to learn the schedules and to make new friends. It was amazing, there was always someone accompanying me and making sure I was doing well.

- *Elena: Excelente, me encanta saber eso. Ahora, la segunda pregunta: ¿hubo algo que no te haya gustado o que cambiarías? De ser así, ¿qué?*

- Elena: Excellent, I love to hear that. Now, second question: was there something that you didn't like or which you'd change? If so, what?

- *Jack: En realidad, mi tiempo acá fue perfecto, no cambiaría nada. Desde el primer momento hasta el último lo disfruté, y también disfruté las instalaciones.*

- Jack: Truthfully, my time here was perfect, and I wouldn't change anything. From the first moment until the last I enjoyed it, and also enjoyed the facilities.

- *Elena: ¿Seguro? De acuerdo. Tercera pregunta para ti: ¿cómo piensas usar esta experiencia para crecer en tu carrera? ¿Le dio esta pasantía un giro a tu vida profesional o simplemente fue un paso más?*

- Elena: Are you sure? All right. Third question for you: how do you plan to use this experience to grow in your career? Did this internship give a new turn to your professional life, or was it simply an additional step?

- *Jack: Interesantes preguntas. Bueno, para comenzar, creo que esta experiencia me ayudará a entender cómo es la vida realmente en las empresas de nuestra industria. Pude ver realmente qué es lo que hacemos y qué voy a hacer en un futuro. Disfruté poder entender mejor mi rol en la industria, además de observar las dificultades de todas las cosas que vienen por delante. Ahora, sí pienso que esta pasantía le dio un giro a mi carrera. Voy a entender mejor lo que debo aprender antes de graduarme y convertirme en un empleado más, y esto me ayudó a prepararme para trabajar en equipo con otros profesionales.*

- Jack: Interesting questions. Well, to begin, I think that this experience will help me understand what life is really like in the companies of our industry. I was able to see what we really do and what I'm going to do in the future. I enjoyed better understanding my role in the industry, as well as observing the difficulties I have coming up ahead. Now, I think that this internship gave a marked a turning point for my career. I'll better understand what I must learn before graduating and becoming another employee, and this helped me learn to prepare myself for working as a team with other professionals.

- *Elena: De acuerdo, quedan solo dos preguntas más. Cuarta pregunta: ¿cuál fue tu momento profesional más memorable dentro de la empresa?*

- Elena: Fine, now there's only two more questions. Fourth question: what was your most memorable professional moment within the company?

- *Jack: Creo que sería el instante en el que entré y recibí una gran bienvenida. Hubo muy buena recepción y, de hecho, los otros tres pasantes que entraron lo disfrutaron igual que yo. Todos estaban muy felices de tenernos acá, y era como una gran fiesta de cumpleaños anticipada. Me sentí como parte de algo especial.*

- Jack: I think that it would be the moment in which I entered and received a great welcome. There was such a good reception, and in fact the other three interns that joined enjoyed it as much as I did. Everyone was so happy to have us here, and it was like a great birthday party in advance. I felt like part of something special.

- *Elena: ¡Que bueno saberlo, Jack! Es algo que intento cultivar en la oficina, un gran trato hacia todos los compañeros, ¡sin importar qué rango o edad tengan! Última pregunta, y esta es la más importante de todas: ¿cuál sería tu evaluación de ti mismo en estos ocho meses de pasantía? ¿Puedes ponerle un valor del uno al diez?*

- Elena: ¡That's amazing to know, Jack! It's something that I try to cultivate at the office, a great treatment towards co-workers, no matter what rank or age they are! Last question, and this is the most important of them all – what would be your evaluation of yourself in these eight months of internship? Can you place a value between one to ten?

- *Jack: ¡Vaya! Esa pregunta sí que es interesante. Bueno, a ver, pienso que merezco un siete de diez.*

- Jack: Yikes! That question sure is interesting. Okay, let's see, I think I deserve a seven out of ten.

- *Elena: ¿Siete? Justifica ese resultado, por favor.*

- Elena: Seven? Justify that result, please.

- *Jack: Pienso que hubo veces que llegué tarde a trabajar y, aunque no fueron muchas, sí sucedió. También tardé un poco en entregar mi informe final y no fue hasta el último día, hoy, cuando lo tuve listo. Además, no logré cumplir todos los objetivos que me propuse.*

- Jack: I think that there were times when I arrived late to work, and although it wasn't many times, it did happen. I also took some time to submit my final report, and it wasn't until the last day, today, when I had it ready. Furthermore, I didn't manage to accomplish all of the objectives I set myself.

- *Elena: Bueno, Jack. Gracias por responder a todo. Quiero que sepas que, a pesar de tu autoevaluación, yo pienso que mereces un diez. Has sido, para mí, el mejor pasante que ha pasado por aquí. Tu actitud profesional ha sido genial, has logrado enormes resultados, y me aseguraré de darte una recomendación para que vengas a formar parte de nuestro equipo apenas te gradúes.*

- Elena: Well, Jack. Thanks for answering everything. I want you to know that, despite your self-assessment, I believe you deserve a ten. You have been, to me, the best intern that has come here. Your professional attitude has been excellent, you've accomplished enormous results, and I'll make sure to give you a recommendation so that you can come and form part of our team once you've gradated.

- *Jack: ¿Es en serio?*

- Jack: Are you serious?

- *Elena: Sí. Así que, ¡sal allá afuera a comerte el mundo! Suerte... y nunca cambies tu actitud.*

- Elena: Yes. Now go out there and show the world what you're made of! Good luck... and never change your approach.

- *Jack: ¡Gracias, señora Elena! ¡Es un enorme honor! ¡Lo haré!*

- Jack: Thanks, Mrs. Elena! It's a massive honor! I'll do it!

Chapter 13 - Explaining a Mistake

- *¡Lo lamento mucho, fue un grave error!* – I'm so sorry, it was a terrible mistake!

- *eso que pasó esta mañana es inaceptable dentro de la empresa* - the event that took place this morning is unacceptable within the company

- *pudiera considerarse un acto criminal* - could be considered a criminal act

- *podría llamar a la policía y presentar cargos, y estarías preso en poco tiempo* - I could call the police and press charges, and you would be arrested in a short time

- *voy a tener que llamar a las autoridades inmediatamente* - I will have to call the authorities immediately

- *todo es un malentendido, ¡puedo explicarlo!* - it's all a misunderstanding, I can explain!

- *no me parece un malentendido* - it doesn't seem like a misunderstanding

- *conductor de montacargas* - forklift driver

- *bajo la influencia del alcohol* - under the influence of alcohol

- *debido a tu estado de embriaguez* - because of your state of drunkenness

- *derribaste numerosas estanterías llenas de mercancía de alto costo* - you knocked down several pallet racks full of expensive goods

- *destrozos valorados en varias decenas de miles de dólares* - destruction valued in several tens of thousands of dollars

- *acabaste con, al menos, una cuarta parte de los electrodomésticos* - you wrecked at least a quarter of the electrical appliances

- *destrozaste muchos equipos que estaban listos para ser entregados* - destroyed many pieces of equipment that were ready to be delivered

- *lidiar con este problema* - deal with this problem

- *es cierto que causé un gran daño a la empresa* - it's true that I caused massive damages to the company

- *esto es imperdonable* - this is unforgivable

- *¡estás fracasando!* - you're failing!

- *¿la mercancía estaba asegurada?* - were the goods insured?

- *no hemos confirmado si el seguro va a cubrir esto* - we haven't confirmed if the insurance will cover this

- *nunca he fallado antes* - I've never made a mistake before

- *lo que hiciste fue demasiado* - what you did was too much

- *hice algo terrible, muy estúpido* - I did something terrible, very stupid

- *estoy pasando por un muy mal momento* - I'm going through a very bad moment

- *me está yendo muy mal* - everything's going so badly for me

- *cada vez tengo más deudas y problemas* - every time I seem to have more debts and problems

- *últimamente estoy más deprimido y sin saber cómo salir de esta situación difícil* - lately I'm more depressed and without having an idea of how to get out of this difficult situation

- *es difícil seguir viniendo a pesar de lo que pasa en casa* - it's difficult to continue coming here despite what is going on at home

- *puede llamar al terapeuta de la empresa y consultarle* - you can call the company's therapist and check it out with him

- *parece que estás sufriendo de una seria depresión* - it seems that you're suffering from a serious depression

- *alcoholismo agudo* - acute alcoholism

- *debo pagar las consecuencias de alguna forma* - I must pay the consequences somehow

- *terminaría de arruinar mi vida* - it would finish ruining my life

- *necesito que recompenses a la empresa por este terrible acontecimiento* - I need you to compensate the company for this terrible event

- *buscaría maneras de reparar los equipos que se hayan dañado con la caída* - seek ways to repair the equipment that has been damaged with the fall

- *espero que se pueda recuperar lo que destruí* - I hope I can help recover what I destroyed

- *jamás volverá a suceder* - it will never happen again

- *gracias por asumir tu responsabilidad* - thank you for accepting your responsibility

Let's see the following dialogue:

- *Bárbara: Edward, voy a necesitar que seas completamente sincero: eso que pasó esta mañana es inaceptable dentro de la empresa y pudiera considerarse un acto criminal. Podría llamar a la policía y presentar cargos, y estarías preso en poco tiempo. Exijo una explicación, o voy a tener que llamar a las autoridades inmediatamente.*

- Barbara: Edward, I'm going to need you to be completely honest – the event that took place this morning is unacceptable within the company and could be considered a criminal act. I could call the police and press charges, and you would be arrested in a short time. I demand an explanation, or I will have to call the authorities immediately.

- *Edward: ¡Espere, por favor! Todo es un malentendido, ¡puedo explicarlo!*

- Edward: Wait, please! It's all a misunderstanding, I can explain!

- *Bárbara: No me parece un malentendido, la verdad. Viniste a tu trabajo de conductor de montacargas bajo la influencia del alcohol y, debido a tu estado de embriaguez, derribaste numerosas estanterías llenas de mercancía de alto costo, causando destrozos valorados en varias decenas de miles de dólares. Acabaste con, al menos, una cuarta parte de los electrodomésticos que teníamos en el almacén, destrozaste muchos equipos que estaban listos para ser entregados a nuestros clientes y ahora debemos lidiar con este problema, con la época navideña acercándose rápidamente.*

- Barbara: It doesn't seem like a misunderstanding, to be honest. You came to your job as a forklift driver under the influence of alcohol, and because of your state of drunkenness you knocked down several pallet racks full of expensive goods, causing destruction valued in several tens of thousands of dollars. You wrecked at least a quarter of the electrical appliances we had in the warehouse, destroyed many pieces of equipment that were ready to be delivered to our clients, and we have to deal with this problem now, with the Christmas period approaching quickly.

- *Edward: Sí, es cierto que causé un gran daño a la empresa y que la noche anterior había consumido una gran cantidad de alcohol, pero era mi cumpleaños y me hicieron una fiesta sorpresa, y...*

- Edward: Yes, it's true that I caused massive damages to the company, and that last night I consumed a huge amount of alcohol, but it was my birthday and they threw a surprise party for me and...

- *Bárbara: ¡No me interesa! Esto es imperdonable. ¿Crees que porque ayer era tu cumpleaños te vas a salvar de las consecuencias? Si esta es tu manera de detenerme de llamar a la policía, ¡estás fracasando!*

- Barbara: I don't care! This is unforgivable. Do you think that because it was your birthday yesterday you're going to be saved from the consequences? If this is your way of stopping me from calling the police, you're failing!

- *Edward: ¡Por favor, espere a que podamos mirarlo desde otro punto de vista! ¿La mercancía estaba asegurada?*

- Edward: Please, wait until we can look at it from another point of view! Were the goods insured?

- *Bárbara: Sí, pero no hemos confirmado si el seguro va a cubrir esto. Esa incertidumbre es la única razón por la que aún tienes trabajo.*

- Barbara: Yes, but we haven't confirmed if the insurance will cover this. That uncertainty is the only reason why you still have a job.

- *Edward: Señora Bárbara, recuerde que tengo siete años trabajando fielmente con ustedes, incluso en días libres, vacaciones y domingos. Nunca he fallado antes, ¡entiéndalo, por favor!*

- Edward: Mrs. Barbara, remember that I've been working here for you faithfully for seven years, even on days off, vacations and Sundays. I've never made a mistake before, understand it, please!

- *Bárbara: Es cierto, pero lo que hiciste fue demasiado. ¿En qué estabas pensando cuando viniste a trabajar en esas condiciones? Fue una estupidez, ¡y mira lo que causó!*

- Barbara: It's true, but what you did was too much. What were you thinking when you came to work in those conditions? It was an act of stupidity, and look at what it caused.

- *Edward: Sí, hice algo terrible, muy estúpido. No puedo justificarlo, yo... estoy pasando por un muy mal momento. Mi cumpleaños, anoche, fue la primera vez que alguien se ha acordado de mí en mucho tiempo —me está yendo muy mal—. Mi esposa me dejó hace dos meses, llevándose a mis hijos, y cada vez tengo más deudas y problemas. Sí, tomé de más, pero fue debido a que últimamente estoy más deprimido y sin saber cómo salir de esta situación difícil. No he querido faltar al trabajo, pero es difícil seguir viniendo a pesar de lo que pasa en casa.*

- Edward: Yes, I did something terrible, very stupid. I can't justify it, I... I'm going through a very bad moment. My birthday last night was the first time somebody has remembered me for the longest time – everything's going so badly for me. My wife left me two months ago, taking my children with her, and every time I seem to have more debts and problems. Yes, I drank too much, but it was due to the fact that lately I'm more depressed and without having an idea of how to get out of this difficult situation. I haven't wanted to miss work, but it's difficult to continue coming here despite what is going on at home.

- *Bárbara: Mmm... no sabía que esto estaba sucediendo en casa. Pero tampoco tengo cómo corroborarlo. ¿Puedes demostrar que todo está ocurriendo de alguna manera?*

- Barbara: Mmm... I had no idea that this was happening at home. But I don't have a way to verify what you're saying. Can you demonstrate that this is all taking place somehow?

- *Edward: Sí, puede llamar al terapeuta de la empresa y consultarle. He estado yendo a consulta con él.*

- Edward: Yes, you can call the company's therapist and check it out with him. I've been going to appointments with him.

- *Bárbara: Lo haré, dame unos minutos... De acuerdo, Edward. Parece que estás sufriendo de una seria depresión, la cual ha provocado un alcoholismo agudo. Esto no suena nada bien. Por un momento, incluso puedo sentir que lo que pasó en el almacén no es tan grave.*

- Barbara: I will, give me a few minutes... All right, Edward. It seems that you're suffering from a serious depression, which has caused a bout of acute alcoholism. This doesn't sound good at all. For a moment, I can even feel that what happened at the warehouse isn't so serious.

- *Edward: No, señora Bárbara, debo pagar las consecuencias de alguna forma. Solo no llame a la policía, por favor. Eso sería lo peor que podría ocurrirme en estos momentos. Terminaría de arruinar mi vida. No quiero que mis hijos sepan que estuve en la cárcel; terminaría de perderlos.*

- Edward: No, Mrs. Barbara. I must pay the consequences somehow. Just don't call the police, please. That would be the worst thing that could happen to me at this moment. It would finish ruining my life. I don't want my kids to know that I was in prison; I would lose them for good.

- *Bárbara: No voy a llamar a la policía, ¿de acuerdo? Pero necesito que recompenses a la empresa por este terrible acontecimiento. ¿Qué sugieres?*

- Barbara: I'm not calling the police, okay? But I need you to compensate the company for this terrible event. What do you suggest?

- *Edward: Sí... puedo pagarlo con trabajo, trabajando horas extra. También ayudaría a arreglar el desastre que causé y buscaría maneras de reparar los equipos que se hayan dañado con la caída. Es lo mínimo que puedo hacer.*

- Edward: Yeah... I can pay it with work, working extra hours. I would also help fix the disaster I created and seek ways to repair the equipment that has been damaged with the fall. It's the least I could do.

- *Bárbara: De acuerdo. Además, deberás recibir un pequeño descuento a tu salario por seis meses. No será mucho, pero será suficiente para que ya no tengas que preocuparte por un problema legal. Yo soy tu supervisora directa, pero si no aceptas y se enteran los gerentes o directores, se acabó todo para ti.*

- Barbara: Very well. Also, you will receive a small discount of your salary for six months. It won't be a lot, but just enough for you not to have to worry about a legal problem. I'm your direct supervisor, but if you don't accept and the managers or directors find out, it's all over for you.

- *Edward: Está bien. Acepto. Voy a necesitar que hagamos un contrato, pero está bien, no tengo otra opción. Gracias, señora Bárbara. No es fácil, y no quería que me afectara así, pero espero que se pueda recuperar lo que destruí. Jamás volverá a suceder.*

- Edward: It's fine, I accept. I'm going to need us to make a contract, but it's okay, I have no choice. Thank you, Mrs. Barbara. It isn't easy, and I didn't want it to affect me like it did, but I hope I can help recover what I destroyed. It will never happen again.

- *Bárbara: No hay problema, Edward. Saldremos de esto, ya verás. Ahora, ve a ayudar a arreglar lo que rompiste y luego tómate el día. Pronto te haré un nuevo contrato. Gracias por asumir tu responsabilidad.*

- Barbara: No problem, Edward. We'll get out of this, you'll see. Now go help fix what you broke, and then take the day off. I'll soon write a new contract for you. Thank you for accepting your responsibility.

Chapter 14 - Firing Somebody

- *Que tengas buena suerte en otra empresa* – Good Luck at Another Company

- *disculpe por llegar un poquito tarde a su cita* - I'm sorry for arriving a bit late to the appointment

- *necesitaba comunicarte algo* - I needed to inform you of something

- *¿es algo serio?* - is it something serious?

- *siento el ambiente algo tenso* - I feel the tension in the atmosphere

- *reestructuración* - restructuring

- *los departamentos han sido reorganizados* - the departments have been reorganized

- *algunos cargos se han cambiado o eliminado por completo* - some positions have been changed or eliminated entirely

- *ilustraban de manera detallada y específica* - illustrated, specifically and in detail

- *las personas de las que vamos a prescindir* - the people we are going to lay off

- *lamentándolo mucho* - with great regret

- *debo informarte que no vamos a requerir tus servicios a partir del final de este mes* - I must inform you that we are no longer going to require your services starting from the end of this month

- *tu cargo ha sido fusionado con el de supervisor* - your position has been merged with that of the customer service supervisor

- *un especialista de la capital* - a specialist from the capital

- *arreglar tus asuntos* - arrange your affairs

- *agradecimiento* - appreciation

- *un bono en tu indemnización* - a bonus in your severance pay

- *creo que nunca he fallado en mis responsabilidades* - I believe I've never failed in my responsibilities

- *me gustaría que reconsideraran esta decisión* - I would like for this decision to be reconsidered

- *mil disculpas* - I beg forgiveness

- *estás entre mis mejores empleados* - you are among my best employees

- *no soy el que decide ni el que da la orden* - I'm not the one who decides or gives the order

- *brindarte una recomendación para tus futuros empleos* - provide you a recommendation for your future jobs

- *actualmente debo cubrir los gastos de mi hogar* - I currently have to cover the expenses at home

- *crisis de desempleo* - unemployment crisis

- *probablemente me mantenga desempleada* - I will probably stay unemployed

- *beneficios del estado para desempleados* - state benefits for the unemployed

- *no podré calificar para esos beneficios* - I won't qualify for those benefits

- *poseo una vivienda y automóvil propio* - I own a home and car

- *baja prioridad* - low priority

- *entre en efecto* - comes into effect

- *decirles a mis hijos que fui despedida* - tell my kids I've been fired

- *¡ha salvado a mi familia!* - you've saved my family!

- *sé que podrás recuperar tu camino* - I know you'll be able to get back on your path

- *todas las historias deben llegar a su fin* - all stories must reach their ending

- *nunca lo olvidaré* - I'll never forget you

Let's see the following dialogue:

- *June: Buen día, señor Harry, ¿cómo está? Disculpe por llegar un poquito tarde a su cita, estaba terminando unas tareas de la oficina. Me avisaron esta mañana que necesitaba verme.*

- June: Good morning, Mr. Harry, how are you? I'm sorry for arriving a bit late to the appointment, I was finishing some tasks at the office. I was informed this morning that you needed to see me.

- *Harry: Sí, June. Gracias por venir. No te preocupes, toma asiento. Así es, necesitaba comunicarte algo.*

- Harry: Yes, June. Thanks for coming and don't worry. Take a seat. That's true, I needed to inform you of something.

- *June: A ver, ¿qué será? ¿Es algo serio? Siento el ambiente algo tenso, la verdad.*

- June: Let's see, what might it be? Is it something serious? I feel the tension in the atmosphere, to be honest.

- *Harry: Bueno, June, es importante que hablemos un poco de la empresa y una reestructuración que se está llevando a cabo en este momento. La directiva de la compañía ha comenzado a cambiar la manera en que hacemos las cosas en esta sede, y los departamentos han sido reorganizados de ciertas formas. Algunos cargos se han cambiado o eliminado por completo.*

- Harry: Well, June, it's important that we talk a bit about the company and the restructuring that is being carried out at this moment in time. The company's board has begun to change the way in which we do things at this branch, and the departments have been reorganized in certain ways. Some positions have been changed or eliminated entirely.

- *June: Entiendo... Bueno, ahora me siento un poco preocupada. ¿De qué vamos a hablar acá?*

- June: I understand... Okay, and now I feel a bit worried. What are we going to talk about here?

- *Harry: El día de ayer recibí un correo electrónico de parte de mis superiores, en el cual ilustraban, de manera detallada y específica, los cambios a realizarse en esta sede, incluyendo una lista de los cargos que serían eliminados, además de las personas de las que vamos a prescindir.*

- Harry: Yesterday, I received an email from my superiors, in which they illustrated, specifically and in detail, the changes to be made at this branch, including a list of the positions that would be eliminated, as well as the people we are going to lay off.

- *June: Oh, ya sé de qué trata esta conversación.*

- June: Oh, I know what this conversation is about now.

- *Harry: Sí, June. Lamentándolo mucho, debo informarte que no vamos a requerir tus servicios a partir del final de este mes, ya que tu cargo ha sido fusionado con el de supervisor de atención al cliente, el cual será llenado por un especialista de la capital. El aviso te llega el día de hoy para que tengas tiempo de arreglar tus asuntos y buscar un nuevo empleo en el mercado. Como agradecimiento, incluiremos un bono en tu indemnización por despido.*

- Harry: Yes, June. With great regret, I must inform you that we are no longer going to require your services starting from the end of this month, since your position has been merged with that of the customer service supervisor, which will be filled by a specialist from the capital. The notice arrives today for you to have time to arrange your affairs and find a new job in the market. As appreciation, we will include a bonus in your severance pay.

- *June: Eso no es lo que quisiera, —me encantaría mantener mi trabajo, sin importar si es en algún departamento nuevo con otro cargo—. He dedicado siete años de mi vida a esta empresa y creo que nunca he fallado en mis responsabilidades. Me gustaría que reconsideraran esta decisión, ya que he sido una trabajadora eficiente y dedicada.*

- June: That's not really what I want – I would love to keep my job, without caring if it's in a new department with another position. I've dedicated seven years of my life to this company, and I believe I've never failed in my responsibilities. I would like for this decision to be reconsidered, because I have been a faithful and efficient worker.

- *Harry: Mil disculpas, June, pero la decisión es final. Me duele mucho tener que darte esta noticia, además de haberla recibido; la verdad es que estás entre mis mejores empleados y eres una de las personas que más ha generado resultados para esta sede. Lamentablemente, no soy el que decide ni el que da la orden, y lo máximo que puedo hacer por ti es brindarte una recomendación para tus futuros empleos.*

- Harry: I beg forgiveness, June, but the decision is final. It hurts a lot for me to have to give you this news, as well as having received it; the truth is that you are among my best employees and are also one of the people who has generated results for this branch. Unfortunately, I'm not the one who decides or gives the order, and the best I can do for you is provide you a recommendation for your future jobs.

- *June: Esto no puede estar pasando, señor Harry. Actualmente debo cubrir los gastos de mi hogar y, con esta crisis de desempleo, no será fácil encontrar otro trabajo. Probablemente me mantenga desempleada por un largo tiempo.*

- June: This can't be happening, Mr. Harry. I currently have to cover the expenses at home, and with this unemployment crisis it won't be easy to find another job. I will probably stay unemployed for a long time.

- *Harry: Podrías probar con los beneficios del estado para desempleados, recuerda que existe esa opción.*

- Harry: You could try the state benefits for the unemployed, remember that the option exists.

- *June: No podré calificar para esos beneficios, ya que poseo una vivienda y automóvil propio, y eso hace que esté en baja prioridad. Realmente necesito que lo reconsidere, señor Harry.*

- June: I won't qualify for those benefits, because I own a home and car, and that makes me a low priority person. I really need you to reconsider, Mr. Harry.

- *Harry: No es posible, June. Ya la decisión fue tomada. Ahora bien, voy a intentar lograr una extensión de emergencia a tu contrato hasta septiembre, es lo máximo que me darán. Jamás lo he tenido que hacer antes, pero lo haré por consideración a ti y a tus hijos. ¿Qué tal suena eso? Les recordaré todo lo que has aportado para la empresa y pediré que el nuevo cargo entre en efecto para el primero de octubre.*

- Harry: It isn't possible, June. The decision has been made. Now, I'm going to try to get an emergency extension of your contract until September, which is the most I can get. I've never had to do it before, but I will in consideration of your kids and yourself. How does that sound? I'll remind them of everything you've provided for the company and will ask that the new position comes into effect on the first of October.

- *June: ¿En serio haría eso? ¡No se imagina cuán agradecida estoy al saberlo! No sería fácil para mí llegar a casa hoy y decirles a mis hijos que fui despedida y que pronto no tendré dinero para cubrir los gastos. Esto mejora un poco mi situación, ya que me da tiempo suficiente para hallar nuevas oportunidades. ¡Ha salvado a mi familia!*

- June: Would you really do that for me? You can't imagine how thankful I am to know it! It wouldn't be easy to arrive home today and tell my kids I've been fired and that soon I won't have money to cover the expenses. This slightly improves my situation, since it gives me enough time to find new opportunities. You've saved my family!

- *Harry: No te preocupes, en serio, es una forma de agradecerte a ti por tus servicios y los resultados que has producido para nosotros a lo largo de los años. Déjame escribir ese correo electrónico ya, antes de que envíen al nuevo trabajador. Esto ha sido todo. Lamento darte esa noticia, pero sé que podrás recuperar tu camino. Recuerda también que voy a recomendarte.*

- Harry: Don't worry, seriously, it's a way of thanking you for your services and the results you've produced for us throughout the years. Let me write this email now, before they send the new worker. This has been all. I apologize for giving you that news, but I know you'll be able to get back on your path. Also remember that I'll be recommending you.

- *June: Sí, señor Harry. Todas las historias deben llegar a su fin. Gracias por tenerme trabajando en esta empresa. Nunca lo olvidaré. Regresaré a mi puesto a seguir trabajando.*

- June: Yes, Mr. Harry. All stories must reach their ending. Thank you for having me work for this company. I'll never forget you. I'll go back to my working station to continue working.

Chapter 15 - Online Learning

Empezemos! (Let's get started!) The quickest way to learn Spanish is to find a teacher. If you can hire an individual tutor, you should do so. Direct instruction, whether it be in a group class or with a private tutor, is one of the best ways to really pick up conversational Spanish. Also, having somebody that insists you to do homework and will hold you accountable can keep you on track. With an experienced tutor, you can receive guidance that's tailored to you providing a very structured approach to your personal goals. This is not the case with typical evening language classes where you will be expected to maintain the pace of the class; not very conducive to learning Spanish quickly.

This should be a fun endeavor for you, and the last thing you want is to end up in a suffocating class that takes away from the exciting discovery of new words and sentences. In most cases, these classes and tutors can be quite expensive, and since you're looking to learn quickly, you may not find many options available for the schedule you need. Consider the trip too. If you have Internet access, you can save yourself a lot of time and money.

If private tutoring and classes are out of the question, or if you want to continue learning outside of class, you can find everything you need on the internet, at the library, or at your local bookstore. Of course, if you have a smartphone, you have access to various instructional materials right at your fingertips.

There are plenty of both paid and free online websites and programs providing all varieties of instructional content for any level of Spanish student. You can find Podcasts, interactive websites, videos, and Apps. With so many options available, it can be challenging to decide which programs are right for you. Let's look at some of the most popular online resources available.

Podcasts

Podcasts are a great way to help build your skills as they allow you to hear native Spanish speakers. Listening to Podcasts can really maximize your learning since you're able to pick up on the pronunciation and phrases they commonly use. You can listen to a podcast while performing menial tasks and passively soak up the new knowledge.

When searching for the right Podcast for you, consider how long they've been on-air. Also, look for Podcasts that break down conversations slowly for beginners, so that you can understand them. While you can find Podcasts online for free, many require that you sign up or subscribe to a platform to access them.

Websites

If you prefer a more traditional approach to learning, some great websites have printable worksheets and interactive quizzes. While it is easy to find many websites that teach you the basics, it can be a challenge finding intermediate and expert Spanish level material. After you've committed some vocabulary to memory and can start stringing sentences together, check out websites that offer tests. Keep in mind most online testing will be focused on vocabulary and grammar; not necessarily speaking and listening.

Practice typing in Spanish with websites that provide a Spanish keyboard that includes accents. That way, you can save time without having to figure out how to type those accents on your standard keyboard. Just perform a search for interactive websites for learning beginners Spanish and take your pick!

Videos

Diversify your Spanish instruction arsenal with videos. You shouldn't have a hard time locating hours of content online with sites such as YouTube. Be sure to bookmark your favorite videos so that you can find them easily when it's time to review. Videos work great because you can stop, pause, or rewind when needed. When watching videos, pay careful attention to pronunciation as well as study the mouth and lip movements of Spanish speakers.

Hidden subtitles can be a handy feature when listening to Spanish speakers — so that you can read along and start to develop an eye for the language as well.

Try searching for a Spanish alphabet song, or even children's content showing numbers, colors, and nursery rhymes that you are already familiar with. Another fun way to get in practice time is to find Spanish games. There are a wide variety of games online, and you can search for games that will target your weakest areas. Reviewing your vocabulary and practicing your translation while under pressure or finding a fun game of simple matching can reinforce what you're learning offline.

Apps

There are many Apps available on your smartphone or tablet that are entirely free for use. Look for Apps that have a very straightforward interface and are easy to use. Using language Apps can help keep you motivated with goal-setting, visual cues to stay on track, and highlighting both strong and weak points. If you're interested in creating simple sentences right away, there are interactive Apps available to get you constructing phrases right away. Keep in mind that most Apps are not meant to be stand-alone courses, but they can make for a great addition to your learning toolbox.

A simple internet search for top language apps will give you multiple lists with recommendations. Finding an app that supplies both visual and audio cues will be the most helpful, and you can even find Apps that have offline learning if you find yourself getting distracted online.

Focus on what you need

Because Spanish is considered one of the easiest languages for an English speaker to learn, you shouldn't have any trouble achieving success with a combination of online/offline materials. Even if you're not entirely convinced that you'll be able to pick up Spanish quickly these methods are available so that you can cut to the chase and focus on learning what you need. If you have any prior knowledge, you can build on what you already know and look forward to what you still need to learn.

To recap what we've learned in this chapter; you'll want to take advantage of as many avenues for learning that you can. While you don't want to overwhelm yourself with too much information, having a wide array available to stimulate new thoughts can really keep you on track. Keep away from materials loaded with grammar theory to start. Instead, try to find things that build your confidence; that could mean taking quizzes in workbooks or online. You need to see results fast so that you stay motivated and continue to be inspired. Develop a strategy so that you have access to the right tool when you need it. It can be easy to get discouraged and give up, just make sure that you always start again so that you do not forget everything that you've learned.

Chapter 16 - Getting To A New Country- Llegando A Un Nuevo País

Alquilar una casa – Rent a House

Spanish

- *Katy: Buenos días, quiero alquilar una casa.*
- *Agente: Buenos días, gracias por preferir nuestra agencia de alquiler. ¿Qué está buscando?*
- *Katy: Quiero un town house o casa de un piso, que tenga tres habitaciones, dos baños, sala de estar, jardín y dos puestos de estacionamiento.*
- *Agente: Con esas características tenemos tres opciones.*
- *Katy: A ver.*
- *Agente: Tiene esta, una casa de un solo piso, tres habitaciones, dos baños, sala de estar, jardín, tres puestos de estacionamiento y derecho al uso de la piscina de la urbanización. Está ubicada a 15 minutos al norte de la estación de autobús de Kendall, con un costo de 650$ mensuales, sin incluir los servicios y debe dar un adelanto de cuatro meses.*
- *Katy: ¿Qué otras opciones hay?*
- *Agente: Tiene este town house, tiene las características que usted pidió, está más al norte de la anterior pero el alquiler son 500$ mensuales, con los servicios incluidos y solo debe dar tres meses de adelanto.*
- *Katy: Me gusta, ¿Y la tercera opción?*
- *Agente: Una casa pequeña, tres habitaciones, dos baños, sala de estar, jardín y un solo puesto de estacionamiento. Cuesta 450$ al mes, incluye los servicios y debe dar tres meses de adelanto igual que en la anterior.*
- *Katy: Creo que me quedare con la segunda opción.*
- *Agente: Excelente elección. Ya hacemos los trámites.*
- *Katy: Muchas gracias por su ayuda.*

English

- Katy: Good morning. I want to rent a house.
- Agent: Good morning. Thank you for preferring our rental agency. What are you looking for?
- Katy: I want a townhouse or a one-floor house, with three bedrooms, two bathrooms, living room, garden, and two parking spaces.
- Agent: With these characteristics, we have three options.
- Katy: Let's see.
- Agent: You have this, a one-floor house, three bedrooms, two bathrooms, living room, garden, three parking spaces, and the right to use the swimming pool of the urbanization. It is located 15 minutes north of the Kendall bus station, at a cost of $650 per month, not including services and must give an advance of four months.
- Katy: What other options are there?
- Agent: You have this townhouse. It has the features you asked for. It is located further north than the previous one, but the rent is $500 per month, with the services included and you only have to give three months in advance.
- Katy: I like it, and the third option?

- Agent: A small house, three bedrooms, two bathrooms, living room, garden, and a single parking place. It costs $450 a month, includes the services, and must give three months in advance as in the previous one.
- Katy: I think I'll take the second option.
- Agent: Excellent choice. Let's do the paperwork.
- Katy: Thank you very much for your help.

Preguntando tradiciones – **Asking About Traditions**

Spanish

- *Rod: Buenas noches. ¿Cómo estás?*
- *Alice: Muy bien Rod, ¿Y tú?*
- *Rod: Excelente Alice. Un poco confundido.*
- *Alice ¿Por qué?*
- *Rod: La gente está contenta, como celebrando algo, pero no se qué.*
- *Alice: Hoy es el tercer lunes de Febrero.*
- *Rod: ¿Y eso que significa?*
- *Alice: Hoy se celebra el día del presidente.*
- *Rod: No sabía, tengo poco tiempo viviendo acá. ¿Qué otras tradiciones tienen?*
- *Alice: El día de Martin Luther King se celebra el tercer lunes de Enero, el Memorial Day se celebra el ultimo lunes de Mayo, el Labor Day se celebra el primer lunes de Septiembre, el Veteran's Day se celebra el 11 de Noviembre y el día de la independencia que celebramos el 4 de Julio, las otras como Navidad, Halloween y acción de gracias si son igual que en los otros países.*
- *Rod: Ya veo, muchas gracias por la explicación.*
- *Alice: Está pendiente de la próxima festividad.*

English

- Rod: Good evening. How are you?
- Alice: All right, Rod. What about you?
- Rod: Excellent, Alice. A little confused.
- Alice: Why?
- Rod: People are happy, like celebrating something but I don't know what.
- Alice: Today is the third Monday of February.
- Rod: What does that mean?
- Alice: Today is President's Day.
- Rod: I didn't know; I don't have much time living here. What other traditions do you have?
- Alice: Martin Luther King Day is celebrated on the third Monday in January. Memorial Day is celebrated on the last Monday in May. Labor Day is celebrated on the first Monday in September. Veteran's Day is celebrated on November 11th and Independence Day on July 4, and the other traditions like Christmas, Halloween, and Thanksgiving are the same as in other countries.
- Rod: I see, thank you very much for the explanation, Alice. Stay tuned for the next holiday.

Preguntando comidas típicas- Asking About Typical Foods

Spanish

- *Martin: Buenos días muchachos, ¿Cómo están?*
- *Luis: Todo bien, ¿Y tú?*
- *Carlos: Estoy bien.*
- *Alex: Muy bien.*
- *Martin: Me alegro. Hoy quería hacer un compartir en mi casa y cenar todos alla.*
- *Carlos: Genial, ¿Qué hay que llevar?*
- *Martin: Como cada uno de nosotros es de un país diferente, pensé que cada quien llevara comida típica de su país.*
- *Luis: Excelente idea.*
- *Alex: Me parece espectacular.*
- *Martin: Como yo soy de Italia, hare distintos tipos de pastas con sus salsas. ¿Cuáles son los platos típicos de sus países?*
- *Carlos: Yo soy de Argentina y los platos típicos que puedo llevar son una provoleta, un poco de chimichurri y unos alfajores para el postre.*
- *Alex: Yo soy de Estados Unidos y puedo llevar unas hamburguesas y un pie de manzana.*
- *Luis: Yo soy de Japón y llevaré sushi, sashimi, udon y un poco de soba.*
- *Martin: Genial, nos vemos en mi casa a las ocho de la noche.*
- *Carlos y Luis: Ok.*
- *Alex: Llegare un poco antes, ¿Hay algún problema?*
- *Martin: Para nada, así me ayudas con los preparativos.*

English

- Martin: Good morning, boys. How are you?
- Luis: All right, how are you?
- Carlos: I'm fine.
- Alex: Very good.
- Martin: I'm glad. Today, I wanted to do a sharing in my house and have dinner there.
- Carlos: Great. What do we have to bring?
- Martin: Since each one of us is from a different country, I thought that everyone should bring food typical of their country.
- Luis: Excellent idea.
- Alex: I think it's spectacular.
- Martin: Since I'm from Italy, I'll make different types of pasta with their sauces. What are the typical dishes in your countries?
- Carlos: I'm from Argentina, and the typical dishes I can take are a provoleta, a little chimichurri, and some alfajores for dessert.
- Alex: I'm from the United States and I can take some hamburgers and apple pie.
- Luis: I'm from Japan and I'll take sushi, sashimi, udon, and some soba.
- Martin: Great, I'll see you at my house at eight at night.
- Carlos and Luis: Ok.
- Alex: I'll be a little early, is there a problem?
- Martin: Not at all. That way, you will help me with the preparations.

Preguntando Sobre impuestos- Asking about Taxes

Spanish

- *German: Buenos días.*
- *Peter: Buenos días, ¿En qué puedo ayudarle?*
- *German: Revise mi cuenta ayer y tengo un montón de deducciones y quiero saber de que son.*
- *Peter: Dame tu número de cuenta.*
- *German: 888877775555559999.*
- *Peter: De acuerdo, esta deducción es por impuesto sobre ingresos, esta es por impuestos sobre la renta y estas por impuestos de seguro social.*
- *German: Entiendo. ¿Sabe cuánto es el impuesto sobre ingresos?*
- *Peter: Si, es del 30% de los ingresos mensuales.*
- *German: Muchas gracias por la información.*

English

- German: Good morning.
- Peter: Good morning. What can I do for you?
- German: I checked my account yesterday, and I have a lot of deductions and I want to know what they are.
- Peter: Give me your account number.
- German: 8888777755555559999.
- Peter: Okay, this deduction is for income tax. This is for rent taxes, and these are for social security taxes.
- German: I understand. Do you know what the income tax is?
- Peter: Yes, it's 30% of monthly income.
- German: Thank you very much for the information.

Comprar una casa- Buy a House

Spanish

- *Nora: Buenas tardes.*
- *Calvin: Buenas tardes, ¿Cómo esta?*
- *Nora: Muy bien, ¿Y tú?*
- *Calvin: Excelente.*
- *Nora: Vi que tiene su casa en venta. ¿Puedo verla por dentro?*
- *Calvin: Seguro, pase adelante.*
- *Nora: Muchas gracias.*
- *Calvin: La casa fue construida hace 20 años y remodelada hace 10, tiene cuatro habitaciones, un cuarto de servicio, un cuarto tipo oficina, dos baños arriba y uno abajo, una sala, garaje, jardín y un jacuzzi.*
- *Nora: Me encanta. ¿Cuánto pide?*
- *Calvin: Pido 70.000$.*
- *Nora: ¿Hay posibilidad de financiación?*
- *Calvin: Quizas.*
- *Nora: Si quiero pagarlos a 5 años, ¿Cuánto tendría que pagar mensual?*

545

- Calvin: *Con intereses del 15%, tendría que pagar 1345$ mensuales.*
- Nora: *Sin inicial, ¿correcto?*
- Calvin: *Asi es.*
- Nora: *La compro.*
- Calvin: *Perfecto, firmemos los papeles y cerremos el trato.*

English

- Nora: Good afternoon.
- Calvin: Good afternoon, how are you?
- Nora: Very well, and you?
- Calvin: Excellent.
- Nora: I saw that you have your house for sale. Can I see it inside?
- Calvin: Sure, come on in.
- Nora: Thank you very much.
- Calvin: The house was built 20 years ago and remodeled 10 years ago. It has four bedrooms, a maid's room, an office type room, two bathrooms upstairs and one downstairs, a living room, garage, garden, and a Jacuzzi.
- Nora: I love it. How much do you want?
- Calvin: I am asking $70,000.
- Nora: Is there any possibility of financing?
- Calvin: Maybe.
- Nora: If I want to pay for 5 years, how much would I have to pay monthly?
- Calvin: With an interest of 15%, you would have to pay $1345 per month.
- Nora: No initial, right?
- Calvin: That's right.
- Nora: I will buy it.
- Calvin: Perfect, let's sign the papers and close the deal.

Comprar un carro- Buy a Car

Spanish

- Alejandro: *Buenos días. Quiero comprar un carro.*
- Vendedor: *Excelente. Pase adelante.*
- Alejandro: *Muchas gracias.*
- Vendedor: *¿Sabe qué tipo de carro quiere?*
- Alejandro: *Quiero un carro familiar, con buena autonomía y que tenga maletero.*
- Vendedor: *Tenemos estos carros grandes, una autonomía de 10 kilómetros por litro, con maletero, aire acondicionado, dirección asistida, frenos abs y luces HID.*
- Alejandro: *Me agrada, pero, ¿No es mejor una van o un SUV?*
- Vendedor: *Tenemos estas, pero la autonomía no es tan buena, la autonomía de esta van es 7.7 kilómetros por litro y de esta SUV es de 8.5 kilómetros por litro.*
- Alejandro: *Ya veo. ¿Cuánto cuesta el carro grande que me dijiste?*
- Vendedor: *Tiene un valor inicial de 10.000$ y puede pedir extras como mejoras en el sistema de sonido, asientos de cuero, rines de lujo, quemacoco, colores especiales y portavasos.*
- Alejandro: *¿Cuánto cuesta con todos los extras?*

- *Vendedor: Su valor final seria 12.599$.*
- *Alejandro: ¿Y para pagarlo en 36 meses?*
- *Vendedor: Tendría que pagar 405$ mensuales.*
- *Alejandro: ¿El costo incluye mantenimiento?*
- *Vendedor: Correcto. Al comprar el vehículo con nosotros usted obtendrá 2 años de mantenimiento gratis.*
- *Alejandro: Excelente. Tenemos un trato entonces.*

English

- Alejandro: Good morning. I want to buy a car.
- Seller: Excellent. Come on in.
- Alejandro: Thank you very much.
- Seller: Do you know what kind of car you want?
- Alejandro: I want a family car with good autonomy and a trunk.
- Seller: We have these large cars, a range of 10 kilometers per liter, with a trunk, air conditioning, assisted steering, abs brakes, and HID lights.
- Alejandro: I like it, but isn't it better to have a van or an SUV?
- Seller: We have these, but the autonomy is not so good. The autonomy of this van is 7.7 kilometers per liter, and this SUV is 8.5 kilometers per liter.
- Alejandro: I see. How much does the large car you told me cost?
- Seller: It has an initial value of $10,000, and you can ask for extras such as improvements to the sound system, leather seats, luxury rims, sunroof, special colors, and cup holders.
- Alejandro: How much does it cost with all the extras?
- Seller: Its final value would be 12.599$.
- Alejandro: And to pay it in 36 months?
- Seller: You would have to pay 405$ per month.
- Alejandro: Does the cost include maintenance?
- Seller: Correct. When you buy the vehicle with us, you will get 2 years of free maintenance.
- Alejandro: Excellent. We have a deal then.

Mantenimiento del carro- Car maintenance

Spanish

- *Adam: Hey, ¿Todo bien Vladimir?*
- *Vladimir: Hey, todo excelente, ¿Tú?*
- *Adam: No me quejo.*
- *Vladimir: ¿Qué haces aquí?*
- *Adam: Vengo a pedirte que le hagas mantenimiento al carro.*
- *Vladimir: Perfecto. ¿Mantenimiento full o normal?*
- *Adam: ¿Cuales son las diferencias?*
- *Vladimir: El mantenimiento full incluye cambio de filtro de aceite, filtro de gasolina, filtro de aire, cambio de aceite, lavado del motor, cambios de discos y pastillas de freno, cambio de bujías y sus cables, alineación y balanceo.*
- *Adam: Ya veo porque le dicen full. ¿Y el normal?*

- *Vladimir: El normal incluye solo cambio de aceite, cambio de filtro de aceite, alineación y balanceo.*
- *Adam: ¿Cuál me recomiendas?*
- *Vladimir: Tienes tiempo sin hacerle mantenimiento, ¿Cierto?*
- *Adam: Asi es.*
- *Vladimir: Creo que es mejor el full entonces.*
- *Adam: Genial, si tu lo dices.*

English

- Adam: Hey, is everything all right, Vladimir?
- Vladimir: Hey, all excellent, you?
- Adam: No complaints.
- Vladimir: What are you doing here?
- Adam: I've come to ask you to maintain the car.
- Vladimir: Perfect. Full or normal maintenance?
- Adam: What are the differences?
- Vladimir: Full maintenance includes oil filter change, fuel filter, air filter, oil change, engine wash, disc, and brake pad changes, spark plug and cable changes, alignment, and balancing.
- Adam: I see why you call it full. And the normal?
- Vladimir: The normal includes only oil change, oil filter change, alignment, and balancing.
- Adam: Which one do you recommend?
- Vladimir: You have time without maintenance, right?
- Adam: That's right.
- Vladimir: I think full is better then.
- Adam: Great, if you say so.

Pidiendo un crédito- **Asking for a loan/credit**

Spanish

- *Daniela: Buenas tardes.*
- *Agente bancario: Buenas tardes.*
- *Daniela: Me gustaria pedir un crédito para comprar una casa.*
- *Agente bancario: ¿Cuánto desea pedir?*
- *Daniela: 50.000$.*
- *Agente bancario: Chequeare su historial de créditos.*
- *Daniela: Esta impecable.*
- *Agente bancario: Eso veo.*
- *Daniela: ¿Si lo aprobara?*
- *Agente bancario: ¿A cuánto tiempo desea pagar el crédito?*
- *Daniela: A cinco años.*
- *Agente bancario: Para ese plazo el interés es de 25%.*
- *Daniela: ¿Y a diez años?*
- *Agente bancario: El interés seria de 35%.*
- *Daniela: Creo que elegiré a 10 años.*
- *Agente bancario: Perfecto.*

- *Daniela: Muchas gracias.*
- *Agente: bancario: Si alguno de los pagos tiene retraso se le cobrara una cuota extra de 10% en dicho plazo.*
- *Daniela: Entiendo.*

English

- Daniela: Good afternoon.
- Bank agent: Good afternoon.
- Daniela: I would like to ask for a loan to buy a house.
- Bank agent: How much do you want to ask for?
- Daniela: $50,000.
- Bank Agent: I will check your credit history.
- Daniela: It's impeccable.
- Bank Agent: That's what I see.
- Daniela: Will you approve?
- Bank agent: How long do you want to pay the credit?
- Daniela: Five years.
- Bank agent: For that term, the interest rate is 25%.
- Daniela: And ten years?
- Bank agent: The interest would be 35%.
- Daniela: I think I will choose 10 years.
- Bank agent: Perfect.
- Daniela: Thank you very much.
- Agent: Banker: If any of the payments are late, you will be charged an extra fee of 10% in that period.
- Daniela: I understand.

Limpiar la piscina- Clean the pool

Spanish

- *Elias: Amor, los niños quieren invitar a sus amigos a jugar en la piscina.*
- *Elizabeth: ¿Cuándo?*
- *Elias: Mañana por la tarde.*
- *Elizabeth: No creo que puedan.*
- *Elias: ¿Por qué?*
- *Elizabeth: La piscina está muy sucia, no se ha limpiado desde hace meses.*
- *Elias: ¿Y qué hay que hacerle?*
- *Elizabeth: Hay que vaciarla, limpiar la losa que ya tiene moho, llenarla, limpiar los filtros, ponerle cloro y todos los detergentes que necesite y reparar el calentador para que el agua no esté tan fría.*
- *Elias: Es mucho que hacer. Pero creo que, si empiezo ya, estará lista para mañana.*
- *Elizabeth: Empieza de una vez entonces.*
- *Elias: Perfecto. ¿Dónde están los utensilios para limpiarla?*
- *Elizabeth: En el depósito.*
- *Elias: Ok.*

English

- Elias: Love, the children want to invite their friends to play in the pool.
- Elizabeth: When?
- Elias: Tomorrow afternoon.
- Elizabeth: I don't think they can.
- Elias: Why?
- Elizabeth: The pool is very dirty; it hasn't been cleaned for months.
- Elias: And what should be done to it?
- Elizabeth: It needs to be emptied, to clean the tiles that already have mold, to fill them, to clean the filters, to put chlorine and all the detergents that it needs, and to repair the heater so that the water is not so cold.
- Elias: It's a lot to do. But I think that if I start now, it will be ready for tomorrow.
- Elizabeth: Start once and for all then.
- Elias: Perfect. Where are the utensils to clean it?
- Elizabeth: In the storeroom.
- Elias: Ok.

Mudanza- Moving

Spanish

- Lucio: Despiértense, hoy es el día de mudarnos.
- Karl: Genial, no puedo esperar a llegar a la nueva casa.
- Lila: Yo no quiero irme de aquí, me encanta mi casa.
- Lucio: Lila, tu hermanita ya va a nacer, y la perra ya va a tener a sus cachorros, necesitamos una casa mas grande. Espera que veas la nueva casa, te encantara.
- Lila: Lo dudo.
- Lucio: Dale una oportunidad.
- Karl: Piensa Lila, un cuarto más grande, un closet más grande, un jardín más grande y estaremos más cerca del centro comercial.
- Lila: Bueno, así no suena tan mal.
- Lucio: El camión de la mudanza debe llegar en media hora, traigan todo su equipaje, sus cajas, sus bolsos, sus almohadas, colchones, traigan absolutamente todo. Una vez que nos mudemos no podremos regresar a buscar nada.
- Lila: Lo sé papa, lo has dicho toda la semana.
- Lucio: Las cajas tienen nombre y número, seamos organizados con la mudanza.
- Karl: De acuerdo.

English

- Lucius: Wake up. Today is the day to move.
- Karl: Great, I can't wait to get to the new house.
- Lila: I don't want to leave here. I love my house.
- Lucio: Lila, your little sister is about to be born, and the dog is going to have her puppies. We need a bigger house. Wait till you see the new house, you'll love it.
- Lila: I doubt it.
- Lucio: Give it a chance.

- Karl: Think Lila. A bigger room, a bigger closet, a bigger garden, and we'll be closer to the mall.
- Lila: Well, that doesn't sound so bad.
- Pike: The moving truck should arrive in half an hour, bring all your luggage, your boxes, your bags, your pillows, mattresses, bring absolutely everything. Once we move, we won't be able to come back for anything.
- Lila: I know Dad; you've been saying it all week.
- Lucio: The boxes have names and numbers. Let's be organized with moving.
- Karl: All right.

Leyes- Laws

Spanish

- *Miley: Buenas noches vecina, ¿Cómo esta?*
- *Lucy: Muy bien mi niña, ¿Y tú?*
- *Miley: Bien, un poco preocupada.*
- *Lucy: ¿Por qué?*
- *Miley: Como usted sabe, me acabo de mudar para acá, y no sé nada de las leyes y normas que hay aquí.*
- *Lucy: Tranquila, las leyes son las más comunes, no hacer mucho ruido en las noches, no manejar ebrios, ser respetuosos, utilizar el cinturón de seguridad, no hacer comentarios racistas ni sexistas, no maltratar a los niños, no robar, no conducir sin licencia y otras normas que son de sentido común.*
- *Miley: Ya veo.*
- *Lucy: Hay muchísimas otras leyes y normas que debes seguir, pero mientras cumplas esas no tendrás problemas por estos lados.*
- *Miley: Muchísimas gracias Sra Lucy.*
- *Lucy: A tu orden joven. Si quieres vienes otro día y te enseño mas sobre leyes y normas de acá.*
- *Miley: Gracias, de todas maneras, yo tomare un curso sobre eso para estar al tanto de todas las leyes lo más pronto posible, no quiero meterme en problemas.*
- *Lucy: Eres una chica muy inteligente.*

English

- Miley: Good evening, neighbor. How are you?
- Lucy: Very well, my child, and you?
- Miley: Well, a little worried.
- Lucy: Why?
- Miley: As you know, I just moved here, and I don't know anything about the laws and regulations here.
- Lucy: Don't worry. The laws are the most common. Don't make too much noise at night, don't drive drunk, be respectful, use your seat belt, don't make racist or sexist comments, don't mistreat children, don't steal, don't drive without a license, and other rules that are common sense.
- Miley: I see.
- Lucy: There are so many other laws and rules that you have to follow, but as long as you follow those rules, you won't have any problems here.

- Miley: Thank you very much, Mrs. Lucy.
- Lucy: At your service, young lady. If you want, you can come another day, and I'll teach you more about laws and rules here.
- Miley: Thanks, anyway I'll take a course about it to be aware of all the laws as soon as possible. I do not want to get into trouble.
- Lucy: You're a very smart girl.

Multas – Penalty fees/ fines

Spanish

- *Policía: Buenas tardes.*
- *Mark: Buenas tardes.*
- *Policía: ¿Sabe usted porque es esta citación?*
- *Mark: Ni idea señor.*
- *Policía: Vamos a quitarle su licencia de conducir.*
- *Mark: ¿Qué? ¿Por qué?*
- *Policía: Es imprudente conduciendo.*
- *Mark: Claro que no.*
- *Policía: Aquí tengo todas las grabaciones de usted cometiendo imprudencias.*
- *Mark: A verlas.*
- *Policía: Aquí condujo a exceso de velocidad, se le colocó una multa y nunca la pagó; aquí pasó un semáforo en rojo, se le colocó una multa y nunca la pagó; aquí está conduciendo ebrio, se le colocó una multa y nunca la pagó; aquí esta cambiándose de carriles sin utilizar las luces de cruce, se le colocó una multa y nunca la pagó; aquí está de nuevo a exceso de velocidad. Creo que hay razones suficientes para quitarle su licencia.*
- *Mark: ¿Si pago las multas no me la quitas?*
- *Policía: Se la tengo que quitar porque tiene muchas multas. Pague las multas, espere su penalización de seis meses sin licencia y puede volver a solicitarla.*
- *Mark: ¿Seis meses sin licencia? Es un abuso. ¿Cómo voy a buscar a los niños al colegio? ¿Cómo iré al supermercado?*
- *Policía: Debió pensar en todo eso antes de cometer esas infracciones.*

English

- Police: Good afternoon.
- Mark: Good afternoon.
- Police: Do you know why this citation is?
- Mark: No idea, sir.
- Police: We're going to take away your driver's license.
- Mark: What? Why?
- Police: You are reckless driving.
- Mark: Of course not.
- Police: Here, I have all the recordings of you committing reckless acts.
- Mark: Let's see them.
- Police: Here, you drove too fast. You were fined and never paid it. Here you ran a red light, you were fined and never paid it. When you are driving drunk, you were fined and never paid it.

When you are changing lanes without using dipped headlights, you were fined and never paid it. When you are speeding again. I think there are enough reasons to take away your license.

- Mark: If I pay the fines, won't you take it away from me?
- Police: I have to remove it because you have many fines. Pay the fines, wait for your six-month penalty without a license, and you can apply for it again.
- Mark: Six months without a license? It's an abuse. How am I going to pick up the kids at school? How am I going to go to the supermarket?
- Police: You should have thought of all that before you committed those violations.

Preguntando sobre colegios- Asking about Schools

Spanish

- *Mia: Hola Abby, ¿Cómo estás?*
- *Abby: Mia, que bueno verte. Ando un poco ocupada, estoy buscando colegios donde pueda inscribir a mis hijos, ¿Sabes de algunos?*
- *Mia: Claro, yo tengo a mis hijos en el Orlando High School, tienen clases todos los días de 8 a.m. a 3 p.m. y ven materias extras como cocina, arte, economía, diseño y algunas otras.*
- *Abby: Suena genial, pero esa me queda un poco lejos, ¿Sabes de alguna más al sur?*
- *Mia: Esta la Plantation High School, mi hermana tiene a sus hijos ahí, el horario es de 8:30 a.m. hasta las 2:30 p.m. y tienen su equipo de natación, de básquet, de beisbol y de futbol; además dan materias extras como música, teatro y jardinería.*
- *Abby: Esa me agrada mas, a mis hijos les encantan los deportes.*
- *Mia: Esa es muy buena, es muy bonita y grande también.*
- *Abby: Puede que vaya a verla en la semana. ¿Me acompañas?*
- *Mia: No creo, estaré ocupada.*
- *-Abby: Este bien*

English

- Mia: Hi, Abby. How are you?
- Abby: Mia, good to see you. I'm a little busy. I'm looking for schools where I can enroll my kids; you know some?
- Mia: Sure, I have my kids at Orlando High School. They have classes every day from 8 a.m. to 3 p.m., and they see extra subjects like cooking, art, economics, design, and some others.
- Abby: Sounds great, but that one's a bit far away. Do you know any more to the south?
- Mia: There is the Plantation High School. My sister has her kids there. The hours are from 8:30 a.m. to 2:30 p.m. and they have their swimming, basketball, baseball, and soccer teams. They also give extra classes like music, theater, and gardening.
- Abby: I like that one better. My kids love sports.
- Mia: That's very good. It's very nice and big, too.
- Abby: Maybe I'll see it this week. Will you come with me?
- Mia: I don't think so. I'll be busy.
- Abby: It's okay.

Preguntando sobre Gimnasio - Asking about a Gym

Spanish

- *Will: Hola hermanito, ¿Como estas?*
- *Wade: Hermano, todo bien, ¿Y tú?*
- *Will: Bien, me alegro.*
- *Wade: Te veo con más músculos, ¿Sigues entrenando en el gimnasio?*
- *Will: Claro, voy todos los días a entrenar, ya es rutina.*
- *Wade: Que bueno.*
- *Will: Deberías inscribirte y entrenamos juntos.*
- *Wade: ¿Tú dices?*
- *Will: Claro, así pasamos más tiempo juntos, tú entrenas y ganas algo de músculo.*
- *Wade: Puede ser.*
- *Will: Así sacas musculo tu también, que ya te veo delgado.*
- *Wade: Jajajaja, ¿A qué gimnasio vas tú?*
- *Will: Al Power GYM.*
- *Wade: ¿Y qué hay allí?*
- *Will: Esta toda la maquinaria necesaria para entrenar todos los músculos como bíceps, tríceps, espalda, hombros, piernas, abdominales y pecho. También hay un salón donde dan clases de muchas cosas como fit combat, TRX, crossfit, boxeo, baile y tae kwon do.*
- *Wade: Listo, el lunes me inscribo y empiezo a entrenar.*

English

- Will: Hello, little brother. How are you?
- Wade: Brother, all right, and you?
- Will: Well, I'm glad.
- Wade: I see you with more muscles. Are you still training in the gym?
- Will: Sure, I go every day to train. It's routine.
- Wade: That's good.
- Will: You should sign up, and we train together.
- Wade: You say?
- Will: Sure, that way, we spend more time together, you train and gain some muscle.
- Wade: Maybe.
- Will: That's how you get muscle too because you're already thin.
- Wade: Hahahaha, which gym are you going to?
- Will: To the Power GYM.
- Wade: And what's in there?
- Will: It's all the machinery necessary to train all the muscles like biceps, triceps, back, shoulders, legs, abdominals, and chest. There is also a classroom where they give classes of many things like fit combat, TRX, CrossFit, boxing, dance, and taekwondo.
- Wade: Ready, on Monday, I will sign up and start training.

Supermercados- Supermarkets

Spanish

- *Rachel: Gracias por la cena, estaba exquisita.*
- *Dom: A la orden. Me alegra que te haya gustado.*
- *Rachel: Quedo muy sabrosa, todos los ingredientes estaban muy frescos y bonitos.*
- *Dom: Muchas gracias.*
- *Rachel: ¿A qué supermercado vas tú? ¿Dónde compraste todas estas cosas?*
- *Dom: En realidad compro en varios supermercados, en el supermercado del norte usualmente compro solo los productos de limpieza porque ahí tienen buenas ofertas en esos productos siempre; en el supermercado del sur tienen todo muy caro así que no compro nada allí; en el supermercado del este compro las frutas y verduras, están a buen precio y siempre están muy frescas, ahí no compro la carne porque aunque esta a buen precio no es tan bonita ni tan fresca como la carne del supermercado del oeste.*
- *Rachel: Recorres mucho para comprar, ¿Cierto?*
- *Dom: Es la mejor manera de comprar buenos productos y ahorrar un poco de dinero.*

English

- Rachel: Thank you for dinner. It was exquisite.
- Dom: On your order. I'm glad you liked it.
- Rachel: It was very tasty. All the ingredients were very fresh and nice.
- Dom: Thank you very much.
- Rachel: Which supermarket are you going to? Where did you buy all these things?
- Dom: Actually, I buy in several supermarkets. In the supermarket in the north, I usually buy only the cleaning products because there they have good offers on those products always. In the supermarket in the south, they have everything very expensive, so I don't buy anything there. In the supermarket in the east, I buy fruits and vegetables. They are at a good price, and they are always very fresh. I don't buy the meat because although it is at a good price, it is not as nice or as fresh as the meat of the supermarket in the west.
- Rachel: You travel a lot to buy, don't you?
- Dom: It's the best way to buy good products and save a little money.

Guarderias- Daycares

Spanish

- *Emma: ¿Cómo estas Gianna? ¿Cómo está tu bebe?*
- *Gianna: Hola Emma; estamos bien gracias a Dios.*
- *Emma: Me alegro.*
- *Gianna: Ya en dos meses debo volver a trabajar y estoy preocupada porque no se con quien dejar a mi bebe.*
- *Emma: ¿Qué hay de tu mamá?*
- *Gianna: Tiene un viaje. Estaba pensando en dejarlo en una guardería, ¿Conoces alguna?*
- *Emma: Donde yo dejaba a mis niños. Es espectacular, tienen una piscina de pelotas, muchas niñeras, el servicio y atención son excelentes. Tienen una página en internet donde puedes*

meterte a ver a todas las niñeras, todas las áreas, los certificados de las niñeras y las opiniones de las otras madres.

- *Gianna: Que bien, pásame el link por un mensaje de texto.*
- *Emma: Eso hare. También tienen una aplicación para teléfonos con la que puedes acceder a las cámaras de la guardería y ver a tu hijo en tiempo real.*
- *Gianna: ¿Qué? Eso es increíble.*
- *Emma: Si, la tecnología avanza muy rápido y ellos supieron aprovecharlo.*
- *Gianna: Me encanta eso. Lo que más me preocupaba era no saber de mi hijo en todo el dia, pero con eso está solucionado.*

English

- Emma: How are you, Gianna? How's your baby?
- Gianna: Hi Emma. We are well, thank God.
- Emma: I'm glad.
- Gianna: In two months, I have to go back to work, and I'm worried because I don't know who to leave my baby with.
- Emma: What about your mother?
- Gianna: She has a trip. I was thinking of leaving him in daycare, do you know any?
- Emma: Where I used to leave my children. It's spectacular. They have a ball pool, a lot of nannies, and the service and attention are excellent. They have a website on the internet that you can visit and see all the nannies, all the areas, the nanny certificates, and the opinions of the other mothers.
- Gianna: Well, send me the link for a text message.
- Emma: That's what I'll do. They also have an application for phones with which you can access the cameras of the daycare and see your child in real-time.
- Gianna: What? That's unbelievable.
- Emma: Yes, the technology advances very fast, and they knew how to take advantage of it.
- Gianna: I love that. What worried me the most was not knowing about my son the whole day, but that solves it.

Seguros Medicos- **Medical Insurances**

Spanish

- *Stevie: ¿Cómo estás?*
- *Francis: Bien, ¿Tu?*
- *Stevie: Bien, saliendo del hospital.*
- *Francis: ¿Y eso?*
- *Stevie: Me caí por las escaleras y me fracturé la muñeca.*
- *Francis: ¿Cuándo?*
- *Stevie: Hace dos semanas.*
- *Francis: ¿Ya estas mejor?*
- *Stevie: Si, fui al doctor y me pusieron un yeso.*
- *Francis: Menos mal.*
- *Stevie: Si, lo mejor es que lo cubre el seguro medico.*
- *Francis: Que bueno. ¿Cuál usa?*

- *Stevie: Yo tengo un seguro privado, pero creo que me cambiare al Trumpcare u Obamacare, este es muy costoso.*
- *Francis: Yo uso el Trumpcare, es bastante bueno.*
- *Stevie: Eso estoy averiguando.*
- *Francis: Tengo un amigo que puede darte información.*
- *Stevie: Genial, te aviso para ir a verlo.*

English

- Stevie: How are you?
- Francis: Good, you?
- Stevie: Good, coming out of the hospital.
- Francis: Why's that?
- Stevie: I fell down the stairs and fractured my wrist.
- Francis: When?
- Stevie: Two weeks ago.
- Francis: Are you better now?
- Stevie: Yes, I went to the doctor, and they put a cast on me.
- Francis: Thank goodness.
- Stevie: Yes, the best thing is that it's covered by medical insurance.
- Francis: That's good. Which one do you use?
- Stevie: I have private insurance, but I think I'll switch to Trumpcare or Obamacare. This is very expensive.
- Francis: I use Trumpcare. It's quite good.
- Stevie: That's what I'm researching.
- Francis: I have a friend who can give you information.
- Stevie: Great, I'll let you know so you can go see him.

Seguros de carros - Car Insurances

Spanish

- *Chris: ¿Cómo estas vecino?*
- *Luke: Bien, todo bien.*
- *Chris: ¿Qué le paso a tu carro?*
- *Luke: Me chocaron el otro día.*
- *Chris: ¿En serio?*
- *Luke: Si, tristemente.*
- *Chris: ¿Y el que te choco no te va a pagar?*
- *Luke: No, me choco y huyo.*
- *Chris: Yo estaría molesto.*
- *Luke: Lo estoy.*
- *Chris: ¿Y el seguro no te lo arregla?*
- *Luke: No tengo seguro, nunca supe cómo funcionaba eso.*
- *Chris: Gran error.*
- *Luke: Si, eso he estado pensando.*
- *Chris: Yo te puedo ayudar con eso.*

- *Luke: Muchas gracias. ¿Tu cual usas?*
- *Chris: El seguro privado que yo tengo tiene servicios como responsabilidad por daño a la propiedad, responsabilidad por daño corporal, pago medico, cobertura de conductores sin seguro, daños por colisión y cobertura completa.*
- *Luke: Suena perfecto, protección para todos los casos.*
- *Chris: Así es, lástima que no sabias.*
- *Luke: Lo tendré muy en cuenta para el próximo vehículo, o para este si logro arreglarlo.*

English

- Chris: How are you, neighbor?
- Luke: Fine, everything's fine.
- Chris: What happened to your car?
- Luke: I was hit the other day.
- Chris: Really?
- Luke: Yes, sadly.
- Chris: And the one who hit you won't pay you?
- Luke: No, he crashed and ran away.
- Chris: I'd be upset.
- Luke: I am.
- Chris: And the insurance won't fix it for you?
- Luke: I don't have insurance. I never knew how that worked.
- Chris: Big mistake.
- Luke: Yeah, that's what I've been thinking.
- Chris: I can help you with that.
- Luke: Thank you very much. Which one do you use?
- Chris: The private insurance I have has services like property damage liability, bodily injury liability, medical payment, uninsured drivers coverage, collision damage, and full coverage.
- Luke: Sounds perfect, protection for all cases.
- Chris: That's right. Too bad, you didn't know.
- Luke: I will keep it very much in mind for the next vehicle or for this one if I manage to fix it.

Servicio de correo- Postal Service

Spanish

- *Charles: Hola Olivia, ¿Estas ocupada?*
- *Olivia: Hola Charles, no mucho, ¿Por?*
- *Charles: Quería preguntarte algo.*
- *Olivia: Claro, dime.*
- *Charles: Compre algo por internet y me gustaría que me llegara a la casa, pero no tengo idea de cuál servicio postal utilizar.*
- *Olivia: Hay muchos, yo uso el USPS, tiene un montón de servicios como correo express, envio de primera clase, correo de prioridad, confirmación de entrega, correo certificado, seguro y respuesta pagada. Es bastante bueno.*
- *Charles: Perfecto, creo que usare ese, tiene bastantes servicios interesantes.*
- *Olivia: Ese es el que yo uso.*

- *Charles: Muchas gracias, te aviso como me va con ellos.*

English

- Charles: Hi, Olivia, are you busy?
- Olivia: Hello, Charles, not much. Why?
- Charles: I wanted to ask you something.
- Olivia: Sure, tell me.
- Charles: I bought something online, and I'd like to have it delivered to my house, but I have no idea which postal service to use.
- Olivia: There are many. I use the USPS. It has a lot of services like express mail, first-class mail, priority mail, delivery confirmation, certified mail, insurance, and paid response. It's pretty good.
- Charles: Perfect. I think I'll use that one. It has quite a few interesting services.
- Olivia: That's the one I use.
- Charles: Thank you very much. I'll let you know how I'm doing with them.

Suscripciones – **Subscriptions**

Spanish

- *Ana: Hola Tatiana buen día, ¿Cómo van con la mudanza?*
- *Tatiana: Hola todo bien, ahí vamos, que bueno que te interese. ¿Crees que me puedas aclarar unas dudas con el asunto de las suscripciones? Sabes que estoy nueva en el país y tengo dudas al respecto.*
- *Ana: Si claro, aprovechemos que aun no llega mucha gente a la oficina para hablar.*
- *Tatiana: ¿Cuáles tienes tú?*
- *Ana: Yo estoy suscrita a servicios de entretenimiento como Netflix, Hulu y Youtube red; estoy suscrita al Amazon prime para compras por internet y estoy suscrita a la revista Home, porque dan buenos tips de cosas para el hogar.*
- *Tatiana: Entiendo, muchas gracias.*
- *Ana: ¿Hay algo que te interese?*
- *Tatiana: He escuchado sobre Spotify. ¿Para qué es esa?*
- *Ana: Esa es muy buena, es para escuchar música. Mucha gente la usa, yo no porque yo uso Apple Music.*
- *Tatiana: Ah está bien. Seguimos hablando luego, ya está llegando gente y hay que trabajar.*
- *Ana: Esta bien, cualquier cosa me avisas.*

English

- Ana: Hi, Tatiana, good day. How are you doing with the moving?
- Tatiana: Hi, everything's fine. Here we are, it's good that you're interested. Do you think you can clarify some doubts with the matter of subscriptions? You know I'm new in the country, and I have doubts about it.
- Ana: Of course, let's take the chance that still not many people have arrived at the office to talk.
- Tatiana: Which do you have?
- Ana: I am subscribed to entertainment services such as Netflix, Hulu, and Youtube. I am subscribed to Amazon prime for internet shopping, and I am subscribed to Home magazine because they give good tips on things for the home.

- Tatiana: I understand, thank you very much.
- Ana: Is there anything that interests you?
- Tatiana: I've heard about Spotify. What's that for?
- Ana: That's very good. It's for listening to music. A lot of people use it. I don't because I use Apple Music.
- Tatiana: Ah, it's good. We'll talk later. People are arriving, and we have to work.
- Ana: All right, let me know anything.

Chapter 17 - Listening and Speaking Skills

Language and Listening

Linguists and language enthusiasts agree that listening is one of the most important things you can do to learn Spanish. It's not very surprising is it when we consider that babies begin to listen to people and can partly acquire language acquisition before even being born. A study carried out by German researchers even showed that babies cry with an accent, based on the language they heard while in the womb.

As adults who learning Spanish, we can learn a lot from children who are more biologically capable of learning languages than we are. Studies have demonstrated that young children are capable of learning languages just from exposure, by listening and imitating native speakers. The reason why children can absorb language faster this way is because their brains are still developing.

While it's true that for us adults, we can't just surround ourselves with a language and expect to master it in a short amount of time, there is still an immense benefit from actively listening to native speakers and imitating their patterns of speech. It helps to remember when you were a kid, having some fun imitating maybe a brother, sister or parent. It's helpful to go back into that headspace as you have fun practicing your dialogs.

And you will be happy to know that you have one great advantage as an adult learning a second language. You can be an explicit student. You are capable of taking the initiative to learn a language. Language experts agree that consistent, routine studying is necessary to achieve your language goals, a discipline that our younger counterparts lack.

As an adult, your hard work and discipline give you a distinct advantage. An example of this is your ability to use the Rote Learning technique to memorize a list of vocabulary with the use of repetition. Another one is an exercise often used by those who stutter to help them speak with confidence. The exercise is to first say what you want to say first in your mind and then out loud. Try it and see how it works for you.

Passive vs Active listening

Now, let's go back to that idea of immersion we discussed in the last chapter. How much good do you think it would do you to go abroad and spend time around native speakers – at the bar or coffee shop, casually listening in on their conversations? Just by listening, this ought to help your Spanish speaking skills, right? Unfortunately, that is not the case. Because, unlike children, we don't have the ability to naturally absorb most of what is being spoken in its entirety.

On the other hand, when we grow up and mature, we now have the ability to actively study the Spanish content. We can listen to native speakers in movies or music, and then actively study it to drastically improve our skills.

Among language learners, this is called passive vs. active listening. Passive listening occurs when you're driving and casually listening to the radio on the car stereo. Or when you're cleaning the house while listening to your favorite music. In actuality, you're hearing it rather than listening to it.

Active listening is when you are paying acute attention to what you are hearing. It's a skill that is most beneficial when holding a conversation, as well as when learning Spanish. The method in this book will help you to hone this skill.

Capitalizing on Similarities Between Spanish and English

Luckily, for Spanish learners, there are many similarities between English and Spanish. First of all, one of the most obvious similarities you've probably already noticed is that they both use the Roman alphabet. Unlike learning Chinese, Korean, or even Arabic, when learning Spanish, you don't have to go through the trouble of learning an entirely new alphabet or thousands of new characters.

Secondly, other than a couple of word-order exceptions (Example: English places the adjective before the noun and Spanish places the noun before the adjective), you'll be surprised to find that most sentences in both languages follow the same basic structures.

And lastly, 30% to 40% of all words in the English language have related and similar-sounding words in Spanish that are called "cognates". An example of some Spanish cognates would be words like "accidente" "elefante" or "familia". Because these words have a similar sound, meaning, and appearance, it will help you transfer your knowledge of English into your Spanish.

Listening vs. Speaking

There is a lively debate in the language community about what's more important; listening or speaking? Arguably both are necessary when learning a language, however, listening proves to be the area of difficulty for most Spanish language learners.

When native speakers don't enunciate, speak slowly, or use unfamiliar vocabulary most language students begin to feel lost in a conversation. I surveyed several dozen of my past students and asked them this very question: what's more difficult: speaking or listening in Spanish? Two-thirds agreed that their biggest challenge was being able to listen and understand Spanish rather than speaking it. Which brings us to the conclusion that listening is key to learning Spanish.

The AGE-OLD Problem

Are you concerned that you're too old to learn a new language? Have you ever heard about the Critical Period Hypothesis argument that language learning is biologically linked to age? In a nutshell, this theory argues that there's a "Critical Period" during a child's development, before the age of 12, when language can be learned. But is there actual evidence for this theory?

The most famous piece of evidence supporting the Critical Period Hypothesis comes from a case in Los Angeles in the 1970s. A young girl nicknamed "Genie" was kept in isolation devoid of any social interaction until the age of 13 when social workers rescued her. She didn't know how to speak, had trouble walking and didn't know how to do a lot of the basic things you'd expect for a girl her age. Social workers and therapists worked with her for seven years to teach her how to talk, but they were largely unsuccessful. She was never able to gain linguistic competence. Genie had missed her opportunity to learn basic linguistic structures like grammar at an early age and therefore was unable to fully develop the necessary speaking skills.

Although this seems to be the case for acquiring your first language, researchers have shown that this hypothesis does not apply to second language acquisition. As mentioned before, even though you cannot simply learn Spanish the same way as young children do, you do have the capability to learn with the above-mentioned skills and the method created within this book.

Conclusion

I once had a Spanish language professor at university who told me, with regards to learning Spanish, "Learn the culture and you'll inevitably learn to speak the language." Now years later, I look back on this piece of advice and realize how true it is. To this day, I'm still amazed of the beauty, magic, and charm of the Spanish language. I'm absolutely convinced that my love for the culture and its amazing people have played a major role in helping me to become fluent in the Spanish language.

We've finally reached the end of this book and I sincerely would like to congratulate you on making it this far. I hope you found the learning experience enjoyable and rewarding. And I hope that you continue using Spanish movies, TV shows, and music to reach your ultimate Spanish speaking goals. As you continue using this method and immersing yourself in the Spanish culture, I'm confident you'll be speaking fluently in no time! I wish you the very best of luck! Thank you for picking up our book to learn and study with. Until next time! *¡Buena suerte!*

Made in the USA
Monee, IL
04 March 2021